THE TRAIL OF HISTORY:

OR,

HISTORY OF RELIGION AND EMPIRE

IN

PARALLEL

FROM THE

CREATION TO THE PRESENT TIME.

WITH A

Valuable Historical Diagram.

BY

REV. T. M. MERRIMAN, A. M.,

Author of "William Prince of Orange."

THIRD, NEW AND IMPROVED EDITION.

BOSTON:

PUBLISHED BY MERRIMAN & STEWART.

1875.

Printed by
J. G. STEWART, Jr.,
19 Sprtng Lane, Boston,
1875.

ADVERTISEMENT.

The plan of this Work is such, that persons will find it will serve a very good purpose as a Reading-book of History for those who have not leisure to make History a study. It will serve equally well the purpose of a Text-book in all institutions of learning, from the College and Sabbath-School to the District School, especially if used in connection with the large Diagram. The fundamental plan and facts of history are so clearly and compactly arranged, as to secure a rapid acquisition of historic information.

A little confusion might be thought to exist by the frequent repetition of the "*Ages*" in the Contents, particularly in the History of Empire. But all is made perfectly clear when we recollect that there are several different empires, and that they begin and end at different points of time, as can be seen on the Diagram. Hence, by taking up any *one* Empire, and following it out, and noting the Periods at which it passes from one "Age" to another, the *apparent confusion* merges into *harmony.*

The division of History into "Ages" is a new one, and very convenient in two respects. First, it separates the chaos of history into a few large and plain features, distinctly marked by the prevailing sentiment of that date. The second advantage is, the whole is so easily remembered.

CONTENTS.

BOOK I.

HISTORY OF RELIGION.

I.—AGE PATRIARCHAL.

FROM CREATION TO THE DEATH OF JOSEPH.

SUBJECT—SACRED HISTORY.

PERIOD I.—FROM CREATION TO THE FLOOD; 1—1656 A. M. AND 4004—2348 B. C.

PERIOD II.—FROM THE FLOOD TO THE DEATH OF JOSEPH; 1656 A. M. AND 2348 B. C., TO 2365 A. M., AND 1639 B. C.

II.—AGE OF WAR FOR POWER.

FROM DEATH OF JOSEPH TO CHRIST.

SACRED HISTORY.

PERIOD I.—FROM THE DEATH OF JOSEPH TO THE DEATH OF JOSHUA; 2365 A. M. AND 1639 B. C., TO 2561 A. M. AND 1443 B. C.

PERIOD II.—FROM JOSHUA TO THE TEMPLE OF SOLOMON; 2561 A. M. AND 1443 B. C., TO 3000 A. M. AND 1004 B. C.

PERIOD III.—FROM SOLOMON'S TEMPLE TO THE BABYLONISH CAPTIVITY; 3000 A. M. AND 1004 B. C., TO 3416 A. M. AND 588 B. C.

III.—AGE OF WAR FOR OPINION.

FROM CHRIST TO THE PEACE OF RELIGION, 1555 A. C.

SUBJECT—ECCLESIASTICAL HISTORY.

PERIOD I.—FROM CHRIST TO THE END OF THE APOSTOLIC AGE; 4004 A. M. AND 1 A. D., TO 4100 A. M., AND 96 A. C.

IV.—AGE OF CONSOLIDATION.

FROM THE PEACE OF RELIGION TO THE PRESENT TIME.

ECCLESIASTICAL HISTORY.

PERIOD I.—FROM THE PEACE OF RELIGION TO THE LANDING OF THE PILGRIMS; 5559 A. M., AND 1555 A. C., TO 5624 A. M., AND 1620 A. C.

BOOK II.

HISTORY OF EMPIRE.

I.—AGE PATRIARCHAL.

SUBJECT—PROFANE HISTORY.

I.—AGE PATRIARCHAL.

BABYLON.—FROM NIMROD TO BELSHAZZAR.

PROFANE HISTORY.

PERIOD I.—FROM NIMROD TO SARDANAPALUS; 1771 A. M. AND 2233 B. C., TO 3184 A. M. AND 820 B. C.

II.—AGE OF WAR FOR POWER.

PROFANE HISTORY.

PERIOD II.—FROM SARDANAPALUS TO BELSHAZZAR; 3184 A. M. AND 820 B. C., TO 3466 A. M. AND 538 B. C.

PERSIA.

PERIOD I.—FROM CYRUS TO DARIUS CODOMANUS; 3466 A. M., AND 538 B. C., TO 3680 A. M., AND 324 B. C.

I.—AGE PATRIARCHAL.

EGYPT.—FROM MENES TO CLEOPATRA.

PROFANE HISTORY.

PERIOD I.—FROM MENES TO THE END OF THE SHEPHERD KINGS; 1816 A. M. AND 2188 B. C., TO 2244 A. M. AND 1760 B. C.

II.—AGE OF WAR FOR POWER.

PERIOD II.—FROM SHEPHERD KINGS TO ALEXANDER THE GREAT; 2244 A. M. AND 1760 B. C., TO 3668 A. M., AND 336 B. C.

PERIOD III.—FROM ALEXANDER TO CLEOPATRA; 3668 A. M. AND 336 B. C., TO 3974 A. M. AND 30 B. C.

I.—AGE PATRIARCHAL.

GREECE—FROM ITS EARLY SETTLERS TO ITS SUBJUGATION BY THE ROMANS.

PERIOD I.—FROM ABOUT 1908 A. M. AND 2096 B. C., TO THE TROJAN WAR, 2820 A. M. AND 1184 B. C.

II.—AGE OF WAR FOR POWER.

PERIOD II.—FROM THE TROJAN WAR TO THE FIRST PERSIAN INVASION; 2820 A. M. AND 1184 B. C., TO 3513 A. M. AND 491 B. C.

PERIOD III.—FROM THE FIRST PERSIAN INVASION TO ALEXANDER THE GREAT; 3513 A. M. AND 491 B. C., TO 3668 A. M. AND 336 B. C.

PERIOD III.—FROM THE COMMONWEALTH TO THE FIRST TRIUMVIRATE; 3495 A. M. AND 509 B. C., TO 3945 A. M. AND 59 B. C.

PERIOD IV.—FROM THE FIRST TRIUMVIRATE TO THE DEATH OF AUGUSTUS CÆSAR; 3945 A. M. AND 59 B. C., TO 4018 A. M. AND 14 A. C.

III.—AGE OF WAR FOR OPINION.

FROM AUGUSTUS CÆSAR TO THE REFORMATION.

SUBJECT—CIVIL HISTORY.

PERIOD V.—FROM AUGUSTUS' DEATH TO THE END OF THE WESTERN EMPIRE; 4018 A. M., AND 14 A. C., TO 4480 A. M., AND 476 A. C.

III.—AGE OF WAR FOR OPINION.

FRANCE—FROM PHARAMOND TO LOUIS NAPOLEON BONAPARTE.

CIVIL HISTORY.

PERIOD I.—FROM PHARAMOND TO PEPIN; 4424 A M. AND 420 A. C., TO 4756 A. M. AND 752 A. C.

PERIOD II.—FROM PEPIN TO THE END OF THE REIGN OF PHILIP IV; 4756 A. M. AND 752 A. C., TO 5817 A. M. AND 1313 A. C.

PERIOD III.—FROM PHILIP IV. TO FRANCIS II.; 5817 A. M. AND 1313 A. C., TO 5563 A. M. AND 1559 A. C.

IV.—AGE OF CONSOLIDATION.

SUBJECT—CIVIL HISTORY.

PERIOD IV.—FROM FRANCIS II. TO THE REPUBLIC; 5563 A. M. AND 1559 A. C., TO 5796 A. M., AND 1792 A. C.

PERIOD V.—FROM THE REPUBLIC FORWARD; 5796 A. M. AND 1792 A. C., TO 5864 A. M. AND 1860 A. C.

III.—AGE OF WAR FOR OPINION.

ENGLAND.—FROM JULIUS CÆSAR TO QUEEN VICTORIA.

SUBJECT—CIVIL HISTORY.

PERIOD I.—FROM ITS EARLY HISTORY TO THE END OF THE SAXON HEPTARCHY; 3949 A. M. AND 55 B. C., TO 4831 A. M AND 827 A. C.

PERIOD II.—FROM THE END OF THE HEPTARCHY TO WILLIAM THE CONQUEROR; 4831 A. M. AND 827 A. C., TO 5070 A. M. AND 1066 A. C.

PERIOD III.—FROM WILLIAM THE CONQUEROR TO HENRY VIII.; 5070 A. M. AND 1066 A. C., TO 5513 A. M. AND 1509 A. C.

PERIOD IV. — FROM HENRY VIII. TO THE END OF THE REVOLUTION; 5513 A. M. AND 1509 A. C., TO 5692 A. M. AND 1688 A. C.

IV.—AGE OF CONSOLIDATION.

IV.—AGE OF CONSOLIDATION.

AMERICA—FROM THE REFORMATION FORWARD.

CIVIL HISTORY.

PERIOD III.—FROM THE INDEPENDENCE TO THE PRESENT TIME; 5787 A. M. AND 1783 A. C., TO 5864 A. M. AND 1860 A. C.

PREFACE.

It would seem almost superfluous to make any addition to the numerous works already published on the great subject of Universal History.

But the vastness of the subject is such, and its importance being equally great, we may rest assured that its merits have not yet been fully set forth, nor all its practical teachings imbibed and cherished.

In order to comprehend a matter, either seeing, or perceiving, is necessary. Experience teaches us that our perception is greatly aided by sight; and just in proportion as we perceive clearly, is our comprehension just, and our knowledge of a matter solid and useful.

If, then, we can array the great drama of the world before the vision, and thereby obtain a clear perception of its facts, and their important relations, we shall be enabled easily to gather up and retain a fund of knowledge not to be despised.

With the hope of facilitating the study of history, and bringing its rich and varied instruction into the foreground of observation, this volume is submitted to a discriminating, thinking, reading, criticizing, and charitable public.

Books enough have been written, and well enough written, on the subject of history; and still the study of it is invariably anathematized as DRY! DRY! DRY! The facts are not dry, *but the method of getting at them* is where the difficulty lies.

One writer gives us a vast quantity of reading, too voluminous for persons of limited time and little patience to peruse; yet what could we do without these same emporiums of historic wealth?

Another selects some portion of the world's history, and pours upon it a light that would seem to set forth its importance above all other parts of the great whole; and such labors are of priceless value. But still the impression returns, after perusing these various stores of wisdom, that we have not compassed the matter yet.

Any aid, therefore, that can be rendered in this difficulty, must be timely, and of use.

An attempt was made some ten years ago, by the author, to overcome this impediment at the door of historic inquiry; and, after much labor and study, the present volume is offered as the result.

The plan is briefly this: to trace out the march of Religion and Empire in parallel. These two great themes have controlled the world; and in their "trail" we can see what has befallen mankind.

In the department of Religion, attention is directed chiefly to the religion which has the *Living God* as its author, and the Bible for its law-book. False and idolatrous religions are only noticed, as they have *perverted* the right ways of the Lord, or attempted to blot out his name and fear among men.

Empire is traced in its principal forms, or in the great empires of ancient and modern times. One great truth in the march of Empire is, that it began in the *East*, and has steadily removed *West*, in no instance going backward, more than the current of a river. *The ark of power* now rests with the extreme western nations. The same is true of Religion, and of the "Ark of the Covenant."

In order to carry out this plan of parallel, the "diagram" is introduced. This is divided first into six parts, of a thousand years each. Each of these is divided into ten sections, each section representing one hundred years of time. The *upper* line of figures shows the number of hundred years from the creation to now; or, the years of the world. The *lower* line begins at the time of Christ, and numbers the same sections to our time, and then begins at Christ and numbers back (to the left) to the creation, showing at a glance any point *before* or *after* Christ, and the year of the world. This is the chronology of the diagram.

The lines crossing the upper part of the diagram horizontally, show the "trail" of Religion. Those on the lower part, that of Empire. The more prominent events are indicated by the names of distinguished persons, in both departments, all located, as nearly as possible, in the time or date at which they lived.

One other important feature of the diagram is its division into ages, according to the prevailing sentiments of those ages, indicated by the colored sections. The First Age is termed the *Patriarchal.* The Second Age, that of *War for Power.* The Third Age, that of *War for Opinion.* The Fourth Age, that of *Consolidation.*

In the course of the work, another set of divisions is introduced, called *Periods*, which take up any portion that falls in the way, conducting it through the age in which it belongs. In each period are introduced as many names of persons or things as are found necessary to hand along the thread or "trail" of history.

This arrangement, it is hoped, will serve two purposes. One is, to direct the *student* of history to any portion of the great subject he wishes to investigate, at a greater length than it is here treated, or can be, consistently with the design of this work. The other is, to give a connected, broad, and compact idea of the great body of history, to persons who have neither time nor money to expend upon large and elaborate histories.

The part devoted to Religion, it is to be hoped, will especially aid in the understanding of the Bible, and in impressing the fact upon all readers, that God has ever had a people to serve him since the world was. Particular pains have been taken to trace this matter through the time from the close of the O. T. history, about four hundred years B. C., to his time, illustrating particularly the fact, that "the sceptre did not depart from Judah until Christ did come."

Also to show that through the "Dark Ages," or the ninth to the twelfth centuries after Christ, there were faithful witnesses, of the true seed, upon the earth. These sections of Religious history are not so easy of access to the general reader, and hence a value will be attached to their being put in the present connection.

A similar use can be made of the history of Empire, illustrating the progress of civil liberty.

What better wisdom can we seek, than that of the ways of Providence with man; and the nature of, means of obtaining, keeping, and enjoying, *Civil and Religious Liberty?*

The History of Religion, before Christ, is called "*Sacred History;*" after Christ, "*Ecclesiastical History.*" That of Empire, before Christ, is called "*Profane History;*" after Christ, "*Civil History.*"

THE

TRAIL OF HISTORY.

LESSONS OF HISTORY.

History is that department of knowledge which refers exclusively to the past. Every act passes into that department as soon as performed. *Written* history is a detail of the *acts* of mankind. The "Trail of History," contemplates the *survey* only of the great highway trodden by the generations of the past.

History is the best adapted of all subjects to meet the tastes of all classes. It is alike interesting to old and young, to the learned and unlearned. It is an enchanting source of amusement, a deposit for profound improvement, and a fountain of desirable and important knowledge.

History gives us an insight into the circumstances and influences which impelled others to do as they have done. Hence we are led to weigh their motives and acts, and also to admire the good and great *wherever* found. It shows us that true goodness and greatness go hand in hand, and that the most deserving of true renown are those who have done most to promote the good of mankind.

History furnishes a true index of the measures best adapted to promote the peace and welfare of individuals, communities, and nations. This is its greatest use.

History teaches us the sad lesson of the instability of human affairs, and that the high and mighty are often more miserable than the lowly. The occasion of all the fluctuations of this inconstant world is found to dwell, tyrant and alone, in the supreme *selfishness* of the human heart.

History unfolds to us in countless ways "the vast designs, the deep abyss of Providence." The Eternal God had a purpose "before the world was;" and when the combinations of men seek to thwart that purpose, He, by a flood upon the world, or a confusion of tongues, or the overthrow of a nation, does vindicate his ways to men.

A knowledge of history will incline us to contentment and cheerfulness with the lot that befalls us; restrain unhallowed and unwarranted ambition; cure us of hero-worship, by finding that all men are "subject to like passions with ourselves;" and that the true duty and station of all men is "to do justly, love mercy, and walk humbly with thy God."

SOURCES OF HISTORY.

Preëminent and above all other books is the Bible as a source of historic knowledge. For 3300 years we have no other written account of any event in that long night of unwritten silence, but what is found in the volume of inspiration by Moses.

Next, in point of time, is Herodotus, styled the "Father of History." He compiled what he could learn of the history of nations from 713 to 479, B. C.

Oral Tradition must have supplied most of the facts penned by these ancient historians.

Historical Poems. These are common among barbarous nations. The Iliad and Odyssey of Homer are regarded as of historic authority, and are the only history extant of the Heroic Age of Greece.

Visible Monuments, as pillars, heaps of stones, and mounds of earth.

Ruins: found in Egypt, the Holy Land, Greece, and Italy; in their ruins of cities, temples, aqueducts, and columns,—giving evidence of the power, opulence, and taste of their architects and projectors.

Names of Countries, Towns, etc. These perpetuate the names of discoverers, conquerers, and founders.

Coins and Medals. The most ancient of these, whose dates can be ascertained, belong to the fifth century before Christ.

Inscriptions on Marbles. The most celebrated of these are now in possession of the University of Oxford, England, called the "*Arundelian Marbles*," brought from Greece by the Earl of Arundel.

BOOK I.

HISTORY OF RELIGION.

I.

AGE PATRIARCHAL.

FROM CREATION TO THE DEATH OF JOSEPH.

SUBJECT—SACRED HISTORY.

PERIOD I. FROM 1—1656, A. M., OR TO THE FLOOD 2348, B. C.

THE BIBLE.—To this priceless volume we owe more than to any other, in a historic point of view. It is not the fountain of romance, but of *positive* knowledge. Being written by men not seeking to establish a lie, its statements are worthy of our implicit confidence. It directs us, as do all other sources of knowledge, to the East, as the birth place of man, and the beginning of empire. Being all the history of religion we have for about 3600 years from the creation, we can do no other way than follow the Bible record.

COSMOGONY.—"In the beginning God created the heavens and the earth." To this sublime and profound statement, nothing can be added nor substituted any more satisfactory on the origin of the world. The absurdity of the attempt need only be mentioned to be seen.

Zenophanes, Strabo, and others, taught that the whole system of the universe was the Deity himself. Pythagoras taught the numerical system of the monad, dyad, and triad, and by means of his sacred quaternity elucidated the formation of the world, and the secrets of nature. Others adhered to the mathematical system of squares and triangles, the cube, the pyramid, and the sphere, etc. Others refer the origin of the globe to the combination of the four elements, air, earth, fire, and water, with the assistance of a fifth, an immaterial, and vivifying principle.

The inspired Shastah, of the Brahmins, records that the angel Bistnoo transformed himself into a great boar, plunged into the watery abyss, and brought up the earth on his tusks. Then issued from him a mighty tortoise and snake, and Bistnoo placed the snake erect upon the back of the tortoise, and then placed the earth upon the head of the snake.

The negroes of Congo affirm that the world was made by angels except their own country, which the Supreme Being constructed himself; that he took great pains with its inhabitants, and made them very black and beautiful, and when he finished the first man, he was so pleased with him, he stroked his face with his hand, which made his nose, and the noses of his posterity, flat.

Darwin, an infidel, in accounting for the origin of the world, *supposes* that the mass of chaos suddenly exploded, like a barrel of gunpowder, and in that act exploded the sun, which in its flight, by a similar convulsion, exploded the earth; and thus by a chain of explosions, the whole solar system was produced, and set in regular motion.

Even Geology leaves us at no better stopping-place, after penetrating into depths unfathomable, than the well-known haven, "In the beginning God created the heaven and the earth."

Creation. — It is plain that a creation must have a creator. The author of all things is neither a cube, a square, a boar, gunpowder, nor Bistnoo, but the eternal Jehovah.

The earth was without form, and darkness was upon the deep, when the spirit of God moved in the silent void, a light was struck, and day and night were created the first day.

"The firmament," or atmosphere, was made the second day.

The division of the water, dry land, and herbage, the third day.

The sun, moon, and stars, made the fourth day.

The beasts, fishes, and fowls, the fifth day.

Man and woman created the sixth day, and also marriage instituted.

The Sabbath instituted, and the Lord rested the seventh day and hallowed it. Every seventh day is the Lord's through all time.

Eden. — The geographical location of the Garden is a matter of conjecture, and also of no real importance. Some place it near Mount Ararat; others at the junction of the rivers Pison, Gihon, Hiddekel, and Euphrates, near the Gulf of Persia. The superior loveliness of the place can be easily believed, when we recollect it was fitted by God for the home and happiness of our first parents.

Adam and Eve. — After the Garden was prepared, the Lord put Adam into it, to dress it, and keep it. He being alone, "the Lord saw it was not good for him to be alone," so to make a "help meet for him," the Lord caused Adam to fall into a deep sleep, when he took a rib from his side, from which he made woman.

To Adam and Eve the Lord gave first, a privilege to eat of every tree in the garden; second, a prohibition, that of the tree in the centre they were not to eat at all. The penalty for disobedience was to be death, — *i. e.*, the introduction of the ills of this life, of which sin is the cause, and death is the last of them.

Temptation. — The devil, in the form of a serpent, insinuates a jealousy into the mind of Eve, against the commandment of the Lord, that it deprived them of very important knowledge. In this way he bewitched her with an uneasiness, which she could not dismiss until she had yielded to Satan's temptation, and disobeyed the Lord, — thus giving the devil's *insinuation* more credit than the Lord's *commandment.* Adam also took of the fruit, and did eat.

Fall. — In the cool of the day, or the evening, the Lord appeared in the Garden. At his approach, Adam and Eve fled from his presence. The Lord called, "Adam, where art thou?" He said, "I am naked, and afraid, and hid myself."

The Lord then asked him if he had eaten of the tree which he was commanded not to eat? He answered, "The woman thou gavest me, she gave me of the fruit, and I did eat." When the Lord asked her why she did this, she said, "The serpent beguiled me, and I did eat." The Lord then proceeded to inflict the penalty, first upon the serpent.

Curse. — A part of that penalty was, the entailment of perpetual enmity between the righteous and wicked.

Upon the woman fell peculiar and aggravated sorrows, as the mother of children, and subjection to her husband: "He shall rule over thee."

Upon the man fell increased difficulties, as thorns and thistles, in cultivating the ground, — also sorrow to additional labor: "In the sweat of thy face shalt thou eat bread, until thou return to the ground."

Expulsion. — The Lord next drove them out of the beautiful garden, and closed up the entrance, by placing a flaming sword to guard the way of the tree of life. Thus by taking of the tree of the knowledge of good and evil, death was placed between them and the tree of life. "Thou shalt *surely die!*"

Cain and Abel. — He was the first-born of the human race, — supposed to have been born in the first year of the world.

Abel is supposed to have been born the next year.

It is evident that their parents followed God's plan, in bringing up their children religiously and industriously. Cain was a farmer, and Abel a shepherd.

"In process of time," — *i. e.*, at some set time of religious worship, — perhaps the Sabbath, — they each brought an offering to the Lord; Cain of the fruit of the ground, Abel of the flocks.

For good reasons, the Lord had respect to Abel's offering, but not to Cain's. Filled with rage at this, Cain fell upon Abel and killed him. Thus Adam and Eve saw "the enmity between the serpent's seed and her seed," spoken of in the curse. God immediately interposed, as in the case of Adam, and inquires of Cain for his brother.

Cain feigns ignorance, and thought it not his business to look after him. "The Lord said: the voice of thy brother's blood crieth unto me from the ground."

The Lord then gave Cain a sign, that no one should kill him, and sent him out into the world a vagabond.

SETH. — At the age of one hundred and thirty years, Adam begat a son, and called his name Seth. He was to be in place of Abel, and through him the line of the godly was to descend. Then began men to be called by the name of the Lord, — or the distinction began to be made between the godly and ungodly. The two classes were also called the children of God, and the children of men.

ENOCH. — As a specimen of the piety of the church before the flood, it is stated of Enoch, that "he walked with God, and was not, for God took him." Thus with great favor, and great honor, the Lord will reward all them that diligently seek him. Enoch lived between 600 and 1000 before the flood.

NOAH. — Little else is known of the church before the flood, except the long lives of some of the Patriarchs, — as Methuselah, who lived to the year of the flood, and was then nine hundred and sixty-nine years old. Noah was born six hundred years before the flood. The deplorable fact that wickedness spread with greater rapidity over the earth than piety, provoked the Lord to administer judgment upon the whole degenerate race. Previous to this, however, he sent Noah on an errand of mercy, as a "preacher of righteousness." By this act God showed the world that his purpose was to pacify and restore men to his favor, if they would repent and turn to him. For one hundred and twenty years Noah labored in his mission with little if any success, as the earth was finally "filled with violence." Seeing no reform in the wicked, the Lord poured out his wrath upon them, and they were all destroyed.

Upon the appointed day, Noah, with his family, and the animals to be preserved, entered the ark, and God opened the flood-gates of heaven, and drowned the world and its people.

FLOOD. — The rain, that caused the flood, continued forty days and forty nights. Such was the quantity that fell, that the water rose to twenty-seven feet above the highest mountains. The waters of the flood continued upon the earth about one year and ten days, when they abated and dried up.

Those who maintain that the flood was only partial, have a few very difficult points to combat; such as the strong language of the Bible: "The windows of heaven being opened, and the fountains of the great deep being broken up." The waters upon the earth at the creation had been gathered into seas, and raised above the atmosphere, and need only be recalled, to cover the earth again.

Besides, it is a matter of great query, if it was only *partial*, how the ark came to rest upon Mount Ararat, its highest peak being ninety-five hundred feet.

Again, why did the Babelites undertake to build a tower up to heaven, as a retreat from another flood, if they got no idea of the waters being above the highest mountains?

The traditions of *all* nations are *against* the caviller. Even the Indians of America relate the wonder of the flood. The event called the deluge, is incorporated into the annals of the Chaldeans, Phœnicians, Assyrians, Greeks, Romans, Goths, Druids, Persians, Hindoos, Burmese, Chinese, Mexicans, Peruvians, Brazillians, Nicaraguans, West-Caledonians, Otaheitans, and Sandwich-Islanders. To dislodge all these concurring traditions, is more than sceptics *can* do.

ARK. — This wonderful boat was built according to the plan Noah received of the Lord. The material was gopher wood (or, as some suppose, cypress wood). Its form was of an oblong square, with a flat bottom, and a double roof, elevated one cubit in the middle. It had neither sails nor rudder, being designed only to lie on the water steadily. It was three stories high, each story eighteen feet in height, and divided into separate apartments. It was also pitched within and without, and thereby water-tight.

It may be computed at five hundred and twelve feet in length, eighty-seven wide, and fifty-two feet high; or thus, equal to one hundred and ten thirty by forty feet barns, with sixteen feet posts, placed three side by side and three high, in an oblong shape.

It rested on Mount Ararat, on the sixth of the month of May. Noah did not leave it until the eighteenth of December following.

PERIOD II. FROM THE FLOOD, 1656 A. M. AND 2348 B. C., TO THE DEATH OF JOSEPH, 2365 A. M. AND 1639 B. C.

NOAH. — After the abatement of the flood, Noah and family came forth from the Ark, to reïnhabit and repeople the world.

It is worthy of notice, that Noah's first public act, after leaving the ark, was the erection of an altar, and offering of sacrifice to

God, as an acknowledgment of the great deliverance of him and his family from the flood.

To this act God had special regard, and was well pleased, and made promise that it was not his design to destroy the world in this manner again, but while the earth remains there shall be seed time and harvest, and day and night.

Being the postdeluvian Adam, God also confirmed Noah in the privileges of our first parents, viz.: to "multiply and replenish the earth, and the right of dominion and use of all animal, fish, and fowl creation."

But whilst God put the lives of all creatures into the hands of men, he expressly forbade taking each others' lives wantonly, making murder a capital offence; "for whoso sheddeth man's blood, by man shall his blood be shed."

The forfeiture of the murderer's life is the penalty for the crime of murder. In the early ages, before civil governments were established, the right of executing the death-penalty belonged to the nearest relative of the person murdered.

God not only made promise to Noah, but also gave him a sign — that of a rainbow in the cloud; so that when we look upon that beautiful thing, it is to remind us that God also looks upon the same as his token and pledge no more to drown the world.

Homer, speaking of the figures on Agamemnon's breast-plate, says there were three dragons, whose colors were "like the rainbow which Saturn (father of time) placed in the cloud, as a sign to short-sighted men." The Scandinavians regarded it as a means of communication, or bridge, between God and man. It was worshipped by the Greeks, Romans, and Peruvians.

Noah immediately betook himself to the business of farming, — showing the propriety of useful employment, and the existence of the curse, that "by the sweat of the face shall man eat bread, until he return to the ground."

Noah planted a vineyard, and at the feast of ingathering, partook too freely, and "erred through wine."

It is evident Noah did not live in times of total abstinence. Neither was he an habitual drunkard; for his getting into this plight was a very great surprise to his family, which shows it to have been an uncommon thing. One son turned it into ridicule, while the other two threw over the scene the veil of charity. If excess of eating were followed by similar effects of excess of wine, we should find gluttony a more common error than drunkenness.

But little else is known of Noah. His prophecy of his sons, has had a very striking fulfilment in the history of their descendants.

The curse of bondage to Shem and Japheth, was pronounced upon Canaan.

The bondage of the Israelites, their captivity, and the enslavement of the sons of Ham, are very striking illustrations of the fulfilment of Noah's prediction.

Noah lived after the flood three hundred and fifty years, to dispense the precepts of the Lord to his posterity, and thereby lay a permanent foundation for the upbuilding of the Church of God among men. This eminent servant of God died in the year 2006 A. M., and 1998 B. C., aged nine hundred and fifty years.

SHEM. — The sons of Noah soon separated into different parts of the country, and their history, and that of their descendants, is various. But from the benediction of their father, and the history of Shem, it is plain that God made Shem and his posterity the channel of religious good to the world. Through his line are to be traced the generations of the righteous.

Shem lived five hundred years after the flood, and was contemporary with Abraham and Isaac, and died about the year Jacob was born, aged about six hundred years.

It is supposed by some that Shem might have been the "Melchizedek" mentioned in the Scriptures. One objection to this is, "we can't know positively." In answer to that it is said, "There is *no other* person on whom we *can* fix the title." Hence, in the absence of *positive* proof, we are at liberty to take the strongest *presumptive* evidence. The presumption is in favor of Shem, he being an antediluvian patriarch and contemporary with Abraham, whom he met and blessed. Again, it is objected, that Melchizedek "had neither beginning of days nor end of life," which Shem had. In reply, it would be as difficult to reconcile this with any other person as with Shem. And as the expression above is applied to the *spontaneous priesthood* of *Melchizedek*, there is not the slightest difficulty in applying the same to Shem.

Since, therefore, it is not known who Melchizedek was, we are robbing no one by bestowing this honorable title upon Shem.

As Shem is the last of the antediluvians, we may here gather up the evidence of the authenticity of the narrative of the creation, flood, etc., down to this date of time. Besides all the others who lived in these times, we have in direct line three credible witnesses, which number is sufficient in all cases to establish a point beyond successful cavil. These three are Adam, Methuselah, and Shem; reliable witnesses, who bring the tradition of the creation down to the time of Abraham, or 2160 A. M., or 1844 B. C., establishing the credibility of the Mosaic Scriptures.

Abraham.—It was the purpose of the Lord that *all men* should be godly, and serve him as faithful children.

But the experiment, thus far, proves that but a small portion of the race were disposed so to do; hence the Lord makes known his purpose to show *special* favor to such as *will* fear and obey him.

Abram, the ninth from Shem, receives a special call to become the "father of the faithful;" *i. e.*, to be the first of those who would heed and obey the requirements of the Lord, in distinction from those who were bent on disobedience. In order to make this distinction the more apparent, the Lord required Abram to leave his relations in Ur, and go and dwell in the land of Canaan, which he and his posterity were to have as theirs. The particular occasion of his leaving his friends was their idolatry, which was directly opposed to the worship of the true God.

On his departure from his friends, Abram took with him his half-sister, Sarai, for his wife, and also his nephew, Lot, as partner in business.

At the first stopping-place in Canaan, Abram built an altar to the Lord, who appeared to him. From this he removed to a spot between Bethel and Hai, and there built another altar unto the Lord, "and there called upon the name of the Lord;" or "preached concerning the name of the Lord." This, then, became a Missionary Station, and Abram, like Noah, was "a preacher of righteousness," or a Patriarchal Missionary. His mission must have been very impressive, when the popular taste was for conquest and spoils, for a man with his retinue to seek to establish the fear of God, and do good to his fellow-countrymen.

But a trial of Abram's *faith* awaited him. The Lord brought a famine on the land, and Abram was obliged to remove to Egypt. Fearing that his sojourn there, with his beautiful wife, might endanger his life, he had recourse to a device of reporting her as his sister, which she was, half-sister, and said nothing about her as his wife. Thus he set out, with faith in a device, and not in the Lord.

Sarai's beauty captivated Pharaoh, as Abram anticipated; but the Lord troubled Pharaoh, until he was led to make inquiry about the matter, when he found she was Abram's *wife*, and immediately restored her, and reproved Abram for not telling him at first how the case stood. The device failing, Abram was led to see that God was his protector, after all.

After a stay of about two years in Egypt, Abram returned to Canaan, 2086 A. M., and 1918 B. C. Abram returned to the spot where he built the second altar, and there called upon the name of the Lord.

The course pursued by Abram, in the dissolution of partnership between him and Lot, exhibits the spirit of Abram as a man of peace. It appears they had each their own servants and cattle all the time, but enjoyed common pasturage, and kept together for mutual protection, assistance, and pleasure.

From some cause, the herdsmen had a "falling out." Abram at once beseeches Lot to discourage all strife between the herdsmen; and then proposes to Lot to take the first choice of all the country before them, and he would take what was left. "If you go to the right, I will go to the left; and if you go to the left, I will go to the right." Lot chose the plain of Jordan, and Abram dwelt in Canaan.

Not long after this, the kings around made war with the kings of the plain; and, among the others, Lot and his family, and possessions, were carried off captive. Abram, with his "trained servants," went in pursuit, recovered Lot and his effects, and brought them back to Sodom. It was on his return from this expedition that "Melchizedek met Abram, and blessed him." Abram's disinterestedness is seen here, inasmuch as he would not retain any of the spoils of conquest, thus discarding the idea that the "father of the faithful" sought to enrich himself by plunder.

The Lord next proceeds to give Abram a prophetic view of the affliction and deliverance of his posterity, which he will overrule for their good. The Lord reäffirms his promise, that of Abram he will make a great people, and as tokens of this, changed the patriarch's name from Abram (*a high father*) to Abraham (*father of a multitude*); and gave him the rite of circumcision, to be observed by him and his posterity. For the same reason was the name of Sarai (my *princess*) changed to Sarah (a *princess of multitudes*).

The Lord further confirms his purpose to carry out his promise, by giving Abraham and Sarah a son, as the beginning of their numerous seed, though he was about a hundred years old, and his wife about ninety. This last extraordinary purpose of the Lord, to fulfil his covenant, was accomplished in the birth of Isaac.

About this time, Abraham interceded the Lord for wicked Sodom. The Lord heard his prayer, and declared he would not destroy the righteous with the wicked; and should there be found fifty in the city, for their sakes he would spare it. But this number not being found, it was reduced to ten, and for their sakes the city should be spared. When not ten righteous were to be found, the city perished. So, to this day, the mark of God's displeasure against a wicked people can be seen in that abiding monument, the "*Dead* Sea."

But a still more severe trial than any before, now awaited the "father of the faithful." In the face of all that the Lord had done to inspire Abraham with the belief that he would make a great nation of him, especially the encouragement that all should come to pass through "the son of his old age," the patriarch is commanded to take that son of promise, and go to Mount Moriah, and offer him up to the Lord as a "*burnt* offering."

Hitherto, the Lord had not laid any grievous burden upon Abraham, but had raised his hopes, and increased his substance, well-nigh to surfeiting. But it is beautifully plain that Abraham did not follow the Lord simply for the goods; for, instead of shrinking from this trying duty, as a faithless man would have done, he at once entered upon the execution of the awful, but divine, command. As soon, however, as Abraham had gone so far in the matter as to satisfy himself, and the world after him, that he was in earnest, and meant to obey, the Lord sent his angel to tell him "It is enough; thy faith is proved; lay not thy hand upon the child."

Hence the just appellation given to Abraham, "the father of the faithful." The crowning act of Abraham's life being now past, he went down to his grave in peace, leaving his example of faith in God's promises to inspire his family to be steadfast unto the end. He died 2182 A. M., or 1822 B. C., aged one hundred and seventy-five years.

Isaac.—According to the custom of the times, Abraham procured a wife for his son, and thus saw his posterity in the right way before his death.

Rebekah, Isaac's cousin, became his wife.

Lot, Isaac, and Rebekah were cousins. It is said of Isaac, that he went out into the field to pray (a fruit of his piety), and while there, his attention was arrested by the coming of the servants with Rebekah. Isaac's marriage occurred at the age of forty years. He, like Abraham, was a man of peace. A strife arose with a party of roving herdsmen, about the right to a well, which Isaac's herdsmen had just dug, when the strife was ended by the latter giving up the well, removing, and digging another. Here they met another tribe of marauders, and this strife ceased, also, by yielding the well, and removing to a third place and digging a third well, which they enjoyed in peace. When those herdsmen remained, he departed.

After these trials, which Isaac bore so patiently, the Lord appeared to him, and confirmed the promises made to Abraham. Whereupon Isaac "builded an altar, and called upon the name of the Lord." Abimelech, also, king of Gerar, and some of his officers, seeing the peaceful conduct of the patriarch, came to him and desired to exchange vows of peace, which was done.

The promise of offspring was abundantly fulfilled to Isaac, by Rebekah's giving birth to a pair of twin sons, Esau and Jacob. On them the hopes of the world rested, and through them the promises to Abraham were to be realized.

But Isaac's time drew near to die; and as the blessing of the patriarch on his successor was of the greatest importance, he prepared to confer the gracious benediction. Isaac's sight having failed him, he found, after the ceremony was over, that he had bestowed his last blessing upon Jacob the younger, instead of Esau the first-born, to whom the blessing belonged, by his birthright. But on finding that the birthright had been transferred to Jacob, he *confirmed* the blessing upon him, as the two belonged together.

Isaac then called Jacob, and charged him not to take a wife of the Canaanites, but of his mother's house, and then gave him his final blessing in the name of the Lord, and confirmed upon him all the promises made to Abraham and his seed forever, to which Isaac had previously succeeded. From this time to Isaac's death, a period of about forty years, nothing is recorded of him, during which time he was without the use of his eyes.

Abraham and Isaac both made the homestead at Hebron, where the latter died. This event took place in 2288 A. M., and 1716 B. C.; aged 180. He was buried by his sons, Esau and Jacob.

Jacob. — Esau and Jacob were the first pair of twins we read of. Eve gave birth to the first man, Rebekah to the first *pair* of men. Little is said of these brothers until the selling of the birthright by Esau to Jacob.

The privileges of birthright are said to have been: 1. Of succession to the government of the family or kingdom. 2. A double portion of the parental estate. 3. The peculiar benediction of the patriarch. 4. The office of the priesthood. But it more probably included the promises and blessings made to Abraham in reference both to Canaan and the Messiah, who was to descend from the line of the first-born. Jacob esteemed the birthright, but Esau thought light of it.

Esau, being a hunter, returned from the field one day, with poor success, hungry and weary, just as Jacob had made ready a boiled dish; when Esau begged his brother to give him some refreshment. Jacob, it seems, was on the watch for a good chance to buy his brother out of the birthright; and so took this opportunity, when his brother was intent upon gratifying his hunger, to make the desired purchase, and was successful.

Some time after this, Isaac, thinking he might die suddenly, told Esau to go get venison and prepare him a choice dish thereof, and he would bless his first-born before himself should die. Jacob, seeing that the *deed* to the birthright he had purchased was about to pass to Esau, informed his mother of his alarms, and she aided him in planning and executing a device by which Jacob obtained the blessing also.

Some have taken exception to this underhanded act of Jacob. It may not all be just right; but the fact of Jacob being under the advice of his mother, and being his mother's favorite, while Esau was his father's, places them all about on the same level, whatever that level may be. But Jacob's act of intercepting his brother to get the blessing, was not so great an error as Esau's attempt to get it after he had sold the birthright to which it belonged.

Esau now seeing that all the blessings promised Abraham were confirmed to Jacob, began to realize the value of the trade now closed in favor of his brother.

It being too late to regain his loss, he resolved to do as Cain did when he was rejected, — slay his brother.

To avoid such a collision in the family, Rebekah hurried Jacob off to tarry with her brother Laban, until Esau's wrath had spent itself, when she would send for him to return again.

Before Jacob's departure, Isaac called him, and reblessed, or confirmed the blessings, promised to Abraham and his seed, upon Jacob and his seed. He also charged him not to take a wife of the Canaanites, but to marry into his mother's family.

Being weary in his journey, Jacob laid down upon the ground, to rest for the night, with stones for his pillow. While he slept, he had a dream, in which he saw a ladder reaching from earth to heaven, and angels going up and down the ladder. At the top of it the Lord appeared, and declared himself to be the God of Abraham and of Isaac, and confirmed the blessing of Jacob's father, saying: "To thee and thy seed will I give this land whereon thou liest." When he awoke, he felt that the place was the very gate of heaven.

Jacob then took the stones he slept upon, made a pillar, and poured oil upon it, and called the place Bethel. He also vowed to the Lord, that if he would prosper him, and permit him to return to his father's house in *peace*, one-tenth of all his fortune should be the Lord's.

As he pursued his journey, he came to a well, and while inquiring of some shepherds for his uncle Laban, behold Rachel, his uncle's daughter, came up with his flock to water. Jacob rolled the stone from the well's mouth, and assisted her to water the flock. He met with a very cordial reception from his uncle and family, as soon as they found he was Rebekah's son.

Jacob's uncle, not wishing to have his services for nothing, immediately proposed to employ his nephew, and asked him his terms. As his father and mother sent him to get a wife, and the custom was to serve a term for a wife, the way was all open now, and he offers to work seven years for Rachel. Laban accepted the offer and said, "Abide with me."

When the seven years were out, Jacob demanded his wife. (He was now over eighty years of age.) Esau had by his own acts, and his brother's, and Isaac's blindness, been disinherited of his birthright; but Laban took good care that his elder daughter, Leah, though not a beauty, should be cared for in her birthright. So, by a device of which Jacob was ignorant, he found in the morning that the "wheel of fortune" had been turned by another *birthright*, and he had *Leah* for a wife, instead of *Rachel.*

As soon as Jacob found out the deception, he complained to Laban, who told him the custom of the land was, never to give the younger before the first-born.

Thus Jacob had a taste of the experience of his brother Esau, who had to bear a similar disappointment in the loss of the blessing, and, because of the law of the land, had to bear his grief as best he could. Jacob could now sympathize with him.

The matter was all got over by a compromise. Laban gave him also Rachel; and in *advance* of the seven years, he was to serve for her also. At the end of this term of service, Jacob began to see the "promises advancing," in a large family born him in fourteen years, among whom was Joseph, son of Rachel.

Jacob now proposes to return to his father's house, asking only his wives and children.

Laban, knowing that Jacob's services had been of benefit to him, proposes now to pay wages for the rest of the time he would stay and left it to his son-in-law to state his terms. These were, that Jacob was to sustain all the losses among the cattle, and have for his share all the spotted cattle, and give his uncle all the red cattle. To this Laban agreed.

Jacob now got the birthright into his hands again, and knew how to use it so as to cause by far the greater number of cattle to be born spotted. By this means, in a very short time, Jacob's share was much larger than his uncle's.

Laban's sons, seeing the turn of affairs, began to murmur. They first insinuated that all Jacob had, he got by using their father's capital; and second, that he had metamorphosed most of that into his own possession, by carrying out, in *spirit* and *letter*, the peculiar contract made with their father.

Laban, seeing the prosperity of his nephew, and hearing the clamor of his sons, and possibly remembering his treatment to Jacob, and the advantage given in the bargain he had made with him, had occasion, as he really did, to become surly.

Jacob observed this change in his uncle's manner towards him, mentioned it to his wives; interpreted his prosperity as God's favor towards him; referred to their father's attempt to take advantage of him at times; and proposed to them that they had better take what they had, and remove to Canaan, — the Lord having warned him so to do.

Jacob's departure was not known, however, to Laban until the third day after. Laban immediately took a company and pursued Jacob, and overtook him at Mount Gilead; but the Lord warned Laban in a dream the night before not to treat Jacob with abuse.

Laban's first accusation was, that Jacob had gone off and not let him know it, that he might have had a feast, and sent them off in good style.

Laban felt that his son-in-law leaving as he did, would look as though he had not treated him well; and, as that was the fact, it would have been a delightful opportunity for him to have made a great spread at Jacob's leaving. By so doing, he could have removed, in a great measure, from the mind of his neighbors, the reports that got out about his misusing his nephew. Jacob being in good business, leaving all at once, and taking only what belonged to him, cast a severe, but just reflection upon his uncle, which the old man felt keenly.

He charges Jacob with taking a foolish course, and says: "I have *power* to injure you, but feared the warning he had of the Lord." Laban then charges his daughters with having stolen his gods.

If those articles had been really objects of worship, Laban could have purchased more if he had not been too covetous; again, if they were, it shows Laban to be an idolater, and hence poor company for Jacob and his family. But if they were only some pictures that had been in the family a good while, and which the daughters had probably had promise of, and when about to leave, could get them in no way but the way they did, and having never received any dowry of their father, and no prospect of any, they took what had been promised them, and left. To treat Jacob as Laban did in getting married, give them nothing but wages, and then pursue them and charge them with theft, was not very fatherly.

After having made search for his trinkets among Jacob's "stuff," and not finding them, Jacob then rehearsed to his uncle what had been done since he went into his family to live. He showed Laban that he had been of service to him, and but for this course, I should have been sent away of you, empty. And as proof of all this, and that I am right, "God rebuked thee yester-night."

Laban finally yielded, and for once treated Jacob as an equal, and proposed to make up and part friends. Accordingly, they erected a heap of stones, and called it Galeed (*the heap of witness*), and Mizpah (*a watch-tower*), that they had become reconciled, and would ever keep their vows to each other. Jacob then offered sacrifice upon the mount, and treated his friends with bread, and encamped for the night. Early in the morning Laban arose, kissed his sons and daughters, and blessed them, and returned to his home.

As Jacob went on his journey, the angels of the Lord met him, and he said, "This is the Lord's host."

The next old grudge Jacob had to prepare to meet, was the one held against him by his brother Esau. The last understanding was, Esau sought his life. Jacob, being on his return to his father's house, must now encounter the old affair about the birthright.

Jacob sent messengers to Esau to inform him of his wealth, of his coming, and of his desire for peace. The messengers returned and told Jacob that Esau was coming to meet him with four hundred men. Jacob, not knowing whether Esau meant war or not, divided his company into two parts, intending to send one on first, and if Esau smote that, for the rest to flee.

Jacob then prayed the Lord to deliver him from the wrath of his brother; claiming the protection the Lord promised him when he called him to return to Canaan; and also that his seed should be great in the earth.

When Jacob went away from his father's, he made a vow to the Lord if he prospered him, one-tenth of all he possessed should be the Lord's. As a fulfilment of this vow, Jacob sends on to Esau 580 cattle, as a present to his brother.

Jacob well knew that all he had came by the birthright, and to use this large share of it to appease the wrath kindled by his having the birthright, was directly included in his previous vow. Thus he vowed, and paid the vow.

Jacob then ordered the rest of the company to advance, following after the present, which was to lead the march, and be offered to Esau, on meeting him, as a present from his brother, who was behind; and if his present was accepted, he would also see him. In the evening of the day of preparation, Jacob took his family across the brook Jabbok, and then returned, and wrestled until break of day with the angel of the Lord, and would not let him go until he blessed him. He prevailed; and for this his name was called Israel (a prince of God). By this he was also taught that he should prevail with Esau.

Jacob's attention was then called to look, and Esau was coming, sure, with his four hundred men. As he drew near, Jacob bowed himself to the ground, when Esau ran and met him, and embraced him, and kissed him, and they wept. And then came the wives and children, and they bowed also.

Esau then inquired what that drove he met was for, and Jacob told him to gain his favor. Esau refused to take it; but, after much importunity, he accepted it. Esau returned to Sier, and Jacob settled in Succoth.

Soon after, Jacob revisited Bethel, where the Lord met him, when he went to Padan-aram, set up the pillar again, and had a pleasant review of all the Lord had done for him in his absence. From this he journeyed on to go to revisit his father; got as far as Ephrath, when Benjamin was born, and Rachel died at the same time.

Jacob now settles in Canaan with his large family. His trials henceforth arise out of his *own* family; the greatest of which was connected with Joseph.

Out of Jacob's family one must be selected to be the successor of Abraham. Joseph is indicated as the one for this great distinction. Envy showed itself immediately, as in the case of Cain, and Esau, when they saw the promotion of their brothers.

The special mark of favor Jacob bestowed upon Joseph, was the "coat of many colors." This, and the intimations of the Lord of his future greatness, being misunderstood by his brethren, they formed a conspiracy against his life.

This they carried out so far as to make their father think, verily, that Joseph was dead. But Jacob afterwards found that, like himself, his son went out from his father's house *for a purpose.*

Jacob lived through many trials to see his son Joseph alive, and the *promises* fulfilling in him.

But the patriarchal blessing was the great platform for foreshadowing the destiny of families. Jacob prepared to administer this last rite before he died.

The predictions and fulfilment of this remarkable charge, as now Jacob called his sons together and delivered to them, stand before the world in such a striking light, that no caviller can doubt that Jacob spoke under the guidance of greater than human wisdom.

His course was different from Abraham's or Isaac's in this; the blessings of the church were confirmed in a *tribe*, instead of a *family*, and a son of that family, as in Jacob's case and Isaac's. Each of Jacob's sons was to be a father of a *tribe*, and all together to be a great nation; but the tribe of *Judah* was to have the distinguished honor of giving birth to the Messiah. "The sceptre shall not depart from Judah, nor a law-giver from between his feet, until Shiloh come, and unto him shall the gathering of the people be."

Jacob, having finished his work, had only to make request about his burial. Being in Egypt now, he makes special request to be buried "with his fathers, in the land of Canaan, in the cave in the field of Machpelah, which Abraham bought with the field, of Ephron the Hittite, for a possession of a burying-place. "There they buried Abraham, and Sarah his wife; there they buried Isaac and Rebekah; and there I buried Leah." And Jacob "yielded up the ghost, and was gathered unto his people." This event occurred in 2315 A. M., and 1689 B. C., Æ. 147.

After the days of embalming and mourning were over, Joseph and his brethren, and Pharaoh and the elders of his house, and all the elders of the land of Egypt, went up to the land of Canaan, and buried Jacob in the Cave of Machpelah, as he had requested. A very imposing funeral. Thus the days and trials of Jacob were ended.

JOSEPH. — Joseph was the first-born of Rachel, Jacob's first and most loved wife. Benjamin, his younger and only brother by Rachel, was not born until after Jacob returned to Canaan from Padan-aram.

The sons of Jacob were, like himself, early set to tending flocks and herds; the older ones had the care, while the younger sons were about, learning the duties and habits of a shepherd's life. The younger ones were also sent to and from the field, as occasion might require. In this latter service Joseph was employed.

Joseph was about seventeen years old when his brethren began to hate him. The occasions for disliking him were several. They found that as he went home from the field, their father was told of some things they had rather he would not know, and Joseph was the medium of the information. This was one charge.

Another was the partiality shown him by his father; specially, in the "coat of many colors." Besides these, Joseph dreamed a dream, that he and his brethren were in the field binding sheaves, and his sheaf stood up. Presently all their sheaves stood up and bowed to his sheaf. Again he dreamed that the sun, moon, and eleven stars bowed to him. This he told to his father and brothers. The brothers took these things as intimations of his exaltation over the rest of the family, and, all things together, they *envied* him; but his father observed and pondered them.

On a time after, as the other sons were out with the flocks, Jacob wished to hear of their welfare, and proposed to Joseph to "go and see whether it be well with thy brethren and the flocks, and bring me word."

But neither he nor his father "dreamed" to what this journey would grow. After coming to Shechem, he was told that his brethren had gone with their flocks to Dothan.

As they saw him coming, they say, "Here comes this dreamer;" and at first proposed to kill him, and see what would become of his dreams. But one of them shrunk from this, and proposed to put him into a pit or dry well, and let him perish there.

They then very deliberately sat down to eat, and probably of some provision, and even dainties, which Joseph had brought them, fresh from home. Joseph was sent to see if any evil hand had been laid on them, and they turn on him with that same evil hand. How hearty Joseph's errand after their welfare, until he finds them! but how base their treachery and cruelty!

But presently there came along a company of Ishmaelites, and they concluded to sell Joseph to them, and so send him far away into Egypt, whence they should hear no more of his dreams. This they did, and now they fancied themselves at rest.

But one thing more remained to be done, and that was to get up a report to send to their father. The plan hit upon was to take that famous "coat of colors" and tear it as beasts of prey would, dip it in the blood of a kid, and send it to Jacob. The next difficulty to be met was, what kind of a story to tell the old gentleman. This was met by telling him, "This we *found;* is it thy son's coat?" And Jacob knew the coat, but not the *beasts* that tore it.

"Surely," said he, in great grief, "an evil beast hath devoured him; Joseph is rent in pieces."

And Jacob mourned for his son many days.

It must have been an exceedingly hard task for Joseph's brethren to have kept up an appearance of innocence, when their father was in such grief for him, and when reference was made, from time to time, of Joseph's death by the wild beasts. But the time drew on, when a revelation of the secret of Joseph's disappearance, and of their perfidy and unfaithfulness to their father and brother, would be made. The last favor done them by Joseph was when he fed them, and the next will be, to *feed* them. Their last cruelty to him was to sell him, their last shift was to submit themselves to *him* in their shame.

Joseph was taken to Egypt, and sold to a captain of Pharaoh's guard. He was too goodly a person to go as a common slave; and from this better place, soon rose to a higher, by the excellence of his character, until his master made him overseer of his entire business.

In this elevated position, his master's wife cast wanton eyes upon him; but Joseph resisted her solicitations, until she took hold upon him, and seeking to clear himself from her, a part of his coat was torn off, and he fled and left it with her. Then, to hide her own guilt in the affair, told her husband that this young Hebrew attempted to insult her, and in defending herself, tore his coat, and he fled. This changed his master's good opinion of him, and believing his wife, cast Joseph into prison.

Poor Joseph was lied out of his life, in his father's opinion; and now by this wanton woman lied out of his character, in his master's opinion. But with such a character as his, he must rise yet. For no sooner is he in prison, than the jailor discovers an unusual spirit in this new prisoner, until he put all *his* business into the prisoner's care. Thus Joseph rises yet.

But the king became wroth with his chief butler, and he was cast into prison. The butler having a dream, of which he knew not the interpretation, was in trouble because no one could interpret it to him. Joseph says: "Do not interpretations belong to God? Tell me it, I pray thee."

He at once told the butler that he would soon be released from prison, and restored to his office before Pharaoh. Soon, indeed, the order for his release came; and as he was about leaving the prison, Joseph simply requests of the butler to "remember me when it is well with thee, and bring me out of this house."

In two years' time after this, Pharaoh had a dream which troubled him, and for which no interpreter could be found among all the magicians of the land. In this dilemma, the butler thought of Joseph, and recommended him to the notice of Pharaoh. Joseph is called. He interprets the dreams as having reference to seven years of unusual plenty, to be followed by seven years of famine.

Pharaoh saw, and was led to acknowledge that such interpretations must come from God, and that the Spirit of God dwelt in Joseph. Pharaoh immediately exalts Joseph to the highest dignity in the kingdom, excepting himself, and that only in the throne. To confirm this in the minds of the people, Pharaoh took off his own ring, or seal, and put it on Joseph's hand; arrayed him in royal apparel; a gold chain on his neck; caused him to ride in the *second* chariot, and made him ruler over all Egypt. In addition to these favors, Pharaoh gave him Asenath, daughter of the Prince of On, to be his wife.

The boy of the coat of many colors is now raised to all the greatness his dreams foreshadowed, and far more. With all the lies heaped upon him by his brethren, and Potiphar's wife, he is exalted higher than being waiter for his brethren, or servant to a captain of the king's guard.

Joseph entered immediately upon the work of storing up the surplus corn of seven years, to supply against the famine that was at hand.

It was this famine which was felt in Canaan that brought Joseph's brethren into Egypt to buy corn, to preserve the family alive.

He knew them when they first came, but they knew not him. As they came to him, they bowed down to him as the governor of Egypt, little thinking that they were fulfilling the dream of the sheaves.

What must have been Joseph's emotions to behold these wicked brothers, whom he never expected to see, driven to him to buy bread, and put so completely in his power, whom they tore from the family circle, and sold into hopeless servitude?

Instead of making himself known to them, he sternly charged them with being spies. This they denied; stating that they were brothers, and had yet one more at home, the youngest, and "*one is not.*" To make them prove themselves not spies, Joseph compels them to leave one of their number in prison, until the others go and carry corn home, and bring their youngest brother.

When this severe measure was agreed to, they began at once to reflect that all this came upon them because of their ill treatment to their brother, who "*was not.*"

They returned, and brought the heavy intelligence to Jacob that the governor of Egypt had demanded their youngest brother to be brought, as proof that they were *true* men. This was a sore demand on the father, who at once said, "*One is dead*, and if this be taken, I must die in sorrow." But go he must, or they could get no more corn. The desperate alternative lay before them. Jacob yielded. He, however, ordered presents to be made, to appease his anger.

When they returned, on approaching Joseph with the presents, they again *bowed* themselves. Joseph then asks if their father, the old man, is yet alive and well. They say yea, and "*bowed their heads.*" He then asks, "Is this your youngest brother?" and said,

"God bless you, my son," and turned away and entered his chamber, and wept there.

Joseph then ordered a meal prepared; and, as a mark of special regard, served out to Benjamin five times as much as any of the rest. He then caused their sacks to be filled, and his silver cup put into Benjamin's sack, and so sent them away home.

But soon an officer overtook them, and charged them with stealing the governor's cup. Surprised at such a charge, they at once declare that if it be so, "he on whom the cup is found shall die, and we will be your servants." The camels were unloaded, search was made, and the cup found in Benjamin's sack. They then reloaded their corn, and returned to the city.

As they came to Joseph, they all *fell before him on the ground.* Joseph asked them what they had done now, and gave them to understand that he could certainly divine. They were in great distress at this affair, and proposed all to remain Joseph's servants. But he would accept of none but the youngest brother, and him he *would* keep.

This threw them into the greatest distress, as it would be such a terrible grief to their father.

They had more regard for their father's feelings now, than when they sold Joseph; and more for Benjamin than for the boy of the dreams.

Judah offers to stay himself, a bondman, if Benjamin can be released; "for how can I behold the evil that will come upon my father, if Benjamin go not up unto him?"

Joseph could carry the matter no further. He caused all to leave the room but his brethren, when he said: "*I am Joseph, your brother, whom ye sold into Egypt*," and wept aloud; and all the Egyptians and the house of Pharaoh heard.

Their consternation was very great at this revelation of their wickedness; but Joseph turns it all into a providence; he does not charge them with the wickedness of selling him, but says, "God sent me here."

This was true; but his brethren could not get rid of the stinging recollection of the *wicked* part they took in this marvellous providence.

Joseph immediately sends for his father and all the family to come down into Egypt, and sojourn. This, and the news of Joseph's life and prosperity, caused the spirit of Jacob to revive, and he says: "Joseph, my son, is yet alive, and I will go and see him before I die."

With what shame must they have been filled, when they told

Jacob that his son was yet alive, to reflect how they had kept this concealed from him all this time! And with what ill grace must they have appeared in the eyes of their father for such perfidy!

Jacob gathered up all his effects and family, and started, and was directed to the land of Goshen, as the part of the country he was to occupy. When Joseph knew of his coming, he prepared his chariot to go and meet Israel. This was a melting time for the old patriarch, to behold his beloved Joseph, safe, and exalted to be Egypt's governor. And Joseph fell on his father's neck, and wept a long time.

Joseph then informed Pharaoh of the coming of his father's house to sojourn in Egypt. He then gave his father an introduction to the king, and told his brethren when Pharaoh should call them and inquire of their occupation, to tell then their business was about *cattle;* for *shepherds* were hated by the Egyptians.

The occasion of this antipathy to shepherds was owing to the oppression of the "shepherd kings" that conquered and tyrannized over them about 250 years, and not a very long time previous to Israel's going into Egypt to dwell.

For Joseph's sake, Pharaoh told him to let his father and family dwell in Goshen, the best part of Egypt.

Here, then, Joseph's dreams are fulfilled. While the Egyptians are forced to sell all that they have, and even their services, to escape from starvation, Jacob and his family are kept in comfortable circumstances, through the mere clemency of Joseph, whose life his brethren had wantonly put in the greatest peril. To this dreamer the eleven sheaves, sun, moon, and eleven stars, had to bow, bow, bow! God's hand was in it for good, but theirs for evil.

Israel's time drew near to die; whereupon he had a private interview with Joseph, preparatory to his last remove. He obtained a promise from Joseph that he would bury him in Canaan, and not in Egypt, in the old patriarchal cave in Machpelah. At another interview he rehearsed the promises of the land of Canaan to his seed, and that they should increase to be a great nation; and then constitutes Joseph's two sons heirs to these promises with his own family, and were after reckoned as Jacob's sons. He then kissed them, embraced them, and blessed them.

In Israel's last blessing on all his sons, he foretells their career, and all that was predicted of Joseph was realized in Ephraim and Manasseh.

Upon the death of Israel, Joseph prepared, after the days of mourning and embalming were over, to bury his father, with all the distinguished honor due to so eminent a servant of the Lord. With his own brethren, and the retinue of the court of Pharaoh, the remains of Jacob were borne to the land of promise, and deposited in the cave of Machpelah, along with Abraham and Isaac.

Thus the faithful and beloved Joseph did to the last, and all that a loving son could do, to cherish and honor the memory of his revered father.

After they had returned from the funeral of Israel, a messenger came to Joseph one day, with an errand from his father: "Thy father commanded us to say unto thee, forgive us, thy brethren, our trespass against thee, and our sin, for we did evil unto thee." This confession, made at the direction of Joseph's father, brought the governor of Egypt to tears again; he wept while they spake to him. Seeing Joseph melted, they fell down before him, saying, "We be thy servants." The eleven stars made obeisance surely.

But Joseph spoke kindly and forgivingly to them, making no charge against them, and giving them no credit for the favorable issue of their plot against him. "It is not ye, but God, brought me to this place to save much people alive."

But Joseph's time to die drew on, and he, like his predecessors, tells his posterity what is for them in the future. "God," he says, "will surely visit you, and bring you out of this land, unto the land which he sware unto Abraham, and to Isaac, and to Jacob."

Having confirmed on them the promises of God, he took a pledge also of the children of Israel that they would also carry up his bones to the land of promise, when they should be delivered and taken thence. And Joseph was gathered with his fathers, the last of the patriarchs, who walked by, and died in, the faith. His death occurred in 2369, A. M., and 1635, B. C.; aged 110 years.

His body was then embalmed, and put in a coffin, — not buried, but kept in readiness for the departure Joseph predicted would arrive. Also, being put in a coffin was then a mark of great distinction. Truly the end of the righteous man is peace.

Job. — Although Job does not appear in the regular trail of events, still the prominent notice he receives in the Bible warrants us in giving him a location and whereabouts, in the time he is supposed to have lived. Although no positive proof can be adduced of the precise time Job flourished, yet it is thought that he lived before the Exodus of Moses; and from the name of Eliphaz the Temanite appearing in the book of Job, and also in the genealogy of Esau, it is concluded that it was also before Moses. Again, being contemporary with Eliphaz, a descendant of Esau, he must have lived between the death of Jacob and the birth of Moses.

Relying upon the authenticity of the Book of Job, we have a beautiful example and confirmation of the faith of the patriarchal times. The belief here of an arch-adversary of all righteousness (the devil) seeking whom he may devour, is as plain as that there was such a man as Job.

His temptation, endurance, and justification, show us well how the grace of God is sufficient for the day of such as trust in him. So Job died, full of faith and full of days, being, as is supposed, 240 years old.

INTERREGNUM. — After the death of Joseph, it would seem that the cause of God must have become extinct. But the seed sown by the patriarchs was then germinating, and preparing to bring forth a hundred-fold.

After the generation of the patriarchs passed away, there arose another king, who knew not Joseph, and so had no faith or interest in the welfare of God's cause.

The first notice he takes of the Israelites is their rapid increase. Although this was one of God's special promises to them, yet he neither knew it nor cared for it.

Fearing that the Hebrews might become numerous, and, perhaps, powerful and dangerous to the safety of the throne, the new king institutes oppressive measures to retard their increase, and break their courage. These measures were to be carried out by putting task-masters over them, to compel them to extraordinary tasks, and so weary them; while the midwives were instructed to select all the male children as soon as born, and kill them.

Little did he think, in this last measure, that he was deliberately fighting against God. Little did he suspect, either, that when he ordered the males destroyed, that the Hebrew women were able to break his power. They had no fear of the king, and even took more pains to save the male children; and God set his approbation upon their course. This course pursued by the midwives, was *the* measure which resulted in the bringing out of the Hebrews from Egypt, as Joseph had said.

II.

AGE OF WAR FOR POWER.

FROM THE DEATH OF JOSEPH TO CHRIST.

SACRED HISTORY.

PERIOD I. FROM THE DEATH OF JOSEPH TO THE DEATH OF JOSHUA: OR 2365 A. M. TO 1639 B. C., TO 2561 A. M. TO 1443 B. C.

MOSES. — During the rigor of the Egyptian infanticide, Moses was born; 2433 A. M., and 1571 B. C. He was born of the tribe of Levi, and being "a goodly child," he was soon put out of reach of the wicked law of Pharaoh. Although hid in the flags of the river, yet precaution was taken to have his sister remain in sight, and watch the fate of the child.

While watching, along came Thermuthes, the king's daughter, with her maidens, to bathe. As the sister of Moses saw them nearing the place where the little ark lay, and fearing that the child would be reported to Pharaoh and slain, ventured to draw near as soon as the ark was opened. Thermuthes at once declared it to be a Hebrew child, when Moses' sister offered to go and get a Hebrew woman to take the child, and nurse it for her. This was agreed to, and Moses' mother was called, and the princess gave orders to her to nurse the child, and she would pay wages for the same. The princess named the boy *Moses*, because she drew him out of the water.

Although Moses was brought up in the court of Pharaoh, yet he learned other wisdom than that of the Egyptians. When about forty years of age, he knew his people and their burdens, and seeing an Egyptian smiting a Hebrew one day, he interfered, and slew him.

The slaying of the Egyptian offended the king, and he sought to slay Moses, who fled to the land of Midian.

While sitting by a well, the daughters of the prince of Midian came to the well with their flocks, *and after* having drawn the water for them to drink, a party of lazy fellows interfered and drove them off, so as to let their own flocks drink.

Moses, not being in the habit of letting such injustice go unrebuked, and being a gentleman in its true sense, interfered in behalf of the shepherdesses, restored their rights to them, and assisted them in drawing the rest of the water for their flocks. Returning home earlier than usual, their father inquired into the cause, and they told him: "An Egyptian delivered us out of the hands of the shepherds, and helped us draw water for the flocks." He reproved them for not inviting him home, and sent them to call him, and let him eat bread.

A contract was at once made between their father and Moses, and he began tending sheep; and, as a token of favor and good-will, gave Moses Zipporah his daughter for his wife.

During this sojourn, the King of Egypt died; and the children of Israel sighed, for their bondage and burdens were heavy; and God heard their cry. And, for the covenant which he had made with their fathers, God had respect unto them, and in answer to their prayers and tears sent them a Deliverer.

One day, as Moses was tending Jethro's flock, near Mount Horeb (and Sinai), the Lord appeared to him behind a burning bush. Seeing the flame, and the bush not burned, Moses drew near, when a voice accosted him, saying, "I am the God of Abraham, the God of Isaac, and the God of Jacob;" and Moses hid his face, and was afraid.

The Lord then informed him that the cry of oppression had reached him from the children of Israel, and that his purpose was to deliver them; and that Moses was to be the agent for that great deliverance; and that, through this great movement, they should be brought into the land of Canaan, promised to Abraham and his seed.

Moses plead insufficiency for this task, when the Lord assured him of his presence and aid, and that he and they should worship in this same mount. Moses inquires, "Whom shall I tell the children of Israel hath sent me to them?" The Lord said, Tell them (יְהוָֹה) I Am, the God of their fathers, hath sent you. At the same time, Moses is told that the King of Egypt would refuse his request, and not let them go; but that he, by the judgments God would send upon him by the hand of Moses, would yield at last, and let them go.

To convince Moses of this call being from the Lord, he was commanded to cast the rod in his hand upon the ground, when it became a serpent. The Lord then told him to put forth his hand and take it by the tail, when it became a rod his in hand again; then to put his hand in his bosom; and when he drew it out, it was leprous; he put it back, and then drew it out, when it was whole again.

Moses then plead his slowness of speech, as being a hinderance in presenting his errand at the court of the king. But Aaron is mentioned as a substitute in this respect; so that he was to be mouth for Moses, and Moses be to Aaron as God, or instead of him.

Moses returns to Jethro, his father-in-law, and gets released from his shepherd's office, and liberty to take his wife and return to Egypt. On his way he meets Aaron, makes known the great commission they had jointly to execute, goes to Egypt and calls together the Elders of Israel, and showed them their errand and authority, which they readily believe, and receive Moses as their deliverer.

Next, Moses and Aaron waited upon Pharaoh, and asked the release of the children of Israel in the name of the Lord. Pharaoh, feignedly or really, knew not who the Lord was; refused their petition, and increased the burdens of the Hebrews by compelling them to make brick without straw, and so serve with increased rigor.

This unfavorable turn of things discouraged both the people and Moses and Aaron. But the Lord encouraged the latter, that by the miracles they should work, and the assistance he would render them, Pharaoh would be forced at last to let them go.

At this they took courage; and, through a long series of wonders and judgments, Pharaoh did at last conclude to let the people go. Preparatory to starting, the Hebrews asked the gift of a variety of jewels, which they obtained without difficulty.

As a final signal of departure, the Passover is instituted. The destroying angel was to go through Egypt that night, and slay all the first-born of the Egyptians; but all who would kill a lamb, and put some of the blood upon the door-posts, the angel would pass over, and not slay their first-born. At midnight, Pharaoh and his servants rose up and made a great cry for the dead among them, and called for Moses and Aaron, and urged them to depart with all possible haste, — even take all their flocks and herds, and be gone; and bless me also.

The greatness of that night's transaction made the Passover an ordinance of perpetual observance. The number that went out of Egypt, as descendants of Jacob, was 600,000 *men*, besides women and children — probably not far from 1,800,000! These, with their flocks and herds, made a vast procession, and a vast impression on the minds of the Egyptians.

They went out in order, five in a rank, and took their course towards the Red Sea. The bones of Joseph were taken along, as they promised him, to be buried in Canaan. In this march the Lord led them by a cloud by day, which became a pillar of fire by night.

The infatuated King of Egypt, however, could not retain the

lessons he had been taught, before the Hebrews left him; so he must harness up his chariots of war, and pursue them. The Lord, however, interfered, and put a cloud of darkness between them and the Hebrews, so that they came not nigh them.

But when the Israelites found the Egyptians were pursuing them, they were in great fear, and wished they had died in bondage, rather than go out into the wilderness to perish. But Moses commanded them to wait and see the salvation of God.

Moses then stretched his hand over the sea, and the Lord caused it to divide, and the waters to stand up on each side, so as to leave a path of dry land through the sea. Into this path the Israelites went, and so passed over to the other side, and thus escaped their enemies.

Pharaoh and his host, "trusting in their *chariots*," attempted the fearful pass. But when Moses got upon the other side, he raised his rod over the sea, and Pharaoh and his host were drowned in the midst.

For this remarkable deliverance the children of Israel sung, with great joy, the song of Moses — rehearsing the interposition of God in their behalf.

After this they took their journey into the wilderness, and, while they were beset with trials and privations on every hand, many began to murmur. But these complaints were in a measure silenced by the Lord sending manna for bread, and giving Moses power to furnish water out of the rock, and thus satisfy all their wants.

Not long after, Moses had to encounter Amalek, a king, in the way they were going. But, as long as Moses was able to hold up his rod, Israel prevailed over their enemies; and when Moses was weary of holding up his hand himself, he was aided by Aaron.

After this success against Amalek, Jethro, Moses' father-in-law, came to him in the wilderness, and brought him his wife and children, who had been at Jethro's during the exodus of the Hebrews from Egypt. Jethro, seeing that the labor of attending to all the civil and religious concerns of so great a people was too much for Moses, suggested a different plan, which was this: Moses was to be the head man, and all important questions were to be referred to him; but, to relieve him from all the little vexing quarrels that might arise, suitable men were to be appointed to act as judges, in sections of tens, fifties, hundreds, and thousands. An appeal could be made, in cases of doubt, from the judge of tens to the one of fifties, and so on to Moses, who sought wisdom of God. This plan was adopted, and is proved to be the best basis for the government of a commonwealth, ever yet devised.

Shortly after this, God gave Moses directions how to prepare the people for receiving the law.

The people were to remain at the foot of the mount (Sinai), and there wait Moses' return. He had been directed to prepare two tables of stone, and bring them up into the mount, and the Lord would write on them his law: this was the giving of the law, or the Ten Commandments. A variety of other directions were given, respecting social life, justice, worship, etc., which served as the laws of the Israelites during their journeyings and after their settlement in Canaan.

In order to keep the worship of God the more easily and constantly before the people, Moses is ordered to make a tabernacle for the purpose. This was to serve as a substitute for a permanent house of worship during the journeyings of the Israelites, and so was constructed on a plan convenient for frequent removals.

In shape, it was forty-five feet long, fifteen wide, and fifteen high. Its material was boards and pillars for the walls, its coverings and partition of finely-wrought curtains. It had two apartments; the first was the ordinary place of worship, while the second contained the "ark of the covenant," and over it was seen the visible glory of God's presence; this was the "holy of holies."

Around the tabernacle was an enclosure of pillars and curtains, eight feet high, one hundred and fifty feet long, and seventy-five wide. Within this enclosure the sacrifices and offerings were made.

When Moses directed the people to bring in their offerings for the tabernacle, such was their liberality, that he had to issue express orders to restrain them; they gave more than was needed.

As soon as Moses had finished the tabernacle, and all its utensils, and consecrated them, the heads of the different tribes made a donation, for the service of the sanctuary, of bullocks, rams, lambs, goats, gold, silver, flour, and oil, to the amount of $636,000.

The pillar of cloud rested upon the tabernacle, and when it stood still, the people stayed in their place; and when that moved, they understood it to be a sign from the Lord for them to follow.

The "ark of the covenant," was an oblong chest, made on purpose to hold the tables of the Law, and was kept with the Hebrews continually, and esteemed as very sacred. It formed, afterwards, a very important article in the sacred furniture of the temple. A great variety of other vessels were made, at great expense, to celebrate the various rites of their imposing worship — the styles and uses of which were communicated to Moses by the Lord.

Upon the tabernacle being set up, the Lord directs Moses to take Aaron and his sons, and consecrate them to the office of the priest-

9

hood. This being done, Aaron proceeded to make the appropriate offering, when the fire descended from heaven and consumed it upon the altar. When the people saw this, they fell upon their faces. In this consecration, the whole tribe of Levi was set apart perpetually to the office of the priesthood, to do the service of the sanctuary.

The Mosaic ritual is very complicated, and would require more space for insertion here than can be afforded, consistent with the design of this work. In the observance, however, of this form of worship, God often manifested his presence and approbation.

In consequence of the disobedience of the people, the Lord caused them to wander in the wilderness forty years, during which Moses was their lawgiver, leader, and mediator between the people and Jehovah. This important post Moses held during life, when he was succeeded by Joshua. As they drew near the Promised Land, Moses rehearsed, in his famous song, the wonders of their deliverance and journey.

Moses followed the example of the patriarchs, in closing up his labors with a programme of the duties of the people, and a prophetic vision of their history as the seed of promise. Thus, after giving the Israelites ample laws, a pure religion, a sure encouragement of possessing the Promised Land, appointed for them a competent successor of himself, and assured them that their prosperity and continuance as a chosen people depended wholly upon their faithfulness to the Lord, he blessed them, and prepared to die.

Through all these long, complicated, and wearisome duties of Moses' eventful life, his natural strength was not abated, nor did his eyesight become dim; yet his time had come to die. It pleased the Lord not to let Moses enter the land of Canaan; this was for some impatience in the midst of trials; but he was permitted to see that his great labors were owned of God, and that the people of Jacob would possess the Promised Land.

Moses now took leave of the children of Israel, all snugly encamped on the plains of Moab. The Lord called him up into Mount Nebo, to the peak Pisgah, and there showed him all the country in sight, to assure him this was the land promised to Abraham, Isaac, and Jacob, and to their seed. Then turning his eyes once more, and for the last time, saw the tents of Israel below, and then closed his eyes in the long sleep of death, aged one hundred and twenty years. This occurred in 2553 A. M., and 1451 B. C. The children of Israel mourned for him thirty days. The place of his grave was never known.

Moses was the first writer of the Scriptures, having written the first five books of the Bible (called the Books of Moses; also called "The Pentateuch)."

JOSHUA. — The entrance of Israel into Canaan not being completed at the death of Moses, Joshua succeeds him as the leader and deliverer of the people.

The first notice we have of Joshua is in the war with Amalek, where he was appointed to the chief command. In this conflict Joshua proved himself valiant and victorious.

As the Israelites drew near the Promised Land, the Lord directed Moses to send one of each tribe into the land of Canaan, as spies, to get a report of it and its inhabitants. Among them were Caleb and Joshua; and they two, of all the company, brought back a good report of the land. They insisted upon its being a land flowing with milk and honey; and that, if the Lord would delight in them as a people, they were abundantly able to go up and possess it at once.

In order to avoid all contention or doubt as to Moses' successor, the Lord directs him to take Joshua and set him before Eleazer the priest, and before all the congregation of the children of Israel, and lay his hands upon him, and give him charge in their sight, so that they might all know of Joshua's appointment. He was further to ask counsel of Eleazer, and thereby a good care of the people would be secured. All things being now ready, Joshua was prepared to take the administration as soon as Moses should die.

Upon the announcement of Moses' death, Joshua's first move was to put the people in motion for the land of promise. None were ordered to march, upon three days' notice, only the armed men; these were to go before.

With the order to march, God also gave Joshua much counsel and encouragement; viz., that if he would keep the book of the law, peruse, and meditate upon it, and do all it required, and be of good courage, none of his enemies should be able to stand before him; for the Lord thy God is with thee, whithersoever thou goest.

Joshua then gave his generals orders to have all things in readiness to pass over Jordan in three days. In reply to these orders, they all declared themselves ready to do and go as he should direct; as they had obeyed Moses, so they would Joshua.

In order not to be taken by surprise, Joshua sent over two spies, to take observations about Jericho. The King of Jericho, hearing of their presence in the country, made a smart attempt to catch them; but they, not without difficulty, escaped from their pursuers, and returned to Joshua.

The report they made to him was respecting their being pursued, and how they were assisted by a woman of the city to make their escape; and that, for this aid, they promised her and her father's family protection, when they should enter the country. Also, that the news of God's dealing with them at the Red Sea, and with the kings in their way, had reached the people over Jordan, and they were full of fear, and their hearts melted in them.

As they came to Jordan, the last signal for advancing was given to the people. This was, that the priests who carried the "ark of the covenant," should go before into the river, and the people were to follow, two thousand cubits (about three-fourths of a mile) behind them.

As the priests stepped into the water, the river parted, and left a dry path for them to pass over.

The priests advanced to the middle of the river, and there halted until the armed men passed over, and then, after them, all the rest of the people. Before the priests moved, twelve men, one from each tribe, were chosen to take twelve stones, one for each tribe, from the bottom of the river, and carry over. This being done, the priests were then ordered to pass over from the middle of the river. As soon as this was done, the water flowed on again as before.

The twelve stones taken out of the river, Joshua took and set up in Gilgal, as the Lord directed, that the generations after them might be reminded that by a mighty hand God had brought them through the river into this great and good land. Not only that they should remember the event, but be taught thereby to fear and serve him, from generation to generation. Here, also, they made their first encampment, after passing over Jordan.

This miraculous event put all the inhabitants of the land in great terror; so that they shut themselves up within their cities, and went not out and in, for fear. Joshua improved this occasion to circumcise the people. The covenant of circumcision was given to Abraham, and had been observed by his posterity; but as all the men of war who came out of Egypt died in the wilderness, and those whom Joshua led over the river had grown up in the journey, and had not been circumcised, it was necessary to attend to it the first opportunity.

This done, they next observed the Passover — the solemn feast established to commemorate the deliverance in Egypt, when the destroying angel passed over their first-born.

On the day following the Passover, they ate of the old corn of the land; and from that time God sent them no more manna. Thus, in just forty years from the institution of the Passover, on that fearful night in Egypt (corresponding to the fourteenth of March), the seed of Abraham are fed and lodged in the land of promise.

The preliminaries of entering Canaan being now over, Joshua turns his eyes to look toward Jericho. As he looked, behold a Man stood before him, with a drawn sword in his hand. Joshua drew near, and asked him, "Art thou for us, or for our adversaries?"

And he said, "Nay; but as the Captain of the host of the Lord, am I come." Then Joshua fell on his face before him, and inquired what word he had to tell him.

The Captain answered him, in the first place, as the Lord did Moses, when he drew near the burning bush: "Loose thy shoe from thy foot, for the place where thou standest is holy." Next, the Captain — *i. e.*, the Lord — gave Joshua directions how to take the walled city, Jericho.

The plan of operation being given him, like all faithful servants of God, Joshua went immediately about its execution. The disposition of his forces was on this wise: A large and heavy body of armed men were to lead in the procession; next to them were to follow seven priests, with seven rams' horns; next, there were to follow the priests, bearing the "Ark of the Covenant;" and behind them a strong rear-guard.

In this order the whole procession was to march around the city, once a day, for six successive days. None of the company was to make any noise in this tramp, only the shrill blast of the priests upon their horns. On the seventh day, they were to compass the city seven times; and at the end of the seventh round, the people were to shout, with the blowing of the horns. With what fearful suspense the people of Jericho must have awaited the interpretation of all this, to them, unmeaning parade! With the miracle of Jordan fresh in their minds, they could be filled with naught but forebodings of evil.

After Joshua had led the people around the city for the last time, and the priests prepared for the final terrible blast, he cries out to them, "*Shout, for the Lord hath given you the city!*" The walls all fell flat, and Jericho, and its people, and all the spoil, fell into the hands of Joshua.

Having taken Jericho, and redeemed the pledge of the spies to Rahab and her friends, Joshua next prepared to take Ai. Spies were also sent to take observations around it, and returned with a report, that "two or three thousand would be quite sufficient, without the whole army being engaged."

The requisite number was sent out, the attack commenced, when the men of Ai sallied forth, and the Israelites were repulsed.

This defeat gave Joshua and the Elders of Israel great distress, so that they fell before the "ark," and put dust upon their heads.

Whilst thus bewailing their reverses, the Lord said to Joshua, Get thee up; why liest thou upon thy face? Israel hath sinned, hence you can never stand before your enemies, until this accursed thing be removed.

An investigation was appointed, by which search was made through all the people, first by tribes, families, and individuals. This course resulted in the detection of Achan, the son of Carmi, of the tribe of Judah. He immediately confesses, that among the spoils of Jericho he saw a goodly Babylonish garment, and a wedge of gold, which he took for himself, and hid them in his tent, and there they are now.

This was specially displeasing to the Lord, as he had commanded the *destruction* of all the spoils, and the dedication of the gold and silver to the treasury of the Lord, for his service. Hence the great offence he committed against the Lord, and his selfishness in trying to better his own condition, by purloining from the common treasure.

But God, the Judge, pronounced the terrible sentence, that whoever was taken, he and all his should be burnt with fire; while the people were made the executioners; and they took Achan, his family, and all his flocks and cattle, and stoned them to death, burnt them, and the goods he had taken, with fire, and heaped upon them a great heap of stones, in the valley of Achor.

Evil being thus put away from Israel, the Lord encourages Joshua, saying, that Ai should be given into his hands; and instructs him in the plan of operation against it. This plan was, to send a detachment in front of the city, as before, and another to go in the rear, by night, and lie in ambush.

When Joshua commenced the assault upon the city, the people of Ai sallied forth, and Israel retreated, as before. The soldiers of Ai, supposing the flight to be a defeat, pursued Joshua's army hotly. The ambush were to enter the city, and set fire to it, as soon as its defenders were gone out, and the smoke thereof was to be the signal to Joshua, to face about and give battle. This unexpected turn of affairs, gave the men of Ai great surprise; for when they turned and saw their city on fire, and the hosts of Israel before and behind them, their hearts melted in them, and that day they became an easy prey to Joshua, the Lord's servant.

Having a little season of repose now, Joshua erects an altar to Jehovah, of whole, or unhewed stones, and offered burnt and peace offerings. He also gathered the people together around the ark, and read to the whole congregation, all the law written by Moses.

The tribes in the hill-country were differently impressed with the successes of Joshua.

The people of Gibeon were put in fear, and prepared themselves with old clothes and bread, as though they had come from afar, and desired conditions of peace, which they accomplished.

Joshua, on finding out the deception, kept his agreement, but made them hewers of wood and drawers of water.

But Adonizedek, King of Jerusalem, stirred up four neighboring kings to join him in revenge upon the important city of Gibeon, for making allegiance with Joshua.

The people of Gibeon being alarmed at this coalition against them, sent in great haste to Joshua for assistance. This circumstance gave Joshua a strong ally, in the city of Gibeon. He made haste and went up, and all the mighty men of valor; the Lord assuring him that none of these men should be able to stand before him. Besides all that were slain by the sword, the Lord sent a shower of hail-stones upon the armies of the kings, which destroyed more than the sword.

But many of them being left yet, Joshua desired to make a further end of the work, and for this purpose he prayed the Lord to let the sun and moon stand still for another day, without going down; and the Lord granted his request. So, by the Lord's help, he completely routed and scattered his enemies. The five kings fled, and hid in a cave at Makkedah.

Their retreat being made known to Joshua, he ordered the cave to be stopped up with great stones, and a guard placed over it, until they could pursue and destroy the rest of their enemies. This being done, the cave was opened and the five kings brought forth, when Joshua's captains put their feet upon the necks of the kings; they were then slain, hanged on five trees until evening, then taken down and buried under a heap of stones.

In this affair, we see the enmity mentioned in the curse upon Eve, between her seed and the seed of the wicked; and how the kings bruised Joshua's heel, but he bruised their heads. That same enmity still exists between the church and the world.

So Joshua slew these kings, and conquered their country: showing that they who fight against God, shall surely be overthrown.

After this, Jabin, King of Hazor, took the same course as Adonizedek had just taken; viz., to form a confederacy with the surrounding kings, against Joshua. But they had not counted the cost, though their men, horses, and chariots, consisted of hundreds of thousands. The Lord was on Joshua's side, and he accomplished the work God told him he should; he slew their men, cut the heel-cords of their horses, and burnt their chariots with fire.

This great battle completed the conquest of the Promised Land —Joshua having taken possession of it, and destroyed thirty-one kings.

The conquest of Canaan being so far gained as to give the people room to dwell, the Lord gave Joshua directions to proceed to the division of the land, among the tribes.

A full account of this survey and division, can be seen in the Book of Joshua; and it need only be added here, that those portions of the country unconquered at this time, were included in the division, with reference to future possession. It is to be observed, also, that the tribe of Levi had no inheritance among the other tribes, as they were wholly set apart to the priesthood. Several cities, however, were granted them by special privilege.

Thus God made large provision for ministers, who should teach, expound, and urge attention to the law of the Lord.

Joshua's work being now about finished, he imitates the patriarchs, by calling the people of his charge together, and delivering his farewell discourse. Feeling the weight of the cause in which he had spent his life, and knowing it to be God's cause, he speaks like a dying man to dying men.

He first refers them to the land in which they were now settled, and ascribes all this success to the special and direct blessing of the Lord; and then aims to impress upon their minds the duty of loving and serving him, with all constancy and fidelity: assuring them, also, *in the most positive manner, that God will not aid them against* their enemies unless they did trust in him.

In a second and last public address to the people, Joshua rehearsed the dealings of the Lord with them, from Abraham's time to his; giving them the same pungent assurance, that it was the Lord God who had cared for them all the way through.

He then urges upon them, in the most pathetic, earnest, and imploring manner, to make choice of the Lord, instead of the idols of the heathen, as their object of worship. After they had vowed solemnly their fidelity to the Lord, Joshua set up a stone under an oak, as a perpetual witness of the oath between them. Thus his last soul-stirring effort was to fix the impression upon the minds of the people, that their refuge was in God; and that if they forsook him, he would assuredly forsake them.

Joshua's work being now finished, and having arrived at the same age as Joseph, he died in 2561 A. M., and 1443 B. C., aged one hundred and ten years.

The interment of Joseph's bones took place about this time, as he requested, and as they promised him, in the sepulchre of his fathers.

Eleazar, the high-priest, died also about this time, just as Aaron, the first high-priest, died near the time Moses did, Israel's first leader; so Joshua, their second leader, and Eleazar, their second priest, passed off the stage together.

Phineas, son of Eleazar, and grandson of Aaron, succeeded his father in the high priesthood.

Being now well established in the country, and having a prospect of peace, the tabernacle is again set up, and divine worship once more enjoyed. It is said the tabernacle stood at Shiloh, about three hundred and twenty-eight years.

It is stated that on a pillar erected by the Carthaginians, near the "Pillars of Hercules" (*i. e.* the Straits of Gibraltar, in Africa), there was seen, in the time of Justinian, an inscription thus: "We are fugitives from the face of Joshua, the robber, the son of Nun."

The allegation of "robber," as applied to Joshua, is void of all truth, when viewed in the light of facts. True, he "drove them out;" but to whom did the land belong? God gave it to Abraham and his seed, as a possession; hence Joshua was an heir to the land — Israel's inheritance. While the Israelites were in bondage, the Canaanites entered the land merely as squatters; or like a man walking into another's house, while he is gone, and taking possession. When the rightful owners came to the land, the squatters refused to *go out*, and so Joshua *drove them out.* With them "*might* was right;" but Joshua only maintained his *right* by might. Hence the apology for the Israelites taking possession of the land of promise. This right was extinguished when "Shiloh" (Christ) came.

PERIOD II. FROM JOSHUA TO THE TEMPLE OF SOLOMON, 2561 A. M., 1443 B. C., TO 3000 A. M., 1004 B. C.

INTERREGNUM. — It pleased the Lord to appoint no successor to the office held by Moses and Joshua. Upon the death of the latter, the management of affairs devolved upon each tribe by itself. The office of high-priest continued in Phineas, while that of commander-in-chief fell into the hands of the Judges. Each tribe was now left, to finish in its own division of the land, the expulsion of its enemies, and the establishment of civil and religious order. In this, sometimes a tribe would prosecute its work under its head, or judge; and sometimes two or more tribes would unite and appoint the most suitable person among them to take the chief command of the enterprise. The Lord, however, was still the guide and counsellor of the people, just as in the days of Moses and Joshua, when they called upon him.

After the death of Joshua, the people inquired of the Lord which tribe should lead in going up against the enemy. The lot fell upon Judah.

The first important point gained, was the city of Jerusalem, which they took with ease; and its king also fell into their hands.

Upon this successful lead by Judah, several of the other tribes made war upon the inhabitants of the land, and gained numerous and important victories. Instead, however, of "*driving out*" the inhabitants of the land, as the Lord had specially directed them, the Israelites were content to subdue their enemies, and keep them in the land, but under tribute.

For this unwarranted departure from the policy Joshua taught them, the angel of the Lord appeared to them, and administered a severe reproof; saying, also, that these nations should remain as the Israelites had chosen to have them, but should be as thorns in their sides. An apparent reform followed this message, as the people wept aloud, and sacrificed to the Lord.

But they soon relapsed into the worship of the idols of the heathen, which caused the Lord to leave them to be overcome by their enemies; and their distress was great. The Lord sent them deliverers, to persuade them to serve him; but as soon as they were at ease again, they departed from him. In addition to image-worship, the Israelites had intermarried with the people of the land, which had been expressly prohibited, and was a great snare.

A very striking affair is mentioned in the last chapters of the Book of Judges, which is supposed to have occurred in the course of the time between Joshua and the Judges.

A Levite returning home from his father-in-law's with his wife, turned aside to tarry all night in Gibeah. In the night the house was surrounded by a party of lewd fellows, of the baser sort, who demanded the surrender of the man's wife into their hands. The man of the house expostulated with them for a time, but was forced to yield to them, when they proceeded to abuse the woman until she died. She was found dead at the door of the house in the morning.

The Levite took her and departed to his own place, and there divided her into twelve pieces, and sent a piece to each tribe, appealing to them for redress. Response to the call was made from Dan to Beersheba, with Gilead, and unto Mizpeh. Delegates from all the tribes assembled.

When all was ready, the case was called, and the Levite related his grievance as above. The decision was, that all the tribes declared they would not return home, until redress was obtained.

The first thing was, to demand of the people of Gibeah the surrender of the vile fellows who committed the offence, to be executed. This they obstinately refused to do, when the sword was drawn, and in three battles there fell on both sides sixty-five thousand men of war, besides women and children. All this to put evil away from Israel. This cut off the women, so that the Benjaminites who were left were without wives; and not being allowed to marry into each other's tribe, a necessity arose, in which a supply must be furnished, or the tribe of Benjamin must be cut off entirely.

A device was got up: at the feast of Shiloh the young men were to lie in wait, and when the maidens came out into the vineyard, each was to seize him a maid, and so supply themselves with wives. Thus the tribe of Benjamin was preserved.

These and other proceedings occupied about thirty years — from Joshua to the first Judge; during which time the generation of Joshua's time passed off, and a new class came upon the stage of action. Eight years of this time the Lord had given Israel into the hands of the King of Mesopotamia, who subdued and oppressed them greatly.

In the midst of this oppression, they cried unto the Lord, and he sent them a deliverer.

OTHNIEL. — He was younger brother to Caleb, and the first of the so-called "Judges of Israel." The Lord was with him by his Spirit, and delivered into his hands the King of Mesopotamia, and thereby gave Israel rest for forty years.

EHUD, — The second Judge, delivered Israel from the oppression of Eglon, King of Moab, and they had rest eighty years. During this time a better state of things prevailed, until a relapse.

SHAMGAR, — The third Judge, ended the oppression of Philista. He slew six hundred Philistines with an ox-goad.

DEBORAH AND BARAK. — Deborah was a prophetess, and fourth in office of Judge. Israel, for their sins, were again in trouble with Jabin, King of Canaan, and oppressed by him. Sisera was general of Jabin's forces, which could boast of nine hundred chariots of iron; while Barak was general of Israel, who was called and commissioned by Deborah, from the Lord, and with ten thousand men was ordered to marshal his forces on Mount Tabor. Sisera, learning that Barak was ready to give battle, put his chariots in motion, and when arrayed, Barak descended upon him, and drove him, and pursued his army and slew them all. Returning to look after Sisera, who deserted his soldiers, he found him in a tent, dead, whither he had gone to hide and rest; when Jael, wife of Heber, took a hammer and drove a nail through his temples while he was asleep.

This ended the oppression of Jabin, King of Canaan, and the land had rest forty years. During these spaces of rest from oppression, were the seasons of religious enjoyment and prosperity. Sad to say, also, repose was but too favorable to the relapses which involved the children of Abraham in the snares of idolatry, and the judgments of the Lord.

GIDEON.—The fifth Judge of Israel, delivered them from the oppression of Midian. In all cases where the people turned to idols, God made the Canaanites thorns in their sides for the same; and when they repented and reformed, he just as soon turned victory on Israel's side.

While Israel cried to the Lord because of the oppression of the Midianites, the angel of the Lord appeared to Gideon in Ophrah, as he threshed wheat, and saluted him thus: "The Lord is with thee, thou mighty man of valor!"

Gideon at once replies, Why, if the Lord be with us, are we thus afflicted? He then demands a sign from the angel, to satisfy him that the message was from the Lord. To obtain this he prepared a kid as a sacrifice, and placed it upon a rock, when the angel put forth his rod and touched the rock, and fire came out of the rock and burnt the sacrifice. This evidence of a call from the Lord, filled Gideon with great emotion.

He was then directed by the Lord to pull down his father's altar to Baal, cut down the grove around it, erect in the place of it an altar to the Lord, take a bullock for a sacrifice, and with the wood of the grove offer up a burnt sacrifice.

When it was found what Gideon had done, the Baalites demanded of his father that Gideon should be slain. But his father, Joash, replied, if Baal *be* a god, let him avenge himself, for the overthrow of his altar.

Gideon then asked another proof of the Lord, that he should deliver Israel. He asked the Lord to allow him to spread a fleece of wool on the ground, and if the dew was on the *fleece* only, then he would believe that Israel would be delivered by him: and it was even so with the fleece.

Then he plead for one sign more only, if the Lord would not be displeased; that he might spread the fleece again, and let the dew be on the ground, and *not* on the fleece, and then he would be satisfied: and that was even so, as he requested.

Gideon then moved forward, and pitched his army in sight of the

Midianites. In order that the hosts of Israel might not fall into the mistake, that because they were so many, they had conquered Midian in their own strength, the Lord reduced the detachment that was to go with Gideon.

In the first place, Gideon was to proclaim, that all that were faint-hearted were to leave the field and return. Twenty-two thousand left at this, and only ten thousand remained with Gideon. The Lord then told him to take these to the water, and all who could not lap water like a dog, were to stay behind, and not go to the war. This reduced the number to three hundred only. Thus the Lord put Gideon to as sharp a test as he had the Lord, with the fleece.

In the evening Gideon and one of his officers, Phurah, went out to view the position of the enemy; and as they came near one of their outposts, or advance guards, they overheard two of them talking.

They listened, and found one was telling the other a dream he had: that he saw a barley-cake come rolling down the mountain, and it struck a tent of Midian, and all the tents fell to the ground. And his fellow answered, "This is nothing else save the sword of Gideon, the son of Joash, a man of Israel; the Lord hath delivered Midian into his hand."

Gideon was now satisfied that Midian would fall before him, as the Lord had said. He returns to his men, divides them into three companies of one hundred men each, furnishes them with trumpets, lights in pitchers, so as to carry their lights unobserved until the moment for use. The stratagem lay, in suddenly presenting to the sight of the enemy a glaring light, with a thrilling blast of trumpets, and a tremendous shout, and so put the enemy into confusion and dismay.

Gideon commanded one division in person, and a signal from him was to engage the whole force. Soon they were on their winding way, and came to the outside of the camp in the beginning of the middle watch, just as the Midianites had put on a new guard. No sooner on the spot than the work began. Gideon and his division blew and shouted, and the other companies did the same, broke their pitchers, and cried, "The sword of the Lord and of Gideon."

Such an unexpected, unusual, and terrific assault, at dead of night, put the whole camp of Midian in such alarm and confusion, that they could only seek refuge in flight, and that in the greatest disorder. Their numbers were as the grasshoppers in the valley; but in their defeat, they were as chaff before the whirlwind.

Having put the enemy to rout, Gideon then sent out orders to the tribes to fall in all around, and pursue them, until they were destroyed.

After returning from the overthrow of Midian, the Israelites desired Gideon to rule over them, and that his sons should succeed him upon his throne. To this Gideon gave the most prompt and decisive refusal; saying, "The Lord shall rule over you."

So Israel was again delivered from their oppressors, and had a space of quiet for forty years; when Gideon also died, in a good old age.

Thus, in the deliverance of Israel again, the Lord so ordered the whole affair, that the glory belonged exclusively to himself. He will have the glory due to him, in all the affairs of men.

ABIMELECH.—He was sixth Judge, but only for a short time. Gideon had refused to reign over Israel, when requested, or have his sons; but Abimelech sought this office unasked, and even acted the usurper, to gratify his ambition.

He was a son of Gideon, and had seventy brothers. These he judged by himself, and imagined that they were designing to assume the reins of Judgeocracy. To this he aspired himself; and to make the way clear, he supposed it necessary to get these brethren out of the way. Accordingly he went to Shechem, and, by his insinuations against his brothers, induced the people of that city to enter into a conspiracy with him to put them to death.

Without stopping to count the cost, the Shechemites second his perfidy, and draw funds out of the treasury of an idol temple there, and give it to Abimelech; and with it he hires a posse of vain and light persons, and proceeds to inaugurate his usurpation.

His first demonstration was to enter his father's house, seize his brothers, and put them all to death, except Jotham, the youngest, who escaped his hands. After this, the Shechemites assembled at Millo, and made Abimelech king, or judge, of Israel, without consulting the other tribes at all.

The Shechemites having thus committed themselves openly to a base scheme, Jotham went there and called them together, and said, "Hearken to me, that God may hearken unto you." He then spoke a parable, thus: The trees went forth to choose a king; the office was tendered to the olive-tree, then to the fig-tree, then to the vine; but all declined (just as Gideon and his sons had done). The offer was then made to the bramble, and accepted, with almost ironical boasting (this was like Abimelech). If you have done well by my brethren and father, then rejoice in Abimelech; but if not, then let him devour Shechem, and let fire come out of Shechem and devour Abimelech. Jotham then fled, for fear of Abimelech.

This opened the eyes of the Shechemites to their folly, and the overthrow of the bramble. They then formed a conspiracy against Abimelech.

This was immediately told to Abimelech, when he turned in wrath towards Shechem — not for the same purpose as before, but to destroy it. He laid siege to it, destroyed it, and sowed it with salt. And finding a large number had fled into an idol temple, he set it on fire, and destroyed them all. Thus fire came forth from Abimelech, upon Shechem.

For some offence given him (for joining the conspiracy, possibly), Abimelech besieged Thebez, a city near by. The people fled to the tower; and, from the top of it, a woman cast a piece of a millstone upon Abimelech's head, and broke his skull.

To escape the stigma of being killed by a woman, he called upon his armor bearer to thrust him through with his sword.

Tola. — After the wicked conspiracy of Abimelech was overthrown, Tola, the seventh judge, succeeded him in the office. Twenty-three years he judged Israel, and enjoyed rest from the disturbances which so often put the nation in commotion.

Jair. — The eighth judge, next held the office twenty-two years. He had thirty sons, who, from having thirty cities assigned them, probably assisted their father in administering a good government.

Jephthah. — He was chosen to be the ninth judge of Israel. The relapse into idolatry, which brought on the oppression of Ammon, was the most general and gross of any on record. The Israelites seem to have lost all sense of gratitude or obligation to God, for the great deliverances he had wrought for them, and turned verily to dumb idols.

When they began to call upon the Lord to deliver them, he, in order to lead them to a more sincere and lasting repentance, turned them away, and told them to go and call upon the gods they chose to serve. He had repeatedly delivered them, but apparently to little effect.

Seeing they were rejected of the Lord, they began to feel their awful condition; and were led not only to ask help against their enemies, but were brought to make humble confession of their sins, with fervent supplication.

Then the Lord pitied and heard them, and Jephthah was indicated as a suitable person to bring deliverance to them.

The choice of Jephthah as judge being approved by all concerned, and a mutual oath of allegiance being taken before the Lord, he proceeded to execute his commission.

He first sends messengers to the King of the Ammonites, asking him for his reasons for prosecuting an unjust war against Israel. He refers Jephthah to the time the children of Israel came into the country, and destroyed the Ammonites, as they went along; and this was just retribution upon the Israelites. Jephthah then refers him to the fact, that they came to the border of the Moabites and Ammonites, and courteously asked the privilege of passing through their territory to their own land; pledging themselves to make good all damages, and defray all expenses. This quiet and reasonable proposition was flauntingly rejected, when Israel took liberty to pass through on their own conditions.

Now, says Jephthah, to the King of Ammon, we both claim the country, and as war is enevitable, I want you to understand this: whomsoever your god, Chemosh, delivers into your hand, must submit, of course; and whomsoever the Lord our God delivers into our hands, must expect to submit, also.

After this message was gone, Jephthah began to feel that he had now appealed his case to the Supreme Court of the Universe; and that should the King of Ammon prevail, then it must go that Chemosh was God, and not the Lord. Jephthah felt now that he must fall into the Lord's hands, or into the hands of the enemies of God and Israel.

In his extreme earnestness for success, he makes a rash vow, "that if the Lord would give him victory, when he returned in peace to his own house, whatsoever cometh forth to meet me shall be the Lord's, for a burnt-offering." The Ammonites were given into his hands to his heart's content; but alas! when he came home, who should come bounding forth to meet him, but his only child and daughter.

This painful occurrence did not deter Jephthah from performing his vow; but it produced so great a sympathy in behalf of the damsel, that the day of her dedication was observed by the daughters of Israel, by keeping four days of mourning for the daughter of Jephthah every year.

He judged Israel six years.

IBZAN. — The tenth judge held office seven years. Nothing special during his administration.

ELON. — The eleventh judge, ruled Israel ten years.

ABDON. — The twelfth judge, ruled eight years in Israel, and died.

Another occasional space of rest seems to have been enjoyed about the time of these last judges, which, sad to relate, was usually unfavorable to the purity of religion; as, in times of quiet, the idolatry of the land crept in among the professed people of God.

SAMSON. — The thirteenth judge, served Israel twenty years. The Philistines oppressed them at this time, because they again did evil in the sight of the Lord.

The choice of Samson as judge, was out of the ordinary course. The angel of the Lord revealed to the wife of Manoah, that she was to be the mother of an extraordinary son. She made known to her husband the message she had received, and Manoah entreated the Lord for another interview with the angel. This was granted; when the directions were given, that the mother should take no wine or strong drink, nor should any razor come upon the head of the child, for he was to be a Nazarite unto God.

Manoah, not knowing who this messenger was, proposed to entertain him as a man, when he was directed to make his offering to God. Upon this, he prepared a burnt-offering, and, while it was burning, the angel ascended in the flame. Then Manoah knew that it was a message from the Lord.

Samson was the son referred to above; and, as he grew up, there were frequent indications, in his actions of bravery and zeal for his nation, that he would some day be of service in breaking the power of Israel's oppressors.

The special gift with which the Lord endowed Samson, was extraordinary physical strength.

When about twenty-two years of age, Samson desired his father (as the custom was) to intercede for him for a wife. But, to the grief of his parents, he sought one from among the Philistines, instead of his own nation. And as no importunity would prevail to turn him from his purpose, his parents both accompanied him to Timnath, to seek him a wife.

On his way Samson met a lion, which he killed as easily as he would a kid, and left it in the field. The woman he went to espouse pleased him well. As twelve months had to elapse after the espousals, before she could be given him, he awaited the time. While on his way again to Timnath, he turned aside to see the lion, and behold, a swarm of bees had hived in the carcass. He took some of the honey and ate as he went.

It was customary for young men, on their marriage, to give a feast. At Samson's there was a good attendance. For the amusement of the company, he put forth a riddle, promising each of the company a suit of clothes, if any of them could tell it. So, out of the lion and the bees he made his famous riddle: "Out of the eater came forth meat; out of the strong came forth sweetness."

Being unable to tell it, they persuaded his wife to get it from him, and tell them. So before the seventh day was out (the length of the feast), they said to him, "What is stronger than a lion, or sweeter than honey?"

Samson, finding they had "ploughed with his heifer," and then asked the reward for telling the riddle, had due revenge upon them, by going and slaying thirty Philistines, and giving them the thirty changes of raiment off the backs of their own countrymen. This was the first blow by which the Philistines began to learn that Samson was to be a scourge to them.

His wife remained behind, and was given to one of those companions. After a time Samson came back for his wife; but the Philistines refusing to let him have her, he set their grain on fire, by fastening burning torches to the tails of foxes, and sending them loose into the fields. So, for this abuse to him, the Philistines made nothing.

They then pursued him, got him bound by the aid of men of Judah; but when the Philistines began to exult over him, he broke the cords, like burnt flax, found a jaw-bone of an ass, and slew one thousand of them.

He then turned into Gaza for the night; and finding the Philistines designed to kill him, he passed out of the gate, taking gates, posts, and bar, and carrying them to the top of the hill before Hebron.

But he was finally snared by a woman, named Delilah. She got hold of his affections, and the Philistines put her up to find where his power lay. After directing her to several things, she began to accuse him of not telling her the truth, until, by much importunity, he yielded; and told her if his locks, which had never been shaven, were cut, he would be like any man. Soon after this was done, he fell before the Philistines.

As soon as they had reduced him, they further bound him with fetters of brass, and put out his eyes.

Then the lords of the Philistines gathered together to have a great rejoicing over their fallen foe, whom Dagon had delivered into their hands. Samson was brought forth to be made sport of, and for their amusement, in his blindness. But as Samson stood between the two main pillars of the building, he took hold of them, and then prayed earnestly to God for his strength once more to come, which was answered, and he bowed himself mightily, and brought the building down. As a vast concourse were assembled, the number killed at Samson's death was more than he killed in his lifetime. Thus, not much was gained in this operation against the mighty man, Samson. He gave the Philistines a few tastes of oppression, which they were in daily practice of inflicting upon the Israelites.

Samson judged Israel twenty years.

The ease with which Samson could pull down the building in which, and on which, the Philistines were gathered, when once his marvellous strength came to him, is seen, when we recollect that it was circular in form, flat roof, and supported in the centre by two main pillars, and upon these he laid hold.

The Book of Judges is supposed to have been written by Samuel.

The story of Jephthah's daughter, Samson's foxes, and of Delilah's cutting off the fatal locks, are all wrought into heathen mythology and fable; even Samson is the very *Hercules* of the heathen.

ELI. — The thirteenth judge of Israel was also priest in the tabernacle at Shiloh. He one day seeing the mother of Samuel in earnest prayer, mistook for drunkenness her silent, earnest petition to the Lord, and reproved her, when he found out his great mistake. In due time she came to Shiloh, and offered an offering before the Lord, and brought also her son, and gave him to the Lord perpetually, as the burden of the petition she offered when Eli reproved her.

This child, Samuel, ministered before the Lord, though the consecrated priests were not required by law to commence before twenty-five, nor continue longer than fifty years old. Eli then blessed the parents of Samuel, and he grew in favor of the Lord and of men.

But Eli had trouble with his own family. His sons were not pious; they were unjust in the sacrifices, and lewd withal; and for their sins Eli reproved them stoutly, but to no purpose. Upon this a prophecy was told to Eli, — that for the sins of his sons, specially in trying to enrich themselves out of the sacrifices, they should be cut off in their prime.

One night, after Samuel came of proper age, the Lord called him, so that he awoke, and went to Eli to inquire what he wished. Eli told him he had not called him, and to lie down; but he soon returned again, and this was repeated three times; when Eli told him at the next call to say, Speak, Lord, for Thy servant heareth. The Lord then showed him what should befall Eli's sons.

Eli, knowing that some revelation had been made to Samuel, would not let him go until he told him what it was. On being informed, he resigned himself to the will of the Lord. And it was known throughout Israel that Samuel was to be a prophet.

After this, Israel went out to war against the Philistines; and, being beaten, Eli's sons, Hophni and Phineas, went into the tabernacle at Shiloh, and took the Ark into the battle-field, thinking that would save them. But Eli's forebodings at this were great; and as a messenger came from the camp and brought the sad intelligence that both his sons were slain, and the "Ark of God" taken, he fell from his seat backward, and, breaking his neck, died.

The wife of Phineas also died, at the sad intelligence of the fate of the battle. Thus, in one day, was Eli, his two sons, and one of their wives, cut off; Israel defeated; the priests slain; the chief magistrate dead, and the Ark of God taken. Surely, "the glory was departed."

Eli judged Israel forty years.

The Philistines supposed, when they had taken the "Ark," that they had obtained a prize, — anticipating that the God of the

Hebrews would now go with them, and give them success against Israel. But upon carrying it into the temple of Dagon, and placing it before their idol, they found next day that Dagon had fallen before it. He was set up again, but next day was fallen again, and his head and hands broken off. This, and other things, troubled the Philistines, until they returned the Ark to its place, and gave an offering with it, so as to be entirely clear from it. How strikingly God showed himself to be the Lord Omnipotent, both to the heathen and to Israel!

SAMUEL. — He is reckoned the fifteenth and last "judge," and the first prophet. After the death of Eli, Samuel called the people together at Mizpeh, and there prayed the Lord for them; and while in the act of worship, the Philistines fell upon them with the sword. The Lord interposed for Israel by a great thunder-storm, and broke them up, so that Israel fell upon them, and so overcame them, that they troubled Israel no more during the days of Samuel. On the occasion of this triumph, Samuel raised the stone he named Ebenezer; for, "hitherto, the Lord hath helped us."

Samuel travelled in a circuit as judge, going from Ramah, where he lived, to Bethel, Gilgal, and Mizpeh, home again. Being well along in years, he appointed his sons to assist him; but complaints were soon made that they were bad judges. Instead of attending to justice, judgment, and the weighty matters of the law, they turned aside to taking bribes, and perverting judgment.

In consequence of this, the people became clamorous for a king, after the manner of the nations around them, and resolved to dispense with the office of judge henceforth.

Samuel being directed of the Lord to yield to their clamor, the rule of the judges passes over into a monarchy in 2909 A. M., 1095 B. C.

From the end of the judgearchy, which terminated with the rejection of Samuel's sons, his history is mingled with that of the kings, as prophet and priest.

Samuel was founder of the "schools of the prophets," where young men were instructed in the duties of the prophetic office.

Samuel died about 1060 B. C. The schools of the prophets were located at Bethel, Jericho, Jerusalem, and other places, and were presided over by Samuel, Elijah, Elisha, etc.

SAUL. — He was first King of Israel, 2909 A. M., 1095 B. C., after the manner of the nations around them. The clamor of the people for a king displeased Samuel, and he laid the matter before the Lord, who directed him to yield to their request; but first to warn them of the nature of the change they were about to bring upon themselves, and then let them choose.

Samuel then told the people that they were about to put out of their own hands the management of affairs, and put them into the hands of an absolute power. That they could no longer choose judges, and so rule the country; but they would have to submit, and not rule.

He then enumerated some of the forms of oppression the monarchy would entail, such as absolute power to draft and put their goodliest sons in the armies; force them to till the ground, and make instruments of war (or build forts, walls, towers, chariots, etc.), under taskmasters, as in Egypt; make cooks and waiters of their daughters; he will take as much as he pleases of your vineyards, olive-yards, and flocks, and ye shall be his servants; and ye shall cry out in that day because of your king. But all this availed nothing; they say, "Nay, but we will have a king."

Saul, the son of Kish, went out one day to look for his father's asses; towards night he drew near to the city where Samuel dwelt, and not finding the asses, said to the servant with him, Let us turn in and inquire of the seer, where we may find them. It happened that the man he inquired of, for the seer, was Samuel himself. The Lord told Samuel, the day before, that the future king would come to him next day; so he immediately invited him home, entertained him with special marks of regard before the company at his own house. On the next day, Samuel went with Saul a little way, and made known to him that he was to be King of Israel. In addition to this, he took a horn of oil and poured it upon him, kissed him, and appointed the day for his coronation.

As Saul was returning, the Lord gave him another heart; and he soon met a company of prophets, joined them, and prophesied. It was a matter of surprise when his former acquaintances heard of this change, and the proverb arose, "Is Saul also among the prophets?"

At the time appointed, Samuel called all the people together at Mizpeh, to the recognition of Saul as their king. Before commencing business, Samuel again rehearsed the condition of affairs: Ye have forsaken God, who brought you out of Egypt, and persist in having a king; now proceed.

The choice falling upon Saul, he was brought forth, and stood head and shoulders above all the people; and when they saw him, they shouted, "God save the king!"

Samuel then gave them a lecture on the administration of the government by a king, and sent them away home.

The sons of Belial were not well pleased with the choice of Saul. But a war soon broke out with the Ammonites, in which Saul was victorious. Upon this, Samuel complained of the Belials as enemies to a prosperous king. But Saul pardoned them, and would not consent to any lives being taken; "for the Lord hath salvation in Israel."

Saul being established as king, Samuel made a formal retirement from office. He appealed to Israel to produce any default in his administration as judge, if they had any such charge. The people, with one voice, exonerated him from any charge of bribery, or injustice; upon which he felt at liberty to speak to them. He then rehearsed the Lord's dealings with them, from Moses and Aaron to their refusal of himself, and choice of a king; and exhorted them, just as earnestly as Joshua and others had done, to be faithful to God, and he would bless their king; but, if they turned aside from him, he would visit them with perpetual affliction.

In several conflicts with the Philistines, Saul and his son Jonathan made very good headway, as long as they obeyed the Lord. But when Samuel came to him with a message to go and destroy Agag, the Amalekites' king, and all the spoil, and his people, instead of carrying out his instructions, Saul went and fought Agag, took him and his princes, and the best of his spoil, and brought them up to offer them to the Lord. For this disobedience to orders, Samuel reproves him sharply; and also told him, that for rejecting the word of the Lord, he had also rejected him from being king.

This filled both Samuel and Saul with great sorrow. But the Lord directs Samuel to arise, and fill his horn with oil, and go to Jesse the Bethlemite, and anoint one of his sons to be king. Samuel made known his errand, when Jesse called one after another of his sons, until all but the youngest, who was keeping the sheep. He being called, the Lord showed Samuel that this was his choice. So Samuel anointed him, and the Spirit of the Lord came upon David, and departed from Saul, and an evil spirit troubled him.

Saul, from this, became gloomy; and hearing that a son of Jesse was a good musician, sent for him to come and drive dull care away. Being pleased with David's music, he sent a request to his father to have his son remain with him. Saul little thought the Spirit of the Lord had left him, and was upon this young shepherd boy.

The Philistines again came out to war against Israel; when Goliath, a giant and champion, defied the Israelites to single combat. To the utter astonishment of both parties, the son of Jesse accepted the challenge, and went out to meet the defiant brag of a heathen army. But, to the greater consternation of the Philistines, and astonishment of Saul, David threw a stone from his sling, which sunk into the giant's forehead, and he fell dead.

From this time, Saul would not part with David, but promoted him in the army, and he gained fast in the esteem of the people and of Saul's officers; and as they returned from the war with the Philistines, the women sung and saluted them as they passed, ascribing to Saul the slaying of thousands, and David his tens of thousands.

This unfavorable comparison of Saul with David, aroused in him the first spirit of jealousy towards his young rival. "What," says Saul, "can he have more, but the kingdom?" Saul still seems not to have known that he was rejected of the Lord, and David chosen; but his popularity made Saul his bitter enemy. Twice Saul made a direct attempt to take his life; but failing, began to fear him, for the Lord was with him.

Saul's prosperity was now waning, and David's was increasing; this only made Saul the more unhappy and surly. His settled purpose was, in some way to dispose of David. But being once put entirely into David's power, and no violence done him, Saul was aroused to a sense of his own baseness, and, on the first opportunity, acknowledged his fault to David and besought him, when he came to the throne, to spare his (Saul's) family, and not cut them off from the nation; to which David readily acceded, as he had no evil intent upon the house of Saul.

From the disobedience of Saul in the matter of Agag, his decline and fall are dated. His final overthrow was in a battle with the Philistines, in which Saul was worsted, for the archers hit him and wounded him sore. Seeing his end was near, rather than fall into the hands of his enemies, he fell upon his own sword, and died.

David. — Notwithstanding the enmity of Saul, upon news of his death, David mourned that the great man had fallen; thus showing his sincere friendship to his constant and open enemy.

David is made king over the tribe of Judah only; while Abner, Saul's general, gets Ishbosheth appointed king over some of the other tribes. This produced a civil war, as the enmity of Saul to David was cherished by his sons and officers. But the house of Saul grew weaker, while David's grew stronger. A quarrel between Abner and Ishbosheth resulted in Abner's deserting him and going over to David, which still hastened the overthrow of Saul's house.

This brought Abner into service of David, side by side with Joab, David's general, and gave Joab an opportunity to take Abner's life, which he did, in revenge for his brother's death, whom Abner slew while prosecuting the cause of Saul's house. Soon after, Ishbosheth was assassinated on his bed, which left the throne of Israel to its rightful king.

The tribes then gathered together at Hebron, to make David King of all Israel. Jerusalem was not entirely subdued until now, and hence the name of that portion the Jebusites had held is called the "City of David."

Being now established in the kingdom, David turns his attention to the cause of God. The first move was to bring up the "Ark" from Kirjath-jearim to the City of David. This was its final recovery and return to Israel, after it was carried into the battle, when Eli's sons were slain and the Ark taken by the Philistines.

Having had great prosperity in war, and being at leisure, David next meditates building a house for the worship of God. Hitherto the worship of God had been held in the tabernacle, surrounded by curtains, and the king thought a better arrangement was required. He laid the subject before Nathan, the prophet, and he bade him go on, and the Lord would prosper the undertaking; and, by a vision, God told Nathan to inform David if he would do this, and be faithful to him at all times, his throne should be established forever.

He did not, however, prosecute the work of building the house of the Lord to much advantage, owing to constant trouble by the invasions of the Ammonites and Syrians. In these conflicts David was very successful in victory, and much of the spoil taken from his enemies he dedicated to the Lord, to be used in the temple.

The dark spot in the history of David is his sin with the wife of Uriah, one of his officers. He saw her washing herself one day; was sinfully smitten with her beauty; sent for her while her husband was away in the army; took her to his own bed, and humbled her. She soon after informed the king that they were both involved in trouble that would be a serious affair.

David then gave orders to Joab, his general, to plan some battle, so that Uriah would have to take a very dangerous post. The king's object was to get him slain, so that his wife would be free to become the wife of David. The plan succeeded, and Uriah was slain.

But this thing displeased the Lord, and he sent Nathan the prophet to rebuke David. By an ingenious parable Nathan obtained David's judgment, which the prophet turned against the king with great force, saying, "Thou art the man!" He further pronounced upon him the curse of the sword as long as he lived, and a variety of other judgments, as the Lord directed him.

This produced in David deep repentance, and confession, and reform. The child that was born to him died.

The next son born to David by Bathsheba was Solomon, afterwards king.

One curse for David's great error was to be trouble in his own house. This was visited upon him, in the first place, by the incest of his son Amnon, with Tamar, his sister. The next domestic judgment was the insurrection of Absalom, David's son. He being a young man of good address, managed to insinuate himself into the good graces of the people by his condescending attentions, and boasts of the impartial administration of justice, if he could only be made judge of the nation; thus he stole the hearts of the people.

When Absalom supposed he had gained a party sufficiently strong to compass his ends, he pretended to David that he had a vow to fulfil to the Lord in Hebron. At the same time he had sent spies through the land, to secure a simultaneous rally around the standard of the king's son. The plan succeeded; the conspiracy was general, and so formidable, that David thought it prudent to leave Jerusalem, without trying to defend it. In this way the ardor of the movement would subside, and time would afford opportunity to compass the schemes of the young usurper.

The insurrection was easily enough started, but *after* that was the time and need for wise counsel. The young would-be king had neither the mature wisdom, nor the safe counsellors, of his father.

Absalom's counsellors differed in opinion, thereby his cause was put in jeopardy; but soon the opposing forces were brought into contact; and the final and fatal battle was fought in the wood of Ephraim. In the confusion that ensued, Absalom came upon some of David's staff, when he fled, to make his escape; and in his flight, passing under an oak, his long, flowing, beautiful hair caught in the limbs, dragged him from his beast, and left him hanging, to the mercy of his pursuers. Joab, hearing of his suspension, hastened to the spot, and thrust three darts through his heart, as he hung in the oak.

The death of Absalom gave his father great sorrow, as well it might, for his presumptuous folly, and swift retribution, that numbered him among the transgressors.

Besides Amnon's and Absalom's defections, which were in his *own house*, David had frequent disturbances to quell among the friends of Saul. The enmity he had towards David was cherished by his sons, relatives, and officers; so that, literally, the sword did not depart from David's house.

But the condition of his kingdom becoming more quiet, David turns his attention to the establishment of the worship of God. He buys a spot of ground, as the site of the proposed temple, erects an altar thereon, and offers a burnt-offering to the Lord, which was accepted, by his sending fire from heaven to consume it upon the altar.

The altar and tabernacle set up at Shiloh had become old, and were left to go to decay, upon the worship being set up in Jerusalem.

David begins to collect iron, and other materials, for the building of the house of God.

Adonijah showing symptoms of usurping the throne, it became necessary that David should appoint a successor. He then issued orders to Zadok the priest, and to Nathan the prophet, to take Solomon and bring him to Gihon, that he might be anointed king. So Solomon was caused to ride upon David's own mule, and was brought to Gihon, when Zadok the priest took a horn of oil out of the tabernacle, and anointed Solomon; and the trumpets were blown, and the people shouted, God save King Solomon!

After arranging matters as to the offices of the priests, and singers, and captains of the hosts, David proceeds to give his final charge to his son. First addressing the people, he declared his purpose to build a house to the Lord, but was denied the privilege, because he had been a man of war; but his purpose would be accomplished by his son. He then urged the people to continue in the law of the Lord, that they might remain in the land, and leave it a possession to generations after them.

And thou, Solomon, my son, know thou the God of thy fathers, and serve him with a perfect heart, and with a willing mind; for the Lord searcheth all hearts. If thou seek him, he will be found of thee; if thou forsake him, he will cast thee off forever. Take heed, now; for the Lord hath chosen thee to build a house for the sanctuary; be strong, and do it. He then passed over into the hands of Solomon a plan of the temple and its furniture, with all the immense provisions he had made for the great work. Besides iron, brass, and other materials, David and his princes contributed in gold and silver to the amount of forty-six thousand tons weight—valued over four thousand millions of dollars!

At such liberality, the people and the king rejoiced together greatly; and David said, Blessed be thou, Lord God of Israel, our Father, forever and ever. He then called upon the people to bless the Lord God of their fathers; and they bowed down their heads and worshipped the Lord. And they sacrificed to the Lord that day, with great gladness.

David reigned over Israel forty years; and he died in a good old age, full of days, riches, and honor, 2989 A. M., 1015 B. C.

Dr. Delany says that David, at his death, had everything that his heart could wish; he died in a good old age, full of days, riches, and honor,—having gained more renown than any other crowned head ever did. He was a true believer; zealous adorer of God; teacher of His law and worship, and inspirer of His praise. A consummate and unrivalled hero; a skilful and fortunate captain;

a steady patriot; a wise ruler; a faithful, generous, and magnanimous friend; and, what is yet rarer, a no less generous and magnanimous enemy. A true penitent, a divine musician, a sublime poet, and an inspired prophet. By birth a peasant, by merit a prince; in youth a hero, in manhood a monarch, and in age a saint.

As Moses died without entering the promised land, so David died without seeing the temple, for which he had done so much.

GAD. — He is mentioned as a prophet. He was God's messenger to David on several occasions. By his advice David left the cave of Adullum, and appeared in Judah. He was sent to David to lay before him three judgments the Lord was about to use, for David's fault of numbering the people; namely, a famine, or flee before his enemies, or a pestilence. He was one of David's biographers.

NATHAN. — A prophet, who shared largely in the confidence of King David. To him David made known his purpose of building a temple to the Lord. The Lord, however, sent Nathan to inform David that he would not be permitted that honor, but his son would.

Nathan was also chosen to admonish David for his sin, in the matter of Uriah's wife. He also wrote the life of David.

SOLOMON. — The kingdom being now confirmed upon Solomon, he at once set about its affairs. His first act was to call out the people, with their captains and leaders, as David had arranged them, and all went up to Gibeon — where the tabernacle and brazen altar yet remained — and there offered a thousand burnt offerings.

The night following, the Lord appeared to Solomon, and asked him what gift he would like. Solomon first requested the fulfilment of the promises made to his father — to establish his throne forever; so much for the nation. Then for himself, he asked the gift of *wisdom and knowledge*, to go out and come in before this people.

The Lord commended Solomon for his wise choice, and because he had not asked for wealth, honor, long life, nor the life of his enemies, he would confer upon him all these, to the extent that no king ever had before him, and none should ever have after him; and all history confirms this promise.

Then all the people returned to Jerusalem from Gibeon. Solomon married the daughter of Pharaoh, of Egypt, and was in peace with him, and with most of the kings round about. His reign was the most peaceful and prosperous of any the Jews ever enjoyed.

A very striking evidence of Solomon's wisdom is seen in the art he used to ascertain which was the real mother of a living child. Two women, with each a child, slept in the same bed, and in the morning it was found that one child was dead. Both claimed the living child, and to settle it, they appealed to the king. He, knowing that the *real* mother would sooner give up the child than have it slain, commanded a sword to be brought and divide the living child between them. To this the spurious mother gladly consented, and urged it; whereupon the king delivered the true mother her child.

Solomon, by his wisdom, and the favor of the Lord upon him, had at this time risen to the enviable summit of kingly and national greatness, — his kingdom extending from the Euphrates to the Great Sea, and to the borders of Egpyt. Hiram, King of Tyre, hearing of his greatness, sent embassies of peace and good-will, both for Solomon's sake and his father's.

Solomon responds, and makes out a contract for cedars from Lebanon, to be delivered in floats at Joppa, for the building of the temple.

He also requests Hiram to send him a skilful artist, that could oversee the ornamenting of the building.

Hiram considered the proposition made by Solomon, and accepted it cheerfully; for the enterprise pleased him, as well as the compensation, which was to supply his house with provisions during the time.

Arrangements being all made, the work of building now moves forward. Hiram furnishes all needful help in getting out the timber, and every part goes on prosperously. The site of the temple was on Mount Moriah (where Abraham went to offer his son to the Lord), on a plot of ground about one-half mile square.

Seven years were consumed in building it, and one hundred and eighty-four thousand six hundred men employed during the time. A minute account of the work, with its various utensils and ornaments, is given in the Scriptures, all of which corresponds with the sumptuous provisions made by King David.

Such care was exercised in the preparation of the walls even, that every stone was fitted for its place in the quarry; so that the whole building went together without the sound of a hammer, or any tool of iron.

The work being completed, next came the solemn ceremony of dedication. The ark was first brought into the temple by the priests (from the City of David), and placed in the holy of holies, still containing the tables of stone given to Moses in the mount. As soon as the ark was put in its place, the glory of the Lord filled the holy place, so that the priests could not stand there to minister.

Solomon then turned toward the people and pronounced the blessing of the Lord upon them, inasmuch as the promise of the Lord to

David, that his son should build a house for Jehovah, was now fulfilled. He then offers the Dedication prayer, most fervently beseeching the Lord ever to be present at this house of prayer.

He prays that the Lord would have pity and forgive, if two Israelites should quarrel; if their enemies should drive them; if famine, pestilence, or the plague, come; in short, for all ills they might encounter; when they pray in this house of prayer, built for God, hear Thou, forgive, and deliver.

Then Solomon offered sacrifices to the amount of twenty thousand oxen, one hundred and twenty thousand sheep; when the holy fire came down from heaven and consumed them.

The Lord heard and answered Solomon, and renewed all the promises to his father, and declared his constant care over him and his people forever, on the all-important condition that they continue in his precepts and obey his commandments: If ye do this, there shall not fail thee a man to sit upon the throne of Israel.

Thus the temple was finished — the most magnificent building in the world — and the dedication continued seven days, commencing with the 30th of October, 3000 A. M., 1004 B. C.

PERIOD III. FROM SOLOMON'S TEMPLE TO THE BABYLONISH CAPTIVITY, 3000 A. M., AND 1004 B. C., TO 3416 A. M., AND 588 B. C.

SOLOMON. — After the temple was finished, Solomon proceeded to erect a mansion for himself, after which the Lord appeared to him as at Gibeon. His was a prosperous reign. Of the inhabitants of the land he made vine-dressers and workmen of various sorts; but of the children of Israel he made him captains and princes, and filled all offices of trust and honor by them.

Three times a year Solomon offered burnt-offerings upon the altar he had built for the Lord; thus, by precept and example, he encouraged the worship of Jehovah. Indeed, never before, nor after this time, did the temple service receive so much attention; all the officers, from the high-priest down, were in their lot and place; and the name of the Lord God of Abraham, and of the whole earth, was hallowed daily and yearly at Jerusalem.

As the peace and piety of a nation become established, commerce and the arts will flourish. So Solomon and Hiram united, and fitted out a navy to go for gold. This shipping was built in the Red Sea, and, it is supposed, sailed around Africa to Spain, and along the way gathered gold, ivory, peacocks, and a variety of precious dust. Not only this, but he traded largely in spices, and other valuable articles, with the merchants of the East. Indeed, his whole retinue was made to dazzle with the lavish use of gold.

His income has been estimated to have been over six hundred million dollars a year, — over twelve million dollars per week, and over one million five hundred thousand per day!

Such was Solomon's fame abroad, that the Queen of Sheba (south of Arabia) came to see him, unsolicited. Solomon made himself very communicative, inasmuch as the queen had taken pains to make him such a flattering visit, merely to see his greatness.

All the wisdom he possessed he used to answer the questions of the queen, and correct any wrong information she had received.

When she had seen all Solomon's wisdom, and the magnificent buildings he had erected, the splendor of his table, his attendants and their apparel, and his cup-bearers, she fainted. She then declared that his fame in her own land was so great, that she would not receive it as truth; but now she said, the half was not told me; thy wisdom and prosperity exceed the fame which I heard. She then pronounced his servants and men (princes) happy to have such a lot; and pronounced the Lord God blessed, who delighted in Solomon, to set him on the throne of Israel.

According to oriental custom in such royal visits, she made a present. Of spices and precious stones; she gave many; and of gold, an hundred and twenty talents — valued at two million seven hundred and three thousand nine hundred and sixty dollars.

Solomon returned the compliment, "out of his royal bounty." Amount not known.

Besides Solomon's practical wisdom, wealth, royalty and power, he is said to have been the author of the Books of Proverbs, Ecclesiastes, and the Song, in the Bible; and also of three thousand other proverbs, one thousand and five songs, and to have written largely on Botany, Natural History, and Commerce. His history is religiously and politically instructive. No monarch ever enjoyed such popularity and prosperity; and yet he was very far from being happy. (See Eccl.)

Strange as it appears, yet even Solomon was afterwards drawn off into idolatry, so far as to favor it, at least. He followed the custom of those times, for kings to have many wives, and these from the nations about him; and they, like Eve, led him to partake of forbidden fruit.

At this the Lord was displeased, in that he had turned away from following the Lord, who had appeared unto him twice, and commanded him that he should not go after *other* gods. Wherefore the

Lord declared, that for this he would rend the kingdom out of his hand, and give it to his servant.

For David's sake he would not take it out of Solomon's hands, but from his son's hand it should be rent; nevertheless, one tribe should remain to Soloman's son, for David's sake, and for Jerusalem's sake, which I have chosen.

Hadad, of Egypt, who had gone there, got into favor with Pharaoh, and married his wife's sister; he held an old grudge against Israel, and went up to trouble Solomon in his latter days.

Jeroboam, a man of valor and industry, was placed over a section of the people, in repairing the wall of the City of David: and feeling elated with his promotion, aspired for more than belonged to him. For this the king sought him, to bring him to justice, when he fled from Jerusalem. As he was leaving, Ahijah the prophet caught hold of his new garment, and tore it into twelve pieces, and told Jeroboam to take ten of them; he then declared to him that thus the Lord would rend the kingdom out of the hands of Solomon, and ten tribes should be given to him. So Jeroboam fled to Shishak, King of Egypt, and remained there until the death of Solomon.

Solomon's work being now done, he was gathered to his fathers, and was buried in the City of David, 3029 A. M., 975 B. C.

The Book of Ecclesiastes furnishes the best comment of the penitence and piety of the great, the wise King of Israel — Solomon, the son of David.

THE TEN TRIBES.

Ahijah. — A prophet of the Lord, who resided at Shiloh. It was he who met Jeroboam, as he was on his way to Egypt, pulled off his new garment, and tore it into twelve pieces, giving Jeroboam ten of the pieces. This act he explained to Jeroboam, to mean that Israel should be rent, as a nation, and that he should have ten of the tribes to rule over; at the same time assuring Jeroboam from the Lord, that if he and his tribes would adhere to the law of the Lord, they should prosper; otherwise, they should be destroyed by the nations about them.

The son of Jeroboam was taken ill, when he sent his wife to Ahijah to inquire whether the child would recover or not. The prophet assured her that the child would die, as the Lord had revealed it to him; and so it was.

Jeroboam I. — The revolt of the ten tribes is here introduced, so as to dispose of them by themselves; after which the history of

Judah will be taken up, from the death of Solomon, and continue to its close.

Jeroboam, it will be remembered, was a disaffected and disloyal officer under Solomon, who, by arousing the displeasure of the king, fled for refuge into Egypt.

After the death of Solomon, and on the occasion of the crowning of Rehoboam, his son, Jeroboam came up from Egypt; and on account of the severity with which Rehoboam declared he should administer the government, the ten tribes were offended, revolted, and chose Jeroboam their king. This was as the Lord had declared by the prophet it should be. Jeroboam made Shechem the chief city of his kingdom.

He soon found that it was easier to get a kingdom, than to keep it. He saw that the habit of going to Jerusalem to worship, was strongly fixed in the minds of the Israelites, and could not be indulged without danger to his authority. A substitute must be devised, or his throne would fall.

Not knowing but a *form* of godliness would do just as well, "*without* the power," he accordingly made two golden calves, and put one in Bethel, and the other in Dan, and then proclaimed to the people that it was too much for them to go to Jerusalem: Behold thy gods, which brought thee up out of Egypt. He also made houses of worship, and appointed the lowest of the people for priests.

But worse than all the other trouble, after he had got this sham in operation, there came along a man of God, and cursed his altar; saying it should be destroyed.

At this, the king put forth his hand to seize the man of God, and it withered, so that he could not take it back; and the altar was rent, and the ashes fell. So he entreated him to ask the Lord to restore him his hand: and it was made as it was before. But Jeroboam reformed not; and for this the curse of God followed his family.

Iddo — Is supposed to be the "man of God" who cursed the altar of Jeroboam. On his return from this errand, he died by the way. The occasion of his death was disobedience. The Lord charged him not to stop to take refreshment from any one, during this trip. But another prophet persuaded him to violate this order, and he was found dead, slain by a lion; the lion and an ass standing near him.

Omri. — We pass by Nadab, Baasha, Elah, and Zimri, who, with Omri, deserve no honorable mention, further than that the latter built Samaria, which thereafter became the capital of the Ten Tribes.

Ahab, — The son of Omri, next came to the throne of Israel. He married Jezebel, a profligate and idolatrous Zidonian; soon fell into her faith; worshipped Baal; made a grove, and built an altar for his service. Ahab did more than any king before him to provoke the Lord.

Jezebel caused a great slaughter among the prophets; one hundred and fifty of whom Obadiah concealed from her fury, and fed them secretly in the caves.

During the three years' famine, foretold by Elijah, Ahab and Obadiah, his governor, and a godly man, went out to find grass by the fountains and brooks, to keep their horses and mules from perishing; and, in their journey, fell in with Elijah the prophet.

He had been instructed by the Lord to go to Ahab, and reprove him for his idolatry. On seeing him, Ahab tauntingly said, "Art thou he that troubleth Israel?" Elijah retorted the charge, and then challenged the king to a proof of their faith. By this means he drew the priests of Baal into the snare of calling upon their god, to answer by fire from heaven. Theirs was a most deplorable failure; while Elijah's God answered by fire, and consumed the sacrifice.

To this proof of the Lord being God, Elijah added a strong assurance that rain was at hand, to put an end to the three years' drought; and it was so.

Ahab, six years after, was obliged to defend himself against Benhadad, King of Syria, who came up with a mighty host and besieged Samaria. But, trusting in his great numbers, he was at his ease; when Ahab sallied forth, while the king was drinking wine in his tent, put his army to route, and Benhadad was obliged to take flight on a horse.

The next year, he renewed the attack; when the Lord favored Ahab, who put them again to flight, slaying one hundred thousand; and a wall of Aphek, where a part of the Syrians had fled, fell, and killed twenty-seven thousand more. Benhadad now begged for quarter, which Ahab gave him, and let him go. For this the Lord sent his prophet to Ahab, telling him that since he had let his enemy go, whom the Lord had given into his hands, Ahab's life should go for Benhadad's, and his people for the Syrian people.

Ahab did not reform, although the Lord, by favors and prophets, sought to win him to the right. He next proposed to buy a vineyard, of Naboth, that lay joining his own property. Naboth preferred not to sell. Ahab was grieved, and took his bed; when Jezebel laid a plot, by which Naboth was put out of the way. Ahab then took possession. But Elijah told him that in the place where dogs licked the blood of Naboth, shall dogs lick thy blood.

Ahab, receiving a visit from Jehoshaphat, King of Judah, proposed an alliance with him, to recover Ramoth-Gilead from the King of Syria, to which Jehoshaphat signified his assent. Ahab then consulted his Baal prophets, and was told to go on. Jehoshaphat wished to consult a prophet of the Lord; this being done, a contrary verdict was obtained. Ahab sent him to prison for his faithfulness, and rushed on to the battle.

For some reason (possibly fear), Ahab went into the battle without his uniform, Jehoshaphat taking the formal command. But this did not shield the Baalite king from the arrow which a Syrian shot from his bow at a venture; for it pierced him, and the blood ran out into his chariot; so he died. As they washed his chariot in Samaria, the dogs licked his blood, as was predicted.

Micaiah, — A prophet of the Lord, whom Jehoshaphat sent for, when the prophets of Ahab advised them to go up together against Ramoth-Gilead.

Micaiah prophesied that evil would befall Ahab, which so wounded his pride that he caused the prophet to be seized, imprisoned, and fed on the bread and water of affliction, until he returned in peace. But Ahab fell in battle, as the prophet had foretold.

Ahaziah, — Son of Ahab, succeeded to the throne. He entered into a co-partnership with Jehoshaphat, in fitting out a fleet, in the Red Sea, to trade with Tarshish. The Lord was not pleased that Jehoshaphat should be thus associated with idolatry, even in commerce; and the fleet was accordingly destroyed in a storm.

Ahaziah had a fall, which injured him, and he sent a messenger to Ekron, to inquire of Baal if it would cause his death. The man met Elijah, who told him the king would die. On hearing this, the king inquired how the man looked. The description answered to Elijah; then the king was enraged, and sent an officer and band of men to *seize* him. Elijah, knowing their errand, as they drew near, fire came from heaven and consumed them. A second party came out, and shared the same fate. A third messenger came and fell before the prophet, begged him to spare *his* life, and come down and see the king. So he did, and told him he would die; and so he did. Neither did this break up idolatry, though God showed so plainly, by fire from heaven, that Baal was no God.

Jehoram, — Second son of Ahab, came to the throne next; but of no particular note.

Jehu. — This king was grandson of Jehoshaphat, King of Judah, but was anointed by a young prophet, to reign over Israel. He was a furious driver of horses, and a terrible scourge upon idolaters.

As he approached the city of Jezreel, Jehoram, the king, sent a messenger to know if he came in peace. He replied, What have you to do with peace? go behind me. It was seen by the sentinel on the wall, that he reached Jehu, but returned not. Another was sent, and went behind also. Then Jehoram went himself, and he met Jehu on the ground of Naboth; and, for his blood, Jehu shot him with an arrow.

As Jehu came into the city, Jezebel, wife of Ahab, painted her face, and looked out of a window; and as Jehu passed, she uttered a most taunting sarcasm, thus: "Had Zimri peace, who slew his master?" — (An allusion to Zimri's usurping the throne, by assassinating Elah: and reigned only seven days. And Jehu had just killed Jehoram: the taunt was very severe.) At this, Jehu called upon some eunuchs near her, to pitch her out of the window, which they did; and she fell down and died.

Jehu went on, and after dinner proposed to go and bury her, as she was a king's daughter; but, on coming to the place, they found nothing but her skull, and the palms of her hands, — the dogs having literally eaten her up.

Thus this idolatrous Zidonian, Jezebel, ruined Ahab; caused a slaughter of the prophets; executed her conspiracy against Naboth, which gave his blood to the dogs, then Ahab's, and then her own, in the very city of Naboth, viz., Jezreel.

Jehu then wrote to those who had the care of Ahab's sons, to select the fittest among them, and make him king. This they were afraid to do, but declared themselves willing to perform any other service for him; when he ordered the sons' heads brought to him; which was done, in baskets; seventy in number. On his way to Samaria, Jehu met Ahaziah, and forty-two with him (a branch of Ahab's family); these he also slew; the last of Ahab's house.

On arriving at Samaria, Jehu proclaimed a general gathering of all the priests, and worshippers of Baal, as though himself would join in offering sacrifice to the idol. A great effort was made by the idolaters to get out to the meeting, partly through fear of Jehu, and partly through hope that he would favor their stupidity; but his design was to get them together, and cut them off too.

The summons was obeyed far more promptly than it would have been had Jehu called them together to worship Jehovah. Jehu ordered them to put all who did not fellowship Baal out of the temple; this the Baalites did, cheerfully, so as to purify the company. Jehu was particular, also, to have it done, so that none who were innocent of idolatry should perish with the besotted dupes.

Jehu then charged those who were to do the execution, to let none of them escape; if they did, life should go for life. The terrible slaughter went on, as was ordered; the image of Baal was thrown down; and offal and filth took its place, in order to pour the utmost contempt upon the pollutions of idolatry. Thus Ahab, Jezebel and their family, the devotees of Baal, and his image and worship, were exterminated from Israel.

This took place as the fulfilment of the curse the Lord pronounced upon Jeroboam's altar, by the prophet. Surely Jehu showed his zeal for the Lord, and the Lord placed his seal of displeasure upon idolatry. Jehu ruled Israel twenty-eight years, and was succeeded by his son.

Jehoahaz, — Son and successor of Jehu. His bad rule left him a prey to Benhadad and Hazael of Syria, and by them was nearly robbed of his kingdom.

Joash, or Jehoash — Grandson of Jehu, recovered from the Syrians the ground lost by Jehoahaz, his father. Amaziah, King of Judah, rather picked a quarrel with Joash; when he roused up finally, drove Amaziah, broke down a part of the wall of Jerusalem, pillaged the temple, and, with large spoil, returned in triumph to Samaria. He soon after died.

Jeroboam II. — Great-grandson of Jehu, raised the kingdom of Israel to its last high pitch of prosperity; recovering all the country of the Israelites, east of the river. He, however, followed all the evil ways of idolatry, — the bane and ruin of the Ten Tribes, and of all who worship idols.

Next came Zechariah, then Shallum; both of little note.

Menahem — Was next, and his reign inglorious; his realm being invaded by Pul (father of Sardanapalus), King of Assyria. Menahem bought peace with Pul, for one thousand talents of silver; and raised the money by direct tax upon his people.

Pekahiah, and Pekah, followed. The idolatry of Jeroboam, son of Nebat, remained — the curse of Israel.

Hoshea — The last of the kings of Israel, or of the Ten Tribes, that revolted. Being weary of the tribute the nation had to pay the King of Assyria (imposed upon it by Menahem), Hoshea withheld it from him that year, and gave it to So, King of Egypt, to unite with him, and throw off the yoke of Assyria from Israel.

Finding out the conspiracy, Shalmaneser seized Hoshea, and put him in prison, and then marched against Samaria, and besieged it; but, by a brave resistance, he was not able to take it, short of three years. It was then taken, and the Ten Tribes carried into perpetual captivity by Shalmaneser, King of Assyria — two hundred and fifty years after they left their brethren, under Jeroboam, and at the same time turned to dumb idols, from serving the Lord.

They vainly supposed that they could escape from such a fate as Rehoboam threatened upon them, by revolt and idolatry; but they found it no better to be joined to idols, and let alone, than to remain in the way of duty, and be corrected. For the sin of idolatry they were slain.

Nothing is known of the Ten Tribes after this, only that they mixed with other nations, and so were lost.

SAMARITANS. — A class of people is often spoken of in the New Testament, by this name.

Their origin was this: After the Ten Tribes were carried off by Shalmaneser, their country was peopled by emigrants from the east, who adopted the Jewish law, to some considerable extent, but did not worship with the Jews, and made Samaria their capital, — and hence are called Samaritans. This, their heathen origin, and the different interpretations of the law from the Jews, made the animosity between them very bitter; — "They had no *dealings* together." Hence how pertinent, in a Jewish ear, the story of the good Samaritan!

TRIBES OF JUDAH AND BENJAMIN.

REHOBOAM —Was the son and successor of Solomon; and through him the line is continued from Abraham, until Shiloh came.

Upon coming to the throne, Rehoboam met some of the prejudices that had grown up, in the last of Solomon's days. At his coronation, the people assembled at Shechem, and before the ceremonies, he was interrogated as to his policy of governing. Jeroboam came up from Egypt, by the advice of his friends, and was made spokesman, to draw out the line of policy of the new king.

Rehoboam asked three days to determine, and then he would report. In the meantime, he sought the advice of his father's old counsellors. They counselled him to rule in a firm but generous manner. Next he called the men of his own age and time. They advised him to rule like a king, and let the people know that the complaints they brought against his father were trifles; that while he ruled with whips, you will use scorpions.

Seeing no disposition in the new king to listen to their petition, the Ten Tribes replied, "What portion have we in David?" So they separated, with Jeroboam as their king, and as has been noticed.

Rehoboam, to test the sincerity of the revolters, in their mad scheme, sent Adoram, the officer of the tribute — knowing if they refused to pay tribute, the die was cast. When Adoram's errand was made known, he was stoned to death. Rehoboam, hearing of this, hastened from Shechem to Jerusalem, and assembled his men of war, determined to force the Ten Tribes to submit. But the word of the Lord came by Shemaiah, expressly forbidding their going up against Israel, and so the expedition was abandoned.

Upon this, Rehoboam turned his attention to building forts, and strengthening himself. Besides this, the priests and Levites in Israel, being put out of office by Jeroboam, — who abolished the worship of the Lord, — these all flocked to the standard of Rehoboam, and thus he was greatly strengthened also. Many others of the Ten Tribes, who were really pious, also came to Jerusalem; and, for three years, Rehoboam was strengthened, and the worship of God flourished.

But, sad to relate, Rehoboam's prosperity did not keep him from forsaking the law of the Lord; but, like Israel, fell into idolatry. For this relapse, the Lord sent Shishak, King of Egypt, to punish Jerusalem, five years after the revolt. At his approach, Judah cried to the Lord; he heard, and pitied, and delivered them from destruction. But Shishak pillaged the temple, and the king's house; he carried off much treasure: even the shields of gold Solomon made. He also put Judah under tribute.

Rehoboam being thus humbled, things went well in Judah. Yet the king did not well, in that he prepared not his heart to seek the Lord.

SHEMAIAH. — Rehoboam having prepared himself for war with Jeroboam, to bring him into allegiance to himself, was forbidden by the Lord, through Shemaiah the prophet, from making war upon Israel. Rehoboam and his princes were also assured by Shemaiah of deliverance from utter destruction by Shishak, upon repentance, and turning to the Lord.

ABIJAM — Son of Rehoboam, reigned three years. He gave battle to Jeroboam, but first tried to persuade him to return to his allegiance to the house of David, restore the priests of the Lord he had ejected from office, and not forsake the Lord God.

But Jeroboam would not listen, but made the assault upon Judah from ambush. Judah then cried to the Lord, who heard and delivered them, because they plead his cause before Jeroboam, and cried to him for help.

Abijam gained the victory — not, however, without a slaughter of five hundred thousand of Israel — and they never recovered from the blow, during Abijam's reign.

Thus again the Lord vindicated himself, and taught those who feared him, that it shall be well with the righteous; but wo to the wicked, it shall be ill with him.

Asa — Was the third king of Judah, and grandson of Rehoboam. He prosecuted the work of reform with much vigor, — demolishing the idol his mother had erected, and cutting down the grove where it stood; also deposing her from the throne. He then gave the most *explicit* orders to Judah to serve the Lord God, and him alone. He next strengthened the strong places, and so arose to a state of great prosperity; — a consequence of seeking the Lord *first*.

No sooner had he strengthened his kingdom, than Zerah, an Ethiopian, came against him, with a million of soldiers. Asa was able to meet him with five hundred thousand, and, calling earnestly upon the Lord for help against this host, was able to repel them, taking, also, much spoil.

The Lord then sent Azariah the prophet to impress upon Asa the importance of earnestly following the Lord; telling him if he sought the Lord, he would be found of him; but if he forsook him, God would also forsake him. Asa then proclaimed a gathering of Judah and Benjamin at Jerusalem; and they offered of the spoil to the Lord, seven hundred oxen, and seven thousand sheep. And they entered into a covenant to seek the Lord with all the heart: and they vowed, with shouting, and blowing of trumpets. And the Lord gave them rest round about. The temple was also replenished of its utensils.

All this prosperity stirred up the jealousy of Baasha, King of Israel; and, to prevent his people from going up to Jerusalem, he commenced a fort at Ramah, — a narrow place in the mountain, on the main road, — so as to keep them back. At this, Asa sent presents to the King of Syria, at Damascus, and solicited him to attack Baasha in the rear, to draw him back to take care of the interior of his kingdom.

While Baasha was thus engaged, Asa demolished the fort at Ramah, and took the timber and stones and built Geba and Mizpah, of Benjamin.

For this resort to the King of Syria, to keep Baasha from spreading idolatry (instead of calling upon the Lord), Asa was reproved by the prophet. Being offended at this, he cast the prophet into prison, and was afterwards a little inclined to oppression. He was taken with a disease in his feet, very severe, in the thirty-ninth year of his reign. But he sought unto the physicians, instead of the Lord, and died more honored of men than of God.

Azariah, — A prophet of the Lord, sent by him to Asa the king, to impress upon his mind the important truth, that if he forsook the law and service of Jehovah, he would also be forsaken of him.

Asa received the message with gladness, and set about removing the idolatrous corruptions of the times; gathered the people together; offered ample sacrifices, and caused the people to vow allegiance and constancy to the Lord.

JEHOSHAPHAT — Was son and successor of Asa on the throne of Judah. His first acts were to garrison his forts, and make the kingdom strong. He then removed the groves, and high places of idolatry. Jehoshaphat had honor, riches, and peace, and lifted up his heart to serve the Lord.

He did a very important work, in calling out all the learned and pious men of the realm, and sending them through the land to teach the law of the Lord. By thus supplying the civil and ecclesiastical offices with the best men of the nation, he raised the kingdom to a great pitch of prosperity, so that the fear of the Lord fell upon the nations round about, and they made no war upon Jehoshaphat.

In a friendly visit to Ahab, King of Israel, the latter proposed to Jehoshaphat to unite with him in taking Ramoth-Gilead from the King of Syria. Ahab's prophets said go; but Jehoshaphat wanted to consult a prophet of the Lord. In doing so he was told not to go, and yet ventured to follow Ahab. He came very near losing his life in the battle; and, besides, Jehu reproved him stoutly for his presumption.

After this, Jehoshaphat renewed his charge to the judges and Levites throughout the land, to be faithful in teaching and obeying the law of the Lord with perfect hearts.

Amariah was chief-priest, and Zebadiah secretary of state, or agent for all the king's matters in Judah.

A confederacy being formed between the Ammonites, Moabites, and others against Judah, Jehoshaphat proclaimed a fast to the Lord, and all the people came together, when the king made a most imploring prayer to the Lord to save them from their enemies. An answer was obtained that they should be delivered, and that without fighting. So they went out to meet the enemy with singing and trumpets, which put them to flight in great panic and confusion. The people of Judah were three days gathering up the spoil the enemy left in their haste.

So the realm was quiet, for God gave it rest. On the whole, Jehoshaphat proved a very godly and wise king, by adhering to the law of the Lord.

JAHAZIEL — The prophet who encouraged Jehoshaphat when he gathered the people together to ask help of the Lord against the invasion of the Ammonites. The Lord saw the humble dependence of Jehoshaphat upon his aid, and so sent the prophet Jahaziel to inform him that he should have the victory even without fighting. And it was even so.

Jehoram — Son and successor of Jehoshaphat. His first public act was to put his brethren and many princes of Israel to death.

He copied after Ahab, and well might, for he took Ahab's daughter, a half Jezebel, to wife.

For his violence he lost his sway over the Edomites, who revolted from him, and also some of his own people. His kingdom was also overrun by the Philistines and Arabians, whom the Lord stirred up to punish him. They plundered his palace and took all the royal family prisoners, except the youngest son. Jehoram died, as the prophet told him he would, with a fearful disease of the bowels, which cut him off in God's displeasure, unlamented and unhonored.

It is supposed by some that this disease was the same as that of Antiochus Epiphanes and Herod Agrippa, who were signally cut off.

Elijah. — Few have ever enjoyed such marked favor of the Lord, as did this eminent prophet. He was first sent by the Lord to foretell Ahab of a three years' drought. He was then told to retire to the wilderness, by a brook, where he stayed until it dried up. During his stay there he was fed by ravens. After the brook dried up, he was sent to Zarephath; and as he drew near the gate, he saw a widow woman, and asked her for a drink of water and a morsel of bread.

She replied, that she had but a little meal, and a little oil, and was gathering sticks to cook it for herself and son, to eat their last and die. But Elijah insisted upon being served first, assuring her that he had come to board with her until the Lord should send rain; and that the cruise of oil and the meal should not fail, and it did not.

During Elijah's stay the widow's son died, whom he raised to life again — ample pay for his board.

Elijah was then told to go and show himself to Ahab. As he was going, he met Obadiah (who hid and fed one hundred prophets in caves, at the time Jezebel, Ahab's wife, made a slaughter among the prophets), and told him to inform Ahab that he wished to see him. His object was to show him the folly of idolatry. In the interview, Elijah challenged the priests of Baal to offer a burnt-offering, and see whose God would answer by fire and burn it. The Baalites tried first, and called, and called in vain; when Elijah prayed to the Lord God, who sent fire and burnt his offering. Elijah then caused the idol-priests to be slain. This took place in Mount Carmel; and before they left, signs of rain were seen, — the three years' drought was over.

Ahab, returning, told Jezebel what Elijah had done, when she vowed his death. Elijah fled into the wilderness, into Mount Horeb; and it was at this time he complained to the Lord "that the prophets had been slain, and he was alone, and his life was sought."

While there in the mount (Horeb), the Lord appeared to him, and sent him by the way of Damascus, to anoint Hazael to be King of Syria, and Jehu to be King of Israel; and also Elisha to be prophet after himself. The Lord also assured him of seven thousand men in Israel who had not bowed the knee to Baal.

As he went he found Elisha ploughing with twelve yoke of oxen, and called him to follow him, which he did.

He next appeared to Ahab, in the field of Naboth, and declared to him the extinction of his family for his wickedness, and that dogs should lick his blood, as they had Naboth's, whom Jezebel caused to be slain.

Ahaziah, son of Ahab, falling from the top of a house, sent a messenger to Ekron to consult Baal whether he would recover. But on his way he met Elijah, who told him the king would die. The king was vexed because *Elijah* had said this, and sent out a posse of men to *seize* him as a prisoner. The prophet seeing them coming, and knowing their intention, called fire from heaven and destroyed them. A second detachment fared likewise; when a third came, and asked him to come down and see the king, which he did. And the king died.

Elijah's time to leave had come, so he and Elisha went to Bethel and Jericho, and took the students from the "schools of the prophets" there, and went away towards Jordan. As the sons of the prophets stood off a little, the prophets went down to the river (probably where Joshua went over), and Elijah took his mantle and smote the waters, when Jordan parted, and they went over. While over there, Elijah says to Elisha, What shall I do for thee before I be taken from thee? He replied, Give me a double portion of thy spirit (much like the choice of Solomon). While they were walking and talking, a chariot and horses of fire appeared, and took Elijah to heaven, and he was seen no more. Thus he passed away, on the other side of Jordan, as Moses did — and as Enoch did, without death.

ELISHA. — At the sight of Elijah's ascension, Elisha exclaimed: "My father, the chariot of Israel, and the horsemen thereof!" Elisha then took the mantle, as it fell from the prophet, and, returning, smote the river, when it parted again, and Elisha went over.

At this the sons of the prophets exclaimed, The spirit of Elijah doth rest upon Elisha!

As Elisha came on his way back toward Bethel, there came out rude boys, saying, "Go up, thou bald-head!"—probably said in allusion to Elijah's ascent; as if they had said, Come, old bald-head, let us see you go up! Similar to "Let him come down from the cross, and we will believe;—he saved others, himself he cannot save," etc., spoken of Christ tauntingly.

For this insult to Elisha, two bears came out of the woods and tore forty-two of them in pieces.

After this, being in company with Jehoshaphat and his army, Elisha supplied them with water, when they must have perished without it.

A widow of one of the prophets came to Elisha one day, stating, as a grievance, that her husband, a godly man, had died in debt, and the creditor had come to take her two sons for bondmen. So the prophet asked what she had in her house. She replied, "Only a pot of oil." He then told her to go and borrow empty vessels not a few, and take her pot of oil and pour out of it until one was filled, and set it away, and so on. This she did, and filled a large number, until the oil stayed.

Then the prophet directed her to sell enough to pay the debt, and she and her sons to live on the rest.

As Elisha came to Shunem one day, a wealthy lady invited him to her home, when she and her husband perceiving him to be a godly man, entertained him in a very cordial manner.

He, seeing their kindness, and that they were rich and pious, yet childless, rewarded them by the promise of an heir, which took place in due time, to their great joy. But the child sickened and died. The woman started at once for Carmel to see the prophet, who, as soon as he saw her, inquired if all was well with her, her husband, and the child.

But her errand was soon made known, and she persuaded Elisha to go to her house and restore the child to life again, which he did.

He next directed Naaman the Syrian to go and wash seven times in Jordan, as a means of cure for his leprosy. He hesitated for a time, when he finally went, and was cured. This so impressed Naaman that there was a God in Israel, that he even professed to renounce idolatry and choose the service of Jehovah.

Elisha wrought several other miracles, such as causing an axe lost in the river to rise to the top and swim, smiting the Syrian army with blindness, etc.

But his last sickness came, and Elisha died; and so he passed away, like all the good before him; having executed the prophetic office over sixty years, with great fidelity and success. The next year the Moabites invaded the country. And as a company were about to bury a man, they looked up and saw a party of the enemy coming, and not having time to finish the burial, hastily thrust the body into the tomb of Elisha; as the body touched the prophet's bones, it came to life and stood up.

Surely, from the history of these two eminent men, every reflecting mind must be persuaded that there is a God in heaven, and that Elijah and Elisha (not Mohammed) were his prophets.

Also, that *all* who work righteousness are accepted of God, and the wicked are reserved to be punished.

AHAZIAH — Son of Jehoram, and King of Judah, was slain by Jehu, at the same time with Joram of Israel.

JONAH. — This prophet is supposed to have lived and prophesied between 862 and 790 B. C. His adventure at sea is related in the book by his name in the Old Testament, and is a most pertinent rebuke on attempts at evading the plain duties of religion.

The King of Nineveh, at the time of Jonah's visit to that wicked city, is said to have been Pul, father of the notorious Sardanapalus.

The fictitious adventure of Hercules, in Grecian tales, being three days in the belly of a shark, cutting and hacking his entrails, and coming out with the loss of nothing but his hair, is founded on the story of Jonah.

JOASH. — Between the death of Ahaziah and the coronation of Joash, Athaliah, wife of Ahaziah, daughter of Ahab (hence half Jezebel), took the reins of government.

The death of her husband by the hand of Jehu stirred up the *Jezebel-Ahab* in her, and she sought vengeance by seeking to put all her husband's children by former wives, to death, and usurping the throne of Judah.

Whilst she supposed she had done this, a sister of her husband had taken Joash, the youngest of his sons and his nurse and hidden them in the temple, until he was seven years old. The sympathies of the people being in his favor, and being disgusted with the usurpation of Athaliah, a plan was readily seconded to crown Joash king.

His coronation took place in the court of the temple, with great pomp and solemnity. But when the wicked Athaliah saw it, she screamed, "Treason! treason!" She did not allude to her own treason, but hoped to arouse the popular fury in her behalf; but, to her astonishment, the popular will retorted the charge of treason, and Jehoiada the high-priest ordered her to be slain with the sword.

Jehoiada then put the king and people under oath, to serve the

Lord God faithfully; whereupon the altars of Baal and his worship were destroyed. Joash, or Jehoash, orders the temple repaired, when Jehoiada takes a chest and bores a hole in the top, puts it by the door of the temple to receive the money given for the purpose. This repair of the temple took place about 3148 A. M., or 856 B. C. Not only the building, but the utensils of the temple were replenished, so that the state of religion was good at the death of Jehoiada, which took place twelve years after — he being of the great age of one hundred and thirty years.

But when Jehoiada died, Joash lost his best friend. For then his courtiers began to fawn and flatter him, and he took it, and was turned to idols; for which Zechariah the priest, son of Jehoiada, reproved him, and warned him of the consequences of forsaking the Lord. Joash flying into a rage, the priest was slain, "between the porch and the altar." Thus fell the son of the man who had saved the king's life, raised him to the throne, and directed him; and now he requites it all by turning to idolatry, and slaying the priest in the temple. While dying, he predicted God's judgment for this.

This was soon fulfilled, by an invasion from the Syrians, with whom Joash bought peace, by giving up the treasures of the temple and the king's palace: and conspirators slew him in his bed.

How strikingly the prediction of the Lord, by Samuel, when the people clamored for a king, is fulfilled, in the excesses and oppressions of both the kings of Israel and Judah! (See 1 Samuel, 8 : 6—22.)

Zechariah. — He was a prophet in the days of Joash, King of Judah. He was son of Jehoiada, who secured his life and throne to Joash. But, notwithstanding that great service done the king by Zechariah's father, and his being sent by the Lord to reprove the people for their sins, Joash flew into a rage at the prophet, and caused him to be stoned to death, between the porch and the altar.

Amaziah — Son of Joash, and eighth King of Judah. He did that which was right in the sight of the Lord, but not with a perfect heart. He put the conspirators to death who slew his father, but spared their children, on the strength of the law, "that the children are not to bear the sins of the fathers."

He early formed the purpose to re-conquer the Edomites, who had revolted during the reign of Jehoram. To do this, he raised three hundred thousand of his own men, and hired one hundred thousand of Israel; but he was directed of God to dismiss the latter, or he would fall before the enemy. This he did reluctantly, and they, taking offence at the dismission, ravaged the cities of Judah as they returned, taking also much spoil.

Amaziah then prosecuted the war with Edom, slaying ten thousand, and taking ten thousand prisoners. Elated with his success, he took their idols, and set them up and worshipped them. For this, the Lord sent a prophet to reprove him for turning away from Jehovah, who had given him the victory. He ordered the prophet be silent; but he closed his speech by telling the king God would surely destroy him for his wilfulness.

He then turns, and gives Joash, King of Israel, a challenge to meet him face to face in war. Joash declined, thinking it unwise to meet in war; but Amaziah forced him to make defence. Being driven to it, Joash made a vigorous resistance, drove the King of Judah back, broke down a part of the wall of Jerusalem, plundered the temple and the palace, and returned.

Amaziah sought this quarrel with Joash, to get revenge for the depredations committed by the one hundred thousand on their return. But having resisted the warning of the Lord to him, and going on the strength of his own wilful ambition, he fell.

Fifteen years after, he was obliged to flee from a conspiracy in Jerusalem, but was pursued and slain in Lachish.

Uzziah, or Azariah. — He was made king upon the death of his father, at the age of sixteen. He began his career in the ways of wisdom, being guided by Zechariah, who had understanding in the visions of God. He was successful against his enemies; improved and strengthened Jerusalem; built towers, vineyards, wells, and was great in husbandry. He very greatly improved the condition of his army, furnishing all the implements and engines of war. His fame was very great with the kings about him.

But his prosperity was his adversity. He became so popular that he entertained the foolish notion monarchs often do, that he had a divine right to usurp any office he pleased. So he went into the temple, and laid hold of the priests' censer, and proceeded to offer incense, when they warned him of his improper conduct; for it pertained to the priests alone to offer incense to the Lord.

At this rebuke, the king was displeased, and persisted in executing the priests' office; when the leprosy arose in his forehead, and he remained a leper until the day of his death.

Amos — Prophesied in the time of Uzziah, between 759 and 734. He was employed in rural pursuits, and called specially to prophesy against Israel, by rebuking their sins, and foretelling the judgments of the Lord that awaited them; yet he exhorted them to repentance and reform, and so peace and mercy would come unto them.

But Amaziah, a priest of Baal, made complaint to the king, Jeroboam II., that a prophet of Judah had come to speak against Israel, and that the land could not bear his words; saying that the sword shall cut off the king, and Israel shall go away, and die captives in a strange land.

So the prophet was obliged to leave the country, and retire to Tekoa, ten miles south of Jerusalem.

The time and manner of his death are unknown.

Thus the Lord sought to save Israel by his prophets; but they would not: hence their rejection.

HOSEA — Also prophesied about the same time, and lived in Samaria. He reproved Israel, and tried to lead them in the right way; but in vain. He also spoke strongly of the coming Messiah, and the glory of his kingdom.

JOTHAM — Son of Uzziah, followed the good, and shunned the bad example of his father. He built largely, and strengthened his kingdom, and put the Edomites under tribute. So Jotham became mighty, because he prepared his ways before the Lord.

Happy would it be for the world, were *all* kings guided by the fear of the Lord. The prosperity of the Jews, and their adversity, all grew out of their fear or scorn of the Almighty. Further; the true fear of God is not confined to any people in particular; for we see the kings of Judah and Israel often changing, alternately from Jehovah to Baal.

AHAZ — Son of Jotham, took the opposite course from his father, on coming to the throne of Judah; he even offered his own children in sacrifice to Baal.

The kings of Syria and Israel formed an alliance, and came up against Ahaz; when the Lord sent the prophet Isaiah to assure the king that, for David's sake, Judah should be spared. During this visit he uttered the memorable prophecy of the coming of Immanuel, — the Shiloh of Moses' time, the Messiah, the Lord our Righteousness.

Still, the kings of Syria and Israel carried off two hundred thousand women and children, after slaying one hundred and twenty thousand men of Judah. On coming to Samaria with this host, Oded, a prophet of the Lord, besought the conqueror of Israel not to retain in bondage his own kindred, and prevailed upon him to liberate them; and putting them in a condition to journey, with beasts and provisions, they returned.

The magnanimity of this act is without a parallel in all the history of the hateful lust of power and conquest.

The Edomites and Philistines uniting against Ahaz, he sent to Tiglath-pileser, King of Assyria, to help him. This he did; but his services, and the large draft on the treasures of the temple and the palace, and the tax on the princes, left Ahaz so that Pileser's aid was no advantage to him.

Besides that, when Ahaz went to Damascus, to acknowledge the favors of the King of Assyria, he saw an idol altar, and taking a fancy to it, sent a draft to Urijah, at Jerusalem, and ordered one made like it, and put in the place of the one there. While at Damascus, he also sacrificed to idols.

After his return to Jerusalem, he mutilated many of the vessels of the temple, took down the laver from the oxen, and despoiled much of the beauty of the holy furniture. In Jerusalem, and in the cities of Judah, he erected idol altars, and provoked the Lord God. He died, and was buried unhonored.

Joel.—This prophet lived about the time of Ahaz, and was contemporary with Isaiah.

The burden of his prophecy was the fearful temporal judgments that were speedily coming upon the nation, and in view of which he exhorted them to repentance, and to seek the mercy and favor of the Lord, while he was yet on the forgiving hand.

He also uttered a prophecy, which had its fulfilment on the day of Pentecost.

Micah — Prophesied in the reigns of Jotham, Ahaz, and Hezekiah, and respecting each of them.

The most important feature of his prophecy is his view of the Messiah,—his birthplace, characteristics, and blessings of his reign on earth.

Nahum—Prophesied in Hezekiah's time, and foretold the overthrow of Nineveh, and so remarkable has been the fulfilment thereof, that even the site of Nineveh has been a matter of dispute for about sixteen centuries.

Hezekiah—The son and successor of Ahaz, led the very opposite course his father pursued. He opened the doors of the temple Ahaz had shut up, caused the temple to be purified, and gave the strictest orders to the priests and Levites to sanctify themselves, and to resume the neglected and desecrated service of the Lord's house. These orders being strictly carried out, religion was put at once in a flourishing condition, and the nation as soon made prosperous and peaceful.

He also proclaimed throughout the whole realm a gathering of the people at Jerusalem, to keep the Passover. This met with a hearty response from the tribes, for they gathered in great numbers, and kept the feast of the Passover fourteen days, instead of seven, such was the joy of the people at the revival of the worship of

Jehovah. Thus Hezekiah had restored the breach made by Ahaz, in leading the nation into gross idolatry.

In the fourth year of Hezekiah, Shalmaneser took Samaria, and carried the Ten Tribes into irrecoverable captivity, and they were swallowed up as a people.

Ahaz having left the kingdom of Judah under tribute to Assyria, Hezekiah was induced to pay it over when Israel was taken away, hoping to turn back the avarice of the King of Assyria; but this only created a thirst for more, and he sent three of his principal men, and an army, to induce the people to revolt from Hezekiah, and join the Assyrians.

Instead of listening to these proposals, the people declared their allegiance to Hezekiah. But not being satisfied with this simply, Hezekiah inquired of Isaiah, the prophet of the Lord, and he assured him that Sennacherib should not hurt him, and should fall by the sword in his own land.

Returning from an expedition against Egypt, Sennacherib, wrote a letter to Hezekiah, in which he blasphemously compared the Lord with the gods of the heathen, and tauntingly boasted that no one could stand before his victorious march. At this Hezekiah became alarmed, not knowing but the Lord was really using Sennacherib as a scourge of wickedness; so he took the letter, and read it, and went up to the house of the Lord, and spread it before him, and prayed earnestly for the interposition of Heaven in his behalf.

He acknowledged the successes of the King of Assyria — that he had destroyed the gods of the nations, but that they were no gods at all. He then cried to the Lord, who could deliver him, if he would but stretch forth his hand in favor of Judah.

Then Isaiah the prophet sent to Hezekiah, saying, "Thy prayer is heard; the Lord will put a hook in the nose of Sennacherib, and a bridle in his mouth, and turn him back by the way he came, so that he shall not come nigh this city; for I will defend it for my own and my servant David's sake, saith the Lord."

All this was fulfilled; for the Lord smote of Sennacherib's army, in one night, one hundred and eighty-five thousand, so that they died; and he himself returned to his own land, and while in the stupid act of worshipping his idol, two of his sons entered and slew him with the sword. Thus fell the blasphemer of the God of heaven.

After this, Hezekiah was taken sick, and Isaiah told him to set his house in order, for he should die, and not live. But the king prayed earnestly that his life might be spared yet longer.

In answer to this prayer, Isaiah told him the Lord would add to his days fifteen years.

Berodach-baladan, King of Babylon, hearing of Hezekiah's sickness and recovery, sent him a present and letter (not of blasphemy against Jehovah, like Sennacherib) but of congratulation. Hezekiah received the flattery, and showed the messengers all his wealth and treasure. For this unnecessary disclosure and acceptance of Babylonish court flattery, Isaiah told Hezekiah that all this wealth, of which he had gloried before men, should be carried away captive into the very palace from which this fawning proceeded, and with which he had been foolishly pleased.

This produced in Hezekiah deep penitence before the Lord, because he had done foolishly. The latter part of his life was passed in tranquillity, and he was gathered unto his fathers full of honors.

Hezekiah was the best king from Solomon's time to his, and all for keeping close to the Lord, and relying upon him for wisdom and strength — the true and unfailing source of prosperity.

ISAIAH — The prophet, lived and prophesied during the reign of the four last-mentioned kings. The city of Rome was founded in his time, 753 B. C. He is said to have been one of the faithful who were sawn in sunder. Wicked as some of the kings were, and idolatrous as many of the people were, yet there were true prophets, and many wise and good men, — some not known to the prophets, as with Elijah, who kept the faith in its purity.

The Book of Isaiah contains, in the first thirty-nine chapters, an account of matters during the prophet's active life; and the rest of the book treats of the finishing up of the Babylonish captivity, and the coming, progress, triumph, and glory of the kingdom of the Messiah. He is also styled the Evangelical Prophet, from the resemblance of his writings to the gospels of the New Testament.

MANASSEH — Son and successor of Hezekiah on the throne of Judah, — was only twelve years old when he became king; but his heart was not established in the right way.

He built altars to Baal, revived the worship of images, and is said even to have placed an image of himself in the temple; and was guided by the familiar spirits, wizards, and enchantments of idolatry.

For such impiety the Lord stretched forth his hand against him, and the King of Babylon carried him off in chains, a captive. This opened his eyes, and brought him to repentance; and by supplication to God, he was set at liberty, and permitted to return to Jerusalem.

Upon his return, Manasseh went about reforming the bad manners of the people, growing out of his former bad example. He built a piece of new wall for the defence of Jerusalem; removed the idol from the temple; broke down the idol altars he had erected, and earnestly, by example and precept, strove to lead Judah back to serve the Lord God.

In this labor he succeeded greatly, yet did no more than turn the tide of his own misdoings, and hardly restored the kingdom to the condition in which his father left it. Still, his last days were his best days.

AMON — The fourteenth king of Judah, did all the evil of Manasseh his father, but not the good. After a short reign of two years, he was assassinated by his own servants.

JOSIAH. — Of no king of Judah have we so good an account throughout, as of this. He began his reign at eight years of age. "He began well, continued well, and ended well." The uprightness of his early life must be attributed, in a great measure, to the influence of his mother, Jedidah, and also of Hilkiah the high-priest, and this extended to his riper years.

He soon manifested an abhorrence of the idolatry of the nation and of his predecessors. In the eighteenth year of his reign, he went about a thorough repair of the temple, as did also Joash. During the repairs, Hilkiah the priest found a copy of the law, by Moses, which gave great joy to the king and all the people. When it was read before Josiah he rent his clothes, and deplored the departure of the nation from its sacred teachings. It is supposed that Ahaz and Manasseh did much to suppress the law and render it scarce, as wicked rulers often do. (Intelligence is dangerous for tyrants.) Josiah assembled the people at the temple, and had the law read in the presence of them all, and vowed himself and the people also to keep the covenant of the Lord.

Josiah next turned his attention to destroying the idols and altars of Baal, throughout the nation. He first ordered the vessels brought out of the temple and burnt, that were put in there for the service of Baal. He emptied the offices of the idolatrous priests forthwith, of their contents and incumbents; he destroyed the houses of ill-fame devoted to idols, and spared no severity upon the altars and idols throughout the land. Even the bones of the idolatrous priests he took out of their sepulchres, and burned them upon the altar erected in Bethel by Jeroboam, as the man of God prophesied.

Josiah next proclaimed the Passover, to be kept by all the people. He first ordered the priests to attend to the part assigned them by the law of Moses. He did not dictate what they should do to please him, but commanded them to obey the law and the testimony. The sacrifices of the occasion consisted of thousands of oxen; the singing, and all the parts of the service, were attended to with great exactness and solemnity; so that from the days of Samuel the prophet there was no Passover kept like that by Josiah; and by the priests and Levites, and all Judah and Israel that were present, and the inhabitants of Jerusalem.

An unfortunate affair turned up, by which King Josiah lost his life prematurely. Pharaoh-Necho, King of Egypt, made war upon the Medes and Babylonians; and, in his march, passed through the territory of the King of Judah. The King of Media and Josiah were allies, and if Josiah had wished to remain neutral he could not, by allowing one of the hostile powers to pass through his territory quietly, thereby forfeiting both alliance and neutrality, and so was forced to oppose Necho.

The battle took place at Megiddo, when Josiah was wounded by the archers, so that he died, and was carried to Jerusalem and buried in the sepulchre of his fathers. No king's death was ever so deeply lamented by the Jews as Josiah's, — showing that, as a nation, they might have been led in better ways than they often were by their wicked kings.

ZEPHANIAH. — A prophet in King Josiah's time, and a little before Jeremiah. His prophecy was designed mainly to excite the Jewish nation to repentance, in view of the judgments that were gathering about them, and encourage the faithful with the assurance of the final triumph of righteousness.

JEREMIAH, — The prophet, lived and prophesied between 628 and 586 B. C. — about seventy years after Isaiah. He was son of Hilkiah, who found the book of the law while the temple was being repaired by Josiah, and was himself a priest. He was in public life about forty-two years.

His faithfulness brought upon him much ill-will and abuse from his wicked countrymen.

But no ill-treatment deterred him from his duty, though calumniated and imprisoned. He exhorted the king and people to submit to Nebuchadnezzar, and become tributary to him, rather than venture on resisting him, as that would only end in the defeat and overthrow of the whole nation.

But swarms of false prophets filled Jerusalem at this time, who contradicted the prophet, and thus led the people in the way they wanted to go, and hence their ruin. After a portion were carried away captive, the false prophets predicted their speedy return; but Jeremiah wrote them that their captivity would be long, even seventy years, and that they had better submit, enter into some business, and pray for their conqueror.

Still he encouraged them to hope, for a day of deliverance would come at last.

When it was found that Jeremiah had written his prophecy on a roll, Jehoiakim caused it to be read before him, and being offended therewith, cut in pieces with a penknife, and caused it to be burnt.

Then Jeremiah delivered it again, and Baruch, his scribe, wrote it again, and many more like words.

So, neither imprisonment, unbelief, nor bribes, could deter the faithful prophet from declaring the sins of the people, and the ruin of the nation.

Such was his devotion, that he even refused the offer of ease and plenty, made to him by the King of Babylon. But his choice to remain with his countrymen did not secure him from their abuse; for, after the murder of Gedaliah (whom Nebuchadnezzar made governor of Judea), the conspirators were in fear of the Chaldeans, and thought to take refuge in Egypt. Jeremiah was consulted to know whether that were best, when he told them by no means would it be best to go.

But they gave no heed to his words, and not only went themselves, but took Jeremiah with them, by force. In Egypt it is supposed he died, and some think a martyr to his faithfulness.

His prophecy relates chiefly to the judgments of God upon the Jewish and other nations, and to the future glory that should arise on the Church of God, and on such as were steadfast in his service; when the "Desire of Nations," or the Messiah, should come, and all flesh should see the salvation of God.

Habakkuk — One of the prophets. He lived in the reign of Jehoiakim, and was contemporary with Jeremiah. He is supposed to have remained and died in Judea.

His prophecy relates chiefly to the invasion of Judea by the Chaldeans, the overthrow of the Babylonian empire, and the final deliverance of God's faithful people. So that the judgments of Judah came not upon them unawares, but in the midst of the most faithful admonitions, and upon a nation persisting in the way to ruin.

Jehoahaz — Son and successor of Josiah. Upon the death of Josiah, the people proclaimed him king — being the youngest son, which was irregular. This being done without the knowledge of the King of Egypt (who had gone against the Chaldeans), when he returned, contrived to get Jehoahaz into his power by stratagem, at

Riblah, and sent him to Egypt in chains, where he died. Necho then filled the throne with his brother.

Jehoiakim — Being subdued by the King of Egypt, and placed upon the throne by his clemency and power, he could do no better than yield to his demand of tribute. So he put the country under tax, to satisfy the forced claim of Necho. This measure was adopted by the King of Egypt, out of revenge for the opposition of Josiah to his marching through his possessions, against the King of Assyria.

Thus Necho, by taking the life of Josiah, putting one of his sons on the throne, and changing his name from Eliakim to Jehoiakim, and laying the whole nation under tribute, made a distinct mark for himself, and had complete revenge.

Nebuchadnezzar, not being pleased that Necho should rob him of the alliance of Josiah and the nation, came against Jehoiakim and took away the tribute to the King of Egypt, and put the nation under tribute to himself. Jehoiakim was carried in chains to Babylon, but was liberated, and permitted to return to Jerusalem and reign as a tributary prince.

His reign of eleven years was a wicked one, and hastened the approaching calamities. Among the captives taken when Jehoiakim was, were Daniel and the three worthies of the fiery furnace.

Jehoiachin — Son and successor of Jehoiakim. In the eighth year of his reign, Nebuchadnezzar came up again and besieged Jerusalem, took the king and his family, the principal part of the nation, with the royal treasures and the temple furniture, and transported them to the proud city of Babylon. Among these captives was the prophet Ezekiel. Jehoiachin was notorious for his wickedness, — precisely the characters whom God devotes to destruction.

Zedekiah. — This is the last King of Judah — her cup is full. The land could now enjoy her Sabbaths, when the profaners are carried off.

The King of Babylon put Zedekiah upon the throne of Judah, as a tributary. He was a son of Josiah, named Mattaniah, but changed by King Nebuchadnezzar to Zedekiah. He was the personification of sin and wickedness, — hence the severe reproofs uttered against him by Jeremiah.

In the ninth year of his reign he revolted against Nebuchadnezzar, when he marched against Judea, took the strong cities first; and at last Jerusalem, by a famine brought on by supplies being cut off by the besiegers, was forced to surrender.

The King of Egypt, hearing of the peril of the King of Jerusalem, marched an army to aid him; whereupon, the Chaldeans raised the siege, and turned upon the Egyptians. In this interval, Zedekiah with his military undertook to escape, and so fled to the plains of Jericho, where he was overtaken, and obliged to surrender to the Chaldeans. He was then brought before the King of Babylon, who, after reproaching him for his perfidy (in revolting), slew his sons before his eyes, and then put out his eyes. He was then loaded with chains, and carried to Babylon, where he died.

In this transaction, two prophecies respecting Zedekiah, so apparently contradictory that Josephus refused to believe either of them, were fulfilled. One was by Jeremiah, who predicted that he should not escape from the King of Babylon, but that they should look each other in the eyes. The other, by Ezekiel, that he should be carried to Babylon and die there, but not see it. The above occurrence completely fulfils them both.

Soon after Nebuchadnezzar had carried off the inhabitants, he sent his general Nebuzar-adan, with the army, to plunder, demolish, and burn Jerusalem, and bring away the treasure, and all the furniture and works of brass provided by Solomon, and carry them away to Babylon.

Thus Jerusalem was destroyed, and Judah carried away captive, in 3416 A. M., 588 B. C., on the 27th August. It occurred in the eleventh year of King Zedekiah; nineteenth of Nebuchadnezzar; four hundred and twenty-four years three months and eight days from the foundation of the temple; four hundred and sixty-eight years from the beginning of the reign of David; three hundred and eighty-eight from the revolt of the Ten Tribes, and one hundred and thirty-four years after *their* captivity.

Nebuzar-adan meeting Jeremiah, told him that these calamities were predicted by himself from his God, for their sins. As for the prophet himself, the general gave him liberty to go to Babylon to be cared for, or remain with those left behind of his own people. He chose the latter.

Gedaliah was appointed Governor of Judea, by Nebuchadnezzar. He tried to persuade the people to submit to the King of Babylon, as had also Jeremiah. But the advice of both the governor and the prophet were spurned by a people panting for their own ruin.

Gedaliah was assassinated, when the perpetrators and many other Jews fled to Egypt through fear, forcibly taking Jeremiah with them, against his will.

Thus Judah was taken captive; but with the prophecies of Isaiah and Jeremiah, that after seventy years they should be set at liberty by Cyrus, and return and rebuild Jerusalem. Even the manner of taking Babylon (by turning the river) was also foretold, and all nearly two centuries before Cyrus was born.

And yet, with such prophets as these in their midst, whom God inspired, it was for their sins and rejection of the Lord the Jews were made captives.

PERIOD IV. FROM THE CAPTIVITY, TO THE DESTRUCTION OF JERUSALEM, 3416 A. M., AND 588 B. C., 4074 A. M., 70 A. C.

DANIEL, — The next after Habakkuk, was also one of the prophets. Though but a youth at the time Judah was carried away, yet he and Shadrach, and Meshach, and Abed-nego, soon attracted special attention for their abstemiousness and piety.

Nebuchadnezzar dreamed a dream in the second year of his reign, which troubled him; but he could get no interpreter, neither by bribes nor threats. Upon this, he flew into a rage, which was pacified only by Daniel's offer to give the interpretation. This being done, Daniel (like Joseph, in Egypt) was promoted to be a great officer in the government of Babylon; and Shadrach, Meshach, and Abed-nego, were officers under him.

Through jealousy and stratagem, the three last mentioned were cast into a fiery furnace, from which God delivered them.

Nebuchadnezzar dreamed again, and Daniel interpreted that also. It was this dream in which the king was shown that he must acknowledge that his glory and greatness were the gift of God, on penalty of wandering in the fields and eating straw (or herbs), like an ox, until he would. Refusing, he was sent out, but in due time came to Daniel's terms, when he blessed, and praised, and honored the Most High. It is thought the king was a true convert, and died in the faith of the God of Israel.

BELSHAZZAR — Successor to Nebuchadnezzar, while holding an impious feast with his courtiers and concubines, and drinking drunk out of the holy vessels brought from Jerusalem, saw a hand writing on the wall, which Daniel was called to interpret. The interpretation was, that the kingdom of Babylon was at an end, — and that night Belshazzar was slain.

DARIUS. — Cyrus the Persian, after taking Babylon, gave it into the hands of Darius, *i. e.*, Cyaxares, for a time; and he, because he saw an excellent spirit in Daniel, and, doubtless, having heard of his wisdom and worth, thought to make him chief officer in the realm.

Jealousy was again fired up among the officers of the king, to sacrifice Daniel to royal displeasure.

The first attempt was made upon his official integrity; but, finding everything right, they despaired of their purpose, unless they could hit him for his religion. To do this, a private bill received the royal signature, prohibiting any one asking a petition of any person save of the king during thirty days.

The devisers of this plot *knew* they could impeach him now, as he was in the habit of turning his face towards Jerusalem, and praying, three times a day. Soon a charge came to the king against Daniel, the president of the presidents. What has he done? He prays to his God, which is asking a petition, contrary to law; and the penalty is, casting into the den of lions. Have him forth!

The king saw the plot then, and would gladly have let him off; but the law on one hand, and the intolerable clamor of office-seekers on the other, induced him to yield. But as Daniel was brought forth, the king said to him, "Thy God, in whom thou trustest, will deliver thee, O Daniel!"

So he was cast in, and a stone placed upon the mouth of the den, and sealed with the king's seal and that of his lords, that the purpose might not be changed concerning Daniel.

Then, "very early in the morning," the king came to the den, and cried, with a "lamentable" voice, Daniel, O Daniel, has thy God preserved thee? Daniel replied, that God had sent his angel and shut the mouths of the lions. Then was the king glad, and ordered Daniel taken out of the den, and those cast in who had tried to injure him; and their bones were broken by the lions, ere they reached the bottom.

The king then proclaimed a royal decree throughout the realm, for all the people to worship the God of Daniel, as he was the true God. Thus Daniel prospered in the reign of Darius and Cyrus.

This eminent man was also favored with visions of a very remarkable kind, showing the fate of the Babylonian empire, the rise and fall of the Persian empire, also the rise and fall of the Macedonian empire, the rise and fall of the Roman empire, and the rise, spread, glory, and eternal duration of the kingdom of Christ, which is not of this world, but is destined to fill the whole earth, and have no end.

The predictions of these holy men, in this age of the world, are truly marvellous, and an overwhelming evidence that they were inspired of God.

Daniel prophesied from 606 B. C.,—the same period, before Christ, as the appointment of the first Pope, 606, after Christ. He died in Chaldea.

Obadiah — Prophesied about this time; and a great similarity can be seen between his and a portion of Jeremiah's writings.

Ezekiel, — The prophet, was among the captives when Jehoiachin, King of Judah, was carried away, and was settled with the colony of Jews on the banks of the Chebar, in Chaldea.

He, like Daniel, had sublime visions of future things. He prophesied between 590 and 540 B. C. Eight years of the first of the time corresponded with the last eight of Jeremiah's time. His prophecy relates to Tyre, Egypt, Edom, and Judea. He spoke in the most solemn and reproving manner against the idolatry, hypocrisy, and rebellion of the Jews, with exhortations to faith, and confidence in God's righteousness, and upon repentance, promises of mercy and restoration.

Cyrus — First King of Persia, becoming master of all the East, had a right to issue such orders as he pleased, with reference to any of his subjects, or any part of his realm. Accordingly, he made a royal proclamation throughout the land, that the Lord God had given him all the kingdoms of the earth, and had charged him to build him a house in Jerusalem. Who, then, is there of all his people? The Lord his God be with him, and let him go up!

Thus, from the very country that the ruin of Jerusalem came, its restoration came also. Besides the influence of God's Spirit upon Cyrus, the mention of his name, in the prophecy of Isaiah, as the future deliverer of the nation, nearly two hundred years before, had a great influence in disposing his mind favorably towards the Jews. The time was most favorable for such a move; the country was all under one king, and he in favor of it. Just as it was in the time of Solomon — a general peace. God selects such times to begin some great work. Another example is, the introduction of the gospel, when the universal empire of Rome was at its zenith. The advocates of the new doctrine had to contend with only one form of government. The present peace of the world borders on some great event.

Cyrus not only made a decree for the return of the Jews, but also delivered up the golden vessels taken from Jerusalem by Nebuchadnezzar, — 5400 in number, — and ordered, also, contributions to the same end, that the work might go on.

Just as the Hebrews borrowed (or solicited) contributions from the Egyptians, on the event of the exodus.

Zerubabel — Was the second Moses, to lead the people in a second exodus (3468 A. M., 536 B. C.), and take them up to Jerusalem. With him also went up Jeshua, or Joshua, the first high-priest after the captivity. He was also son of Seraiah the high-priest, whom Nebuchadnezzar put to death, and others, at Riblah, when Zedekiah was taken.

The number who went up at this time, was not far from fifty thousand. On arriving at Jerusalem, they found it in ruins truly; but began the work they went to do, by making a contribution for the temple, which amounted to four hundred and forty-four thousand dollars. Their next step was to erect the altar of burnt-offering, which they did upon the same old foundation laid by Solomon, and offered the daily burnt-offering. They also revived the feast of tabernacles, and so set up the worship of God again at Jerusalem.

The next step was to engage workmen to get cedars from Lebanon to Joppa, in floats, as in the building of the first temple, by Solomon. The work was vigorously prosecuted, so that the ceremony of laying the corner-stone took place in the course of the next year after their arrival at Jerusalem, 3469 A. M., 535 B. C. This was a very imposing and thrilling scene. The priests, with their trumpets and cymbals, were arranged in rows, so as to sing and play alternately, and by responses. The most affecting part of the ceremony was the sobbing of the old men, who remembered the glory and worship of the first temple; and the shouting for joy of the young men, at seeing the prospect of a new temple; — the sobbing and shouting so intermingled, that they could not tell at a distance which prevailed.

When the Samaritans, or Cutheans, who settled in the country from which the Ten Tribes were carried off, heard that the Jews were rebuilding the temple, under the authority of Cyrus, came up to Jerusalem, and proposed to Zerubbabel and the chief men, to unite with them in the enterprise. Being pagans, of course the Jews declined the offer; whereupon, the Samaritans took offence, and at once bribed some of the king's councillors to excite his prejudice. against the Jews, and get him to interfere, and stop their building.

So these hired liars entered devotedly upon their foul work, and prosecuted it to a successful issue, when a decree was passed by King Artaxerxes; so, with authority, and probably with a detachment of the army, they went up, and with force and power stopped the work during the life of the king.

In the second year of Darius, the prophets Haggai and Zechariah encouraged the Jews to go on with the work, in utter disregard of the "bribe decree" of Artaxerxes. This had the desired effect — to bring the matter before Darius, through the renewed complaints made by the Samaritans to him, by his officers, against the Jews, warning him if he permitted them to go on, they would get strong, and reject his authority, which would damage the tribute.

Government "pap" is no insignificant article in seasoning the loyalty of government officials, and in prompting them to acts of great solicitude for the revenue of the lord who divides liberally with his faithful servants.

The king informs Zerubbabel of the complaints made against him and his people, when a reply is at once made out and sent to the king, in which they acknowledge the sins and judgments of their forefathers—all of which were charged in the complaint. But reference is also made to another matter, omitted in the complaint; viz., that the God of heaven had showed them favor in the days of King Cyrus, when a royal decree was passed for the Jews to return and build their city. Now, if it please the king to have search made in the public records, he will find it so; and hence the apology for our persisting in the work; and let the king send us his pleasure concerning the matter.

Search being made, and the decree of Cyrus being found, the decree to stop the building was changed, and authority to go on renewed; grants made, out of the revenue beyond the river, to assist them; and if any man interfered to prevent the work, let his house be pulled down, a gallows made of the beams thereof, and he hanged upon it! Let all this be done speedily, that they may offer sacrifices to the God of heaven, and pray for the life of the king.

A motive for toleration among the heathen kings was, that they might have the prayers of persons professing all religions.

The work now went on rapidly, and was completed, and the temple was dedicated in the sixth year of Darius, King of Persia; or 3489 A. M., 515 B. C. The dedication and feast lasted seven days, with great joy; and they offered one hundred bullocks, two hundred rams, four hundred lambs, and twelve he-goats for a sin-offering. The appointments for the priests were filled up according to the law of Moses—purification observed. And so the Jews were restored.

HAGGAI—The prophet, is supposed to have been born during the captivity, and returned with the colony under Zerubbabel. His prophecy was uttered after the return from the captivity, and abounds in encouragements and reproofs, respecting the building of the second temple. His design was, to nerve the people to prosecute the work, in spite of their enemies. He also spoke of the coming, spread, and glory of Christ's kingdom.

Some have thought his reference to the glory of the latter house over the former, took in the fact that the Messiah should appear and teach in the second temple.

The Jews were strong in the belief that the Messiah would appear in this temple, even until its destruction by the Romans;

and to make their rejection of Christ consistent, they resorted to the alternative of pretending that a third temple is to be built, in which their deliverer will appear.

ZECHARIAH — The prophet, lived and wrote in Haggai's time; he returned from the captivity under Zerubbabel. His purpose was to encourage the Jews in reëstablishing their national institutions and ancient glory. He also spoke explicitly of the coming of Christ.

ESTHER. — Under Ahashuerus (Artaxerxes Longimanus), King of Persia, about 3544 A. M., 460 B. C., another plot was laid against the Jews, from the fury of which they were delivered by Queen Esther the Jewess. Failing to defeat the building of the temple, the enemies of the Jews sought to cut them off at a blow. The king, on a great feast day, sent for the queen to appear before him, which she refused to do; for which the king rejected her, and offered her place to the most *beautiful* woman in the realm. At this, Mordecai, one of the captives of Judah, persuaded Esther, his niece, and an orphan, to make a trial of her charms before the king. To the astonishment of herself and uncle, she won the king's favor for her beauty, and was proclaimed queen, instead of Vashti; still, it was not publicly known that Esther was a Jewess.

Mordecai, being one of those who sat at the king's gate, discovered a conspiracy, formed against the king, made it known to him through Esther, when the conspirators were taken and hanged, and the king's life saved.

But there was one Haman in the king's employ, an Amalekite, a descendant of Agag, whom Saul was sent to destroy, who hated Mordecai, as he did all the Jews. But Mordecai refused to bow to Haman, as the other servants of the king did, when he passed; and for this, Haman resolved to destroy Mordecai, and all the Jews. To aid him in his purpose, he represented to the king that there was a people in the realm diverse in laws and religion from the king and his people, and that the safety of the realm required their destruction; and, upon this showing, obtained a royal decree for the same, and offered to bear the expense of its execution himself.

When this was known to Esther, she ordered Mordecai to call a meeting of the Jews, and, by fasting and prayer, ask the Lord to give her favor before the king, in a petition she was about to ask. This being done, she ventured before him with her request, which, at first, was simply a special request to the king and his favorite, Haman, to a private banquet with the queen. At this supper the king pledged himself to grant Esther her request, let it be what it would, under a forfeit of half the kingdom.

Esther, however, only made request for the king and Haman to come again to a similar entertainment next day.

This royal attention greatly flattered Haman's pride, so that he made much boast of it to his wife and friends; yet he felt that even this honor availed but little, while Mordecai the Jew sat in the gate and refused to bow to him: this stung him to the quick. His wife and friends at once suggested a plan to get rid of this grief to his mind: "Let a gallows be erected fifty cubits (about ninety feet) high, and let Mordecai be hanged thereon." So the gallows was erected, and stood waiting for its victim.

That night the king could not sleep. He took it as an omen, and so ordered his records to be read, to see if any neglect of his could be discovered. When the account of the detection by Mordecai of the conspiracy against the king was read, he inquired if any reward had been made him for this loyalty. When he found that nothing had been done, Haman was called before the king, not knowing what had just transpired.

The king then asked Haman what should be done to the man whom the king should delight to honor. (Now, thought Haman, is the time for me to seize upon royal favor.) He replied, Let the royal apparel be put upon him; let him sit on the king's horse, and let the crown royal be placed on his head, and let one of the king's most noble princes lead the horse through the city and proclaim, Thus shall be done to the man whom the king delighteth to honor!

To Haman's inexpressible consternation, all this was to be done to Mordecai the Jew, and Haman was to lead the horse. On returning to his home, he was not half so elated as before, having been humbled before the man he so much hated. His wife and friends then told him, that if Mordecai be of the seed of the Jews, before whom thou hast begun to fall, your ruin is at hand.

But the messengers came for Haman to hasten to the queen's banquet. Being seated with the king and queen at table, and Haman still not knowing that Esther was a Jewess, the king called for her request.

She modestly begins: "If I have found favor in thy sight, O king, and if it please the king, let my life be given me at my petition, and my people at my request." She then referred to the diabolical plot, already ripe, for their and her destruction, and that it drew nigh. She concealed the fact that it was a plot against them as Jews, so that the king should have no time to allow any prejudices Haman might have instilled into his mind against Mordecai to influence his judgment or decision.

The king was aroused, and asked at once, Who is he? or, Where is he that dares presume on such a deed?

Now the timid Esther has courage to speak. "The adversary and enemy is this wicked Haman!" These words fell like thunder upon the wretch, who thought to revel in innocent blood.

This aroused the king to wrath and vengeance; and an order was issued at once for Haman to be hanged on the very gallows he had erected for the execution of Mordecai the Jew.

The decree had already gone forth for the execution of the Jews, on a given day, and could not be revoked by a royal proclamation. But means were set on foot at once, to inform the Jews what had taken place at the capitol, and that liberty was granted them by the king to put themselves in an attitude of self-defence on the fatal day, which they did, and gave a successful repulse to their enemies, and so were delivered by Esther, the queen, God's agent for that merciful purpose. Then was Mordecai (like Joseph) next to the king, and a blessing to his people, the Jews.

The annual festival of the Jews, called *Purim*, held in remembrance of this event, has been kept by them from that time to the present, without interruption. Similar occasion to the Passover. Haman was hung on his own gallows; — so the inventor of the guillotine, in Paris, was among the first to suffer by it.

Ezra. — The second colony of Jews left Babylon for Jerusalem, under Ezra, about fifty years after the completion of the temple. He was a descendant of Seraiah, who was put to death at the time Zedekiah had his eyes put out. He was a priest, and a ready scribe (*i. e.*, expounder) in the law of Moses, and received his commission from Artaxerxes Longimanus.

The king fitted out Ezra with contributions for his work; gave him the office of chief civil magistrate beyond the river, with power over the officers, and power to appoint civil officers, and to inflict any punishment, even to death, for the violation of any of the laws of Ezra, or of the king.

All this he conferred upon Ezra for the sake of the Lord his God, whose house was in Jerusalem.

Before starting, Ezra collected the people together, and besought the Lord to take care of them in their journey, which lay through an enemy's country.

Ezra thus felt his dependence upon God, for he was ashamed to ask a guard of soldiers, after he had told the king that the Lord's face was towards them that trust in him, and against all those who turn from him. The Lord heard their cry, and brought them safe to Jerusalem, having delivered them from the enemy all the way.

The treasure they brought with them amounted to over a million of dollars, which was all put into the treasury of the Lord, in charge of the priests.

No sooner had Ezra taken his office as governor, than he was informed of a very glaring violation of the law by the people, in taking wives from among the heathen — a thing expressly forbidden by the Lord himself. This gave Ezra much grief, so that he rent his clothes, and plucked off the hair of his head and beard, and sat astonished and heavy-hearted till the evening sacrifice. When the people were then gathered together, he fell upon his knees, and spread his hands toward heaven, and made a most solemn, humble confession before God.

At the close of this prayer, the people gathered around Ezra in great numbers, and wept very sore.

Thus the work of reform was gloriously begun by prayer, humility, confession, and tears. The work of separation from these unlawful marriages continued about three months, when the whole matter, as far as could be, was arranged according to the law of the Lord.

From this time, and after, Ezra was superseded by Nehemiah in office of governor. He turned his attention to the reformation of true religion among his countrymen. One very important measure was that of collecting the sacred books — especially the historical and other portions — from Chronicles forward, covering a space of about one hundred years — from 3450 to 3550 A. M. His services in this particular, by one so competent, shows the value set upon the Scriptures by the ancient people of God; and posterity reaps the inestimable fruits of his labors.

Ezra exceeded even King Jehoshaphat (who sent fit men throughout the realm to teach the people the law of the Lord), by originating the custom of building *synagogues* throughout the land, where the people might easily get together and offer prayers, and listen to the reading of the law.

This, unconsciously and undesignedly, introduced the dissolution of the established worship at Jerusalem, preparatory to the introduction of the glorious reign of the universal kingdom of the Messiah. So Christ declared, that the time had then *come* when men should worship God acceptably everywhere.

The custom introduced by Ezra, is still kept up in the practice of building meeting-houses throughout the land; and no better way can be devised than this to diffuse a knowledge of the law of the Lord and his Christ.

NEHEMIAH — One of the captive Jews, remaining still cup-bearer to the King of Persia (Artaxerxes Longimanus), receiving a visit from one of his brethren from Jerusalem, inquired after their state.

Upon learning of their low condition, and the hinderance of their work by their enemies, he became very sad. Not only sad, but he betook himself to earnest, humble supplication before God, in their behalf; making confession of their sins, as a nation, and imploring the forgiveness of God, and their return to him, by obedience.

Such was his deep solicitude, that the king observed his countenance had changed, and inquired of him the cause of his sadness. He told him it was anxiety in behalf of his oppressed countrymen; and he made request to the king to return to them.

His request was granted, and letters of rights given, and instructions to the king's officers beyond the river (Jordan), and a military escort sent to accompany Nehemiah to Jerusalem, — 3559 A. M., 445 B. C.

He immediately surveyed the walls of the city, and, finding them all out of repair, aroused the people to commence at once the building of the walls of Jerusalem. The spirit of opposition had not died out, notwithstanding the interposition of the decree of King Cyrus, and the overthrow of the plot of Haman; for no sooner did they begin the walls, than Sanballat, Governor of Samaria, interposed every obstacle to prevent them.

But the people were disposed to do as Nehemiah had proposed; and to this end portioned out different sections of the wall, and appointed overseers to prosecute the work with vigor and speed.

They also put themselves in an attitude of defence, by wearing their swords while at work; and Nehemiah, taking the oversight of the whole, had a trumpeter close by him continually, to give warning, so that the enemy could not have time to fall upon them, ere they were ready for battle. So, by day and night, they kept strict watch, not even putting off their clothes, except for washing. And, during the building of the wall, when the opposition increased, they called the more earnestly upon the Lord, and put their hands the more vigorously to the work, until the walls were finished, to the great joy of the Jews, and the great grief and mortification of their enemies.

Shortly after, the people collected together — about fifty thousand of them — when Ezra the priest stood upon a pulpit of wood, and read and expounded the law of Moses unto all that could understand. This caused them to lift up their voices and weep, and cry Amen! amen! to the holy law they had neglected.

Next followed a reform, by confession of all the people, revival of neglected rites, general consecration to the cause of God, and dedication of the wall.

On the return, however, of Nehemiah, from a visit to his old friend Artaxerxes, and the court of Babylon, for five to ten years, he found the priesthood had become secularized, from the people neglecting to provide for their support; — the Sabbath had become desecrated by many, and remnants of mixed marriages, all of which he had aimed to regulate and reform. Having regulated all things as well as he could, according to the law of the Lord, he closes up his labors with this earnest prayer: "Remember me, O my God, for good."

Nehemiah has been styled, and with good reasons, the first patriot, or father of patriots.

"For disinterestedness, philanthropy, patriotism, prudence, courage, zeal, humanity, and every virtue that constitutes a great mind, and proves a soul in deep communion with God, Nehemiah will ever stand conspicuous among the greatest men of the Jewish nation; and an example worthy of imitation by the first of every nation under heaven."

With the Book of Nehemiah the Old Testament history closes, — about 3595 A. M., 409 B. C. After the death of Nehemiah, Judah became a province of Syria.

In his time flourished Herodotus, the "Father of History," and Thucydides. These are the most ancient profane historians whose works are extant; so that where sacred history ends, profane begins, — a fact worthy of special note. Hence to religion and letters we are indebted, under God, for a knowledge of the past. Plato and Socrates lived about the same time.

MALACHI — The last also of the ancient prophets, is supposed to have flourished in Nehemiah's time, or about 3595 A. M., 409 B. C. In his book he administers sharp rebukes for the relapses of the nation, after the reformation by Ezra; specially for intermarriage with the heathen, withholding tithes, and general coldness and indifference to the worship of the good and great Jehovah.

He seeks to intensify his exhortations, by declaring the Messiah to be near, and foretells of his coming by the heralding of the news by John the Baptist; and thus sought to speed them on in true reform and true piety.

It is remarked that the composition of the Book of Malachi betrays signs of decay in the elegance and vigor of the Hebrew language. Be it so. God took good care, just as this noble tongue was passing out of common use, to *stereotype* his Holy Word therein, for generations unborn to read. In like manner was the Greek language ripening into a similar use, in which might be written, as with a pen of iron, the New Testament. Also the Latin, though for a less important purpose, became the depository of the thoughts of the "Fathers" of the early Christian Church.

LIST OF THE PROPHETS, AND DATE (B. C.) IN WHICH THEY FLOURISHED AND WROTE. CLASS I. BEFORE, II. DURING, AND III. AFTER THE CAPTIVITY.

Class	Prophets	B. C.
I.	Samuel, Gad, Nathan,	1165—1000
	Ahijah, Iddo, Shemaiah, Azariah, Micaiah, Jahaziel,	1000—897
	Elijah, Elisha,	909—825
	Zechariah,	878—840
	Jonah,	862—790
	Amos,	787—762
	Hosea,	785—725
	Joel,	690—660
	Micah,	750—710
	Nahum,	713—691
	Isaiah,	810—698
	Zephaniah,	640—609
II.	Jeremiah,	629—588
	Habakkuk,	612—598
	Daniel,	606—534
	Obadiah,	588—583
	Ezekiel,	595—570
III.	Haggai,	520—518
	Zechariah,	520—518
	Malachi,	436—420

From the close of the Old Testament history, which is with Nehemiah, we may rely upon the Apocrypha for most of the history of the Jews, to the time of Christ.

During the period from the return from Babylon to Christ, we shall use the high-priests as guides to the History of Religion for that period.

JESHUA — Was the high-priest who returned with the first colony of Jews under Zerubbabel.

JOIAKIM — It is supposed, succeeded him, 483 B. C., during whose term of office, of thirty years, Ezra returned with the second colony of captives from Babylon.

Eliashib — Succeeded him in office, 453 B. C. He departed from the law in marrying a heathen wife (daughter of Sanballat); and for this Nehemiah deposed him from the priesthood, and drove him from the nation. In addition to the above offence, he gave up a part of the temple, devoted to sacred purposes, to Tobiah, for his own personal and secular use.

Joiada — Succeeded him, 413 B. C., as high-priest.

Jonathan I. — Came next in the office, in 373 B. C. In the eighth year of his serving, in the reign of Artaxerxes Mnemon, King of Persia, Bagoses, Governor of Syria and Palestine, meddled with that which was none of his business, by appointing Joshua, brother of Jonathan, to the priesthood, for the purpose of superseding him. This interference of a heathen ruler in the ecclesiastical affairs of the Jews, exasperated them to resistance. Joshua attempted the prerogatives of the office by force, when the assumption was rejected by force, and in the affray, Joshua was killed in the temple.

Bagoses vented his wrath upon the Jews, by an impost of about six dollars on every lamb offered in sacrifice. This would be a double infliction, as the expenses of lambs for sacrifices had for some time been provided for out of the revenue of the Persian government.

Jonathan, however, retained the priesthood.

In this affair we see the glaring incongruity of having the civil rulers invested with any power whatever over any religion whatever, to interfere with its peace and purity. Also the stupid folly of its ministers, in seeking government pap.

Jaddua — Succeeded to the priesthood, 341 B. C. About this age flourished some of the most celebrated philosophers of antiquity. But by wilfully closing their eyes to the possibility that the Jews had a knowledge of the true God, or of his revealed will, they went about to establish their own righteousness, blindly seeking God where he was not.

Even Socrates, with all his wisdom, only arrived at a *conjecture* that "there is something remaining for the dead, and that then it will be better for good than for bad men;" and even this was received with such ill favor by his countrymen, that they took his life for heresy. Virgil, in speaking of Tartarus and Elysium, — the heathen for future misery and happiness — says: "The whole was a mere fable." The Pythagoreans, Platonists, Peripatetics, and Stoics, the four most renowned schools of philosophers, *taught* the doctrine of future rewards and punishments, but disbelieved it at heart.

Plato avowed to his intimate friends, that "*mankind must be deceived;* there are truths the people are not to know; the world is not to be trusted with the true notion of God." The doctrine of the Jews was, that men must have the true notion of God, and woe to those who neglect and despise him.

Philosophy and Sanballat unite in the sneer, "What do these feeble Jews?"

While Alexander the Great was engaged in the siege of Tyre, he sent to Jaddua for supplies; but the Jews returned answer that they were under allegiance to Persia, and could not reasonably comply with his request. As the conqueror drew near Jerusalem, the priests, fearing his wrath, determined to go out in procession, dressed in white robes, and seek to appease him. When Alexander saw them approaching him, with the high-priest, Jaddua, at their head, he hastened to meet them; and to the surprise of his staff and the Jews, made obeisance to the high-priest. "This sight," he said, "I saw in a dream, in Dios, Macedonia, and this priest bade me advance, and assured me of success."

Alexander entered the city, and ordered the priests to offer sacrifices, according to the Jewish ritual.

Jaddua then showed him the prophecy of Daniel, and assured Alexander that it referred to him, and that Persia would fall into his hands.

On his departure he granted the request of the Jews, which was, that they might be permitted to live according to the law of their fathers, and be exempt from tribute on every seventh year, when they were forbidden to cultivate their land.

The integrity of the Jews to their faith, is seen in the refusal of some of them to obey the orders of even Alexander's officers in Babyl'on, in repairing the heathen temple of Belus.

For this refusal the officers caused some of them to suffer military punishment, and others even death.

Complaint being made to Alexander, he inquired into the circumstances, and finding that the Jews refused obedience because of the work being an idolatrous enterprise, he released them from their tasks and abuses, and gave them liberty to return to Jerusalem with honor.

Herodotus speaks of this people as "adhering closely to their law, choosing to suffer death rather than break its precepts." He speaks of their captivity; that "they had only one city, and in the midst of it a stone enclosure (the temple), with two doors, and inside a square altar of unwrought stone. Near this altar is a building, in which is a large golden candlestick, which has a light night and day. They have no image, no grove, and the priests are there continually, performing certain purifications, and drink no wine in the temple."

These statements above show the Jewish Church to be in a very tolerably prosperous condition at this time.

The high-priest Jaddua died 321 B. C.

ONIAS I. — Succeeded him, and died about 300 B. C., and was succeeded by his son.

As no warrior of this age could be content without subduing the Jews, Ptolemy Lagus next besieged Jerusalem; and taking advantage of the Jews' regard for the Sabbath, — on which day they would not defend themselves, — he entered the city without opposition, B. C. 320. At first he treated them with rigor — taking one hundred thousand of them prisoners; but after a time allowed them liberty, and appointed many to offices of trust and importance.

SIMON "THE JUST" — Next in the office of the high priesthood, was so called from the holiness of his life, and the integrity of his actions. He repaired and fortified Jerusalem, and benefited his nation greatly.

The greatest work of Simon the Just was the completion of the canon of the Old Testament, by adding the Books of Chronicles, Ezra, Nehemiah, Esther, and Malachi. This took place under the sanction of the men of the great synagogue, by which name a succession of elders — one hundred and twenty in number — who lived after the Babylonish captivity, were called, the last of whom was Simon the Just. He was the last high-priest who acted as president of the Sanhedrim, or council; hereafter the offices were distinct.

The origin of the Sanhedrim is variously stated, — some claiming it to be the continuation of the assistants appointed to help Moses, at the suggestion of Jethro, his father-in-law; others, that it originated after the captivity, to serve as a congress of the nation. It consisted of seventy-two members, and was in active operation until the time of Christ, and was the supreme court of the Jews. After the subjection of the nation to the Romans, the Sanhedrim was deprived of the power to inflict capital punishment, and hence the reason why the Sanhedrim delivered Christ to Pilate to be crucified.

Simon, dying 291 B. C., was succeeded by

ELEAZAR I., — His brother, in the high priesthood.

During his priesthood, Antigonus Socheus, a learned and pious man, was president of the council.

In urging men to the service of God, from motives drawn from the abstract conception of his holiness and perfections, — upon his followers misunderstanding and misconstruing his meaning, — a new sect sprung up under Sadok, one of his disciples. Sadok denied the resurrection of the dead, future rewards and punishments, the existence of angels and spirits, and declared death to be an eternal sleep. From him sprang the sect known in the time of Christ by the name of Sadducees. This sect of blasphemers and atheists were practical antinomians, — literally urging each other to "eat and drink, for to-morrow we die."

The Egyptian kings showed much favor to the Jews, both in Egypt and in Jerusalem. Ptolemy Philadelphus, the reputed founder of the Alexandrian Library, requested a copy of the Hebrew Scriptures, at the suggestion of Demetrius Phalereus, his principal librarian, to put into his library. Aristeas and Andreas were sent by the king to Eleazar the high-priest to make the request.

Upon this the Sanhedrim appointed six men for each of the Twelve Tribes — making a board of seventy-two — to translate the Bible into Greek, for the use of the Jews in Egypt, who then spoke Greek, — it being the prevailing language of the time. This work is called the "Septuagint," or Greek Version of the Hebrew Scriptures; translated about 286 B. C.

Unlike the philosophers of Greece, the wise men of the Jews thought it safe to unfold to the people and the world the true notion of God. Those ancient priests of God's altar deemed it safe to allow the common people not only to have the Scriptures, but even translated them into the common tongue, that they might read and know God's will. The Septuagint was the first *translation* of the Scriptures; it was done by Alexandrian Jews. The favor of the king made a fine opportunity for Bible introduction and distribution in heathen Egypt.

Manasses, — Brother of Eleazar, came to the office of high-priest 276 B. C. For some time the Jews enjoyed quiet, until the wars between the kings of Syria and Egypt, foretold by Daniel.

Onias II., — Son of Eleazar, succeeded Manasses in the high priesthood. Being of a sordid and selfish soul, he refused the annual tribute to the King of Egypt, of twenty talents of silver, — though Euergetes still favored the Jews, and made large offerings to the temple on his visit to Jerusalem, 245 B. C. The king sent a demand for the arrears, and a pledge of prompt payment in future, accompanied with a threat of vengeance in case of refusal. Onias still persisted in his refusal to pay, when, by the timely interference of one Joseph, who gave pledges for the sum due, the nation was saved from the wrath of an offended king and his army. Joseph, however, was permitted to use the army himself, to bring Onias to terms, but spared the nation further harm.

Simon II. — Came into the office of the high-priest 217 B. C. In a few years after, Ptolemy Philopater came to Jerusalem, and, as a return for the preservation of his life by a Jew, in a late battle, he ordered sacrifices to be offered, and made presents to the temple.

Philopater then wished to enter the temple, and even the holy of holies, where none went but the high-priest, and that only once a year. On being refused, he claimed that he entered other temples, and insisted on proceeding, when, by the prayers of the priests, the king all of a sudden fell upon the floor, powerless and speechless, and was quickly carried out by his attendants.

At this the king was filled with wrath, threatening vengeance on the Jews. He took away their national privileges, drove from his court all who did not sacrifice in heathen temples, and degraded them to the rank of slaves, and resistance was punished with death; to which was added the brand of the ivy-leaf, with a hot iron, on their bodies, — the badge of the votaries of Bacchus, the god of wine.

Then, with bribes, tempted as many as he could to forsake the religion of their fathers; and those who refused, were put to death, as "enemies of his government."

The king next sent orders throughout the land to gather the Jews to Alexandria, threatening death on any who should conceal one, thrust them into the hippodrome (a large place for shows and games), where he ordered them trodden to death by five hundred elephants, made furious by wine and frankincense. Whilst awaiting their doom, the Jews prayed unceasingly to God for deliverance; and when the hour of doom arrived, the elephants turned upon the spectators and soldiers, and slew more of them than of the Jews, though forty thousand of the latter perished.

The king was so terrified at this Divine protection, and the recollection of his fall in the temple, in answer to the prayers of the priests, that he revoked his infernal decrees, and restored the Jews to liberty again.

Praying Daniels can move the arm of God, and the hearts of kings.

The Jews suffered much by a war, in which Philip of Macedon and Antiochus the Great intended to make spoil of Egypt, when the Romans interfered, and forbade the execution of their designs. Antiochus, wishing to gain the allegiance of the Jews, colonized many of them from Babylon to Lydia and Phrygia; so the Jews whom the apostles found in Asia Minor, were descendants from these colonies.

Onias III. — Succeeded to the priesthood on the death of Simon II., 195 B. C. Onias was a worthy man, but lived in troublous times. In 187 B. C., Joseph, the collector of the revenue, now very aged, sent an embassy to Egypt, to congratulate Ptolemy Epiphanes on the birth of a son.

Joseph's elder sons declining the embassy, Hyrcanus, his younger son, twenty years old, undertook it.

Instead of drawing upon his father's agent there for *ten* talents, he took a thousand, and purchased two hundred beautiful slaves, and, with a large sum of money, presented them to the king and queen, and gave large gifts to the courtiers, by which he obtained his father's office as collector of customs. His brothers were offended at his perfidy, gave him battle on his return from Egypt, in which Hyrcanus was victor, and two of them slain. The principal Jews at Jerusalem refused to have intercourse with him.

His father dying soon after, a contest arose between him and his brothers about the property; when Hyrcanus was obliged to flee to a fortress east of Jordan, until the accession of Antiochus Epiphanes, when, being threatened for his doings, destroyed himself.

Onias favored him so far as to take charge of his treasures, and deposit them in the temple.

Simon, oldest son of Joseph and governor of the temple, getting at variance with Onias, instigated the King of Syria to seize the treasures of the temple, and so get the money belonging to Hyrcanus. This paved the way for terrible sufferings upon the Jewish nation shortly after.

In 176 B. C., the King of Syria sent his treasurer, Heliodorus, to seize the treasures of the temple. This threw all Jerusalem into a panic, and many were the prayers offered up to God to deliver the temple from the plunderer, who sought the sacred treasures, as well as those of Hyrcanus, which he was wickedly sent to take also.

At this juncture, a strange sight presented itself to Heliodorus: a horse, with a terrible rider upon him, and he came fiercely towards him, striking at him with his forefeet; and the rider's armor appeared to be of gold.

Besides, two young men stood one on either side, having strength, beauty, and splendid apparel, who scourged him continually, and gave him many sore stripes. He also fell down straightway, he and his guard, being greatly astonished and overcome by the sight.

On returning, the king asked who would be a proper person to send again. If, said he, you have an enemy, or traitor, send him; you will doubtless receive him again well scourged, if, indeed, he escape with his life; for in that place there is a special presence of God, who watcheth it, and beateth back all who come near to hurt it.

But corruption in the nation, and force outside of it, did it harm. Onias was deposed from the priesthood by Epiphanes, and succeeded by

JASON — His younger brother, as high-priest. This he obtained by a bribe of four hundred and forty talents, as purchase money, in addition to the tribute. Jason having acquired a taste for Grecian manners, erected a gymnasium at Jerusalem, in which the Jewish youth were taught the games and sports of the heathen, which lead to a neglect of the law. Onias was detained at Antioch, so that his influence might not be felt against these innovations and sins.

Epiphanes, making a visit to Jerusalem, was received with great attention by Jason, who was soon, however, made to hang upon the same gallows he had erected for Onias III. Jason sent Onias, his younger brother, to Antiochus on business, who assumed the Grecian name Menelaus, and offered the king three hundred talents more for the high-priest's office, which was granted him, 172 B. C.

Being unable to drive Jason from Jerusalem, Antiochus sent an army to assist Menelaus, when Jason fled to the Ammonites.

MENELAUS. — Menelaus being unable to raise the money to pay his bribe, sold off the golden vessels of the temple to do it.

For thus sacrilegiously obtaining the high priesthood, Onias III. reproved him; whereupon he hired Andronicus, ruler of Antioch, to put the aged priest to death, which was done in the temple of Daphne, where Onias had fled for protection. This act so displeased Epiphanes, that he caused Andronicus to be put to death.

A deputation of Jews, from the Sanhedrim, made complaint to Antiochus of the sacrilege of Menelaus, which was clearly proved; but through the influence of one Ptolemy Macro, he persuaded the king, and secured him, so the apostate high-priest was acquitted, and the deputies put to death.

Omens of ill, and of distress for the devoted remnant of Israel, multiplied rapidly.

A report of Antiochus's death, while in Egypt, reached Jason, when he raised an army and drove Menelaus to take refuge in the stronghold of Zion. Thinking that this was a general revolt of the Jews, Antiochus hastened to Jerusalem, took it by storm, and, in a massacre of three days, forty thousand were slain, and as many taken captives and made slaves.

Guided by the apostate Menelaus, the Syrian king (unlike Cyrus), entered the sanctuary and carried away all the gold and silver he could find. To make the desecration more complete, Antiochus caused a sow to be sacrificed on the altar, and the liquor in which swine had been boiled, was sprinkled through the whole temple.

A Phrygian was appointed Governor of Jerusalem; Menelaus reäppointed high-priest; while Jason, failing of the reward for his treachery, fled, first to Arabia, then to Egypt, and finally to Sparta.

How hateful is kingly interference in the affairs of religion, when vile men obtain its offices, and are sustained by viler men as kings! Away with Church and State united, or even confederated!

Antiochus Epiphanes being obliged to yield to the orders of the Roman Senate, and leave Egypt, in 167 B. C., resolved to pour out his wrath upon the Jews.

Apollonius, his chief collector, was sent with an armed force to Jerusalem; entered it under pretence of peace, and then, on the Sabbath, when the Jews would not fight, let his soldiers loose, to massacre and plunder. Some of the Jews were slain, and many sold for captives; the buildings near Mount Zion were demolished to make the fortress into a citadel. So in June, 168 B. C., the daily sacrifices ceased.

An edict of Epiphanes followed this, enforcing obedience and uniformity to certain heathen rites throughout his dominions. By this intolerant measure, the observance of the Jewish religion was suppressed; the temple at Jerusalem was dedicated to Jupiter; an idol set up, and sacrifices offered to it on the great altar. An old Athenian priest was appointed to perform the service, the temple filled with all the pagan abominations, and idols set up in the towns throughout Judea.

Thus, as in the days of Ahab, true religion appeared to be obliterated; but the smoke of hundreds of altars ascended to heaven to form a cloud of wrath to return upon the oppressor. Besides, there were many Jews, pious and praying, who were waiting for the consolation of Israel, though both the Jewish polity and religion were almost every vestige of them obliterated. Nor did they wait in vain.

MACCABEES. — These deliverers were of the tribe of Levi, descendants of Asmoneus; and hence their reign, of one hundred and twenty-six years, is called the Asmonean dynasty.

At this time, 167 B. C., Mattathias, an aged priest, was head of the family, of the course of Joarib, descended from Phineas, son of Aaron. He was much esteemed for his virtues and piety, and had five sons, — Johanan, Simon, Judas, Eleazar, and Jonathan. Their residence was in Modin, near Joppa, and the battle-ground of David and Goliath. The city was on the peak of a high hill, and hence a strong place of defence.

Epiphanes sent Apelles to Modin, to see the edict of conformity carried into effect. He found Mattathias mourning over the miseries of his nation, but attempted, by the strongest bribe, to persuade him to set the people an example, by performing the heathen rites prescribed by the king. Mattathias stoutly declared, though all the nation forsook the religion of the fathers, yet he would not.

It is related, that when an apostate Jew came forward to sacrifice upon the altar at Modin, in obedience to the king, Mattathias could contain himself no longer, and sprang forward and slew the apostate on the altar. He also put Apelles, the king's commissioner to death, and tore down the altar he had caused to be polluted. Very like Jehu and Moses.

Mattathias, knowing that he had now exposed himself to the wrath of the king, went through the streets of Modin, and cried, "Whoever is zealous for the law, and maintaineth the covenant, let him follow me!" He then left his home and property, and, with his sons and a few — only ten in all — fled to the mountains.

Others fled to the mountains, but the heathen soldiery pursued them. Finding a body of Jews, about a thousand in all, the cowardly ruffians attacked them on the Sabbath (knowing that the Jews would not fight on that day), and massacred them in cold-blooded fury.

This event convinced Mattathias and his followers that resistance would be in vain, unless they stood on the defensive, Sabbath days and all. They were then joined by many like-minded with themselves, by the names "Assideans and Zaddukeans," afterwards Pharisees and Sadducees.

Antiochus was full of wrath at the intelligence from Palestine, and hastened thither to enforce his edict with increased rigor. Many were the faithful witnesses during this persecution, among whom were an aged priest, seven brothers, and their mother.

Eleazar, one of the principal scribes, had swine's flesh forced into his mouth, but spit it forth, choosing to die rather than eat it. An attempt was then made to induce him to take such flesh as he could eat, and prepare it, and then pretend before the people that he was yielding to the king's command. But, "taking on him a discreet consideration," he chose rather than disgrace his age, or leave a perverse example to the young, to yield to torture and death, than be a dissembler in the law of the Lord; and while being beaten to death, yielded his spirit up to his God.

Mattathias and his followers increased in numbers, boldness, and victories, by demolishing altars, routing their persecutors, and circumcising the children of Jews. In the following year, 166 B. C., Mattathias was gathered with the fathers. In his dying charge, he encouraged his followers to trust in God, and he would prosper them. He suggested that his son Simon act as counsellor, and Judas as captain of the forces — known as Judas Maccabéus.

The term Maccabees, is said to be derived from the letters borne on the standards of the Asmonean troops; viz., M. C. B. J., the initials of four words, meaning, "Who is like unto Thee, O Lord, among the gods?"

Similar is the origin of the term *Whig*, which is made of the initials of the four words, "We hope in God."

Judas soon earned a reputation in arms which placed him in rank with Joshua, Gideon, and David, by dispersing his enemies, enlarging his people, and making his name great as a man of war.

Epiphanes was attending a debauched festival of Jupiter Olympus, his favorite idol, which gave the Maccabees a good opportunity to enlarge themselves. Their first success was against Apollonius, Governor of Samaria, whose sword Judas obtained, and used it in his subsequent battles. Soon after, he defeated Seron, Governor of Cœlo-Syria, whose army was composed of many Samaritans and apostate Jews. The Samaritans had allowed, at this time, their temple on Mount Gerizim to be dedicated to Jupiter Xenius, thus turning away from the alliance they wished to form with the Jews in the days of Nehemiah.

In the battle with Seron, the armies met on the heights of Bethlehem. The smallness of the numbers of the Maccabees well-nigh discouraged them when they saw the hosts of the enemy; but Judas made an appeal to them, to trust in the God of battles, who had and still could give the battle to few as well as many, if his help was sought. Seron was overthrown.

The successes of the Maccabees put the wrath of Epiphanes into a seven times hotter state than usual, when he resolved on the extermination of the Jews. His treasures being exhausted, word was given out that the prisoners would be sold cheap, so as to induce buyers to be present; and with an army of fifty thousand, well supplied with able generals, the march begins.

The Jews, knowing the wrath of the king, gathered together at famous old Mizpah, as in ancient times, and fasted; put on sackcloth; cast ashes on their heads; opened the Book of the Law; brought in their tithes, and then cried unto the Lord for their desolations, and asked him earnestly how they could stand before their enemies, except thou, O God, be our help.

Judas then made ready for battle; and, finding that he was to be attacked in the night, retreated to the mountains, — the Syrians supposing they had fled. The Maccabees fell upon them early in the morning, and put them to flight; — Nicanor, the general, making his escape in the garb of a slave. In the following year Judas gained further success against Lysias, whereupon Judas and his brethren resolved to cleanse the sanctuary at Jerusalem.

So all the host assembled at Mount Sion. Great were their lamentations when they saw the desolation; the altar profaned; the gates burned down; the shrubs growing in the courts, as in the forest. Judas then set a detachment of the army to protect them, while the priests cleansed the sanctuary. Not knowing what to do with the altar, which had been defiled by Antiochus's sacrifice of a sow thereon, but fearing it might be a reproach to them, it was removed, and piled away, until a prophet should arise to instruct them what to do with it. They then built a new altar, and supplied the temple with the candlestick, shewbread, and vessels, and so set up again the temple service. Thus the daily sacrifices were resumed, just three years after the dedication to Jupiter, on the 25th of December (Christmas), 165 B. C. This dedication of the new altar, and re-dedication of the temple, lasted eight days.

The prophet referred to above was evidently the one spoken of by Moses, Deut. 18:18.

Thus the Jews were again delivered from their oppressors, and, by throwing off the Syrian yoke, rendered the nation independent. They were further set at rest by the sudden death of Antiochus, who, enraged at other disasters in the east, started once more to exterminate the Jews; when, being suddenly seized with a terrible disease in the bowels, he fell from his chariot and broke his neck.

Thus once more the Lord made the wrath of man to praise him, and the remainder he restrained. The eleventh chapter, twenty-first to thirtieth verses, of Daniel, are thought to refer to the events of this reign. Indeed, infidel Porphyry thought the prophecy so minutely descriptive of the events, that he declared it must have been written after the events, instead of before, which, however, was not so.

Judas Maccabeus next found it necessary to weaken the strength of some of his nearer neighbors. About this time, the government was separated from the ecclesiastical office. Being successful in quelling his neighbors, Judas made a gathering to provide sacrifices for a sin-offering, in accordance with the law; his purpose being to deplore before the Lord the slaughter of the people for their sins; and thus "made reconciliation for the dead, that they (the living) might be delivered from sin." Similar to Joshua, at Mount Ebal (Joshua, 8:30, 31); or Jephthah (Judges 11:32, etc.).

This circumstance of Judas is taken as authority for the practice of praying for the dead. Rather slim authority for a grave religious tenet.

The citadel of Acra, being still held by the Syrians, was a source of great annoyance to the Jews in Jerusalem, it being on Mount Zion, and very strong. Judas made an attack upon it, when a Syrian army was sent to its relief, composed of one hundred and twenty thousand men, three hundred chariots, and thirty-two elephants. It is said, "When the sun shone upon their shields of brass and gold, the mountains glistened therewith, and shone like lamps of fire."

Against this host, Judas was successful in a night attack; but Eleazar, his brother, after stabbing an elephant, on which he supposed the king was riding, the animal fell upon him and crushed him to death. Being a Sabbatical year, which the Jews had observed since their return, and provisions failing them, they were obliged to abandon the assault of Acra, and retreat to Jerusalem.

Thither the Syrians pursued them; but, by timely aid from Philip of Antioch, Lysias, and Eupator, were compelled to offer peace to the Jews.

Menelaus, the wicked high-priest, joined the enemies of his country; but Lysias, thinking him the cause of this unsuccessful war, threw him into a tower of ashes, used for punishing criminals; the wheel was put in motion, and he was immediately smothered — 163 B. C.

Thus his perfidy ended in his ruin and death, like the conspiracy of Absalom against David.

Alcimus. — The title of high-priest was next conferred upon Alcimus, an apostate Jew, and as wicked as Menelaus, — a specimen of the wisdom wicked kings exercise in the bestowment of ecclesiastical dignities.

Upon this the lawful high-priest, Onias, son of Onias III., turned in disgust from the corruptions at Jerusalem, and built a temple at Heliopolis, in Egypt. In this he officiated according to the Jewish rites, and to it many Jews resorted. This temple stood as long as the one at Jerusalem. Both were destroyed in the reign of Vespasian.

Demetrius coming to the throne of Syria, Alcimus, whom the Jews disliked, accused them of disloyalty to Syria, when an army was sent by Demetrius, under Bacchides, 161 B. C., to confirm Alcimus in the high priesthood. The new high-priest, after slaying many righteous Jews, who went forth to reason with him peaceably, made himself odious by further acts of cruelty; whereupon he was obliged to flee to Demetrius to escape the indignation of Judas, who was again aroused to redress his nation's wrongs.

Alcimus labored to convince Demetrius that there could be no peace in Judea so long as the Maccabees existed, when Nicanor was sent into Judea to destroy Judas and his followers. Becoming enraged at their resistance, like Sennacherib, he used blasphemous threats against the nation, city, and temple of the Jews, which ended in his head and right hand being suspended from the walls of Jerusalem, about 160 B. C.

The land now had an interval of rest, when Judas made a league with the Roman senate, to impose a restraint upon Demetrius, and stop his operations against Judea. The Jews were the first eastern people who were freed by the Romans; and at last these same Romans proved to the Jews their first utter destroyers.

Demetrius, anticipating this interference of the Romans, resolved on one more attempt upon Judea; and Bacchides was again sent with a large army against Judas. Judas, being elated with his past successes, and the prospect of aid from Rome, resolved, with a few, only eight hundred men, to attack the Syrian host. They charged the Syrian horse, broke their right wing; but the vast numbers closed in upon the little band, and Judas Maccabeus, the greatest deliverer of his nation since the time of David, fell.

His appeal to his soldiers was to resolve to die manfully, and not stain their honor.

He had failed to appeal to the God of his fathers for aid, and so was left to the protection of an arm of flesh, when military valor proved a snare. In that, he more resembled Leonidas the Spartan, than Gideon the Judge of Israel.

Jonathan and Simon, his brothers, buried him in the sepulchre of his fathers, in Modin, and all Israel made great lamentation over him.

After Judas' death, the nation suffered great affliction, through the ascendency of Alcimus the apostate over the righteous Jews. But their sufferings drove them, as under Judas, to resolve on self-defence, and they chose Jonathan, the youngest son of Mattathias, to be their leader. He, with his brothers Simon and John, and many followers, retired to a strong position near Jordan, in the wilderness of Tekoa, with the river on one side and a morass on the other.

Here Bacchides attacked them on the Sabbath, thinking they would allow him to butcher them in cold blood; but the Jews followed the example of Mattathias, and gave the Syrians battle; but, being overpowered by numbers, the rest of the Jews retreated, by swimming across the Jordan. The Syrians dared not follow them into that trap, remembering Pharaoh. Alcimus died shortly after this, being struck with palsy while engaged in profanely removing some of the sacred walls of the temple, 160 B. C.

SEVEN YEARS VACANCY. — The removal of Alcimus threw the apostate Jews into a decline, when Jonathan soon caused the force of his wisdom to be felt, and he was soon acknowledged, by both Jews and Syrians, as the rightful prince of Judea.

Upon the appearance of Alexander Balas, as the rival of Demetrius for the Syrian throne, it became an object for each of them to secure the favor of the Jews, as their power could easily turn the scale between the rivals. Hence the Jews had rest, and became pets with the kings, each vieing with the other in generous offers of aid and comfort to them.

Jonathan seized upon this repose to improve and strengthen Jerusalem. Balas sent a purple robe and a crown to Jonathan, and a commission to rule as Ethnarch, or Prince of Judea; and also appointed him to the high priesthood, which had been vacant seven years.

JONATHAN II. — He was of the course of Joarib, who was of the first class, or course, of Aaron, and hence lawful priest. He accepted the priesthood, and officiated at the feast of tabernacles, 153 B. C.

Demetrius also followed up with his magnificent offers, which, from their greatness, and his enmity to the Jews formerly, led them to suspect him not honest, and so inclined to Alexander Balas. In an encounter between the rivals Demetrius was slain, and thus the Jews were delivered from a hurtful enemy, 150 B. C.

A splendid marriage next ensued at Ptolemais, between Balas and Cleopatra, daughter of Philometor, King of Egypt, to which Jonathan was specially invited, and treated as a very distinguished guest.

A number of changes occurred in Egypt and Syria at this time, all of which conspired to strengthen Jonathan and Simon. Upon this, Jonathan sent another embassy to Rome, to renew his friendship with that power. On their return they visited Sparta, and ascertained that "the Lacedemonians and Jews were brethren, and of the stock of Abraham." (?)

In reporting their fortunes to the Spartans, they expressly declared that aid was granted them from Heaven, — showing that the Jews had not lost wholly the knowledge or fear of the true God of heaven.

Tryphon, in plotting for the throne of Syria, aimed at getting Jonathan out of the way. He marched into Palestine, and, being met by a large force of the Jews, declined giving battle; but Jonathan was brought by him into a snare, by offering to put the Jews into possession of Ptolemais. By this, Jonathan was induced to leave all his army but a thousand, who went on with him; and as soon as they entered the city, Jonathan was seized as a prisoner, and his followers massacred.

Simon then roused the Jews to avenge their wrongs, when Tryphon again declined a battle, and pretended he only detained Jonathan until one hundred talents, due him, was paid. This being done, he still kept Jonathan, and harassed the Jews with an army. Bad weather forced the Syrians to retire into Gilead, where Jonathan was put to death, 143 B. C. Simon buried him in Modin, the sepulchre of the Maccabees.

SIMON III. — Under Simon, the independence and prosperity of the Jewish nation were achieved, so that "the Jews and priests were well pleased that Simon should be their governor and high-priest forever, until there should arise a faithful prophet."

None, however, did arise until the one like unto Moses, and he it is to whom the gathering of the nations shall be.

Thus, in 143 B. C., the triumph of the Maccabees was made complete, which was begun by Mattathias. Simon had many privileges confirmed to him, among which was the coining of money, specimens of which are still in existence.

The faithless Sidetes, hearing of the wealth and magnificence of Simon, sent an army to plunder his treasure, which was defeated by the Jews under Judas and John, sons of Simon. Treachery was then brought to bear, when a son-in-law of Simon invited him to a banquet in the castle Docus, where he caused him to be murdered, with his sons Judas and Mattathias, at the instigation of Sidetes.

Thus fell the last of the five sons of Mattathias the elder.

JOHN HYRCANUS. — An attempt was made upon the life of John, the last of Simon's sons (called Hyrcanus from his exploits in Hyrcania, under Demetrius), but he defended himself, and defeated the assassins.

Sidetes, hearing of the death of Simon, marched against Jerusalem; but, during the siege, Hyrcanus asked a truce, to keep the feast of tabernacles, which was granted. Hyrcanus then applied for peace, when Sidetes, through fear of the Romans, offered terms by which it was concluded.

Hyrcanus was now established as ruler of the Jews, and high-priest also, 131 B. C. The changes in the governments around him all operated to his advantage.

He improved his opportunities further, by subduing the Greek colony, planted in Samaria by Alexander the Great; also the Samaritans, by taking Shechem, and destroying the temple on Mount Gerizim; and also the Edomites, many of whom embraced the Jewish religion. Indeed, he enlarged the kingdom, until it was equal in extent to the days of David and Solomon.

At Jerusalem he built the castle Baris, which was made the royal residence of the Asmonean princes. When Herod repaired the temple, he cased this fortification over with polished marble.

The Asmonean dynasty was now at the zenith of its prosperity. The two sects, the Sadducees and Pharisees, had become two political parties, the latter fast gaining the ascendency. Hyrcanus was a Pharisee; but, from an attempt by them to reproach him by an unfounded charge that his mother was a prisoner of war, — which, if true, would unfit him for the high priesthood, — he left them, and went over to the Sadducees.

Hyrcanus died in the year 106 B. C., after having ruled the Jews thirty years, as their prince and high-priest. In his reign the Book of Ecclesiasticus (in Apocrypha) was translated from Hebrew into Greek.

Now follows the Jewish monarchy under the Asmonean kings, which is lost in the Herodian dynasty, in which Christ was born. The religious character of the Jews at this time was better represented by the Egyptian Jews than those of Jerusalem.

Hyrcanus died without appointing his successor, yet left three sons, Aristobulus, Antigonus, and Alexander. The eldest assumed the title and diadem of king, also the high priesthood; but he esteemed the crown above the mitre.

ARISTOBULUS I. — He was the first Jew that wore a crown after the captivity, though the state displayed by Simon and Hyrcanus had a strong bearing towards aping the style of Roman and Grecian kings. Aristobulus imprisoned his mother, and three younger brothers. Antigonus was his favorite; but, it being represented to the king that Antigonus intended to seize the government, Aristobulus commanded him into his presence, *without* arms, on pain of death. Antigonus was falsely told, by his enemies, that the king wished to see him *with* his armor on; and while approaching, was slain by the guards. Anguish of mind, and bodily disease, soon ended the days of Aristobulus.

His queen soon released his brothers (his mother having previously died in prison), when

ALEXANDER JANNEUS — Was made king. He made a few efforts to strengthen himself, but with poor success. He being a Sadducee, the Pharisees strove to make him unpopular. Their hatred broke out openly in 94 B. C. When about to officiate as high-priest at the feast of tabernacles, the Pharisees stirred up the people to insult him with reproachful language, calling him the son of a slave, and pelting him with citrons they carried at the festival. Janneus, indignant at this, caused a massacre by his guards among the people, and afterwards kept a strong guard of hired foreigners about him.

The opposition to the king, however, continued, until he asked what would appease them, when they replied, "Nothing, but for him to cut his own throat."

It is said that, in less than six years, over fifty thousand Pharisees were slain by the Sadducees.

In 88 B. C., the Pharisees induced Eucerus the Syrian to aid them against their king, which he did, and Janneus was obliged to flee; but the Pharisees were glad to rejoin their king, to rid the country of the Syrians.

In 86 B. C., in a skirmish with the Pharisees, he drove them into a fortress, took them prisoners to Jerusalem, and caused eight hundred of them to be crucified in one day, in presence of their wives and children.

Being successful in a campaign beyond Jordan, his popularity increased, when he gave himself up to drunkenness, which brought on ague, from which he suffered three years, and died 77 B. C. His wife, Alexandra, being with him, asked his advice as to her future course, when he advised her to conceal his death, embalm his body, and after the surrender of Bagoda, then under siege, to conduct the army to Jerusalem; then to summon the chief of the Pharisees before her, and offer to be guided by them in the affairs of the government, and deliver the remains of Alexander Janneus to them, to be treated with ignominy.

So pleased were they to get control of a power they had so long coveted, that they gave the half-decayed remains of the king a magnificent funeral, and established Alexandra as ruler, being content to rule in her name.

Hyrcanus. — Alexandra being established as ruler, she appointed her son Hyrcanus to be high-priest. He was indolent, which gave the Pharisees the sway. Upon this, Aristobulus, the younger of the princes, with many Sadducees, came to his mother and desired the privilege of going into voluntary exile, or be permitted to occupy some strong fortress, where they could protect themselves from their enemies.

The latter request was granted, and he was afterwards appointed to the command of the army.

In 69 B. C., Queen Alexandra died. Previous to this, Aristobulus planned for the chief power. His friends joined him, hoping to check the influence of the Pharisees; the queen would not interfere, when, after her death, the Pharisees declared Hyrcanus king. A battle was fought between the armies of the brothers, when Hyrcanus was defeated; his soldiers then joined Aristobulus, who became sole ruler, — Hyrcanus resigning the crown to him.

The resignation of the unambitious Hyrcanus was not pleasing to his supporters, particularly Antipater, father of Herod the Great. Antipas, Governor of Idumea under Janneus and Alexandra, and father of Antipater, supported Hyrcanus, and made him believe his life was in danger, and induced him to flee to Petra, and seek protection from Aretas, an Arabian prince.

Soon an army returned, with Hyrcanus, toward Jerusalem, which was joined by the Pharisees, when Aristobulus was driven into the temple and a fortress near for defence. The victors committed many outrages, among which was the refusal to supply animals for the passover sacrifices, after Aristobulus had paid the sum demanded for that purpose. Baskets were lowered from the wall, with the money, which the besiegers took, and filled the baskets with pigs.

Among the Jews who fled from this civil war, was one Onias, revered for his piety, whose prayers are said to have caused rain in time of drought. He was discovered, and brought back to the camp, and required to pronounce imprecations upon Aristobulus and his followers, for their immediate destruction. Being compelled to speak, he said: "O God, the King of the whole world! since those that stand by me now are thy people, and those that are besieged are thy priests, I beseech thee that thou wilt neither hearken to the prayers of those against these, nor bring to pass what these pray against those." At the close of his prayer, the zealous observers of the law stoned him to death.

Aristobulus was relieved from his peril by the Roman generals, while his army defeated Aretas, the Arabian chief, in his retreat. Aristobulus was losing influence in Rome. On a golden vine he had sent to be placed in the temple of Jupiter, in the capitol of Rome, the senate ordered his father's name to be put, instead of his own.

Pompey listened to the charges made by the rival parties against their respective leaders, Aristobulus and Hyrcanus. He finally ordered Aristobulus into his presence, when he was required to order his fortresses to surrender, and was then dismissed.

Aristobulus then hastened to Jerusalem, and prepared against a siege; but he hesitated, and again submitted; but his followers refused to admit the Romans into Jerusalem.

Pompey then ordered Aristobulus put in chains; marched to the city, when the friends of Hyrcanus permitted them to enter, and the siege of the temple and its fortress began. The garrison held out three months, and would have done so longer, but for the regard for the Sabbath by the Jews. They would have defended them selves, if attacked on that day, but would not oppose the works of the besiegers; so Pompey was active in forwarding his engines of destruction. At last the works were completed, and the temple taken by storm, when most of those within were slaughtered. The friends of Hyrcanus gave vent to their ill-will against their brethren by great cruelty. Even the priests were slain while performing the solemn services of the temple, choosing thus to perish rather than fight; hence mingling their blood with the sacrifices, by their slaughtering brethren and foes.

After the massacre, Pompey, with his principal officers, entered all apartments of the temple, even the holy of holies, to the grief of the Jews; and from this time, it is remarked, his decline began, which ended with his fall before Julius Cæsar. Pompey, however, refrained from robbing the temple of its treasure, that the services thereof might be immediately resumed, and even ordered the temple cleansed from the horrid results of war.

Hyrcanus was confirmed in the office of high-priest and prince of the Jews, but forbidden wearing a crown; while Aristobulus and his family were carried to Rome, to grace Pompey's triumph, celebrated, two years after, with great splendor.

The Jewish cities taken by the Syrians were restored to the Roman province.

Hyrcanus was now established as ruler of the Jews, with Antipater as his principal adviser.

Alexander, the son of Aristobulus, escaped from his guards on their way to Rome, and, returning to Judea, excited fresh troubles, which, however, resulted in a change of the Jewish monarchy into an aristocracy. Some of the principal Jews objecting to a monarchical rule, had their wishes gratified by the appointment of five councils, one at each of the following places: Jerusalem, Jericho, Gadara, Amathus, and Sephoris, each ruling a certain district.

In 57 B. C., Aristobulus, with his son Antigonus, escaped from Rome, returned to Judea, and excited a new revolt; but the father was soon retaken prisoner to Rome, and the son liberated.

Hyrcanus and Antipater retained the chief sway, and favored Gabinius, the Roman Prefect of Syria, by whom they had been assisted. During Gabinius' absence in Egypt, Alexander, son of Aristobulus, made another effort to regain the throne of Judah, when, upon the return of Gabinius, Antipater was confirmed in the power, after a battle Alexander lost on the plains near Mount Tabor.

Gabinius was recalled, and Crassus sent as the Prefect of Syria, in 54 B. C. He came the same year to Jerusalem, and plundered the temple of its treasures. Eleazar the priest obtained a solemn pledge from him, that he would leave all the treasures in the temple upon Eleazar giving up a large bar of gold, worth about fifteen thousand dollars, hid in a beam of the temple. But, upon obtaining this, he at once seized the rest of the treasure, amounting to ten millions of dollars.

Thus the *aid* the Romans gave the Jews before, now turns to *plunder*.

Crassus, however, fell into the hands of the Parthians, who poured melted gold into his mouth, to gratify his thirst for the article.

Upon Julius Cæsar getting into trouble in Egypt, Antipater marched to his aid, with a body of Jewish troops.

Antigonus, son of Aristobulus, applied to Cæsar to be restored to the privileges of his father, and at the same time complained of Hyrcanus and Antipater. But Cæsar, remembering the services rendered him while in Egypt by the two latter, confirmed on them the offices of priest and prince, — thus doing away the councils of Gabinius. Antipater then appointed his sons Phasaelus, Governor of Jerusalem, and Herod (the Great), of Galilee.

Some of the Jews, who envied Antipater, induced Hyrcanus to summon Herod before the Sanhedrim, to answer to the charge of putting men to death without a fair trial. Herod came with a letter from the Roman governor, Sextus Cæsar, forbidding his punishment; he also came in robes of state, and with guards, not as a culprit.

These things intimidated the council, so that they dared not proceed, except Sameas, who stood forth and reproved Herod alone, and also the council, telling them if they quailed thus before Herod, he would be made an instrument to inflict on them the Divine displeasure. Hyrcanus dismissed the council.

Not many years afterward, Herod caused all the council to be put to death, except Sameas and one other.

Some of Cæsar's last acts were favors to the Jews. Hyrcanus was confirmed as high-priest and ruler; tribute remitted in the Sabbatical year; permission to repair the walls of Jerusalem, destroyed by Pompey, and privileges to the Jews at large throughout the Roman Empire.

Malichus, an aspiring Jew, plotted the death of Antipater, that he might rule under Hyrcanus. He succeeded in his design, by bribing the chief butler of Hyrcanus, who gave a poisoned cup to Antipater at a feast: he died. Malichus seized the government, then tried to persuade Phasael and Herod, Antipater's sons, that he was innocent of the atrocity.

But Herod and Malichus being called to attend Hyrcanus to Tyre, on public business, with Cassius, Herod obtained a party of Roman soldiers of Cassius, who went out and slew Malichus as he drew near Tyre.

The Pharisees, lately headed by Malichus, made an attempt against the sons of Antipater, and, being favored by Hyrcanus, were confident of success. But Phasael and Herod being successful, they reproached Hyrcanus for requiting their father's kindness with evil upon his sons. The rupture was quieted by Hyrcanus promising Herod his beautiful grand-daughter Mariamne as his wife.

Antigonus, son of Aristobulus, again set up his claims, but was worsted by Herod; Antony then applied to Hyrcanus to know who were fittest to govern, when he replied, Phasael and Herod.

Antigonus then applied to the Parthians to assist him, when Jerusalem was taken. Herod escaped; but Phasael, fearing his enemies, took his own life, while Hyrcanus was delivered into the hands of Antigonus, whom the Parthians made king.

Hyrcanus's life was spared, but his ears were cut off, to disqualify him for the priesthood. He afterwards resided with the Parthian Jews.

Herod proceeded at once to Rome, and proposed that Aristobulus, brother of Mariamne, should be made king, and Herod to govern under him; but the senate proposed to make Herod himself king at once.

(In the year 40 B. C., so great was the expectation that a mighty personage was about to appear in Judea, among both Jews and pagans, that Virgil is said to have ascribed the fulfilment of this great hope to the birth of a son to Pollio, the Consul of Rome. The son soon after died. Notwithstanding, Virgil wrote a poem declaring the fulfilment of the long cherished hope.)

In 38 B. C., Herod effected his marriage with Mariamne, thinking thereby to gain favor with the Asmonean family. The next year the last battle was fought by Antigonus, the last monarch of the Asmonean family, in the siege of Jerusalem, which was taken and plundered by the Romans.

Antigonus was taken and sent to Antony in fetters, who put him to death by the scourge and the axe of the lictor. This he did at the request of Herod, who thought thereby to lessen the reverence of the Jews for the Asmonean family.

Herod ascended the throne 37 B. C. He further poured out his vengeance upon the Sanhedrim, by putting them all to death except Pollio and Sameas; — they urged a surrender of Jerusalem to the Romans, while the rest of the council opposed it.

Pollio and Sameas are regarded by Jewish writers as among their most learned doctors, and are known by the names Hillel and Shamaiai. Hillel was the father of Gamaliel, the instructor of Paul; also last president of the council before Simeon. Luke 2:25—35.

Aristobulus II. — Herod promoted Ananleus, an obscure priest of Babylon, to the high priesthood, which displeased Mariamne and the Asmoneans; they considering Aristobulus, her brother, as the rightful incumbent of the office. The change was so made.

Fearing the influence of the aged Hyrcanus, Herod made very flattering propositions to him, to return to Jerusalem and dwell. The Parthian king warned him to beware of the snare Herod was laying for him. But the old priest, suspecting no harm, returned to the holy city, but only to meet the fate of the snare. Herod disposed of him.

"Uneasy lies the head that wears a crown."

Herod saw in the movements of Alexandra, the mother of Aristobulus, a desire to obtain the *crown* also for her son. And while officiating at the feast of tabernacles, Aristobulus performed the public ceremonials in such a manner as to delight the people, and excite their applause. Herod then resolved on his death. Accordingly, Herod invited Aristobulus to a feast, at the close of which several entered the bath, among them the young high-priest, who was decoyed into the refreshment of the bath only to be drowned, — being held under water in pretence of sport.

Fresh troubles sprang up in Herod's family, in consequence of an order he left with his uncle, Joseph, on his departure with Antony; viz., if in his absence he should be taken prisoner, or killed, that Mariamne his wife should be put to death. This bred discontent in her mind, that ended in sorrow.

Joseph disclosed this plot to Mariamne, as a mark of affection for her in Herod; but she thought otherwise. On Herod's return, his sister Salome accused Mariamne of getting hold of his order for her death, by criminal intercourse with Joseph. The secret of Salome's hatred was the noble descent of Mariamne from the Asmoneans, while her own was from Antipater, an Idumean Jew. Herod allowed his wife to clear herself from the charge of infidelity to him, but he flew into a rage at her resenting his conduct towards her, in the order for her death.

Octavius becoming sole emperor, Herod thought it wise to visit him in person to obtain the crown, and again left his wife and her mother in the care of a confidant of his, with orders for her death in case of his, and for Pheroras his brother to declare himself king.

Mariamne finding out this second plot against her life, again received

Herod, on his return, with coldness and dislike, which so alienated his love for her, as to give the malignant Salome space to compass her ruin.

Upon Herod's return from Egypt, whither he had followed Augustus Cæsar, Mariamne refused to be reconciled, at the same time reproaching Herod with the death of Hyrcanus, Alexander, and Aristobulus — her grandfather, father, and brother.

The tyrant was enraged, and, at the solicitations of his own mother and sister, he caused his innocent wife to be accused as an adulteress, before judges who dared not clear her, and thus secured her condemnation.

Mariamne was then led forth to execution, and as she passed along was taunted by her persecutors; but with undaunted fortitude, she submitted to death, by decapitation, 29 B. C. She was an ornament to the nation — religious, and innocent.

Thus perished the last of the Asmoneans, or Maccabees, from Mattathias to Mariamne, the last dynasty of the royal Jews. They lived and reigned between the desolation and tyranny of Antiochus Epiphanes, and Herod.

Herod was soon filled with remorse for his wicked proceedings against Mariamne. He sought to drown his grief in the intoxicating cup, but even in his distracted fits he would call for his murdered queen. He never recovered his cheerfulness of mind afterwards.

Lord Byron thus expresses Herod's grief, in one stanza of his poem on the death of Mariamne:

"She's gone who shared my diadem;
  She sunk, with her my joys entombing;
I swept that flower from Judah's stem,
  Whose leaves for me alone were blooming;
And mine's the guilt, and mine's the hell,
  This bosom's desolation dooming;
And I have earn'd those tortures well,
  Which, unconsumed, are still consuming."

The sceptre was not yet departed from Judah, nor was it to depart (Genesis 49:10) until Shiloh come. Herod, though not an Asmonean, was still a Jew, and Judea was still a kingdom, under its own laws, and with its own king. The family of Antipater was now upon the throne, with little to fear from the Asmoneans. The sceptre was preparing to depart. Herod was made the stepping-stone between the last of the royal Jews and Shiloh, to pass the sceptre over to him.

Herod's next enterprise was to erect stately buildings at Jerusalem and elsewhere. But he was decidedly unpopular among the Jews.

As an example: a party that informed of a plot to poison Herod, was torn in pieces in a popular tumult. He, however, took the liberty to appoint whom he would to the office of high-priest, and accordingly removed Joshua, and appointed in his stead

SIMON IV. — Herod had married Simon's daughter, Mariamne by name. His sons Alexander and Aristobulus, by the first Mariamne, were sent to Rome for their education — the emperor receiving them with great favor, and even assigning them rooms in the palace.

Herod's next attempt to please the Jews and make himself popular, was the repairing, or rebuilding of the temple. It had fallen into decay through the commotions of war. He first proposed the undertaking at the feast of the Passover, 19 B. C.

Fears being expressed that if he tore down the present structure it might not be rebuilt, he gave assurances not to begin until adequate preparations were made. For two years he employed many thousand laborers, and the work was begun 17 B. C.

In a year and a half, the sanctuary was rebuilt from the foundation; in eight years the courts were ready, and the other works continued, until it was said by the Jews to Christ, "Forty and six years was this temple in building." It was still called the second temple by the Jews.

It was, however, a much more magnificent structure than the one built after the return, and on a much larger scale than that of Solomon.

The day of the dedication of the temple was on the festival day of the king's inauguration. Herod sacrificed three hundred oxen, and others did as much as their ability would permit. The king constructed an underground passage from the capitol to the temple, so that he might go to and from the temple, safe from any sedition of the people against him.

All the works about the temple were not discontinued until 62 A. D., when many thousands were thrown out of employ, which led to the wars with the Jews and Romans, brought about, in eight years after, the destruction of this splendid edifice.

In 16 B. C., Herod went to Rome to visit his sons; they accompanied him home to Judea. The youths were popular among the Jews, which circumstance excited the fears of those who had been instrumental in causing the death of their mother, Mariamne, lest they might some day seek revenge. The intrigues set on foot resulted in alienating the father and sons, and hence of plans to rob them of their succession to the throne of their ancestors. Herod finally obtained of Augustus authority to take some measures against the sons of Mariamne. A council of Roman governors and tributary kings was assembled at Berytus, before whom Herod accused his sons. His complaints were regarded, and power given him by the council to take the lives of his sons, if he saw fit so to do. The two Asmonean princes were strangled at Sebaste.

As we now draw near the New Testament history, it may be mentioned that about this time a very general persuasion was abroad, among sacred and profane men, that a great personage was to appear in Judea. The heathen writers all looked for a temporal monarch; and even Tacitus, a Roman historian, mentions the anticipations of the Messiah.

The Jews were so blinded by the worldly policy they had so long adopted, that they fell into the same grovelling explanation of the coming of the Just One.

Josephus, even, writing the history of his nation for the Greeks and Romans, speaks of this "great personage," mentioned in their sacred books; but, with little of the spirit of Daniel, and much of the spirit of a court sycophant, applies all to Vespasian.

But there were those who were truly waiting for the Consolation of Israel; for, while Zacharias was officiating at the altar of incense, the angel Gabriel appeared, and assured him that his wife should bear him a son whose name should be John, and who should be the forerunner of the Messiah. And as evidence of this, the angel told him he should be dumb until the event. When the child was to be named, he wrote on a table the name John, and immediately his tongue was loosed, and he praised God. The advent of the Saviour was also foretold; so that none need be in doubt upon so important a point.

We will now continue the history of the Jews, to the destruction of Jerusalem, and then return to the birth of Christ, and proceed with ecclesiastical history.

A plot for poisoning Herod being discovered, in which Mariamne his wife was accused of having a part, Herod divorced her, deposed her father, Simon, from the high priesthood, and appointed in his stead

MATTATHIAS I. — The sceptre had now well-nigh departed from Judah, for Herod their king was now almost wholly under the power of Rome. He held Judah's sceptre, but with Roman authority. The end of Judah, as a nation, came in Herod.

Hence it was in obedience to the decree of Augustus Cæsar that Joseph went to Bethlehem with Mary his espoused wife, to be enrolled for taxation, — a new Roman law, obeyed under the *shadow*, but not the *authority*, of Judah's sceptre. During this journey, Christ the Saviour was born.

Herod, being impressed with this event, adopted the rash measure of causing all infants about him under two years old to be put to death, in order to compass the death of the "King of the Jews."

Some suppose Herod really thought Christ to be the Messiah, and so instituted this bold measure. But it would seem more in keeping with another supposition: that he suspected this as a *device* to bring up one of the Asmoneans, by-and-by to sit upon the throne of Israel. Any way, it shows his baseness.

Being now sixty-nine years of age, his end drew nigh. He made one more change in the priesthood, deposing Mattathias, and appointing, instead,

Joazar I. — His brother-in-law. Being sick at Jericho, and the event of his death being pretty certain, some of the Jews pulled down a golden eagle which Herod had caused to be placed over the eastern gate of the temple.

Herod, knowing his end was near, and that his death would be hailed with pleasure by the Jews, determined to give them one more blow while he could. Hence he summoned the principal Jews to attend him at Jericho, where he was, and, on their arrival, had them thrust into the circus until his death, when the soldiers were to be ordered to massacre them. This horrid design was intrusted to Herod's malignant sister Salome, and her husband Alexas, for execution; but, instead of carrying it out, upon Herod's death she released them all, and allowed them to return to their homes in peace.

Thus died Herod, about 3 B. C. His sons who succeeded him in office, were children by a Samaritan wife, hence no Jewish blood; and truly the sceptre passed away from Judah, then and forever.

A contest then arose between Herod's sons, which threw the whole country into confusion, as to who should have the throne. This was brought to a conclusion by an edict from Rome, confirming Archelaus in Judea; Herod Antipas, Tetrarch of Galilee and Petrea; and Batanea, Auranitis, and Trachonitis, to Philip. Archelaus removed Joazar from the high priesthood, and appointed his brother,

Eleazar II. — Who was in turn supplanted, and

Jesus I. — Son of Siva, appointed in his stead.

Archelaus obtained the throne by supplanting Antipater, and so, as things went then, he was summoned to Rome, where matters terminated in the dethronement and banishment of Archelaus to Vienne, in Gaul, and Judea became a Roman province.

The sceptre being now gone from the Jews, a semblance of authority was still exercised by their council, or Sanhedrim. Of this body the high-priest sat as president. This council was the supreme court of the Jews, having power to inflict even capital punishment. This power it soon lost, and so acted as a kind of senate, or mediation between the Jews and the tribunal of Pilate. Hence they only held the mock trial of the Saviour; judged him worthy of death, and then denounced him at Pilate's bar, and asked for his crucifixion by the Roman Government.

Thus that often persecuted people turn against the Messiah, their long expected prophet, and invoke a heathen governor to put him to the death of the cross, even when Pilate himself could find no fault in him.

The religious sects of the Jews were chiefly Pharisees, who were noted for external observance of the law of Moses and the dogmas of their own devising; the Sadducees, who admitted a divine providence among men, and were extremely severe in the infliction of the law upon its violaters, and denied the future existence of the soul; the Essenes, a monastic order, deeming the subjection of every natural enjoyment the perfection of virtue.

Numerous other vain conceits of men had an existence at the time, showing how likely it was that a true prophet and pure teacher would be rejected and put to death for the all-important purpose of pleasing the priests and appeasing Cæsar.

An order being issued for a census of persons and property throughout the Roman realm, the spirit of the Jews was terribly stirred at this last step in their degradation.

JOAZAR II. — But Joazar, who reäppears in the office of high-priest, succeeded in pacifying the moderate Jews into quiet submission. But the fiercer Jews found a leader in one Judas, who sought rather to inflame than pacify their rage; when not only the proud, but the fierce and foul, rallied around his standard.

Like the Maccabees, they declared themselves the subjects of God alone, as King; but though the *cry* was the same, those who *made it* were changed, and other circumstances were so changed that they could not rise.

They made a strong party for some time, but their principal influence was felt, in disturbing the harmony between the Jewish people and the Roman Government; and to this party Josephus ascribes most of the subsequent insurrections, which finally brought on the ruin of the city and temple.

Quirinius, Prefect of Syria, having disposed of the confiscated goods of Archelaus, removed Joazar, who had become unpopular, from the priesthood, and

ANANUS, OR ANNAS — Was appointed high-priest in his stead, and Quirinius returned to Syria. During Augustus' life the governors of Judea were often changed; but upon his death, Tiberias Cæsar pursued a different course — appointing only two during twenty-three years; viz., Valerius Gratus, 15 A. C., and Pontius Pilate, 26 A. C.

Gratus did but little of note; still took great pains to gratify his contempt for the Jews, as most tyrants did. His great feat was changing the high-priests to suit his fancy.

ISMAEL — Son of Tolu, was appointed, and Annas removed.

ELEAZAR III. — Son of Annas, was next appointed.

SIMON V. — Son of Camith; and, lastly,

JOSEPH CAIAPHAS — Son-in-law of Annas.

Pilate removed the winter-quarters of his troops from Samaria to Jerusalem, when the Jews besought him not to display their standards, on which were images of the eagle and the emperor. Pilate at first refused to comply, giving as a reason, that it would be disrespectful to the emperor; but finally, as a matter of prudence, yielded to their wishes.

He then seized a part of the treasury of the temple, to build an aqueduct to supply the city with water, from a distance of twenty-five miles. The populace were offended at this sacrilege, and interrupted the work; whereupon Pilate ordered his workmen to wear long frocks, and carry swords concealed; and with these they made great slaughter among the Jews.

Still, when Jesus Christ was brought before him, he was for releasing him, "finding no fault in him." The Jews cried out, "Condemn him, or you are not *Cæsar's friend!*" When he saw that he could both please the Jews, and show loyalty to Cæsar, he delivered him unto them to be crucified.

The malignant Jews, under the direction of Caiaphas, the high-priest, with consent to execute the death penalty from Pilate, under the protection of Roman soldiers, and the mob crying, "Crucify him! crucify him!" had it all their own way. Pilate was, not long after, called to Rome and disgraced.

Vitellius, President of Syria, then visited Jerusalem, conferred some favors upon the Jews by releasing them from a tax on the sale of the fruits of the earth, and restoring the high-priest's robes, which had been kept in the fortress or Antonia, and was now the Roman armory, to the depository in the temple.

He also removed Caiaphas from the high priesthood, and appointed

JONATHAN III. — Son of Annas, in his stead.

Herod Antipas, son of Herod the Great, repudiated his wife, and married Herodias, his niece, wife of his *living* brother Philip, for which he was reproved by John the Baptist; and thereby John was cast into prison and beheaded.

His repudiated wife being sister to Aretas, King of Arabia, the latter sought revenge, and Herod's army was cut off. Herod invoked aid of Tiberias the emperor, when Vitellius was again sent with an army to chastise Aretas.

Vitellius and Herod and his friends, while the army was moving on across the Jordan, went the second time to attend the Passover at Jerusalem. He then removed Jonathan from the priesthood, and appointed

THEOPHILUS — His brother, in his stead.

The accession of Caligula to the emperorship of Rome, gave a new start to Agrippa "the Great," son of Aristobulus, one of the two sons of Herod the Great, by the second Mariamne.

Agrippa was at first assisted to means by his sister, the wicked Herodias. But in time his favor with the emperor excited her displeasure towards her brother, who was rising above her husband. Through a regular course of court intrigues, Herod Antipas was banished to Lyons in Gaul, and Agrippa made king.

Agrippa's presence in Rome at the critical moment of Caligula's assassination, was of great service. He controlled by his advice the senate and army, and encouraged the imbecile Claudius to accept the purple.

His services were amply repaid by the emperor, by the bestowment of nearly all the territory of the ancient Jews upon Agrippa. The edict was registered on a tablet of brass in the capitol, with a high eulogium on Agrippa. A treaty was formally concluded between the emperor and Agrippa, in the forum at Rome.

Agrippa returned in great splendor to his kingdom, paid great respect to the national religion, and hung in the temple the golden chain given him by Caligula, — equal in weight to one of iron Agrippa wore while in prison.

He inherited Herod's taste for building and display; and to please the Jews, put James to death and cast Peter into prison, and such little playful acts of a would-be popular sovereign.

He exercised his power in removing and replacing the high-priests. Theophilus was removed, and

SIMON CANTHERUS — Substituted. Not long after, he offered the dignity to Jonathan, son of Annas, who declined it.

MATHIAS — His brother, was then appointed. Before the close of his reign, however, Agrippa appointed

ELIONAEUS — Son of Simon Cantherus, high-priest.

On a set day Agrippa appeared in the theatre clothed with a robe of silver, and was greeted with the applause of, "A present god!" He accepted the adulation; but, like a mortal, he was smitten with a disease in the bowels, which bred worms, and he died.

Fadus was next sent to be Governor of Judea. He thought the high-priest had a trifle too much influence, and undertook to interfere a little, when Herod, King of Chalcis, brother of Agrippa, obtained the sovereignty over the temple. He removed Cantherus, who had gotten again into the office, and appointed

JOSEPH I. — During Fadus' term of office, Theudas disturbed the country; but he was taken, his head cut off, and sent to Jerusalem.

Tiberius Alexander, an apostate Alexandrian Jew, succeeded Fadus. He caused James and Simon, sons of Judas the Galilean, to be crucified, for disseminating their father's doctrines.

Herod of Chalcis died about this time, having made one more change in the high priesthood.

ANANIAS — Son of Nebid; for Joseph, son of Camith.

Quadratus, the Prefect of Syria, took occasion, for some disturbances, to implicate Ananias, the high-priest, and Annas, the captain of the temple, and sent them in chains to Rome.

JONATHAN IV. — Who was next high-priest, under the sway of the dissolute Felix, attempted to do the wretch good by exhorting him, as Paul did; but to little effect. Felix rather identified himself with the banditti of the land; and having bribed Doras (an intimate friend of Jonathan), and a company of outlaws, at the instigation of Felix, they went with Jonathan into the temple, with daggers under their cloaks, and mingled with the attendants of the high-priest, and in an unsuspecting moment struck him dead.

King Agrippa, son of Herod Agrippa, being promoted, his influence at Rome helped the condition of the Jews a little.

ISMAEL II. — Son of Fabi, was appointed high-priest by Agrippa. It is probable that the office was filled by Ananias, though irregularly, after the assassination of Jonathan. Ananias' release from Rome was through the influence of Agrippa. It was this Ananias who commanded them to smite Paul on the mouth, while speaking to the people. So Paul's cutting reply to him was not so far out of the way as they pretended; for Ananias was only bogus high-priest, and his order to smite the prisoner was bogus justice.

Darkness succeeded darkness; for, besides the contests without, feuds of the worst kind began to break out among the priests, even to robbing each other of the tithes, and that by force.

But the final blow was to be struck in Cesarea, the inhabitants being a mixture of Syrian Greeks and Jews. The Jews contended that the city was founded by Herod their king, and intended for a Jewish ruler; while the heathen claimed that the temples and statues of Herod showed his design for a heathen influence.

Tumults and bloodshed ensued; and an order for the soldiery was given by Felix, which so exasperated the Jews, that an appeal was made to Nero. A decree followed, through the influence of bribes, depriving the Jews of equal citizenship. This made the Greeks more insulting, and the Jews more exasperated, as time went on.

Agrippa resided at Jerusalem at this time, in the palace of the Asmoneans; and in order to have an opportunity to view the temple courts, and the ceremonies of worship, and lie on his couch at the same time (too lazy to go to meeting!), he raised a tower high enough to overlook the whole.

The priests, displeased at this, raised a wall so as to hide the view. This resulted in an appeal to Nero, to decide the quarrel.

Agrippa and Festus agreed to this, when a deputation of ten was sent, headed by Ismael, the high-priest, and Hilkiah, the treasurer of the temple. Through the influence of Poppea, wife of Nero, the wall was permitted to stand; but Ismael and Hilkiah were detained in Rome. Agrippa seized upon the opportunity to fill the vacant office of high-priest, by the appointment of a son of Simon Cantherus.

Joseph II., — Named Cabi. Soon after he removed Cabi, and put in his place the fifth son of a former high-priest, Annas, who, with himself, his five sons, and son-in law Caiaphas, had filled the office. Their names were, Annas (the father), Eleazar, Joseph Caiaphas (son-in-law), Jonathan, Theophilus, Mathias, and Ananus (sons); seven in all.

Ananus. — Being a Sadducee — and the sect were vindictive in spirit and deed — this Ananus put James the Just to death, to please the Jews, and also killed others of the Christians at the Passover. This, however, displeased Agrippa, and soon he removed him from office,

Jesus — Son of Dammai, succeeding. Festus dying, Albinus succeeded him as governor. Ananias the elder contrived to keep the governor and high-priest in good pay, and so, by rapacity and violence, succeeded in laying up wealth. Agrippa began some public work for himself in Cesarea Philippi, and made large outlay, with the intention of moving there, which displeased the Jews.

The removal of the high-priest from his office, and the appointment of

Jesus — Son of Gamaliel, increased the general discontent. Upon this, strifes multiplied between the rival priests, and they scrupled not to take might for right.

Upon a petition of the Jews to Agrippa, to expend the surplus treasure of the temple (fearing the banditti would get it), Agrippa ordered them to use it in paving the city with stone. He afterwards removed Jesus, son of Gamaliel, and appointed

Mattathias, — The *last* legitimate high-priest of Jerusalem.

Fall of Jerusalem. — The time drew near; Christ, though unheeded by many, had told of the fall, to rise no more, of the devoted nation of the Jews.

Appalling omens began to appear, such as a comet, in shape of a sword, that hung over the city for a whole year; at the feast of unleavened bread, a bright light shone about the altar and temple for half an hour; a cow, while led forth to sacrifice, brought forth a calf; the inner gate on the east, made of brass, and so heavy as to require twenty men to shut it, bolted into the stone posts with strong iron bolts, suddenly opened of itself, and was with difficulty closed; on an evening, just before sunset, chariots and armed squadrons were seen encircling the city; on Pentecost, as the priests entered the temple by night on duty, a sound of a host was heard, and a voice saying, "Let us depart hence." Josephus attests these things to be so, and that they would be incredible had they not been confirmed by eye-witnesses, and subsequent events.

A countryman, son of Ananus, began to cry out in the temple, "*A voice from the East! a voice from the West! a voice from the four winds! a voice against Jerusalem and the temple! a voice against the bridegrooms and brides! a voice against the whole people!*" No attempts to silence him were of any avail. He resented no insult; thanked nobody for any favor. For four years before the war, and particularly on festivals, he continued to cry, "*Woe, woe, to Jerusalem!*" At last, during the fatal siege, he cried, "*Woe, woe, to myself!*" when a stone struck him, thrown from a balista.

The cup of Divine wrath, now full, was soon to be upset, and its contents poured upon the heads of those whose sins had dictated its fulness and fierceness.

The old feud at Cesarea broke out into a flame of civil war, which proved to be a war of extermination to the Jewish people.

Nero had assigned the magistracy of the city to the Greeks, which placed the two parties in direct antagonism.

The Jews had a synagogue, but the land around it belonged to a Greek. The Jews offered a much larger sum for the land than its actual worth, but it could not be bought — malice being sweeter than gold. In order to annoy the Jews still more, the owner proceeded to erect some mean shops close to the synagogue, so as to make the passage to and from it as narrow and difficult as possible. The indignant Jewish youth interrupted the workmen. John, a publican, collected the large sum of two hundred thousand dollars, and sent it to Florus, the governor, as a present, to get him to interfere and stop the building. He took the money, made fair promises, and then left Cesarea for Sebaste, so as to give full scope for the riot.

On the next day, the Sabbath, as the Jews were crowding to the synagogue, some Greeks overset an earthen vessel in the way, and made a mock offering of birds upon it. This was intended for an insult upon the Jews; they were accused of being anciently driven out of Egypt because they were lepers, and birds were the offering for leprosy. This act was a malignant insult. The Jews took it as such, and fell upon the Greeks, who were already armed, and took this way to provoke a fight. The Jews being worsted, took their sacred books and went out of the city, to Narbater, seven and a half miles distant.

John the publican, with twelve of the highest rank, went to Florus, beseeching him to protect them, and reminding him of the little purse he received, when the wretch cast them all into prison.

The news flew to Jerusalem, and put the city in a panic; and the measures taken after this all turned out to hasten the downfall of the Jews.

Space cannot be afforded to insert in detail the events which now follow to the destruction of the city. Contentions among the Jews themselves were carried to such an extent, that the wrath of Rome was at last excited against them, as a whole. At first their contention was with their governor, but at last they were brought to face the legions of Rome.

As soon as the affair came to Nero, he at once despatched Vespasian, his ablest general, to quell the disturbance in Palestine. Vespasian sent his son Titus to Alexandria, to put the fifth and tenth legions in motion for the seat of war.

The capture of Jotapata was one of great difficulty to the Romans, from its strength, and hence a great point gained. And by no means the slightest advantage to Vespasian was the capture of Josephus, the intrepid and brave Jewish commander, afterwards a favorite with Titus, and still better known as the historian. A minute detail of this war is recorded in his history.

The death of Nero called Vespasian to the chair of empire, when the command of the expedition against Jerusalem was put into the hands of his son Titus.

Upon the death, during the siege of Jerusalem, of the high-priests Ananus and Jesus, Josephus dates the ruin of the holy city.

The siege was now pressed. Titus, wishing to save the city, made offers of peace repeatedly, but they were rejected by the Jews with the utmost contempt.

Affairs within the city were daily becoming horribly worse and worse. It is stated that one mother killed, cooked, and ate of her own child, to save herself from starvation.

This circumstance coming to the ears of Titus, his indignation and horror were excited, and he declared that, "Soon shall the sun never more dart his beams on a city where mothers feed on the flesh of their children; and where fathers, no less guilty than themselves, choose to drive them to such extremities, rather than lay down their arms."

Titus' wish was to save the temple; but, while asleep in his tent, a soldier, "*pushed on by Providence*," as Josephus says, climbed upon the shoulders of his comrades, and threw a blazing fire-brand into one of the apartments that surrounded the sanctuary, and soon it was in flames. Then followed the destruction and sacking of the city, that horrible scene, the contemplation of which never fails to make the heart sicken and relent.

The number slain is estimated to have been over one million one hundred thousand, and ninety-seven thousand taken prisoners. Simon, son of Gioras, being the resolute defender of Jerusalem, was at last taken; and thus fell, and forever, the metropolis of the Jewish State, at the same season of the year, autumn, that the first temple was destroyed by Nebuchadnezzar — the latter, 70 A. C.

What a scourge is war! And yet God permits it, as a lesser evil than wickedly departing from his law, and persisting in such alienation.

From the day in which the Roman general led his triumphant legions from Jerusalem, the Jews have been "without a king, without a prince, and without a sacrifice; without an altar, without an ephod, and without divine manifestations."

All was swept away; a dispensation which had existed for ages; a nation, as such, blotted from being, which had outlived some of the proudest monuments of antiquity.

The Jews are now dispersed through the world, — despised and hated by many, — persecuted, and yet upheld; lost among the nations of the earth, and yet distinct, they live as monuments of the truth of Christianity, to convey to the world the solemn lesson, that a nation cannot reject the Incarnate Son of God with impunity.

The history of the children of Abraham is ended.

The Hebrews, or Jews, began in Abraham, and were associated together, under the patriarchal discipline, until Joseph; thence in Egyptian bondage until Moses; thence the exodus and settlement in Canaan, until Joshua; thence under judges (the Theocracy) until Saul, the first king; thence under their kings, during which time the Ten Tribes went off, and were lost, until the Babylonish captivity;

in captivity seventy years; then continued about one hundred and forty years under the auspices of Persia; then under Alexander; then under Egypt; then under Syria; then, independent, under the Maccabees; finally, subject to the Romans, when the sceptre departed. Though under different governments, they were only in allegiance to them, all the time retaining their identity as a civil community, until this peculiarity was blotted out by the Roman emperors, as God had declared.

III.

AGE OF WAR FOR OPINION.

FROM CHRIST TO THE PEACE OF RELIGION, 1555 A. C.

ECCLESIASTICAL HISTORY.

Leaving, or rather closing, the history of the Jews, as of any importance in the history of Religion, at 70 A. D., we now return to the beginning of the gospel of the Son of God, or Ecclesiastical history.

As heretofore, the names of prominent men, of different times, will make our divisions, instead of chapters and verses; yet a general division will be made into periods, for convenience.

PERIOD I. FROM JOHN BAPTIST TO THE END OF THE APOSTOLIC AGE, 4000 A. M., AND 4 B. C., TO 4100 A. M., AND 96 A. C.

John Baptist. — In the fulness of time the Messiah was to appear; and at the time of his coming, many were looking for him, but saw him not, because they overlooked him. Many, however, did see him, with great joy.

While Zacharias, a devout priest, was officiating at the altar of incense, the angel Gabriel, who spoke to Daniel and others, appeared, and stood beside the altar. Zacharias was filled with fear at the sight, when Gabriel informed him that his wife should soon give birth to the *herald* of the Messiah. Upon asking for proof of this, the angel replied, "For not believing my words, this shall be the sign: you shall be dumb, and not able to speak, until these things be fulfilled."

And so it was until the day of the circumcision of the child, when the friends proposed to name him for his father. Zacharias objects at once, and called for a tablet, and wrote, "His name shall be called *John*," as the angel directed.

Immediately after this his tongue was loosened, and he spoke again.

This shows that God had still, in the old Jewish Church, those with whom he held counsel. Zacharias' lack of faith about a son being born to him, finds an example in a similar event, in the family of the old patriarch Abraham.

Not far from the same time, Gabriel appeared to Mary, cousin to Elizabeth, wife of Zacharias, and informed her that she, although a virgin, should be the honored mother of the true Messiah, as predicted by the prophet Isaiah; and that his name should be called *Jesus*.

John, for his faithfulness in reproving Herod for his unlawful marriage, lost his head by Herodias. (See also Kilian, and Fredric.)

Jesus Christ. — While at Bethlehem, for the purpose of being enrolled for taxation, under a decree of Augustus Cæsar, Mary is delivered of a child, which was called a "Saviour, Christ the Lord." Such was the crowded state of the city, that no room could be found in the inn, when her accouchement took place in the inn barn, or manger, 4000 A. M.

But the announcement of this event by angels, to the shepherds, soon brought them, guided by a star, to Bethlehem, where the child was; and soon a stir was made that the Messiah was born.

When he was brought to Jerusalem, to do to him after the manner of the law, old Simeon, a devout man who was waiting for the consolation of Israel, seeing the child, took him up in his arms and exclaimed: "Lord, let now thy servant depart in peace, for mine eyes have seen thy salvation!" At the same time, one Anna, a prophetess, coming in, concurred with Simeon, that the Great Deliverer had come.

Herod the Great, fearing in him who was called the "King of the Jews," a rival on the throne of Judah, issued and executed an edict for the destruction of all children under two years old, thinking to compass the death of Christ.

An angel directed Joseph, who took Mary and the child and fled into Egypt, until the death of Herod, which took place in a year or two after the massacre.

At twelve years old Christ accompanied his parents to Jerusalem, to the feast of the Passover; and on that occasion manifested such wisdom as to astonish and confound the Doctors of the Law.

When about thirty years of age, he began his public ministry. As a prelude to this, he sent before him, as his herald, John the Baptist, son of Zacharias and Elizabeth, to announce his advent as the Messiah.

Upon this John went forth, preaching to the people that they should repent and believe on him who was shortly to appear as the Saviour of the world.

Soon he came from Galilee to Jordan, and was baptized of John in the river; and immediately the heavens were opened, and the Holy Spirit descended upon him in the form of a dove, and a voice declaring, This is my beloved Son, in whom I am well pleased.

We now find him publicly teaching, and confounding the would-be instructors of the people in such a masterly way as to convince all, even his opposers, of his divine mission. He healed the sick, unstopped the ears of the deaf, opened blind eyes, and in every possible way ministered to the good of the people, by teaching them wisdom and healing their diseases.

As a religious teacher, he confirmed all the moral precepts of the Old Testament, and explained and enforced their application to social life.

He assumed to be the Messiah, and to have such connection with Divinity, as made the Jews accuse him of blasphemy. He exposed the vain and lying teaching of designing men, often reproving the Pharisees and Doctors of the Law as false and hypocritical, and in such a manner as to make them feel its force.

His disciples he instructed with the greatest fidelity and tenderness, assuring them of the perpetuity of the kingdom which he came to set up, and that its subjects were to be the children of the Most High God. In order to become subjects of his kingdom, all must be made new creatures by repentance and faith. Hence his object was to bring man back from his apostasy from God, and thereby be fitted to serve and enjoy him here and forever.

He further taught the abolition of the Mosaic ritual, — declaring that Jerusalem, even, should be henceforth no better place than any other to worship the Lord God in spirit and in truth; and as evidence that these things should be so, both Jerusalem and the temple itself were to be destroyed, and not one stone left upon another.

He also defined the position of his kingdom and people in the body politic. They were directed to keep the peace, obey their rulers, and submit to wholesome laws; and illustrated this by paying taxes, as the law required; thus recognizing the propriety and necessity of civil government.

At the same time made exception, that the conscience was to be reserved for God; and when the laws of the land require what God forbids, they are to refrain from obeying such laws.

This sentiment is couched in his ever memorable words, "Render unto Cæsar the things that are Cæsar's; but unto God the things that are God's." It, however, took, as we shall see, sixteen centuries to get that principle adopted in the civil affairs of the world. In the event of a clash between Cæsar and the conscience, the disciples' alternative was, "Fear not those who kill the body, and after that have no more that they can do; but fear Him who, after death, has power over both *soul* and body: yea, I say unto you, fear him."

Thus a very pertinent distinction is made between duty to magistrates, and duty to God.

But neither the sanctity of his life, the wisdom of his teaching, the blessings of his miracles, nor even his faultless demeanor, could shield the Saviour from the malice of men. Of the twelve persons he chose to succeed him, and put his church in due form and operation, one of them was bribed to deliver him into the hands of his enemies. The signal by which the police were to be guided to the identical person, was one of affection: "Whom I shall kiss, that same is he; hold him fast!" And Judas, one of the twelve, drew near, and said, "Hail, Master!" and kissed him. Then they laid hold of him.

Being taken, they led him before the Sanhedrim, Caiaphas being high-priest. A court was then held, to get proof of some evil he had done. Accusations were brought, but nothing could be proved. At last two came forward, and testified that he said he was able to destroy the temple of God and build it in three days.

Making no reply, Caiaphas tauntingly asked him, why he did not answer the charge. Jesus making no reply, Caiaphas then asked if he were really the Christ, the Son of God. He replied, "Thou hast said." Caiaphas took this at once as an affirmative answer, and immediately seized upon it, and founded upon it a charge of blasphemy, and for this he was condemned as worthy of death.

The Sanhedrim being deprived by the Roman Government of the power of inflicting the death penalty, they then took Jesus before Pilate, the governor, and asked him to pass the death sentence. Pilate demurring, as he could see no ground for such a sentence, a tumult was raised at once. Referring the case to Herod Antipas, who beheaded John the Baptist, to whose jurisdiction Jesus belonged, Pilate and Herod were friends at once; and as the Jews had accused Pilate of being no friend to Cæsar if he let Jesus go, he yielded, and delivered him up to them, to do with him as they saw fit. In an instant they set up the cry: "Let his blood be upon us and our children!" Pilate passed no sentence, yet authorized them to do it, or not, as they pleased.

Immediately they led him away to Calvary, and crucified him between two thieves.

The crucifixion of Christ occurred in the eighteenth year of the reign of Tiberius Cæsar, A. D. 34.

After his death and burial, it occurred to the Scribes that Jesus Christ had said he was to die, but would rise again. Fearing what might happen, they aped a great concern for the welfare of the people, and suggested to Pilate the propriety of having a guard set at the tomb, lest his disciples steal him away, and then say he was risen.

As it happened, this very precaution was of the utmost service to the world; for, upon his actual resurrection, they were put to the difficult and unwelcome task of *covering up* the fact.

Their vain and perfidious attempt to still throw the stain upon his disciples, of stealing him while they slept, with his actual appearance afterwards among his disciples, put the fact of his resurrection beyond a doubt.

Having remained with his disciples forty days after this, and instructing them in their future duty, he took leave of them, upon the Mount of Olives, and ascended into heaven, A. D. 34, from whence he is to come again, at the end of the world.

Before leaving his disciples, he assured them that an effusion of the Holy Ghost should be granted them, to fit them for the great work before them and their successors. The fulfilment of this promise took place at Pentecost, a feast of the Jews, fifty days after the Passover. On this occasion, great numbers embraced the faith taught by Christ and his apostles.

APOSTLES.

Of the history of Christ's twelve apostles, the following is a brief summary:

1. Peter. — He was among the foremost to advocate the doctrines and cause of Christ. He charged, in the most vehement manner, upon the Jews, the crime of maliciously shedding the innocent blood of the Messiah. The civil and ecclesiastical authorities, taking offence at him, charged him to desist, which charge he persistently disregarded, telling them he should "obey God rather than men."

He was a very bold preacher: at Pentecost three thousand were converted under his preaching. He was delivered from prison by an angel, in answer to the prayers of the church, — having been cast into it by Herod Agrippa. He preached in several places in Asia Minor, and finally came to Rome, where he suffered death, under Nero, — being crucified, head down, about 64 A. D.

2. Andrew. — He was brother of Peter. He travelled through Asia Minor, and along the shores of the Black Sea to Constantinople, where he founded a church, ordaining Stachys bishop, whom Paul calls his beloved Stachys.

From thence he travelled into Achaia, to Patras, where he was killed for Christ's sake. He was fastened to a cross in the form of the letter X, by means of ropes, to make his death more lingering.

During two days he preached from the cross, and many believed Hence this form of cross has received the title of Saint Andrew's cross.

3. James.—He and John are called Sons of Thunder. James preached to the Jews; was apprehended and imprisoned by Herod Agrippa, and then slain by the sword; which so pleased the Jews that Herod thought to slay Peter also; but he was delivered from the expectation of the Jews.

4. John,—The brother of James, with his brother and Peter, saw the transfiguration of Christ. He penetrated as far as Parthia in Asia, preaching the gospel. After, took up his residence at Ephesus. During the persecution under Domitian, he was taken to Rome and thrown into a caldron of boiling oil, from which he escaped unhurt. He was then banished to the Isle of Patmos, where he wrote the Revelation. In the reign of Nerva he returned to Ephesus, where he wrote his Gospel, A. D. 97 or 98. He also wrote three Epistles. He died, aged one hundred years, A. D. 100.

5. Philip.—He preached in Upper Asia and Scythia. On coming to Hierapolis, a city of Phrygia, where the people worshipped a huge serpent, called Jupiter Ammon, he preached the gospel; many believed, and, as is usual, opposition arose. Such was the fury of the wicked, they thrust him into prison, scourged him, and then hanged him by the neck to a pillar.

6. Bartholomew.—He is supposed to be Nathaniel, whom Philip sought. He travelled much with Philip. A copy of the Gospel of Matthew, in Hebrew, found many years after by Pontianus, a Christian philosopher, in Arabia Felix, was called Bartholomew's; left there by him when he planted the gospel there.

He would have suffered at Hierapolis with Philip, at the same time (being then bound to a cross), but an earthquake so terrified his persecutors that they released him through fear.

At Albanopolis, in Armenia, the governor of the city apprehended him, and condemned him to crucifixion. On his way to execution he exhorted the disciples to faithfulness. He was crucified head down.

7. Matthew—Was a tax-gatherer. He preached in Judea for several years, and, it is supposed, in other parts. Author of the Gospel. It is said he suffered martyrdom at Naddabar, a city in Ethiopia.

8. Thomas—Called also Didymus. He is said to have preached the gospel to the Persians, Medes, Carmanians, Hyrcanians, Bactrians, and other people.

He then penetrated into the East Indies, as far as Ceylon, or Sumatra. At Meliapour he was about building a place of worship, when the prince of the city forbade it; after a time, he and many of the nobility were converted, and the house was built.

This so exasperated some of the people, that, while Thomas was one day preaching in a solitary place, one of them stabbed him with a spear.

9. James the Less — Brother of Simon and Jude. He was Bishop of Jerusalem, and called by Paul a pillar in the church. He was killed by a blow from a fuller's club, under Ananias, the high-priest, A. D. 62.

The Epistle of James was written by him.

10. Simon — It is said, preached in and about Egypt, and finally suffered martyrdom in Persia.

11. Jude. — He was author of the Epistle; called, also, Thaddeus. Is said to have preached in Mesopotamia, Syria, Idumea, and Arabia, and suffered martyrdom at Berytus, A. D. 80.

12. Judas Iscariot — "Went to his own place."

From this account it is clearly seen that the apostles and others were true missionaries, having gone over nearly all the missionary ground of the different ages since; and all but one laid down their lives for Christ's sake and the gospel's.

Stephen. — The opposition to the gospel increased, and the malignity of the rulers was excited, until, near the close of the year A. D. 35, Stephen, a holy man, was called to be the first to follow Christ, as a martyr to the gospel. He was stoned to death.

Saul. — In the year 36, occurred the conversion of Saul, which added greatly to the prosperity of Christianity. He was president of the mob at the stoning of Stephen. Being instructed in the law of the Jews, by the celebrated Doctor Gamaliel, his zeal was even greater than his knowledge. He not only espoused the cause of the Pharisees, but turned the sword of persecution against the Christians. Whilst going from Jerusalem, with authority from the chief-priests, to bind and send thither all that were of that way of worshipping in Damascus, the Lord met him on his way. Saul, being overcome by a light exceeding that of the sun, which felled him to the ground, he was led to inquire what he should do; when a voice from heaven directed him to go to Damascus, and it would be told him what to do.

Ananias, a Christian man in Damascus, was warned of the Lord of the condition of Saul, and assured that he was called to do a great work for Christ, but was now awaiting instruction, which Ananias must impart. He went and laid his hands on him, calling him "Brother Saul." He then told Saul that Jesus, who appeared to him on his way, had revealed to him that Saul was a chosen vessel, to bear the gospel to the Gentiles. His eyes were opened (for he was blinded from the time he saw the light until now), and he arose immediately and was baptized, as the custom was then.

Saul (after this he was called Paul) went into Arabia for three years, on a missionary tour, when he went up to Jerusalem and offered himself to the church there. The church, being a little fearful that all was not right, hesitated about receiving him, until they were assured of his conversion and adherence to Christianity, when they gladly gave the reformed persecutor the right hand of fellowship.

None of the apostles were so eminently successful in spreading the gospel as was Paul; throughout Asia Minor and Greece, he labored with great success. Some have even conjectured that he preached in Britain. He was finally carried prisoner to Rome, where he lived and instructed all who came unto him, and wrote most of his epistles. He is supposed to have suffered martyrdom, under Nero, about A. D. 64.

Timothy is said to have been the founder of the church in Alexandria, which makes a very conspicuous figure in the early history of Christianity.

Luke was author of the Gospel by his name, and of the Acts of the Apostles. He was a Syrian, and, it is said, was hung on an olive-tree in Greece.

PERSECUTIONS.

Besides the frequent disturbances, and destruction of the lives, peace, and property of the early Christians, there were ten seasons of general and terrible persecution. The *first* was under the Emperor Nero. Such was the rapidity with which the gospel spread over the world, that its disciples attracted universal attention, simply from their numbers.

The cause of this persecution was a charge made against the Christians, of setting Rome on fire. Hearing of their belief, that the world would one day be set on fire, Nero was impatient to see it. Having set the city on fire, he went into a tower to view the conflagration, and played on his harp, imagining that the scene resembled the burning of ancient Troy, and declared he "wished the destruction of all things before his death." To cover the odium of this wanton act, he very early laid the crime at the door of Christians, as they believed the destruction of the world would be by fire.

In order to make a fair show of the enormity of the crime of firing Rome, Nero tempered the punishment accordingly. Some were covered with the skins of wild beasts and exposed to be torn in pieces by dogs; others were crucified; others hung upon a sharp stake by the chin, to keep them upright, and then covered with wax and other combustibles and set on fire, to serve as lamps in the night.

Nero offered his garden for the occasion, had a horse-race, and was present in the attire of a charioteer. This persecution extended as far as Spain.

No computation can be made of the depth and extent of this terrible scourge upon the bosom of Christ's infant church.

A moment's reflection would have shown Nero that he was himself author of both the fire and the persecution. Such were the times and the rulers who domineered over the church.

The Christian Church escaped for a few years the fire of persecution, during which time many labors of love were performed. The venerable John of Patmos went about among the distracted churches, encouraging and regulating the dejections and disasters resulting from the persecution. He was the last of the apostolic veterans who set up the true tabernacle of God among men.

Domitian coming to the throne after Titus, and inheriting the brute disposition of Nero, began, in 95 A. D., the *second* persecution.

The cause of this was the atheism of the Christians; *i. e.*, their refusal to offer incense to idols; and, having no altars, idols, nor sacrifices, were considered as having no religion at all, and hence, fit only to be put to the sword. Upon the death of Domitian, Nerva came to the throne; being an old man, and inactive, the persecution ceased.

This brings us to the close of the Apostolic Age — a fit point to halt and meditate.

It is astonishing to see the rapidity with which the gospel had spread, in the space of one hundred years. Unaided by court favor, but rather opposed; planted and flourished side by side with Judaism; ignoring pomp and worldly aggrandizement, and even opposing the temple worship, and all kinds of idolatry to which the whole world was addicted, both noble and ignoble, sage and fool, officers and tools, — in the face of all these it spread itself from Sumatra to Britain, from Egypt to Constantinople. Its followers were peaceable and mild, in an age of treachery and brute force; they neither had nor sought civil power, and yet were formidable for numbers.

But when we consider it to be "the Lord's doings, well may it be marvellous in our eyes."

At this point it may be well to throw together a brief synopsis of the history and contents of the Bible. All the New Testament was written during the first century after Christ.

The Law was first given on Sinai, on tables of stone prepared by Moses, and written by the finger of God. Moses afterwards wrote the first five books of the Old Testament. The rest were written as records of the nation of the Jews, and predictions of its inspired prophets. The canon was completed by Simon the Just, about three hundred years B. C., and soon after, the translation of the Septuagint occurred.

These writings formed the Jewish Scriptures. To them Christ referred, as containing predictions of himself and his mission; of them he spoke, and from them he taught.

To these were added the writings of the evangelists and apostles, making the New Testament; both together constitute our Holy Bible.

The Apocrypha is not inspired, but is a valuable historical document, respecting the affairs of the Jews between the Old and New Testament times, giving the connection.

Following is a list of the books of the Bible, their contents, and date when written: the Old Testament before Christ, the New Testament after Christ.

BOOKS.	CONTENTS.	DATE — B. C.
Genesis,	The Cabinet of Antiquities,	1491
Exodus,	The Departure, and Moral Law,	1491
Leviticus,	The Ceremonial Law,	1490
Numbers,	Enumeration and Continuation,	1451
Deuteronomy,	Rehearsal and Explanation,	1451
Joshua,	The Wars and Settlement,	1427
Judges,	History of the Governors,	1406
Ruth,	The Widow and her Daughters,	1312
Samuel and Kings,	History of the Kings,	1055, 990
Chronicles,	Record of the Times,	1015, 1004
Ezra,	The Restoration of Israel,	457
Nehemiah,	The Reformation of Israel,	434
Esther,	The Wonderful Deliverance,	509
Job,	The School of Patience,	Uncertain.
Psalms,	The Height of Holy Aspirations,	"
Proverbs,	Ethics, Metaphysics, Politics,	1000
Ecclesiastes,	The Vanity of Man,	975
Song of Solomon,	. . . .	1013
Isaiah,	The Evangelical Prophet,	698
Jeremiah and Lamentations,	The Devout Mourner,	588
Ezekiel,	The Captive Prophet,	574
Daniel,	The Historical Prophet,	534
Hosea,	Faith and Repentance,	740
Joel,	Awful Threatenings,	800

BOOKS.	CONTENTS.	DATE — B. C.
Amos and Obadiah,	Keen Reproofs,	787, 587
Jonah,	Disobedience Reproved,	862
Micah and Nahum,	Israel's Sins and Dangers,	750, 713
Habakkuk,	Comfort for Captives,	626
Zephaniah, Haggai, and Zechariah,	Preparations for Sad Times,	630, 520, 520
Malachi,	The Last of the Prophets,	397
		A. C.
Matthew, Mark, Luke, and John,	Life and Sayings of Christ,	38, 65, 63, 97
Acts,	Establishment of the Church,	64
Romans,	Foundation Doctrines,	58
1st and 2d Corinthians,	Christian Deportment,	56, 57
Galatians,	Epitome of the Truth,	52
Ephesians,	Cautions and Encouragements,	61
Philippians,	Commendations and Rejoicings,	62
Colossians,	Faith and Manners,	62
1st Thessalonians,	Practical Theology,	52
2d Thessalonians,	Controversial Theology,	52
1st and 2d Timothy,	Pastoral Theology,	64, 65
Titus,	Clerical Counsel,	64
Philemon,	The Wanderer Restored,	62
Hebrews,	The Sacrificial System Illustrated,	63
James,	Faith shown by Works,	61
1st and 2d Peter,	Theological Summary,	64, 65
1st John,	Heresies kindly Refuted,	69
2d John,	The Christian Matron,	69
3d John,	The Liberal Christian,	69
Jude,	False Prophets,	70
Revelation,	Future Things,	96

These books constitute the holy Bible. At first these writings were composed like letters. Their first division into chapters and verses is attributed to Stephen Langton, Archbishop of Canterbury, in the last of the twelfth, or first of the thirteenth century. Cardinal Hugo divided the Old Testament into chapters, as they now stand. In 1661, Athias, a Jew of Amsterdam, divided the sections of Hugo into verses, as they now stand. Robert Stephens, a French printer, divided the New Testament into verses in 1551, as they now stand.

PERIOD II. FROM APOSTOLIC AGE TO CONSTANTINE THE GREAT, 4100 A. M., AND 96 A. C., TO 4310 A. M., 306 A. C.

Now follows what is called The Age of the Fathers; or the first laborers in the gospel after the apostles.

Simeon. — No sooner was one pastor cut down at his post, than another was ready to fill it.

The pastorate at Jerusalem was filled by Simeon, upon the death of James by Herod Agrippa.

Upon the death of Nerva, the old man emperor, Trajan came to the throne, when the *third general persecution* was begun, and lasted nineteen years.

The celebrated letter of Pliny, to Trajan, furnishes some excellent evidence of the character of the early Christians.

Nonconformity was the crime laid against the Christians, and for which they were persecuted.

As to Simeon, he was accused to Atticus, the Roman governor. He was about one hundred and twenty years old at this time. After being scourged several times, without yielding in any degree, his persecutors, astonished at his endurance, ordered him to be crucified; and thus ended his days.

Clemens Romanus — Was born at Rome, — a fellow laborer of Paul; was bishop of the church at Rome, and distinguished both as a minister and defender of the faith.

Of his writings none remain, except an Epistle to the Corinthian Church, which is esteemed next to Holy Writ, as an ancient ecclesiastical relic. Clemens died at the advanced age of one hundred years.

Ignatius — Was bishop of the church at Antioch, and in many things resembled the apostles. In A. D. 107, Trajan marching through there, to the Parthian war, Ignatius, fearing for the safety of the church, presented himself to the emperor, offering to suffer in their stead. This frankness of the good man exasperated Trajan, and he ordered him sent to Rome at once, to be thrown to wild beasts, for the amusement of the people. Being hurried forward to Selucia, and thence by ship, they stopped at Smyrna. While the ship was detained there, he was allowed to visit Polycarp, bishop of the Christians there. They had been fellow-disciples of the apostle John. The mingled emotions of joy and grief experienced by these holy men, can hardly be conceived.

The intelligence of his arrival and condemnation spread quickly through the church, and many flocked to see and console him, and catch a few of his parting words. He wrote seven letters to various churches, four of which were written at this time, from Smyrna. At length the hour of separation came, and Ignatius was torn from his friends and hurried to Rome, where he was thrown alive to hungry lions; and this for the amusement of the polished (?) Romans! A few bones only were left, which the deacons who attended him carefully gathered up, and buried in Antioch. Such were the tender mercies of imperial Rome, in its glorious days.

SYMPHOROSA. — Not pastors only were made to feel Trajan's brutality; but a widowed mother, of the name above, with her seven sons, being ordered by him to sacrifice to the heathen deities, refused. The emperor, enraged at this, ordered her carried to the temple of Hercules, where she was scourged, and hung up by the hair of her head; then taken, and a stone tied to her neck, and thrown into a river. The sons were tied to seven pillars, and being drawn by pulleys until their limbs were dislocated, still were unshaken in their resolution. They were then martyred; the oldest was stabbed in the throat, the second in the breast, the third in the heart, the fourth in the navel, the fifth in the back, the sixth in the side; the seventh was sawn asunder.

The power of the gospel was such, as to enlighten its possessors in the midst of the heathen darkness of the times, and enable them to endure even to death the reproach of Christ.

A. D. 117, Trajan died, when a more pacific season for the church ensued, under Adrian.

He listened to appeals in behalf of the Christians; and his orders did much to check persecution in the provinces.

QUADRATUS — Was bishop of the church at Athens, and presented an apology for the Christians to Adrian, while he was there. Aristides, also, a Christian writer of Athens, presented an apology.

But what most decided him in favor of the Christians, and which these apologies had prepared him to receive, was a letter from Serenus Granianus, Proconsul of Asia, in behalf of the Christians. He said, "that it seemed to him unreasonable, that the Christians should be put to death, merely to gratify the clamors of the people, without trial, and without any crime being proved against them."

Granianus being shortly after removed, Adrian replied to his letter, addressing it to Minutus Fundanus.

After referring to the letter of Granianus, he takes into grave consideration the wrong of accusing and punishing innocent persons, the great evil which would naturally grow out of such a bad policy, and charges Fundanus to take good care that justice be administered, and only actual crime punished.

He closes thus: "But, by Hercules! if the charge be a mere calumny, do you estimate the enormity of such a calumny, and punish it as it deserves."

Persecution abated somewhat.

JUSTIN MARTYR, — So called, from being a martyr — was a Greek, brought up in and attached to Grecian philosophy. Walking one day along the sea-shore, Justin was met by a venerable person, who conversed with him upon the claims of Christianity. This led to his conversion, 132 A. D., and subsequent usefulness in the church.

Charges of atheism and impiety, and of being the cause of earthquakes, being made against the Christians in the time of Antoninus Pius, Justin wrote his first apology for the Christians, and presented it to the emperor, 140 A. D.

Whereupon Pius wrote to the common council of Asia, to let the Christians alone, since it much more concerned the gods, whom they refused to worship, to punish them, than for civil magistrates; that the Christians seemed to gain their point when they gave up their lives, rather than violate their faith. He charged the council with living in neglect of the worship of the supreme God, and persecuting those who did worship him.

He renews the sentiments of his "divine father, Adrian," to punish those who accuse the Christians, *merely as such*, and let the accused go free. Similar letters were sent to other parts of the empire.

Justin wrote another apology to the Emperor Marcus, and the senate of Rome, 166 A. D., which, however, irritated rather than appeased. Crescens, a philosopher of abandoned life, whom Justin had reproved, accused him in such a manner before the prefect of the city, as to procure his imprisonment. Justin, with six others, was brought before the prefect, and required to sacrifice to the gods; but upon refusal, Rusticus, the magistrate, sentenced them to be scourged and beheaded. On going back to prison, they rejoiced in the prospect of martyrdom.

The sentence being executed, Christian friends took up their bodies and buried them.

Thus fell Justin, a man of distinguished powers, and the first man of letters in the church, since the time of Paul. Though he continued in the profession of philosophy and letters, still he was ardently attached to the gospel: defended it when calumniated, and, rather than abandon it, gave up his life for it.

POLYCARP. — This eminent servant of God had been bishop of the church in Smyrna about eighty years, and was truly a father in the church. He and Ignatius were disciples of the apostle John.

As the fury of the *fourth* persecution spread, his friends persuaded him to retire to a neighboring village, to escape his enemies. After searching for him in vain, some of the church were put to the torture, to draw from them the place of his concealment. This being made known to him, he could not endure the thought of others suffering for him, and voluntarily gave himself up.

After being permitted to spend two hours in prayer, he was placed upon an ass, and brought to the city. Efforts were made when he was brought before the proconsul, to induce him to abjure his faith, and swear by the fortunes of Cæsar. This he peremptorily refused to do, when he was threatened with being thrown to wild beasts. "Call for them," said he; "it does not well become us to turn from good to evil."

The proconsul then threatened him with fire, when the populace asked that a lion might be let out against him. Surviving this, he was then ordered to the flames. After binding him, he prayed aloud; and when he said "amen," the fire was kindled; but an officer standing by, impatient for his death, plunged a sword into his body.

With such representative men as Polycarp, we may safely infer the excellent character of the Christian Church in this age, 166 A. D.

Irenæus — Was a disciple of Polycarp, and bishop of the church in Lyons, France. It is not certainly known by what means the gospel was first planted in Lyons and Vienna (Pothnias was bishop of the church in the latter city), though, doubtless, their commercial intercourse with the East made it not difficult for missionaries to go there.

Of the many works which issued from the pen of Irenæus, only five are preserved. Escaping the fury of this persecution, which was violent in France, he wrote an account of it to the brethren in Asia and Phrygia, by which we gain our information respecting it. Every cruelty that could be inflicted, by fire, sword, and wild beasts, was inflicted upon those guilty of nothing but the faith and patience of saints.

One Blandina, a female, who had been exposed to wild beasts, which refused to touch her, was again brought forward, with a youth of only fifteen years of age, and after refusing to acknowledge idols, they were put to torture of scourging, and the hot iron chair. Ponticus, the youth, expired. Blandina, surviving, was put into a net and exposed to be tossed by a wild bull. Enduring even this for a time, she was despatched by a sword, — the spectators even *admiring* such fortitude in a woman.

What generosity, on the part of Roman upper-tendom, to condescend to applaud a *martyr's fortitude!*

Irenæus escaped the fourth persecution, but in the *fifth* he perished, about 203 A. D.

A singular respite was allowed the church under the Emperor Commodus, in which the gospel flourished greatly, and many of the nobility of Rome, with their families, embraced it. The mildness of Commodus towards the Christians is attributed to one Marcia, his favorite concubine, who used her influence over him to extend his favor to the gospel and its disciples.

CLEMENS ALEXANDRINUS — Was born at Alexandria, and celebrated for employing his vast learning in defence of Christianity. He was long and highly revered in his native city.

TERTULLIAN. — He was by birth a Carthaginian. He was formerly a heathen lawyer, but afterwards embraced the Christian religion; he, too, possessed great abilities and varied learning, which he used vigorously in defence of Christianity.

It was during the *fifth* persecution, under Septimus Severus, which began in 202 A. D., and spread into France again, and also into the African provinces, and especially into Carthage, that Tertullian was induced to write his apology for the Christians. In that he gives a pleasing view of the spirit and behavior of Christians in his day, and of their adherence to the faith, order, and discipline of *still more primitive* times. (It was in this persecution Irenæus was martyred.) Tertullian is styled one of the ablest Latin writers. Being of a melancholy disposition, and measurably deficient in judgment, his standard of principle was somewhat lowered in the latter part of his life.

ORIGEN. — He was born at Alexandria, A. D. 185, and was one of the most noted characters in the age in which he lived. In his youth he saw his father beheaded for Christianity, and all the family estate confiscated.

But the Lord put it into the heart of a rich lady of the city to take him under her patronage. He soon acquired great stores of learning.

He was a very popular instructor, and master of the Alexandrian school. At the age of forty-five he was ordained, and delivered theological lectures in Palestine.

Upon being often met with the objection from the Jews, that the quotations from the Greek and Latin versions of the Bible did not agree with the Hebrew, Origen determined he would arrange them all, verse against verse, that they might be easily compared. To do this he made six columns, the Hebrew first, Septuagint next, and so on, according to their date. The whole filled fifty large volumes. It was found, fifty years after his death, in the public library of the city of Tyre. It was called *Hexapla*.

His great theological blunder was, that Scripture was not to be explained in a *literal*, but an *allegorical* manner. The *hidden* or *figurative* sense he often gave, but at the expense of truth. This led to many and great errors afterwards, by being adopted, as the standard method of interpretation.

He is said to have been the author of textual sermonizing; *i. e.*, of taking a single text as the subject of a discourse. He suffered martyrdom, under Decius, A. D. 254.

With the exception of three years' persecution under Maxamin, the *sixth* of the ten, the church enjoyed about forty years of great repose and freedom from peril. Maxamin vented his wrath upon the pastors of the churches, for their suspected friendship to his predecessor, Alexander Severus.

Philip was the first Roman emperor who embraced Christianity.

Towards the middle of the third century is marked as the first great and general declension in the church. The repose it had enjoyed was more detrimental to its prosperity than persecution; so that, when the *seventh* persecution, under Decius, broke out, vast numbers apostatized; or, "having no root in themselves, endure for a while; but when tribulation and persecution ariseth, because of the Word, by-and-by they are offended."

Eudemon, Bishop of Smyrna (where Polycarp had preached and suffered for the truth), apostatized, to the great grief and damage of the church there.

During this persecution the foundation of *monkery* was laid, by one Paul, of Egypt. At the age of fifteen he was left an orphan, but entitled to a large estate. His sister's husband, wishing to get his estate, took advantage of this time of persecution (as Paul was decidedly a Christian) to get his life taken, and so cover his design with his zeal for *heretical* blood.

Paul, being apprised of this, fled to the deserts of Thebias, to evade the storm of persecution; where, acquiring a love for solitude, he remained in seclusion from the age of twenty-three to one hundred and thirteen years. From his example sprung the delusion of hermitage: not designed on his part, though indirectly sanctioned, and by others directly adopted.

Cyprian. — He was preëminent, at this age, in preserving the church from ruin.

Cyprian was by birth of family note and of fortune. Bred to the bar, liberally educated, and an orator; converted in 246 A. D., he then devoted himself and his substance to the cause of Christ.

In 248, just before the reign of Decius, he was chosen bishop of the church at Carthage. His first effort was to restore the discipline of the church, which had run down during the declension heretofore referred to. Scarcely had he got under way, when the flames of persecution burst upon them in all their fury. Carthage soon became the scene of great distress. At the urgent solicitations of his friends, in order to save his valuable life, he was induced to repair for two years to a retreat they had prepared for him.

The church at Carthage endured great affliction; but Cyprian continued to send forth letters of encouragement to his distressed people.

During his concealment, the "Novatian Schism" arose, in the churches of Carthage and Rome. Novatus, an officer in the church at Carthage, had been censured for conduct not worthy his station, just before the retirement of Cyprian. Novatus took advantage of his absence, and raised a party, who proceeded to the appointment of Fortunatus as bishop, to the exclusion of Cyprian.

Fearing the return of Cyprian, Novatus fled to Rome, where, with Novatian, he succeeded in forming a party holding the severest sentiments in reference to those who had apostatized, showing them no favor, however sincere their repentance and reform.

No little part of this was intended for Cyprian. At this time, and for some time past, Rome had no bishop, it being considered unsafe to appoint one. Being fearful to what the disturbance of Novatian might grow, the church thought it best to proceed to the election of a bishop, and, with the assistance of the neighboring churches, ordained Cornelius to the office. At the same time, Novatian's party appointed him to the same office. The difference between these two prominent churches was, at Carthage discipline was too severe, at Rome not severe enough.

At this juncture, Cyprian returned from exile; soon after, assembling his church and deputies from other churches, Fortunatus and Novatian were disfellowshipped, as schismatics, and excluded from the fellowship of the church in general.

Fortunatus' party at Carthage soon divided, while the Novatians, under the name *Cathari* (signifying pure), continued to exist and flourish until the fifth century in most of the provinces where the gospel had been received. Novatian sealed his faith by martyrdom, under Valerian.

Under Gallus a short season of persecution ensued, when Cornelius was sent into banishment. Lucuis, his successor as Bishop of Rome, was also banished, but permitted to return in 252. Shortly after, he was put to death, and succeeded in office by Stephen. The bishop's chair at Rome, at this time, seems to have stood very near the door of martyrdom.

Cyprian was spared to do many noble deeds for the church, until the year 259, while residing near his native city, orders from Valerian came to put all ministers to death. Upon this Cyprian was seized and led to a spacious plain surrounded with trees. On his arrival he laid aside his mantle in great composure, fell upon his knees, and, after having worshipped, bound a napkin about his eyes; his hands were tied behind him, and a sword severed his head from his body.

SIXTUS — Bishop of Rome, was the first person of distinction who suffered death in the *eighth* persecution, by Valerian, from 257, and lasted three years.

On his way to execution, Laurentius, his chief deacon, followed him, saying, "Whither goest thou, father, without thy son?" To which Sixtus replied, "You shall follow me in three days."

LAURENTIUS. — A report got into circulation that the church at Rome was in possession of great treasure. The prefect of the city sent for Laurentius, and ordered him to deliver up the spoils.

"Give me time to set things in order, and I will render an account," said the deacon.

Three days being allowed, he gathered together all the poor who were supported by the church, and going to the prefect, invited him to "come and see a court full of golden vessels."

On seeing these he was filled with wrath, and turning upon Laurentius, said, "I know you value yourself for contemning death, therefore it shall be lingering and painful." He was then stripped, and bound to a gridiron, to be broiled alive.

After broiling some time on one side, he said, "Turn me over, I am done enough on that side." Being turned, he said, "I am done enough, serve me up." Then lifting his eyes to heaven, he prayed for the conversion of Rome, and expired.

The fate of Valerian is a striking instance of the frown of God upon those who glut themselves in the blood of the saints.

Sapor, King of Persia, took him prisoner, detained him for life, made him stoop for the king to step on to mount his horse, and at last had him flayed alive and rubbed with salt. So death was to him "*lingering and painful*," as well as to Laurentius.

In Gallienus, who succeeded his father Valerian in A. D. 260, the church found a friend. He not only stayed the persecution of his father by his imperial edict, but issued letters of license to the bishops to return from their dispersion to the care of their respective pastoral charges. During another respite of nearly forty years, which succeeded the ninth persecution, another decline was visible. The third century added but little to the real vital power of Christianity; but, on the other hand, worldlymindedness crept in and paralyzed, to a great degree, the apostolic energy of the first and second. Nominal Christianity increased, but it was too much of a form without the power.

This repose, however, was only the slumberings of a more fearful outburst of the fire of persecution, preparing to deluge the church again in blood.

The accession of Dioclesian, in 286, opened the way for the *tenth and last persecution.* Associating with himself Maximian, Galerius, and Constantius in the government, a term of blood followed; all but the latter are represented as "monsters of horrible ferocity." Galerius being brought up a bigoted pagan, imbibed in full that spirit; and Dioclesian surrendered himself up, to be guided in those matters by that wretched bigot.

The first blow was struck upon the place of worship in Nicomedia; the doors were burst open by a party of soldiers, the sacred writings burned, the house plundered of its valuables, and then the building demolished.

The day following, edicts were issued by the emperor, depriving Christians of all honor and dignity, and dooming them to torture.

Galerius caused the palace to be set on fire, and, Nero-like, laid it to the Christians. Thus imbued with pagan madness, the work of death went on with a faithfulness that was carried to an extent that decency forbids mentioning.

Victor, Tarachus, Probus, and Andronichus — Were four eminent examples, in this persecution, of faith and Christian steadfastness. The great effort made was to induce them to worship idols and abjure their faith.

Victor, who converted his jailors while being kept by them, was brought out, and an altar set up for him to offer incense upon; but when ordered so to do, he stepped forward and kicked over both altar and idol.

Maximian, the Roman emperor, immediately ordered that foot cut off, and Victor thrown into a mill to be crushed by the stones.

The others, after refusing to apostatize, and after wild *beasts* — to which they were exposed — refused to devour them, the heartless *brute*-emperor caused their heads to be struck off by the sword.

Many apostatized, as all ages show there will in persecution; but there must have been a vast multitude of the faithful, when we learn that throughout the empire the persecution prevailed, except in France, where Constantius ruled, and in severity exceeded all that had gone before.

One writer computes, "that not less than seventeen thousand Christians were put to death in one month; and that during the persecution in the province of Egypt alone, no less than one hundred and fifty thousand persons died by the violence of their persecutors, and five times that number through the fatigues of banishment, or in the public mines to which they were condemned." By this fire the churches were purged of much dross, but by no means destroyed.

This was the tenth and last general persecution, within two hundred years, visited upon the churches of Christ by imperial Rome, for the offence of calling no man master, in faith, but Christ.

From the character of their bishops, or ministers, and from the vast numbers of Christians in every part of the empire, and the nature of the proceedings of their enemies against them, we may infer the integrity of their profession and lives. A very striking resemblance is found between these and the Apostolic times.

But the scene now changes.

PERIOD III. FROM CONSTANTINE TO CLAUDE, OF TURIN, THE FIRST REFORMER, 4310 A. M., AND 306 A. C., TO 4821 A. M., AND 817 A. C.—A PERIOD OF ERRORS.

The removal of Galerius by death, helped open the way for Constantine to become sole emperor.

Galerius, like Herod, died of a disease that bred worms in his frame, until even his bones and marrow became a mass of rottenness and putrefaction. He was conscious of this being sent upon him for his persecution of the Christians, and so revoked his edicts against them, and solicited their prayers for his own welfare and that of the empire: at the same time granting them the freest exercise of their religion. This important edict was set up at Nicomedia, where the persecution began.

Maxamin, too, began to relax his severity towards the Christians, but not until his cup of iniquity was also full. He was afflicted with a terrible disease that no medicine could cure, and the internal fever was so great as to make his eyes start from their sockets. He took poison to hasten his miserable end.

CONSTANTINE — Being called upon by the Roman people to deliver them from the oppressions of Maxentius, was marching towards Rome, in 311, for that purpose, when, it is said (but with some doubt), that he saw a *cross* in the heavens, exceeding bright above the sun, and bearing the inscription, "*Conquer by this.*"

The expedition, at all events, turned in his favor, and Constantine found himself sole emperor of the Roman world, which had not been for many years under the entire sway of one man.

He immediately proceeded to do for Christianity what he doubtless thought the greatest favor it ever received from mortal man, but which proved to be otherwise, and was never finally undone until the standard of religious liberty was raised in Rhode Island, about 1636.

Christianity was now universally established; no other religion being tolerated throughout the empire.

By Constantine's order, the pagan temples were demolished, or turned into Christian churches; the priesthood disbanded, and idols destroyed; large and costly places of worship were erected, and old ones repaired and enlarged.

The ministerial office was honored with great favors, and enriched with vast endowments; the form of service had many additions, and the habiliments of the clergy were pompous, — so that the whole Christian worship had the appearance of worldly display and court show.

At first view, we might conclude that all this favor to Christianity must result in its exaltation and glory; soon every knee must bow, and every tongue confess to God. The whole royal power of Rome in its favor, who can be against it to any advantage? But, alas! it has proved that religion, nursed by the world, corrupts its very breath.

While the lamp of religion was trimmed by the sword of persecution, it gave its light; but when its oil became consumed, its light was darkness. Formerly, there had been too much opposition from court; now, there was too much favor.

The ostentation introduced into Christian worship, the emoluments bestowed upon the clergy, destroyed the humility, self-denial, and brotherly kindness so peculiar to true Christianity.

The government of the church was soon modelled after the form of that of the state. The emperor assumed the title of bishop, and claimed for himself and successors the right to regulate its internal affairs; and hence at the councils the emperor must preside, and, finally, determine all matters of dispute.

The assumption of power to *enforce* obedience to one form, and *prohibit* the exercise of another form of worship, are equally false positions for the civil magistrate. Hence while Constantine intended the greatest possible good, he actually made just as great a blunder as a man could make.

Donatus. — A controversy arose, about this time, called the Donatist, from the above man. According to some, it arose on the question, whether those who gave up their sacred books, during the tenth persecution, should be received again to communion. Donatus and his friends, thinking they should not, found fault with Mensurius, Bishop of Carthage, on this point, and refused to hold communion with him.

Others find the more immediate cause of this rupture in the election of Cæcilian as Bishop of Carthage, the neighboring bishops only being invited to assist and sanction the appointment. This offended Brotus and Celesius, both presbyters of the same church, and both aspirants to the bishopric, and also the Numidian bishops, who had always before been invited to the ordination of the Bishop of Carthage.

These discontented ones called another council, and Cæcilian was deposed by them, and Majorinus appointed. This divided the church at Carthage, each division adhering to its bishop. It also divided most of the churches throughout the country, so that in many of the cities there were two parties, — one for Cæcilian, as the bishop chosen by the church, the other favoring Majorinus.

At length the Donatists laid their cause before Constantine. He became impatient, and banished some, and put some to death who were refractory. He had, in 313, with several bishops, examined the subject, and decided in favor of Cæcilian. In a second and much more numerous council, in 314, the same result was declared.

Upon this the Donatists appealed directly to the emperor, when he confirmed the decision of the two councils. Hence his resort to severity, as above, but with little effect.

Here is the danger of having an emperor-bishop in the church, or in the churches. But more mischief grows out of it.

Under Constans a battle was fought at Bagnia, when the Donatists were defeated, which weakened their cause: the first battle after the union of church and state, and which grew out of that unholy alliance. A variety of fortunes ensued under the different emperors, until Augustine took the pen against the Donatists, which hastened their decline and fall.

Not long after that of the Donatists, arose, also, the "Arian controversy." This originated in the church at Alexandria. Arius, a presbyter in the church, disputed with Alexander, the bishop, about the Sonship of Christ; affirming that there was a time when Christ was not; that he was capable of virtue and vice, and mutable, as other creatures.

Not being able to reclaim Arius, and being alarmed for the truth, Alexander invited about one hundred bishops to sit in council on the matter; when Arius was deposed and excommunicated.

Retiring to Palestine, he wrote letters, and succeeded in gaining to his cause the Bishop of Nicomedia, and other men of distinction, influence, and authority in the church.

Constantine, finding Alexander and Arius were getting farther apart, summoned the bishops of the several provinces of the empire to meet at Nice, in Bithynia, 325 A. D. In this council of three hundred and eighteen bishops, a multitude of presbyters deacons, and others, the emperor himself presided. Grand spectacle!

After a session of two months, Arius was deposed and excommunicated; and at the same time was adopted the "Nicene Creed."

Here is the first ecclesiastical congress, and the first promulgation of human devices to guide men to an understanding of the Bible. This is only the first of many, however.

The creed above was ordered to be subscribed by all, upon pain of banishment. State power in church matters. Woe, woe, woe!

In addition to the above, it was decreed that Easter should be kept in all the churches on the same day; that celibacy was a virtue; new converts should not be introduced to orders; a certain course of penitence should be enjoined upon the lapsed, etc. A good foundation was here laid for the traditions of men to be exalted to the level of Scripture.

Constantine was prevailed upon, finally, to recall Arius from banishment, repeal the edicts against him and his followers, and even favored his cause; so much so as to require Athanasius, Bishop of Alexandria (successor of Alexander), to receive him to communion. Athanasius refusing, the emperor banished him to Gaul.

Arius pretended to subscribe to the Nicene creed, whereupon the emperor ordered Alexander, Bishop of Constantinople, to receive him to communion. Alexander betook himself to prayer, that God would prevent such a man from returning to the church, who was only a disturber of its peace, and hypocritical in his profession.

The day was fixed for his restoration; but, while on his way to the church, Arius was seized with a terrible disease of the bowels, and died 330 A. D.

Constantine died 337, not having received baptism until during his last sickness, and then at the hands of his favorite bishop, Eusebius, of Nicomedia.

The order of things Constantine introduced fostered rivalry among the bishops. Those of Antioch, Alexandria, and Rome, had been promoted to a kind of superiority over all others; but to these he also added Constantinople. These four cities were erected into "*Metropolitan*" bishoprics, and hence how easy to give names to other places and ministers. The bishops of these cities soon became patriarchs, and so the distinctions pontiff, patriarch, metropolitan, archbishop and bishop, were soon made. From this platform, how easy to shape it around, until some one of the bishops is exalted to be chief over all!

Lactantius. — He was an African by birth; gained an early and great reputation in rhetoric; so much so, that Constantine appointed him tutor to his son Crispus. He was styled the "Christian Cicero," on account of his attainments as a writer and speaker. His "Divine Institutions," composed in defence of Christianity, about 320, are all of his works that have reached us.

Eusebius — Was born in Palestine 267, educated there, and elected Bishop of Cæsarea 313. He bore considerable part in the Arian controversy, which at first he defended, thinking Arius was misused.

Eusebius was honored with special marks of Constantine's favor, being frequently invited to his table, and often receiving letters from the emperor. He was the emperor's favorite bishop. Among other works, he wrote an ecclesiastical history, from Christ to Licinius, 323; also, a life of Constantine.

Athanasius. — He was of heathen parentage, but was taken at an early age, by Alexander, Bishop of Alexandria, and educated by him, and appointed deacon. Alexander took him along to the Council of Nice, when he showed himself an able disputant against Arianism. Upon the death of Alexander, he was appointed bishop of the church, at twenty-eight years of age. After Arius' recantation, Athanasius was required by the emperor to reädmit him to communion; but resolutely refusing, he was banished into France.

Thus the bishops had fallen into the hands of the emperor.

He was recalled, and again exiled; but died in 373, having been bishop forty-six years.

Anthony is considered the leader of the monastic orders, which sprang up in the fourth century. Retiring into solitude, for greater sanctity of life, was by him, and many who imitated his example, considered the climax of piety.

Females, catching the enthusiasm, devoted themselves to the same austere life, but soon collected into groups; and thus nunneries had their origin.

It has now become customary, not to say necessary, to locate monks and nuns nearer together than formerly.

St. Simeon, a Syrian monk, took his post on top of a pillar, and only changed his place to occupy others, which he did four times. On the last, which was sixty feet high, and only three feet broad on top, so that he could not lie down, he remained standing fifteen years, without intermission, day and night, summer and winter. He remained in meditation from morning till three in the afternoon, when he harangued the people, who flocked from all parts to hear him, until sundown.

Athanasius is said to have encouraged monkery. Basil called it an angelic institution. Jerome declares the monks and nuns to be the very flowers among all the ornaments of the church.

The prayers of these saints (?) became worth paying money for, and so it flourished.

Benedict thought a little more order was needed, and hence arose the Benedictine monks of the sixth century. In the eighth and ninth centuries, the monks rose to the highest eminence. In the tenth, arose the contemptible order of the congregation of Clugni. In the eleventh and twelfth, flourished the Cisterians, and Carthusians. In the thirteenth, arose the Mendicants, instituted by Innocent III. They contemned wealth, and lived upon charity; they became very popular. From them arose four orders, under the auspices of Gregory: the Dominicans, Franciscans, Carmelites, and Hermits of St. Augustine.

Taking the origin of this system, being purely of men, and not all pure men either, and the baneful influence it has exerted upon the world, every intelligent man, and Christian especially, will place the whole scheme of monkhood very low in the scale of importance. It is not a *popish invention;* still of very impure birth and life.

Constantius, third son of Constantine, becoming sole emperor, through his favor Arianism had the ascendency during his reign. The Scriptures had now ceased to be the standard of faith; and whatever was received as orthodox or heterodox, was determined by fathers and councils. The bishops had departed from the simplicity of the gospel; and avarice, ambition, temporal grandeur, high preferment, and large revenues, were the ruling passions. Two parties existed now, Orthodox, and Arians; and either party that could get the ascendency threatened the other with intolerance and even persecution. Hence the condition of the church was no better under its professed Christian emperors than under paganism, since the sword was again taken up to afflict any of an opposite faith to those in power, or any not in favor of the civil power.

Another hideous feature of state religion was brought out on the accession of Julian, the *apostate.* Constantine was orthodox, and persecuted the Arians and pagans. Constantius was an Arian, and persecuted the orthodox and pagans. By Julian (called the apostate, as he returned to paganism), the rights and privileges of the pagans were restored, and those of the Christians suspended. How uncertain and corrupt is the course of state religion!

By way of reproach, Julian called the Saviour the Galilean. In a war with the Persians, being mortally wounded by a lance, he caught a handful of his blood, and throwing it indignantly into the air, exclaimed, "O Galilean! thou hast conquered."

It was during his reign that an attempt was made to rebuild

Jerusalem, but the work was broken up and abandoned, by fire bursting out of the ground. So God stopped the mad design.

BASIL — Is counted one of the lights of this age. He was born in Cæsarea, in Cappadocia, 226. After studying at Antioch, Constantinople, and Athens, he was converted to Christianity. Upon the death of Eusebius, he was chosen bishop in his stead, 370. He suffered much opposition from the Arians. He was greatly beloved by his people, who bewailed his death. He died after uttering these his last words: "Into thy hands I commit my spirit."

HILARY — Was a native of Poictiers, France. In 355, he was made bishop of his native town. He was distinguished for his attachment to the gospel in its simplicity, and was a man of penetration and genius. He openly arrayed himself against the Arians. Through their influence, however, with Constantine, he was banished to Phrygia, where he wrote twelve books on the Trinity. Being afterwards restored, it is said that France was freed from Arianism by Hilary alone. He died 367.

AMBROSE — Was born in Gaul, 333. Being appointed governor of several provinces, he settled at Milan. In 374, the bishop of that place dying, a contest arose between the Orthodox and Arians about a successor. As governor, he interposed to keep the peace; and while addressing the people, they cried out with one voice, "Let Ambrose be bishop!"

It will be observed that the power of appointing bishops in primitive times lay wholly in the breasts of the individual churches, and each bishop presided in his own church and no more.

Upon this he yielded to the wishes of the people; was baptized, and ordained bishop of Milan. He died in 397, leaving several works of merit on religious subjects. The hymn "Te Deum" is ascribed to him.

About the middle of the fourth century is marked as the time of the rise and increase of the power and influence of the bishop of the church at Rome. This was manifest in the splendor of his church, his revenues, his attendants or ministers, credit with the people, and sumptuous style of living. This led Prætextatus, a heathen magistrate of the city, to say: "Make me Bishop of Rome, and I'll be a Christian too!"

In 363, Jovian came to the throne, when Orthodoxy again triumphed, and Arianism and Paganism fell back. In 375, Valens was emperor, and he favored Arianism again, and persecuted the orthodox. A company of eighty ecclesiastics, who refused to embrace the Arian faith, being ordered into banishment, Valens caused them to be put on board a ship, and when out of the harbor, it was set on fire. Such was the tender mercy of an emperor-bishop.

In 378, Gratian and Theodosius were associates in the government. They changed the state religion again, when orthodoxy was supported, and the other two rejected.

Like Constantine, Theodosius called a council in 383, consisting of nearly two hundred bishops, which met at Constantinople. This council ordered that the Nicene creed should be the standard of orthodoxy, and that all heresies should be condemned.

Soon after two edicts were issued by the emperor, in both of which all meetings, whether public or private, were forbidden to heretics (*i. e.*, Arians).

In 390, he issued another against paganism, designed for, and it proved, the death-blow to it; for it fell to rise no more.

Christianity (?) was again established by law.

JEROME — Is reckoned as one of the Fathers of the fourth century. He was born of Christian parents, and his father took the greatest possible care of his education. Being placed at Rome, he had masters in rhetoric, Hebrew, and divinity, who instructed him in all parts of learning, sacred and profane. He then spent a while in travel, went as far as Syria, and then returned to Rome. Having retired to a desert, he spent four years in devotion, study of the Oriental languages, and of the Scriptures, which he is said to have committed to memory. He was inclined to monasticism; his principal work was the translation of the Bible into Latin.

AUGUSTINE. — This name adorns the pages of Christianity. His mother was a woman of distinguished piety and virtue. His father designed him for some of the learned professions, and early sent him to school. But having no taste for study, he wasted his time in gaming and idleness, hiding his indolence with false stories.

His father next sent him to Carthage, where he acquired a taste for rhetoric; and returning to his native place, gave lectures upon the subject. But he was still irreligious, and even a heretic.

He, however, was determined to visit Rome; but on his way called at Milan, and attended the preaching of Ambrose. His sermons made a deep impression upon Augustine's mind, and induced him to espouse the cause of the orthodox party, 384. He was shortly after converted, and became one of the most sincere and ardent Christians of his time. He was chosen Bishop of Hippo in 391.

From this time he set himself for the defence of the gospel. From his writings a body of theology was composed, which served for centuries as a guide to those who desired to escape the errors of the times, and abide in the truth. He died 430, aged 76.

John Chrysostom. — He was born, of a noble family, at Antioch, about 354. His education was entrusted to the care of his mother, who attended to it strictly; and while quite young he inclined towards Christianity. He became contaminated with the monasticism of the times, and so spent six years of his life in seclusion, at the end of which he returned to Antioch.

His reputation, sometime after, opened the way for him to be appointed Bishop of Constantinople. He immediately began to reform things in the church, which gave offence to both the laity and clergy of the times, particularly the most wealthy part, through whose influence Chrysostom was seized, by order of the emperor, and exiled to a port on the Black Sea. But such a tumult ensued, that the emperor deemed it prudent to recall him.

No sooner was he released than he showed his apostolic zeal, and redoubled his efforts to root out corruption. His enemies redoubled their zeal also, and implored the emperor to banish him to Caucasus, in Armenia; but, not satisfied with that, he was sent still further to Pictyus, on the Black Sea. On his way, however, to the latter place, from fatigue in travelling, and abuse from the soldiers, he fell into into a violent fever, and died 407, A. D.

Chrysostom ranks amongst the ablest preachers, of which Christianity has had many. With great strength of mind, a lively imagination, fine powers of elocution, an able commentator, and constitutionally ardent, he was a man of influence and reputation. A marked man among the corrupt and designing, and hence met with bitter persecution, which brought him to his grave.

Let it be observed that the union of church and state, by Constantine, created a transition movement in the church. By the emperor's putting himself at the head of the clergy, and using his power to help them, the tendency at once was, to substitute one of their own class, clergy, in the place of the emperor, but still hold both ecclesiastical and civil dominion. Hence we may look for the emperor-bishop to be transformed into a bishop-emperor. This process is at work.

In the breaking up of the Roman Empire, west, by the northern nations, about this time, they generally agreed to support, as the state religion, that form they found in pompous blast at Rome.

They, however, generally adopted the Arian system, and hence the advocates of the Nicene creed met with bitter persecution. The *established* form of religion was a form without the power; and yet the northern idolaters abandoned their own superstitions, and embraced those of the conquered. There were those who, in spite of the general corruption, maintained the purity and simplicity of the gospel; and through these alone can we trace the life and continuance of true Christianity until the Reformation, which, however, was yet a thousand years ahead.

Patrick. — Efforts had been made to introduce Christianity into Ireland, by Cælestius, Bishop of Rome, who sent Palladius there for that purpose, but with small success.

Patrick, a Scot, and one of the bishops of Scotland, being taken prisoner of war, and carried to Ireland, devoted himself, with great zeal, to the conversion of the people. Like Paul, he turned his capture to the conversion of his keepers. His influence long survived him in Armagh. He died in 460.

Clovis, — A king of the Franks, is said to have been converted about 496. His wife, Clotilda, was a Burgundian, of a people who had received Christianity; and she had labored without success to convert her husband. Although the Burgundians were Arians, Clotilda adopted the Nicene creed. It is said while Clovis was engaged in a battle with the Alemans, finding the Franks giving ground, and the foe advancing, he implored the assistance of Christ, and solemnly engaged to worship him as God, if he would give him victory. Clovis was conqueror; and the following year, after being instructed in Christianity, he, with three thousand of his soldiers, was baptized at Rheims, 495, A. C. The credit this affair deserves stands upon the same platform of Constantine's vision of the cross; yet his espousal of religion was a great comfort to those professing the Nicene creed.

From this conversion of Clovis originated the title of "Most Christian Majesty," usually applied to the kings of France.

Gregory. — Christianity was introduced into Britain in the times of the apostles. But, at this time, almost all traces of it were obliterated by the reigning idolatry. The people paid their homage to such gods as the Sun, Moon, Thuth, Odin, Thor, Frigga, and Surtur, from which the English derive the names of the days of the week. Still, with the prevailing idolatry, there were many who adhered to the simplicity of the gospel.

But the circumstance which most favored the introduction and spread in England of the then prevailing form of Christianity, was the marriage of Ethelbert, King of Kent, to Bertha, a pious descendant of the house of Clovis. She, like Clotilda, wife of Clovis, labored hard, and prevailed at last, in bringing her husband to embrace the gospel.

Before Gregory was chosen bishop of the church at Rome, he was one day walking in the market-place, and seeing several youth of handsome appearance exposed for sale, he inquired whence they were? On being informed that they were pagans from Britain, his compassion for them was stirred, upon which he offered himself to the bishop, to go as missionary to the island. His proposition not being accepted, he abandoned the project for the time.

But no sooner was he chosen bishop, than he renewed his purpose respecting Britain. In the year 597, he sent Augustine, with forty assistants, to go and preach the gospel in England. It was at this point that the royal patronage of Queen Bertha was of such great service. She, knowing the nature of Christianity, prevailed upon the king to allow the missionaries to enter the country and preach.

It is to be regretted that the form of Christianity was of the pompous and domineering kind. Not long after, Gregory was under the necessity of checking the ambition of Augustine, who not only sought to be elevated above all the clergy of the island, but threatened, and even inflicted, some chastisements upon the people for not yielding to him.

But a still graver subject turned the attention of Gregory homeward. The rivalry among the metropolitan bishops had become narrowed down chiefly between those of Rome and Constantinople. A crisis was approaching; one or other of these two must ere long become first. The level existing among the bishops of the N. T. must now yield to, "Who shall be greatest?"

As early as 588, John, Bishop of Constantinople, had *assumed* the title (so bewitching had its contemplation become) of Universal Bishop. His successor assumed the same proud name. Gregory the Great, being contemporaneous with John's successor, took great umbrage at the boldness of the Bishop of Constantinople for *assuming* a title that, by precedence, belonged to the Bishop of Rome; though Gregory's conscience would not permit him to take it himself. But Gregory was relieved of all his troubles by death, in 604.

Boniface III., — The successor of Gregory, had less conscience than he had, and was not only willing to receive the great title, but coveted it, and even asked it of the emperor, with the privilege of transmitting it to his successors.

The profligate emperor Phocas, in order to gratify the inordinate ambition of this court sycophant, deprived the Bishop of Constantinople of the title, and conferred it upon Boniface, at the same time declaring the church at Rome to be the head of all other churches.

Boniface III. thus became Universal Bishop, and the church at

Rome the Head Church of Christendom.(?) Here, then, is the first Papa, or Pope.

This Universal Headship in the church and its bishop at Rome, is the direct and legitimate result of union of church and state by Constantine. As he was head of the state, so naturally, and of consequence, a head of the bishops must accrue. An emperor at Rome, with governors throughout the provinces and empire, must be imitated by a universal bishop at Rome, over all the bishops throughout the world! Now let this bishop have temporal power, and we have church and state — Constantine's state and church — inverted; with a bishop-emperor, instead of an emperor-bishop. And, when either or both degenerate so far as to use their power to persecute for conscience' sake, what are they better than Nero the pagan?

Whilst we can easily trace the growth of this gigantic state-church, through a few succeeding centuries, to its zenith and decline, we shall also be obliged to follow the true spirit of Christianity into the mountains, dens, and caves of the earth, until its triumphant rise to victory, as Constantine's church loses power and recedes before the glorious Reformation.

The ignorance, superstition, and corruption of the times, were favorable circumstances for the growth and popularity of prelatical assumption.

The corresponding means, used to the same end, were, preference given to human composition over the Bible, efforts to convert the heathen, introduction of the worship of images, coöperation with monkery, veneration for the relics of saints, absolution and indulgences, purgatory, and the Inquisition. The object of the abettors of this system was absolute sway, and they well-nigh attained it.

The year 609 is given for the rise of the Mohammedan imposture. Mohammed was a descendant of the princes of Mecca. His father's name was Abdallah. At the age of twenty, he entered the army under command of his uncle, and gained considerable notoriety as a soldier.

At the age of twenty-five, he engaged in the service of Cadijah, a rich widow of the nobility of Mecca. After spending three years in Damascus, and about one in Syria, as her agent, to her entire satisfaction, she rewarded him for his fidelity, with the gift of her hand and fortune. This gave him a standing.

In announcing his religion to the world, he claimed for himself to be a prophet of God. In order to conciliate the Jews and Christians, he acknowledged Moses and Christ to be prophets, but himself to be above them both. Setting aside the Scriptures, he claimed a special revelation from God, which, by the assistance of an angel, he embodied in the "Koran," the Bible of the Mohammedans.

The religion of Mohammed consisted of *faith* and *practice*. The items of faith are: Belief in God, in his angels, in the Koran, in his prophets, in resurrection and final judgment, and in God's absolute decrees. The *practice* consists of prayer, with washings, alms, fasting, pilgrimage to Mecca, and circumcision. With this faith, he ventured before the world.

For a time success lingered. At length, however, he began to rally, and an opportunity presenting itself to unite the civil power to his religion (like Constantine), Mohammed added the sword to the crescent, and then, like the power represented by the sword and the cross, hastened to conquest.

The fates and fortunes of ambition followed Mohammedanism through wars extending into France, Spain, Italy, Persia, and Asia; until the Turks, finally, with an army of thirty thousand troops under Mohammed II., during the reign of Constantine XII., took Constantinople, putting an end to the Eastern Roman Empire, and making that city the capital of the Mohammedan power, in 1453, and so remains to the present day.

A very striking and truthful instance of the tendency of the union of church and state, resulting in intolerance and tyranny.

The seventh century presents a great contrast between the East and the West. In the East, ambition flourished, while the true spirit of the gospel was hardly to be seen, except as discovered here and there among the humble, and now and then a faithful and fearless bishop; and these had each but little influence beyond his own immediate parish.

The most was done in this century for true religion in England, France, Germany, Denmark, and vicinity. It is recorded, that in this century, a glorious effusion of the Spirit was enjoyed in England, so that great numbers turned from idols to the living God. Many who were inclined to favor a superintending power at Rome (not dreaming of a hierarchy), labored in all simplicity and faithfulness in the cause of evangelical religion. Such was their success that the British King Edwin, with all his nobles, and many of his subjects, were baptized, and so openly avowed their adherence to vital Christianity. Even among the monks, who were increased and increasing at the time, there were some godly and earnest men in the faith of the gospel. Among them was Paulinus, who preached in Lincolnshire, where the governor and all his house were converted through his preaching. Many instances of the kind are on record, showing the existence of evangelical labor and faith, in spite of the growing and absorbing tendency of Constantinianism.

True to itself, this revival of religion stirred up a missionary spirit in the subjects of grace.

Many, in companies and single-handed, went over to the continent, to spread the truth in Friezeland, and about in the north of Europe.

Kilian — an Irish missionary, received a commission from the Bishop of Rome to preach; he came to Wurtsburg on the Maine, where the pagan duke, Gosbert, was governor. The duke received the gospel, and was baptized, many following his example. But, like Herod, he had married his brother's wife. Kilian deferred admonition on this point, until the duke appeared settled in the faith; when, like John the Baptist, he reproved him for the connection. Gosbert promised to obey, after returning from an expedition. In his absence, Geilana, the *German* "Herodias," desired Kilian's head; and so, like John the Baptist, for *similar faithfulness*, he and his companions shared a *similar fate*, 688.

The similiarity in these events and the Scripture narrative, is sufficient to establish an identity in preachers, and the gospel preached.

Willebrod — An Englishman, and eleven of his countrymen, went over into Holland to labor among the Friezelanders; but being ill-treated by the king, who put one of them to death, they retired to Denmark. Returning into Friezeland in 693, they propagated divine truth with success. Willebrod was ordained Bishop of Wilteburg, by the Roman prelate (a departure from the ancient practice, for each church to ordain its own bishop), where he labored in his diocese until his death; while his associates spread the gospel into Westphalia, and the neighboring countries.

Bede — An Englishman, flourished about 700; was so much distinguished for his humility and piety, that he acquired the surname of "Venerable." He was educated in a monastery, and, being inclined to a monastic life, spent much of his time in his cell, devoted to writing. His principal work was a history of the church, from the time of Christ to his own time.

In one of his letters to the Archbishop of York, he says: "Above all things, avoid useless discourse, and apply yourself to the Holy Scriptures, especially to the Epistles of Timothy and Titus, to Gregory's Pastoral Care, and his homilies on the gospel. Have always those about you, who may assist you in temptation; be not like some bishops, who delight to have those about them who love good cheer, and divert them with trifling and facetious conversation." Not a very popish piece of advice for any age.

Winfred — Was co-laborer and successor of Willebrod, in Friezeland. Daniel, Bishop of Winchester, wrote to Winfred, about A. D. 723, for advice how to deal with the pagans. In reply, he says: "Do not contradict, in a direct manner, the account of the genealogy of their gods; allow that they were born from one another, as mankind are; this concession will give you the advantage of proving that there was a time when they had no existence. Ask them who governed the world before their gods were born; ask them if their gods have ceased to propagate. Argue thus with them, not in the way of insult, but with temper and moderation; taking opportunities to contrast their absurdities with the Christian doctrine; inform them that idolatry did once prevail over the world, but Jesus Christ was manifested, in order to reconcile men to God by his grace."

A much more scriptural doctrine, and Christian spirit, than appeared in the second Council of Nice.

Winfred seems to have been the master agent in diffusing the spirit of the gospel in those parts. He was devotedly attached to Friezeland; so much so, that he often induced individuals to go over there from England; and when he visited Rome, his ambition was to enlist volunteers for his German mission.

The chief instrumentality used for the protection of this mission, was the favor shown it by the French kings.

It seems a strange medley for France to favor both popery and Christianity, protect the latter from destruction by the former; and that some of the evangelical bishops of the time, who were spreading the truth and light, directly opposed to the idolatry and worldliness of Rome, were ordained and commissioned by the Pope himself!

Winfred was one of them, and he even induced Englishmen from Rome to aid him in his mission, by accompanying him to his field of labor.

Having appointed a day for confirming his new converts, and while awaiting their arrival, who should appear but a troop of armed pagans, who fell upon him and his company and slew them, fifty-two in number, in 755.

Paulicians; — A class of Christians having its origin about 660. They are said to have derived their name from Paul. They were earnest, zealous, unassuming teachers of the Scriptures and a pure faith.

Their origin seems to have been, not from any sects of the times, but spontaneous, or by the influence of the Spirit of God calling them from darkness to light. They were perfectly free from image-worship; were simply scriptural in the use of the sacraments; disregarded relics, and knew no other mediator but the Lord Jesus Christ.

A Greek officer, Simeon, was sent, by imperial authority, to destroy the Paulicians. Sylvanus, the leader, was taken, and stones were put into the hands of some of his followers, with the order to stone him to death, as the price of their own deliverance.

To this order but one obeyed; Justus (should have been called Judas) bought his life by stoning to death the pastor of the Paulicians, who had labored among them twenty-seven years. Simeon, the officer, convinced of their piety, embraced their faith, preached the gospel, and himself died a martyr.

They existed from the latter part of the seventh to the former part of the ninth centuries; spread their doctrines nearly all over Asia Minor, and flourished greatly; were the objects of the most bloody persecution by the popes, until, weary and despised, they were eaten up by their enemies, and their dispersion completed about 845.

The great revival in England and on the continent, in the eighth century, is the chief feature of the true church in this age. It may be denominated a missionary age; for no age, since the apostolic, bears a more marked feature of the missionary spirit than this. Indeed, God seems to have poured out his Spirit afresh, as an antidote to the growing assumptions of Rome.

Nothing will so effectually withstand the machinations of evil, in any and all forms, as the presence of the Holy Ghost.

The growth of the papal monopoly was so subtle, and ran so near in parallel with the times, that all might have been lulled into image-worship, had not God preserved a seed to serve him, animated by his Spirit.

Leo. — For some time previous to 727, there had been a growing regard for images, as aids to devotion, on the part of the Roman Church and its adherents. In 727, Leo, the Greek emperor, began openly to oppose this idolatry; but no sooner had he made known his opposition to images, than Germanicus, Bishop of Constantinople, and Gregory II., Bishop of Rome, opposed *him*, — many in both churches supporting the two idolatrous bishops.

What a change! In Nero's time, the emperors venerated idols, and the bishops despised them; now, the emperor despises idols, and the bishops venerate them!

In 730, Leo issued an edict against images, deposed Germanicus, and ordered the removal of an image, which had been set up in the palace at Constantinople. While an officer was performing this work, some women pulled down the ladder on which he stood, and murdered him on the spot. An insurrection ensued, which the emperor only quelled with blood.

The news flew to Rome; the images of the emperor were pulled down and trodden under foot; all Italy was thrown into confusion; the Bishop of Rome favored an attempt to elect another bishop, in spite of the emperor, and absolved the Italians from paying tribute to Leo any longer.

Fine successor of Christ! who paid tribute and commanded his disciples to do so also. Fine bishop, to oppose the *righteous* proceedings of an emperor, and favor idolatry!

Gregory II. died in the midst of the confusion, and was succeeded by Gregory III., who assembled a council in 732, in which he excommunicated all who should speak contemptuously of images.

In 741, both he and Leo died. Constantine, son of Leo, succeeded him as emperor, having all his father's zeal *against* images, while Zachary was chosen Bishop of Rome, with all of Gregory's zeal *for* images.

At this time, Childeric, a weak prince, occupied the throne of France. Pepin, son of Charles Martel, his prime minister, aspired to the throne; and, to strengthen his purpose, asked the advice of Pope Zachary, "Whether it would be just in him to depose his sovereign and usurp the throne?" The Pope answered in the affirmative, and Pepin ascended the throne.

Doubtless Zachary foresaw the advantage it would be to his cause to favor Pepin's design, and thereby gain an ally: at least, put the King of France under obligation to the See of Rome.

Stephen, the successor of Zachary, finding himself in danger from the Lombards, applied to Constantine, his legal sovereign, for protection; but, failing to obtain it, he was obliged to look to Pepin for aid. In this emergency, Pepin could not refuse, since he owed all he had to the advice of a former Pope.

The struggle resulted in confirming, as a possession to the Pope, the Exarchate of Ravenna, and twenty-one cities, 755, A. D.

Here, then, we get the "*bishop*-emperor," having the *sceptre* united to the *keys;* indeed, Gregory himself proposed to *withdraw* his allegiance to the Greek emperor, Leo, and bestow the consulship of Rome upon Charles Martel, father of Pepin, if he would aid and protect him.

Surely we can now reckon the Bishop of Rome among the civil mountebanks of the age.

All we need to add to the See of Rome now, to place it back on a level, not with Constantine, but the *pagan emperors*, is to attach idolatry to her creed and practice, with persecution, and we shall then have papal-paganism.

Constantine VI. assembled a council of three hundred and thirty-eight bishops, in the year 754, to decide the question of images. This council condemned their use: showing that Rome had not triumphed yet, and that even at this time, the influence of the gospel was considerable.

Leo, his son and successor, died in the year 780, when his wife, Irene, assumed the government, and at once signified to Pope Adrian her entire willingness to coöperate with him in the establishment of image-worship, notwithstanding the opposition to it by her husband and predecessors. (Another Jezebel!)

Having lost sight of the doctrine of *justification* by *faith*, the popes were eager to seize upon any subterfuge, that would exalt their sway over the minds of men.

At length, in the year 787, the second Council at Nice was held, under the auspices of the Empress Irene, in which the worship of images was established.

In taking Christian (?) notice of the previous council, at Constantinople, this language was used: "Long live Constantine, and Irene his mother! Damnation to all heretics! Damnation on the council that roared against venerable images! — The holy Trinity hath deposed them."

Compare the winding-up of the council held by the apostles, at Jerusalem. — Acts 15:28, 29.

Thus, in less than five centuries from Constantine's *destruction* of idolatry, it is reëstablished by his own state and church device: showing the retrograde and corrupt tendency of *state* religion.

ALCUIN. — While the East had gone over to idolatry, the great revival in England and the west of Europe, preserved the light for some time after. As soon as Adrian had obtained the decrees of Irene's council, he transmitted them to Charlemagne, Emperor of France, for him to obtain the assent of the bishops of the West to them.

In this he was disappointed. Alcuin, an Englishman, whom Charlemagne respected highly, had a great influence over his mind, in the opposite sentiment, it being the sentiment of the West generally. The British churches execrated the Council of Nice. So far was the emperor from receiving these decrees, that he requested the bishops of the West to examine the merits of the question.

The result was the issue of the Carolin (*i. e.*, Charlemagne) books, in which Alcuin took a prominent part. In these books they condemned, in very free terms, the *worship* of images (though permitting their presence in the churches), using very pointed Scripture arguments, still in a respectful tone.

These books being presented to Pope Adrian, by order of Charlemagne, elicited from him a very weak and tame reply. This was owing chiefly to the fact, that Adrian, as well as his predecessors, were dependent upon France for support and protection. Charles and the French churches, however, took a middle course, allowing the presence of images, but abhorred the adoration of them. In A. D. 794, a council was held in Frankfort on the Maine, consisting of three hundred bishops, in which the second Council of Nice, and the worship of images, were condemned.

PERIOD IV. FROM CLAUDE OF TURIN, 4821 A. M., 817 A. D., TO THE PEACE OF RELIGION, 5559, A. M., 1555 A. D.

CLAUDE.—Hitherto the growing assumptions of Rome had not been resolutely opposed. Contrary opinions had been proclaimed, and objections made; a middle course pursued by some, admitting the presence, but not the worship of images, etc.; and the devout had turned in disgust to a more excellent way; but the assault upon the popedom was left to be made by Claude, Bishop of Turin.

He was born in Spain, and became chaplain to the Emperor Louis I. of France. This monarch, observing the deplorable ignorance of a great part of Italy, of the gospel, and desirous of providing the churches of Piedmont with some one who would stem the growing torrent of image-worship, promoted Claude to the bishopric of Turin, A. D. 817.

True to his trust, he made a decided, bold, and persevering attack upon the Man of Sin, whereby he is justly styled the *first* reformer; so that, before the Papacy had attained its growth, it began to feel the "smooth stones" from the Davids of the Reformation.

The emperor was not disappointed in Claude; and God owned and blessed him, and the Church of Christ to-day honors him. He removed the images from the churches; reproved with severity the elevation of tradition to a level with the Bible; insisted upon the *fallibility* of "the church;" contended for the equality of all the apostles with Peter, and denied the authority of the popes; denounced the idolatry and superstition that everywhere prevailed through their influence; and maintained that Jesus Christ was the only proper Head of the church, and that we must be saved by faith only.

The providence of God shielded Claude from the storm of popish wrath that lowered upon him, in the favor of the Emperor of

France, who, strange to say, at different times favored Rome and opposed it.

In some of his reasonings about idols, he says: "If they who have quitted the worship of devils, honor the images of saints, they have not forsaken idols, they have only changed the names; for, whether you paint upon a wall the pictures of Saint Paul or Peter, or those of Mercury, Jupiter, or Saturn, they are all dead, and are now neither gods, apostles, nor men. . . . . If the cross ought to be adored because He was nailed to it, so ought we to adore mangers, for He was laid in one; and swaddling clothes, because he was wrapped in them. . . . Ye fools, who run to Rome to seek the intercession of an apostle, when will ye be wise? Shall we not believe God, when he swears that neither Noah, nor Daniel, nor Job shall deliver son or daughter by their righteousness? What would St. Augustine say of you, whom we have so often quoted? The apostolic, that is, the pope, is not he who fills the see of the apostle, but he who discharges its duties."

The faithful and successful labors of Claude were felt in the tenth century, and had their influence even to the times of the Waldenses. Thus God's church was preserved from extinction through the dark ages; from this to the fourteenth century.

Besides the tremendous onslaught of Claude upon the Church of Rome, he set an example which many, in after-times, hesitated not to imitate, and apply to the common enemy of truth.

GOTTECHALUSS — Has rendered himself worthy of notice for his vindication of the doctrines of *predestination* and free *grace.* His enemies, not being able to confute him, implored the interference of civil pains and penalties to induce him to recant. But all being in vain, he was thrown into prison, where he died A. D. 869. After his death, however, many defended his doctrines; and in several councils they were variously supported and condemned.

CYRIL, and METHODIUS. — Constantine, called Cyril, and his brother, Methodius, were the instruments of introducing the gospel among the Bulgarians, though perhaps in a less pure state than in apostolic times, yet infinitely superior to the paganism they professed.

They also invented and taught letters to the Moravians; and the Sclavonian tongue, invented by them, is to this day used in the liturgy of the Moravians, or United Brethren. Cyril died a monk; Methodius was Bishop of Moravia 880.

FREDRIC — Of Devonshire, and nephew of Winfrid, being appointed Bishop of Utrecht, was one day dining with Louis I., the Meek, when the emperor exhorted him to discharge his office with faithfulness and integrity. Pointing to a fish on the table, Fredric inquired "whether it were proper to take it by the head, or by the tail."—"By the head, to be sure," replied the emperor. Said the bishop: "Then I must begin my career of faithfulness with your majesty," and proceeded to reprove him for being in an incestuous connection with the Empress Judith; and, like John the Baptist to Herod, and like Kilian to Gosbert, Fredric said to Louis, "It is not lawful for you to have her." So in like manner as did Herodias, and Geilana, did Judith also compass the death of the bishop. Thus did John, Kilian, and Fredric, perish for reproving the same sin in high places; and in each instance by the *woman's* hand who was implicated. See Kilian, page 200, and John, page 168. He died in 833.

HAYMO, — Chosen Bishop of Haberstadt in 841; was a scholar of Alcuin, and relative of Bede; took great pains to preach to the people.

Says he: "By the Book of Life, we ought to understand the divine predestination as it is written. The Lord knoweth them that are his. Faith, remission of sins, and all the gifts of God, are freely given to believers."

ANSCARIUS, — The apostle of Denmark and Sweden, did a great work for those parts, and died in 865. Having obtained the favor of *Eric*, King of Denmark, he found it of great service to him. See mention of the family name "*Eric*," in the history of Empire.

ALFRED, — King of England, though a Catholic nominally, was not blind to the corruptions of the Papacy, nor to the truth of the gospel. In speaking of wealth, life, and power, he says: "All thy happiness would but work thy misery, *unless thou could purchase thee Christ*."

In speaking of the translation of the Scriptures into the vulgar tongues, he says: "I called to mind how that the law was at first found written in the Hebrew speech; after that the Greeks had learned it, they turned it into their own speech; and then the Latin people, through wise interpreters, turned it into their own language; and all other Christian people have turned some part of it into their tongue."

He lamented the irreligion and ignorance of his times, and proved himself a reformer. Ministers the most pious and apt to teach, were patronized by him. One-third part of his time he spent in translating the best foreign books into English. He is said to have been the founder of the University of Oxford. He flourished about 900 A. C.

Hence we gather good evidence, and the student of history can find much more, that, in the age of the growing assumptions of Popery, the truth as it is in Jesus was held, preached, and practised by a vast number, in spite of popes.

The tenth century is called the *leaden* age of the church — the darkest epoch in the annals of mankind. Mosheim says: "The history of the Roman Pontiffs that lived in this century is a history of so many monsters and not of men; and exhibits a horrible series of the most flagitious, tremendous, and complicated crimes, as all writers, even those of the Romish Community, unanimously confess." One Roman writer admits that this was an iron age, barren of all goodness; a leaden age, abounding in all wickedness; a dark age, remarkable above all others for the scarcity of writers and men of learning.

This description better suits the emperors of pagan Rome than Rome under Christian bishops. But when it is remembered that these bishops had added temporal to spiritual power, become princes as well as priests, embraced the worship of images, and were seeking aggrandizement by worldly wars, adding persecution, withal, against those who refused to adore idols, and being equally sunk in voluptuousness, we can hardly recognize anything but pagan emperors in the papal bishops.

In the year 909, at a council held in Trosle, in France, expression was given to Christian doctrine, without mixture with peculiarly popish notions.

Councils, from time to time, ventured to act in contempt of the Pope. A remarkable instance of the kind occurred in Rheims, in which a council deposed a bishop without consent of the Pope.

Arnulphus, — The president of this council, and Bishop of Orleans, addressed it as follows: "O deplorable Rome, who in the days of our forefathers producedst so many burning and shining lights! thou hast brought forth in our times *only* dismal darkness, worthy of the detestation of posterity. What shall we do, or what counsel shall we take? The gospel tells us of a barren fig-tree, and of the divine patience exercised toward it. Let us bear with our primates as long as we can, and in the meantime seek for spiritual food where it is to be found. Certainly there are some in this holy assembly who can testify that in Belgium and Germany, both which are near us, there may be found real pastors, and eminent men in religion. Far better would it be, if the animosities of kings did not prevent, that we should seek in those parts for the judgment of bishops, than in that venal city, which weighs all decrees by the quantity of money. What think you, reverend fathers, of this man, the Pope, placed on a lofty throne, shining in purple and gold? Whom do you account him? If destitute of love, and puffed up with the pride of knowledge only, he is Antichrist sitting in the temple of God."

Thus, in the tenth century, the Pope would have been rejected wholly, but for his unrighteous assumptions, which he claimed and enforced with the sword. There was enough of the true church left to *know* him and *despise* him.

OTHO.— Papal Rome had now sunk to equal depths of shame with pagan Rome, when Alaric the Goth made his descent upon it, and emptied the sinks of iniquity; so at this time, Otho I., King of the Germans, entered the "venal city" with the sword, and probed its festering corruption.

The civil order he restored so put the popes at bay, that, had there been some Claude, or other valiant man for the truth, to have directed the emperor at this juncture, the popedom might have been overthrown; but none arose. Otho's zeal was, doubtless, the result of the influence of missions in Germany in previous years.

His efforts, seconded by his empress Adelaide, to purify the outward church, to promote learning, to erect bishoprics, to endow churches, and propagate the gospel among the barbarous nations, were truly laudable,— all such efforts were so entirely at variance with the spirit and policy of the popes; also, being so rare an exception to the princes of the times, who were fast bowing to the Man of Sin.

GYLAS.— This Hungarian chief is said to have embraced pure Christianity, and was baptized at Constantinople. He encouraged the labors of Hierotheus, the bishop who returned with him among the Hungarians, which proved salutary.

Geysa, chief prince of Hungary, married Sarolta, daughter of Gylas, and by her influence Geysa embraced Christianity, and by her means was the gospel once more introduced into that desolate region. Stephen, son of Geysa, embraced Christianity, and was baptized, and through his zealous labors almost the whole of Germany was evangelized.

ADALBERT.— That this archbishop, born in 956, had some sense of religion, is evident from his remark: "It is an easy thing to wear a mitre and a cross, but an awful thing to give an account of a bishopric before the Judge of quick and dead."

UNNI,— Archbishop of Hamburg, with associates, went into Denmark and Sweden, and traversed over much of the ground on which Anscarius had formerly labored, and was abundantly successful in reviving the work, and extending it even beyond where it had hitherto spread. He died at Birca, in A. D. 936.

Indeed, throughout the North, and at remote places from Rome, there is a vast amount of evidence of the existence of vital godliness. The doctrines of regeneration, justification by faith, headship of Christ over the church, in short, a good understanding of the gospel, and a faithful profession of it and obedience to the same.

So, while left to itself, the gospel has enough of leaven to keep alive the germ of spiritual life in the hearts of its friends, and animate Christian men to go forth among idolaters, and turn them from idols to the living God.

But, under the influence of the "Universal Bishop," the spirit of piety was rooted out, and that of ambition, pride, and worldly pomp, entered in.

Theophylact — Bishop of Constantinople, speaks very clearly on several important points.

On filial obedience, he says: "If thou wouldst have thy sons obey thee, instruct them in the Divine Word. It is for thy own interest that thy children be well versed in Scripture; thence they will learn to reverence their parents."

Not very popish to teach *children* the *Scriptures.*

Of the state of man after the fall, he says: "Some, indeed, are found to be good-tempered and benign by nature, none by exercise and meditation. And though some be reckoned good men, yet they adulterate every action by vain glory."

On justification, he says: "The righteousness of God preserves us, not our own; for what righteousness have we, who are altogether corrupt? for God justifies us not by works, but by faith. The righteousness of God is by faith."

On the abundance of grace, Rom. 5, he says: "Suppose a person thrown into prison, with his wife and children, because he is deeply in debt, and then should be not only freed from the prison and the demands of the law, but also receive at once innumerable talents; be introduced into the royal palace; be presented with a kingdom, and accounted worthy of the same, and be reckoned the son of a king; this is the abundance of grace."

Of Christian faith, he says: "He who believes with great affection, extends his heart to God. His heart, inflamed, conceives a strong assurance that it shall gain its desire. We all know this by experience, because Christ hath said: Whatever ye ask in prayer, believing, ye shall receive. He who believes gives himself wholly to God; he speaks to him with tears, and in prayer holds the Lord, as it were, by the feet."

Such sentiments, in the tenth century, are noble. They savor very little of priestly confession, absolution, indulgences, and what not, taught by the Universal Bishop of Rome.

NILUS — Was of Greek extraction, born in 910, in Calabria. After the death of his wife, he entered a convent in 940.

In 976, the Bishop of Calabria, and a lord of that territory, named Leo, with many priests, made him a visit, rather with a view to try his skill, than to derive any benefit from his instructions. Nilus treated them civilly, prayed with them a short time, and then put into the hands of Leo a book concerning the small number of the *saved.*

The company expressed dissatisfaction with the harshness of the doctrine. This induced Nilus to bring proof of his position from the Fathers, Paul, and the Gospels. Said he: "These maxims seem terrible, because they condemn your practices. Unless you be sincerely holy, you cannot escape everlasting torments."

One of the company, whom Nilus knew lived in open sin, asked him if Solomon were saved or not? "What is that to us?" said he. "It is sufficient for you to know that Christ pronounces damnation against all workers of iniquity. I should think it would be a more interesting object of injuiry for you to consider whether you shall he saved or not."

This short account exhibits clearly who were of the true Church of Christ, and who of the apostate Church of Rome. Christ's people were at this age scattered like sheep among wolves, — wolves in sheep's clothing. The gospel was loved, believed, and practised in this night of sin.

The eleventh century was visited with a little impulse of learning, but confined chiefly to the monks and established clergy.

In the Papal Church, a contest arose between the popes and the emperors, particularly in settling the question, who should appoint the popes. The power of doing this important work was finally taken from the emperors, and lodged in the college of cardinals, where it still remains.

The celibacy of the clergy, and the doctrine of transubstantiation, were fully recognized and established; in short, Popery reigned triumphant in the high places.

This century is noticed for the separation of the *Eastern* and *Western*, or Greek and Latin churches. The desire of each to rule, had not been extinguished since the time John, of Constantinople, *assumed* the title of Universal Bishop; and the time when Phocas wrested it from John's successor, and bestowed it upon Boniface III., of Rome.

The point of contention now was, respecting the source of the Holy Ghost. The Latin Church maintained that the Spirit proceeds from the Father *and* the Son; the Greek Church maintained that the Spirit proceeded from the Father, *through* the Son. On this rock they split.

It seems a curious affair, that the division of the seat of empire, between Rome and Constantinople, should have finally rent both the empire and church of Constantine.

In 1054, an attempt was made to reconcile these differences, and legates were sent to Constantinople by the Roman pontiff. But both parties were too proud to yield, and the effort ended abruptly.

The Roman legates, however, closed the affair, by meeting in the Church of St. Sophia, and publicly excommunicating the Greek patriarch and all his adherents.

No attempts since have been of any avail in harmonizing the breach, then completed, and so they remain separate to this day. Rome was now left to pursue its idolatry and domination.

Berengarius. — The most considerable opposition made to the errors of Rome, in this century, were the writings of this man, against the doctrine of transubstantiation. The doctrine so called, consists in the belief, that in the Lord's Supper, the real, actual presence of Christ's incarnate body is in the bread and wine. Against this, Berengarius made so strong opposition, that the popes were obliged to take notice of it. This shows that some sense of truth prevailed amid the general error, 1050 A. C.

So strong was the opposition he endured, that, for a time, he was compelled to bend before it; but, greater numbers beginning to rally for his defence, he again set his face against his foes. His writings proved a formidable weapon, in the hands of the lovers of truth, against the errors of Rome.

Stephen, — King of Hungary, showed himself a zealous patron of the gospel. Under his auspices, Astricus came into Hungary, opened a school, and educated ministers; while Boniface, one of his disciples, preached the Word in Lower Hungary. Stephen's zeal was much stimulated by his pious queen, Gisla, daughter of the Emperor, Henry II. He often accompanied the preachers, and pathetically exhorted his subjects. He suppressed barbarous customs, and restrained open crime.

His excellent code of laws is to this day the basis of the laws of Hungary. In it he forbids all impiety, the violation of the Sabbath, and irreverent behavior in the house of God. He lived to see all Hungary become, externally at least, Christian. He died in A. D. 1038.

Many efforts were made, from time to time, to convert the pagans, which proved unsuccessful; yet they show beautifully that the propagation of the gospel, a spirit so peculiar to itself, was in existence even in these dark ages.

Godeschalus, — Duke of the Vandals, revived among his subjects a regard for the gospel, which they had once embraced, but afterwards neglected.

Boniface, — And eighteen others, set out from Germany, to labor among the Prussians; but were all massacred by that barbarous people.

Olaus II. — King of Sweden, made request, in 1001, for missionaries to be sent over from England, to preach the gospel there. Success attended their labors in East and West Gothland, the pagans often making great opposition.

Elfric — Supposed to be the predecessor of Alphage (1006 A. C.) had it inserted in one of the canons, published by a council at which he presided, that every parish priest should be obliged, on Sundays, and other holidays, to explain the Lord's Prayer, the Creed, and the gospel for the day, before the people, in the English tongue. Such an order as this is worthy of special notice, published by a council in the eleventh century: showing that withholding the light from the people was not a universal practice, though a strong power sought to bring it into force.

Alphage, — Archbishop of Canterbury, refused to leave his post, during a furious invasion of the Danes, saying, "The hireling leaveth the flock when he seeth the wolf coming." Whilst they were putting children and women to the sword, Alphage went forth, and besought the soldiers to humanity, saying: "Many of your troops have been brought over to the faith of Christ, through my means, and I have frequently rebuked you for your acts of injustice." Exasperated at his boldness, the Danes threw him down and stoned him to death, 1013.

Ulfrid, — An Englishman, preached the faith first in Germany, then in Sweden, under the patronage of Olaus, and many were converted, till, in 1028, while preaching against the idol Thor, and hewing it down with a hatchet, he was slain by the pagans.

Olaus, — King of Norway, in retiring from England, after assisting the Danes against the English, took with him several priests. This prince also used to travel with zealous preachers, exhorting his subjects, and destroying temples. He abolished idolatry in Norway, Orkney, Iceland, and Greenland, 1030 A. C.

Nearly all this northern part of Europe was very largely and favorably influenced, and proverbially elevated in the spirit and temper of their minds, and all attributable to the spread of an anti-pagan and anti-Roman Christianity; *i. e.*, the true gospel of Jesus.

Under William the Conquerer, Popery received encouragement in England; he, seeing it to be a good tool of despotism, used it.

MARGARET, — Queen of Scotland, was a person of rarest piety; and through her influence Scotland received great blessings, by the spread of the gospel. "She was a character fitted to throw a lustre on the purest ages."

ANSELM — The most important character at this time, was born in Aoust, Piedmont. He was made Archbishop of Canterbury, England, in 1092.

His works evince considerable evangelical spirit. He was, perhaps, the most devoted to the gospel of any public character of his age.

His inclinations were in favor of the Pope, and not the king, disposing of ecclesiastical affairs.

In a council, at Bari, called to settle the dispute with the Greek Church, about whence the Holy Ghost proceeded, Pope Urban called upon Anselm to express his opinion. It was so clear and pungent, as to silence the Greeks. His views were with the Latin Church on this point.

Such was his desire for holiness, that he is reported to have said: "If he saw hell open, and sin before him, he would leap into the former to avoid the latter!"

Great as was the darkness and tyranny of this age, we still find a multitude moved by the Spirit and truth of God. Among these, many of whom were zealous propagators of the pure gospel, we must look for the true church, and the truth as it is in Jesus.

Pilgrimages to Jerusalem had come, in this century, to be of great account in the Church of Rome. An idea sprang up, that the thousand years spoken of in Revelation 20:2—4, were nearly fulfilled, and the end of the world at hand.

A great excitement prevailed; numbers forsook their pursuits, left their families, and hastened to the Holy Land, where, they imagined, Christ would suddenly appear, to judge the living and the dead.

Jerusalem had now been in the hands of the Saracens since 637; during which time the pilgrims were permitted to visit the holy places, by the payment of a small tribute. The Saracens were followers of Mohammed, — a people who inhabited the north-western part of Arabia. The Ottomans, afterwards called Turks, inhabited the north shores of the Caspian Sea; were converted to Mohammedanism by the Saracens.

In 1065, the Turks took possession of Jerusalem, and the pilgrims were no longer safe. They were insulted, their worship derided, and their effects plundered.

Peter the Hermit, a Frenchman, returning from a pilgrimage in 1095, seeing the annoyances to which the pilgrims were subject, conceived the project of arming the sovereigns and people of Europe, for the purpose of rescuing the holy sepulchre from the hands of the infidels.

Accordingly he went from province to province, exciting princes and people to embark in the holy enterprise.

Pope Urban II. espoused the cause of Peter; called a council, at which four thousand ecclesiastics and thirty thousand people assembled, and declared for the war, but still slow to engage. A second council was held the same year, at Claremont, at which the Pope addressed the people in person; at the close of which, they exclaimed: "*It is the will of God! It is the will of God!*"

Persons of all ranks flew to arms furiously.

Eternal salvation was promised to all who should go forth to the help of the Lord. Nobles, bishops, and even women entered the ranks in disguise. Robbers, murderers, and incendiaries embraced the opportunity to secure a place in paradise.

Peter, in the spring of 1096, at the head of an undisciplined multitude of three hundred thousand, commenced his march towards the East. Outrage and murder marked their course. Scarcely one third of them reached Constantinople, and these were utterly destroyed, in a battle at Nice, by the Sultan Solyman.

A formidable body of disciplined troops were, however, in the rear, and soon neared the city. Godfrey commanded, assisted by several other distinguished generals and princes of Europe. Arriving at Nice, he reviewed his troops, and found his army composed of one hundred thousand horse, and six hundred thousand foot. City after city fell before them; and at Antioch, they vanquished an army of Saracens, of six hundred thousand strong. Arriving at Jerusalem, in 1099, reduced by killed, and detachments of protection by the way, the army consisted of only one thousand five hundred horse, and twenty thousand foot; while the garrison of Jerusalem consisted of forty thousand men.

A siege of five weeks, ending with an assault, carried the city, and all within were indiscriminately put to the sword, and the crusaders' flag waved in triumph over the battlements of holy Jerusalem.

Godfrey was saluted king. He only wore the crown a year, having to resign it to the Pope's legate, who claimed it as the property of the Roman See.

Foolish as was the crusaders' undertaking, yet the success was a most glorious achievement of arms. To march an army from France to Jerusalem, and take it in the first attempt, was carrying the crusaders' flag in triumph over the graves and battle-fields of the Cæsars, Hannibals, Pompeys, Alexanders, Dariuses, and Antiochuses of ancient war.

TWELFTH CENTURY.

The Turks soon fell upon the kingdom of the crusaders, threatening it with ruin. A *second* crusade was deemed necessary. St. Bernard took the place of Peter the Hermit, and succeeded in raising an army of three hundred thousand men from among the subjects of Louis VII., of France, and Conrad III., of Germany. The army, headed by these monarchs, took up its march for Jerusalem, in 1147. After enduring incredible hardships, and loss of their troops, they returned in disgrace to their own country.

In 1187, Saladin, sovereign of Egypt, Arabia, Syria, and Persia, invaded Palestine, and annihilated the kingdom of Jerusalem.

The news of this catastrophe reaching Europe, filled it with grief and consternation. Pope Clement III. immediately proclaimed a *third* crusade. The principal sovereigns of Europe eagerly enlisted in the cause; Philip Augustus, of France, Richard I., of England, and Frederick Barbarossa, of Germany. This effort also proved a failure, — the Infidels retaining the holy places.

For nearly two centuries, Europe was convulsed with what was (falsely) called holy wars. Besides the wreck of families and fortunes at home, two millions of Europeans were buried in the East.

Great wealth accrued to the Roman pontiffs, but every million they obtained cost Europe ten millions; so that the enriching of Rome, was the impoverishing of Europe.

Beneficial results are, however, reckoned indirectly, accruing to society from these barbarous expeditions, in respect to its political condition, manners and customs of the people; to commercial intercourse; to literature, and, in the end, to religion itself.

Such, in brief, were the crusades, or holy (unholy) wars.

It is plain that the history of the dominant Church of Rome is not the history of the true Church of Christ. We must look for it among the scattered and peeled, seeking a resting-place, with a few noble exceptions, where the prowlings of Popery could not find or devour them.

They were known by the names Cathari, or pure; Leonists, or poor men of Lyons; Albigenses, from Alby, a town in France; Petro-brussians, from Peter Bruys, an eminent preacher; Waldenses, from *Valdesi* (Italian for valley), as they lived in the valleys of Piedmont, — afterwards called Waldenses, from Peter Waldo.

Evervinus wrote a letter to Bernard, in 1140, inquiring what to do with certain persons who held very obnoxious doctrines to the Papacy. Their heresies were: "One of their bishops, and his companions, openly opposed us in the assembly of the clergy and laity, in the presence of the Archbishop of Cologne, and of many of the nobility; defending their heresies by the words of Christ and the apostles." *What audacious heretics!*

"They further asked for an opportunity for their teachers to discuss their doctrines publicly, promising to return to *the church* if their opponents could confront their masters; but that otherwise, they would rather die than yield their opinions. Upon this last declaration, they were seized by the people, in the excess of zeal, and burnt to death; and, what is very amazing, they came to the stake and bore the pain, not only with patience, but even with joy. Were I with you, Father, I should be glad to ask you how these members of Satan could persist in their heresy with such courage and constancy, as is scarcely to be found in the most religious believers of Christianity?"

Very astonishing, indeed, friend Evervinus! Wonder if St. Bernard could solve the mystery!

"Their heresy is this: — They say that the church is only among themselves, because they alone, of all men, follow the steps of Christ, and imitate the apostles, — not seeking secular gains. The apostolical dignity, say they, is corrupted by engaging in secular affairs while sitting in the chair of Peter. They put no confidence in the intercession of saints; and all things observed in the church, which have not been established by Christ himself, or his apostles, they call superstitious." Monstrous!

"Those of them who have returned to our church, told us that great numbers of their persuasion were scattered almost everywhere, and that among them were many of our clergy and monks."

Such were the true believers, and the true church; and yet Evervinus calls these same men monsters! In the twelfth century, there were those who disowned the Pope!

St. Bernard says: "If you ask them of their faith, nothing can be more Christian; if you observe their conversation, nothing can be more blameless; and what they speak, they prove by deeds."

Egbert, a monk, says: "I have often disputed with these heretics; they are they who are commonly called Cathari."

It will be observed that all who deny the Roman Church, are indiscriminately, and by *that* authority, called *heretics.*

"They are armed with all those passages of holy Scripture which seem to favor their views; and with these they know how to defend themselves, and oppose the Catholic truth. They are increased to great multitudes throughout all countries; their words eat like a canker."

In a work called "The Noble Lesson," written by one of the Cathari, he says: "If a man love those who desire to love God and Jesus Christ; if he will neither curse nor swear, nor act deceitfully, nor live in lewdness and injustice, nor avenge himself of his enemies, they presently say, 'The man is a Vandes.'"

These extracts, from the enemies of the Christians in the twelfth century, resemble, very strikingly, Pliny's letter to Trajan, A. D. 106.

Popery, at this time, was reaching its zenith; people, prelates, and princes were made to bow before its dominant sway. Every symptom of opposition was hunted, and silenced if possible. Fluentius, Bishop of Florence, taught publicly that Antichrist was born and come into the world: on which account Pope Paschal II. held a council there in 1105, reprimanded the bishop, and enjoined upon him silence on that subject; thereby proving himself to be the very Antichrist.

Henry II., of England, crouched to the Pope, and even aided the King of France in persecuting the Cathari. Thirty of them, men and women, from Germany, came into England in 1159, and were there brought before a council of clergy at Oxford.

Gerard, their teacher, a man of learning, said that they were Christians, and believed in the doctrine of the apostles. They abhorred the doctrine of purgatory, of prayers for the dead, and of the invocation of saints.

Henry, in conjunction with the council, ordered them to be branded with a hot iron on the forehead; to be whipped through Oxford; to have their clothes cut short by their girdles, and to be turned into the open fields; and likewise forbade any one, under severe penalties, to shelter or relieve them. It was in the depth of winter, and they all perished through cold and hunger. These poor Germans consoled themselves in their distress, with the promise, Blessed are they that are persecuted for righteousness' sake, for theirs is the kingdom of heaven. Gerard had an additional brand on the chin.

Galdinus, Bishop of Milan, who had inveighed against the Cathari for eight or nine years of his episcopacy, died in 1173, of an illness contracted through the excess of his vehemence in preaching against them.

Surely papal and pagan Rome were not unlike each other.

The power of the clergy grew at last to be so great and intolerant, that Henry undertook to restrain it somewhat, when he received the most determined resistance from Thomas à Becket, first chancellor, afterwards Archbishop of Canterbury. Such was his insolence and domineering conduct, that he was finally slain before the altar, whither he fled for protection.

Becket is represented by some as a hero and a martyr; by others, as a hypocrite and a traitor.

JOACHIM, — Abbot of Calabria, asserted that Antichrist was born in the Roman State, and would be exalted to the Apostolic See.

Good proof of this is seen in a bull issued by Innocent III., in 1197, declaring it was not fit that any man should be invested with authority who did not revere and obey the holy See.

ARNULPH, — A presbyter, came to Rome and declaimed against the Papacy. Knowing that his life was forfeited thereby, he said: "Nor is it to be wondered at, that you should kill me, a sinful man, who speaks to you the truth, since if St. Peter himself were to rise from the dead and rebuke your multiplied enormities, ye would not spare him."

Arnulph was secretly murdered, 1135.

BERNARD — Is noticed as a great character in this age, but it requires some skill to harmonize the elements of his greatness; for, pious, learned, and influential as he was, he threw it all into the fanaticism of the crusades, and the persecuting to death of the scattered sheep of Christ, whenever the wolves of the Papacy could find them. — 1145 A. C.

Such, with a variety of other incidents not here related, go to show what was the domineering, persecuting character of Constantine's church in the twelfth century. It had continued to gain strength, power, influence, and awe, over the whole of Europe, causing thrones to tremble before it, unless they rendered it obeisance and tribute. Thus it not only mingled civil and ecclesiastical matters, but domineered in both, and persecuted all who would not acknowledge her authority.

On the other hand, those who strove to spread the peaceable fruits of righteousness among the benighted and barbarous, and maintain the simplicity of the truth, as taught by the Saviour and his apostles, were by the Roman Hierarchy denominated heretics, and put to far greater torture and ignominy than murderers and all vagabonds.

Still, among these very despised people, the Lord preserved the holy seed in the world; and through them, in the dark ages, from Claude of Turin, to Peter Waldo, was the light of divine truth, and all the semblance to the apostolic faith and manners, preserved. No reformers are found in this period, though there were many who loved, believed, and preached the truth boldly, and many more who counted not their lives dear unto them.

So that, in England and Europe, through all this ecclesiastical night, the truth and life of Christianity were not extinguished; neither had it been up to the time of Claude, nor do we find it henceforth.

In future we shall find not only those who hold the truth, but spread it; not only stand aloof from the Church of Rome, but combat and demolish some of her strongholds, though she, at the same time, doubles her diligence to extend and establish her dominion.

PETER WALDO. — This eminent servant of God stands next to Claude of Turin, in the class of reformers: second only in time, not in zeal or love for the cause, nor in sacrifice and devotion.

Waldo began his labors in 1160. He is said to have been an opulent merchant of Lyons, in France. One evening, after supper, as he sat conversing with a company of his friends, one of them suddenly fell and expired. Such a lesson on the uncertainty of life, forcibly impressed the mind of Waldo, and led to that serious reflection on divine things, which resulted in his conversion.

Religion, true to itself, not only filled the mind of the merchant with joy, but inspired him with evangelical and godlike desire for the salvation of others. To this end he gave up mercantile life, distributed his goods among the poor, as occasion presented, and devoted his energies to extending a knowledge of the one thing needful.

Looking in vain for the knowledge of divine things he longed after, he at last found the treasure in the Scriptures. But he was not satisfied merely with possessing and reading the Bible himself, which was in no more common language than the Latin, and that not understood by common pople; his countrymen must have it too.

Upon this, he gave his efforts to the work of translation, — not afraid, as no good man and true is, to allow the people to have the Bible. In the translation of the Scriptures, Waldo stands next to Jerome,— the Septuagint being the first translation of the Scriptures, the Vulgate the second (by Jerome), and the French the fourth (by Waldo).

Athelstan, a king of England, caused a third translation of the Bible to be made, in the tenth century, into the Saxon tongue.

A careful study of the Bible revealed to him the enormities of the Church of Rome. He could see the difference between the simplicity of the apostolic faith and practice, and the complicated superstitions of the Papacy. Upon this, he lifted his voice in fearless denunciation of Rome, raising, in contrast, the standard of revelation.

His preaching, and the distribution of the Scriptures, had the effect, under God, of multiplying believers greatly. His labors and success did not long pass unnoticed. One of his enemies said of him, by way of accusation, "Being somewhat learned, he taught the people the text of the New Testament." A crime of which the popish clergy were entirely innocent.

A fearful storm of persecution was raised against him and his disciples, on account of which they were compelled to flee from Lyons, in A. D. 1163.

Ireneus was Bishop of Lyons, and was martyred there in 202.

Waldo and his followers were driven out of Lyons, by order of Pope Alexander III., who ordered the archbishop of the city to proceed against him with the utmost rigor. O, apostolic Pope!

The scattering of the Waldenses was similar to that of the church at Jerusalem, in the persecution of Stephen; and the effects were much the same. For, like the primitive disciples, the Waldenses "went everywhere preaching the Word." Some of his followers united with the Vaudois, of Piedmont, carrying the rich treasure of the Scriptures in the native tongue. Waldo himself, it is thought, never visited Piedmont.

He retired into Dauphiny, where his doctrines took deep and lasting hold of the people.

His disciples, who were many then, were called Leonists, Vaudois, Albigenses, and Waldenses. Meeting the spirit and power of persecution in Dauphiny, he was driven into Picardy; from thence he was driven into Germany. At length settling in Bohemia, he remained there until his death in 1179, after a ministry of nearly twenty years.

So passed away this great light in a dark age; but the results of his labors were felt for a long time after.

WALDENSES. — The dispersion of the Waldenses served the purposes of God far better than it did of their enemies. Extermination was *their* aim, while, under the fostering care of God, they spread their principles abroad, and multitudes became obedient to the faith. In the south of France, in Switzerland, Germany, and the Low Countries, thousands embraced their sentiments. In Bohemia alone, it is computed, there were eighty thousand of these Christians, in the year 1315.

The sentiments of those Christians, found by the Waldenses in Piedmont, Germany, and elsewhere, were so nearly the same, that they all merged together when near each other, and soon they all passed by the same name among their enemies; showing that the Bible produces the same fruits in those that believe, whether preached by John, Paul, Claude, or Waldo.

The Waldenses were traduced by their enemies, and had heaped upon them all manner of invectives, such as — "Poor men of Lyons," "Dogs," "Cut-purses," "Insabaths," — for not keeping saints' days as Sabbaths. In Germany they were called "Gazares," "flagitiously wicked," "Turlupins," "livers with wolves," "Arians," and "Ribalds," "dissolute men," etc., etc.

But their enemies, speaking of them, say: "Heretics are known by their manners; in behavior they are composed and modest, and no pride appears in their apparel." "It much strengthens the Waldenses, that, their heresy excepted, they generally live a purer life than other Christians." "I say that in morals and life they are good: true in words and unanimous in brotherly love; but their faith is incorrigible and vile, as I have shown in my treatise."

Hold! Mr. Witness: "By their *fruits* ye shall know them."

Rienerius, a cruel persecutor of the Waldenses, says: "They frequently read the holy Scriptures, and, in their preaching, cited the words of Christ and his apostles concerning love, humility, and other virtues."

Jacob de Riberia says, he "knew peasants who could repeat the Book of Job by heart; and several others who could repeat the whole New Testament perfectly." Some learned men sent to dispute with the Waldenses, on return, would declare that they had learned more of the Bible from the answers they would receive from them, than they ever knew before. Thuanus says of them: "Their clothing is skins of sheep; . . . . they live in houses with their cattle, having a fence between; they have, besides, two caves; in one they conceal themselves, in the other their cattle, when hunted by their enemies. . . . . One thing is astonishing, that persons externally so savage and rude, should have so much moral cultivation. They can all read and write. They understand French, so far as is needful for the understanding of the Bible and the singing of psalms. . . . They pay tribute with a good conscience, and the obligation of this duty is peculiarly noted in the confession of their faith."

Are not these Christ's flock?—in "sheep skins," in "dens and caves," afflicted and tormented?

As to their doctrines, the foregoing testimonials are enough to show them to have been uncorrupt. They, with all Protestants, took the Scriptures for their only and all-sufficient rule of faith and practice.

And from their connection with the true Church of Christ, as has been shown all along, their separation from Popery, and abhorrence and opposition to it unceasingly, we may regard them and the Scriptures as "two witnesses clothed in sackcloth," or God's true people, cast down but not destroyed,—a standing witness against Antichrist.

"Before they go to meat, the elder among them says: 'God who blessed the five barley loves and two fishes before his disciples in the wilderness, bless this table and that which is set upon it, in the name of the Father, Son, and Holy Ghost.' After meat, he says: 'The God which has given us bodily food, grant us his spiritual life; and may God be with us and we with him always.' After their meals they teach and exhort one another."

Rienarius, their enemy, declares that "a certain Waldensian heretic, with a view of turning a person from the Catholic faith, swam over the river in the night, and in the winter, to come to him to teach him the novel doctrines."

Not quite so bad as to have burnt him alive, in order to persuade him over, as Rienarius would have done!

The persecutions they endured were the more violent, inasmuch as kings had become subject to the Pope. In 1162, two years after Waldo began to preach in Lyons, Louis VII. of France, and Henry II. of England, holding the bridle of the horse of Pope Alexander VII., walking one on one side and the other on the other side, conducted him to his habitation. "Exhibiting," says the Romish author, Baronius, "a spectacle most grateful to God, to angels, and to men."

Thus the kings of the earth gave their "power and strength to the beast;" and so, princes and people being enslaved to the popedom, true Christians were persecuted with savage barbarity.

The increase of the Waldenses was a matter of notoriety and alarm to the Pope and his adherents. Measures of the greatest violence were resorted to, in order to check and reduce them. In 1181, Pope Lucius III. issued his edict anathematizing them, and all who should give them support. In 1194, Idelfonso, King of Spain, followed the Pope's fiendish example, adding to it, that it was high treason to be present to hear their ministers preach.

Thus matters stood at the close of the twelfth century, ripening for the climax of iniquity in the next. What striking examples of the power of delusion are to be seen in the growing monstrosities of the Papacy!

Century thirteenth gives us a view of the highest elevation to which the papal power arose. God's purpose in permitting this great apostasy to continue and grow so long, was, evidently, to make it crush itself; and then, during its ruin, "build his church, against which hell shall not prevail."

The popes found that edicts, anathemas, and fire and sword, were not sufficient to prevent the increase of the Waldenses, and that still more vigorous measures must be adopted in order to suppress them.

The new measure adopted was, the appointment of a number of persons, who *inquired* out (and from this were called *inquisitors*) the number, strength, and riches of heretics, and reported them to the bishop in whose diocese they were found, for him to anathematize, banish, or chastise. But the bishops were not all hearty enough in the work; they moved too slowly to answer the Pope's desires.

The concentration of this important work into fewer hands, was evidently what must be done. A character was found, equal to the task, who should be entrusted with the command of this new scheme of extirpation. *Dominic*, a Spaniard by birth, was appointed chief *inquisitor;* and now an independent instrument is brought into play, known by the name of the *Holy* (all but the holy!) *Inquisition.* Being taken out of the hands of the bishops, and put under the control of the Pope, with Dominic as his agent, it soon began to send up the smoke of its torments.

The Inquisition was established in 1206, under the sanction of Pope Innocent (if *innocent*) III., — just six hundred years from the appointment of the first Pope, Boniface III., 606, by Phocas.

The birth of the Inquisition being secured, its baptism soon followed; and that, too, in the blood of the Waldenses. The holy (?) instrument received the sanction of popes and princes, and at its work it went. The order of Dominicans has furnished the world with a set of inquisitors, in comparison with whom all who had dealt in tortures in former times were but novices.

Papal bishops and Pagan emperors on a level.

An epitome of the inquisitorial proceedings will suffice as a clue to their general character always. The persons in charge of this infernal machine were men from whose hearts the last feeling of compassion had departed, and blindly and brutally devoted to the interests of the Papacy.

Falling into the hands of such characters, nothing but their tender mercies, which are cruelty, could be expected. At first, the prisoner (who is any one whom the suspicions of inquisitors may indicate) is seized, remanded to jail, and searched and robbed with impunity and indignity. When brought before the tribunal, he is asked what he will have done. A trial is asked. In reply, the inquisitor says: "Your hearing is this: confess the truth, conceal nothing, and rely on our mercy."

If he confesses anything, that establishes his guilt; if he refuses, then he is an obstinate heretic. So he is guilty anyhow. What mercy "our mercy" is!

If any confess they are heretics (*i. e.*, Christians), then they are condemned; if they confess they are Catholics, then they are required to answer a list of questions verbally, without premeditation;

the answers being taken down in writing. Then the list is to be answered in writing by the person himself; and if there is not a perfect agreement between the verbal and written answers, then he is accused of dissembling; he is guilty. If there is an agreement, then he is charged with premeditated artifice; then he is guilty. So it is impossible to escape.

The sentence of those they *do find guilty*, is either to be whipped, violently tortured, sent to the galleys, or sentenced to death; and in *either* case (*i. e.*, all cases) their effects are confiscated. After sentence is passed, a procession is formed to the place of execution, which ceremony is called "Auto da fe," or Act of Faith. Shades of Peter!

Kings were compelled to be present and witness these executions, and the chief inquisitor conducted the whole affair in such a way as to indicate that his authority and dignity were above those of the king.

The Christian heroism of those who suffered, often drew from the amazed spectators the lamentation that such heroic souls *had not been more enlightened!* Very like the scenes in the amphitheatre of pagan Rome in the third century.

The humane (?!) inquisitors only allowed the torture to be used *three* times, — death, or decrepitude for life, being the result.

The condemned was taken into a cell with stifled walls to deaden his cries, immediately seized by six wretches, placed upon his back upon a table, an iron collar put about his neck, one on each wrist and ankle, and then two small ropes put around each arm, and each thigh, and the ends passed through holes in the table, and all drawn tight by four of the men, at the same instant, on a given signal; thus cutting the flesh in such a manner as to draw blood at eight places. If no confession is made, this tightening of ropes is repeated four times. This is the first torture.

The wretches finding, after a few weeks, that all their trouble has the effect only to make the prisoner pray the more fervently for aid from Heaven to endure his trials, he is again brought to torture.

He is then taken, and, by means of cords, his arms are drawn backward until the backs of the hands touch behind him; the shoulders are dislocated; the blood runs from the mouth of the heretic.(?) This is repeated three times, if no confession is made. He is again remanded to his dungeon, where the physician adds to his pain by brutally setting his dislocated limbs. This is the *second* torture.

In two months after, the prisoner was again taken and placed upon a board, with a chain around his body, crossed upon his breast, extended to the wrists, and then attached to pulleys, so that, when drawn, the breast was bruised in proportion as the chain was tightened,—the wrists and shoulders being dislocated. This was repeated twice. This was the *third* and *last* torture; the *laws* of the *institution allowing only three!* The above is from the statements of one who passed through the infernal portico, and was released at an "Auto da fé."

Females were put to the same excruciating tortures, with the addition of the most shocking indecencies.

Branches of the "Holy Inquisition" were soon scattered over the country, like post-offices, wherever the Waldenses were to be found, and put into full blast.

An account of the Apostolic Inquisition is shorter; thus: "Knowing, therefore, the *terrors* of the *Lord*, we *persuade* men." Dominic says: Knowing, therefore, the *terrors* of the *Pope*, we *torture* men. Who would suppose the latter to be a successor of the former?

Other modes of torture were added, from time to time, by way of improvement, — racking, burning, etc.

An effort was made about 1206, to reduce the Albigenses of Toulouse, France, then under the government of Count Raymond. Disputants were sent to confound and disprove the doctrines of the Albigenses, and also a demand to Raymond to expel them from his dominion. This he refused to do, as they were good subjects; hence he was interdicted, and force was to succeed the use of milder means. The Albigenses, seeing the turn things were about to take, gave the disputants of the Pope a challenge to a public discussion.

Montreal was the place chosen for the discussion. Arnold Hot appeared for the Albigenses, and Eusus for the Pope, accompanied by Dominic, and two legates. The points Arnold proposed to prove were, that the Mass and Transubstantiation were idolatrous and unscriptural; that the Church of Rome was not the spouse of Christ; and that its polity was bad and unholy.

Eusus asked fifteen days to answer, which was granted. At the appointed day he appeared, and brought with him a large manuscript, which he read in the conference. Arnold wished to reply by word of mouth. He discoursed for four days, with such fluency, readiness, and with such order, perspicuity, and strength of argument, that a powerful impression was made on the audience.

During the debate, the umpire of the papal party declared there could be nothing determined, on account of the coming of the Crusaders.

The instructions given by Pope Innocent to the army, were: "We exhort you, that you would endeavor to destroy the wicked heresy of the Albigenses, and to do this with more rigor than you would use towards the Saracens themselves. Persecute them with a strong hand; deprive them of their lands and possessions; banish them, and put Roman Catholics in their room." The persecution of the Albigenses continued until 1281.

In 1229, a council was held at Toulouse; one of the canons passed was, that the laity should not be allowed to have the Old or New Testament in the vulgar tongue; and *it forbade men even to translate the Scriptures!*

In the council at Lambeth, in 1281, the *cup*, in the Communion, was denied the laity, for the very grave reason, that Christ was given all and entire in the bread. This was a prop to transubstantiation.

Query: If Christ is to be had entire in the bread, *why does the priest need any wine?*

This is the first popish denial of the Scriptures to the laity. Protestants and reformers translate and distribute them, while Papists and inquisitors burn and prohibit them. Without entering into detail of the sufferings of the Albigenses, suffice it to say, that one can scarcely conceive the scenes of baseness, perfidy, barbarity, indecency, and hypocrisy, over which Innocent III. and his immediate successors presided.

During these persecutions, many of the Albigenses crossed over the Alps, and settled in some of the Spanish provinces, where they flourished for several years. They built churches, and their ministers preached their doctrines publicly and boldly. But, in due time, the inquisitors followed them, and for a century and a half preyed upon them like hungry wolves upon the flock.

An attempt was made to introduce the Inquisition into Piedmont; but the proceedings of that infernal thing in France, opened the eyes of the people, and they, with their princes, steadily refused it admittance.

Of the Waldenses it can be said, that they are the seed of the primitive churches; and though persecuted by, yet never bowed to the dominion of the Church of Rome, and never observed its idolatrous rites.

Dominic was also the inventor of the Rosary. The practice of repeating prayers had already obtained, and was often made use of. A certain privilege, as the priest might direct, could be attained by the repetition of so many "Pater-nosters," or Ave-Marias;" and again, certain penances could be discharged by the same rule; hence how vastly important the principle, for both priest and people.

In order to secure exactness among the people, and relieve them of remembering the number and order of their prayers, the rosary (or "beads") was invented. By holding this in the hand, and repeating a prayer to each one, it is easy to know when duty is done.

Cardinal Hugo wrote comments on the whole Scriptures, and honestly exposed the impiety and wickedness of the ecclesiastics of his time; is said to have been the inventor of concordances, — of vastly more value to the world than the rosary.

Grosseteste was another character similar to Bernard: a man of genius, of godly phrases, of pungent reproofs to popes; but merged all his greatness into the interests of Popery.

No one would, seemingly, be and do all these opposite and contradictory things, unless he were a coward, hypocrite, or a dupe. If, however, it be possible for a man to endorse the popish faith, and be a true man of God, doubtless Grosseteste was such an one.

CENTURY FOURTEENTH.

The year 1300 marks the highest summit of papal arrogance. Its tendency, as shown hitherto, has uniformily been to wax worse and worse, in presumption and assumption. But even such a growth, like a putrefying sore, must either break itself and heal, or leave the patient to languish, or take life at once. So Popery came to its full measure, and was checked.

The See of Rome having been vacant for two and a half years, Celestine, a monk, was unanimously chosen Pope, on account of his chastity. No Pope since Gregory had entered the office with more purity of intention. But, not having the talents of Gregory for business and government, and the Papacy being full grown with corruption, Celestine was bewildered with his lot. He accepted the office reluctantly, held it tremblingly, and left it joyfully.

Celestine asked the opinion of Cardinal Cajetan, if the Pope could *abdicate*. Being answered in the affirmative, he retired. Before retiring, however, he made a constitution, providing for the abdication of the Pontiff at pleasure. No Pope since, however, has availed himself of the provisions of that instrument.

Cajetan contrived to empty the chair of Peter, and then contrived to fill it with himself, and took the title of Boniface VIII. His name stands at the summit of the papal force; beginning with him also, a decline, above which it has never since risen.

Fearing that Celestine might change his mind and purpose of abdication, Boniface sent him to the Castle of Fumone, under a guard of soldiers, where he was kept and annoyed, until a fever ended his days.

Of Boniface it is said, he entered the pontificate like a fox, lived like a lion, and died like a dog.

Like Celestine, he also left a constitution, as follows: "That the Roman Pontiff ought to be judged by none, though, by his conduct, he draw innumerable souls with him to hell." Shades of St. Peter! Not much like Celestine, and still less like the apostles.

But the most remarkable encounter, and fatal blow, Boniface received, was from Philip IV. of France.

It is a singular circumstance that the kings of France were the first to uphold the popes, and do so from time to time, and also the first to abuse and confront them, and that, too, from time to time, from Pepin to Bonaparte.

Philip was distinguished for ambition, dissimulation, perfidy, and cruelty, and engaged in continual contests; just the man, however, for the age. He attempted to raise money from the *clergy* as well as the people. This brought Boniface to his feet. He entertained such attempts by Philip with the most haughty disdain; wrote him the most insulting letters, declaring that "The Vicar of Christ is vested with full authority over kings and kingdoms on the earth; and that he and all other princes were, by a divine (Boniface's) command, obliged to submit to the authority of the popes, as well in political and civil matters as those of a religious nature." The "divine command," to which Boniface did *not* refer, is this: "Render, therefore, unto Cæsar the things that are Cæsar's; and to God the things that are God's."

Philip, indignant at the insolence of Boniface, denounced him as an impostor, heretic, and Simoniac, and declared the See of Rome vacant. He sent a party who seized the Pope, and compelled him to ride a horse without saddle or bridle, and his face turned towards his tail! The mortification of this affair, with the loss of his treasure, threw Boniface into a frenzy, of which he died.

Philip then managed to get a Frenchman appointed Pope, and transferred the seat of the Papacy from Rome to Avignon, in France, where it continued for seventy years. The Italians called this "The Babylonish Captivity of the Holy See."

Thomas Bradwardine — Is reckoned a great light in his day. He was Proctor of the University of Oxford in 1325. He appears to have been a pious, modest, studious man. His writings were particularly directed against a rationalism of his time, interwoven strongly with Pelagianism.

Besides his polemical theology, he wrote on the leading doctrines of evangelical faith. He did much to render the doctrine of human merit less popular, and exalting justification by faith.

Hence, as God had overruled that Popery should poison itself with its own fangs, he took care also to nourish trees of his own right hand's planting.

In 1378 occurred the great WESTERN SCHISM.

The *Eastern Schism* was the rupture at Constantinople, about the source of the Holy Ghost, or division of the Latin and Greek churches, in 1054.

The Western Schism was the election of two popes at the same time, one at Avignon and one at Rome; each Pope and his party claiming the real succession.

From this time to 1414 the Papacy continued to have *two* and sometimes *three* different heads, each claiming to be the real Pope, and all forming plots and thundering out anathemas against each other.

Surely, the Catholics were for once afflicted with that Protestant *infelicity*, "quarrelling among themselves." And whether the Pope chosen at Rome, Urban VI., or the one at Avignon, Clement VII., were the real one, is *still* a matter of *dispute*.

In this whole affair, the papal power received an incurable wound.

Kings and princes, who had formerly been the slaves of the lordly pontiffs, now became their judges and masters; and the people, even among the more stupid, came at length to despise the popes for their disputes.

Did ever the apostle Paul get into such a freak with Nero, as Boniface, Paul's pretended successor, did with Philip? The fusion of church and state is utterly impracticable.

The authority of the Pope gained some ground in England at this time. Upon King John the Pope succeeded in fixing an annual tribute, thus reducing him to the condition of a vassal. Ashamed of vassalage, it was denied, in name, yet the tribute was paid until Edward III., when it was ripped up, the tribute withheld, and those outlawed who dared appeal to Rome.

WICKLIFFE.—A mightier champion than Bradwardine or Bernard, appeared *for* truth and *against* error, in the person of John Wickliffe, born in Yorkshire in 1324. He did not, like them, claim to teach purer doctrine than the clergy, openly rebuke them for their errors and crimes, and still continue with them, favor their persecutions and share the spoils; but, rather, numbered himself with Claude and Waldo, as an earnest reformer. For, placing them as they justly belong in the scale, as first and second, Wickliffe deserves to be ranked as third.

He was not only one of the "Fathers of the Reformation," by his numerous writings, fearless and successful exposure of the wicked and unchristian pretensions of the Popes and prelates, and the extreme corruption of the Roman Church, but especially as he was the first to translate the Scriptures into the English tongue. Like Waldo, he translates the Scriptures into the *spoken* language.

Wickliffe was a prodigy of learning in that dark age. He was Professor of Divinity at Oxford, which university he defended against the insolent pretensions of the mendicant friars. He boldly remonstrated with the Pope on account of his exorbitant tithes, which, upon various pretences, it is said amounted to much more than the nation paid in taxes to the king. He rendered the greatest possible service to true religion, by translating the whole Bible into English, by which the Scriptures were unfolded to the people, and a permanent foundation laid for the upbuilding of the cause of Christ, and the uprooting of papal superstition. The revival (as a consequence of an appeal to the Scriptures) of the great doctrine of justification by faith, through the redemption, that is in Christ Jesus, made his whole labors permanently lasting and useful.

Every possible effort was made by popes and prelates not only to silence him, but to destroy him; but he was defended by the Duke of Lancaster and the people. The more he did to bring the Pope and clergy into odium for their abominations, the higher their wrath arose; and for the same reasons, and in equal proportion, did the tide of parliamentary and popular favor swell, so that Wickliffe was able to do bravely, and in safety, the work of reform. More than once his judges quailed before the popular favor shown the valiant reformer. He spent his last days in the discharge of pastoral duties, as Rector of Lutterworth, in Leicestershire, where he died in peace, A. D. 1387.

But the death of Wickliffe was not the death of his doctrines; they were God's truth, reüttered and bravely defended in spite of envious priests, and hence would live and thrive.

The old farce of "sealing the tomb, and making it fast and setting a watch," was acted over. In a popish council, at Constance, in 1415, by order of Pope Martin V., his doctrines were condemned, and about two hundred volumes of his books were ordered to be burnt; and also, that if his bones could be distinguished from the rest, they were to be dug up and burnt to ashes; which last was executed by Fleming, Bishop of Lincoln, about twenty years after.

One writer observes, that, while they burnt his bones to ashes, and cast them into the Severn, which conveyed them to the ocean, his ashes thus became the emblem of his doctrine, which spread all over the world.

All this did not avail the Papists much, for his works were sought, copied, and circulated all over Europe. Another compliment, bestowed upon him by the University of Oxford, made the burners of his bones still more infamous.

It was as follows: "That all his conduct through life was sincere and commendable; that his conversation, from his youth upward to the time of his death, was so praiseworthy and honest, that never, at any time, was there a particle of suspicion raised against him; and that he vanquished, by the force of the Scriptures, all such as slandered Christ's religion. God forbid that our prelates should condemn such a man as a heretic, who has written better than any others in the university, on logic, philosophy, divinity, morality, and the speculative arts."

Such is an epitome of the life of this great reformer,—for such praise he merits, and all others, who not only differed from Rome, but actually raised the standard of the gospel, and also used just and severe weapons and measures against "Antichrist, and his clerks." A great man, and a great light in the fourteenth century.

Passing into the fifteenth century, we shall find the doctrines and followers of Wickliffe, and the persecutions of their enemies. The term "Lollards," by which the followers of Wickliffe were known, is derived from the German *Lullen*, which signifies singing, or singers; arising from their custom of "speaking to each other in psalms, hymns, and spiritual songs."

The fury of persecution against the Lollards was much stayed through the protection of the Duke of Lancaster, their "political father," and Ann, consort of Richard II., and sister of Wenceslaus, King of Bohemia. She is said to have possessed the Gospels in the English language, with four learned commentaries on them; and is said, also, to have been very pious. Hence this queen was a nursing mother to the persecuted Lollards.

The principal charge brought against the Lollards was that they held "*speculative errors*." Quite harmless! But they were made to feel something more than speculative restraint from Henry IV., and Arundel, Archbishop of Canterbury. Henry, like Pepin of France, usurped the throne, and Arundel, like Pope Zachary, said it was all right; and so the latter couplet, like the former, united to crush the reformers.

William Swarte—Was a clergyman of London, who openly taught the doctrines of Wickliffe, and opposed the abominations of Popery. For these two unpardonable crimes he was burnt at the stake.

Henry IV. was the first English king who burnt his subjects for their religious opinions; and was son of the Duke of Lancaster, who protected Wickliffe. Swarte was the first martyr under English kings.

Henry V., succeeding to the throne in 1413, also seconded the purposes of Arundel, in extirpating the Lollards by penal coercion.

Lord Cobham. — In the first year of the new king's reign, this archbishop collected a universal synod of all the bishops and clergy of England, at St. Paul's Church, London. The object was to suppress the growing sect; but the special object of the resentment of the whole synod was Lord Cobham (or Sir John Oldcastle).

This nobleman made no secret of his opinions, and openly opposed the abuses of Popery. At great expense he had collected, transcribed, and distributed the works of Wickliffe among the common people; and he even maintained itinerant preachers in the dioceses of Canterbury, Rochester, London, and Hereford.

But Lord Cobham was a favorite of both the king and the people, and his overthrow required caution. The first attempt was to send delegates to Oxford, to ascertain which way the influence of that great seat of learning would be thrown; and, to the mortification of the prelates, it favored Cobham, as it had done Wickliffe. But, nothing daunted, the enraged archbishop proceeded to burn a copy of each of Wickliffe's works, and among them one by Cobham. This volume proved Cobham to be a Lollard, and the bonfire was intended to influence the people against him.

Previous pains having been taken to prejudice the people against him, it was suggested very gravely in the synod that the young king better be consulted upon the measures they had in view, before they proceeded any further; accompanying their *inquiry* with a very urgent request, that his majesty would consent to the persecution of so incorrigible an offender.

To this request the king listened; but, in consideration of the high birth, military rank, and good services of Lord Cobham, the king desired the synod to delay a few days, that he might personally attempt the restoration of the lord to the church, without rigor or disgrace.

The king made the effort, and, after using all his persuasion in vain, Cobham replied as follows: "You I am always ready to obey, because you are the appointed minister of God, and bear the sword for the punishment of evil doers. But as to the Pope and his spiritual dominion, I owe him no obedience, nor will I pay him any; for as sure as God's word is true, to me it is fully evident that the Pope of Rome is the great Antichrist foretold in holy writ, the son of perdition, the open adversary of God, and the abomination standing in the holy place."

At this, Henry left Cobham to the malice of his enemies. Being cited by the archbishop to appear, Cobham paid no attention to it.

In the issue, he was arrested by the king's express order, and lodged in the tower of London.

Cobham's distinction between the civil and ecclesiastical authority above, is precisely the same in spirit as Christ's injunction, "Render unto Cæsar," etc. The reformers, and Christians in all ages, have recognized the same, and sealed it with their blood. The *lord* was far wiser than the *king*.

At the first examination, the primate told the lord that he was before him convicted, but that clemency would be shown him should he meekly ask for it.

In reply, Cobham took out a paper and read the substance of his faith, which contained a firm, yet not insolent, denial of the dogmas, of transubstantiation, penance, image-worship, and pilgrimages; and then passed it to the archbishop. His reply to Cobham was little else than to reäffirm the importance of those popish dogmas.

After disclaiming the offer of absolution from Arundel, Cobham kneeled down and prayed fervently to God for absolution; rising, he exhorted the people to beware of these false teachers.

This bold speech threw the court into some confusion; but, recovering their self-possession, they went on to question him: "Do you believe that after the words of consecration, there remains any MATERIAL bread?" Says Cobham: "The Scriptures make no mention of MATERIAL bread; the bread is the thing we see with our eyes; but the body of Christ is hid, and only to be seen by faith." Upon which, with one voice, they cried, "Heresy! heresy!" One in particular said: "It is a foul heresy to call it bread." Cobham replied, smartly: "St. Paul, the apostle, was as wise a man as you, and perhaps as good a Christian, and yet *he* calls it BREAD." After reproving them sharply for their superstitions, Dr. Walden exclaimed: "What rash and desperate people are these followers of Wickliffe!"

Cobham then declared that until he knew the doctrine of Wickliffe, he was very sinful; and would have remained so, finding no such grace in all your pompous instructions. Walden was surprised, that he found no such grace until he heard the devil preach. Cobham said: "Your fathers, the Pharisees, ascribed Christ's miracles to Beelzebub, and his doctrines to the devil."

A friar asked him, if he would worship the real cross on which Christ was crucified. Said he: "Where is it?"—"But suppose it were here," said the friar. "What sort of worship do I owe it?" says Cobham. "Such as St. Paul speaks of," said the friar: "God forbid that I should glory, save in the cross of Christ." Cobham replied that it was not the *material* cross he meant, but Christ's sufferings and death, in which Paul gloried.

It is said the court were brought to a stand, "their wits and sophistry so failed them that day."

But Arundel exhorted Cobham to weigh well the dilemma he was in; for "you must either submit to the ordinances of the church, or abide the dangerous consequences."

Cobham replied: "My faith is fixed, — do with me what you please."

Arundel then pronounced him "an incorrigible, pernicious, and detestable heretic," and delivered him up to the civil authority.

Cobham then cheerfully declared that all they could do was only to the body, and that God would take care of his soul; then exhorted the people to beware of these men, "for they will lead you blindfolded into hell with themselves." He then prays for the court: "Lord God Eternal! I beseech thee of thy great mercy to forgive my persecutors, if it be thy blessed will."

He was then sent back to the tower, under guard.

Cobham, "for his integrity, was dearly beloved by the king;" yet given over to his tormentors.

Such was the popularity of Lord Cobham, that after the sentence was passed, Arundel, through fear of the people, asked the king to defer the execution for fifty days. Posters were then put up, declaring his recantation, so as to diminish respect for him.

Ere they were aware, the prisoner (like Peter) made a very sudden and mysterious disappearance. Fleeing to Wales, he concealed himself for four years. His enemies then manufactured a report that he was secretly instigating a revolt, among the Lollards, against the king and government of England.

To give this lie some plausibility, a plot was laid to apprehend a meeting of Lollards, in a thicket called St. Giles' Fields, where they often met at dead of night, as they were obliged to do to escape disturbance. On the evening of January 6, 1414, while gathered there for worship, a detachment of soldiers was sent against them, and the solemn farce of dispersing and apprehending the conspirators was fully carried out.

From this time Cobham was represented as a traitor, and branded as guilty of high treason. And finally a bill of attainder passed the Commons against Cobham, through royal influence. The king set a price of a thousand marks upon his head, and a promise of perpetual exemption from taxes, to any town that should secure him. Through the (fiendish) diligence of Lord Powis and his semi-devils, Cobham was taken, near the end of 1417, and brought to London.

He was now in the hands of a power that had declared him a heretic and traitor, and his fate was soon determined. He was dragged to St. Giles' Fields, suspended alive in chains upon a gallows, and burned to death, with circumstances of aggravated and disgusting cruelty.

Chicheley became Archbishop of Canterbury upon the death of Arundel, 1414, and continued to be until 1443. For his cruelty and rashness he was notorious, "and deserves to be called the fire-brand of the age." Many were the worthies who suffered under the persecutions of those times.

It is almost incredible, that persons should be committed to the flames for such slight causes; as, for example, the case of John Brown, of Ashford, in Kent. He suffered under William Wareham, Archbishop of Canterbury. His detection and offence were as follows: Brown, happening to sit near a priest, on board a Gravesend barge, was rebuked by the inquiry: "Dost thou know who I am? Thou sittest too near me; thou sittest on my clothes." (!) Brown says: "No, sir, I know not what you are." — "I tell thee I am a priest."—"What, sir, are you a parson, a vicar, or a lady's chaplain?" — "No, I am a soul-priest. I sing for souls;" —*i. e.*, sing for their deliverance from Purgatory.

Says Brown: "Where do you find the soul, when you go to mass?" — "I cannot tell thee."—"Where do you leave it, when mass is over?" — "I cannot tell thee," said the priest, again. "How, then, can you save the soul?" asked Brown. — "Go thy way; thou art a heretic. I will be even with thee!" said the stupid fellow.

Three days after, while Brown was bringing a mess of pottage to his table for some guests who were dining with him, a party of the bishop's servants entered his house, took him out and put him upon his own horse, tying his feet under the horse's belly, took him to Canterbury, and kept him in close confinement forty days. Wareham, the archbishop, and Fisher, Bishop of Rochester, had caused his bare feet to be placed upon hot coals, until they were burnt to the bones. To his wife he then said: "The bishops, good Elizabeth, have burnt my feet until I cannot set them on ground, to make me deny my Lord; but, I thank God, they will never be able to make me do that. Therefore, I pray thee, continue as thou hast begun, and bring up thy children in the fear of the Lord. Thy husband is to be consumed at the stake to-morrow."

Thus were the Lollards treated by England's kings and archbishops.

JOHN HUSS. — From England the writings of Wickliffe were carried, by an officer of Oxford, into Bohemia, where they were read by Huss, Rector of the University of Prague. These writings opened Huss's eyes; and, being a man of great boldness and decision of character, he at once began to lay the axe of truth at the root of the upas of papal corruptions. His labors were successful in bringing many in Bohemia, and especially in the university, to embrace the doctrines of Wickliffe.

How providential, that the great seats of learning were disposed to favor the cause of the gospel! Their authority in those dark times was so nearly equal to the Pope's, that true religion was greatly aided by their means. But "great boldness in the faith" always stirs up fiery opposition.

The introduction of Wickliffe's writings into the university, gave great offence to the Archbishop of Prague, and he at once began a war upon Huss. The archbishop, feeling the need of help, applied to the Pope, who ordered Huss to be cited to appear before him at Rome. Huss declined the citation, when excommunication followed. At this Huss redoubled his vigilance, both in the pulpit and by his pen.

The archbishop then ordered all persons having Wickliffe's works to deliver them to him forthwith. Upon this demand, some two hundred volumes, finely written, adorned with costly covers and gold borders, were committed to the flames. This, however, had the opposite effect from what was intended; for, thereupon, both the writings of Wickliffe and the disciples of Huss abounded, and became more and more numerous.

"So mightily grew the word of God, and prevailed."

In the year 1414, the Council of Constance was called, remarkable for three things: the adjustment of the Papal Schism, and the condemnation to the flames of John Huss, and Jerome of Prague.

There were at this time three dignitaries scuffling for St. Peter's chair. The council thought best to put them all out, and chose a fresh successor to the apostolic (?) See of Rome — Martin V. In their haste to heal the schism, the council decreed the superiority of councils over popes. So that, while they healed the schism, it left the Pope with his right arm of power firmly bound. The world had begun to think. This decree also gave the reformers, a few years after, a tremendous advantage.

But Huss was summoned before the Council of Constance for believing, preaching, and circulating the doctrines of Wickliffe, though Rector of the University of Prague, Chaplain to the Queen of Bohemia, and an eminently useful preacher among his countrymen.

Being fearful of what might befall him at the council, he wrote a farewell letter to his friends, exhorting them to continue steadfast in the faith of Christ. After having received assurance from the Emperor Sigismund, under whose auspices even the council was assembled, to the effect that "he required all his subjects to suffer Huss to pass and repass secure, AND, FOR THE HONOR OF HIS IMPERIAL MAJESTY, IF NEED BE, TO PROVIDE HIM WITH GOOD PASSPORTS," he departed.

Accordingly Huss set out for the council, in the charge of Count John de Chlum, relying upon the emperor's "safe-conduct." Chlum immediately informed the Pope of Huss's arrival, and bespoke clemency in his behalf. This the Pope promised, and even removed his previous excommunication.

But no sooner had Huss arrived at the palace, than he was seized and thrust into prison. Chlum made loud complaints to the Pope, but in vain. Incensed at the imprisonment of Huss, he wrote to Sigismund upon the subject. The emperor immediately sent express orders to his ambassadors to cause him to be set at liberty, and even to break the gates of the prison in case of resistance. But Huss was not released; the Pope's clemency, the emperor's safe-conduct and express order to fetch him out, had no effect.

Ah! Sigismund was told that his conscience ought not to be burdened with this matter; that he was excused from keeping faith with a heretic; and that for him to acquiesce in the desires of the venerable council was the proper line of conduct for an obedient and "good son of the church."

And it was decreed that no promise ought, by human laws or divine, to be kept with Huss, to the prejudice of the Catholic faith! Holy fathers!

Huss was warned of this betrayal; but he, in hope, had ventured all for the cause of divine truth.

It may be considered quite sufficient to say, respecting Huss's doctrines, to show them to have been scriptural, that they were condemned by the Council of Constance. Huss's views shared the same fate there as did Wickliffe's, and as would Peter Waldo's, Claude's, and others.

A few specimens of his treatment while on trial may suffice also, without minute detail. One of their calumnies raised against Huss was, that "he exhorted the people to take up arms against those who opposed his doctrine." Huss replied, he exhorted the people "to put on the whole armor of the gospel, and fight the fight of faith."

Sigismund then exhorted him to retract his errors, and that, rather than support him in his heresy, he would with his own hands kindle the fire to burn him! Sigismund's "safe-conduct!" "Punic faith!"

At the close of the third day's examination, Chlum followed him to his prison. Huss exclaimed: "Oh! what a comfort was it to me to see that this nobleman did not disdain to stretch out his arms to a poor heretic in irons, whom all the world, as it were, had forsaken."

Few realize how much we of the nineteenth century are indebted to those noble reformers for the liberties we enjoy.

Huss, deeming his end to be at hand, wrote letters to his flock, entreating them to adhere solely to God's word, and not to follow him if they had seen anything in him not agreeable to it. He begs them to be grateful to Chlum, and another nobleman, who had been faithful to him in his sufferings. He adds: "I hear no news from Jerome, except that he is a prisoner, like myself, waiting for the sentence of death."

In reference to his books being burned, he remarked, that "Jeremiah's books shared the same fate."—Jer. 36:23.

Huss was finally brought before the council, in the presence of the emperor, the princes of the empire, and an incredible concourse of people. In attempting to speak, he was interrupted, when he begged the privilege of speech, that he might justify himself before the people; "after which you may dispose of me as you shall see fit." But the prelates refused; when Huss knelt down, and, with a loud voice, recommended his cause to the Judge of all the earth.

After a short space to speak, he closed by saying: "I came voluntarily to this council, under the public faith of the emperor here present." As he uttered these last words, he looked earnestly at Sigismund, who blushed at the unexpected rebuke. Imperial tool!

Sentence was now passed against both Huss and his books, and the mock ceremony performed, of clothing him with priests' garments, and then taking away one by one, pronouncing with each one an appropriate (?!) curse. As the Jews arrayed and mocked Jesus, so did the prelates.

A paper coronet was put upon his head, on which they had painted three devils and "Arch-Heretic," with the salutation, "We devote thy soul to the infernal devils."

Huss replied: "I am glad to wear this crown of ignominy, for the love of Him who wore a crown of thorns."

The final sentence of the council was: "The Holy (?) Synod of Constance declares, that John Huss ought to be given up to the secular power, and does so accordingly give him up, considering that the Church of God has no more to do with him."

Sigismund committed the execution of Huss to the elector Palatine. Huss, walking amidst his guards, declared his innocence to the people. On arriving at the place of execution the elector prevented his addressing the people, and ordered him burned. Huss exclaimed: "Lord Jesus, I humbly suffer this cruel death for thy sake; and I pray thee forgive all my enemies."

Quite different sentiments from the council's: "We devote thy soul to the infernal devils!" when Huss had done them no harm, but reprove their sins. Oh, the malignity of infernalism!

The elector withdrawing, the fire was kindled, and Huss, calling upon God as long as he could speak, was soon suffocated.

JEROME OF PRAGUE — Was a gentleman of fortune, and a man of eminent learning, which he had increased at Oxford. He encouraged Huss in going to Constance, promising to follow and assist him if he got into trouble. This promise he fulfilled, and went there; but, finding Huss in such bad hands that he could render him no service whatever, he returned to Bohemia.

This act of favor to a "heretic," was enough to send his soul also "to the infernal devils," after having been first judged (?) by incarnate fiends. Besides, he seconded Huss's endeavors to promote a reformation in Bohemia.

Soon after his return, he was seized, led in chains to Constance (by the successors of Peter!), and brutally treated for a whole year.

At his trial, a doctor of Cologne said: "You vented several errors in our university." — "Be pleased to name one." The doctor replied: "My memory fails me." Grave error! Several pertinent and impertinent things were said, and when the prelates' "memories all failed them," they set up a roar, and voices from all quarters burst forth: "Away with him! away with him! To the fire! to the fire! Away with him! away with him! Crucify him! crucify him!" This was "nothing new under the sun."

Jerome stood aghast, and cried aloud: "Since nothing but my blood will satisfy you, I am resigned to the will of God." In a few hours after, Wallenrod, Archbishop of Riga, caused him to be conveyed to St. Paul's Church, where he was bound to a post, his hands chained to his neck, and so he remained ten days, fed upon bread and water.

The examinations of "heretics" before the council, were only so many tirades of abuse. Being permitted to speak, he referred them to the unjust condemnation of ancient worthies, as Moses, Joseph, the prophets, John the Baptist, and the Saviour, and most of his apostles, and that himself was about to suffer at their hands an unrighteous sentence. "Ye have determined to condemn me unjustly; but after my death I shall leave a sting in your consciences, and a worm that shall never die."

He voluntarily put the mitre on his own head, for the sake of Him who wore a crown of thorns.

He sang cheerfully as he went to the stake, and there knelt and prayed. Being bound, he sang a hymn:

> "Hail! happy day, and ever be adored,
> When hell was conquered by great Heaven's Lord," etc.

The executioner, so as not to be seen of Jerome, came behind him to light the fire. "Come forward, and put fire to it before my face," said the martyr.

When almost smothered in the flames, he was heard to cry out: "O, Lord God! have mercy on me, have mercy on me." Jerome's death occurred in A. D. 1416, the next year after Huss's.

Between their deaths the Bohemians held an assembly, and addressed a letter to the Council of Constance, signed by sixty principal persons, barons, noblemen, and others, in part as follows:

"We know not from what motive ye have condemned John Huss, bachelor of divinity, and preacher of the gospel. Ye have put him to a cruel and ignominious death, though convicted of no heresy. We wrote in his vindication to Sigismund, King of the Romans, ... but ye burnt it, we are told, in contempt of us. . . . : John Huss was a man very honest, just, and orthodox: that for many years conversed among us with godly and blameless manners; . . . after all our inquiry . . . . we find in him everything pious, laudable, and worthy of a true pastor. . . . . Ye have not only disgraced us by his condemnation, but have also unmercifully imprisoned, and perhaps already put to death, Jerome of Prague, a man of most profound learning and copious eloquence. . . . . We are resolved to sacrifice our lives for the defence of the gospel of Christ, and of his faithful preachers."

L'Enfant, a Papist, after complimenting John Huss for having all the good qualities of a gentleman, scholar, hero, and Christian, said: "There is one thing, after all, that might expose him to condemnation with some show of justice, and that is, HIS INFLEXIBLE OBSTINACY."

The very words of Pliny to Trajan, in the first century: ". . . . yet for their *inflexible obstinacy*, certainly deserved punishment." Christianity is the same in all ages, and so is paganism, prelacy, and Popery.

Poggius, Secretary to Pope John XXIII., who was present at the trials and deaths of these two men, says of Jerome: "I never saw the art of speaking carried so near the model of ancient eloquence.

. . . . With surprising dexterity, he warded off every stroke of his adversaries.

('It shall be given you in that hour what ye shall say.')

". . . . Nothing escaped him; his whole behavior was truly great and pious.

". . . . He lamented the cruel and unjust death of that holy man, John Huss, and said he was armed with a full resolution to follow the steps of that blessed martyr.

". . . . It was impossible to hear this pathetic orator without emotion. . . . . Throughout his whole oration, he showed a most amazing strength of memory. . . . . His voice was sweet and full, and his action every way proper. . . . . If there be any justice in history, this man will be admired by all posterity. I call him a prodigious man, and the epithet is not extravagant. I was an eye-witness of his whole behavior, and could easily be more prolix on a subject so copious."

Thank you, Poggius. Still they burnt those fellows!

Aretin, to whom he wrote these things, says: "You attribute to this man more than I could wish. You ought at least to WRITE more cautiously of these things."

Who can fail to see that these martyrs were the true followers and apostles of the Lord? The gospel has never, up to this time, been without disciples and advocates.

Some considerable show at reformation of abuses was made by the council, but in such a way as to give no offence, and still quiet outsiders with the idea, that there was no need of such men as Huss, when the church was doing the clean thing. (?)

Like St. Bernard, make much ado, and yet do nothing. Or thus: Repent, and reform of your enormities, ye holy sons of the church.

In 1418, the Council of Constance closed; having, as the result of their labors, deposed three popes; decreed that councils hold authority above popes; showed themselves the veriest knaves, in violating safe conducts; kindled freely the fires of martyrdom; condemned the doctrines of Wickliffe; made a mock at reform; chosen a new Pope, Martin V., and then dissolved.

HUSSITES. — Whenever the Papists had disposed of any prominent leader, they next turned upon his followers. This was the fearful doom of the Hussites.

Their memorial to the Council of Constance only brought them directly under the set purpose of the council, to extirpate all who should favor the doctrine of Huss. Upon this, orders were issued to all the friends of the Papacy in Bohemia, to assist in exterminating heretics.

This opened afresh, and at large, the horrors of persecution. Burning, drowning, and torture were the papal arguments to recantation. A Hussite clergyman, with three farmers and four boys, was laid upon a pile of wood; when called upon to abjure, he replied: "God forbid! We would, if it were possible, endure death not once only, but an hundred times, rather than deny the truth of the gospel, solemnly revealed in the Bible." Clasping the children in his arms, he began a hymn of praise, in which all joined, till they were suffocated by the flames. From Bohemia, the savage spirit of persecution followed the Hussites into all places, wherever they were to be found.

Two years after the Council of Constance, Pope Martin V. issued an edict accusing the Hussites of the most damnable heresies, and called upon emperors, kings, and princes, "for the sake of the wounds of Jesus, and their own eternal salvation," to assist in their extirpation.

The Hussites, conscious of the purity of their motives and practices, afflicted with the treatment Huss and Jerome received at Constance, — and public opinion had so far advanced into the light as to see the unwarranted assumptions of the See of Rome, — concluded that forbearance had ceased to be a virtue, and so determined to resist the minions of the Pope by force of arms.

They found a leader competent to the task in a man of noble family, brought up at court, and renowned for his love of country and fear of God, in the person of John Ziska. To him multitudes flocked, until their number amounted to forty thousand. They encamped on Mount Tabor, about ten miles from Prague; and from this circumstance were called Taborites.

Ziska boldly defended his cause, even declaring war against Sigismund, and defeating the emperor's troops in several battles. He first began by attacking and putting the sumptuous palaces, churches, and costly robes of the priests to some other use; demolished their images; discharged the monks, who, he said, were only fattening like swine in sties; reduced the power of the emperor, and gave laws to Bohemia, till the time of his death, in 1424. It is said when Ziska found he was about to die, he ordered that his *skin* should be taken off, after death, and converted into a *drum*.

This order was fulfilled, and the drum was used for a long time as a symbol of victory to his followers.

In the above line of policy, Ziska imitated John and Judas, the Maccabees. If it be affirmed that he was a rebel, what were those against whom he so victoriously rebelled? Sigismund was not a "*terror to evil doers*," and a "*praise* to them that do *well*," but the contrary; and hence not the "minister of God."

Procop became the Hussite general after the death of Ziska. The Hussites got divided into two parties, known as Calixtines and Taborites. The former obtained, finally, a grant of the cup to the laity, in the communion, which was denied them at Constance, and was about all the Calixtines cared for in shape of reform, and did even persecute the Taborites.

But the latter, and the pious part, too, desired a much greater reform; and for this purpose assembled a kind of council at Lititz, in 1456, and proceeded to form a system of church government, in conformity with that of the primitive Christians.

They assumed the name of the United Brethren, and are known by that, and Moravians, to this day. From this time they increased rapidly. Many of the ancient and scattered Waldenses united with them, finding in each other a kindred spirit.

The "United Brethren" were the first church among the reformers: showing a great advantage gained, since they could do this with some degree of safety and success, notwithstanding the fearful odds against them.

Scarcely had they got their arrangements made, ere another crusade broke upon them. The papal wrath was poured out; the Brethren were driven from their homes, and obliged to perish from cold and hunger; the public prisons were filled; many were inhumanly dragged at the tails of horses and carts; others quartered, or burnt alive. Such as escaped, fled to the woods and caves, where they held religious meetings, chose their own teachers, and labored to edify and strengthen each other.

In their distresses and wanderings, sympathy and a friendly union was formed between them and the Hussites and Waldenses, owing to the similarity of their views and treatment from their common foe. These persecuted people were the seed of the true church, and humble followers of the meek and lowly Jesus.

In 1440, the noble art of printing was invented, which gave to the world, and particularly to the Church of Christ, a weapon of aggressive and defensive war upon the rotten system of Popery, which neither the councils, inquisitions, nor armies of the Pope could evade, destroy, nor capture. The reformers found an agent, in the press, which the hootings and clamors of archbishops and emperors could not gag, nor by safe-conducts ensnare, nor much fire consume, nor many waters drown.

Learning was cultivated to some purpose, and its influence upon the public mind was most salutary.

Towards the last of this century, Erasmus appeared on the theatre of action, and aided greatly in preparing the way for the Reformation.

By his labors, monastic superstition received a wound which has never since been healed; and mankind were furnished with critical skill and ingenuity, which they seized and used with a force and application far beyond what Erasmus himself ever anticipated.

In 1487, burst out another horrid persecution of the Waldenses in Piedmont, in which all the barbarities of former times were reäcted, at the relation of which the heart sickens. This persecution continued, with greater or less severity, until relieved by the glorious Reformation, for which God at this time was preparing the way.

So much was the world getting its eyes open to the corruptions of Popery, that authors and preachers were fast multiplying. Among the number was Wesselus. He was denominated the *light of the world.* More properly called the forerunner of Luther.

In a preface to one of Wesselus' works, Luther thus speaks: "By the wonderful providence of God, I have been compelled to become a public man, and to fight battles with those monsters of indulgences and papal decrees. All along, I supposed I stood alone. . . . I have utterly despaired of making any impression upon these brazen foreheads, and iron necks of impiety. But I am told that even in these days, there is a secret remnant of the people of God; nay, I rejoice to see a proof of it.

"Here is a new publication by Wesselus. . . . It is very plain that he was taught of God, as Isaiah prophesied Christians should be (Isa. 54:13). . . As to myself, I not only derive pleasure, but strength and courage from this publication. . . I am in no doubt now upon the points I have inculcated, when I see so entire an agreement in sentiment, and almost the same words used by this eminent person." Wesselus died in 1489.

Though we will not detract from the well-earned and richly-deserved fame of Martin Luther, yet we cannot close our eyes to the faith and sufferings of those dear people who maintained the truth and cause of God through the long night of the dark ages. "They *endured* the *contradiction* of *sinners*," Luther *rebuked* sinners; and God in all was glorified, and we benefited.

MARTIN LUTHER. — It is very remarkable that God so often raises up some prince to be a "nursing father" to the church, when he calls some eminent man into his vineyard.

For example: Claude of Turin was promoted to that place by Lewis of France; and, under his protection, Claude was shielded from harm.

Peter Waldo was not so specially favored; yet he was not so sharply exposed, so that the times were favorably tempered.

Wickliffe received the aid and protection of the Duke of Lancaster, or his days would have been cut off prematurely. The burning of his *bones* did neither him nor his cause any harm, nor his enemies any good.

Huss labored successfully, and under the protection of Sigismund, and the princes of his nation, and obeyed the summons to the Council of Constance, under the "*safe conduct*" of the emperor, who was bribed to turn traitor to Huss, and deliver him up to his enemies; not, however, until he had sown the seed of the truth.

So we shall find the prosperity of Luther is, under God, attributable to the protection of Frederic the Wise, Elector of Saxony.

It is related of Huss, that he foresaw the Reformation. While wandering in the fields of Bohemia, after being driven out from Prague, and surrounded by those who followed him, he said: "The wicked have begun by preparing a treacherous snare for the *goose.* (Hüss, in Bohemian, signifies *goose.*) But if even the goose, which is only a domestic bird, a peaceful animal, and whose flight is not very high in the air, has, nevertheless, broken through their toils, other birds, soaring more boldly towards the sky, will break through them with still greater force. Instead of a feeble goose, the truth will send forth eagles and keen-eyed vultures."

John Hilton, who suffered great insults and imprisonment from the monks, declared to them that "*another man would arise in the year of our Lord* 1516; *he will destroy you, and you shall not be able to resist him.*"

These predictions were both fulfilled in Luther's life, labors, and astonishing success.

Luther's parentage was humble, that the glory might be of God, and not of men. John Luther, and Margaret, were his parents' names. He was born in Eisleben, Germany, November 10, 1483, on St. Martin's eve; and hence his name, *Martin* Luther. His father was a miner, but a man of strong mind.

Luther's father resolved on giving him an education; and accordingly sent him to a Franciscan school at Magdeburg, at the age of fourteen. Without the means of support, he was obliged to go at times, with groups of boys, singing from door to door for his daily bread. They used to sing, in four parts, songs about the infant Jesus, born at Bethlehem.

He was frequently repulsed, to his great grief. In about a year his father removed him to Eisenach, to a school there, hoping his son would find assistance. For a time his fate was the same, until a lady saw him in the street, and, having heard him sing before, opened her door and took him in. From that time he had a home there, and went on with his studies. This event strengthened him in confidence in God, not to be shaken. This noble woman was the wife of Conrad Cotta.

Some years after, when he had become the first Doctor of the age, one of Conrad's sons came to Wittemberg to study. Luther received him to his table with joy, and gave him a home under his roof, as part pay for a similar favor shown himself.

Luther's good understanding, lively imagination, and retentive memory, enabled him to excel in study.

From this Luther was removed to the University of Erfurth, in 1501. Here he plunged into study with unparalleled zeal. But one day, while in the library, looking over volume after volume, to see their titles and authors' names, he comes upon a strange book, the like he had never seen before. He paused, and gazed, and read, and wondered. The Bible! what is the Bible? and soon he found it to be the word of God — a new book to him.

Luther at this time was twenty years old. His father designed him for a lawyer; but he had already had very strong religious convictions, and was very much agitated about his own personal salvation. "To pray well, is the better half of study," said he. A severe fit of sickness, and a dangerous cut from a sword he wore, in both which he came near dying, with the reading of the Bible, made a very deep impression upon his mind of the importance of personal salvation in his own case; though at this time he knew no other intercessor but Mary. He found no rest. He had learned that God is angry with the wicked every day, and that he was not prepared to meet God in peace. Such thoughts filled his mind with the keenest terrors.

In 1505 he visited his parents; and, while returning to Erfurth, was overtaken by a terrible thunder-storm. The lightning flashed, the bolt fell at his feet. Luther threw himself upon his knees. Here, as he says, "encompassed with the anguish and terror of death," he made a vow to the Lord to devote himself to his cause, if he would spare him. Now his thirst for holiness was as great as it had been for learning. How to become pure in heart, was his perplexity and inquiry. He resolved to enter a monastery, and there become holy.

Thus God brought Luther, as he did Paul, by a special interposition, to vow to live for him.

Entering Erfurth, he avowed his intention to his friends; and, leaving behind him his clothes and books, except Virgil, and Plautus, an epic poem and comedies, — as yet he had no Bible, — he repairs, in the darkness of night, to the convent of the hermits of St. Augustine. The gate opens and closes. Luther is secluded from the world. This event took place August 17, 1505, he being then a little past twenty-one.

This event gave Luther's father great distress, and even stirred up his anger, that his son should enter a convent; but at length he became reconciled to it.

The attempt of the monks to discourage the young Augustine from study, had to be abandoned in a short time, as no restrictions could quench the flame that burnt in his soul for knowledge. A chained Bible in the convent was his most delightful study. Here his faith found something to nourish it.

He soon began the study of the Greek and Hebrew, and used all helps to a knowledge of the word of God. Among these were the learned commentaries of Nicholas Lyra, who died in 1340. From this circumstance Pflug said: "*Si Lyra non lyrasset, Lutherus non saltasset.*"—If Lyra had not lyred, Luther had never danced.

John Staupitz was a very important character at this period. He, like Luther, had wandered in darkness, and writhed under conviction, but had found permanent relief through faith in Christ.

Staupitz had become a friend and confidant of Frederic the Wise, and under his direction, Frederic founded the University of Wittemberg. Staupitz was the first dean of the theological faculty of that school, from which the light was shortly to proceed to illumine the nations.

In Staupitz's visit to the monastery as vicar-general, his attention was directed to Luther, which resulted in a private interview that was of incalculable benefit to the young monk. The vicar directed him to Jesus, as the Saviour of sinners, and that, too, by faith. This gave Luther peace. Staupitz told Luther that God had raised him up for great purposes; and, as a guide to his future usefulness, exhorted him "to make the study of the Scriptures his favorite occupation;" and, to seal all his advice, gave Luther a Bible for his own, to his great joy. To the study of this he added the works of Augustine only; and now the work begins.

Little did either Staupitz or Luther realize the importance of that visit. And little did Augustine think of the important use that would be made of his works, while writing them a thousand years before.

Luther was ordained a priest in May, 1507. Staupitz, who had led Luther out of darkness to Christ, the true light, led him also out of the convent to a professorship in the University of Wittemberg. He was appointed to this post by Frederic the Wise, in the last of 1508.

Luther's life was one of strides. From the law, he fled to the monastery; thence he went to the university; then chose theology, in preference to philosophy. He had now arrived at the goal of his desires, — to study and teach the oracles of divine truth. His lectures took deep effect, astonishing some, and strengthening others.

Among the latter was his friend Staupitz, who asked him to preach in the church of the Augustines. From this Luther recoiled, but at length consented. In the middle of the square at Wittemberg stood an ancient wooden chapel, thirty feet long and twenty wide, whose walls, propped up on all sides, were falling to ruin. An old pulpit, made of planks, and three feet high, received the preacher. It was in this wretched place that the preaching of the Reformation began.

Seven monasteries getting at variance about their views, agreed to refer their matters to the Pope; and together chose Luther as their representative to his Holiness in the affair.

This journey to the seat of papal Christianity was a most fortunate or providential affair to the cause of the Reformation. It revealed to Luther what he would not have believed, only upon *being* an eyewitness, and ignorant of which he would not have felt so deeply the importance of his work.

At his entertainment in a convent on the Po, he saw the profligacy and corruption of the priests, to his utter astonishment, but profit. In Rome itself, where he felt *sure* of finding a purer state of manners, behold it was worse and worse.

But while there, he availed himself of an opportunity of increasing his knowledge of the Bible, by which Rome was to fall. Thus his faith in Popery was weakened, and in the Bible strengthened.

But the finishing touch of death to his blind faith in works was given while he was ascending (on his knees) Pilate's Staircase at Rome. When part way up, the truth he had before discovered came to him with renewed and irresistible force: "The just shall live by faith." Luther arose upon his feet, then no more to bow to the Pope.

On his return to Wittemberg, he was made Doctor of Divinity, October 18, 1512. On that memorable day, he was armed champion of the Bible. The oath he took was: "I swear to defend the evangelical truth with all my might." Thus called by the university, his sovereign, and the See of Rome, and bound before God with the most solemn oath, he now became the herald of the Word of Life.

Besides all this, his own undaunted courage all combined to give weight to his character, security to his person, and hence success to the Reformation. He thus declares: "I, Doctor Martin Luther, unworthy herald of our Lord Jesus Christ, confess this article: that *faith alone, without works, justifies before God;* and I declare that it shall remain forever in despite of the Emperor of the Romans, the Emperor of the Turks, the Emperor of the Tartars, the Emperor of the Persians; in spite of the Pope and all the cardinals, with the bishops, priests, monks, and nuns; in spite of kings, princes, and nobles, and in spite of all the world, and of the devils themselves; and that, if they endeavor to fight against this truth, they will draw the fires of hell upon their heads.... I am determined, in God's name, to tread upon the lions, to trample dragons and serpents under foot. This will begin during my life, and will be accomplished after my death."

Such was the position and determined purpose of Luther, in bringing about the great Reformation.

Having given a little sketch of the start Luther got, up to his becoming Doctor of Divinity, and thoroughly a public man, his individual history will now be dropped, and only noticed with the leading events of the Reformation.

The immediate cause which led Luther to a pointed and fierce attack upon Popery, was the sale of Indulgences by Tetzel, under the sanction of Pope Leo X. Tetzel came into Germany in all the pomp and show of a prince, and with the effrontery of an arch-apostate, offering, without let or hinderance, certificates of pardon for all sins, to the living or dead, and even for crimes which any one *intended* to commit.

Tetzel's great text was: The moment the money tinkles in the chest, the soul for whom it is paid mounts from purgatory.

"Tetzel's Indulgence-Box" is still to be seen in the Church of St. Nicholas, in Jutterbogk (near Berlin). It stands conspicuously near the centre of the church, very unlike a modern "contribution-box" in its dimensions.

"It is a great log, dug out of oak, ten feet long, three feet broad, and two and a half deep, strongly hooped with iron, the front covered with iron ornaments. The lid is a heavy, two-and-a-half-inch plank, with a large slit in the middle for the money to drop through, secured by stout hinges and three strong hasps. The padlocks are gone, so are the keys, so is *Tetzel.* When filled, it was a load for four strong horses."

A nobleman, Hans Von Hacke, asked him if he could grant an indulgence for a sin which a man *intends to commit in future.* "Surely," said he, "upon the actual payment of the sum required." "Well," said the nobleman, "I am desirous of taking a slight revenge on one of my enemies, without endangering life; for such an indulgence I will give you twenty crowns."—"Not short of thirty crowns," said Tetzel. The sum was paid, and the indulgence granted. As Tetzel was about leaving the place with his chest of money, a party sprang upon him, from ambush, headed by this nobleman, seized him, beat him (slightly?) with a stick, took his treasure, and let him go. Tetzel invoked the civil authority; but, upon showing the indulgence, Duke George ordered the nobleman released from custody. This, however, did not destroy the traffic; for in 1709, even, there was captured, at Bristol, England, a budget containing five hundred bales of bulls of indulgences, with sixteen reams in a bale. Estimated worth, £3,840,000 ($19,200,000)!

Such was the anxiety of Tetzel and others for money, that the people themselves said: "Pay! pay!—that is the head, belly, tail, and contents of all their sermons."

Luther, hearing of Tetzel's enormities, was aroused, not wholly at him, but at the effrontery of the Roman See in sanctioning such impunity. In his telling way, Luther declares: "If God permit, I will make a hole in his drum." When people came to Luther to confession, he warned them to break off their sins by righteousness; but they refused, and to prove their right to do so, showed their indulgences. At this Luther saw that Tetzel was playing under him, rendering his authority as a priest null and void.

Luther was aroused; he preached a sermon, attacking the traffic of indulgences in such a manner as to shake even the strong hold it had upon the base prejudices and passions of the populace.

A curious dream, by Frederick the Wise, is worthy of notice. On retiring, and being in great distress about souls in purgatory, he begged of God to direct him and his people in the way of truth. "I fell asleep and dreamed that God sent a monk, a true son of Paul, and with him all the saints. They asked my permission for the monk to write on the chapel door at Wittemburg. I consented. As the monk began to write, lo! the extremity of his pen reached even to Rome, and pierced the ears of a lion there (Leo X.), and shook the triple crown on the Pope's head. The cardinals ran to hold it on. They besought me to oppose the monk, as he lived in my dominions. The princes, with myself, hastened to Rome, and tried to break his pen; but it even grew stronger. I then asked the monk where he got the pen, and how it was so strong. He said: 'This pen belonged to a Bohemian goose (Huss), one hundred years old. I had it from one of my old schoolmasters. It is so strong, because no one can take the pith out of it, and I am myself quite astonished at it.' On a sudden, I heard a loud cry: . . . . from the monk's long pen had issued a host of other pens. I awoke, and it was daylight."

The interpretation of this dream was difficult at the time, but has since been abundantly explained and confirmed.

The work of piercing the lion's ears, and of writing on the door of the Wittemburg chapel, begun in ninety-five propositions Luther composed and put up on that door, October 31, 1517, against indulgences. This drew out from Tetzel one hundred and six in reply.

Before they came to their public discussion, each reviewed the other's "theses," publicly and severely. In reference to Tetzel, Luther says: "Let him call me heretic, schismatic, slanderer, and whatever he pleases, I shall not be his enemy for that, and I shall pray for him as for a friend. . . . . But I cannot suffer him to treat the Holy Scriptures, our consolation, as a sow treats a sack of oats."

Luther's boldness, in publishing his theses, struck some of his warmest friends with a little trembling, lest he had over acted; and Luther didn't know but he had. But in after-years he banished all such misgivings. And so he should. A bold man was needed. Luther was the man for the times. All Germany was in a panic.

The affray with Tetzel had reached the "ears of the lion at Rome," and Luther was summoned to appear before the Pope. But at the request of the University at Wittemburg, he was permitted to have a hearing in Germany. The legate, De Vio (surnamed Cajetan), fishing after popularity, solicited and obtained the management of Luther's case, and Augsburg was the place for the meeting.

The brief of the Pope, which accompanied the summons, was found to contain Luther's condemnation also, and was written even before the summons reached him. What must the court be, if the summons and judgment reach the prisoner before the trial? Luther said: "They forgot to take hellebore to clear out their heads, before resorting to such trickery."

Fearful apprehensions were now entertained by Luther's friends. He was now about to face the same power as did Huss, for the same fault, and a similar fate was suspected. Luther, however, was tranquil, saying: "My wife and my children are well provided for (*having neither to leave to suffer*), and my poor life is but little for them to take."

Luther set out for Augsburg, without a safe-conduct even, and on foot, turning a deaf ear to friends who entreated him not to put his life in the hands of his enemies. "Let Christ live; let Luther die," said he. At Nuremburg, two of his friends, Link and Leonard, went with him to Augsburg, where they arrived October 7th.

Next day, Luther was waited upon by Cajetan's feeler, Serra Longa, to ascertain the spirit of Luther. Finding that he had come without a safe-conduct, Longa told him it was of no use to have one, and urged his immediate appearance before the legate. Fine trap, if he could have gotten Luther into it. His friends having obtained a safe-conduct, he appeared before Cajetan, in answer to the Pope's summons.

In coming before the legate, Luther prostrated himself; at his order he rose upon his knees; at another order he stood up. Cajetan then addressed him as a dear son that had disturbed all Germany, and then read Father Leo's billet to him, which was: *First*, own your faults, retract your errors, propositions, and sermons; *second*, abstain in future from propagating your opinions, and, *thirdly*, bind yourself to behave with greater moderation, and avoid everything that may grieve or disturb the church.

Luther tried to talk with the legate, but was answered by taunting and effrontery. He even condescended to ask Luther if he would like to have him grant him a "*safe-conduct to Rome?*"

No doubt he would have been conveyed safely there!

At the second interview, the legate was even more insulting than before, speaking all the time, hardly giving Luther time to speak. Luther was satisfied that nothing could be done with Cajetan. All he sought was to compel him to say, "I retract," and that he never would do nor say. Luther now prepares to take issue with the legate.

The third interview took place October 14th; Luther, with the Elector's councillors, appeared before the legate. Luther advanced and laid his protest before the legate, who received it with contempt and sneers. Luther had asked him to present his paper to the Pope in his behalf. Railing followed railing, until Cajetan wound up by the blurt: "Recant, or return no more!" Luther bowed and left, the councillors following him, to the astonishment of the legate and his posse, who did not look for that.

All at once the legate and his courtiers became quiet, but had hitherto been very alert. This attracted the notice of Luther's friends, and alarmed them for his safety. They looked upon it as the calm before the storm; they remembered the fate of Huss. The messenger to Rome had a positive errand; an order might come any moment for the delivery of Luther to the custody of Cajetan.

Two devices were laid to thwart the evil purposes of the legate. One was, for Luther to write, and leave for presentation to him, an appeal from him to the Pope. The other was, for Luther to flee, secretly and immediately, from Augsburg, which he did.

Mortified and vexed at losing his prey, Cajetan wrote to the Elector, either to send Luther to Rome, or expel him from the German States.

Frederick refused to do either; and but for this firm protection, Luther would — like Huss, Jerome, Cobham, and others — have been speedily burnt, and the Reformation quashed for the time.

The failure at Augsburg gave great dissatisfaction at Rome, and De Vio gained nothing in the favor of the Holy (?) See. But, in order to stir up Luther to fresh attacks on Popery, and give new occasion for proceeding against him, Leo issued a bull, reäffirming the goodness of indulgences. He studiously refrained from calling any names, yet took special pains to mention the particular points Luther had condemned.

But the reformer was a little ahead of the Pope; for, anticipating what would come, he had, on November 28, 1518, a few days before the bull, in the chapel of *Corpus Christi*, at Wittemburg, appealed from the Pope to a general council of the church. "This," he said, "I am obliged to do, as the only means of safety against that injustice which it is impossible to resist."

The failure of Cajetan to restore Luther, induced the Pope to send a man of milder turn, to try what the offer of a cardinal's hat would do towards luring the obstinate reformer. For a time, kindness and clemency won Luther's attention, and great hopes were entertained by Miltitz, the Pope's envoy, of a reconciliation. But when recantation, or the mummeries of Popery were urged upon Luther's faith, he was as far from yielding as ever.

Doctor Eck, a Papist, managed to draw Luther into another public debate, at Leipsic, in 1519. Eck had rather worsted Carolstadt, a friend of Luther's, and so sought to meet the champion himself. This Eck did, to his sorrow. Luther laid him out.

That discussion had another good effect: Philip Melancthon was present, and from that time espoused warmly the cause of the Reformation. With scholarship equal to Erasmus, and integrity in a far greater degree, he became, what is very rare, a *useful ornament* to the cause of Christ.

About the same time arose Zuinglius, in Switzerland, who resisted the indulgence hawkers in a similar way to that of Luther. He did a glorious work there, in breaking the papal thraldom, and exalting the word and worship of the living and true God.

Thus the work advanced, and God was glorified.

Eck and De Vio, being badly whipped, went growling back to the den at Rome, and stirred up the old lion afresh, whose *ears Luther's pen had pierced.*

They induced Leo X. to issue a bull of excommunication against Luther, unless he threw himself, within sixty days, upon the sovereign mercy of the Court of Rome. Inviting proposition!

The bull was forthcoming, June 15th, 1520. But, on the tenth of December, 1520, Luther caused a pile of wood to be laid outside the walls of Wittemburg, *when he took the bull of excommunication and laid it upon the pile, and placing fire beneath it, reduced the whole to ashes.*

Bold push, that; and few but Luther would have done it. But it must be done, and by this act he declared himself free from the Papal Church; and, taking the *bull* by the horns, whose roar had terrified so many, he taught the Pope and the world that the bull that pushes with the horn shall be destroyed.

The Emperor Maxamilian I. died in 1519, and was succeeded by Charles V. The Pope besought Charles to proceed against Luther, with the utmost rigor. Charles wanted to retain the favor of the Pope, and yet he could but have some regard for Luther, on account of his patron, Frederick the Wise, by whom Charles obtained the crown of Germany. So Charles had to take a half-way course. To please the Pope, he consented to the burning of Luther's writings; and to please Frederick, refused to do Luther any harm.

But Charles ordered a general Diet to be held at Worms, to settle the disputes.

It was to this diet Luther's friends tried to persuade him not to go; when he replied, if he "met as many devils at Worms as there were tiles on the houses, he would not be deterred."

At this diet, Charles required Luther to appear. Here he was permitted to speak upon his cause for two hours. Great efforts were made to induce him to recant, but to no purpose. Charles then ordered him to leave Worms.

When pressed beyond measure to retract, he declared the words of Scripture were so strong he could not, and uttered his memorable words: "Here I stand; I cannot do otherwise. God help me. Amen." The prelates clamored with Charles, to let slip his safe-conduct to Luther, and let him fall into their hands. Charles chose not to imitate the perfidy of Sigismund towards Huss, and told them he "did not care to blush with his predecessor."

Yet, while Charles sent Luther away under a safe-conduct, he remained, and gratified the Pope by condemning him as a heretic and an outlaw.

Luther was now in the greatest danger; he had now come to the precipice, and awaited being thrown over it. But his friends succeeded in concealing him for ten months, in the Castle of Wartberg.

During his concealment, he labored at a translation of the New Testament, into German. Hearing of some hasty moves by his friend Carolstadt, in breaking down the images of the saints, he rushed forth, and appeared again at Wittemburg, and restored order.

The Pope still sought Luther's life; but the corruptions of the church were such, that he could not get Luther destroyed for opposing enormities so palpable. Hence, at a diet at Nuremburg, the execution of the sentence was suspended, until a meeting of a general council. But the Reformation was spreading into the countries round about.

In 1525, Frederick the Wise (to whom more is due, under God, than to any other prince up to his time, for his aid to the cause of truth) died. But his brother John espoused the cause, with even more zeal than Frederick.

Luther's marriage occurred June 11th, 1525. He married Catharine Bora. He had been a monk, and she a nun. This circumstance created a great sensation throughout Europe. Amongst other things that were said was, that the offspring of a monk and nun would be antichrist. To which Erasmus replied: "If that be so, the world is full of antichrists already."

Luther was very happy in his married life. His wife Katha, as he familiarly called her, relieved him of all household cares, encouraged him when desponding, and so aided him variously, that he declared that "the best gift of God, is a pious and amiable wife."

Charles again issued orders for a diet, which assembled at Spires, in 1526; but, fearing an invasion from the Turks, and, more than all, a treaty between France, England, and the Pope, against him, he ordered that "every state take its own course in matters of religion, until a general council could meet and determine the matters in dispute."

Thus religious liberty gasped once, after the fearful travail through which Doctor Luther brought it to birth. Glorious child of the daughter of Zion! thou shalt yet breathe again and live. Hallelujah!

Charles and the Pope becoming friends again, between them another diet was called, at Spires, in 1529, which revoked the decree of the previous diet, and substituted, that all departure from the Catholic faith was forbidden until the great council. This was an attempt to strangle the child mentioned above.

Upon this, the German princes entered their solemn *protest* against this enormity; and from this circumstance the reformers were called "*Protestants.*"

Thus they tore off the strangling-cord, and religious liberty breathed again.

In 1530, another diet sat at Augsburg, to settle all disputes. Luther was requested to draw up a summary of Protestant doctrines, to be presented to the diet. This is known as the *Augsburg Confession.* The prospect was fair, at the opening of the diet, for the cause of reform; but the emperor was so pressed by the Papacy, at last, as to agree to the passage of an edict establishing papal supremacy, and submission to it, upon pain of imperial wrath.

Upon this, the Protestant princes saw no hope, only in self-defence. Accordingly, they met at, and formed the *League* of *Smalcald*, and intended to invoke France, England, and Denmark to unite with them. This alliance, and the invasion of the Turks, forced Charles to conclude a peace with them, in 1532, in which the decrees of Worms and Augsburg were revoked, and religious liberty established, until the council.

This may be termed the swaddling-bands of religious liberty.

Luther was not a little disturbed by a work, published about this time, purporting to be written by Henry VIII. of England. In this, Henry wrote upon the sacraments, defending them in the way the Pope taught, and treating Luther's views in a very summary, unceremonious, and sarcastic manner. Luther replied in his usual manner, and no *less* severe than usual.

Charles, seeing that nothing could be done now, until the long expected council should sit, was impatient to have Clement VII. name the time and place. He died, and Paul III. became Pope. Charles pushed him to make the appointment, when Trent was the place fixed upon. To this place the Protestants were unwilling to go, being so near the Pope's dominions. But Charles was in favor of *Trent*, and declared war against all who should refuse to attend the council, or abide by its decisions.

But, while the world was in commotion, the great reformer made his last journey to his native city, Isleben. He fell suddenly ill; his last word was (in answer to the question, whether he still trusted in Jesus Christ, the Son of God, our Saviour and Redeemer?): "Yes." Lying for a quarter of an hour with his hands clasped, soon his features turned pale, and he fell asleep in Jesus, "without a struggle or a sigh," between two and three, on the morning of February 18th, 1546, Æ. 62.

Thus died the great Luther. He lived to see the cause of the Reformation set on a level with Popery, as it had a right to be. He had, by God's help, broken the power of the Pope beyond the possibility of repair, and seen Protestant states take the ground he had cleared, determined to maintain it. This was the most he expected to do; "but," said he, "after my death, it will be completed." Religious liberty was now dressed, and breathed freely.

Council of Trent.—Luther "being dead, yet speaketh." He

had appealed to a general council; it had been agreed to, and Trent was the place for it to be held. In the very year Luther died, the Council of Trent assembled.

It was soon seen that, like all other diets and hearings, the Council of Trent was to be entirely monopolized; and hence, instead of a general council, it was only a popish council. Besides this, Charles V. had taken arms against the Protestants, defeated them, and had taken the Elector of Saxony — the very patron of the Reformation — and others prisoners. He then attempted to compel the Protestants to agree to abide by the decisions of the Council of Trent. This was nothing less than to ask them to submit to the Pope in toto.

Great confusion and alarm ensued; when, at this critical moment, Maurice, son-in-law to the elector, found Charles in a weak condition of defence, at Innspruck, fell upon him, and compelled him to agree upon a peace.

At a diet in Augsburg, September 25th, 1555, a treaty was formed, called "*The Peace of Religion.*" Charles served the interests of either party, just as *force of circumstances* compelled him. In the present position of affairs, the Papacy saw the immense advantage the Protestants were about to gain, and the unparalleled loss they themselves were to sustain. Indeed, it was the triumph of the Reformation.

Hence, in their panic, they cried out, that "in things pertaining to the faith, NO MAN'S CONSCIENCE SHOULD BE FREE. But when any man departs from the common consent of the church, he ought to be punished and restrained."

On the other hand, the FAMOUS decree was passed, that "neither the Emperor, nor the King of the Romans, nor any other princes or states of the empire, should, in any manner whatsoever, hurt or injure any man for the profession of the Augustan, or PROTESTANT, doctrine, religion, and faith; nor should they, by command, or by any other means whatsoever, force any man to forsake or change his religion. That all persons should be suffered freely to profess the Protestant faith, as it then was, or should thereafter be instituted, and quietly to enjoy their rights and property; also, that no attempt should be made to settle controversies in religion by any other than pious, friendly, and quiet ways." Similar engagements were made by the Protestants, as to their conduct towards the Romanists. This was the PEACE OF RELIGION.

The Council of Trent continued from 1546 to 1563, during which time it held no less than twenty-five sessions. Its decrees now stand, as the creed of the Roman Catholic Church.

The Peace of Religion was established during the Council of Trent; and hence that august assembly was spurned by the Protestants, ere it had roared its dragon decrees. The fearful struggle made to establish Protestantism, shows the fearful and tremendous assumption of the rights of men Popery had absorbed. But in the Peace of Religion we see religious liberty, in pantalettes, smiting the *man of sin.* All previous struggles with the Papacy had been quashed, but in this the tide of affairs is completely turned.

IV.

AGE OF CONSOLIDATION.

FROM THE PEACE OF RELIGION, 1555 A. C., TO THE PRESENT TIME.

ECCLESIASTICAL HISTORY.

PERIOD I. FROM THE PEACE OF RELIGION, 5559 A. M., 1555 A. C., TO THE LANDING OF THE PILGRIMS IN AMERICA, 5624 A. M., AND 1620 A. C.

FROM the Peace of Religion, onward, we shall find the struggles for religious liberty confined to the limits of the different states. It will there be found grappling with the same difficulties as heretofore, only with the State power, instead of the Papal, as the world-wide opponent of all reform. Still, in most cases, the state powers, when opposed to reform, were more or less under the control of Popery. But the division of the papal forces, necessary to guard so many points, was favorable to the causes of civil and religious liberty. Hence the gradual *consolidation* of the political and religious elements of society into their present form; being the combination of Patriarchy, Power, and Opinion. This seems to be the age for which all other ages were made.

The history of religion will now be followed through the different sects, or denominations, as they appear.

THE ROMAN CATHOLIC CHURCH.

Being now shorn of the proud title conferred upon the Bishop and Church of Rome by the Emperor Phocas, Papists are now obliged to stand on a level with others, only a sect among sects. This was Luther's aim, to pull down the Pope, and raise up the Church of Christ; and he did it effectually.

Conscious of their tremendous loss, and still waning power, the Catholics felt that some effort must be made to save what was left, and regain something.

IGNATIUS LOYOLA — Brought the plan to light, in 1540, that was finally inaugurated as a "restorer of the breach."

He was the founder of the "Order of the Jesuits;" *i. e.*, the Order of Jesus, which was, after some hesitation, confirmed by Paul III. The order was under the direction of a general, chosen for life by the Pope, and who had the entire control of the whole party. Every member was at his disposal, and subject to his commands.

They laid aside the monkish notion of *seclusion*, and mingled among men in *disguise*. They became lawyers, physicians, mathematicians, painters, and artists, to gain the more ready access to every class. Jesuits were known by Jesuits; but to the eye of the world they passed unsuspected as to their real character. With this arrangement, they went forth, with Saul-like zeal, to prop up and extend the reign of the Pope.

They took "the field to be the world;" and into the East, and South America, they carried their conquests, as far as man could be found. St. Francis Xavier was the Paul of the Jesuits. Other missionary societies were formed amongst them, to serve in the all-absorbing work of "*Propaganda fide*,"— propagation of the faith.

This led to the reconstruction of their whole former machinery of operation. The Reformation remodelled Popery. The laws and courts of the Inquisition were revised and corrected; colleges and schools established; youth trained in the art of disputing, and of defending the doctrines of the Roman Catholic Church, and high distinctions conferred on the most zealous partisans. Thus was infused into the Jesuits all the energy conceivable; but its efforts were more like death-throes than life from the dead.

But the device in which Rome has most delighted, and spent her most pious (?) hours, was not laid aside, and could hardly be improved; namely, persecution of the Protestants.

One of the first bursts of wrath, under the limited sway of the Pope, was upon the Waldenses of Calabria, a province of Italy. Reformed pastors from Geneva had been sent among them, and they had been strengthened, and had formed a junction with the Calvinists at Geneva.

As the Peace of Religion gave each state the right to regulate its own internal matters on religion, the Pope took that liberty in Italy. The business of regulating, (?) in that wretched country, continued over a hundred years. In short, and nothing short of all the horrors of a war upon defenceless people by a brutal soldiery, set on by the instigations of inquisitorial fiends, who loved blood more than mercy, characterized their operations.

Milton's sonnet upon their woes commences thus:

> "Avenge, O Lord, thy slaughtered saints! whose bones
> Lie scattered on the Alpine mountains cold;
> E'en those who kept thy truth so pure of old,
> When all our fathers worshipped stocks and stones,
> Forget not."

They also found generous sympathy in the great heart of Oliver Cromwell.

But the ripest and most bitter fruit of Jesuitical perfidy was the massacre of St. Bartholomew, in Paris, France, Aug. 24, 1572.

Catharine de Medicis, mother of King Charles IX., was the real sovereign of France, *i. e.*, by her influence.

Cate was a fit tool for the purpose contemplated. Her heartlessness and audacity were equal to any emergency.

The Protestants at this time were numerous and influential, having for their patrons two young princes of the blood, Henry, King of Navarre, and the princes of Condé.

Catharine had the art to court the favor of either party, as the end she had in view might require. At last she resolved to dispose of the Protestants ("Huguenots"), so as to have but *one* party to please and control.

The fiendish device was covered up, under a proposed marriage between her daughter and Henry of Navarre, and so unite and reconcile the two parties. Accordingly, Protestants and Catholics were invited to the wedding, and much pains was taken to have the Huguenots present.

Admiral Coligny, high in rank and merit, also a Protestant, was specially invited and flattered.

The marriage passed off with great pomp. But on Sunday morning following, at twelve o'clock, the tocsin for the slaughter was rung. The first blow struck was the assassination of Admiral Coligny. A posse was sent to his room; they entered it; one Berne, a German, addressed him: "Are you not the Admiral?"—"I am," he replied; when Berne plunged his sword into his breast. A call was made below, to throw his body out into the street. Guise, leader of the forces, examining the body, said: "Yes, it is he himself;" gave him a kick, and led off his minions to the slaughter.

The scene that followed beggars description. The blood of ten thousand defenceless Huguenots drenched the streets of Paris; and thus passed another scene in the drama of "Who is Head of the Church?—Christ, or the Pope?"

News of this papal Pentecost was received in Rome with unbounded exultation and joy.

The slaughter spread into other parts, until not less than sixty thousand Protestants perished by the hands of the Papists, under the sanction of the Pope.

Peace and concord by no means followed this perfidious transaction, though it led to a relief for a time.

In 1593, Henry IV. (a Huguenot) ascended the throne of France; and in 1598 he established the Edict of Nantes, by which the Protestants had free toleration.

Religious liberty drew one breath more, after the massacre.

The papal party, however, manifested their regard for Henry, by procuring his assassination in his carriage. Under the Edict of Nantes, the Protestants flourished until 1685, when Louis XIV. revoked the Edict of Nantes, requiring the Reformed Churches to return to the Papal Church. This measure drained France of from five to eight hundred thousand of her best citizens. Protestantism was finally crushed. Thus did Rome redouble her efforts to destroy the Reformation.

Yet, as the kings of France were always doing, first build up the Pope, and then pull him down, so did Louis XIV. By his order, a council of the Gallician Church, in 1682, declared that the power of the Pope is only spiritual, that a general council is superior to him, and that his decisions are not infallible.

Thus Louis "pierced the ears of the lion" at Rome.

But this down-hill course of the Jesuits did not stop here. They had shown the world what they would do, could do, and did do; and it was enough.

This order of creeping fiends was suppressed in England, and expelled in 1604; from Venice 1606; from Portugal 1759; France, 1764; Spain and Sicily, 1767; and finally abolished by Clement XIV., July 21, 1773.

Thus this "right hand" of Popery, in two hundred and thirty years, had become "an offence even to the Church of Rome! and was "cut off and cast from her."

But Popery was doomed to feel yet another blow from a successor of Pepin. The revolution of 1793 brought her humility. Of her fate it is said: "Her priests were massacred. Her silver shrines and saints were turned into money to pay troops. Her bells were converted into cannon, and her churches and convents into barracks for soldiers. From the Atlantic to the Adriatic, she presented but one appalling spectacle. She had shed the blood of saints and prophets, and God now gave her blood to drink." Upon the appearance again of a regular government, "Liberty of conscience and freedom of worship" were declared to be the law of the land.

The child Religious Liberty yet lives and flourishes.

Napoleon deposed the Pope, and the whole system of monkery. In less than four years he dispossessed the Pope of his ecclesiastical state, and reduced His Holiness to a mere cipher in the political world. Shades of Pepin! In a speech to the magistrates of Madrid in 1808, he says: "I have abolished the Court of the Inquisition, which was a subject of complaint to Europe and the present age. Priests may guide the minds of men, but must exercise no temporal or corporal jurisdiction over the citizens."

Constantine and Pepin! what shall be done with Philip IV. and Bonaparte?

But still more recently, the arms of liberty stood before the door of the Vatican, when Bonaparte III. ran to the rescue, and with French bayonets propped up the crumbling power of His Holiness.

The next wave that sweeps over Rome may be the breath of the Almighty. If so, the cry and shout will be: "Babylon the Great is fallen"!

LUTHERANS. — The sect bearing this name are the followers of Luther. They date the rise of their church from his excommunication by the Pope. The *Augsburg Confession*, drawn up by Luther in 1530, consisting of twenty-one articles, forms the standard of faith in the Lutheran Church.

Although strenuously Protestant, the Lutheran Church does not take a foremost rank among evangelical churches.

Swedenborg, author of Swedenborgianism, or the New Jerusalem Church, was a Lutheran bishop, born in Stockholm, 1688.

CALVINISTS. — This sect derive their name from John Calvin, a Frenchman, who forsook the fellowship of the Church of Rome in 1534, and in 1541 settled at Geneva, where his influence did much in advancing the cause of the Reformation. He was the author of the Presbyterian form of church government.

Calvin is reckoned next to Luther, as a promoter of the Reformation. He did much to revive learning in Geneva and Germany. The fault of the age was Calvin's, namely, intolerance. He lent his influence against Servetus, a learned Spaniard, for his views of the Trinity. Servetus was condemned to be burnt, in 1553.

The Calvinistic doctrine consists of Predestination, Particular Redemption, Total Depravity, Effectual Calling, and Perseverance of the Saints.

During the life of Zuinglius, the Swiss churches adopted the sentiments of that distinguished reformer; but after his death, many became Calvinistic. The Calvinists suffered, with others, the rigors of papal persecution; the term came to mean much the same as "Protestant."

James Arminius, from being a Calvinist, turned so far as to reject Predestination and Grace, as explained by Calvin. They each got upon the opposite extreme in some things, yet each had his arguments and advocates.

But the worst feature of the case was, that the Arminians were subjected to persecution from the other reformed churches, showing that the reformers themselves did not understand how to use the liberty they claimed of the Roman Church.

CHURCH OF ENGLAND.

The rise of this sect has its date in 1534, during the reign of Henry VIII., who had a rupture with the Pope. Extremes often meet.

Henry took great pains to write a work against Luther, in *defence* of Popery, and received, as a reward of merit from the Pope, the title of "*Defender of the Faith.*"

Afterwards, wishing to obtain a divorce, Henry applied to the Pope; he refused the king's request. Upon this, Henry applied to the universities of Europe, and they granted it. Exasperated at this refusal of the Pope, Henry determined to have revenge.

He accordingly declared himself the head of the Church of England, and disclaimed the authority of the Pope. He caused the Scriptures to be translated, and favored such measures as were opposed to Popery and favorable to reform.

He next suppressed the monasteries, beginning with the smaller convents. From these he acquired some £40,000. Proceeding to the larger ones, in two years he destroyed six hundred and forty-five monasteries, ninety colleges, two thousand chantries, five chapels, and ten hospitals; all their wealth — lands, silks, jewels, etc. — flowed into the royal coffers.

This raised the ire at Rome. Henry's title was annulled, he excommunicated, his kingdom laid under an interdict, and he cited to appear at Rome. Henry regarded all this raving as idle wind.

EDWARD VI. — Succeeded Henry, and favored Protestantism, to the great joy of its friends and the grief of the Papacy. Edward soon relaxed the severities of Henry's reign. One of the acts passed in his reign was the *bloody statute*, designed to favor popish sentiments.

Cranmer was the guiding star to Edward. About this time was

drawn up forty-two *articles of religion*, thirty-nine of which, known as the "Thirty-nine Articles," still form the code of faith and discipline in that church.

The reformers wanted to complete the reform, by rejecting all popish garments, such as the cap and surplice. Edward was willing, but Cranmer and Ridley would have them worn.

Among those who would not conform to these orders, were Latimer, Coverdale, and John Rogers; and for this they were called *non-conformists.* Cranmer cast Hooper into prison, for refusing to wear the little cap.

Cranmer, and other reformers, (?) persecuted and put to death the Anabaptists, among whom was one Joan Bocher, of Kent. Edward declined signing her death warrant, but was forced to by the intolerant solicitations of Cranmer. On yielding, Edward said, with tears in his eyes: "If I do wrong in yielding to your authority, you must answer for it to God." Edward died in 1553, and bequeathed the crown to Lady Jane Grey, who was soon beheaded, and Mary, sister of Edward, a bigoted Papist, ascended the throne. Popery now triumphed again.

The tables were soon turned. It was Cranmer's lot, now, to feel what he had caused others to feel; he, being opposed to Popery, was imprisoned. Cardinal Pole received England back into the bosom of the Catholic Church, and removed the interdict.

Bonner, who had been imprisoned by Cranmer, now had his liberty, and is said to have "behaved more like a cannibal than a Christian." Cranmer had the pleasure and honor of martyrdom, being burnt at the stake March 21, 1556.

He signed a recantation, but the Papists were bent on his death. In the flames he regretted this, and held the offending hand in the fire, saying: "This unworthy hand!" But no mention of Joan Bocher.

John Rogers, and Hooper, suffered death by fire the year before.

Puritans — Had their rise in Frankfort, Germany, 1554. They consisted first of English Protestants, who fled from the rigor of Mary, and took refuge at Frankfort. They were non-conformists, and, aiming at a still further improvement and simplicity in worship, were called by their enemies, as a term of reproach, "Puritans." John Knox was the pastor of these exiles.

Elizabeth, sister of Mary and Edward, came to the throne in 1558. She did but little until the meeting of Parliament in 1559. Protestantism was restored. The principal act passed was one establishing the *supremacy of the sovereign, and uniformity of common prayer;* — the exact views of her father, Henry VIII.

She avowed Protestantism, but, by keeping the popish garments, took issue with the non-conformists; and now for the scenes of Rome to be reënacted. The Pope was shut out, and the non-conformists shut in.

In the act of supremacy was a clause which gave rise to a new court, called the "Court of High Commission." This consisted of persons appointed by the queen. Power was given them "to visit, reform, and amend all errors, heresies, schisms, abuses, offences, and enormities whatever."

This was a Protestant Inquisition.

If the person apprehended refused to take oath, he was imprisoned for contempt; if he took oath, his own confession thereby convicted him; and the term of imprisonment was wholly at the pleasure of the court.

Dominic and Elizabeth do well agree!

Jesuitical plots not a few were laid to dispose of this prelatical queen. Prelacy and Popery were now at strife, alternately the victims of each other, while the Puritans were victims of both.

The "*Spanish Armada*" was fitted out for the purpose of dethroning Prelacy and establishing Popery, but was blown in pieces by a tempest; the providence of God requiring it so to be.

In 1581, a sect arose among the Puritans, called Brownists, who adopted the *independent* form of church government. A church of this sect afterwards removed, in 1625, to Plymouth, New England.

JAMES I. — Came to the throne in 1603, and gave the Puritans high hopes of favor at his accession. But, though educated a Presbyterian, he soon went over to Prelacy. James' religion consisted purely of "kingcraft."

In reply to a petition of one thousand Puritans, for redress of grievances they suffered from the bishops, James' favorite maxim was: "No bishop, no king;"— meaning that those who opposed the bishops, opposed the king.

Still, upon this petition of the Puritans, James appointed a meeting at Hampton Court, to hear their cause.

The first day, the bishops and king met in private. The second day, the Puritans had a hearing in the presence of the king and prelates. During their defence and plea, they were frequently interrupted and insulted.

James closed his speeches to the Puritans, with his new and pious ejaculation: "No bishop, no king."

In rendering his verdict, he said: "If this is all your party have to say, I will make them conform themselves, or else I will harrie (dog) them out of the land, or else do worse, — only hang them, that 's all!"

Vive Cajetan and James! The Puritans were disfranchised, imprisoned, and denied Christian burial.

In 1605, was discovered the *Gunpowder Plot* (another Bartholomew). It was got up by the Catholics, to cut off Parliament at a blow; but, being discovered and defeated in it, they, Nero-like, laid it to the Puritans.

The interview at Hampton Court resulted in one very important measure, suggested by the Puritans. This was, the translation of the Scriptures into English, published in 1611.

To annoy the Puritans still further, Bishop Moreton drew up, in 1618, in obedience to the king, the so-called "Book of Sports." It recommended that those who came to church (prelates,) twice on Lord's day, should, after divine service, "recreate themselves, by dancing, archery, leaping, vaulting, May games, whitsun-ales, morrice dances, May-pole dancing, and other sports of a like kind." And special pains were taken to do all these nice things where it would most annoy those who wished to keep the day. Hence the secret of the aversion of the Puritans to "dancing, and other sports of like kind."

James died in 1625. Bishop Burnet calls James I., "The scorn of the age; a mere pedant, without true judgment, courage, or steadiness; his reign being a continued course of mean practices."

What could be expected that such a man would do for religion?

Archbishop Laud. — The affairs of the church were directed, under Charles I., by this flaunting and intolerant prelate. He gloried in the privileges and practices of the "Court of High Commission."

Colonel Lillburne, for refusing to answer all inquiries the "court" might put, was fined five thousand pounds, and whipped through the public streets. For speaking against the tyranny of the bishops, he was gagged, and laid in irons for life, in Fleet Prison.

Doctor Leighton, for writing a book entitled "Zion's Plea against Prelacy," was sentenced by the Star Chamber. At the giving of the sentence, Laud pulled off his hat and gave God thanks for the decision of the court.

In his private diary, Laud makes the following record, with evident pleasure: "November 6th. 1st. He (Leighton) was severely whipped before being put in the pillory; 2d. Being set in the pillory, he had one of his ears cut off; 3d. One side of his nose slit; 4th. Branded on the cheek, with a red-hot iron, with the letters S. S. In sevennight, the rest of the sentence was applied to the other cheek also."

From under these severities, thousands fled to America; and these persecutions drained England of half a million of her citizens. The nation became exasperated at the conduct of Laud, and the horrors of the "court." Laud was at length accused of treason, and, after a long imprisonment, he was beheaded, and Episcopacy itself abolished.

Cranmer and Laud had to drink of the cup they gave others to drink.

OLIVER CROMWELL. — Under this great protector of religion and the rights of men, Presbyterianism gained the ascendency in England. Toleration was granted to all, except Catholics and prelaters. Against this toleration the Presbyterians complained; but Cromwell, better understanding religious liberty, would not listen to their clamors.

Religious Liberty has got to be quite a promising young man.

At this time flourished Goodwin, Owen, Flavel, Charnock, Poole, Howe, and Baxter.

Cromwell showed his love for true religion, in the interest he took in the poor persecuted Waldenses, and his uniform respect for the rights of conscience, by which all were equally protected in the free exercise of public worship. Cromwell died in 1658.

CHARLES II.—Upon his restoration, Episcopacy was reëstablished, when the persecution of the Puritans was recommenced. Among other disgraceful acts he passed, was the "Act of Uniformity."

This was designed to bring all ministers to adopt the Book of Common Prayer, wear the popish garments, in short, yield to prelacy. It took effect on St. Bartholomew's day, August 24th, 1662.

Heavy was the trial the Puritans had to pass, when, on the fatal day, being Sunday, they were taking leave of their congregations and parishes, rather than yield to the intolerant and unrighteous act of the king. Turned out of home and employ; exposed to hunger, nakedness, and the fury of their persecutors; and all "for righteousness' sake."

But the "Conventicle Act" was found necessary, to check the operation of the Act of Uniformity.

By the first, the ministers were ejected, and the people followed them; the Conventicle Act was designed to break up all their private meetings; and whoever was found at any meetings, except where they used the form of Common Prayer, the magistrate was empowered to levy five pounds upon each person, or imprison for three months, for the first offence; ten pounds for the second offence, or six months in prison; for the third offence, one hundred pounds, or be transported for seven years; and if they returned, or escaped, death, without benefit of clergy. The jails were quickly filled.

And to prevent even family religion, informers (spies, prelatical Jesuits), were well paid for informing against the Puritans. They were driven at last, according to Christ's words, and as many before them had been, "into the dens and caves of the earth."

The "Five Mile Act" forms the climax of Charles the Second's devices for persecution. It aimed at depriving the Dissenters of the means of living. An oath was first required, which some noble lords then said, "no honest man could take." In case of refusal, it restrained all ministers from coming within five miles of any place where they had ever preached, on penalty of forty pounds for every offence: one third to the king, one to the poor, and one to the informer. O, prelacy! prelacy!

The Earl of Castlemain, a Roman Catholic, said: "It was never known that Roman Catholics persecuted, as the bishops do, those who adhere to the same faith with themselves, and establish an inquisition against the professors of the strictest piety among themselves; for, however bloody the persecutions of Queen Mary, ... under their persecution above treble have been rifled, destroyed, and ruined, in their estates, liberties, and lives; being, as is most remarkable, of the same spirit as those who suffered under Queen Mary." During the reigns of Charles II. and James II., eight thousand perished in prison, and seventy thousand families were ruined in England.

Judge Jeffries. — Under James II. and Jeffries, were enacted the last scenes of infernal prelacy. James sought to enforce Popery on the realm, when the nation united and dethroned him; putting in his place his son-in-law, Prince of Orange.

Petitions poured in, in behalf of friends in prison, guilty of no offence whatever, except want of *conformity to the rites of the Church of England.* No one was safe from apprehension and imprisonment.

Of Jeffries' circuit through the western counties, Bishop Burnet says: "In several places in the west, there were executed near six hundred persons; and that the quarters of two or three hundred were fixed on gibbets, and hung on trees, all over the country for fifty miles around, to the terror of travellers."

Jeffries himself, in his savage, brutal, infernal glory, boasted that he had "hanged more than all the judges of England, since the time of William the Conquerer." Upon his return from his bloody work, he was rewarded with the title of "Lord High Chancellor." O, England! England!

But this is the finale: Jeffries has the honor (?) of being the last practical butcher of saints.

Upon the accession of William, Episcopacy was declared the established religion; Catholics were excluded from holding any office in the nation; but *free toleration* was granted to all dissenters from the Church of England, except Socinians.

Religious liberty triumphant in England, over both Prelacy and Popery!

Archbishop Tillotson, of Canterbury, is said to be the author of the custom of preaching with notes. Origen was the author of the custom of taking a single text for the subject of a sermon.

CHURCH OF SCOTLAND.

The progress of events in England, had their influence in Scotland, and need not be rehearsed.

Only a few things in addition will be noticed.

Patrick Hamilton. — The tocsin of reform was first rung in Scotland, by the death of Patrick Hamilton, a youth of noble descent, who, returning from a stay in Germany of two years, began to propagate the new opinions.

To check this bold fellow, the papal party put him to death, in 1528. Hamilton's death appearing unjust to the Scots, they were determined to know what these "new doctrines" meant.

This inquiry led to the conversion of many of them, and further aroused a spirit of inquiry in the nation, that Popery could not check.

John Knox. — He was designed, in early life, for the ministry; and so, when young, gave great attention to the study of divinity. The persecution then raging in the country, compelled him to flee elsewhere.

During his exile, he learned of Calvin, at Geneva, and from him adopted the Presbyterian form of church discipline and order.

In 1559, however, he was in his native land, laboring zealously and successfully in promoting the cause of the Reformation. Like Luther in Germany, Knox, in Scotland, infused his spirit into the nation. He was styled the "Apostle of Scotland." He died November 4th, 1572. In his eulogium, pronounced as he was laid in the grave, was the following: "*There lies he who never feared the face of man.*"

Still, Knox had the fault of prelates, popes, and of too many Puritans (?); viz., a spirit of persecution. In *responding* to a sharp rebuke he received, for cherishing such a spirit, to which he could not *reply*, he said: "I will not now so much labor to confute, by my pen, as my full purpose is to lay the same to thy charge, if I shall apprehend thee in any commonwealth where justice against blasphemers may be ministered, as God's word requireth."

This is the papal argument, when wit and wisdom fail.

The Scots early adopted for their platform the "Westminster Confession of Faith." The attempts of prelacy to force the liturgy and popish garments upon the Scotch clergy, met with the most determined resistance.

Charles II. attempted, by sword and surplice, to bend the Scots to prelacy, but was at last obliged to desist, and Presbyterianism prevailed, in 1648.

An example of the Scotch spirit is given, on an occasion when an English prelate was sent into Scotland, to conduct worship out of the "Book of Common Prayer." Taking it as an imposition, immediately followed proper resentment. As soon as the reading began, an old lady arose, took the stool on which she sat, and hurled it, with laudable zeal, at the prelate's head. Quickly followed the cry: "Pope! Antichrist! Stone him! stone him!" and the stones flew, to the great interruption of the prelate.

Neither British armies nor British prelates could subject the Scotch to the mummeries of superstition.

Scotland shared with England in the establishment of free toleration in 1688, — about one hundred and thirteen years after the Peace of Religion, — since which time, she, with other parts of Christendom, has shared the blessing of God.

MORAVIANS, OR UNITED BRETHREN.

This branch of Christians has been noticed. They had their origin in the fifteenth century, under the labors, examples, and sufferings of Huss and Jerome.

They were the first church of Reformers; the first who renounced the Church of Rome, and formed themselves into a separate communion. They continue to the present time. (See Hussites.)

PERIOD II. FROM LANDING OF PILGRIMS, TO THE PRESENT TIME.

CONGREGATIONALISTS.

This sect sprung up in England, and, being desirous of a *purer* church, separated from the English Establishment about 1602,—

resolved, "whatever it should cost them," to enjoy liberty of conscience.

The first church had for its first pastor, Mr. Richard Clifton. The second pastor was Mr. John Robinson, a convert under Mr. Clifton's preaching, and Mr. William Brewster, elder and teacher.

At this time intolerance was rife, and soon such a class as this were made its victims. Exile alone promised shelter from the menaces of prelacy; and even this was difficult, as the emigration of Puritans was strictly forbidden. The prelates meant to *keep* them, and *crush* them.

Their departure was attended with difficulty.

Once they were betrayed by seamen, although they had paid them large fees for their services. At another time, they got on board a ship, the master sailed a little way and returned, delivering them up to their enemies. The next year they made another attempt. A few had got on board, with none of their effects though; their wives and children were coming in a barque. At this juncture, a posse of armed men came upon them, when the captain, fearing trouble, set sail, leaving the women to fall into the hands of English Lauds, Jeffries, etc. No persuasion would induce him to return.

In their voyage, a fearful storm arose, which raged seven days, without intermission. They were driven upon the coast of Norway. The sailors' cry arose: "The ship is foundered! She sinks! she sinks!" But the pilgrims' cry arose: "Yet, Lord, thou canst save! — yet, Lord, thou canst save!" Soon, to the astonishment of all, the ship began to rise, and outrode the storm. On their arrival at Holland, they gave most devout thanks to God for their safety.

During the twelve years they lived in Holland, they enjoyed peace; still, sighing for a better land, this side the heavenly. It was finally concluded that Mr. Brewster, and a part of the church, should go to America, designing that Mr. Robinson and the rest should follow; but his death occurred before time to emigrate. His family, and the rest of the church, followed in time.

Preparation being made for removal, one hundred and one souls sailed from Plymouth, England, on September 6th, 1620. Upon an island in Plymouth harbor, they hallowed the first Christian Sabbath in New England.

On the 22d of December, 1620, they stepped upon the strand at "Plymouth Rock." Upon their bended knees they thanked the God of Heaven, who had preserved their number entire, and permitted them to land safely.

Their number was also increased by one during the voyage.

Ralph Smith. — This church in the wilderness was without a regular pastor for nine years, though having the labors of Mr. Brewster. In 1629, Ralph Smith became its pastor: the first New England pastor.

Soon others began to flock to America, where to enjoy liberty of conscience, and settled at Salem, Charlestown, Roxbury, and around about.

In August 6th, 1629, the first Church of the Pilgrims was formed, in Salem, the church at Plymouth sending delegates, by invitation — Mr. Skelton, the pastor. August 27th, 1630, a church was formed at Charlestown; soon after, one at Dorchester; the fourth, at Boston. Soon after, one in Roxbury; one in Lynn, and one at Watertown. In less than two years from the formation of the first church in Salem, there were seven in the colony: like "*seven golden candlesticks.*"

As might be expected, the increase of numbers in the colony would be likely to bring in diversity of sentiments. The first case of this kind occurred in the church at Salem, 1634.

Roger Williams, one of its ministers, advanced sentiments uncongenial to the settled opinions of the colonists, and, being unwilling to "*recant,*" the magistrates, disregarding his rights of conscience, banished him beyond the limits of the colony, to seek in exile, as they had done, freedom to worship God.

Sad tale, yet true: the *fire* — yes, *fire* — of persecution was lighted in Salem. The ashes of martyrs were sown on the virgin soil of America.

This is a problem hard to be solved. For a people who, only twenty-five years before, had been chased into exile like pirates, for conscience' sake, and fled to America to escape prelacy, should inflict the same diabolism upon one of their own friends and ministers, for opinion's sake! Where is Jeffries?

Religious liberty, in coming to America, came near getting murdered. Efforts at oneness of sentiment were made, in shape of platforms and covenants, with persecutions, until a better day dawned.

In 1646, at Cambridge, was formed the "*Cambridge Platform;*" in 1657, at Boston, the "*Half-way Covenant;*" in 1708, was formed the "*Saybrook Platform.*"

As soon, however, as it was discovered that persecution for conscience' sake was contrary to the Scriptures, it was abandoned; and now religious liberty adorns the churches and the nation.

BAPTISTS.

This sect of Christians claim their origin to have been in the time and person of John the Baptist.

Whilst they claim that churches existed in the times of the apostles, and have ever since, holding similar views with themselves, yet they do not place so much stress upon the argument of *Apostolic Succession*, as, that their aim and purpose is, to maintain the apostolic order in church matters. They aim, very earnestly, at skilfulness in understanding the things "written to the churches;" calling no one master but Christ, and admitting no code of faith and discipline but exactly accords with the Bible.

Doctor Mosheim says: "The true origin of the Anabaptists (as he calls them), is hid in the remote depths of antiquity, and is, of course, extremly difficult to be ascertained. There were some among the Waldenses, Albigenses, Petro-brussians, and other ancient sects, who appear to have entertained the notions of the Anabaptists."

In the days of the Reformation, they bore no little share of malignity and persecution from the enemies of truth; and even from the great Reformer himself, they were compelled to feel the force of his disapprobation.

During the reign of Henry VIII., some of them fled from persecution at home, and took refuge in England. But here they were cruelly persecuted, and many of them put to death. Every faith, under the reign of Henry and Cranmer, except Prelacy, felt the weight of their intolerance. In the reign of Elizabeth, they were banished from England, and took refuge in Holland.

In 1608, some of the Independents in England separated from their own communion, sent one of their number to Holland to be baptized by the Dutch Anabaptists; returning to England, he baptized the rest of the society, about fifty in number. From this time they put away the *Ana*, attached to their name, and adopted that of Baptists.

For many years the English Baptists suffered in common with the other dissenters, especially during the reign of the infamous Court of High Commission and the Star Chamber; and in 1662, by an act of uniformity, of Charles II., were ejected from their pulpits.

The year 1684, is the period of Bunyan's death.

At the Revolution, in 1688, on the accession of William of Orange, the Baptists, with other "dissenters," gained a legal toleration, which they have enjoyed to the present time.

But America proved, in those troublous times, the asylum for the oppressed.

The banishment of Roger Williams from Massachusetts, though an act of persecution, was overruled, in the providence of God, for the greatest possible good to mankind.

Driven from the sheltering care of the pilgrims, to seek a home where he could, in the wilderness and among the red men of America, he wandered about, until he saw human forms in Providence Bay; and putting the question to them, "What cheer?" was answered, "Good cheer;" he landed.

The beautiful city of Providence, Rhode Island, marks the spot where the pilgrim set foot from the troubled ocean, and from the raging waves of persecution; and, in gratitude for heavenly guidance and care, he named the hallowed place "*Providence.*"

In 1636, Roger Williams, having purchased territory of the Indians, commenced to found a colony, on the express principles of *religious liberty.* In 1638, others having joined him, and purchased the territory of the present State of Rhode Island, a voluntary government was formally instituted, by a solemn covenant of all, to "submit to the order of the major part, *in civil things only.*"

Behold the child, Religious Liberty, born in 1526, under Doctor Luther, now come of age, and set up for himself, under his last guardian, Roger Williams.

Here are dissolved the banns of wedlock, solemnized by the Emperor Constantine, between the Roman Empire and the Christian Church, in 306, divorced by Roger Williams, in 1638.

This was the first State Constitution ever formed upon the principle of perfect religious liberty.

This is putting into practice the great sentiment of Jesus Christ: "Render unto Cæsar the things that are Cæsar's; and to God the things that are God's."

The first Baptist Church in America was formed in 1639, at Providence, Rhode Island, by Roger Williams.

Bancroft has justly said: "If Copernicus is held in perpetual reverence, because on his death-bed he published to the world that the sun is the centre of our system; if the name of Kepler is preserved in the annals of human excellence for his sagacity in detecting the laws of planetary motion; if the genius of Newton has been almost adored for dissecting a ray of light, and weighing the heavenly bodies in a balance, — let there be for the name of *Roger Williams* at least some humble place among those who have advanced moral science, and made themselves the benefactors of mankind."

If Claude of Turin be regarded as the author of the Reformation, certainly Williams of Providence was the finisher.

The Baptists are still the earnest defenders of the Bible, as the rule of faith, and religious liberty, as the inalienable right of *all men.*

METHODISTS.

JOHN WESLEY. — This sect owe their origin to John Wesley, a native of England, born 1703. While a tutor in the University of Oxford, 1729 (where the celebrated Wickliffe was Professor of Divinity, in about 1350), Wesley became impressed with the importance of a deeper attention to spiritual things.

Being joined by some students, among them George Whitefield, their devotion and reserve in manners soon gained for them, by way of derision, the name of "*Methodists*," none thinking to what this little band would grow.

Though the Methodists had their rise after the fearful battles for religious liberty were fought, and the Peace of Religion established, yet they have the honor of being the first sect of great note that arose after the Reformation; and were also the leaders in the first general revival of religion, on both sides of the Atlantic, after freedom to worship God was obtained.

The popularity and increase of the Methodists was such, that Mr. Wesley was invited to accompany a new colony to Georgia, under General Oglethorpe, as spiritual guide, and also to preach to the Indians.

Mr. Wesley found, soon after his return from Georgia, a large number who acknowledged him as their religious leader, and whom he gradually organized into a distinct sect. The first society was organized in London.

Wesley died in 1791, aged eighty-seven, and the sixty-fifth of his ministry; having travelled three hundred thousand miles, and preached forty thousand sermons.

The year 1766 marks the introduction of Methodism into America. In 1784, the American Methodists became independent of those in England. The first American Bishop was Francis Asbury. The increase of this zealous people has been very rapid.

GEORGE WHITEFIELD.— Meanwhile, Mr. Whitefield was preaching with great success in England. He was ordained in the Church of England, June 30th, 1736. At this time he received letters from Wesley, to come to America, which he did, in 1736. He returned in the following year to England, received priest's orders, and, for want of churches, commenced preaching in the open air, with great success.

Whitefield visited America again in 1739, and returned to England in 1741.

During this absence, Mr. Wesley had changed his views somewhat, upon the doctrine of Perfection, and against Election, which caused a separation between him and Whitefield, which is continued to this day between their followers.

Whitefield, nevertheless, continued to preach, both sides of the ocean, with unabated popularity and success. He closed this life at Newburyport, Mass., 1770, having crossed the Atlantic fourteen times, and been the means of bringing thousands to embrace the gospel and the Lord Jesus Christ.

He never formed his followers into a distinct sect, but continued a member of the English Establishment himself, and advised them to follow his example. After his death, however, they formed a union, and are known by the name of *Whitefield*, or *Calvinistic Methodists.*

Mr. Whitefield said in his will: "I leave a mourning-ring to my honored and dear friends and disinterested fellow-laborers, the Reverends John and Charles Wesley, in token of my indissoluble union with them in heart and affection, notwithstanding our difference in judgment about some particular points of doctrine."

MISSIONS.

The eighteenth century was one pregnant and prolific of great men and measures for the advancement of the Church of Christ among all the nations of the earth.

Missionary Societies, Sabbath Schools, Bible and Tract Societies, all rushed to the glorious work of giving to the nations of the earth the treasures of the Word of Life.

Indeed, the night of despotism, with here and there a twinkling star, had continued from the creation to the Peace of Religion, or until the invention of printing, and the revival of Bible faith and Bible reading. No measure ever did half so much for the establishment of civil and religious liberty in the world, as the free circulation of the Bible among all nations, and in all the dialects of the earth. The Lord speed and establish the knowledge of himself throughout the earth!

JUDSON. — Much had been done in behalf of Missions in England previous to Judson's time; but his name stands at the head of the missionary enterprise in America.

Having, with others, imbibed the desire to go forth to the benighted, no discouragements nor persuasions would induce him to yield the darling purpose. This purpose was laid before the Massachusetts General Association.

In accordance with a suggestion of Doctors Worcester and Spring, the American Board of Commissioners for Foreign Missions was agreed upon and chosen, June 29th, 1810.

Judson was immediately sent to England, to ascertain if a connection could be formed with the London Missionary Society. Finding them reluctant to make the connection with the Board in America, he then solicited an appointment as missionaries of himself and colleagues, by the London Society, in case the American Board should fail to send them.

This being done, Judson returned to America, full of hope, and reported the result of his visit to London. The Board were not prepared to send them at once, and the London Society declined the proposed union.

An alternative presented itself: the Board must *send* them, or *lose* them. The faith of the Board was hardly equal to the task; and yet they must do something. At this juncture, the ardent and hopeful spirit of Judson manifested a little independence of manner towards the Board. Relying upon his appointment by the London Society, he intimated to the Board that his way was clear, and that their coöperation was not essential.

It was not altogether the most agreeable condition to be placed in, for the power of destiny to be so completely monopolized by these youths, and the fathers put at bay; but God here had a purpose to fulfil.

The Board stepped forward to the task of sending them; and from this event arose the spirit of Missions in America.

On the fifth of February, 1812, Mr. Judson, and Miss Ann Hasseltine, were married. On the sixth, he was ordained at Salem, in company with Messrs. Nott, Newell, Hall, and Rice.

On the nineteenth of February, 1812, Mr. and Mrs. Judson, and Mr. and Mrs. Newell, embarked at Salem, in the brig *Caravan*, Captain Heard, bound for Calcutta. Nott, Hall, and Rice sailed in the *Harmony*, from Philadelphia.

This was the inauguration of Missions in America. Soon it pervaded all branches of the Christian Church, and great good has been done thereby.

During Judson's last days, he said: "The salvation of six thousand Burmans amply rewards all my feeble toil."

In review, no student of the History of Religion can fail to see that God has ever had a people and a cause, in all ages of the world; and can easily conceive, that no emergency can arise more difficult than has already been; and hence, finally, that God ever will have a name and a people while the world stands.

So let it be. AMEN.

BOOK II.

HISTORY OF EMPIRE.

I.

PATRIARCHAL AGE.

FROM THE CREATION TO THE FLOOD.

SUBJECT — PROFANE HISTORY.

Empire has a history as well as religion; still we find that God has not been so careful to preserve in existence any distinct civil community, from the creation down, as he has a people to serve him "in spirit and in truth."

Religion is first in time, as well as in importance, to individuals and nations.

Caindom. — The beginning of empire, before the flood, was with Cain. After his rejection from the Lord, he took his wife and went into a section called "Nod," *i. e.*, wandering and vagabondage, so named because he was to be a wanderer and vagabond while he lived; — his punishment for the murder of Abel. He was not cut off from having children, for he knew his wife, and she bare him a son, and called his name Enoch. Soon Cain founded a city, and called it after his son, Enoch, — the first city ever built.

This formed a nucleus, from which similar enterprises originated, and the march of empire took its course.

Jabal. — The early necessities and fancies of mankind were similar to what they are now. Hence we find Jabal applying himself to the raising of cattle; and, instead of building a city and locating himself, he lived in movable tents, thus originating the shepherd's mode of life, still kept up by the Arabs. The convenience of a wandering mode of life for plunder and piracy, by land and sea, has caused it to be prolific in those high crimes.

Jubal. — Such is the innate character of music, that we find, within two hundred years from the Creation, it was reduced by Jubal both to a *science* and an *art*. He invented, and could *handle*, the *harp* and *organ*, and was doubtless the first music teacher and player.

Tubal Cain. — He seems to have discovered the art of working the metals, particularly brass and iron. Implements of husbandry, hunting, and warfare, were doubtless the first made and used. Tubal Cain is supposed to be the *Vulcan* of mythology, — "the blacksmith of hell." Also Naamah, his sister, is the *Venus* of mythology.

Parties. — Thus inaugurated, we may easily imagine the world would go on, much as in later times. "There were giants in those days, ... mighty men, ... men of renown." Such characters would naturally attract attention, and draw followers after them. A little pride of party would soon grow into boasting, which would lead to a challenge, and that to a fight. The fight over, those who were victorious would exact something of the vanquished, which would humble them, and gratify the pride of the conquerors. Out of this would naturally grow a government of chiefs, — the first and most natural form of government.

Pride of conquest would next inflame the breasts of these chiefs, and hence, as we find stated, "violence and wickedness" would fill the earth.

In the trail of conquest is generally found all that debases. Hence God, "seeing the thoughts of the imagination of man's heart were evil, and that continually," which would be the case in the study and pursuit of warfare, determined to put an end to conquest and empire by a deluge.

Noah's Family. — After the flood, God renewed the privileges to Noah and his family that he granted to Adam, namely, of dominion over the animals, and possession of the world.

Accordingly, we find them rapidly spreading over the East, each tribe bearing the name of its progenitor, *e. g.*, Assyrians, from Asshur; Elamites, from Elam; Lydians, from Lud; Medes, from Madai; Ionians, from Javan; Thracians, from Tiras; Gauls, from Gomer; Axenus, or Euxine Sea, from Ashkenaz; Moguls, and Muscovites, from Magog; Palestine, from Pathrusim; Jerusalem, from Jebus; Padanaram, from Aram. Shem's descendants peopled the East; Ham's, Africa, Palestine, and Arabia. Japheth's, peopled Europe.

I.—AGE PATRIARCHAL.

BABYLON.

PERIOD I. FROM NIMROD, 1771 A. M., 2233 B. C., TO SARDANAPALUS, 3184 A. M., 820 B. C.

Babel. — Soon after the flood, an attempt was made to build a tower on the plain of Shinar, "whose top should reach to heaven."

The enterprise being offensive to God, he put an end to it by the "confusion of tongues," which disabled the builders for prosecuting their work, and a dispersion followed.

NINEVEH. — This was the first city founded after the flood; — 1775 A. M., 2229 B. C. Asshur, son of Shem, is said to have been its founder.

It grew to be fifteen miles in length, nine broad, and forty-seven in circumference. On the walls, which were one hundred feet high, three chariots could pass abreast. It had on the walls fifteen hundred towers, each two hundred feet high. In the time of Jonah, its inhabitants amounted to six hundred thousand.

BABYLON. — Nimrod, grandson of Ham, is said to have been the founder of this city. He is supposed to be the "Belus" of profane history; hence the first man who was made an object of worship.

Chedorlaomer, a king of Elam (or Babylon), was repulsed by Abraham.

Babylon and Nineveh, though separate, were, from time to time, made alternately the seat of empire.

NINUS, — Son of Belus, or Nimrod, succeeded his father as sovereign, or chief. Becoming enamored with the wife of one of his officers, he married her after her *husband's death.* He was a warrior, and made several conquests.

SEMIRAMIS. — She is said to have been the wife of Ninus (mentioned above, but very doubtful); she took the throne after the death of her husband. She was possessed of exquisite beauty, and an heroic soul. She enlarged and beautified Babylon, making walls around the city, quays, bridge, a lake, canals and banks for draining the river (possibly the means Cyrus used to take Babylon), the palace, hanging gardens, and the temple of Belus.

To do all these works, she employed two millions of men.

Babylon stood four square, with the points of compass; the Euphrates divided it equally from north to south. Its walls were eighty-seven feet thick, three hundred and fifty feet high, and sixty miles long, and stood in an exact square. On each side of this great square were twenty gates of solid brass. From each gate ran streets, crossing each other at right angles — in all, fifty. Next the walls, inside and around the city, was a street two hundred feet wide, the rest being one hundred and fifty wide. The city was thus cut into squares; these were surrounded with houses, three and four stories high. The areas within the squares were filled up with yards, gardens, and pleasure grounds.

Her last attempt at conquest failed. This she made upon an Indian king. He disputed the passage of the river Indus with her, in a bloody battle; but she finally drove him. Leaving sixty thousand men to guard a bridge, made of boats, she pursued him into the country. After retreating as far as he cared to, he faced about, gave her battle, and drove her back. In this battle, more bloody than the first, he received two wounds. She returned with only one-third of her army (a type of Napoleon's campaign to Russia).

Finding, soon after, that Ninias, her son, was plotting against her, she abdicated; or, as it is thought, Ninias procured her assassination.

NINIAS.—He was unlike his predecessors; instead of being a "mighty one," he was intent on pleasure. He lived in retirement, and held power by keeping trusty officers, and changing his soldiers yearly, to prevent conspiracies between them and the officers.

SARDANAPALUS.—He is represented as one of the most effeminate of mankind. He adopted the dress of females, spun with them, and spent his time with his women and eunuchs. His city being besieged, he gathered his women, eunuchs, and treasures, into his palace, set fire to it, and all perished together. His kingdom fell into the hands of the conspirators, who had become disgusted with him, namely, Arbaces, became King of Media; Belesis, of Babylon; and Pul, of Assyria.

II.

AGE OF WAR FOR POWER.

PROFANE HISTORY.

PERIOD II. FROM SARDANAPALUS, 3184 A. M., 820 B. C., TO BELSHAZZAR, 3466 A. M., 538 B. C.

PUL. — Supposed to be the King of Nineveh, who, with his people, repented at the preaching of Jonah. He also made war upon Menahem, of Israel, and exacted of him a heavy tribute.

TIGLATH-PILESER. — He conquered that portion of Israel east of Jordan, and carried off many captives.

SHALMANESER. — He put an end to the Ten Tribes of Israel, carrying them into captivity, and repeopling their country with Cuthites.

SENNACHERIB. — He invaded Judah, wrote a most blasphemous letter to Hezekiah, and prepared to besiege Jerusalem. But the angel of the Lord destroyed one hundred and eighty-five thousand of his army in one night, whereupon he returned to his own country in disgrace. His two sons murdered him, in his temple of Nisroch, in Babylon.

NEBUCHADNEZZAR I. — About one hundred and eight years after Sennacherib, he ruled in Babylon. Destroying Nineveh, and putting an end to the Assyrian Monarchy, he made Babylon the seat of empire.

NEBUCHADNEZZAR II. — He destroyed Jerusalem, robbed the temple, and carried the Jews captive to Babylon.

BELSHAZZAR. — He succeeded to the throne, and was the last of the Kings of Babylon. During the siege of the city, he held a sumptuous feast with his court.

Whilst engaged in his riotings, profanely using the golden vessels of the temple taken by Nebuchadnezzar, he was surprised by a hand writing on the wall of his "house of feasting."

Regardless of what was going on without, Cyrus, the Persian, had now succeeded in turning the river Euphrates, and marched his army through the arch in the wall, and entered Babylon in triumph. In that night Belshazzar was slain, and the Persian Monarchy set up.

How insignificant is empire, unaccompanied with some direct measure for the benefit of mankind!

PERSIA.

PERIOD I. FROM CYRUS, 3466 A M., 533 B. C., TO DARIUS CODOMANUS, 3680 A. M., 324 B. C.

The first inhabitants of Persia were called Elamites, From Elam, eldest son of Shem. Little is known of them for sixteen centuries. Chedorlaomer, interfered with the King of Sodom, and was repulsed by Abraham.

Dejoces, is mentioned as the first king of the Medes, 690 B. C. Astyages and Cyaxares II. are mentioned also as kings of Medes. The former marrying his daughter to Cambyses, King of Persia, Cyrus was the issue.

Cyaxares (Cyrus' uncle) and Cyrus united against Babylon, and, by cutting deep and large ditches beside the Euphrates, opened the gates and drained the river, and thereby took the city.

Cyrus. — After two years' associate reign with Cyaxares, Cyrus was sole monarch of the most important countries of the East. Cyrus is represented as a very amiable and temperate youth, refusing even to taste wine, when acting as cup-bearer, on a visit to Astyages, his grandfather.

Among the captives of Cyrus, was Crœsus, King of the Lydians. After Crœsus was taken prisoner, he was condemned to be burnt alive. While being led to the funeral pile, he exclaimed aloud: "Solon! Solon! Solon!"

On being asked why he repeated that celebrated philosopher's name with such vehemence at that time, he said that Solon's remark, that "no mortal could be esteemed happy till the end of life," had forcibly recurred to him. Cyrus was so struck with this sentiment, that he released Crœsus from his fate, and ever after treated him with great respect. This was the wealthy person about whom the proverb is made: "*Rich as Crœsus.*"

The name of Cyrus is memorable for the famous edict he passed in the first year of his reign, for the return of the *Jews*, and the rebuilding of their temple at Jerusalem. His reign is said to have been a model one. In an expedition against the Scythians, he was surprised and slain by an ambuscade, 529 B. C.

Cambyses. — Cyrus was succeeded by his son Cambyses, called in Scripture Artaxerxes. He added Egypt to the Persian realm, and it remained so one hundred and twelve years.

He took Pelusium, the "Key of Egypt," by the stratagem of

placing a drove of animals, considered sacred by the Egyptians, in front of his army, and so entered the city without resistance.

DARIUS. — After the usurpation of Smerdis, of seven months, Darius was elected to the throne. He renewed the edict for the rebuilding of the Jewish temple, after the work had been hindered.

Acmetha, where the rolls were found containing the decree of Cyrus for the return of the Jews, is thus described: The building of the city is ascribed to Semiramis by some. "It was surrounded by seven walls, strong and ample, built in circles, one within another, rising one above the other by the height of their respective battlements, each distinguished by a different color, — the first white, the second black, the third purple, the fourth blue, the fifth orange, the sixth plated with silver, the seventh with gold. Within the inner circle stood the king's palace and the royal treasury." The circumference of the outer wall was two hundred and fifty furlongs.

The Asiatic Greeks attempted to throw off the Persian yoke, and were assisted by the Athenians. Whereupon Darius marched his armies into Greece, purposing its entire conquest. He was beaten at the celebrated battle of Marathon.

XERXES. — He was the son of Darius, and made the second invasion of Greece, with the largest army ever known. During this campaign, the battle of Thermopylæ was fought. After several severe losses, Xerxes returned, having suffered a total defeat.

DARIUS NOTHUS. — Under him, the tenth King of Persia, the Egyptians recovered their government from Persia.

ARTAXERXES MNEMON. — So called from his prodigious memory. He is said to have retained the name of each one of his soldiers, and remembered every act of his life. (See Adrian, of Rome.) His brother Cyrus employed ten thousand Greeks to aid in obtaining the Persian throne. Cyrus was killed. The Greek general being also killed, the army chose Xenophon to conduct them home: called the "Retreat of the Ten Thousand."

DARIUS CODOMANUS. — He was the fourteenth and last king of Persia, and was overthrown by Alexander the Great, 331 B. C. So ends the second great empire of antiquity.

I.—AGE PATRIARCHAL.

EGYPT—FROM MENES TO CLEOPATRA.

PERIOD I. FROM MENES, 1816 A. M., 2188 B. C., TO THE END OF THE SHEPHERD KINGS, 2244 A. M., AND 1760 B. C.

Menes. — He was the founder of Egyptian empire, and is supposed to be Mizraim, one of the sons of Ham.

He appears to have been very popular, — his wisdom and abilities rendered him so. He built the tower of Memphis. After his death, he was worshipped as a god, as was Nimrod. His children divided the realm into four kingdoms — Thebes, Thin, Memphis, and Tanais.

In the kingdom of Thebes, Athothes I. reigned at an early period. He was afterwards worshipped as Mercury.

Thebes is mentioned by Homer, under the name Hecatompylos; *i. e.*, having one hundred gates. In the time of its splendor, it could send into the field, by each of its gates, two hundred chariots, and two thousand fighting men. Its extent was fifty-two miles. So great was its wealth, that, after it had been plundered by the Persians, seven and a half millions of dollars in gold, and one and a half in silver, were gathered as gleanings.

Tosorthros reigned in Memphis not long after Menes. From his knowledge of physic, he was styled Esculapius. He also invented the arts of building and writing.

Timaus. — He is the last of the Menean kings; as, under his reign, Egypt was invaded by a fierce race of shepherds, from the east, who conquered the country.

Shepherd Kings. — These were literally shepherds, who invaded Egypt, about two thousand years before Christ. Like most conquerors, they destroyed the strong men, so as to weaken the nation for war, and reduced the women and children to slavery. Indeed, whatever was necessary to render themselves masters of the country, they failed not to do.

They very soon fortified a place called Avaris (and "The Pass," also Pelusium), and garrisoned it with two hundred and forty thousand soldiers, as a protection against the Assyrians, who, they feared, might follow their own example of conquest.

Cheops. — Wishing to keep the natives employed, and so quiet, Cheops, or *Ruchma* — so surnamed from his immense wealth — commenced the first of the pyramids, those standing monuments of ancient ostentation and tyranny.

He shut the temples, and reduced the people at once to the condition of slaves. Some were sent into the Arabian mountains to hew stones, and drag them to the Nile; others set to transport them in boats to the edge of the Lybian Desert.

In this service one hundred thousand men were employed, being relieved every three months. Ten years were spent in preparing the hill on which the pyramid was built, and in excavating chambers under ground, and preparing a causeway on which to transport the stones, — the latter being covered with polished marble, ornamented with the figures of animals.

The pyramid itself was a work of twenty years. It is of square form, and rising to a point in the centre, the base covering eleven acres of ground, and its height five hundred feet. After being laid in very strong cement, it was coated from the top downwards. The items of expense were recorded in Egyptian characters upon the structure; one item of which was for radishes, onions, and garlic, consumed by the workmen, amounting to forty millions of dollars.

Cephrenes. — He was brother of Cheops; pursued the same policy, and built a smaller pyramid. The aversion for these two kings was such, that the Egyptians mentioned their names, even, with the greatest reluctance.

This circumstance explains the allusion of Joseph, when directing his brethren to report themselves to Pharaoh as cattle-men, instead of shepherds; "for every shepherd is an abomination to the Egyptians."

After ruling Egypt about two hundred and fifty years, the Egyptian princes rebelled against these tyrants, and drove them out.

The shepherds, however, retreated to Avaris, where the Egyptians found they could not be taken, and, by a treaty on both sides, the shepherds were allowed to depart peaceably. About two hundred and forty thousand souls left Egypt, and, fearing Assyria, they settled in Judea, and built Jerusalem. From the words *pali* (shepherds), and *stan* (land), it is easy to see that *Palistan*, or Palestine, is meant. Hence the "Shepherd Kings" were the progenitors of the more modern "Philistines."

Besides the pyramids, Egypt boasts also of its Thebes, with one hundred gates; its Labyrinth, with one thousand chambers, and its vast mummy-pits.

A domestic custom among the Egyptians, was to mix their *dough* with their *feet*, and temper their *mortar* with their *hands*.

II.—AGE OF WAR FOR POWER.

PERIOD II. FROM SHEPHERD KINGS, 2244 A. M., AND 1760 B. C., TO ALEXANDER THE GREAT, 3668 A. M., 336 B. C.

Mœris.—He is a renowned King of Egypt. His great work was an artificial lake, bearing his name, fifty miles in length, and ten in width. Its design was to take up the surplus waters of the Nile, and return them gradually at low water.

Egypt exhibits great advance in the knowledge of mechanics, medicine, and astronomy. Yet, with all this "light of nature," they were confirmed and stupid idolaters.

Nitocris.—She is supposed to have begun to reign 1678 B. C. She had revenge upon some of her subjects, for the death of her brother, by inviting a large number of them to a feast, in an underground room, and then turning the river, through a secret passage, upon them. She was then obliged to flee to a tower, to escape the rage of the people. She was extremely beautiful, and equally cruel.

Sesostris.—He is the first Egyptian conqueror. He formed the design of conquering the world, and set out with six hundred thousand foot, twenty-four thousand horse, and twenty-seven thousand armed chariots. His conquests were extensive, and he returned laden with spoils. He enriched his country with useful works and magnificent edifices.

He was very insolent to the kings and chiefs he conquered, having harnessed some of them, four abreast, to his car, to draw him to his temple, instead of horses. In his old age he lost his sight, and, weak and wicked, laid violent hands upon himself.

Apophis.—He is supposed to have been the Pharaoh drowned in the Red Sea.

Amosis.—He abolished human sacrifices, and conquered Heliopolis.

Hermes Trismegistes.—He is celebrated for his philosophical writings. He added five days to the year, which before consisted of three hundred and sixty.

Actisanes—King of Ethiopia, united Egypt to his kingdom. He hunted the Egyptian robbers, cut off their noses, and banished them to Rhinocolura, in the desert, a town he built for the special benefit of the *noseless*.

Cetes—Refused hospitality to Paris and Helen, in their elopement.

SHISHAK, — King of Egypt, besieged and pillaged Jerusalem, in the reign of Rehoboam. He built many temples and cities, and dug canals.

RAMASES. — His peculiarity was avarice. He did nothing, either for the gods or the people, by way of munificence. His private treasure amounted to ten thousand millions of dollars.

Amenophis and Thuoris, who succeeded, were of little note.

SABBACON, OR SO. — He was an Ethiopian; conquered Egypt. While there, acquired a reputation for wisdom and integrity. He voluntarily relinquished the sceptre of Egypt, and returned to Ethiopia. This was the So, King of Egypt, with whom Hoshea, King of Israel, made a league against Shalmaneser, King of Assyria.

THARACA. — He is called, in Scripture, Tirhakah. He made war with Sennacherib, King of Assyria. After him, there was an anarchy of two years, and an aristocracy of twelve governors, for fifteen years.

PHARAOH-NECHO. — He made war upon the Assyrians, under Nebuchadnezzar. To do this, Necho had to pass through the territory of Josiah, King of the Jews. The Assyrians and Jews being at peace, Josiah felt that he would be countenancing Necho's invasion if he allowed him to pass through his territory, against his ally, without opposing him.

In giving battle to Necho, at Meggiddo, Josiah was slain. On his return from Assyria, Necho revenged himself upon the Jews by taking Jerusalem, dethroning Jehoahaz, Josiah's oldest son, and putting Jehoiakim, his youngest son, upon the throne of Judah; put the land under tribute; carried Jehoahaz in chains to Egypt, where he died.

PSAMMENITUS. — Nebuchadnezzar repaid, in some measure, the invasion of Necho.

Cyrus conquered the Egyptians, and held them with an easy sway. Taking advantage of his clemency, they attempted a revolt. But, under Psammenitus, the Egyptians were humbled by Cambyses, son of Cyrus the Great. He took Pelusium ("The Pass," the same as Avaris), by putting sacred animals before his army.

Psammenitus, manifesting some desire to rid himself of the conquerer's yoke, was compelled to drink bull's blood, and died miserably.

Thus was inaugurated the first Persian administration. For a series of years after the subjugation of Egypt by Cambyses, it passed through a variety of changes and revolts. It finally regained its independence, 413 B. C., through

AMYRTHAEUS. — Egypt continued independent for sixty years,

under eight kings. It was able to maintain this independence by the aid received from the Greeks.

NECTANEBIS. — Under him, ancient Egypt lost, and has never yet recovered, its independence. It was then reduced again to the Persian yoke, by Artaxerxes Ochus, and remained so until Persia was overthrown by Alexander the Great.

PERIOD III. FROM ALEXANDER, 3668 A. M., AND 336 B. C., TO CLEOPATRA, 3974 A. M., 30 B. C.—ABOUT THREE HUNDRED YEARS.

PTOLEMY SOTER. — He was placed upon the throne of the Pharaohs by Alexander, and is said to have been the son of Philip, by a concubine, hence half brother to Alexander.

This is called the Ptolemean dynasty. "Soter" signifies saviour, a name given him by the Rhodians, in gratitude for the protection he afforded them.

Soter is represented as an eminent general and statesman, a man of learning, and a patron of literature. He founded the famous *Alexandrian Library*, erected the tower of Pharos, one of the seven wonders of the world. He built new cities, repaired old ones, rendered the canals again navigable, restored prosperity to Egypt, and conquered Syria. He reigned thirty-nine years.

PTOLEMY PHILADELPHUS. — Called "lover of his brother," in derision, for putting his two brothers to death. Son of Soter.

He followed the example of his father, in public works, and finished the canal from Suez to the Nile. His court surpassed all others of the age, as a seat of learning, politeness, and the arts; and was illustrated by Theocratus, and other men of genius. During his reign, the celebrated version of the Old Testament into Greek, called the *Septuagint*, was made, after the request (at the suggestion of Demetrius, his librarian) had been made for a copy of the Jews' sacred book, for the Alexandrian Library. This was the first translation of the Bible.

PTOLEMY EUERGETES, — Or Benefactor; so called for restoring the idols to Egypt, carried away by Cambyses. He made a successful expedition against Antiochus of Syria.

PTOLEMY PHILOPATER — Or, "lover of his father," in derision, for having put his father to death. He was cruel, sanguinary, and persecuting. He undertook to penetrate into the "holy of holies," at Jerusalem, against the most earnest remonstrances of the priests.

But, as he pressed forward to enter the sanctuary, he fell, palsied and senseless, upon the floor, and had to be carried out.

Indignant at this repulse, he determined to have revenge upon the Jews in Egypt. So, collecting a multitude of them in the hippodrome, he let loose upon them five hundred elephants. They, however, turned upon the spectators, and slew more of them than of the Jews, though forty thousand of *them* are said to have perished.

The other Ptolemies were all surnamed: as, *Epiphanes*, or, Illustrious, though his was a weak and inglorious reign; *Philometer*, Lover of his Mother, and is said to have hated her; *Physcon*, Big-bellied, or deformed; *Chick-pea*, from a bunch, like a pea, on his nose; *Auletes*, or, Flute-player.

PTOLEMY DIONYSIUS. — He came to the throne at the age of thirteen, and had his sister Cleopatra for his queen. She caused him to be murdered, and then assumed the sole rule.

CLEOPATRA. — She has the reputation of being both famous and *in*famous. She was the last of the Ptolemies.

Her personal charms, polite learning, brilliant wit, musical voice, high station, and voluptuous manners, rendered her a bad specimen of true womanly excellence.

When summoned to appear before Mark Antony, to answer to the charge of favoring the conspiracy against Cæsar, she came decked in all the emblems of a queen of love, and was successful in turning the attention of the Roman emperor from her cause to herself. From this time, Antony revelled in pleasure with the beautiful Egyptian queen, till the death of both.

Possessed of immense wealth, they vied with each other in giving sumptuous feasts, Cleopatra taking the palm. At one time, she, to be sure to excel, caused one of her ear-pearls, worth two hundred and fifty thousand dollars, to be dissolved in an acid, and then drank it.

After the battle of Actium, Octavius tried to persuade her to take Antony's life; this she refused to do, but offered to deliver him and her kingdom to Octavius. Antony became indignant at the perfidy of the queen, and sought her life; but she eluded his purpose, and took refuge in a monument she had erected for her safety, and gave out that she had killed herself. Upon this news, Antony's fondness for the queen returned, and he resolved to follow her example, and die a Roman (fool's) death. At the moment he had fallen upon his sword, news came that the queen was alive. Weltering in his blood, he wished to see her. After being pulled up by ropes where Cleopatra was, he died in her arms, bedewed with her tears, and nearly stifled with her caresses. Cleopatra, through fear of being taken at last by Octavius, and suspecting his intention of wounding her pride by putting her among his captives, and leading her thus in triumph to Rome, procured an asp, in a basket of fruit; applying it to her bosom, the bite threw her into a fatal lethargy, and Cleopatra was no more. Thus passed the Ptolemies away.

I.—AGE PATRIARCHAL.

GREECE—FROM ITS EARLY SETTLERS, TO ITS SUBJUGATION BY THE ROMANS.

PERIOD I. FROM ABOUT 1908 A. M., AND 2096 B. C., TO THE TROJAN WAR, 2820 A. M., 1184 B. C.

The size of this renowned country is about half that of the State of New York. Small as is its geographical importance, yet, in its relations to taste and philosophy, it fills a space much larger than any of the mighty empires of antiquity.

For renown in genius, learning, and arts, the Greeks are excelled by none, and, in many respects, they have been the teachers of all succeeding ages. In religion they were idolaters; in government they were decidedly inclined to republicanism.

PIONEERS.—Its first people were descendants of Japheth. For a long time they remained rude savages, living in caves, eating fruits and nuts, and wearing skins of beasts for clothing.

INACHUS.—He is supposed to have been a Phœnician. He came into Greece in 2148 A. M., 1856 B. C., and founded the city of Argos.

The fables of this early period are many, and most of them unimportant. But Uranus, afterwards worshipped as the heavens, is said to have had a large family, called Titans. They dethroned their father. Saturn, who took his father's place, fearing lest *his* children might do the same, caused them to be put to death as soon as born. Jupiter, when his mother saw he was a "proper child," hid him, and sent him to Crete, where he was educated. (Not very unlike the story of Moses.) Jupiter, after dethroning Saturn, began to reign in Thessaly. After expelling the Titans, he divided his realm with his brothers, Pluto and Neptune. His own part he governed with great wisdom; having his palace, and holding his courts, on Mount Olympus, which the poets call heaven, and where Jupiter was worshipped as a god. A very good clue to this fable is the account of Moses receiving the Law on Mount Sinai.

Lacedemon, or Sparta. — This state, founded by Lelex, and Messina, were the only two founded by native Greeks. Each village had its petty tyrant, king, or chief, and for a long time everything depended upon the wills of those chiefs, as they had no laws. The oracles of Apollo and Jupiter were consulted in difficult cases, but could be construed to fit the case, turn as it would. Why might not this custom of consulting oracles have originated in the patriarchs asking council of the Lord, or even from Moses?

Athens. — Cecrops founded this famous city, and first gave it the name of Cecropia, 2448 A. M., 1556 B. C.

He, and the colony with him, built twelve cities, Athens being one of them. Cecrops gave them laws, divided them into twelve tribes, and instituted marriage among them. He raised the first altar in Greece, and that to Jupiter. The third king of Athens was Amphictyon, the author of the celebrated Amphictyonic Council. This grew to be a congress, composed of two representatives from each of the twelve states. Its object was to settle differences between states, and punish violations of the laws of nations. Its vernal session was at Delphi; the autumnal, at Thermopylæ.

Ericthonius taught the Greeks agriculture, and was raised to the throne for this eminent service, instead of Amphictyon.

Thebes. — This city was founded by Cadmus, a Phœnician. He introduced letters into Greece; he thus laid the foundation of the literary distinction of the Greeks.

Theseus. — This man laid the principal foundation of Athenian greatness. He formed the twelve cities of Attica into a confederacy, making the first republic. Yet Grecian fickleness banished even Theseus.

II. — AGE OF WAR FOR POWER.

Argonauts. — The "Argonautic Expedition" is called the first great enterprise of the Greeks, 1263 B. C. Jason was the leader. It is supposed to have been either a mercantile, military, or piratical expedition. In it were some of the most illustrious young men of Greece. Among them were Hercules, Theseus, Castor and Pollux, Orpheus, Æsculapius the physician, and Chiron the astronomer. These, with the rest, made fifty-four renowned captains in the company. They were called Argonauts, from the ship *Argo,* in which they sailed — being the first sea-vessel ever built. Their destination was Colchis, on the shore of the Euxine Sea, in Asia Minor.

The object of the cruise, by Jason, was to avenge the death of his kinsman Phryxus, and to recover his treasures, which had been carried off by the King of Colchis. Hence the representation in fiction, that the object was to recover the *golden fleece* of a ram, which originally belonged to Greece. It was guarded by bulls that breathed fire, and by a dragon that never slept.

On their voyage, they attempted to land, for refreshments, near Troy, but were prevented by Laomedon, king of that city, for which they took ample revenge, on their return, by pillaging the place.

On their arrival in Colchis, Medea, the daughter of the king, fell in love with Jason, and, through her assistance, the Argonauts succeeded in obtaining the "*golden fleece*." Upon their return to Greece, Hercules instituted the Olympic Games.

TROJAN WAR. — This celebrated war was caused by Helen, daughter of Tyndarus, King of Sparta. She was reputed the most beautiful woman of her age, and, as a consequence, her hand was solicited in marriage by the most illustrious princes of Greece. Her father, to settle the claims of her many suitors, proposed to the princes that they should abide *her* choice, and the rest take oath that, should she be stolen from her husband, they would assist, with their utmost strength, to recover her. *Menelaus* was the favored choice of Helen, and, after the nuptials, Tyndarus resigned the crown to his son-in-law.

Troy, the capital of Phrygia Minor, was founded 1546 B. C., by Scamander, who colonized it from Crete. Troas, the fifth king from him, enlarged the city, and named it Troy, after himself. Paris, son of Priam, King of Troy, being promised by Venus the most beautiful woman of the age for his wife, paid a visit to Greece. Being a Trojan prince, he took the liberty to visit Menelaus, King of Sparta, and was received by him with every mark of respect.

Shortly after, and on a sudden, the prince and the queen were missing, together with a considerable treasure. An "elopement in high life" had taken place. They fled to Troy. Though Helen had *eloped*, instead of being *stolen*, yet the Grecian princes were all astir for her recovery by force. A confederacy was immediately formed, and Agamemnon, King of Argos, and brother of Menelaus, was appointed commander-in-chief of the expedition. A fleet of twelve hundred open vessels conveyed one hundred thousand Grecian warriors to the Trojan coast.

The Trojans were commanded by Hector, son of Priam, assisted by Paris (his brother) and others.

The Greeks, on landing, found nearly all Asia Minor leagued with Priam, and they spent the first nine years in subduing his allies; then the siege of Troy began, and heroic deeds on both sides were performed.

Achilles became the hero of the Greeks. He slew Hector, tied him to his chariot, and dragged him around Troy. Achilles fell by the hand of Paris himself; and he was after shot by an arrow. The Greeks at last gained possession of the city, by the stratagem of a large wooden horse, filled with soldiers, which the Trojans found left by the Greeks, purposely, not suspecting its contents. When within the city, they burst forth, and turned the victory in favor of the Greeks. The city was utterly destroyed, so that no vestige of it remains. Priam was slain, and his family led into captivity. Such was the Trojan war.

CODRUS. — He was the last Athenian king. With the close of his reign, royalty was abolished at Athens, 1069 B. C.

Upon going into battle with the Heraclidæ, Codrus was told by the oracle that the army would be victorious whose chief should perish. Devoted to his country's good, he, with a brave and chosen few, threw himself into the midst of the hottest of the fight, but conquered when he fell. His two sons fell into a dispute about the succession, when the Athenians took the matter up, and settled it for them, by *abolishing royalty*, yet putting Medon, one of the sons, at the head of the state, with the title of Archon.

For three centuries this office was held for life; then for ten years; finally, for one.

PERIOD II. FROM THE TROJAN WAR, 2820 A. M., AND 1184 B. C., TO THE FIRST PERSIAN INVASION, 3513 A. M., AND 491 B. C.

HERACLIDÆ. — The next principal event was the "return of the Heraclidæ," about eighty years after the destruction of Troy.

Hercules, King of Mycenæ, a city of Peloponnesus, was driven from his dominion, with his family, by the usurper Atreus, son of Pelops. After a century, the descendants of Hercules returned to Peloponnesus, conquered the country, and retook it from the usurpers. This revolution disturbed the affairs of the country, changed the government, caused new divisions among the people, and checked the progress of the arts and civilization. A long period of civil war followed, when Greece became, through the rivalry of petty tyrants, a prey to oppression and anarchy.

HOMER.—This renowned poet of antiquity flourished about 906 B. C. He was a poor blind man, and used to travel from place to place, singing his verses; but his genius was transcendent.

Homer is styled "the father of poetry," and is generally admitted to be the most ancient of all profane *classical* writers. The place of his birth is unknown, though several cities claim the honor; for

> "Seven cities of Greece boast of Homer *dead*,
> Through which living Homer begged his bread.

His greatest poems are the *Iliad*, and *Odyssey*.

Their first appearance in Greece was about two hundred years after the supposed time of the bard. Pisistratus, tyrant of Athens, was the first who arranged the Iliad and Odyssey in the form in which they now appear to us. Greece owes much of its greatness and refinement to the influence of Homer's poems.

LYCURGUS.—The two leading states of Greece were Athens and Sparta. After the return of the Heraclidæ, the government of Sparta was divided between the two twin sons of Aristodemus, whence arose a double monarchy, that continued about eight hundred and eighty years. Polydectes and Lycurgus were sons of one line of these kings.

His brother dying, left Lycurgus successor to the crown; but his sister-in-law being with child, he resigned it to the heir prospective.

She, however, intimated to Lycurgus, that if he would marry her, the child should be destroyed as soon as born. In order to save the child, he proposed to her to send it to him, and he would take care of it (as though he seconded her plot). But, on a time when Lycurgus was at supper with a company of nobles, the royal infant was brought in. He took it, and held it up before them, saying, "Spartans, behold your king!" The child was named Charilaus. The queen, being disappointed, was also disaffected; and, in order to have revenge upon Lycurgus, circulated calumnies about him, when he resolved upon voluntary exile. In his travels, he made it his object to acquire knowledge, especially in reference to the best means of government. During this journey, he found the poems of Homer, which he carefully preserved.

He was recalled to Sparta, 886 B. C., and on his return, brought the poems of Homer with him. Their effect on the national spirit and literature of the Greeks, was highly propitious. Finding the state of political affairs very bad, he was earnestly solicited to set about a reform. This he did, by first instituting a senate of thirty members, to make and execute the laws. The two kings were *ex-*

officio members of it, and acted as presidents of the senate, generals of the army, and high priests of the nation. He also divided the territory of the republic into thirty-nine thousand equal shares, among all the free citizens. He extended this division even to furniture and clothes; abolished commerce; distinction in dress; substituted iron money for gold and silver. All the citizens, with the kings, were required to eat at the public tables, black broth being the principal article of food. Some opposition arose at so many extreme measures, but soon ceased.

Every citizen was wholly devoted to the service of the state, whether in time of peace or war. Deformed infants were exposed to perish, and the well-formed delivered to the care of public nurses; at seven years of age, they were introduced into the public schools, and all educated on the same plan. Letters were taught for use, and not for ornament, and hence arose the term "*laconic speech*." The Spartans were not eminent as scholars; no book has ever reached us written by a genuine Spartan. The young were taught respect for the aged, ardent love of country, a high principle of honor, and keen sensibility to honor or shame, and inured to hardship. The institutions of Lycurgus were adapted only to make a nation of soldiers. To be terrible to their enemies was their highest ambition. The softer virtues, and domestic affections, were sacrificed to the heroic virtues; while such as patriotism, public spirit, courage, fortitude, contempt of danger, suffering, and death, were cherished. Even theft was encouraged, if it could be done without detection. A boy was brought into court for stealing a fox; he denied the theft, though holding the fox under his cloak at the same time, and the animal gnawing at his vitals, until he fell down dead. He died a *true Spartan*.

The manners of the Spartan women were loose and indelicate. They were taught the more masculine traits, to the neglect of modesty, tenderness, and sensibility. They were fond of military glory. Mothers exulted when their sons fell honorably in battle. In bidding them adieu for war, they used the laconic words: "Return with your shield, or on your shield." In examining for their wounds, their concern was, whether they were in their *backs* or *breasts*.

Sparta and Messenia being adjacent, were often at war, until the subjugation of the latter by the former. The first war was 743 B. C. There were two other wars after this.

In one of these wars, the Spartans had bound themselves never to return, until they had conquered the Messenians; but, despairing of this, they sent word to the Spartan women to recruit the population by promiscuous intercourse with the young men who were too young to take the oath when the war began. The offspring of this singular order were called Partheniæ, or Sons of the Virgins.

The extreme attention given to sterner virtues, and the unpardonable neglect of the moral and social ones, were defects in the system of Lycurgus, that eventually caused it to fall into disuse. Still, while brother states were torn by internal dissensions, Sparta acquired solidity, and caused her power to be felt everywhere. Lycurgus, having established his laws, obtained a pledge of the Spartans that they would maintain them during his absence. He then went into voluntary exile, not intending to return, and died. His laws, however, remained in force, in some degree, for five hundred years. Many are the characters far more to be desired than the Spartan.

DRACO. — The first code of laws the Athenians ever possessed, was written by Draco. These soon passed out of use, as he punished every offence, trifling and malignant, with death.

SOLON, — One of the wisest men of Greece, being raised to the archonship, was directed to form a new code of laws. He followed neither of the last two law-givers, but undertook to accommodate his laws to the condition of the people, instead of raising them up to a higher standard. Of his laws he said: "If they are not the best possible, they are the best the Athenians are capable of receiving." He divided the people into four classes, according to property; the fourth class were the very poor. All the offices of the state were confined to the rich; yet all freemen, of thirty years of age, were allowed to vote in the Areopagus, or assembly of the people.

In this assembly all the laws were enacted, every public measure determined, all appointments made, and to it an appeal lay from all courts of justice. In the public addresses before this court, was the place where the talents of the orators of Athens were drawn out, and their fame acquired,—"where Pericles *thundered*, Æschines *charmed*, and Demosthenes *ruled* the hearts of men."

Solon also instituted a senate of four hundred (after increased to six hundred), in which public measures were first discussed, before being proposed to the Areopagus. So between the Senate and Areopagus, he sought to balance the popular interest. Commerce and agriculture were encouraged; industry and economy enforced; disobedience to parents, and opprobrious language were punished; and the father who neglected to teach his son a trade, could have no claim upon him for support in old age.

Solon once witnessed Thespis act various characters in plays, and asked him if he was not ashamed to speak so many lies. Thespis replied: "It was all in jest." Solon, striking his staff on the ground violently, said: "If we encourage ourselves to speak falsely in jest, we shall run the chance of acquiring a habit of speaking falsely in serious matters."

The different law-givers of Athens and Sparta wrought in the people as different characters. At Athens, peace and refinement were the taste of the people; at Sparta, war, military and athletic display. Athenians were luxurious, Spartans frugal; Athenian virtues were agreeable, Spartan severe. They were both, however, equally jealous of liberty, and brave in war.

Pisistratus. — About 560 B. C., Pisistratus, a rich, eloquent, and ambitious citizen, so operated upon the popular mind, in various ways, as to raise himself to the supreme power of the nation, in spite of Solon. He and his sons retained the rule for about fifty years.

Pisistratus exercised a munificent and splendid reign, and is said to have founded the first public library known to the world. It was he who first collected the poems of Homer into one volume. He left the government to his two sons, Hippias, and Hipparchus. They, after a time, abused their power, and were overthrown by Harmodius and Aristogiton, and democracy was again restored. Hipparchus was slain; Hippias fled to Darius, King of Persia, who was then meditating an attack upon Greece. Hippias seconded the designs of Darius, and was afterwards killed in the battle of Marathon, fighting against his countrymen.

Sappho. — She was a Greek poetess, author of the Sapphic verse, so called. Flourished about 600 B. C.

She was born in the island of Lesbos. Talent and beauty were hers. She fell in love with Phaon, a youth of Mytilene; but, being disappointed, she threw herself into the sea, from Mount Lucas.

Æsop, — The Father of Fables, flourished about 580 B. C. He was originally a slave, and had several masters, but procured his liberty by the charms of his genius. He was enfranchised by an Athenian philosopher. He travelled considerably, but resided much at the court of Crœsus, King of Lydia, by whom he was sent to consult the oracle at Delphi. His sarcasms upon the Delphians so offended them, that they accused him of some act of sacrilege, and threw him down from a rock.

PERIOD III. FROM THE FIRST PERSIAN INVASION, 3513 A. M., AND 491 B. C., TO ALEXANDER THE GREAT, 3668 A. M., AND 336 B. C.

MILTIADES. — Darius, King of Persia, was now meditating the invasion of Greece. His subjects in Asia Minor had made an attempt to rid themselves of his control, and were assisted by the Greeks; but Darius succeeded in quelling the disturbance there in a short time; and then for revenge upon Greece.

Darius sent heralds into Greece, demanding earth and water; the indignant Greeks threw some of them into wells, telling them there "to take earth and water." Thebes, and some of the other Grecian states submitted, but Athens and Sparta resisted.

The first Persian army was destroyed by a storm, in passing around the promontory of Athos, and three hundred vessels lost. Another soon followed, in six hundred vessels, with five hundred thousand men. This army ravaged the Grecian islands, whilst another entered Attica by land, consisting of one hundred and ten thousand men. The Grecian generals were entrusted with the command, but the rest agreed that Miltiades should be chief. The two armies met on a narrow plain by the sea side, at the town of Marathon. Here, with a good position, and a better arrangement of his troops, Miltiades met the Persian host, and, after a terrible battle, drove the routed invaders to their ships, with a loss of six thousand three hundred, while the Greeks lost only one hundred and ninety-two.

The glittering honors Miltiades won at this battle, stirred up the jealousy of his rivals to seek his ruin. Failing in an attack upon the island of Paros, not long after, this was seized upon as a ground of accusation against him for treason, which failed of proof; still he was sentenced to pay a fine of fifty thousand dollars. He was thrown into prison, where he died in a few days of his wounds, received at Paros. His son Cimon paid the fine.

Such was Grecian gratitude (?) to Grecian heroes.

LEONIDAS. — The death of Darius postponed the war of Persia for several years; when Xerxes, ascending the throne, was eager to conquer Greece. He spent four years in collecting an army, — the greatest the world ever saw. The army and fleet consisted of two millions fighting men; including the retinue, the whole multitude exceeded five millions! The fleet consisted of twelve hundred galleys of war; and, for the conveyance of the army, two bridges of boats were made across the Hellespont. Xerxes, upon a review of his vast army is said to have wept at the thought, that all would be still in death in one hundred years. His army was then put in motion towards Athens.

Leonidas, King of Sparta, undertook the defence of the celebrated pass of Thermopylæ, a narrow defile in the mountain, on the coast between Thessaly and Phocis. With his six thousand brave soldiers, Leonidas awaited the approach of the Persian hosts. A Persian herald was dispatched first to bribe him; failing of this, he demanded his arms, in the name of Xerxes. The Spartan replied, in a short, laconic speech: "Let him come and take them." The bravest of the Persian troops were repeatedly sent against the Spartans, but as often driven back in disgrace. For two days they held the Persians at bay; but a wretch at last informed them of a secret path over the mountain. This they entered, and in the morning began to pour down upon the Greeks like a torrent.

Leonidas saw he was betrayed; but, as the laws of Sparta forbade its soldiers, in any case whatever, to flee from an enemy, he, with three hundred Spartans, resolved to abide their fate, and were all cut off.

A monument was erected on the spot, with an inscription by Simonides: "O, stranger! tell it at Lacedæmon that we died here in obedience to her laws."

Themistocles. — The Persians, having forced the pass of Thermopylæ, poured down upon Attica. Finding Athens deserted, they pillaged the city and burnt it.

The Greeks, having removed their women and children to the islands for safety, had fled to their ships. A great naval battle was now approaching.

The Persian fleet consisted of twelve hundred galleys, that of the Greeks of three hundred, commanded by Themistocles and Aristides. The engagement took place in the Straits of Salamis, where the Persians could bring but few of their vast fleet into action, and were defeated with immense loss.

Xerxes, who had seated himself upon an eminence in the firm expectation of victory, alarmed at the loss of this battle, fled for his own dominions. The hero of this great naval battle, with all his honors, was not thereby shielded from the spleen of his countrymen. He was suspected of participating in the treason of Pausanias, who, like Hippias, proposed to betray the government of Greece into the hands of Persia, provided he could be made governor thereof, under Persia. Under this suspicion, he was banished by the ostracism.

Proceeding to Asia, he wrote a letter to King Artaxerxes, saying: "I Themistocles come to thee, who have done thy house most ill of all the Greeks, while I was of necessity repelling the invasion of thy father; but yet more good, when I was in safety, and his return was endangered." He was permitted to live in Persia, in great splendor. Ambition, however, was his god. On being asked the occasion of his dejection, after the battle of Marathon, he said, the trophies of Miltiades would not let him sleep.

On one occasion, when he was high in power, he laughingly said his son was "greater than any man in Greece." — "How is that?" said a friend. He replied: "The Athenians govern Greece; I command the Athenians; his mother commands me, and this boy commands his mother."

Cimon. — Upon the flight of Xerxes, he left his general, Mardonius, with three hundred thousand Persian soldiers, to complete the subjugation of Greece.

In the following year, the combined forces of Athens and Sparta, under command of Aristides and Pausanias, met the Persians, with only one hundred and ten thousand men, at Platæa, and defeated them, with tremendous slaughter. Mardonius was killed, and nearly all his troops. On the same day, a naval battle was fought at Mycale, near Ephesus, under Leotychides the Spartan, and Xanthippus the Athenian, when the remainder of the Persian fleet was destroyed. Thus the "mad schemes" of Xerxes were frustrated.

Affairs now took a "turn about." The Greeks assisted the *Asiatic* Greeks to throw off the Persian yoke, when Cimon (son of Miltiades), assisted by Pausanias and Aristides, took the island of Cyprus from Persia, and set it free; then took the city of Byzantium, plundered it, and returned with immense booty. After the banishment of Themistocles, and the death of Aristides, Cimon was left with the sole direction of public affairs. He maintained the political influence and military power of Athens, and was very successful in repelling the Persians, — gaining two victories over them in one day, near the mouth of the Eurymedon, in Asia Minor.

A party at length arose, with Pericles for their leader, and procured the banishment of Cimon by the *ostracism*. He was, however, recalled after five years, and invested again with the command of the army. He was again victorious over the Persians, but died, finally, of a wound received at Citium, in Cyprus. The Persian war was now closed.

During the war with the Persians, the Athenians, under their celebrated generals, Miltiades, Themistocles, Aristides, and Cimon, rose to the summit of their military renown, and even attained the supremacy in Greece, which Sparta had hitherto enjoyed. This last circumstance gave rise to the Peloponnesian war, or the war between Athens and Sparta.

Pericles. — After the death of Cimon, his brother-in-law, Thucydides, became the competitor of Pericles for popular favor. A war of eloquence ensued, which ended in the banishment of Thucydides by the ostracism, when Pericles came into power, and held it, almost undisputed, for twenty years. He governed Athens with arbitrary sway, yet adorned it with masterpieces of architecture, sculpture, and painting; patronized the arts and sciences; celebrated splendid games and festivals, making his administration one of great splendor and magnificence. But he exhausted the public revenue, and corrupted the manners of the people.

A complaint being made by some, that he was spending too much of the public money in beautifying the city, he one day asked, in a public assembly, "If any thought so?" The people said, "Yes." Pericles answered: "Then place the expense to my charge, instead of yours; only let the new buildings be marked with *my* name, instead of *yours*. To this they replied: "Let him use as much of the public treasures as he pleases." Athens was at this time in the height of her glory, both in military renown, and of cultivation and refinement.

After the close of the Persian war, the union that had existed between the Grecian states while repelling their outward foes, gave way to the old jealousies and ambitious views of the rival states — Sparta feeling specially mortified at the renown and supremacy of Athens, gained in the Persian war.

The Peloponnesian war, so called, was precipitated upon the country of Greece, as follows: In a treaty between Athens and Sparta, Corinth was ceded to the latter. The Corinthians waged a war upon the people of Corcyra, whereupon both parties solicited the aid of Athens. The Athenians aided the people of Corcyra, which act the Corinthians interpreted as a violation of the "treaty," and made it the pretext of war, which the Spartans were eager to commence; and an appeal to arms soon involved all the states of the Peloponnesus in a *terrible* "civil war." In the third year of this war, when his eminent services were most needed, Pericles was swept off, with others, by a terrible plague.

On his death-bed, his friends were recounting his wonderful deeds, for his consolation, when he replied, that what most consoled him was, that none of his fellow-citizens had been obliged, by any act of his, to put on a mourning robe.

Lysander.— After the death of Pericles, Cleon and Alcibiades held very poorly the reins of the Athenian government. But the

Athenian fleet being utterly defeated at Ægos Potamos, on the Hellespont, by Lysander, the ablest of the Spartan generals, Athens was reduced to the last extremity. The Spartans blockaded the city by sea and land, and its reduction was left to the sure operation of famine.

The Athenians, forseeing their fate, chose to surrender on almost any conditions. Those they were compelled to accept, were, to demolish their port, with all their fortifications, limit their fleet to twelve ships, and in future to undertake no military enterprise, except under the command of the Lacedæmonians (Spartans). Thus the Peloponnesian war ended with submission of Athens to Sparta.

After the reduction of Athens, Lysander abolished the popular government, and substituted an oligarchy, consisting of thirty Spartan captains, whose power was absolute, and, from their atrocious cruelty, were styled the *Thirty Tyrants*. They were rejected by the people, and the democratic form of government restored (in three years), 403 B. C. To Lysander is charged the first breach in his country's constitution, by the introduction of gold coin into that republic, which had been studiously kept out for nearly five hundred years, or since the time of Lycurgus.

SOCRATES. — About this age of Greece, appeared a class of eminent men, — their memory at once the boast, and, in some instances, the reproach of the nation. Among those who received evil at the hands of their countrymen, none is more prominent, or excites more sympathy, than Socrates.

He was a native of Athens, and followed the employment of his father, which was that of statuary, for some time. The statues of "The Graces," are said to have been the work of his own hands. Called from this honorable employment by a friend, philosophy soon became his study. He served his country with boldness and intrepidity in the field of battle. But his character is more to be admired as a philosopher and moralist, than as a warrior.

He attended but little to physical science, but introduced *moral philosophy*, by teaching mankind to govern their passions, and to consider their actions and their duties. From this circumstance, it was said of him, that he drew down philosophy from heaven to earth. His investigations led to a knowledge of the Deity, the Creator of the universe, and to the belief of a future state of rewards and punishments. He directed the powers of his mind against the atheists, materialists, and skeptics of his own and former times, turning their metaphysical speculations into ridicule.

This provoked the subjects of his sarcasm to seek revenge; and while they could not stand before him in the field, meanly accused him of making innovations in the religion of the Greeks, ridiculing the gods whom the Athenians worshipped, and corrupting the Athenian youth. Through such means his enemies procured his condemnation, by the Assembly of Athens, to death by poison.

Upon this, he was thrown into prison for thirty days. During this time, he conducted himself with the greatest dignity, refusing to escape when he might, conversed freely with his friends upon topics of moral philosophy, particularly the immortality of the soul. One of his disciples lamenting before him that he was to die innocent, "Would you have me die guilty?" replied Socrates, with a smile.

The fatal potion was a liquor resembling the juice of hemlock, which was to cause death by its coldness. When the hour arrived, the philosopher drank the fatal cup, and, with composure, kept up his conversation till the last moment of his life. When too late, the Athenians were made aware of the mistake to themselves, and the gross injustice done this sage, in his wanton destruction. His instructions were wholly given in conversation, not in writing. He was attended by a number of illustrious pupils, among whom were *Plato* and Xenophon, and to them are we indebted for a knowledge of the doctrines, character, and fate of Socrates.

The philosophy of Socrates formed an important epoch in the history of the human mind; and from him arose, soon after, the Platonic, Stoic, and Peripatetic schools of philosophy, besides some others.

HERODOTUS. — He is styled the "Father of History," and holds the same rank among historians that Homer does among poets. His history describes the wars of the Greeks against the Persians. This he publicly repeated, at the Olympic Games, when the names of the Muses were given to his nine books. He lived about 450 before Christ.

PINDAR — The chief of the Grecian lyric poets. His compositions were extremely popular with statesmen and princes, and his hymns were repeated in the temples, and at the celebration of festivals. Horace calls him "inimitable." His statue was erected at Thebes, and viewed with pleasure by Pausanias, the geographer, six centuries after.

PHIDIAS. — He was an Athenian. His statue of Jupiter Olympus passed for one of the wonders of the world. That of Minerva, in the Pantheon at Athens, was thirty-nine feet in height, and was made of gold and ivory. He died 432 B. C.

EURIPIDES. — An eminent tragic poet of Greece.

It is said he used to shut himself up in a gloomy cave near Salamis, where he composed some of his best tragedies. Upon hearing some of his audience object to certain lines of a piece he was representing, he stepped forward and told them he came there to instruct them, not to receive instruction. As a poet, he was very apt in expressing the passions of love; and common expressions have received a perfect polish from his pen. His works abound in moral reflections and philosophical aphorisms.

Euripides was such an enemy to the fair sex as to have merited the appellation of "woman-hater;" yet he married twice, but was so unhappy, as to divorce both his wives. The ridicule and envy to which he was exposed in Athens, caused him to retire to the court of Archelaus, King of Macedon, where he was entertained with great munificence. But the tragic *writer* came to a tragic *end.* While out in one of his solitary walks, the hounds of the king attacked him, and tore him in pieces.

Sophocles. — He was born 497 B. C., and was a rival and competitor of Euripides. He was distinguished as a poet, statesman, and general, and filled the office of Archon with applause. He died at the age of ninety-one, through excess of joy at having obtained a poetical prize at the Olympic Games.

Thucydides — Wrote a history of the Peloponnesian war. Extremely well written.

Hippocrates — Was an eminent physician. Died at ninety-nine years of age.

Xenophon. — Upon the death of Darius, his son, Artaxerxes II., came to the Persian throne. Cyrus, his brother, undertook to dethrone him, and for the purpose employed over ten thousand mercenary Greeks, under the command of Clearchus.

Cyrus and Clearchus both being slain, the Greeks made a retreat of sixteen hundred miles, through the enemy's country, and with difficulty reached the Euxine. Choosing Xenophon for their leader, he has the honor of conducting what is known as the "*Retreat of the Ten Thousand.*"

Xenophon has written a very interesting account of this retreat. He also wrote a life of Cyrus the Great, collected the Memorabilia of Socrates, and continued the history of Thucydides. The simplicity and elegance of Xenophon's style, have won him the name of the Athenian Muse, and the Bee of Greece. He followed Agesilaus in some of his expeditions, and acquired much wealth.

Agesilaus. — The Greek cities of Asia having taken part with Cyrus, the Spartans, under their king, Agesilaus, undertook their defence, and thus became involved in war with the Persians.

The King of Persia, by bribes, induced Athens, Thebes, Corinth, and other cities, to join in a league against them, which compelled

Agesilaus to return to the defence of his own country (similar to Asa, inducing Benhadad, King of Syria, to attack Baasha in the rear, to draw him away from building Ramah). After the Spartans had defeated the confederates at Cornea, then, in turn, the Athenians, under Conon, defeated the Spartan fleet near Cnidus, and after several other turns of the fortunes of "glorious war," all parties became weary of it, and a treaty of peace was at last concluded, called the *Peace of Antalcidas*, the Lacedæmonian.

The conditions of which were, that all the Grecian cities of Asia should belong to Persia, and that all others should be completely independent, except that the islands of Lemnos, Scyros, and Imbros, should belong to Athens.

Agesilaus acted a prominent part in the war with Thebes. Not long after the peace that followed the Theban war, the Spartans, under Agesilaus, went into Egypt to assist Tachos, king of that country, against Nectanebus.

Receiving some affront from Tachos, he turned against him, and raised Nectanebus to the throne. Having set sail for Sparta, he died on the coast of Egypt, leaving a high reputation as a statesman and warrior.

Thus, after the formation of the twelve cities of Attica into the first Republic, by Theseus, and having gone through all the forms of tyrannical, anarchical, aristocratic, democratic, united and divided government, the Greeks settled down upon the platform of six hundred years before!

Retrograde movement truly, when we reckon on so long an experience, and so many renowned law-givers, statesmen, and warriors, as lived and flourished during this period, in Greece itself.

Epaminondas. — Sparta, after enjoying for a long time the honor of being the leading state in Greece, was forced to see Thebes fast rising to be not only a rival, but a conquering state. The Spartans, jealous of her rising greatness, took advantage of some internal dissensions, and seized upon her citadel. This they held four years, when a party of Thebans, headed by Pelopidas, putting on women's clothes to hide their armor, entered a feast given them by the Spartans, and cut their principal officers to pieces.

Archias, the chief Spartan, had a letter put into his hands that very day, giving information of the plot, but he laid it aside, saying, "Business to-morrow." He was the first man killed, and the Spartans were routed, and war ensued. The two armies met, and fought the battle of Leuctra. In this battle the Thebans lost three hundred, and the Spartans four thousand, together with their king, Cleombrotus.

This was the most mortifying defeat the Spartans had suffered for ages, sustaining poorly the renown of Marathon and Thermopylæ. The victorious Thebans, headed by Epaminondas, entered the territories of Lacedæmon, and overran them with fire and sword, to the very suburbs of the capital. This had not happened to Sparta for six hundred years; and the boast of the inhabitants, that "the Spartan women had never seen the smoke of an enemy's camp," was now taken away.

The Theban general, having completely humbled the power of Sparta, returned to Thebes with his victorious army. But not long after, the war being renewed, Epaminondas met the Spartans, under Agesilaus, at the battle of Mantinea, and gained another great victory over them. He fell, pierced with a javelin, in the moment of victory; and, though in extreme agony from his wound, was anxious how the battle went. When informed that the Thebans conquer, he exclaimed: "Then all is well."

With Epaminondas Thebes *rose*, with him she *fell*. See the same of Charlemagne, and his New Western Empire.

Philip. — While Sparta, Athens, and Thebes, were declining, through internal discord, Macedon, in the north, was rising; thus bringing a new and fourth state of Greece into the struggle for power and supremacy. Macedon had been a separate state for four hundred years, but acquired no distinction until its throne was occupied by Philip.

Macedon had hitherto formed no portion of the Greek Confederacy, and had no part in the Amphictyonic Council. Its inhabitants claimed a similar origin with the Greeks, but were considered by them as barbarians. Philip, when only ten years of age, was sent to Thebes as a hostage, and there enjoyed the advantage of an excellent Grecian education, under Epaminondas. At the age of twenty-four, he ascended the throne. Being possessed of great military and political talent, he meditated the conquest of all the Grecian states.

In order to secure his main design, he first subdued his immediate neighbors, the Thessalians, Pæonians, and Illyrians. On his return from one of those expeditions, in which he had been successful, a messenger soon after arrived with the news of his general Parmenio's success; another came with the news that his horses had won at the Olympic Games; and yet a third came, and informed him that his wife Olympias had brought forth a son at Pella. All these being taken as a bad omen, Philip exclaimed: "Great Jupiter! in return for so many blessings, send me a slight misfortune!" Another device of his to gain all Greece, was the employment of pensionaries in all the states, to excite dissensions among them, with a view of having every public measure directed to his advantage. Finally a pretext for war arose, such as Philip wished to see.

The Phocians had long cultivated the Chirrhæan plain, which, it was now claimed, had been in a former age consecrated to the Delphian Apollo; and the Amphyctionic Council had forbidden its further use by the Phocians, under penalty of a heavy fine. The Phocians treated the order of the council with contempt, which brought on the *sacred war*, and this involved nearly all the Grecian states in the contest for ten years. Philip, having attained some renown, proposed to use his influence in carrying out the wishes of the council in compelling the Phocians to submit to its decree. In order to make the most of the case, he proposed to have the Phocians ejected from the council, and the State of Macedon, which had never had a seat in the council, fill the vacancy. This being done, he was also styled the *Amphictyonic General*, which was all he could ask.

The Athenians, suspicious of his designs, refused to acknowledge the election; and, after having their jealousies excited to the utmost by the thundering "Philippics" of Demosthenes, they were plunged into an unavailing war with their powerful and victorious rival and neighbor. A second *sacred war* drew Philip again into Greece. The Locrians trespassed on the sacred ground of Delphi, and, refusing to obey the order of the council, Philip was called upon to vindicate their authority by force of arms.

The Athenians and Thebans, roused to the utmost enthusiasm by the eloquence of Demosthenes, united to resist the growing power of Philip; but in vain. The two armies met at Chæronea (the battle-ground of Agesilaus), and, after a most obstinate fight, Philip gained a decisive victory, which gave him the entire ascendency in Greece.

He did not, however, treat the Greeks as a vanquished people, but permitted them to retain their separate and independent governments, while he controlled all the public measures.

Philip's next project was the invasion of Persia. He, with all Greece, longed for revenge upon that nation, for the repeated efforts of her monarchs to subdue the Greeks, although they had failed to do it. In order to have complete success, Philip called a council of all the states, laid before them his project, which was highly popular, and he was chosen commander-in-chief of the united forces of all the states of Greece. He made formidable preparations for the expedition, and being just ready for his departure, was assassinated by Pausanias, a captain of his guards, from private resentment, while solemnizing the nuptials of his daughter!

The news of Philip's death was received with tumultuous joy by the Athenians, who indulged the vain hope of again recovering their liberty.

Plato. — Among other great men of the time, appeared the eminent Grecian philosopher, Plato, called by the Greeks, "Divine." He was born about 429 B. C. His name, Aristocles, was changed to Plato, from the largeness of his shoulders. He was eight years the pupil of Socrates, after which he travelled for a time in foreign countries. He then retired to the groves of Academus, where he was attended by a crowd of illustrious pupils.

Plato's learning and virtues were topics of conversation in all parts of Greece. His manners were elegant, and he partook only of innocent pleasures and amusements.

His works, which were written in dialogue style, were numerous. They have been regarded, by ancients and moderns, as possessed of unusual depth of thought and merit. Among other things, he taught the immortality of the soul. The school of philosophy he founded is deserving of the most merit of any of those times.

Diogenes. — He lived about this time, and is celebrated as the clown, or cynic philosopher. He seemed to despise the ordinary ways of mankind.

For example, he is said to have lived in a *tub*, instead of a house, or cave. One day he was seen searching around among a crowd, with a lighted candle. On being asked what was the object of his search, he replied: "I am looking for an honest man." His oddities were many and pertinent. He received a visit from Alexander, when he asked Diogenes if he wished any favor of him. He replied: "Yes; I want you to stand out of my sunshine, and not take from me what you cannot give me."

Apelles. — He was Greece's most celebrated painter. Alexander would suffer no one else to draw his picture. His picture of Venus rising out of the sea, was purchased by Augustus, and placed in a temple at Rome.

Aristotle. — He is said to have possessed one of the keenest and most inventive and penetrating intellects ever known. His writings treat of a great variety of important topics: as Moral and Natural Philosophy, Metaphysics, Mechanics, Grammar, Criticism, and Politics.

His eloquence was remarkable; moderate in his meals; slept little, and indefatigably industrious. That he might not over-sleep, he always lay with one hand out of bed, holding in it a ball of brass, which, by its falling into a basin of the same metal, would awake him. Though educated in the school of Plato, he differed from his master, and at length formed a new school.

He taught in the Lyceum. He is said to have had a deformed countenance, but his genius was an ample compensation for this defect. As he expired, he is said to have uttered this sentiment: "I entered this world in impurity; I have lived in anxiety; I depart in commotion of spirit. Cause of Causes, pity me!" He died Æ. 63.

Demosthenes. — His father died when he was only seven years of age; and his guardians, proving unfaithful to their trust, squandered his estate, and neglected his education. He was then left to his own industry and application, for the discipline of his mind.

Demosthenes was afflicted with weak lungs, difficulty of pronunciation, and uncouth habits of body; still, he became the greatest orator of the age.

To cure his stuttering, he used to declaim with his mouth full of pebbles. To break himself of hunching up his shoulders, he used to stand before a mirror, with a sword suspended, point down, just above his shoulder. To get control over himself, and secure presence of mind, he would stand by the sea-shore, in a fearful wind, and declaim to the waves; and that he might devote himself the more closely to his studies, he confined himself to a retired cave, and shaved one half of his head, so that he could not appear decently in public.

His abilities as an orator soon placed him at the head of the government, and in this capacity he animated the Athenians to resist Philip. He also resisted Alexander. After Alexander's death, he attempted again to arouse the Athenians to throw off the Macedonian yoke. But, finding that Alexander's troops were approaching the city, Demosthenes fled for safety to the temple of Neptune, and there took poison, to prevent himself from falling into their hands, in his sixtieth year, 322 B. C.

Euclid. — He was a mathematician of Alexandria, and flourished about 300 B. C.

He distinguished himself by writing on Music and Geometry, but particularly, by fifteen books on the Elements of Mathematics, which consist of problems and theorems, with demonstrations. His Elements have gone through innumerable editions. He was greatly respected by antiquity, and his school at Alexandria became the most famous in the world for mathematics.

Zeno. — He was a native of Cyprus. In early life he followed commercial pursuits; but, during a shipwreck, he took up a book to read, to divert his mind. It happened to be one written by Xenophon; and he was so captivated with it, that from that time he devoted himself to the study of philosophy.

Zeno, becoming perfect in all branches of knowledge, opened a school at Athens, and delivered his instructions in a porch, in Greek, called *stoa*, from which was derived the name stoic. He taught that men should be free from passion, unmoved by joy or grief, and submit without complaint to the unavoidable necessity by which all things are governed. He was austere in manners, but his life was an example of moderation and sobriety. He instructed in philosophy forty-eight years, and died in his ninety-eighth year, 264 B. C. A stranger to indisposition and diseases, virtue was his chief good.

Archimedes.—He was a native of Syracuse.

At the siege of Syracuse, under Marcellus, the Roman consul, Archimedes constructed machines by which he sunk some of the Roman ships; and others he set on fire by burning-glasses,—supposed to be reflectors, made of metal, capable of producing this effect at the distance of a bow-shot.

Marcellus, learning of his extraordinary abilities, when the city was taken, gave orders to have Archimedes conducted to him in safety. So intent was he upon his studies, that he was unconscious that the city was taken, until a soldier entered his room, and bade him follow him. Archimedes requested him to allow him to finish his problem first. The soldier, thirsting more for blood than for science, took the philosopher's *request* as a *refusal* to obey his order, drew his sword, and killed him on the spot, 208 B. C.

PERIOD IV. FROM ALEXANDER, 3668 A. M., AND 336 B. C., TO THE SUBJUGATION OF GREECE BY THE ROMANS, 3857 A. M., 147 B. C.

Alexander—Known also as the Great, was son of Philip, King of Macedon. His early education was committed to Aristotle, and under him the young prince soon manifested a desire to distinguish himself. He read much; Homer's Iliad he especially studied, and is said to have slept with it under his pillow in after-life.

His wonderful feats with the fiery war-horse Bucephalus, which no one else could ride, exhibit his early and natural daring.

This horse was afterwards his special favorite animal. Among other marks of distinction shown him, he built a city and named it "Bucephala," in honor of his admirable steed.

He attended his father in battle, and early manifested not only valor, but skill, and once had the happiness of saving his parent's life, when in great danger from an enemy. The death of his father raised him to the throne, at the early age of twenty years.

Upon Alexander's coming to the throne, Demosthenes again attempted to rouse his countrymen to throw off the Macedonian yoke. But the young king, having extended his dominions somewhat in the north, turned his arms upon Greece. The Athenians submitted, but the Thebans resisted him. Their defeat, however, was accompanied with great slaughter, the burning of Thebes to the ground, and thirty thousand of her inhabitants sold as slaves. These severe measures brought all the Grecian states into submission to Alexander.

He then assembled deputies, at Corinth, from all the states, and renewed his father's proposed invasion of Persia; it was approved, and he, like his father, was appointed generalissimo. He had for his companions in arms, Parmenio, and other distinguished officers, who served in the wars of his father.

With an army of thirty thousand foot, and five thousand horse, the sum of seventy talents, and a single month's provisions, he set out to have revenge on old Persia, for her repeated (though unsuccessful) attempts to subdue Greece. After crossing the Hellespont, he proceeded to the site of Illium, or Troy, and offered sacrifices to the spirits of the heroes who fell in the Trojan war, — particularly to Achilles, whom he pronounced the most fortunate of men, in having Patroclus for his friend, and Homer for his panegyrist.

Darius Cadomanus, King of Persia, resolved to crush the "mad boy" (as he termed him) at once, and so gave him battle, on the banks of the Granicus, with an army of one hundred thousand foot, and twenty thousand horse. The Persians were defeated, with a loss, according to Plutarch, of twenty-two thousand men, while the Macedonians lost only thirty-four. In this battle, Alexander was saved from having his head split open with a battle-axe, by Clytus, who run the officer through with a spear. This victory was of great importance to Alexander, as Sardis, with all its riches, and all Asia Minor fell into his hands.

Early the next spring, 333 B. C., was fought the battle of Issus, when the Persian army, numbering six hundred thousand men, was defeated, and one hundred and ten thousand killed, while the Macedonians lost only four hundred and fifty. The battle took place in a narrow defile, like Thermopylæ,— a Grecian stratagem of war.

The mother, wife, and two daughters of Darius, fell into Alexander's hands, who treated his royal captives with the greatest delicacy and respect. Darius, hearing of the kind treatment of his family, sent an embassy to Alexander, offering for their ransom the sum of ten thousand talents (about ten millions of dollars), proposing a treaty of peace and alliance, with the offer of his daughter in marriage, and all the country between the Euphrates and the Ægean Sea as her dower. (Fine offer to the "mad boy.") This proposition being laid before Alexander's council, Parmenio said: "If I were Alexander, I would accept the terms." — "And so would I, if I were Parmenio," replied Alexander.

His reply to Darius intimated that he had invaded Asia to avenge the unprovoked aggressions of the Persian monarchs; that if Darius would come to him, and ask for his wife and family, he would willingly deliver them to him; but if he proposed to dispute the sovereignty, he would find him ready to oppose him.

Coming to Tyre, he demanded admittance to the temple, to offer sacrifice to the Tyrian Hercules. Being denied this, he became enraged, and resolved on the destruction of the place. This he accomplished in seven months, causing two thousand men to be crucified; many he put to the sword, and others he sold into slavery.

He then proceeded to Gaza, which he took, after an obstinate resistance; sold ten thousand of its inhabitants into slavery, and tied Betis, its brave defender, alive to his chariot wheels, and dragged him around the city, in imitation of Achilles dragging Hector around Troy. Hector, however, was dead, while Betis was dragged alive.

Alexander next visited Jerusalem, where he was kindly received, and treated the Jews kindly in return. (See page 133.)

Egypt, which was subject to Persia, readily submitted to his authority. He was as vain as he was cruel. Through incredible difficulties, he led his army across the Lybian desert, to visit the temple of Jupiter Ammon, and was there flattered with the title of "*Son of Jupiter.*" While in Egypt, he founded the city of Alexandria. Returning from Egypt, he again received liberal proposals from Darius; but these he haughtily rejected, telling him, "the world could no more admit of two masters than two suns." What a "mad boy!"—he could neither be beaten nor pacified.

Next ensued the famous battle of Arbela, on the banks of the Tigris, 331 B. C. Alexander crossed the Euphrates with an army of only fifty thousand men, and met the Persian army of seven hundred thousand. A fearful fight ensued, in which the Persians were defeated with a loss of three hundred thousand men, while Alexander lost only five hundred. This great battle changed the tide of the world's affairs. Europe has ever since maintained the superiority over Asia, which was then acquired. Then, for the first time, was the *ark of power* removed from its old native home Westward, from whence it has never gone back. Hence the proverb,

"Westward, empire makes its way." Darius, having first escaped into Media, and thence to Bactria, was there betrayed by Bessus, the satrap of the province, and murdered; and soon the whole Persian empire submitted to the "mad boy."

Not satisfied with his victories, Alexander projected, in 328 B. C., the conquest of India. In a great battle, he defeated Porus, a king of that country, who, upon being taken prisoner, and brought to Alexander, was asked by him how he wished to be treated? He replied: "Like a king!" This so pleased Alexander, that he released Porus, and restored his kingdom to him.

Alexander's soldiers becoming weary of war, and seeing no probable end of the ambitious schemes of their leader, resolved to return. Being unable to overcome their reluctance to follow him further, Alexander yielded to them, and returned to Babylon. Hence it does not appear that he had "conquered the world, and wept because there were no more worlds to conquer." There were nations still east of where he went, besides formidable old Rome, and her tormenting rival, Carthage, in the west, still unconquered and uninvaded.

This renowned conqueror of antiquity made Babylon the seat of his empire. Though usually accustomed to self-control, his brilliant career, with the extravagant adulations of the sycophants who surrounded him, he became at length intoxicated with his glory; believed himself a son of Jupiter, and a god; believed he could do no wrong, and that his will should be the supreme law of his subjects; and hence very soon ruled, not like a god, but like a depraved tyrant.

It is said that Antipater, whom he left to govern Macedonia during his absence, wrote a long letter to Alexander, complaining in many things of Olympias, his mother; when he said, with a smile: "Antipater does not know that one tear shed by a mother will obliterate ten such letters as this." On the other hand, Parmenio, his best general, he caused to be assassinated on mere suspicion. Clytus, who saved his life at the Granicus, he ran through the body with a spear (precisely what Clytus did to *save* him), when heated with wine. He caused the philosopher Calisthines to be cruelly put to death for refusing to worship him as a divinity.

He ran his career of conquest in six short years, dying in Babylon, from a fever brought on by a drunken debauch, in the thirty-third year of his life, and the thirteenth of his reign.

ALEXANDER'S SUCCESSORS. — He left his vast empire, without appointing any one to succeed him. On his death-bed, he gave his ring to Perdiccas; and upon being asked to whom he left his empire, replied: "To the most worthy."

A scramble followed, among his soldiers, for a share in the spoils they helped to gather; but the empire was finally divided among thirty-three of his principal officers. This was done after the fruitless attempt to place upon the throne his son Hercules, by Bassine, one of his wives. His brother, Philip Aridocus, and a son, born after his death, named Alexander, were soon put to death; and so his family was cut off.

A series of wars and assassinations ensued, which put his kingdom into the hands, ultimately, of four of his generals, 312 B. C. Ptolemy had Egypt, Cassander had Macedonia and Greece, Lysimachus had Thrace, and Seleucus had Syria. These were each in turn absorbed by Rome.

Antipater. — Several attempts were made by the Greeks, in Alexander's absence, to throw off the Macedonian yoke, but were all suppressed by Antipater, who was left in charge. The Spartans and Athenians made resolute efforts to gain their liberty, but were subdued, and Athens was obliged to purchase peace by giving up ten of her public speakers, among whom was Demosthenes, who had excited the Athenians to resistance.

Phocion. — The news of Alexander's death gave great joy to the Athenians, whom Demosthenes tried to arouse to resistance; but he was strongly opposed by the incorruptible Phocion, who was a strenuous advocate of peace, and whose language was: "Since the Athenians are no longer able to fill their wonted glorious sphere, let them adopt counsels suited to their abilities, and endeavor to court the favor of a power which they cannot provoke but to their ruin."

The spirit of turbulence could not rest in Athens; after the death of Antipater, the Athenians proceeded to put those to death who had been friendly to his rule, among whom was the venerable Phocion, now upwards of eighty years of age. He had been forty-five times chosen governor of Athens, besides performing eminent services for the country. To a friend who lamented his fate, he said: "This is no more than what I expected; this treatment, the most illustrious citizens of Athens have received before me."

The following message he sent to his son, just before taking the hemlock: "Tell him that I desire he will not remember the injustice of the Athenians."

Athens enjoyed twelve years of quiet and prosperity under the rule of Demetrius Phalereus, to whom the Athenians testified their gratitude by erecting three hundred and sixty statues to his memory. After him, the glory of Athens wasted away; "Ichabod" eclipsed her renown. Following immediately upon the invasion of

Greece by the Gauls, under Brennus their king, was that of Pyrrhus into the states of the Peloponnesus. He was King of Epirus, and the greatest general of his age. Besides an unsuccessful attack upon Sparta, he was slain at the siege of Argos, with a tile thrown by a woman from the top of a house. See Abimelech.

Achæan League. — The last effort of the Greeks to save themselves from annihilation, was the union of twelve of the smaller states into the Achæan League.

The government of this confederacy was committed to Aratus, with the title of Pretor. He designed establishing the independence of all Greece; but the jealousy of the larger states rendered the scheme abortive.

Aratus was succeeded by Philopœmen, a man of abilities, but with the unenviable title of "The last of the Greeks," as Greece produced no man of note after him. He committed a wanton butchery upon the people of Sparta, when they fell into his hands; but was himself taken by the Messenians, and compelled to drink hemlock.

Sparta had at this time a miserable king, named Nabis. He banished most of the wealthy citizens, that he might seize upon their estates. He also invented a machine, resembling his wife, the breasts, arms, and hands of which were full of iron pegs, covered with magnificent garments. If any one refused to give him money, he was introduced to this machine, which would lay hold of him, and, by her terrible hugging, compel him to give Nabis money. (A similar instrument was used in the dungeons of the Inquisition, in Spain, to extort confessions from the Waldenses.)

The first step of the Romans towards the subjugation of Greece, was in giving aid to the Ætolians, against the Macedonians. (They probably thought as little that they were inviting their conquerors into the country, as did the Persians, when they employed the ten thousand Greeks. Both those expeditions gave the subsequent conquerors the desired knowledge of the enemy's country). This invitation the Romans promptly accepted, and their army, under command of Quintius Flaminius, defeated Philip, King of Macedon, at Cynocephale, and proclaimed liberty to the Grecian states.

Nearly thirty years after, or 167 B. C., a second Roman army, led by Paulus Æmilius, entered Greece, defeated Perseus, son of Philip, in the battle of Pydna, and he was led captive to Rome. Macedonia was reduced to a Roman province.

The Romans, jealous of the Achæan League, sought to weaken it, by corrupting its principal citizens, and cherishing divisions among the states. At length the Spartans invoked the aid of Rome against the League. Metellus led his legions into Greece, and gained a complete victory over the Achæan forces. The remainder of the army shut themselves up in Corinth; the Roman consul, Mummius, finished the conquest by taking and destroying the city. The Achæan constitution was soon after dissolved, and all Greece reduced to a Roman province, under the name of Achaia.

Greece, though conquered by the Roman arms, yet maintained a silent superiority, in the influence of her learning, taste, genius, and arts. The most distinguished Romans were educated in the Grecian schools of philosophy; so that the victors became the disciples of the vanquished.

In reviewing the history of Greece, if we take our stand where we can see their genius, taste, learning, patriotism, love of liberty, and heroism, the Greeks stand renowned and unrivalled among the nations of antiquity. But if we look at the fickleness, ingratitude, and injustice, shown towards some of her most worthy citizens, they appear in a light in which no true man would consider it either safe or honorable to be their public servant. Conquest was the ruling passion of the Greeks; and living in the age of "war for power," they not only partook of the spirit of the times, but contributed, in no small degree, to lend honor and glory to the wicked trade of war.

From their own writings it is evident that the boundaries of right and wrong, justice and injustice, honesty and dishonesty, were little determined by any generally received principles; but that "*might made right*," especially in public transactions, was a tenet generally avowed and practised. Hence the best specimens of self-education and self-culture ever furnished the world (in the history of the Greek nation), having failed of making even themselves a model specimen of humanity, justice, and piety, we instinctively turn from them, to look for some better guide for man than *human* wisdom has been able to afford him, either as a member of society, or as a being formed for immortality.

About one hundred and fifty years after this, the much desired wisdom was brought to light, in the Life, Teachings, Death, Resurrection, and Ascension of the "Desire of all Nations."

II.—AGE OF WAR FOR POWER.

SYRIA—FROM 3703 A. M., AND 301 B. C., TO 3939 A. M, AND 65 B. C.

Syria presents but very little worthy of notice; and all the reason we have for noticing it here, is simply because of hostility shown by some of its kings to the Jewish nation. No conqueror ever showed them more favor than Alexander, and none ever showed them more ill-will than his successors in Syria.

SELEUCUS. — Antigonus, one of Alexander's generals, succeeded to his Asiatic dominions, but was supplanted by Seleucus (son of Antiochus, one of Philip's generals), also Alexander's general.

Antigonus was slain in the battle of Ipsus, when Seleucus founded the kingdom of Syro-Media, 312 B. C., which continued about two hundred and forty-seven years. It was governed by twenty-three kings, called "Seleucidæ," from the founder. Seleucus was a great general, an able and popular sovereign, surnamed Nicator, or Conqueror, on account of twenty-three battles in which he gained the victory. He founded sixteen large cities, the most famous of which were Antioch, Seleucia, Apamea, and Laodicea. Antioch became the capital of the kingdom, and was called the "Queen of the East," and the "Eye of the Christian Church."

ANTIOCHUS THE GREAT. — He was the sixth of the Seleucidæ, 223 B. C. He reigned thirty-six years, and was as much distinguished for his faults and misfortunes, as for his qualities and successes. He was visited by Hannibal, the great Carthaginian general, who endeavored to persuade him to make war upon Rome. Instead of this, he invaded Greece, was defeated by the Romans, and compelled to retire to Asia. Being pursued by the Roman army, under Scipio Asiaticus, and defeated at Magnesia, he was compelled to accept a peace on very humiliating terms, and was afterwards put to death by his own officers.

ANTIOCHUS EPIPHANES. — This was the eighth king of Syria under the Seleucidæ.

Epiphanes was a monster of cruelty. After being ordered out of Egypt by the Roman consul, he returned to Jerusalem, and vented his wrath upon the Jews, nearly annihilating their existence as a nation, and almost obliterated their ancient form of worship. Returning from Syria, for the purpose of crushing them utterly, he died in his chariot, singularly, suddenly, and terribly. Several other kings of Syria did much to injure the Jews as a people; but, in spite of them all, they were wonderfully preserved as a nation. See Judas Maccabeus.

TIGRANES.— He was the twenty-second king of the Seleucidæ, 83 B. C. The Syrians, becoming weary of the dissolute reigns of the Seleucidæ, determined to put an end thereto; whereupon they invited Tigranes, King of Armenia, to accept the government at their hands. This he did, and swayed the sceptre of Syria for eighteen years, in perfect peace. Engaging afterwards in war with the Romans, he was defeated by Lucullus, the Roman consul, 69 B. C.

After this, Antiochus XIII. (or Asiaticus, the last of the Seleucidæ), was acknowledged King of Syria, until it was reduced to a Roman province by Pompey, 65 B. C.

II.—AGE OF WAR FOR POWER.

CARTHAGE—FROM DIDO, 2844 A. M., AND 1160 B. C., TO ITS DESTRUCTION BY THE ROMANS, 3857 A. M., AND 147 B. C.

The first impulse given this famous city of old, was by Dido, a Tyrian princess. She was daughter of Belus, King of Tyre, and married her uncle Sichæus. Pygmalion, her brother, being the successor of Belus, coveting Sichæus' property, ran him through with a spear, while out in a chase. Dido, suspecting her brother's design, asked the privilege, and the assistance of a few ships, to remove her effects to a small city between Tyre and Sidon, where she might live with her brother Barca. Her brother and others favoring her *real* design, as soon as she got her property on board, she set sail for Cyprus; and there taking in a large number of young women, she sailed for Carthage, where she arrived somewhere from 1150 to 900 B. C.

Pygmalion, being defeated in his schemes, was about to send a fleet after the fugitives, but was dissuaded by the tears of his mother, and the threatening predictions of the oracle. The beauty of Dido, as well as the fame of her enterprise, gained her many admirers. Being threatened with war by Iarbas King of Mauritania, her subjects wished to compel her to marry him. Dido requested three months to consider the matter. During the time, she erected a funeral pile, under pretence of appeasing the spirit of Sichæus, to whom she had vowed eternal fidelity. When her plans were completed, she ascended the pile in presence of her people, and stabbed herself; for which feat she is called "*Dido*," or valiant woman. The term "dido," a trick, is also named from her. She was noted for valor and tricks. Wishing to purchase a piece of land in a very important location, she could only have a piece "as large as she could cover with a green hide." She obtained the largest one she could find, had it cut in very small strings, and, by tying them together, drew the whole around a very nice patch of ground.

The government of Carthage, at first monarchical, afterwards became republican; and was commended by Aristotle, as one of the best of antiquity. The religion of the Carthaginians was a cruel superstition, and human victims were offered in sacrifice.

In the time of the "Punic Wars," Carthage was the most commercial, wealthy, and one of the most splendid cities in the world. It had under its dominion about three hundred smaller towns in Africa, a great part of Spain, and also of Sicily and other islands. The Carthaginians worked the gold mines of Spain, and were devoted to commerce. The Romans, who were their rivals and enemies, represented them as wanting in integrity and honor. Hence the ironical phrase, "*Punica fides*" (Punic faith), to denote treachery. Carthage produced few men of distinction, either in philosophy or arts. Her greatest generals were Hamilcar, and his sons, Asdrubal and Hannibal. The latter had instilled into his mind by his father, at an early age, mortal and unceasing hatred to the Roman name; and Hannibal proved the most formidable enemy Rome ever had.

Several things will be omitted here, in the history of this ancient people, that will appear in the history of Rome, and her wars with Carthage. But the final destruction of Carthage may be here briefly described. At the close of the third Punic war, Carthage was humbled, and her people were ready to offer any submission, even to acknowledge themselves subjects of Rome. Besides this, the Romans demanded a promise of implicit obedience, and three hundred hostages, as a security for its fulfilment.

In compliance with this, they gave up their own children as the hostages. Next, they were required to deliver up their arms, ships, and munitions of war; this they did also. But when the last demand was made, to complete their degradation, which was to vacate the city, that it might be razed to the ground, their old Carthaginian pride was aroused. They resolved to fight or die, or both. Robbed of all means of defence, they were at first able to do but little, yet enough to astonish the Romans.

Their vessels of gold and silver were converted into weapons of war, and the women cut off and twisted their fine hair into bowstrings; and such was the desperate, and even successful resistance they offered, it is thought that the city would not have been taken, had not one of her own officers basely gone over to the enemy.

Scipio Æmilianus cut off their supplies of food, blockaded their port, and destroyed their army placed outside the walls, consisting of eight thousand; he then broke through the walls, demolishing and setting on fire the houses and public buildings. Asdrubal delivered himself and the citadel to the conquerors. Devastation and ruin spread on every hand. The burning of the city continued seventeen days, consuming the habitations of seven hundred thousand people, who either delivered themselves prisoners of war, were massacred, or perished in the flames. The scenes of horror were such as to force tears from the eyes of the Roman general. The same year, both Carthage and Corinth were destroyed, and their interests absorbed in Rome.

II.—AGE OF WAR FOR POWER.

ROME.—FROM JANUS TO HONORIUS AND CONSTATINE XII.

PERIOD I. FROM JANUS, 2715, A. M., 1289 B. C., TO THE FOUNDING OF ROME, 3251 A. M., 753 B. C.

Janus.—The very early history of Italy is involved in obscurity. But we have an account of a king named Janus, who arrived there from Thessaly, as early as 1289 B. C., and planted a colony of Greeks on the banks of the river Tiber. Italy was divided into several small states, of which Latium was one, and of this Janus was king.

Latinus.—The fourth king from him was Latinus, in whose reign Æneas arrived in Italy, with a band of exiles from the burning of Troy. Latinus hearing of this arrival, and being already engaged in war with the Rutuli, immediately marched to meet the strangers, expecting to find a posse of banditti. But Æneas, though commanding a body of hardy veterans, held out the olive of peace. Latinus listened to their melancholy tale, and, pitying the misfortunes of the Trojan exiles, granted them a portion of land, on condition of their joining him against the Rutuli.

Æneas eagerly embraced the offer, and rendered such excellent service to the Latins, that the king bestowed on him his only daughter, Lavinia, in marriage, with the right of succession to the crown.

Æneas. — This Trojan prince, though obliged to flee from the destruction of his once proud and valiant city, met a very pleasant fortune in Italy, by being engrafted into the royal family of the Latins.

From this time, for four hundred years, the line of succession continued in his family, through fifteen kings.

Numator. — This was the fifteenth king in the direct line from Æneas. Amulius, the king's brother, being ambitious for the throne, usurped the government, drove Numator into exile, caused the king's only son to be murdered, and compelled Rhea Sylvia, his only daughter, to become a vestal ("nun").

His object in this was to cut off all possibility of his brother's family ever furnishing an heir to the throne. But this was not so to be; for Sylvia, though a *vestal*, in the process of time became also a mother, giving birth to a pair of twin boys, named Remus and Romulus.

Amulius hearing of this breach of vestal vows (forgetting the "beam in his own eyes," as a murderer, usurper, and oppressor), immediately ordered the execution of the penalty of burning alive, imposed on erring vestals; but was prevented from so doing, by the intercessions of his own daughter.

The infants were thrown into the Tiber, by his order. The basket in which they were enclosed floated, and bore them to the foot of the Aventine Mount, where it stranded. It is fabled that a she-wolf nursed them and reared them; but this mistake arose from the circumstance, that the woman's name who found them was *Lupa*, which means "she-wolf." (Not wholly unlike the story of Moses, hid in a basket, and not impossible that it was fabricated out of the story of the Hebrew child.)

The two brothers became shepherds, were fond of hunting wild beasts, and finally went to opposing the bands of robbers that infested the country. Having been informed of their (*half*) royal birth, and of the treatment of their mother and grandfather, and the attempt upon their own lives, they turned their arms against their uncle Amulius, and killed him. Numator, after forty-two years of exile, was again seated upon the throne by his grandsons. To these brothers Numator granted a section of territory, and the liberty of building a city on the hills where they had fed their flocks, and permitted such of his subjects as chose to resort thither and aid in the work.

A difference of opinion arising between the brothers, about the precise spot to begin the city, Numator advised them to watch the flight of birds. They took their stations on different hills; Remus saw six vultures, Romulus saw twelve. Both claimed the victory, — one had the *first* omen, the other the more *complete*. A contest was the result; when Remus, jumping over the walls of the city, was struck dead on the spot by Romulus, who declared that no one should insult his rising walls with impunity.

Romulus, now only eighteen years of age, was left to pursue the enterprise alone. (One is reminded here of the case of Cain and Abel.) He fixed on the Palatine hills as the spot, and enclosing about a mile of territory in extent with a wall, he filled it with one thousand houses or huts. To this beginning he gave the name of *Rome*, after himself, 3251 A. M., 753 B. C. At first, he peopled it with the tumultuous and vicious rabble which he found in the neighborhood. Though nearly destitute of laws, it soon became a regulated community.

PERIOD II. FROM THE FOUNDING OF ROME, 3251 A. M., 753 B. C., TO THE COMMONWEALTH, 3495 A. M., 509 B. C.

ROMULUS. — Having been elected king, he introduced order and discipline among his subjects. The course he pursued so commended itself to observers, that great numbers of men from the small towns around Rome flocked to the city, so that it increased daily in power and extent.

He is said to have divided his people into three tribes, and each tribe into three wards. He further divided them into two orders: patricians and plebeians. He instituted a senate of one hundred members, afterwards increased to two hundred. At first, they were chosen from the patricians, but the plebeians were afterwards raised to that dignity. In hope of uniting the two orders, he established the connection of *patron* and *client*. Each plebeian had a right to choose a patrician for his patron, whose duty it was to protect him from oppression, and who received from his client certain services. The king was attended by twelve lictors with fasces (*i. e.*, an axe tied up in a bundle of sticks), and a guard of three hundred horsemen, called knights.

The division of the people into patricians and plebeians, was a very unwise and unnecessary one, beside being a very injurious one. It was the source of more discontent and strife than any other.

Indeed, the experience of the Romans on this point establishes the importance of "*the equality of all the citizens before the civil authority*." The opposite course will work its own repeal, or the nation's political ruin that adopts it.

The most celebrated affair that occurred during the reign of Romulus, was the "Rape of the Sabine women," as it is called. The people who gathered around him at first were men, and soon they all began to feel the truth of the divine maxim, "It is not good for man to be alone." Upon this, Romulus proposed intermarriage with the Sabines, his neighbors. His offer was rejected with scorn, upon which he had resort to artifice and force. A magnificent display was gotten up in the city, and the neighboring tribes were invited to attend as spectators, when it was found the Sabines, with their wives and daughters, were among the foremost to be present. At a given signal, the Roman youth rushed in among the crowd with drawn swords, seized the youngest and most beautiful of the women, and carried them off by violence. This bold intrusion gave great offence to the virgins at first, *but for some cause*, they finally became reconciled to their new situation.

The Sabines resented the affront, and flew to arms. Under their leader, Tatius, they entered the Roman territories; and having, by stratagem, gained some advantage, they kept up the war at pleasure. At length both parties prepared for a general engagement. In the midst of the fight, the Sabine women, who had been carried off by the Romans, rushed in between the combatants, and exclaimed: "If any must die, let it be us, who are the cause of your animosity; since, if our parents or our husbands fall, we must in either case be miserable in surviving them." This step had the desired effect; and a compromise was agreed upon, which was, that Romulus and Tatius should reign jointly in Rome. Also, that one hundred Sabines should be admitted into the senate, and that as many of the Sabines as chose should enjoy the privileges of Roman citizens.

Tatius survived this affair but five years, when Romulus was again left with the supreme power in his hands. In attempting to usurp the liberties of his people, it is said the senators tore him in pieces in the senate house. The fable in the case, however, is, that while in the act of giving instruction to the senators, he disappeared from their sight. An eclipse of the sun occurring at that time, was used to favor the rumor that he was taken up to heaven.

The above device for obtaining wives might have been an imitation of a like occurrence at Shiloh, when the Benjaminites obtained wives in a very similar manner. (See page 75.) The fable of the translation of Romulus is doubtless founded upon that of Elijah the prophet, page 106.

The Romans paid Romulus divine honors, under the name of Quirinus, and ranked him among the gods.

Compare his fate in the senate, and Julius Cæsar's.

NUMA POMPILIUS. — He became the next king of Rome, in about a year after the death of Romulus, — nearly seven hundred and fifteen years before Christ. He was a Sabine, and the wisest and best of the Roman kings. When offered the throne, he declined accepting it, until overpersuaded by the people; he gave up his own wishes to comply with theirs. He is said to have been a wise and virtuous man, and before coming to the throne, lived contentedly in private. He multiplied the national gods, built temples, and instituted different classes of priests, and a great variety of religious ceremonies. A kind of Solomon.

The Romans received great benefit from the counsels of Numa. He softened their fierce and warlike dispositions, by cherishing the arts of peace, obedience to the laws, and respect for religion. He built the temple of Janus (probably in honor of Janus of Thessaly), which was open during war, and closed during peace.

TULLIUS HOSTILIUS. — He was the third king of Rome, 672 B. C. His disposition was warlike, and by his arms several of the neighboring states — among them were the Albans and Fidenates — were added to the dominion of Rome. The Sabines, now disunited from the Romans, became their most powerful enemies. Tullius reigned thirty-three years, and is said to have been killed by lightning. The remarkable battle between the Horatii and Curatii occurred during his reign.

The story is as follows: In a war between the Romans and Albans, as the two armies were about to engage in battle, the Alban general proposed that the dispute should be decided by single combat, both parties to abide by the issue. To this the Roman general consented. The Horatii and Curatii were six in number, the sons of two sisters, each three at a birth, the former in the Roman, and the latter in the Alban army, — both parties renowned for their valor. Both armies were drawn up in battle form. When the signal was given, the six combatants rushed to the fight. Soon the Curatii were all wounded, and shouts of victory ran along the Roman lines. But soon, again, two of the Romans fell dead; then the shout ran along the Alban lines. Quick as thought, the only surviving Roman fled. The Curatii followed in pursuit, and the Romans hissed him in his flight. But as soon as Horatius had drawn his pursuers after him, at distances from each other, measured by the severity of their wounds, he turned upon them, and, as he met them one after another, laid them dead at his feet. The hisses of the Romans were soon changed.

But behold the end of earthly glory. Horatius, returning to Rome with his laurels, found his sister weeping over the death of the Curiatii, one of whom she was engaged to marry. In a moment his anger arose, and he killed her on the spot. Horatius was condemned to die for his crime; but, appealing to the people, he was pardoned; but his fame departed. (The challenge to single combat reminds us of the like, between David and Goliath.)

Ancius Martius. — He was the fourth king of Rome. He inherited the virtues of his grandfather, Numa, besides being a warrior. He conquered the Latins, and built the fort of Ostia, at the mouth of the Tiber.

Tarquin the Elder. — He was the son of a Corinthian merchant, and was elected the fifth king of Rome. He embellished the city with works of utility and magnificence; built the walls of hewn stone; erected the circus, or hippodrome; founded the capitol; and constructed immense sewers, or aqueducts, to convey the rubbish and superfluous waters into the Tiber.

Servius Tullius. — He was the son of a captive female slave. He ruled with political wisdom. He attained the vacant throne by his own address, and the assistance of his mother-in-law. He married the daughter of Tarquin. He established the *census*, by which, at the end of every fifth year, the number of citizens, their dwellings, number of children, and amount of property, was ascertained. (Similar to David's numbering the people.)

Servius had two daughters; the elder was gentle and submissive, the younger, haughty and ambitious. In order to secure the throne, he married them to two sons of the late king, named Tarquin and Aruns, whose different dispositions corresponded to those of his daughters, — taking care to cross their tempers, hoping they would correct each other in these repects. Servius, having arranged the succession, intended to retire to private life.

But, alas! his violent-tempered daughter Tullia coveted her sister's husband, and he reciprocating her affection for him, they murdered their partners, and the violent Tullia and Tarquin were united.

They next plotted the death of Servius himself. And no sooner had Tullia heard of the death of her father, by the hand of Tarquin, than she ordered her chariot, and went to salute him as prospective king. And while driving her on this base errand, her coachman, seeing her father lying dead in the street, was about turning down another street, to spare her the horrid spectacle of her mangled father's corpse; but the base woman bade him drive on, and she saluted the wretched Tarquin while her chariot wheels were red with the blood of her gray-haired father. But of this cup, Tarquin and royalty had to drink the dregs.

Tarquin the Proud. — He was the last king of Rome, son of Tarquin the Elder, and son-in-law to Servius, and a tyrant.

Having usurped the throne, he began his reign by putting to death the chief senators, and governing in the most arbitrary manner; but his excesses soon disgusted his subjects, and he became the object of universal dislike. But his son Sextus having greatly indulged in detestable vices, became the occasion of his own and the king's ruin.

He and Collatinus, a noble Roman, and some officers, while with the army besieging the town of Ardea, in the height of a drunken frolic were boasting what excellent wives each possessed. Collatinus contended that his was best; and to carry on the joke, the young men mounted their horses and rode home, to see how their wives would be employed, taken by surprise. The ladies were all found visiting, and passing their time in amusements, except Lucretia, the wife of Collatinus. She was industriously spinning wool among her maidens at home.

Sextus, smitten with love for the beautiful Lucretia, and, upon returning to camp, stung with the triumph of Collatinus over them all, plotted a terrible blow — one that would gratify his own lust, and inflict a deep wound upon Collatinus. Returning to the house of Collatinus, Sextus found Lucretia, who received him hospitably, as a prince and a companion of her husband in arms. But when the pall of night was spread, the vile Sextus brutally ventured upon the deed known in history by the title, "Rape of Lucretia."

The unhappy Lucretia immediately sent for her husband and father, who brought with them Junius Brutus, and other friends. To them she related her mournful story, enjoining upon them to avenge her injury; and being unable to survive her dishonor, she plunged a dagger into her bosom, and expired.

Brutus, whose father and brother had been slain by Tarquin, had feigned himself insane, waiting an opportunity for revenge. That time had now come.

Snatching the dagger from the wound of the bleeding Lucretia, he swore upon the reeking blade: "Be witness, ye gods, that from this moment I proclaim myself the avenger of the chaste Lucretia's cause!" This energetic speech and action, in one who had been reputed a fool, astonished Rome. Her corpse was carried to the public square; the vengeance of the people was aroused; and, by the strenuous exertions of Brutus, the senate pronounced sentence of perpetual banishment against Tarquin and his family.

Collatinus and Brutus then raised an army, and drove Sextus and his infamous father from Rome. The tyrant being expelled from his capital, and abandoned by his army, was never able to gain re-admission into the city. With the expulsion of the royal family, followed that of royalty also. Thus ends the line of the Roman kings, 3495 A. M., 509 B. C. The reäction of the violence done Lucretia, swept away both the throne of the Tarquins and the royalty of Rome.

PERIOD III. FROM THE COMMONWEALTH, 3495 A. M., AND 509 B. C., TO THE FIRST TRIUMVIRATE, 3945 A. M., 59 B. C.

Brutus and Collatinus. — The government of Rome now passed from a regal to a republican form; though for a time it was controlled by the aristocracy. But setting aside the king, they chose in his place two persons annually, from the patrician families, as presidents of the Republic, called *consuls*. The first consuls of Rome were Brutus and Collatinus, who had been so active in ejecting the royal family.

Tarquin, as a matter of course, vowed revenge. Fleeing to Etruria, he succeeded in enlisting the two powerful cities, Veii and Tarquinii, in his behalf. A large party existed also in Rome, who favored royalty; and a plot was formed, by which the gates were to be secretly opened, and let Tarquin and his army into the city. The plot being discovered, and the agents apprehended, what must have been Brutus' surprise to find two of his own sons among the conspirators. He, however, acted the part of a Roman consul, and ordered them beheaded in his presence, and remained unmoved during the execution.

All hope from within being cut off, Tarquin was now left to seek aid *outside* the city. A battle ensued between his forces and the Romans, under Brutus and Valerius (chosen consul in place of Collatinus). In this battle, Brutus and Aruns (son of Tarquin) met, and so deadly was the strife, that they both fell dead together.

The Roman matrons honored the memory of Brutus, by wearing mourning for him a whole year. He was further honored as the "Father of the Republic." Valerius was the first Roman who enjoyed the reward of a triumph, which was given him on his return to the city.

Valerius. — He having become arrogant, from the honors bestowed upon him, his popularity began to decline. With a view to save his sinking fame, he proposed a law, termed from him the *Valerian law*, which gave every citizen condemned by a magistrate the right of appeal to the people. This gave the first blow to the aristocracy of the Romans.

Horatius Cocles. — Tarquin, after his second defeat, fled for aid to Porsenna, King of Clusium, who marched toward Rome with a large army, and would have entered it, but for the valor of one man.

Horatius Cocles, while standing as sentinel on a bridge, saw the enemy approaching, and the Romans retreating. He eagerly besought the latter to remain and demolish or burn the bridge, while he should face the foe and hinder their advance. The Romans seconding his proposal, Horatius then advanced, and fought desperately in the midst of his enemies, until he heard the crash of the bridge, when he turned and fled. Leaping into the river, he swam safely across, having effectually stopped the enemy, and saved Rome.

Mutius Scævola. — This bold Roman youth obtained liberty of the senate to go in disguise into the camp of Porsenna, for the purpose of assassinating him.

Entering his tent, and seeing a man there very richly dressed, he supposed him to be the king, and laid him dead. It proved, however, to be only the king's secretary. In trying to make his escape from the camp, Mutius was taken, and brought before Porsenna, who threatened him with severe torture if he did not reveal the schemes of the Romans. Mutius, to show him the little effect torture would have, put his own hand into a fire near him, and held it steadily there. Porsenna, seeing this fortitude, leaped from his throne, pulled the hand from the flame, and dismissed him without further harm. He doubtless inferred from this, that Roman courage was no trifle. Upon this incident peace was concluded, and so ended the third attempt of Tarquin to regain his throne.

Mamilius, son-in-law of the Tarquins, excited the Latins to espouse their cause, and make war upon Rome. The city was again in danger; but the plebeians refused to aid in repelling the enemy, unless the senate would release them from their debts to the patricians, by whom they were oppressed. The consuls found they could do nothing by pressing them into service, as the Valerian law gave them a right to appeal to the people, and so escape them.

An extraordinary emergency now arose. All orders by the consuls could be thwarted by appeals. Hence the necessity for an office and officer, available on such critical occasions. This demand was supplied by the appointment of a *dictator*, to hold office not over six months, and only during the danger. He had authority to make peace and war, to levy taxes, appoint all public officers, and to dispense with the laws, without consulting the senate or people.

Titus Lartius. — He was the first dictator of Rome, and was raised from being consul to this high office. He immediately raised a large army, and by his firmness and moderation, having restored tranquillity, resigned the dictatorship. See also Cincinnatus, Sylla, and Diocletian.

Pothumius. — War having again been excited by the Tarquins, Pothumius was appointed to the dictatorship. Under him the Romans were victorious, and the sons of Tarquin were slain.

But peace without, did not secure peace within Rome. The old feud between the creditors and debtors was again revived. On an alarm of war, the plebeians refused to take up arms in defence of the republic. Their plea was, "Of what consequence is it to us, whether our chains be forged by our enemies or our fellow-citizens? Let the patricians, since they alone have the reward of *victories*, encounter the *dangers* of war." At length, finding no relief from their oppressions, the whole army abandoned their officers, and encamped on Mons Sacer, about three miles from the city, and were soon joined by the greater part of the people. (A natural result from the egregious folly of dividing the people into the two classes, — honorable and mean.)

This was full as effectual a measure on the part of the plebeians, as the dictatorship on the part of the patricians. It had the desired effect. The senate took alarm, and deputed ten of the most respectable of their number, with authority to grant redress. Menenius Agrippa, one of the senators, is said, in his speech to the people, to have related with great effect the celebrated fable of the *belly* and the *members*. A reconciliation was brought about. The debts of the plebeians were abolished, and, for their future security, they had the privilege of choosing annually from their number, five magistrates, styled "*tribunes*," who should have power of annulling, by a single *veto*, every measure which they should judge prejudicial to their interests. By them the aristocracy was held within bounds, and the fury of the populace was regulated.

Coriolanus. — The old feud of party was not, however, settled yet, nor could it be while impolitic distinction was kept up. The revolt of the army caused a neglect of agriculture, which brought on a famine. Relief, however, was obtained by an arrival of corn from Sicily.

But the contemptible aristocrat, Coriolanus, a man of some talent, and who had distinguished himself in the war against the Volsci, revived the old broil afresh. He proposed to withhold the corn from the plebeians until they should restore the *rights* (?) of the senate, and abolish the office of the tribunes. This base proposal excited the resentment of the people, and, as a consequence, the interference of the tribunes was called out, charges made against Coriolanus, and he was sentenced to perpetual banishment. He then went over to the Volsci, and though he had fought them as a Roman, yet they appointed him their commander. These powerful enemies of Rome he led against the city, bent on its destruction.

Several embassies were sent to meet him, and if possible turn him from his purpose, but to no avail. Finally his wife, Vergilia, and his mother, Veturia, with his children and the principal matrons of Rome, started to meet and dissuade him, if possible, from his mad scheme. They were successful.

Before their tears and entreaties his proud spirit drooped, and his warrior's arm fell. In her agony, his mother exclaimed: "Had I never been a mother, Rome had still been free!" In reply, he said, "O, my mother! thou hast saved Rome, but lost thy son." With this inglorious surrender the Volsci were displeased, and he was summoned before the people of Antium; but the clamors of his enemies were such, that he was murdered on the spot appointed for his trial. (Tyrants must expect a thorny path, who deliberately and maliciously trample on the rights of the people.)

To show their sense of Veturia's merit and patriotism, the Romans dedicated a temple to Female Fortune.

Agrarian Law. — This law was designed to meet the objection of the plebeians to enduring the fatigues of the wars and not sharing the spoils. It contemplated the division of the lands, obtained by conquest, among the people, and which were to be the joint property of all the citizens.

But it proved to be a bone of contention, not from its impropriety, but from the unwillingness of the patricians to yield even a fair share of the spoils to the plebeians, who did the fighting and endured the toils of the camp. The strife, however, ended in the triumph of the people.

Volero. — The monopoly and abuse of the supreme power by the patricians, worked its own cure. The frequent compliances on their part with the demands of the people, and as frequent violation of good faith, destroyed all confidence in their integrity, and hence no peace could be permanent until they were deprived of the power they held only to abuse.

Through the influence of the tribune Volero, this important end was secured. A law was enacted, that the election of tribunes should be made, and the chief public business discussed, in the Comitia, or public meetings of the tribes, and not, as before, by the centuries and wards. By this law the supreme authority was taken from the patricians, and put into the hands of the plebeians, and Rome became a democracy, about 471 B. C.

QUINCTIUS CINCINNATUS. — Troubles arising from the operation of the "Agrarian Law," and the threatened invasions of the Æqui and Volsci, the Romans again had recourse to the despotic measure of choosing a dictator, when Cincinnatus was chosen, 456 B. C.

He was fixed upon, as the wisest and bravest man of the commonwealth. He cultivated a small farm of *four acres* with his own hands. The deputies of the senate found him ploughing in one of his little fields, and approaching him, begged him to put on his gown and hear the message of the senate.

Cincinnatus anxiously inquired if all was well, and then requested his wife Racilia to bring his gown from their cottage. After wiping off the dust, with which he was covered, he put on his robe and went to the deputies. They saluted him Dictator, and bid him hasten to the city, which was in the greatest peril.

A handsome barge had been sent to carry him over the river, for his farm lay on the opposite side of the Tiber. His three sons, with his friends, and several of the senators, were ready to receive him as soon as he landed in Rome, and carry him in pompous procession to his head-quarters.

The next morning he began to fortify the city and marshal the soldiers for battle. He very soon gained a complete victory, and caused the officers of the enemy to pass under the military yoke of disgrace. He then entered the city in a splendid triumph, resigned his office, and in sixteen days returned again to his retirement, to labor upon his farm.

Many years after this, in the eightieth of his age, he was again called to the office of dictator, and acted with his own peculiar vigor and wisdom.

DECEMVIRI. — Hitherto, the Romans had never had a written code of laws. Under the kings and consuls, the exercise of justice and the public weal were at the mercy and caprice of these high functionaries. The frequent abuse of power by them, led the people to desire some standard by which they might expect, and demand, a fair and uniform administration of the government.

Three commissioners were accordingly chosen, and sent to Greece, in order to procure the laws of *Solon*, and such others as were deemed useful in forming a suitable code. Upon the return of the commissioners, ten of the principal senators, styled *decemvirs*, were appointed to digest a body of laws, and put them in execution for one year. This was the origin of those celebrated statutes, known by the name of the "Laws of the Twelve Tables" (being written on the twelve tables, and placed in the most conspicuous part of the city), and are still in repute in some parts of Europe.

Nine crimes, of very different complexion, were punishable by death, one of which was *nightly meetings*. The decemvirs were invested with absolute power, and during their term of office all other magistrates were suspended. Each decemvir, by turn, presided for a day, and had the sovereign authority, with its insignia, the fasces. The nine others acted as judges, to determine law-suits and correct abuses. During the first year, the decemvirs governed with so much moderation and equity, that they obtained a new appointment. But they soon became tyrannical, and the office was speedily terminated.

Appius Claudius. — He was the leading member of the body, and by two flagitious acts of his, the office of the decemviri sunk in disgrace.

One of these acts was his procuring the assassination of Sicinius Dentatus, a Roman tribune, who, on account of his valor and exploits, was styled the Roman Achilles. The other was an attempt to get into his possession a young maiden named Virginia. Having seen her as she was going to a public school, he fell in love with her, and proposed marriage to her. She declined his offer, as she was already engaged to marry Icilius, formerly a tribune.

Appius, bent on his purpose at all hazards, employed a miserable dependent of his to claim her as a daughter of one of his female slaves. This the vagabond did; and, bringing his case before the infamous decemvir, obtained a decision, putting the beautiful girl into the hands of Appius and his minion.

Virginius, her father, then at a distance with the army, being informed by Icilius of what was going on in the city, hastened thither with all possible despatch. Finding all was lost, and this wretch was about to tear his daughter from him by the strong arm of law, he resolved upon one more desperate attempt to liberate her. He begged, as he could not rescue her, the privilege of embracing her for the last time, before they parted.

This request being granted, he clasped his child in his arms, while she clung round his neck, wetting his cheeks with her tears. As he was tenderly kissing her, before raising his head he suddenly plunged a dagger into her bosom, saying, "O my child! by this means only can I give thee freedom!" He then held up the bloody instrument before the now pale and frighted Claudius, and exclaimed: "By this innocent blood, Appius, I devote thy head to the infernal gods!"

An uproar followed. Icilius showed the dead body to the people, and roused their fury. Virginius hastened to the camp, bearing the dagger reeking with his daughter's blood, and instantly the camp was aroused. Neither the decemviri nor the senate could still the tumult.

Appius died shortly after, in prison, by his own hand, and the other decemvirs went into exile. Public tranquillity was restored by the consent of the senate to abolish the decemviri, and to restore the consuls, together with the tribunes of the people.

Intermarriage. — The division of the people into patricians and plebeians, the bane of Roman jurisprudence, always disturbed the state, as soon as war outside was hushed. Such a distinction exhibits the *ignorance* of its originators and abettors; and its unsoundness as a line of policy, is seen in the spontaneous and endless feuds it generates among those who are its victims.

Growing out of this most unstatesmanlike division of the people by Romulus, was the refusal of intermarriage between the patricians and the plebeians. (The Romans had probably forgotten, at this time, where their forefathers got their wives, and how. See "Rape of Sabine Women.") The point was however, after a long struggle, conceded, in hope that this would satisfy the plebeians to remain quiet, and allow the aristocracy to go on unmolested in their schemes of aggrandizement and oppression.

Consulship. — The plebeians, however, were not content with any nor all concessions made to them, so long as there remained any *mutual* interest which was monopolized by the patricians. Equality before the civil authority shall extend to all classes alike, was their motto.

The restriction of the office of consul to the patrician order, furnished another source of uneasiness, which nothing but its removal could quiet. Military tribunes were substituted, three from each order, to take the place of the consuls, but were soon laid aside, and the consuls restored.

Regular Pay to the Troops. — In order to avoid the evil which arose from the people's frequently refusing to enlist in the army, the senate introduced the practice of giving "*regular pay to the troops.*" This opened the ranks to both orders, to enlist or not; and, as all were paid, the complaint of unequal division of spoils was stopped. The army was under the control of the senate, and the ranks could be easily filled at all times. From this event, about 400 B. C., the Roman system of war assumed a new aspect. The art of war was improved, and it now became a profession, instead of an occasional employment. The enterprises of the republic were more extensive, and its success more signal and important. This new mode of originating and keeping up armies is still adopted throughout the world. It was a new and very important era in the mode of warfare.

CAMILLUS. — The inhabitants of the city of Veii, long the proud rival of Rome, equal in extent and population, had repeatedly made depredations on the Roman territories, and it was decreed that Veii should be destroyed, whatever it might cost.

After some time, in order to carry on the siege with more vigor, Camillus was appointed dictator.

The Romans had nearly despaired taking the city, until the prosecution of the work was given up to Camillus.

He at once conceived the project of entering the city by a mine, which he caused to be wrought, and which opened into the midst of the capital. He then gave his soldiers directions how to enter the breach — the place was soon filled with his legions, to the utter confusion of the besieged, when the city was plundered and destroyed. Thus, like a second Troy, was Veii taken, after ten years of glorious (?) war. Camillus was honored with a splendid triumph, in which he was drawn by four milk-white horses.

Two years after, he led the Roman army against the city Falerii. During the siege, a schoolmaster betrayed into the hands of Camillus all his scholars, expecting to receive a large reward for his treachery, giving him to understand that a large sum would be paid for their ransom, being the sons of the nobility of Falerii. Camillus, shocked at this perfidious action, sent back the boys in safety to their parents, and, giving each a rod, bade them whip the traitor into town. This generous behavior accomplished more for Camillus than his arms,— the place immediately surrendering, and leaving the terms to the Roman, which were very mild. Some time after these things, an accusation was brought up against Camillus, charging him with appropriating to his own use a part of the plunder of Veii. Indignant at the ingratitude of his countrymen, he went into voluntary exile.

Rome was destined now to feel the weight of the Gothic power.

Her successes were turned into reverses. Under the command of their king, Brennus, the Gauls laid siege to Clusium, a city of Etruria, when its people implored the assistance of the Romans.

The senate despatched three of the patricians of the Fabian family on an embassy to Brennus, to inquire what offence the citizens of Clusium had given him. To this he sternly replied, that "the right of valiant people lay in their swords, and that the Romans themselves had no other right to the cities they had conquered.

The ambassadors having obtained leave, entered Clusium, and assisted the inhabitants against the assailants. This so incensed Brennus, that he raised the siege, and immediately marched for Rome. After defeating the Romans with great slaughter, the Gauls entered the city, and after the general massacre, pillaged it, and then reduced it to ashes, and razed the walls to the ground.

They next besieged the capitol, in which some of the brave young Romans had taken refuge, determined to resist to the last. At length, having discovered footsteps leading up to the top of the Tarpeian Rock, on which the capitol stood, a body of Gauls undertook to ascend it in the night, which they did, while the Roman sentinel was asleep. At this moment, the cackling of some geese in the temple of Juno, awoke Marius Manlius, who, with his associates, immediately threw the Gauls headlong down the precipice.

From this time the hopes of the Gauls began to decline; and they soon after agreed to quit the city, on condition of receiving one thousand pounds of gold. But after the gold was brought, the Gauls weighed it with false weights, and the complaint of this, made by the Romans, was treated with insolence by the Gauls. At this juncture, Camillus, who had been reäppointed dictator, appeared at the gates with an army, and, being informed of the deception and insolence of the Gauls, ordered the gold carried back to the capitol, and ordered them to retire; adding, that "Rome must be ransomed by steel, and not by gold." Upon this a battle ensued, when the Gauls were entirely routed, and *Camillus was honored as the father of his country, and the second founder of Rome.*

Manlius was amply rewarded for his heroism (after being awakened by the geese); but at length, envying the fame of Camillus, he abandoned himself to ambitious views, and being charged with aiming at sovereign power, he was sentenced to be himself thrown from the Tarpeian Rock. Thus, for aiming to rule Rome as the Gauls did, like them also he paid the same penalty. On this rock he built his fame and shame.

Lucius Sextius. — About 367 B. C., the plebeians gained admittance to the consulship; so that one of the two consuls was chosen from their order.

This long-desired end was at last attained, by the discontent of a young woman. Fabius Ambustius, having married his two daughters, one to a plebeian and the other to a patrician, the wife of the plebeian, envious of the honors of her sister, pined with discontent. Her father and brother, learning the cause of her unhappiness, promised her the distinction she desired. By their joint endeavors, and after much tumult and strife, the long-contested point was gained; and now a *plebeian* might be a *consul. Lucius Sextius* was the *first* plebeian consul, and Licinius Stolo, the husband of the plebeian lady, was the second.

Lucretia caused the overthrow of the Roman kings; Virginia caused the overthrow of the Decemviri; and the daughter of Ambustius, the overthrow of the distinction between the patricians and plebeians. Behold woman's power!

ROMAN CONQUESTS. — From the time of giving regular pay to the army, and the admission of the plebeians to the consulate, the extension of the Roman Empire began in good earnest.

After the Gauls were repulsed, and the Hernici, Æqui, Volci, etc., were subdued, a war of fifty years' length, brought the Samnites under the Roman dominion; not, however, without the Romans being obliged to pass under the military yoke of disgrace (which is made by two spears being set up astride, and another bound across them), once at least. This compliment the Romans turned upon the Samnites soon after, and finally subdued them.

The Latins next yielded submission.

A painful incident occurred under the consul Titus Manlius, during the war with the Latins. He had ordered the Roman soldiers not to quit the ranks without permission, on pain of death. A son of the consul happened, with his detachment, to meet a troop of Latins, led by Metius.

Metius dared the young Roman commander to single combat. Titus, forgetful of the order of his father, or indignant at the mocking Latin, sprang forward and slew him. Then gathering up the armor of the fallen foe, he ran and threw it at his father's feet, and told the story of his triumph.

The consul turned from him, and, ordering the troops assembled, thus addressed him in their presence:

"Titus Manlius! You this day dared to disobey the command of your consul and the orders of your father. You have thus done an injury to discipline and military government, and must by your death expiate your fault. Your courage has endeared you to me, but I must be just; and if you have a drop of my blood in your veins, you will not refuse to die when justice demands it. Go, lictor, and tie him to the stake."

The young Roman calmly knelt down beneath the axe.

If this be Roman virtue, let it perish from the earth. The consul's fault was greater than his son's.

The Tarentines, who were allies of the Samnites, called in the aid of Pyrrhus, King of Epirus, the greatest warrior of his age. He hastened into Italy, with an army of thirty thousand men, and twenty elephants. This mode of warfare astonished the Romans greatly, being wholly unaccustomed to it. But the bravery of the Romans astonished Pyrrhus even more, as his memorable saying indicates: "Oh, with what ease could I conquer the world, had I the Romans for soldiers, or had they me for their king."

The physician of Pyrrhus wrote to Fabricius, the Roman general, that for a suitable reward he would poison him. Fabricius dismissed the base proposal, saying: "We should be honorable even to our enemies;" and immediately informed Pyrrhus of the treachery. Pyrrhus, admiring the generosity of his enemy, exclaimed: "It would be easier to turn the sun from his course than Fabricius from the path of honor."

Not willing to be outdone in magnanimity by the Roman, Pyrrhus released all his Roman prisoners without ransom. With the defeat of Pyrrhus, followed the submission of all Lower Italy to Rome. The different states of Italy, however, though conquered, stood in different relations to the parent state. Some were entirely subject to the Roman laws; others were allowed to retain their original institutions; some were tributary; others, allies. The spirit of conquest being now fully aroused in the breasts of the Romans, and not being satisfied with *owning all that joined them*, they began to look with longing eyes to the regions beyond. As yet they had made no naval conquests, and possessed no fleet.

Carthage, bearing the aspect of a rival, was looked upon by the Romans as an object worthy of their attention. A pretext was found in a charge, that Carthage had assisted the enemies of Rome in the south of Italy, in her previous wars, and hence Carthage herself was judged an enemy of Rome, and must be chastised. Thus began the *first* Punic War. The zeal of the Romans was not abated in this war, from the circumstance that the Carthaginians were rich in merchandise, silver, and gold.

A better knowledge of maritime affairs was found necessary by the Romans; and a Carthaginian vessel, being driven ashore in a storm, furnished a model; and in two months a fleet of over one hundred vessels was prepared; and, under command of the consul Duillius, a naval battle was fought, and the Carthaginians were defeated, with a loss of fifty vessels. This victory put Syracuse into the hands of the Romans.

A second naval battle soon followed, under Regulus, off the coast of Sicily, in which the Carthaginians, under Hanno and Hamilcar, lost sixty vessels. They then proposed peace, but it was rejected.

Encouraged by this success, the Romans pushed across the sea into Africa, and took the small town of Clypea. Regulus, the leader, was ordered to remain there as pro-consul, and command the troops; but he was unwilling so to do, wishing to return and take care of a small estate of seven acres. Being assured that this should be done, and his family provided for, he consented to remain. He led the Roman army before the gates of Carthage.

But the Carthaginians had obtained Xantippus, a Spartan, to take the command, and under him the Romans were defeated, and Regulus taken prisoner. Having been kept a prisoner for several years, Regulus was finally sent with the Carthaginian ambassadors to Rome, to procure peace, with this oath upon him: that if the negotiation failed, he would return.

Upon his appearance in Rome, the people were willing to purchase his freedom by granting the request of their enemies. But Regulus saw that it would be a disgrace to his country to do so. He therefore besought the senate to send him back (though he knew that death by torture would be the result), and to refuse the demands of the Carthaginians, and retain their prisoners. The senate consented to this proposition with great reluctance, and, in spite of the tears of his wife, the embraces of his children, and the entreaties of his friends, Regulus returned to Carthage.

The Carthaginians put him to death by torture.

But at length the Romans overcame the Carthaginians, even on sea, and they were compelled to sue for peace on very humiliating terms. One condition was, the surrender of Sicily to the Romans, and to pay them three thousand two hundred talents of silver, and release their captives.

The Romans next made a conquest of Cisalpine Gaul. The peace between Rome and Carthage lasted twenty-three years. During part of that period the temple of Janus was shut, for the first time since the reign of Numa.

The *second* Punic war was begun by Hannibal, son of Hamilcar, the commander during the first one. Hannibal's father had caused him to take an oath when only nine years old, declaring himself the eternal enemy of the Romans; and scarcely did they ever have a more terrible foe. At the age of twenty-six, he was raised to the command of the Carthaginian army. He began the second Punic war by besieging Saguntum, a city of Spain, in alliance with Rome. After a siege of seven months, the inhabitants set fire to the city, and perished in the flames.

Hannibal then resolved to march his army over the Pyrenees, and afterward over the Alps, into Italy. This achieved, he gained four great victories over the Romans, the most important of which was that of Cannæ, the most memorable defeat the Romans ever suffered. Over forty thousand of their troops were left dead on the field, together with the consul Æmilius. More than five thousand Roman knights were slain, and Hannibal sent over three bushels of gold rings to Carthage, taken from their fingers.

Why Hannibal did not advance directly to Rome, after this great defeat of the Roman army, is not known. Instead of pushing his advantages to a successful issue, as he might have done, he lay at ease, comparatively, all the time losing ground, both in the energy of his troops, and the assaults of the Romans from time to time.

While Fabius was continually harassing the Carthaginians, Scipio had made an entire conquest of Spain. At this juncture Scipio suggested to the senate the propriety of his going over into Africa, and thereby draw Hannibal from Italy. This suggestion being favorably received, he invaded Africa, and spread terror and victory towards Carthage. Hannibal, who had now been absent for sixteen years, was recalled to save Carthage from impending ruin.

Hannibal and Scipio met on the plains of Zama, and great was the day and its battle. These two greatest warriors of the world gazed upon each other with mutual awe and admiration. Hannibal strove hard to procure an honorable peace, but the youthful Roman answered him with pride and disdain; when the two armies prepared for battle. The contest was dreadful, and fatal to Carthage. She lost forty thousand men in killed and prisoners, and was obliged to conclude a fatal peace, the terms of which were as follows: Carthage was to surrender all the islands of the Mediterranean, abandon Spain, give up all their prisoners, and their whole fleet, except ten galleys, and in future undertake no war without the consent of the Romans. Thus the end of the second Punic War resulted in humbling Carthage.

Hannibal survived this battle several years; but, being hated and hunted by the Romans, said, at last, "Let us relieve the Romans of their fears, by closing the existence of a feeble old man;" and ended his life by suicide.

The battle of Zama was 201 B. C. Syracuse, which had taken part with Carthage, and which was defended for three years by the inventive genius of the celebrated mathematician Archimedes, surrended to the prowess of Rome under Marcellus. Between this time and the third Punic war, Rome made conquest of Macedonia, in the defeat of Perseus, at the battle of Pydna; also of Asia Minor, under Scipio Asiaticus, in the defeat of Antiochus the Great, at the battle of Magnesia.

About fifty years after the close of the *second* Punic war, the Carthaginians attempted to repel the Numidians, who made incursions into the territory of the former. The Romans seized upon this act as a breach of the last treaty, — to undertake no war without the consent of the Romans, — and so came on the *third* Punic War. Porcius Cato, who now swayed the decisions of the Roman senate, had long cherished the savage design of annihilating Carthage, and was in the habit of closing his speeches with the expression, "Delenda est Carthago," — *Carthage must be destroyed.*

The Carthaginians saw the gathering storm, and, conscious of their inability to resist the Romans, sent two deputations to appease them, and avert, if possible, the threatened evil.

They offered every submission; yielded up their ships, their arms, and munitions of war. Three hundred hostages were demanded as a pledge of future good behavior, and they yielded up their children to meet this demand.

But, to complete their degradation, they were required to leave their city, that it might be levelled to the ground. This demand was heard by the inhabitants with a mixed feeling of indignation and despair. The spirit of liberty and independence not yet being extinct, was roused to make the last effort for themselves, resolved to sacrifice their lives rather than obey this barbarous mandate. After the most desperate resistance for three years, the city was at last taken by Scipio, the Second Africanus, and being set on fire, the flames continued to rage for seventeen days. Such of the inhabitants as disdained to surrender themselves prisoners of war, were either massacred or perished in the flames.

Thus was Carthage, with its walls and buildings, the habitations of seven hundred thousand people, razed to its foundations. The scenes of horror were such as to force tears even from the eyes of the *Roman general!* So complete was this final destruction, that even the place where it stood cannot now be discovered. This city was twenty-four miles in circumference. All the cities that befriended Carthage shared her fate, and the Romans gave away the lands to their friends. The same year (146 B. C.) in which Carthage was destroyed, Corinth was also taken, and Greece reduced to a Roman province.

Brave and irresistible as were the Romans, they suffered a most humiliating defeat, by the Numántines, in Spain. Four thousand of the latter conquered thirty thousand Romans, under the consul Mancinius. Scipio, however, being sent into Spain, soon redeemed the Roman name and honor.

Gracchi. — The spirit of conquest being somewhat satiated (as well it might, with most of Europe, Africa, and Asia Minor, including proud Greece, at its feet), the Romans began to cast about for a new feature in bloodshed. This they soon found, in the renewal of civil strife.

The Gracchi were sons of Cornelia, the daughter of Scipio Africanus, conqueror of Hannibal. She was left a widow with eleven children. A lady once visited Cornelia, and after gratifying her pride in showing her her jewels, asked to see Cornelia's in return. Cornelia waited until her boys returned from school, when she said to her guest: "Behold, madam, — these are my jewels." Tiberius Gracchus distinguished himself by filling the office of tribune according to its virgin intention, though by it he lost his life.

Attalus, King of Pergamus, having by his last will made the Romans his heirs, Tiberius proposed that the money be distributed among the poor. He also attempted to check the power of the patricians, by reviving the *Licinian Law*, which ordained that no citizen should possess more than five hundred acres of the public lands. This blow of abridgment upon the power and estates of the patricians, coming from a plebeian tribune, threw the aristocratic element into a great excitement, and consequent opposition. Happening to raise his hand to his head, in a public meeting, his enemies laid hold upon that slight circumstance to accuse him of desiring a crown, and in the tumult that ensued he lost his life, together with three hundred of his friends, who were killed in the forum by the senators.

Upon the death of Tiberius, the populace put his brother, Caius Gracchus, at their head, who was only twenty-one years of age at this time. He had lived in great retirement, yet did much good, and caused the enactment of many useful measures. He was temperate and simple in his food, and of an active and industrious disposition. His love and respect for his mother were manifested in withdrawing, at her request, a law he very much wished to have passed. So much was he esteemed, that a statue was erected to the memory of his mother, with the inscription: "Cornelia, the mother of the Gracchi."

The fatal issue of his brother's efforts did not deter Caius from pursuing a similar career, in maintaining the rights of the people against the encroachments of the senate; and, like his brother, fell a victim to the cause he aimed to serve. Caius, with three thousand of his adherents, was slaughtered in the streets of Rome, by Opimius, the consul. The tumults attending the efforts of the Gracchi, to remove the corruptions of the aristocracy at their own expense, were only the prelude to those civil disorders which hastened the downfall of the commonwealth.

How palpable the folly, in the history of Rome, of dividing the people into patricians and plebeians, or noble and ignoble, the privileged and restricted, the high and the low! All the "barbarians" that ever surrounded Rome, under all the four winds of heaven, never did her the damage that this false basis did, dictated either by the consummate ignorance, or more detestable haughtiness and pride, of Romulus. It wrought the downfall of Rome, as it will all civil governments which allow a part of the commonwealth to be disfranchised before the civil authority. A *common protection*, or a *common ruin*, must be the history of every nation.

JUGURTHA.—He was the grandson of Masinissa, who took part against Hannibal. He sought to usurp the crown of Numidia, by destroying his cousins, sons of the late king, Micipsa. Having succeeded in putting Hiempsal, the elder of the two princes, to death, Abherbal, the younger, fled to Rome, and sought her aid. The senate, being bribed by Jugurtha, divided the kingdom between them.

Jugurtha then made war upon his cousin, whom he defeated and slew, and then usurped the whole kingdom. This disregard of the senate, drew upon him the displeasure and vengeance of the Romans. Metellus, the consul, was sent against him, and in the course of two years he was defeated in several battles, and forced to negotiate a peace, which, however, was kept with *Punic faith*, and the war was continued.

Marius, who had risen from a poor family to be of some note, managed to supplant Metellus, both in the consulate and command of the army against Jugurtha. Being a man of extraordinary stature, incomparable strength, and undaunted bravery, he soon pressed the campaign, so well advanced under Metellus, towards a successful termination. Bocchus, King of Mauritania, at first assisted Jugurtha; but, fearing lest he might at last provoke the Romans to take his crown from him, and finding that he could secure their favor by betraying Jugurtha, did so. The Numidian usurper being now betrayed, became the prisoner of the Romans, whom he had insulted and fought, and was led in chains to Rome; where, after gracing the triumph of the conqueror, was condemned to starve to death in a dungeon. Who, in all this war, was the greatest traitor?

Social War. — After a short war with the Teutones and Cimbri, in which Marius slew several hundred thousands of them, the Romans had next to encounter a war with the states of Italy. The conditions on which they became connected with Rome were various and unequal (see page 343), and hence arose an inequality of privileges. This condition of things gave rise to the "Social War," which was waged to obtain the rights of citizenship, 91 B. C.

This war closed with the grant of those rights to all the states that would return to their allegiance. This social reform cost the lives of three hundred thousand of the flower of Italy, — showing again the vital importance of *civil equality* among the confederate states and all the citizens.

Sylla. — The social war was soon followed by the Mithridatic war, 89 B. C.

Mithridates was a powerful and warlike monarch, whose empire, at this time, embraced Cappadocia, Bithynia, Thrace, Macedon, and all Greece. He was able to bring into the field two hundred and fifty thousand infantry, and fifty thousand horse. He had also a vast number of armed chariots, and in his port four hundred war-ships. He had formed the design of uniting the northern and eastern nations in a confederacy, and, at the head of their united forces, of overrunning Italy. He began the war by causing eighty thousand Romans, who dwelt in Asia Minor, to be massacred in one day. Contrary to general expectation, and to the great mortification of Marius, Sylla obtained the transfer of the command of this war from Marius to himself.

Rivalry in Rome was now transferred from parties to leading men. Sylla was a favorite of the aristocracy and senate, while Marius was an enemy of the aristocracy, and a favorite of the people. Marius, now seventy years of age, had been distinguished for nearly half a century for his warlike genius and exploits, and had been honored with two triumphs and six consulates. But his ambition could not endure to have the command given to Sylla, and he managed to get it transferred to himself.

Sylla had now made such headway against Mithridates as to force him to desire peace; and at the same time, he received the news of the transfer of his command to Marius, and an order from the senate to return to Rome. This order he at first refused to obey; but his army desired him to march them to Rome, that they might inflict vengeance on his enemies. Sylla then granted the peace Mithridates desired, and improved the respite in marching his army to Rome.

He was met by the forces of Marius, which soon yielded and fled from the city. Now that Marius had fled, Sylla immediately surrounded the senate-house, and compelled that body to issue a decree declaring Marius an enemy to his country.

Having driven his rival into Africa, and poured out his wrath upon Marius' supporters (thus putting Rome into a state of safety and peace, as he supposed), he returned to Asia to finish the Mithridatic war. He soon found that in keeping his eye so steadily on Marius, he had overlooked Cornelius Cinna, who, as soon as Sylla was gone, espoused the cause of the exiled general.

Cinna was of the nobility, ambitious and daring, and had the address to raise an army with which to oppose the supporters of Sylla. At this juncture of affairs, Marius returned, with his son, to the gates of Rome. An army of veterans and slaves flocked to his standard, and, after a bloody battle, Marius and Cinna entered Rome as conquerors, when the massacre begun. Every enemy they could find they put to death, especially the senators who had yielded to Sylla's demand in decreeing Marius an outlaw and enemy.

Marius having satisfied his ambition and revenge, he and Cinna *assumed* the consulship, without the formality of an election. (The first example of the kind in Rome, but soon followed by others.) In a month after this triumph, Marius died in a drunken fit; while Cinna, who was preparing to meet Sylla in arms, perished by an unknown hand, in a mutiny of his own soldiers. What an eclipse of earthly glory!

Sylla soon after returned from his victorious campaign against Mithridates, and on his way met the forces of Cinna, under command of the son of Marius, also a large body of Samnites, who opposed his approach to the city. But, triumphing over them all, and leaving fifty thousand of victors and vanquished on the field, he entered Rome at the head of his army. A long list of Roman senators and knights, besides an innumerable multitude of the citizens, were the victims of his vengeance. Having obtained the dictatorship for an unlimited time, he could, with some show of justice, make the streets of Rome flow with the blood of her citizens.

Sylla was now vested with absolute power, and without a rival. He controlled elections, and caused all offices to be filled with his own creatures; and thus was despotism inaugurated in ancient Rome. To the surprise of all the world, Sylla voluntarily resigned the dictatorship, after three years. He then retired to a small villa at Puteoli, where he spent the remainder of his days in licentiousness, and died of diseases contracted by his debauchery, "a loathsome and mortifying object of human ambition." He composed his own epitaph, in substance as follows: "I am Sylla the Fortunate, who have surpassed my friends by the good, and my enemies by the evil, I have done them." In the civil wars between Marius and Sylla, one hundred and fifty thousand Roman citizens were sacrificed, including two hundred senators and thirty-three ex-consuls.

O Rome! Rome!

Roman Feuds.—Roman liberty was now trembling on the brink of ruin. Though Marius and Sylla were dead, yet their old dissensions were kept alive. Catulus and Lepidus, the two consuls, entered the arena, the latter supporting the cause of Marius. A few years after occurred the servile war, which was excited by Spartacus, a Thracian shepherd, who had been kept at Capua as a gladiator. Escaping from his confinement, he soon raised an army of forty thousand, and maintained for three years a vigorous war in the heart of Italy, and even meditated attacking Rome. His forces were defeated by Crassus, and himself slain. The commonwealth had now disappeared in *fact*, and Rome was on the verge of absolute despotism.

PERIOD IV. FROM THE FIRST TRIUMVIRATE, 3945 A. M., 59 B. C., TO THE DEATH OF AUGUSTUS CAESAR, 4018 A. M., 14 A. C.

Julius Cæsar.—The old patrician and plebeian feuds, inaugurated by Romulus himself, were now removed from the masses of the people, and kept in ferment by the rivalry of ambitious public men. Cæsar espoused the *plebeian* cause.

The confinement of the strife among the public men, soon led to a new form of government, by which the whole Roman nation was schooled in the grace of *submission* to *absolute* power. One of these master spirits was Julius Cæsar.

Julius was the son of Caius Cæsar, one of the nobility of Rome. At sixteen years of age he lost his father, when Sylla sought to have him put out of the way, fearing the ambitious youth. But his friends succeeded in saving him from this plot.

Sylla, however, warned them to beware of that loose-girt boy (alluding to the loose manner of girting his tunic about him), "for I see many a Marius in that dissolute youth." This treatment from Sylla, together with marrying the daughter of Cinna, who joined Marius, turned Cæsar's sympathy in favor of the latter.

With his great name and connections, his eloquence and powers of mind, his tall, slender, and delicate person, with the reputation of being the handsomest man in Rome, he became very popular. His habit of running his fingers among the curls of his hair, when in public, led Cicero to remark, that one "would hardly imagine that under so fair an exterior there was hatching the destruction of the liberties of Rome." By his address he obtained the office of high-priest of the nation. For his bravery and talents in the siege of Mytilene, under Thermus, Prætor of Asia, 80 B. C., Cæsar was rewarded with a civic crown. All things together made him a character to be noticed, respected, and feared in the nation, and a fair candidate for any important office. After being entrusted with the governorship of Spain, he returned to Rome, where he was appointed to the important office of consul.

Pompey. — After a few years of peace with Mithridates, war broke out again about 72 B. C.

He repulsed the successor of Sylla in command of the army, and it became necessary to send a more able general into the field; especially since Mithridates had formed an alliance with Tigranes, King of Armenia. Lucullus was accordingly sent, and soon gained several important battles, and caused both these kings to feel the weight of the Roman power; and peace would soon have followed, had not Lucullus been supplanted by intrigue, and Glabrio appointed to the command. This change was favorable to Mithridates, as he soon began to gain advantage against the Romans. Pompey, now the favorite hero of Rome, was next sent out, with almost the sole management of the Mithridatic war.

During the war, Pompey offered terms of accommodation to Mithridates, but they were rejected.

Gathering up an army of the fragments of his former one, he was about to carry war into Armenia.

Pompey came upon him, and he was obliged to flee; and before he could pass the Euphrates, was forced to engage in battle. It being by moonlight, the archers of Mithridates discharged their arrows at the shadows of the Romans, through mistake, and he was overthrown with great loss. He however escaped, sought aid of several princes, and even at this time meditated the invasion of the Roman Empire. This project coming to light, a mutiny ensued, promoted by his own son. Mithridates fled to his palace, and from thence sent to his son for permission to come out. This was refused him; and now, seeing that a Roman captivity awaited him, he called for his family, and, together with them, took his own life.

After defeating Mithridates, Pompey reduced all Syria, Pontus, and Arabia, to Roman provinces. After a siége of three months, he took Jerusalem, twelve thousand of its defenders — inhabitants —

having lost their lives. After gratifying his curiosity with the holy things of the place, he restored Hyrcanus to the priesthood, and took Aristobulus with him to grace his triumph, 61 B. C., which was the most splendid that ever entered the gates of Rome. In it were exposed the names of fifteen conquered kingdoms, eight hundred cities taken, twenty-nine cities repeopled, and one thousand castles made to acknowledge the authority of Rome. The treasure he brought home amounted to over twenty millions of dollars, while the trophies and other splendors were displayed in most magnificent profusion.

Sergius Catiline. — One more death-throe of the selfish, domineering, patrician party, and Roman *liberty* falls.

A conspiracy was formed by Catiline, a patrician by birth, and of profligate life, associated with a similar class, to work the downfall of the country. The plan was, a simultaneous outbreak in all parts of Italy and Rome, the principal citizens to be put to death; and so Catiline thought to sway the sceptre of Rome, standing on its ruins. But, through the vigilance of Cicero, the orator and consul of Rome, the diabolical project was defeated. He caused the conspirators in Rome to be seized and put to death. Catiline escaped, and, raising an army, attempted to seize by force what he failed to get by plot; but, coming in contact with the forces of the Republic, himself and his whole army were put to the sword. So ended this crushing patrician manœuvre.

Triumvirs. — Renown, wealth, and popularity, had each her candidate for sole power in Rome, in the persons of Pompey, Crassus, and Julius Cæsar. Each of them, desirous of that enviable distinction, laid his plans for it. Pompey and Crassus were each intent upon having the command of the Republic; Cæsar paid court to both, and had the address to unite them, thus avoiding making himself an enemy to either of them, and enjoyed the favor of both. From a regard to their mutual friend, Pompey and Crassus agreed to a partition of power with Cæsar, and thus was formed the *First Triumvirate*, 59 B. C.

This coalition between Pompey, Crassus, and Cæsar, originated a power distinct from the senate or the people, and yet dependent on both; it proved very detrimental to the public liberties. Cæsar was chosen consul, and greatly increased his popularity by a division of lands among the poorer classes (the very measure by which the Gracchi lost their lives). He further strengthened his alliance with Pompey, by giving him his daughter *Julia* in marriage.

Another act of Cæsar's, less generous, though he thought safe, was the banishment of Cicero. This was done by intrigue. Cæsar employed Clodius the tribune, to obtain the enactment of a law, that any one who had condemned a Roman citizen unheard, should himself be banished. This was brought to bear against Cicero, in the summary course he took with Catiline the conspirator; and he was banished four hundred miles from the city, his houses demolished, and his goods set up for sale. (Great abuse, after being the means of saving the very city over which Cæsar himself was so proud to rule.) Pompey concurred in this ungenerous act, but afterwards saw his mistake; and, seeing the growing influence of Cæsar, procured Cicero's recall from banishment, to aid in propping up his falling fame.

The Triumvirs distributed the foreign provinces among themselves. Pompey had Spain and Africa, and remained in Rome; Crassus chose Syria, which was the richest; Cæsar took Gaul. Crassus, in a war with the Parthians, was defeated and slain, which soon left the empire in the hands of Pompey and Cæsar, who then grew jealous of each other, as both wanted the sole rule.

Cæsar entered immediately upon his charge, and made rapid conquest of the nations in the west of Europe. In 55 B. C., he invaded Britain. On approaching the island, he found the shores covered with native warriors, and he had no small difficulty in repulsing them, so that he could land. Having obtained several advantages over them, he bound them to conditions of submission, and returned to the continent for winter quarters. The Britons, being fond of liberty, and feeling that their obligation was only to a *conqueror's* yoke, determined to resist the Roman power. This led Cæsar a second time into Britain. Having overcome them again, they were obliged to make peace.

Thus, in the course of nine years, Cæsar had conquered all the country between the Mediterranean and German Sea, together with Britain, taking eight hundred cities, subdued three hundred states, overcame three millions of men, one million of whom fell in battle, and the remainder made prisoners of war, besides making himself the idol of his army, by sharing with them every danger, and by his great liberality, affability, and clemency, and being in favor of the great body of the Roman people.

Pompey, on the other hand, had all this time remained at Rome, managing to keep the principal offices throughout the country filled with his favorites. He had the good-will of the consuls and senate, and, with a few legions of soldiers at his command, he imagined himself safe and strong. Cicero, however, being a little suspicious of the growing popularity of his rival, expressed his surprise to Pompey that he did not put himself in a better attitude of defence, in case of war. To which Pompey replied: "I need only stamp my foot on the ground, and an army will arise." Thus the two master spirits of the empire stood, both ambitious, both powerful, both popular, though not equally so. An opportunity for trying titles was all that was wanting to start the issue, who shall rule — Pompey, or Cæsar?

Cæsar's term of office being about to expire, he made application to the senate to be continued in his authority. But the senate being under the control of Pompey, he thought this the time to humble his rival, and so induced the senate to deny Cæsar's request. Now the tug of war begins. Cæsar, knowing the source of this refusal to extend his authority, resolved to maintain it by force. For this purpose, he bound his devoted army to him by an oath of fidelity; he then led them over the Alps to Ravenna, where he made a halt.

From this place he wrote to the Roman consuls, declaring that he was ready to resign all command, if Pompey would do the same.

Pompey vainly supposing an order from the senate would bring Cæsar to his knees, induced that body to answer Cæsar's proposal with a demand for him to *lay down* his command, and disband his army within a limited time, on penalty of being declared an enemy to the commonwealth.

Cæsar, knowing the author of this insulting demand (Julia's death having some time previously broken the last bond of union between the two heroes), immediately marched his army to the banks of the Rubicon (a small river forming the boundary between Gaul and Italy), the extent of Cæsar's command, and across which the Romans had devoted to the infernal gods, and branded with sacrilege and parricide, any person who should presume to pass with an army, a legion, or even a single cohort.

On arriving at this famous stream, Cæsar paused, and for a time weighed the momentous step before him.

Turning to Pollio, one of his generals, he said: "If I pass this river, what miseries I shall bring on my country; if I do not pass it, I am undone." In a little time he exclaimed: "The die is cast!" and, putting spurs to his horse, plunged into the stream, and was soon followed to the opposite shore by his soldiers.

News of this movement excited the utmost terror in Rome, and the citizens began to heap reproaches upon Pompey for his supineness. One of the senators asked him, in derision, "Where now is the army that is to rise at your command? Let us see if it will come by stamping." Pompey, aware of his inability to cope with Cæsar, fled into Macedonia, followed by the consuls and a great part of the senate. He took measures to levy troops, both in Italy and Greece.

Cæsar, having made himself master of all Italy in sixty days, entered Rome triumphantly, amid the acclamations of the people, and possessed himself of the public treasures and the supreme authority without opposition. He made a great display of clemency, and allayed the fears of the people that another *Sylla* massacre was at hand, saying, "the very thought of it" made him shudder. Pompey's lieutenants being in possession of Spain, Cæsar started in a few days, for the purpose of conquering his forces there. Marching his army over the Alps again, all Spain submitted to him in forty days, and he returned victorious to Rome, where he was created dictator and consul.

During this time, Pompey had secured the friendship of several of the sovereigns of the East, who offered him aid; and he had, by *stamping*, or some other means, succeeded in raising a large army. His cause was considered that of the commonwealth, and he was daily joined by crowds of the most distinguished nobles and citizens of Rome. He had in his camp at one time upwards of two hundred senators, among whom were *Cicero* and Cato, themselves a host. Cæsar stayed in Rome only eleven days, not feeling easy until the strife between him and Pompey was brought to an issue. Coming in contact with him at Dyrrachium, the relation of the two armies was such as to make a battle necessary, which resulted in nothing very decisive, but on the whole in favor of Pompey, who then led his troops into the plains of Pharsalia.

Pompey had chosen an advantageous position, which led Cæsar to the artifice of decamping, in order to draw the enemy after him, and so provoked a general battle. Seeing the success of his stratagem, with joy he informed his soldiers that the hour they had so long wished for had come, that which was to crown their glory and terminate their fatigues. The contest was an exciting one. The two armies, composed of the best soldiers in the world, commanded by the two greatest generals of the age, and the prize at stake nothing less than the Roman Empire. Pompey's army consisted of forty-five thousand foot, and seven thousand horse; while Cæsar's numbered only twenty-three thousand foot, and one thousand horse. Pompey's soldiers were confident of success, and the spoils, while Cæsar's were well disciplined, and intent on fighting. Every heart was fired, and every arm nerved. The armies were both addressed by their commanders, and exhorted to sustain their reputation for bravery, both being Roman.

The battle commenced on the part of Cæsar. He, foreseeing the strength of Pompey's cavalry, laid his plan to break them as soon as possible. He accordingly sent out a detachment sufficient to draw out Pompey's cavalry to repulse them, but they were not to attempt to drive back the horse. Six cohorts were ready to receive the charge of Pompey's cavalry, with express orders to discharge their javelins at the *faces* of the horsemen. Pompey's cavalry was made up mostly of the younger part of the Roman nobility, who prided themselves upon their personal beauty, and dreaded a scar in the face more than a wound in the body.

This unexpected mode of attack had the desired effect; the flower of the nobility were wounded in their pride and power, and driven from the field; and thereby the day was lost to Pompey and to the Republic. The battle, which lasted from early in the morning till noon, was now won by Cæsar, with a loss of only two hundred men, while Pompey lost fifteen thousand killed, and twenty-four thousand prisoners. Thus ended the famons battle of Pharsalia, in Thessaly, 48 B. C.

Cæsar added to his laurels as victor, by his clemency and moderation. The soldiers he took as prisoners, he incorporated into his own army, and the senators and Roman knights he set at liberty. While gazing upon the battle-field, covered with his fallen countrymen, he relieved himself by uttering the expression: "They would have it so."

Pompey's fall was from a high place to a low one. Accustomed to victory for thirty years, and master of the Republic, robbed of it all in one day, and reduced to a miserable fugitive. As Pompey fled, Cæsar pursued him. Pompey's first meeting with his wife Cornelia, after his misfortune, was distressing to the last degree. The tenderest expressions of affection and grief were mutually uttered. Pompey fled to Egypt, to seek the protection of Ptolemy, whose father he had befriended. But the ministers of Ptolemy, wishing to befriend Cæsar, agreed to receive Pompey, but to assassinate him before he should get ashore.

This treacherous plot was carried out, and just as the conquered Roman arose to go ashore, Septimus (a Roman by birth), in sight of Cornelia, stabbed him in the back, and his body was thrown upon the sand. His freed man, who attended him, took up the body of his master, and, gathering together a scanty funeral-pile, burnt it to ashes, and buried them, with this inscription over the spot: "He whose merits deserve a temple, can now scarcely find a grave." Cæsar soon landed in pursuit, when the head of his rival, which had been saved, was presented to him; but he turned his face from it in horror, shedding tears on the remembrance of their former friendship. He ordered a splendid monument to be erected to his memory. ("Pompey's Pillar.")

Cleopatra, who aspired to undivided authority, and was in a quarrel with her brother, who was associated with her on the throne, invoked Cæsar's aid to settle the question. By the aid of her *personal charms*, he was induced to decide in her favor. After the reduction of Egypt, during which Ptolemy was killed, Cæsar, conqueror of the world, was conquered with the arts of love by the Egyptian Queen, and abandoned himself to pleasure with Cleopatra. He was however drawn from this reverie by the revolt of Pharnaces, son of Mithridates, who had seized upon Colchis and Armenia. The ease with which he quelled this revolt was expressed in his message to the senate: "Veni, vidi, vici." — I came, I saw, I conquered.

Cæsar's presence was next called for in Rome, where Antony, his deputy, had caused disturbances which Cæsar alone could quell. A strong party, adhering to Pompey's interests, was in arms, which Cæsar soon reduced. No sooner was this done, than news came that Pompey's two sons, with Cato and Scipio, assisted by Juba, King of Mauritania, were in arms in Africa. Going thither, he soon overthrew them.

Cæsar now returned to Rome, master of the Empire, and almost of the world, 45 B. C., and celebrated a most magnificent triumph, which lasted four days; the first for Gaul, the second for Egypt, the third for Asia, and the fourth for Africa. On this occasion he distributed liberally rewards to his veteran soldiers and officers, and to the citizens. He gratified the people with combats of elephants, and engagements between parties of cavalry and infantry, and entertained them at a public feast, where he placed twenty thousand couches for the guests.

With these allurements, the people readily yielded up their liberties to the great Cæsar. The people and senate vied with each other in acts of servility and adulation. He was hailed as *father of his country*, created perpetual dictator, and received the title of *Imperator*, or *Emperor*, and his person declared sacred. The state of affairs in Spain called for Cæsar's presence there. Labienus and the two sons of Pompey had raised an army against him there; these he completely defeated in the bloody and obstinate battle of Munda, which decided the fate of the adherents of his rival.

With all that ambition could ask, and what many heroes had longed, fought, and died for, but never attained before, Cæsar now returned to Rome. But no conqueror ever used power with such moderation and wisdom. In one of his speeches, he remarked: "I will not renew the massacres of Marius and Sylla, the very remembrance of which is shocking to me. Now that my enemies are subdued, I will lay aside the sword, and endeavor, solely by my good offices, to gain over those who hate me." Without making any distinctions between parties, friends, or enemies, he devoted himself to the prosperity and happiness of the people. He embellished the city, and made a variety of magnificent and useful improvements.

But, alas! there is a summit to all things. The dizzy height to which Cæsar had now attained was more difficult to keep than acquire. Though he had often refused the crown, when offered him by Mark Antony, yet he was accused of aiming to be *king*. The Romans could not endure the thought, that royalty should again be restored in Rome, nor that a conqueror should rule them with absolute sway. The circumstance that finally fixed in the minds and prejudices of his enemies that Cæsar was inclined to royalty, was that of his not rising from his seat when the senate was conferring upon him some special honors.

Immediately some sixty of the senators formed a conspiracy to deprive him of his life. A rumor got afloat that he was to have the crown conferred upon him on the Ides (fifteenth) of March, when they fixed upon that day to excute their vile design. A few friends, learning his danger, managed to convey a note of warning to him, by the great philosopher, Artemidorus; but Cæsar gave it, with other papers, to one of his secretaries, without reading it. (Like Archias, see page 311.)

As soon as he had taken his seat in the senate-house, the conspirators drew near him, under pretence of saluting him. Cimber, one of them, pretending to sue for his brother's pardon, approached him in a suppliant posture, and so near as to take hold of the bottom of his robe, by which he was to prevent Cæsar from rising. This was the signal agreed upon among the assassins. Casca, who was behind, stabbed him in the shoulder. Cæsar immediately turned, and wounded him in the arm. By this time the others were in motion, and surrounded him with drawn daggers. He received a second stab in the breast, while Cassius wounded him in the *face*. He defended himself with vigor for a time, till on a sudden he discovered his former friend Brutus (whose life he had spared at the battle of Pharsalia), among the conspirators, and, seeing that he was betrayed, gave up in despair. After uttering the memorable sentence, "*Et tu Brute*," — *And you too, Brutus!* — he muffled up his face in his mantle, and fell, pierced with twenty-three wounds. Thus perished Julius Cæsar, in his fifty-sixth year, having enjoyed only about five months the distinguished position it had been the object of his life to obtain. 44 B. C.

His brilliant career, and tragic end, make him one of the most notable characters of antiquity. He appears in the three-fold character of warrior, statesman, and historian. He is said to have corrected the calendar. The world has scarcely seen a more able or amiable despot. In passing a small village, on his way to Spain, before the triumvirate, he was heard to say, he "would rather be the first man in that village than the second man in Rome." He often repeated a favorite sentence from Euripides: "That if right and justice were ever to be violated, they were to be violated for the sake of reigning."

Besides his great achievements on the battle-field, Cæsar was reckoned the greatest orator in the world, next to Cicero; set a pattern to all historians, which has never been excelled; wrote learnedly on the sciences of grammar and augury; and left, at the time of his premature death, memorials of his great plans for the extension of the empire, and of legislation for the world. In Cæsar's triumph is represented the ascendency of the *plebeian* over the *patrician* faction of Rome. With his death ended the first triumvirate.

SECOND TRIUMVIRATE. — The end, or ends, sought by the sixty senators, which were their own aggrandizement, and the overthrow of their conqueror, were far from being realized by the death of Cæsar. For upon the ruins of the first triumvirate arose a second, under whose iron rule Rome was enslaved, and the plebeianism of Romulus obtained the sway. And from this same date may we continue to reckon the decline of Rome; so that facts demonstrate that *Romulus destroyed Rome.*

Cæsar's bleeding body was carried to the Forum, and there exposed to the gaze of the people; when Mark Antony delivered a most artful and exciting oration, while unfolding the bloody robe and showing them the great Cæsar. The effect of this speech was to arouse the people against the conspirators, who were obliged to flee from the city to save their lives.

Upon this the second triumvirate was formed, resembling in no slight degree the first. Antony, a man of great military talents (corresponding exactly to Pompey), Lepidus, immensely rich (like Crassus), and Octavius, another Cæsar (adopted heir by Cæsar, and his sister's grandson, now in his eighteenth year). In this concert of the supreme power, each of the triumvirs gave up such of his friends to the malice of the others as were demanded. Antony gave up his uncle Lucius; Lepidus, his brother Paulus; and Octavius gave up the great Cicero, to gratify the hatred of Antony. He caused his head to be cut off, run through by the blade of a military spear, and the spear set up on end in public,—a spectacle which drew tears from the eyes of all virtuous citizens. Then followed another horrible proscription (like Sylla), when three hundred senators, two thousand knights, and many of the citizens were sacrificed.

Two of the conspirators, Brutus and Cassius, had fled to Thrace, where they were at the head of an army of one hundred thousand men. Antony and Octavius pursued them with a still greater army, and in the battle that ensued at Philippi, they were victorious. Brutus and Cassius escaped captivity by voluntary deaths,—a measure they had mutually agreed upon beforehand.

But the second triumvirs, like the first, did not long live in harmony, each aspiring to undivided sway. Lepidus was soon deposed and banished. (Like Crassus, the rich one in each triumvirate was disposed of first.) Antony took his way into the East, and spent some time at Athens in philosophic retirement. After this, he passed from kingdom to kingdom, attended by a crowd of sovereigns, exacting contributions, and giving away crowns, with "capricious insolence." (So Pompey made a great figure in the East.) Octavius all this time was using, with consummate art, his wealth and talents to gain the favor of the people, with his eye on supreme power. (Like Cæsar.)

Antony having summoned Cleopatra to Tarsus, to answer the charge of aiding the conspirators against Cæsar, she obeyed, and came, decked in all the emblems of a queen of love, in a galley decorated in the greatest splendor. With his royal and beautiful prisoner at the bar, Antony forgot his cause, being captivated with her charms. He forgot ambition and empire, and abandoned himself to the pleasures of passion with the Egyptian queen. Octavius saw in this the presage of his ruin.

On Cleopatra he lavished the provinces of Rome, for which he was declared an enemy to his country, which gave Octavius sufficient reason for declaring war against him.

Like Pompey, Antony had married the sister of his associate in power; but she being divorced for Cleopatra,—not dead like Julia,—this tie was broken between them, as between Pompey and Cæsar. In the engagement which soon came on, near Actium, now called Nicopolis, Antony had one hundred thousand foot, twelve thousand horse, and five hundred ships of war; while Octavius had only eighty thousand foot, twelve thousand horse, and two hundred and fifty ships, but they were better manned and built. Only the navies of the two generals were engaged. The fate of the day was decided by the flight of Cleopatra (who had joined Antony with sixty galleys of war), when Antony soon followed, and his soldiers submitted to Octavius.

Octavius pursued him into Egypt. (As Cæsar did Pompey.) Antony, hearing that Cleopatra was dead, fell upon his own sword, and expired. (So, also, Pompey died in Egypt.) Octavius, like Cæsar, was now left master of the world, with the title of Augustus Cæsar, 31 B. C.

Cicero. — A few prominent men of these times, celebrated for learning, may be here introduced. It is not a little remarkable, that Demosthenes and Cicero, the two greatest orators of antiquity, lived, the one in the times of Philip and Alexander, the other in the times of Cæsar and Octavius, — two as turbulent epochs, in civil matters, as are on record.

Marcus Tullius Cicero was the father of Latin eloquence, and the greatest orator Rome ever produced. He was the son of a Roman knight; and, showing promising abilities at an early age, his father procured for him the most celebrated masters of the times for his instructors. He served one campaign under Sylla, and returning to Rome, he appeared as a pleader at the bar, where the greatness of his genius, and his superior eloquence, soon raised him to notice.

After passing through the minor honors of the state, he was chosen consul in the forty-third year of his age. To the wise and energetic administration of Cicero, belongs the honor of suppressing the conspiracy against Rome, under Catiline. After breaking up the foul plot, Cicero received the thanks of the people, and was styled the father of his country, and, with Romulus and Brutus (the first Roman consul), the third founder of Rome. Being opposed to the arbitrary measures of Cæsar and Pompey, he was sent into banishment, but very unjustly. A law was enacted, that "whoever had condemned a Roman citizen without a trial, should himself be banished." This was made to apply to Cicero in his summary proceedings against Catiline, and hence the baseness and ingratitude of the sentence. In vain did he remonstrate against the injustice of the sentence. He bore his exile with the greatest impatience.

Pompey, finding his own popularity was on the decline, recalled Cicero, after sixteen months' time, to aid in propping up his sinking fortunes. This news of recall filled Cicero with the utmost joy. After much hesitation, he espoused the cause of Pompey, against Cæsar. But after Cæsar's victory at Pharsalia, he was reconciled to Cicero, and treated him with great humanity; and still he countenanced the murder of Cæsar, and by so doing incurred the enmity of Antony, who wished to succeed in power. Upon the formation of the second triumvirate, in the proscription of friends agreed upon, Octavius labored two days to deliver Cicero from Antony's vengeance, but in vain. He gave him up at last. In attempting to escape, Cicero was overtaken by a party of soldiers, who cut off his head and right hand, and brought them to Antony: 43 B. C., Æ. 64.

Cicero's foible was vanity. He sought not only to be the greatest orator of Rome, but to be thought the greatest *jester* also. His conduct was not always that of a patriot, and was frequently accused of being cowardly. But as a statesman, an orator, a man of genius, and a scholar, he has few, if any, equals.

CATO. — He also espoused the cause of Pompey, against Cæsar. Fortifying himself in Utica, he thought of resisting Cæsar; but finding his followers irresolute, he died as many great (fools) Romans did.

When he found it in vain to arouse his soldiers against Cæsar, after supping cheerfully, he went into his bed-chamber, laid down and read with deep attention, for some time, Plato's dialogue on the Immortality of the Soul. Finding that his sword had been removed from the head of his bed, he began to make an ado among his domestics about it, when his son, who caused it to be removed, came forward and entreated him, with tears, to abandon his purpose; but, receiving a severe reprimand, he yielded to his father's maddened wishes.

His sword being at length handed him, he entered his room, and exclaimed: "Now am I master of myself!" He then took up the book, and read it twice over, and fell into a profound sleep. Upon waking, he made some inquiries about his friends, and shutting himself up in his room alone, stabbed himself. The wound not being immediately mortal, with the most ferocious resolution he tore out his own bowels, and died as he had lived, a Stoic.

CATULLUS. — He was a Roman epigrammatic poet. He directed his satire against Cæsar, whose only revenge was to invite the poet, and hospitably entertain him at his own table.

SALLUST. — He is considered as the first philosophical historian. He gained some note as consul. He married Terentia, the divorced wife of Cicero, and hence the immortal hatred between the orator and the historian. Little remains of his writings, except his narrative of the conspiracy of Catiline, and the wars of Jugurtha.

VARRO. — He is styled the most learned of the Romans. He wrote three hundred volumes, all of which are lost, except a treatise on De Re Rustica, and another, De Lingua Latina. The latter he wrote in his eightieth year, and dedicated it to Cicero. In the civil wars he was taken and proscribed by Cæsar, but escaped. His erudition and extent of information were a matter of wonder and admiration to Cicero and St. Augustine. He died in his eighty-eighth year, 28 B. C.

Cornelius Nepos. — He enjoyed the patronage of Augustus, and was an intimate friend of Cicero. He composed several works, but his lives of illustrious Greeks are all that remain.

Virgil — Having lost his farms in the distribution of lands to the soldiers of Augustus, after the battle of Philippi, he repaired to Rome, where, through the influence of Mecænas, he obtained an order for their restoration. Upon showing his order to the centurion who was in possession of them, he nearly killed Virgil, who escaped only by swimming across a river.

In his Bucolics, or Pastorals, he celebrates the praises of his illustrious patrons. He undertook, in his Georgics, to encourage the study of agriculture. The design of his Ænead was to reconcile the Romans to a monarchical form of government. By his talents and virtues, he acquired the friendship of the Emperor Augustus, and of the most celebrated personages of his times. He died at Brundusium, aged 51, 19 B. C., and was buried near Naples, where his tomb is still to be seen. He is styled the prince of Roman poets.

Horace. — The greatest of the Roman lyric poets.

He was educated at Athens, attended Brutus to the civil wars, and fled from the battle of Philippi. Repairing to Rome, he begun writing verses, and there lived on terms of intimacy with Virgil, Mecænas, and Augustus. He died aged 57, 8 B. C.

ROMAN EMPERORS.

Augustus Cæsar. — The commonwealth had now passed away, and the Republic of Rome was converted into an Empire. The patrician order was finally outdone, and the plebeian element gained the ascendency, despite all the intrigues of those who had all the wealth and blood of the nation on their side. Inequality of classes, before the civil power, must either give way to an equality, or the triumph of one party over the other, or the ruin of the nation. In the case of Rome, we see the triumph of one party over the other, and eventually the ruin of the whole. For although we see the triumph of the plebeian order in the Roman emperors, we also see the downfall of Rome, brought about by their profligacy and abuses.

The battle of Actium, put Augustus Cæsar at the head of the Empire, and master of the world. He was now in possession of *Universal Empire*, that mighty thing for which thousands had longed and bled, — seeking it on the battle-field, in senate-halls, and on the rostrum. Though ambitious of power, yet he was also aware of its dangers. For this reason he consulted Agrippa, one of his chief advisers, as to the policy best for him to pursue. His advice was, by all means to restore the liberties of the people. He next consulted Mecænas, his prime minister, who advised him to govern others as he would wish to be governed, had it been his destiny to obey; and further suggested, that under the title of *Cæsar*, he could enjoy all the influence of a king, without offending the prejudices of his countrymen.

Augustus, like Rehoboam, accepted of that advice which was most congenial to his desires, and which he had it in his power to follow. Although his line of policy was fatal to liberty, yet the absolute restraint he exercised tended to general tranquillity.

He claimed the title of emperor, to preserve his authority over the army; caused himself to be created tribune, to quiet the people, and prince of the senate, so as to hold control over that body. In this way he managed to govern with absolute sway, under the names and forms of the republican constitution, which already lay prostrate at his feet. He cultivated familiarity with the people, and even appeared at the bar as an advocate. One of his veteran soldiers entreated his protection in a law-suit. He advised him to employ an advocate; to which the soldier replied: "Ah! it was not by proxy I served you at the battle of Actium." This reply so pleased the emperor, that he plead his cause in person, and gained it for him.

Augustus cherished the arts of peace, embellished the city, erected public edifices, pursued the policy of maintaining order and tranquillity throughout his vast empire; so that the temple of Janus was again shut — for the first time since the second Punic War, and only the third time since the foundation of the city. The emperor, and Mecænas his minister, were both patrons of learning and the arts, in an eminent degree; so that this is celebrated as the Augustan Age of Roman Literature. Some of the characters who illustrated this reign, were *Virgil*, *Horace*, *Ovid*, and *Livy*.

But the most august event of the Augustan Age was the birth of our Lord and Saviour Jesus Christ.

This event took place in the twenty-sixth year of the reign of Augustus Cæsar, and four years before what is commonly termed the beginning of the *Christian Era*.

Augustus was so affable as to return the salutations of all classes. A person one day approached him, with a petition, in a very crouching posture, when the emperor reproved him for it, saying, "Friend, you seem as if you were offering something to an elephant, and not a man; be bolder."

Augustus was less happy in his domestic than in his imperial fortunes. His wife Livia was an imperious woman, and controlled him at her pleasure. Her son Tiberius, by a former husband, so annoyed him by his obstinacy, that he banished him at a distance from Rome for five years. But his own daughter Julia, by a former wife, afflicted him more than all the rest, by her extremely immodest behavior. A favorite son of his was taken off, it is supposed by poison, lest he should supplant Tiberius.

Augustus was often heard to say: "How happy should I have been, had I never had a wife or children!" He died of dysentery, during an absence from Rome, at Nola, in the seventy-sixth year of his age, the forty-first of his reign, 14 A. C.

III.

AGE OF WAR FOR OPINION.

FROM AUGUSTUS CÆSAR TO THE REFORMATION.

SUBJECT — CIVIL HISTORY.

PERIOD V. FROM AUGUSTUS' DEATH, 4018 A. M., AND 14 A. C., TO THE END OF THE WESTERN EMPIRE, 4480 A. M., 476 A. C.

It is worthy of notice, that the summit of Roman prosperity was the time selected by Providence for the advent of the Redeemer of men. Hence the universal Empire of Rome was made the vehicle for the early and almost universal spread of Christianity. The closing of the temple of Janus, because of a universal peace, was a delightful time for the Prince of Peace to introduce himself to the world, with the chant, "Glory to God in the highest! Peace on earth, and good-will to men!"

TIBERIUS. — He was named in Augustus' will as his successor. He was son of Livia, by a former husband, and hence only step-son to Augustus. Tiberius inaugurated his reign with blood. Among the victims was the celebrated general Germanicus, at whose death the people indulged in unbounded grief.

He then took into his confidence one Sejanus, a Roman knight, who persuaded him to remove from Rome to the island of *Caprea*, where he indulged in the most infamous debaucheries. Sejanus so abused the power in his hands, that he was soon put to death by the senate, for his cruelties, and his body ignominiously dragged through the streets.

In the eighteenth year of the reign of Tiberius, occurred the crucifixion of *Jesus Christ.* Small were the favors any virtuous cause received at the hands of this brutal emperor.

At the age of sixty-seven he was quite bald in front; his face was disgustingly ulcerated, and covered with plasters; his body was bent forward, while its unnatural tallness and leanness increased its ugliness. He appointed two of his gluttons to the first posts in the empire, for sitting up with him two days and nights without sleep. The most eminent women of Rome were obliged to sacrifice their virtue and honor to the brute.

His extreme jealousy prompted him to put to death distinguished citizens, upon the slightest pretences. At the place of execution, dead bodies, putrefying, lay heaped on each other, and friends were denied the privilege of weeping. Of certain senators he said, "Let them hate me, as long as they obey me." Cruelty and lust now characterized the Roman people. Death by wild beasts, and various tortures, formed a part of the entertainment at Roman festivities. It gave Tiberius a burst of joy he was unable to repress, on finding that the Roman people and senate had sunk even below his own baseness. He is said to have been poisoned by one of his favorites, 37 A. C.

Caligula. — He succeeded Tiberius; was his grand-nephew, and son of Germanicus. His debaucheries need not be related, only that they exceeded, as far as possible, those of Tiberius. Old and infirm men, and poor decrepit house-keepers, he cast to the wild beasts, to relieve the state of such unserviceable citizens.

He once wished "that all the Roman people had but one neck, that he might dispatch them at a single blow." He caused temples to be built, and sacrifices offered to him, as a god. He employed many inventions to imitate thunder. He built a stable of marble for his favorite horse Incitatus, with furniture to entertain his horse's visitors; frequently invited his horse to his own table, and would have appointed him to the consulship, but death prevented. In one year's time, he squandered eighteen millions pounds sterling, left by Tiberius. In the fourth year of his reign, he was dispatched, through the influence of a tribune of the prætorian bands, 41 A. C. Seneca said of him: "He was an example of what could be produced from the greatest vice, supported by the greatest authority."

Claudius. — After the death of Caligula, the *senate* manifested a little desire to restore the liberties of Rome; but the *army* preferring an emperor, one was accordingly chosen. The choice fell upon Claudius, uncle of Caligula, grandson of Mark Antony and Octavia, the sister of Augustus. He is reported as below mediocrity in talent, and so became the dupe of his attendants, especially of his profligate wife. Her, however, he put to death, with thirty-five senators, three hundred knights, and a vast many other citizens. Among others who perished, was Petus, who was condemned to die by his own hands. His loving wife attended him to the last; and, seeing her husband was timid, she took the poniard and stabbed herself in his presence, and then handed it to him, saying, "It gives me no pain, my Petus."

The most remarkable enterprise in the reign of Claudius, was the invasion of Britain, 43 A. C. He visited it in person, but left soon, and his generals, Plautius and Vespasian, continued the war with various success.

Caractacus, the king, was taken prisoner, and carried to Rome; and on beholding the magnificence of that city, exclaimed: "How is it possible that men possessed of such magnificence at home, should envy Caractacus a humble cottage in Britain?"

Claudius had five wives; the fourth, Messalina, he put to death for her profligacy, when he married Agrippina, who was equally practised in vice, and who poisoned him in the fourteenth year of his reign, and sixty-fourth of his age, to make way for her son Domitius Ænobarbus (Nero), by a former husband. Rome contained, at this time, the enormous and almost incredible number of seven millions of inhabitants; and was sunk in the greatest effeminacy, luxury, and vice.

NERO. — Like other Roman emperors, he at first put on a show of moderation and justice; but no sooner did he begin to feel the strength of his position, than he began to show forth his depravity. He had the advantage of a good education, under the tuition of Seneca the philosopher, and with the wise counsel of Burrhus, prefect of the prætorian guards, he was put in a way to rule well. But he soon broke away from all these salutary restraints, and proved himself a *Roman*.

Some one happening to say, in his presence, that the world might some day be burnt, he replied: "Nay, let it be burnt while I am living." So he caused the city to be set on fire, and, taking his position on a high tower, he indulged the sight with ferocious pleasure, imagining that the scene resembled the burning of Troy. In order to shield himself from the odium such an act would bring upon him, he charged the crime upon the Christians, and proceeded against them with as much rigor as though they were verily guilty of it. This was the first of the *ten persecutions* they suffered from the Roman emperors. It is supposed that Paul was beheaded, and Peter crucified, at this time.

A conspiracy formed against him, by Piso, was detected, and for this Rome was nearly deluged with blood. Everything that a fierce soldiery could do, besides inducing children to destroy their parents, and slaves to revolt against their masters, was brought to bear on all whom he suspected. Crowds of innocent victims were daily led to the gates of the palace, to hear their doom from the lips of the tyrant. The reason for the endurance of all this cruelty by the Roman people, was the bribes paid the rabble, in corn, money, and raw flesh. The times of tyranny were golden days for them.

A revolt of the Britons took place under Nero, in which seventy thousand Romans were slain; but they were in turn subdued, and eighty thousand Britons paid the penalty with their lives. A conspiracy was at last formed against this more than brute monster, headed by Vindex in Gaul, and Galba in Spain. The senate having also passed sentence against him, he avoided falling into their hands by a voluntary death. Too cowardly, after all his brute ferocity, to kill himself, he died by the hand of a slave, aged thirty-two, after reigning fourteen years; 69 A. C.

GALBA. — At the commencement of the revolt against Nero, Vindex proclaimed Galba emperor, and this was sanctioned afterwards by the senate and army. Compared with former emperors, Galba was deservedly esteemed; and, with the exception of cruelty, he had fewer excessive faults than his predecessors. His administration was rendered unpopular, by his attempting to restrain the corruptions, and economize in the expenditures, of the state. Such changes, in those times, could not be brought about at once, without causing dissatisfaction in the minds of those who had been permitted to roll in lust and affluence, having former emperors for examples, and their money freely spent for the indulgence of the people. For some disrespectful treatment towards him from a body of citizens, he ordered a troop of horse attending him to ride in among them, and seven thousand of them were killed.

Instances of his parsimony are related. He is said to have groaned at having an expensive soup served up for him at his table. To a steward, for his fidelity, he one day presented a plate of beans. A famous flute-player, named Canus, having greatly delighted him, he drew his purse and gave him five pence, telling him it was *private*, not *public* money. Through his love of money, notorious villains purchased their liberty. Seeking the good of the country, Galba nominated the virtuous Piso as his successor. This gave offence to Otho, who anticipated the nomination, and flew to arms. In the affray, both Galba and Piso were slain, after reigning only seven months.

OTHO — Being raised to the throne, and receiving the usual titles bestowed by the senate, he began his reign with several acts of mercy and justice. Otho's character improved after his promotion, — a circumstance of rare occurrence with the Roman emperors. In private life he was all that was detestable; but when he became emperor, he was courageous, benevolent, and humane.

Vitellius, who had been proclaimed emperor by his army in Germany, gave Otho battle, near Mantua, when the latter was defeated, and, in a fit of despair, like a Roman, stabbed himself, after holding the power he had wrested from Galba and Piso only ninety-five days.

VITELLIUS. — He came to the throne 69 A. C., and retained his usurpation only eight months. He chose Nero for his model. Going to visit a friend in a violent fever, he gave him poison in a cup of water, with his own hands, that he might obtain his friend's possessions. Those who had lent him money were put to death if they dared ask him for it, and then he took their estates. A Roman knight, upon being dragged to execution, cried, that he had made the emperor heir to his estate. Vitellius asked to see the will; when he found another person mentioned also as heir, he caused them both to be executed, and took the whole. His favorite sin was gluttony. In order to be able to eat often and much, he acquired the habit of vomiting up his food, so as to be ready to take more. His entertainments were so expensive, that it was said, should he reign long, the whole empire would not be able to maintain his table.

Vespasian, who was at the head of the Roman army in Egypt, being proclaimed emperor by his legions, entered Italy, and a great part of it submitted to him; and even Vitellius meanly resigned the empire to him, to save his own life. Indignant at such cowardice, the people compelled him to oppose Vespasian, by force; but, falling into the hands of a party of the enemy, he was ingloriously put to death. "They that take the sword (by violence), must perish by the sword."

VESPASIAN. — He having been declared emperor, by the unanimous consent of the senate and army, was received at Rome with the greatest joy. He was not of noble birth, yet was far more noble, as emperor, than many of better blood, so called. He reigned ten years, with great popularity, and was distinguished for clemency, affability, and frugality. Avarice was his fault. It took some time to restore peace and security to the empire; and when this was attained, he began to correct the abuses that had grown up under the tyrants. He restrained the licentiousness of the army; degraded unworthy senators; shortened the tedious and dilatory process of justice, and extended his care to the whole empire. He built the celebrated amphitheatre, or Colosseum, whose ruins still attest its grandeur. He cherished the arts, and patronized learned men, — among whom were Josephus the Jewish historian, Quintilian the orator, and Pliny the naturalist.

It was during the reign of Vespasian that the city of Jerusalem was destroyed, and the once favored people of God were blotted out as a nation.

He is said to have died by disease — a very unusual occurrence with the emperors of Rome. Taken with indisposition at Campania, he said it would prove fatal; but, in the spirit of a pagan, said, "Methinks I am going to be a god!" He died supported in a standing posture, thinking it most becoming for an emperor.

Titus. — Titus succeeded to the empire upon the death of his father, 79 A. C. His character as a prince is represented as very humane, just, and generous. He so devoted himself to acts of beneficence, that, recollecting one evening that he had done none during the day, he exclaimed: "O, my friends! I have lost a day!" He obtained the enviable appellation of "The Delight of Mankind." He conducted the expedition against Jerusalem with as much clemency as the nature of war will admit. By his hand was the prediction of ruin against that doomed city and people executed.

He is said to have relinquished the hand of his beloved Bernice, sister of King Agrippa, a woman of the greatest beauty and most refined allurements, because the connection displeased the Roman people, notwithstanding their mutual affection. He took upon himself the office of high-priest, so as to keep his hands undefiled with blood, so tender was he of the lives of his subjects. He had a very happy disregard for censure and abuse. He said: "When I do nothing worthy of censure, why should I be displeased at it?"

In his reign Rome was three days on fire. He repaired the loss out of his own private resources. A plague also broke out, when ten thousand were buried in one day. In these distresses he acted as a father to his people; — a more noble spirit than actuated Nero or Caligula.

The eruption of Vesuvius occurred in his reign, in which Herculaneum and Pompeii were overwhelmed, and Pliny lost his life, by venturing too near the volcano.

When Titus was taken ill, he retired to his father's house, in the country of the Sabines. There his indisposition was increased by a burning fever. Seeing that his end drew nigh, and being destitute of the hope the gospel inspires, he murmuringly complained of his fate, in being thus removed from the world, where he had been so well employed in making a grateful people happy. He died in the third year of his reign, and the forty-first of his age, and under strong suspicion of his being poisoned by his brother Domitian.

Domitian. — He assumed the purple after the death of his brother, 81 A. C., and reigned fifteen years. The beginning of his reign promised fair for the continuance of the happiness of the Roman people. But his tyranny and ferocity were soon felt. He condemned to death the most illustrious Romans, and gazed upon their agonies with ferocious pleasure. He caused himself to be styled *God and Lord*, in papers presented to him. He had some learning himself, but banished the philosophers from Rome. In his reign occurred the second general persecution of the Christians, in which forty thousand were destroyed.

During his reign the Romans conquered the South part of Britain, under their general, Agricola, sent there by Vespasian. Domitian gained no renown for it, owing to his abuse of Agricola.

He hated both the senate and nobility, frequently threatening to extirpate them all. He delighted in terrifying and ridiculing them. On one occasion, he invited the senate to a public entertainment. After receiving them at the entrance of his palace, they were conducted into a gloomy hall, hung with black, and lighted with a few glimmering tapers. Nothing was to be seen but coffins, with each senator's name thereon, and instruments of execution. While all were thus wrapped in silent agony, a body of men burst into the room, dressed in black, with drawn swords and flaming torches. After a fearful suspense, orders came from the emperor for the company to retire. At another time, he called a special meeting of the august body of the senate, to ask them in what kind of a vessel a turbot might be most conveniently cooked. The astrologers having predicted his death, he was filled with tormenting inquietude; and, becoming more and more terrified by day and by night, in the same proportion he grew fierce and cruel.

His wife Domitia, having accidentally discovered her name on a list with others who were to suffer death, she concerted with those whose doom was written, and, by hasty and well-devised plans, he was despatched at midnight, in one of the most secret recesses of his palace, where he had gone to rest. With Domitian ends what are called the "Twelve Cæsars," beginning with Julius Cæsar.

NERVA. — He was chosen emperor by the senate, 96 A. C. He was the first Roman emperor of foreign extraction, being a Cretan. Being old, and of an easy disposition, he was unfit for a *Roman* emperor, but did quite an act in selecting a competent successor, after having reigned sixteen months. He made some feeble efforts at reform, in retrenchment of court expenses.

TRAJAN. — He came to the throne in 98 A. C. He has been called one of Rome's best emperors. His virtues were, affability, simplicity of manners, clemency, and munificence. He was also called the greatest general of the age. In presenting a sword to the prætorian prefect, he charged him thus: "Make use of it *for* me, if I do my duty; if not, *against* me." The senate surnamed him *Optimus*, or *Best;* and for over two hundred years, the senate hailed every new emperor with the sentiment: "Reign fortunately as Augustus! virtuously as Trajan!"

His first campaign was against the Dacians, whom he conquered, and reduced their territory to a Roman province. On his return, he entered the city in triumph, and the celebration of his victories lasted for one hundred and twenty days. He afterwards turned his arms eastward, and, after conquering Mesopotamia, Chaldea, Assyria, and Parthia, he sailed down the Persian Gulf, and penetrated even into the Indies. The infirmities of age prevented his pushing conquest to the "confines of the earth;" and while preparing to return to Rome, in unparalleled magnificence, he died in the city of Seleucia, leaving, like Alexander, his vast dominion without nominating a successor, after reigning nineteen years.

"Trajan's Pillar," still to be seen in Rome, was erected by the emperor himself. He was a patron of literature, and in his time flourished Pliny the younger, Juvenal, and Plutarch. But, with all his (Roman) virtues, he exhibited one *infelicity* during his reign — the slight circumstance of fostering that piece of pagan, bloody cruelty, *persecution against the Christians.* The third general persecution of the ten, was under Trajan.

ADRIAN. — He succeeded Trajan, 118 A. C. Trajan's wife forged a will, after the emperor's death, nominating Adrian, his nephew, as his successor. The nomination was seconded by the army, and so the matter was settled.

Judging the empire to be too large, he abandoned the remote provinces, conquered by Trajan, and bounded it on the east by the river Euphrates. Still he was apt in military discipline, but he chose to cultivate the arts of peace, and promote the welfare of his subjects. He spent thirteen years in visiting all parts of the empire, dispensing peace, justice, and order, as he went. While in Britain, he caused a wall of earth and wood to be erected across the island, from Carlisle to Newcastle, to protect the Britons from the incursions of the Scots.

The Jews, becoming exasperated at the privileges granted to the pagans and Christians, provoked the emperor to send an army into Judea, when one thousand of their best towns were destroyed, and nearly six hundred thousand men were slain. He then built a city on the site of Jerusalem, called Aelia Capitolina.

He is said to have excelled all the Roman emperors in his acquirements, being an author, orator, mathematician, musician, and painter. His memory was so retentive, that he recollected every incident in his life, and knew all the soldiers of his army by name. (See Artaxerxes Mnemon, page 289.) He was the first emperor who wore a long beard, and that he did to cover the warts on his face. His successor adopted it as an ornament. As infirmity gained upon him, he often exclaimed: "How miserable a thing it is to seek death, and not be able to find it!" Paganism is a comfortless faith!

TITUS ANTONINUS PIUS. — He succeeded to the empire 138 A. C. His virtues caused him to be highly esteemed, and made him a blessing to mankind. His taste was for justice, peace, and clemency; also a lover of the religion of his country. One of his favorite maxims was: "He would rather save the life of one citizen, than put to death a thousand enemies." Another, with reference to the Christians, was, that "Whoever molested them on account of their religion, should undergo the same punishment as was intended against the accused."

He was a distinguished rewarder of learned men, whom he invited from all parts of the world, and raised to wealth and honor. Among them was Apollonius, the famous Stoic philosopher, whom he sent for to instruct his son-in-law Marcus Aurelius. Upon his arrival at Rome, the emperor desired his attendance; but the Stoic replied, that "it was the business of the pupil to call upon the master, and not the master upon the pupil." Pius replied, with a smile, that "it was surprising how Apollonius, who had no difficulty in coming from Greece to Rome, should think it so hard to go from one part of Rome to another," and then sent Aurelius to him. Pius was taken ill in the midst of his labors, in rendering his subjects happy, and died in the seventy-fifth year of his age, and the twenty-third of his reign.

MARCUS AURELIUS ANTONINUS. — He ascended the throne 161 A. C., and is considered a worthy successor of his father. He is esteemed as the best model of pagan virtue among the Roman emperors; and "appeared like some benevolent deity, diffusing around him peace and happiness." His attachment to the Stoic philosophy was ardent, and he embodied his views in a work called "Meditations."

It is thought that the persecution of the Christians under the Antonines must be attributed to the pagan priests, rather than to the emperors. It is related, that while Aurelius was with the army, beyond the Danube, they were decoyed into a place where they could neither fight nor retreat. At this juncture, a legion of Christians in the service began praying, and soon arose a refreshing shower that revived the thirsty and weary troops; and from the same cloud issued a fearful shower of hail upon the enemy, that so dismayed them that they became an easy prey to the Romans. (See page 69.) From this circumstance, the emperor immediately caused the persecution against the Christians to cease. To each of the Antonines Justin Martyr presented an "Apology for Christianity."

Aurelius was the last of the so-called "Five Good Emperors." From this time Rome declines rapidly to its fall, through the reckless management of its rulers.

COMMODUS.— He was son of Aurelius. His career was after the pattern of Nero, and Faustina his mother. History has it, that the most detestable of all emperors was son of the best. He came to the throne in 180 A. C. His amusements were in the circus, amphitheatre, hunting wild beasts, boxing, and gladiator fights. His administration was weak, contemptible, and tyrannical. He spent the day feasting, and the night in debauchery. For sport, he would cut off men's noses, under pretence that he was shaving them; but, through fear of his own throat being cut, he was obliged to be his own barber.

In imitating Hercules, with his club and lion's skin, he would dress up a company of beggars like giants and monsters, and, giving them sponges instead of stones to throw at him, he would furiously fall upon them and beat them to death. Marcia, his favorite concubine, finding her name among a list of victims whom he intended to destroy, conspired with others to assassinate him by poison and strangulation.

PERTINAX.— He, having been fixed upon as successor by the conspirators, was joyfully proclaimed by the prætorian guards, 193 A. C. Applying himself with too much earnestness to the reformation of abuses, he alienated the affections of a corrupt people, and was deposed and murdered, by the same guards who put him upon the throne, in three months' time.

DIDIUS JULIANUS.— The empire having been put up at auction by the prætorian guards to the highest bidder, Didius bought it. He was a man of consular rank, and the richest citizen of Rome. He gave to each of the guards a sum nearly equal to nine millions of dollars.

At this time, several commanders in the distant provinces were proclaimed emperors by their respective forces, all of whom lost their lives but Septimus Severus. The confusion that ensued, and the various and perplexing counsels he received, so overwhelmed Didius, that he was unable to direct or control either them or himself. The senate, seeing his irresolution, determined to set him aside, and declare for Severus. Didius plead that he ought to be permitted to enjoy what he had purchased during his natural life, as he had been convicted of no crime. But the executioners obliged him to stretch his neck forward, as the custom was, and immediately struck off his head.

SEPTIMUS SEVERUS.— He succeeded to the empire 193 A. C. He

was an African by birth, ambitious, and despotic. His first act, even before he entered Rome, was the degradation of the prætorian guards, and their banishment one hundred miles from the city. They had taken too conspicuous a part in public affairs.

The most terrible battle in Roman history, was fought between the forces of Albinus, a competitor of Severus, and the forces of the Empire. It lasted from morning till night, without cessation, with no decided advantage to either party, until a reserve came to the aid of Severus, and gave him the victory. He also signalized the Roman arms in the East, and returned in triumph to Rome. In his expedition into England, he built a stone wall, nearly parallel with that of Adrian, twelve feet high and eight broad, planted with towers, one mile apart, and communicating with each other by pipes of brass in the wall, which conveyed intelligence from one garrison to another with incredible despatch.

He now began to feel the weight of his cares and labors, and knew that his end drew nigh. But what most wore upon him, was the irreclaimable life of his son Caracalla. Calling for the urn in which his ashes were to be preserved, he addressed it thus: "Little urn! thou shalt now contain what the world could not contain!" Severus died at York, England, in the eighteenth year of his reign.

Caracalla. — The empire was left to him and his brother Geta, — the latter mild, and the other fierce. Geta was soon despatched. He came to the throne in 211 A. C. He was assassinated, and so the world was freed of a monster, who was neither fit to govern an empire, nor fit to live, nor fit to die.

Macrinus. — He instigated the death of Caracalla, and ascended the throne 217 A. C. He attempted a restraint upon the licentiousness of the army, who became restive at the slightest correction. This circumstance was laid hold of by the grandmother of Heliogabalus, and, by her artifices, she alienated the affections of the army from Macrinus; and, in the struggle to retain his power, he lost his life. He reigned only fourteen months.

Heliogabalus. — He was raised to the throne, upon the death of Macrinus, by the army, the people and senate concurring, when only fourteen years of age. He was the natural son of Caracalla; a beautiful youth, loved by the army, but of the Nero stamp. In four years he married six wives, and divorced them all. He even assumed the dress and circumstances of a woman, and married one of his officers. He afterwards married a slave, who beat him, to which he submitted meekly, saying: "A woman should submit to her husband."

His supper generally cost six thousand crowns, and often sixty thousand. He always dressed in cloth of gold and purple, enriched with precious stones, and never twice put on the same habit. He caused his path to be strewed with gold and silver dust, from his door to the place of mounting his horse. The poorest people were invited to his feasts, and being seated on bellows, full of air, they were suddenly emptied, and the people thereon dropped down among wild beasts, to be torn in pieces for his amusement. He undertook to foretell future events by the entrails of human victims, and for this purpose he sacrificed the most beautiful youths in Italy. At length, perceiving that the affections of the army were set upon his successor, he meditated revenge. The soldiers, suspecting his intentions against them, watched him, caught him, and, having despatched him, treated his body with indignity, and then threw it into the Tiber. What a Roman emperor!

ALEXANDER SEVERUS.—He was cousin to Heliogabalus, and succeeded to the throne in 222 A. C. He became emperor at the age of sixteen, and was at that time possessed of premature wisdom of age: his judgment solid; an excellent mathematician, geometrician, musician, painter, sculptor, and poet. The first part of his reign was spent in reforming the abuses of his predecessors, particularly in restoring the senators to their rank and influence. In the tenth year of his reign, he conducted a victorious expedition against the Persians and Parthians, and, with several victories by his generals in other parts, restored the limits of the empire. But this expansion of the declining strength of the nation rather hastened its fall.

He lived on plain diet, faring like the common soldiers. He was at one time instructed by the famous Origen in the principles of Christianity; but no evidence is given that he embraced the gospel. He nevertheless loved good men, and reproved the lewd and infamous. A dispute once being referred to him, about a piece of ground which the Christians claimed for a place of public worship, and was claimed also by a company of grocery-men, he decided, that, "It is better that God be worshipped there, in any manner, than that the place should be put to the uses of drunkenness and debauchery." This virtuous emperor was cut off, in the fourteenth year of his reign, and twenty-ninth of his age, by a mutiny among his own soldiers, instigated by Maximinius.

MAXIMINIUS.—Having effected the death of Severus, he ascended the throne, 235 A. C. He was a son of a Thracian shepherd, and a man of gigantic stature and herculean strength,—being eight feet high, and perfectly symmetrical in form. Though possessed of some merit before his elevation to the throne, yet, after, he became brutal and ferocious. He warred with the Germans, converting hundreds of miles into a waste. He caused many noble Romans to be put to death, on suspicion that they despised him on account of his mean origin.

When apprised of the acts of the senate, appointing others to the supreme power, he howled and raved like a wild beast, and beat his head against the walls of his palace. But he soon changed from these demonstrations to those of revenge. In this career he was soon stopped, being assassinated by his own soldiers while asleep in his tent, as he was too formidable to attack while awake. His strength was such, that he could break in the teeth of a horse with a blow of his fist, and break its thigh with a kick of his foot. This giant ate forty pounds of flesh, and drank six gallons of wine, every day.

Balbinus and Pupienus. — The senate next raised these two to the throne. But, being disliked by the prætorian guards, they were soon despatched; and the guards, finding a grandson of Gordian, a former aspirant for the throne, they proclaimed him emperor.

Gordian. — He accordingly assumed the government, 238 A. C. He was only sixteen at this time, but possessed of some merit. The invasions of the Goths and Persians were repulsed by his arms.

The discontent with his reign, which began to manifest itself about the time Philip, an Arabian, was chosen prætorian prefect, was cherished by the latter, until he thought it safe to venture upon the execution of Gordian.

He reigned only six years. So fond was Gordian of learning, that he collected sixty-two thousand volumes in his private library.

Philip. — From 244 A. C., he reigned five years, and was assassinated.

Decius. — He began to reign 249 A. C. His activity and wisdom might have saved the empire, if human agency, in the hands of Providence, had been so used. But the profligacy and luxury of the times, the disputes between the pagans and the Christians, and the inroads of surrounding nations, were wasting the strength of the empire beyond recovery.

In his reign was the seventh persecution of the Christians. Decius was cut off, in a war with the Goths, by the treachery of his general, Gallus, after reigning two years and a half.

Gallus. — He was raised to the throne, 251 A. C., by the army. He reigned two years and four months. He was a vicious sovereign, and during his reign the empire suffered incalculable misery. In his reign a dreadful pestilence spread over the earth, threatening its depopulation.

Valerian. — He was commander of one of the armies, and succeeded to the empire 254 A. C. In the early part of his reign he showed more favor to the Christians than had been done by any of the other emperors; but his treatment towards them suddenly changed, through the advice of unworthy favorites, and then began the eighth general persecution.

Valerian was finally taken prisoner by Sapor, King of Persia. He used to make Valerian crouch down, so as to serve as a footstool for him to mount his horse. After serving a term of seven years prisoner, Valerian had his eyes put out; he was then flayed alive, and rubbed with salt; — a retributive death for a malignant persecutor. His skin was dyed red, and exposed in a temple.

Gallienus — Son and successor of Valerian, came to the throne 260 A. C. For a time he thought of revenge for his father's death, but soon forgot that, in his base pleasures and the interests of the empire, which was attacked without, and distracted within. Thirty pretenders arose at one time, contending for the dominion of the state. Gallienus died by violence.

Flavius Claudius. — He was next invested with the purple, 268 A. C., agreeably to the wishes of the army and the whole Roman people. The valor of his arms stayed a little the decline of the empire. Among his victories in the north, he destroyed an army of three hundred thousand men. He died a natural death, after reigning less than two years.

Aurelian. — He was made emperor, by the army, 270 A. C. He was the most valiant commander of the age, and has been compared with Julius Cæsar, for his military skill. Besides repelling the invasions of the north, he made a conquest in the east of Zenobia, Princess of Palmyra, called Queen of the East, whom he brought in triumph to Rome, bound in chains of gold, and overloaded with a profusion of pearls and diamonds. She had laid claim to the throne of Egypt, as an heir of the Ptolemies.

In his reign occurred the ninth general persecution of the Christians. On one occasion, in signing certain edicts against the Christians, a thunderbolt fell so near him that his escape was almost miraculous, and deterred him from the act. He fell in a conspiracy raised by his subjects.

Tacitus. — Several months elapsed before a new emperor was chosen. Tacitus at length consented, and began to reign 275 A. C. He died of a fever in six months after.

Florian. — A minority of the army chose him, a brother of Tacitus, to succeed. But upon the establishment of Probus in the empire, Florian sought a voluntary death. He reigned two months.

PROBUS. — He was constantly engaged with the invaders of the north, and quelling the factions within the empire. He was generally the first man to scale the walls of an enemy, and to burst into his tent. In a war with the Germans, he slew four hundred thousand men. Bonosus, who rebelled against him, was a great drunkard, and, being overcome, hanged himself in despair. Probus, seeing him shortly after, said: "There hangs, not a man, but a bottle." For obliging his soldiers to dig a trench, for draining purposes, they took offence, and slew him.

CARUS. — Being prætorian prefect to the deceased emperor, he was chosen to succeed him, 282 A. C. He associated with him his two sons, Carinus and Numerian. Carus was killed by lightning in his tent.

NUMERIAN. — He, through excess of weeping for his father's fate, was obliged to be carried in a close litter. In this situation, his ambitious father-in-law, Aper, slew him.

CARINUS. — He was slain in a contest with Diocletian, who had been chosen emperor.

DIOCLETIAN. — He began his reign 284 A. C. In two years after, he associated with himself in the empire, his general, Maximian; and in 292, they took two colleagues, Galerius and Constantius, each bearing the title of Cæsar. So the government was now in the hands of four men, — two *emperors*, and two *Cæsars*, — Diocletian being the ruling spirit. Although Diocletian had no regard for religion, his wife and daughter cherished a secret regard for it, and many officers of court openly avowed it.

Galerius was brought up by his mother (a bigoted pagan) to hate the Christians, as Hannibal was to hate the Romans, and he was no less true to his training. Constantius, being persuaded to displace all the Christian officers of his household, would not allow of their being persecuted; and when some offered to renounce their religion, he rejected them, saying: "Those who were not true to their God, would never be faithful to their prince." All of these men, except Constantius, are represented as "monsters of horrible ferocity." Galerius, who is said to have exceeded the rest in cruelty, ensnared the prejudices of Diocletian against the Christians, and persuaded him to second his fiendish designs in persecuting them. Hence commenced the *tenth* and *last* general *persecution*, about 303, and continued, in some parts of the empire, for ten years. Except in France, where Constantius ruled, the persecution pervaded the whole Roman Empire, and in severity exceeded all that had gone before. The emperors who have the honor (!) of cherishing the "ten persecutions" of the Christians, were Nero, Domitian, Trajan,

Antoninus, Severus, Maximinius, Decius, Valerian, Aurelian, and Diocletian.

Diocletian, while at the head of the Roman Empire, like Sylla, voluntarily abdicated the throne, 304 A. C., built a magnificent palace near Salona, where he amused himself in cultivating his garden. He was often heard to say, that he enjoyed this mode of life better than to wear the purple of Rome. "Now it is that I live; now I see the beauty of the sun." (See like instances in Sylla, page 350; Cincinnatus, page 337, and So, page 293.) He died 312 A. C. Maximian perished 310 A. C.

Constantius died in York, England, 306 A. C., leaving his son Constantine as his successor. Galerius died four years after, of a terrible and incurable disease.

Constantine. — He, being proclaimed emperor, 306 A. C., had to meet with a little competition. Maxentius, son of Maximian, had proclaimed himself; and in 307, Galerius, who was always slow to acknowledge Constantine, had proclaimed Licinius. In marching to meet Maxentius in battle, it is said that Constantine saw a pillar of light in the heavens, in the form of a cross, with the inscription on it: "*Conquer by this!*"

In consequence of this impressive sight, he caused a royal standard to be made, with the insignia of a cross upon it, and to be carried before him in his wars. He soon after espoused the cause of Christianity. Entering Italy, he routed the forces of his rival, and in making his escape, Maxentius fell into the Tiber, and was drowned. In 314, a war broke out between Constantine and Licinius, which soon ended in a peace. But in nine years after, hostilities were again commenced, when Licinius was compelled to abdicate, leaving Constantine sole master of the Roman world.

Constantine, more than all other men before him, and for a long time after, changed the tide of human affairs. Rome had for many years been tottering to its fall, and its crumbling rottenness was only held together by the mighty bands of despotic power. Constantine cut those bands in sunder, and hence hastened the fall of Rome. The Roman armies had become filled up with aliens from the surrounding nations; and Constantine, to prevent mutinies among the soldiers, reduced the size of the legion from five thousand to one thousand, or fifteen hundred. This measure, while it might prevent mutiny, so weakened the Roman forces, that they were easily repulsed by the invasions of the North. Another bold stroke by Constantine, was the change of the gods of the nation. Christianity, which had hitherto been persecuted to the death by paganism, he made the religion of the state, and prohibited both persecution and even the exercise of pagan rites. The operation of this change in the religious world, is traced in the History of Religion, which see, page 187, etc.

Another very important change introduced by Constantine, was the removal of the seat of empire from Rome to Byzantium. He had made choice of Chalcedon, in Asia Minor, for the new capital; but in laying out the ground-plot for the new city, an eagle caught up the measuring-line, and flew across the Bosphorus, over the city of Byzantium. This led him to change his plan, and select the latter place for his new seat of empire. After having built a capitol, an amphitheatre, many churches, magnificent edifices, and public works, giving it the name of *Constantinople*, after himself, he then dedicated it to the God of Martyrs, and removed there with his whole court.

Thus, by changing the religion of the Empire, and the seat of government, he dealt the mortal wound to both *pagan* and *imperial* Rome. In an expedition against the *Persians*, Constantine died, at Nicomedia, in the thirtieth year of his reign, and the sixty-third of his age.

CONSTANTIUS.—Before his death, Constantine divided the Empire between his three sons, Constantine II., Constans, and Constantius II., and two nephews, who were named *Cæsars*. Their reign began 337 A. C. Soon after coming into power, Constantius found means to destroy the two Cæsars, with five others of his cousins, and two of his uncles. Shortly after this, Constantine and Constans quarrelled, and the former was killed. In a few years more, Constans was killed, while quelling a revolt among his subjects, which left Constantius sovereign of the whole empire. He was much engaged in theological controversy, but to little purpose.

At first, he caused the *Persians* to retire before him, but finally they beat him back in nine signal battles. Constantius created his cousin Julian, Cæsar, but afterwards regarding him with jealousy, and hearing that he had been proclaimed emperor, marched against him, but died on the way, aged forty-five.

JULIAN.—The senate recognized him, in 361, as emperor. He had been previously proclaimed by his soldiers, much against his will; but, upon being required to submit himself to Constantius, as supreme head, he resolved upon maintaining his dignity by arms. The death of the former ended the strife.

He is called the "*Apostate*," for rejecting his Christian education, and restoring the worship and functions of pagan superstitions; reöpening the heathen temples, and giving paganism the favor of the state; he removed the Christians from all offices of the state, and refused them the benefits of the laws. He employed his pen and wit in ridiculing the Christian religion, — satire being his taste. In 363, he attempted to rebuild the temple of Jerusalem, for the purpose of contradicting prophecy, and so furnish a *standing* argument against the truth of Revelation. The blasphemous attempt was defeated by the eruption of fire from the earth, which drove the workmen from the mad design, which leaves Revelation *true*, and Julian a liar.

His "Cæsars," is the most famous of all his compositions, being a satire on all the Roman emperors, from Julius Cæsar to Constantine. Gibbon calls it "one of the most agreeable and instructive productions of ancient wit."

In the year 363, while pursuing a routed Persian army, he received a mortal wound. In conversation with a philosopher, in his last moments, he expressed his expectation of being united with heaven and with the stars. Upon the death of Julian, the race of Constantinus Clorus became extinct, and the Roman world was without a head, and without an heir.

Jovian. — In this situation, the army finally fixed upon Jovian, a Pannonian, as his successor, 363 A. C. He made peace with the Persians, rather as a matter of necessity, as well as policy, by the cession of five provinces. He sought to restore tranquillity to the church, by displaying the banner of the cross, and reversing the edicts of Julian against Christianity.

While on a march to rescue the palace of Constantine, his wife hastened with an imperial train to meet him, carrying their infant son; and while the happy moment of embracing her husband seemed just at hand, the heavy news of his sudden death, by suffocation from charcoal, quickly turned her hour of joy into one of grief. He reigned only seven months; during which time he recalled Athanasius, who had fled before Julian.

Valentinian I. — He was made emperor, by the army, 364 A. C. In one month after, he associated with himself in the empire his brother Valens, to whom he gave the eastern provinces. From this time the empire was divided into Eastern and Western, though still considered as one body. The main business of the emperor now was, in repelling the invasions from the North, in which he was successful.

He favored the Christian religion, and his domestic administration was equitable and wise.

He died, in an expedition against the Alemanni, 367 A. C. Being successful against them, they sent ambassadors to sue for peace. Their policy had been such, however, as to provoke the emperor beyond endurance; and in the interview with them, his anger rose to such a pitch, and his tones and gestures were so violent, that he ruptured a blood-vessel, and expired on the spot.

GRATIAN.—He was son of Valentinian, and came to the throne in 367 A. C. Valens still presided in the east—only as an associate, however. In 376, he permitted vast hordes of the Goths, who had been driven from their country by the Huns, to settle in Thrace. They soon fell to plundering the country, given them as an asylum, when Valens marched to oppose them. He was defeated in the famous battle of Adrianople, two thirds of his army being cut to pieces. Valens was also mortally wounded, and after being carried into a cottage near by, it was set on fire and burnt by the Goths, they not knowing that it contained the Emperor of the East. The death of Valens left Gratian at the head of the whole empire, when he took Theodosius as associate and Emperor of the East.

Gratian undertook to destroy the remains of paganism, and about the same time there was a severe famine in Rome. This was ascribed by the pagans to the gods, as a judgment upon the nation for the destruction of idolatry; and a general belief of that delusion stirred up a general dissatisfaction. Maximius, who commanded at that time in Britain, took advantage of this disturbance, by causing himself to be proclaimed emperor. Gratian, marching into Gaul to oppose him, was deserted by his soldiers, and killed, at Lyons, 371 A. C.

VALENTINIAN II.—He was the lawful successor of his brother Gratian; but, being dispossessed by Maximius, he threw himself upon the protection of Theodosius in the east, who restored him to his throne. After wearing the crown for several years, he was strangled by a Goth, named Arbogastus, 392 A. C., who, after destroying Valentinian, proclaimed Eugenius as his successor.

THEODOSIUS.—Having defeated and slain Eugenius, he succeeded to the whole empire, 379 A. C. He was the first Emperor of the East who succeeded to the Empire, and the last who presided over both the east and west.

In his reign, the finishing work of destroying paganism was done. First, by a grand council, he established the Nicene Creed as the standard of orthodoxy. Then an edict was issued, prohibiting all meetings of heretics, under the severest penalties. In 390, an edict was issued, prohibiting the worship of any inanimate idol, or the sacrifice of any victim thereto, on pain of death. "Upon this," says Gibbon, "so rapid, and yet so gentle, was the fall of it, that only twenty-eight years after the death of Theodosius, its faint and minute vestiges were no longer visible to the eye of the legislator."

Previous to his decease, he divided the Empire between his two sons, assigning the west to Honorius, and the east to Arcadius. This division of the empire so weakened it, that it became a much easier prey to the hordes of the North, that poured down upon the empire like swarms of bees, for multitude. The names of these formidable tribes, bordering on the north of the Roman Empire, were Huns, a tribe that emigrated west from the north borders of China; Alains, an Asiatic tribe; Vandals, came from Scandinavia, now Sweden; Goths, from the same; Visigoths, were West-Goths; Ostrogoths, were East-Goths; the Heruli were emigrants from Sweden.

Honorius. — Stilicho, a famous warrior, had been appointed minister to Honorius during the minority of the latter, and did him great service in repelling the Goths. Alaric, their king, had spread his devastations to the walls of Constantinople, filled Greece with the terror of his arms, and then penetrated into Italy with a large army, where he was defeated by the Romans, under Stilicho.

Stilicho having become the object of jealousy among his rivals, Honorius basely caused him to be beheaded.

Soon after this event, Alaric again invaded Italy, with three hundred thousand men, and carried his conquest to the very gates of Rome. He was only prevented from razing it to the ground, by the promise of enormous sums of gold and silver, and an incredible number of precious articles. These conditions not being fulfilled, Alaric became indignant, and the work of sacking Rome began in earnest. After hedging them in on all sides, famine set in with all its horrors (when human flesh was sold in the market), to do what Gothic arms could not do. What such means failed to do, treachery accomplished, so that the besiegers were triumphant. A Roman sentinel opened the Salarian gate at midnight, when the inhabitants of Rome were aroused by the tremendous sound of the Gothic trumpet.

This mighty city (which had not been visited by an invading army for over six hundred years, during which time she had sat mistress of the world, and had gathered into her treasures and magnificence, the riches of all nations) now lay at the feet of the Gothic king, who said to his soldiers: "All the riches of the world are here concentrated: to you I abandon them; but I command you to spill the blood of none but those you find in arms, and to spare such as take refuge in churches." The pillage lasted for six days. Alaric died soon after, of a short illness.

Instead of rallying to recover his losses, Honorius entered into a treaty with Ataulfus, Alaric's successor, by giving him his sister Placidia in marriage, and ceding to him a portion of Spain. By this and other similar acts, Honorius hastened the destruction of the Empire. He died 422 A. C.

Valentinian III. — He was crowned emperor in 424 A. C., and was seven months an associate with Honorius. The revolt of Count Boniface in Africa, took that country away from Rome. Resisting the army first sent against him, under Ætius, he feared his ability to do it the second time, and so invited to his assistance Genseric, King of the Vandals. He readily went to Boniface's assistance, and, after defeating the Romans, took possession of the country himself, and held it.

The Huns, under Attila their king, overran nearly all the northern provinces, and soon after invaded Gaul, with an army of five hundred thousand men, threatening the destruction of the empire. The Romans, under Ætius ("The Last of the Romans"), met this host on the plains of Chalons, when the Huns were defeated, with a loss of one hundred and sixty thousand men. Attila soon rallied again, and invaded Italy, marched to the gates of Rome, wherein he shut up Valentinian, who was obliged to purchase a peace with an immense dowry, and giving his sister Honoria to Attila in marriage. This "scourge of God" died soon after.

It is said the body of Attila was enclosed in three coffins, — the first of gold, the second of silver, the third of iron, — and that the men who dug his grave were put to death, lest his place of burial should be revealed.

Ætius, who had done so much for his country, was made an object of jealousy by Heraclius the eunuch, and Valentinian stabbed him with his own hand. The next year the emperor himself was assassinated.

Maximus. — He instigated the murder of Valentinian, and was raised to the throne 455 A. C. His *excuse* for this was (*pretended or real*), revenge for the dishonor Valentinian cast upon his wife. He married Eudoxia, the widow of his predecessor, to whom he imprudently revealed his guilt in the murder of the emperor. To revenge this deed, she called in Genseric, King of the Vandals. Upon his arrival in Italy, Maximus fled, and, for his cowardice, his people stoned him to death.

Eudoxia found Genseric no more agreeable company than Maximus. After responding to her call, he concluded to stop and help himself, as he did when Boniface asked him into Africa to help him. After taking Rome, and giving it up to pillage for several days, he took Eudoxia and her two daughters back with him in triumph to Carthage.

Avitus. — He was proclaimed in Gaul, by his troops. Having

made Ricimer, a senator, general of his armies, the latter soon after entered into a conspiracy against his benefactor, whom he arrested and deposed, and who soon after died, while on his way to Italy, 457 A. C.

MAJORIAN.—He was next proclaimed after the deposition of Avitus. He made an unsuccessful attempt against the Vandals in Africa. Gaining a reputation for wisdom and virtue, by publishing some good laws, Ricimer was jealous of him, and so deposed and slew him, 461 A. C.

SEVERUS.—He was created emperor by Ricimer himself, who governed under him. Getting sick of that, he found it convenient, after four years, to poison the nominal master of himself and the empire.

ATHEMIUS. — He was called to the empire, by the united suffrages of the senate, the army, and the people, 467 A. C. In order to attach Ricimer to his interest, as he had become formidable, he gave him his daughter in marriage.

Ricimer soon found occasion to quarrel with his father-in-law, besieged and pillaged Rome, during which the emperor was murdered.

OLYBRIUS. — He was sent with an army, by Leo, Emperor of the East, to assist Athemius against Ricimer; but he was seduced by Ricimer to assist him rather, and was proclaimed emperor, but died three months after, 472 A. C. Thus Ricimer disposed summarily of five emperors.

JULIUS NEPOS. — Glycerus, an obscure soldier, aided by a Burgundian prince, assumed the title of Emperor, at Ravenna; but Leo had conferred it upon Julius Nepos, who took Glycerus prisoner, and had him consecrated Bishop of Salona, 473.

Julius Nepos was proclaimed at Rome, in 474. The next year, Orestes, a Panonian, whom he sent into Gaul, revolted and besieged the emperor in Ravenna. Nepos escaped into Dalmatia, where, in five years, he was assassinated.

ROMULUS AUGUSTULUS. — He, son of Orestes, was made emperor by his father. After a reign of eleven months, he was taken prisoner by Odoacer, chief of the Heruli, who assumed the title of *King of Italy*, 476 A. C. Augustulus was sent into Campania, where he lived privately, in splendor.

Thus ends the Western Empire of Rome. A little fanciful, that the *last emperor* of Rome, should adopt both the names of the *first king* of Rome and the *first emperor* of Rome.

PERIOD VI. FROM THE END OF THE WESTERN EMPIRE, 4480 A. M., AND 476 A. C., TO THE END OF THE EASTERN, 5457 A. M., AND 1453 A. C.

The history of the Eastern Empire will be traced very briefly, since it, as well as most of the nations of the East, has but little interest, so far as pertains to the design of this work.

ARCADIUS.—He was son of Theodosius, the last sovereign of the East and West, hence brother of Honorius, the first emperor of the *Western* Roman Empire, and himself the first emperor of the *Eastern* Roman Empire.

JUSTINIAN I.—He was the eighth Emperor of the East. The Eastern Empire was at its zenith during his reign, and hence he is surnamed the *Great.* He published a *code* of *laws*, prepared by an eminent lawyer of that age, named Tribonian. That code is said to be the foundation of the jurisprudence of modern Europe. The "Laws of Solon," the "Laws of the Twelve Tables," and the "Laws of Tribonian," form distinct epochs in the history of jurisprudence among the ancients. Justinian built the church of St. Sophia, now a Mohammedan mosque.

The greatest injustice done by this emperor was, his ungrateful treatment to Belisarius, his general. On the plains of Dara he defeated the Persians, with great slaughter, in three sanguinary battles, in different years. In a riot between two factions in Constantinople, Justinian was about to flee for safety, when Belisarius appeared for his relief, with a body of veteran soldiers. These he led against the populace, and it is computed that not less than thirty thousand persons perished in the carnage. In an expedition against the Vandals in Africa, Belisarius was victorious. But Justinian, being jealous of him, recalled him; but his victories and prompt obedience secured him a triumph. He was popular all the time the emperor was abusing him.

In 537 Belisarius was sent into Italy, against the Goths. Upon hearing of his approach, the Gothic king retired, showing no resistance. Belisarius nearly revived the ancient fame of the Roman arms. The retreat of the Goths proved to be only a respite, as their king soon attacked Rome with a hundred thousand warriors. Belisarius, however, met him, and turned him back, after a siege against Rome, and finally drove him from the country. No sooner was this done than the emperor recalled him to Constantinople, and, though deprived of a triumph, the favor of the people was equal to one.

Belisarius was again sent to the East, and saved it by his arms.

Italy being again overrun by the brave Totila, Belisarius was again sent thither, and as soon as the prospect of driving the Gothic king was flattering, he was called off to some less important war, as a disgrace, and superseded in his command by Narses. The declining years of this great general were spent in Constantinople, and even at that late period he saved the ungrateful Justinian and his capital from the ravages of the Bulgarians. In extreme old age, he suffered for the comforts of life; for a time, from the false imputation of conspiracy. (Well might the emperor fear him, — he ought to.)

PHOCAS. — He seated himself upon the throne 602 A. C., and was the twelfth Emperor of the East. A revolt of the army occurring, Phocas was proclaimed emperor beyond the Danube, when he marched to Constantinople. Taking Maurice, the emperor, prisoner, he caused his five sons to be murdered before his eyes, when the tragic scene closed with the execution of the emperor himself, falling upon the dead bodies of his children. Phocas' cruelty towards the family of his predecessor, ended with the murder of the innocent Empress Constantia, and her three daughters, at the same place where her husband and sons suffered three years before.

To him also belongs the distinction of robbing John, Bishop of Constantinople, of his assumed title of *Universal Bishop*, and conferring it upon the court sycophant, Boniface III., of Rome; and at the same time declaring the "*Church of Rome to be the head of all other churches*," — 606 A. C.

At last, Heraclius Governor of Egypt, sent his son against Phocas, with a fleet; and, upon his arrival at Constantinople, the cruel Phocas was forsaken of his people, beheaded, and his body treated with the greatest indignity.

CONSTANTINE III. — He was the fourteenth Emperor of the East, 672 A. C.; and during his reign, the Saracens, or Mohammedans, besieged Constantinople for seven months, but were obliged to retire. But, though defeated, they returned every year for seven years in succession, and were every time repulsed by Calinicus, who invented an inextinguishable fire, by which he destroyed their ships.

The Greek, or liquid fire, was composed of naphtha, or liquid bitumen, mixed with sulphur, and pitch taken from green firs. Water, instead of extinguishing, quickened this powerful agent of destruction. It could only be damped by sand, wine, or vinegar. It remained a secret with the Greeks for four hundred years, when the Mohammedans finally discovered and stole it. It was used in war down to the middle of the fourteenth century, when gunpowder took its place. The "Greek liquid fire" was a step in advance of Archimedes' "burning-glasses," in destructive implements of war.

The Eastern Empire was ruled by some thirty-nine emperors, from Constantine III. to the eleventh century. The magnificence of their palaces, scattered upon the coasts and islands of Asia and Europe, and the splendor and luxury in which they lived, had no small attractions to the envious potentates round about. Italy was swept away by the Normans, and the Turks had knocked out many of the Asiatic props of the Empire. Still, Thrace, Macedonia, Greece, Cyprus, Rhodes, Crete, and the fifty islands of the Archipelago, were within its limits. Finally Constantinople was taken by the crusaders, and held in their possession for sixty odd years, during which time the Greek emperors made Nice the seat of their power.

MICHÆL PALÆOLOGUS. — In 1261, this man was found possessed of the requisite ambition and ability to retake Constantinople from its Latin conquerors, and restore it to the successors of Constantine. It continued to drag on a precarious existence until 1453, when it was taken by the Turks.

CONSTANTINE XII. — He was the last Roman emperor, when Constantinople was besieged by Mohammed II., at the head of three hundred thousand Turks. At this time it was attacked with cannon, — not "liquid fire," but *fire and brimstone*. This event put an end to the Eastern, and so to the whole of the Roman Empire; and thus the might of the great Cæsars was brought to nought.

From Janus to Constantine XII. the Empire had lasted, during all its changes and disasters, two thousand seven hundred years, — the greatest length of time of any empire on record.

"DARK AGES."

From the seventh to the fourteenth century is the time usually called the "Dark Ages." They are so called, from the general prevalence of superstition and oppression.

The ruling influences in both Church and State were averse to civil and religious liberty; and hence the dark, leaden, iron, horrid character of those times.

CRUSADES.

One enterprise (if it be worthy of the name) was the Crusades, or Holy Wars, so called. The occasion of these *curse*-ades (more properly called) was as follows. It became a matter of great importance to the Papal Church, to encourage its votaries to go on pilgrimages to Jerusalem, for the purpose of visiting the tomb of Christ, and other places of religious interest in Palestine. While the Saracens, or Mohammedans, retained the control of the country, the "Christians" (?) were permitted to go unmolested on their pilgrimages to the Holy Land.

When the Turks got possession of Jerusalem in 1065, the pilgrims were no longer safe, but exposed to insult and robbery. This aroused the Christian powers of Europe to wrest the Holy Land from the grasp of the infidels. Vast and imposing armies were raised by Peter the Hermit, and sent on this pious errand; and for years an untold amount of suffering, blood, and treasure were expended, and all in vain, as the effort had to be abandoned, and the holy places even yet remain in the possession of the infidels. The Saracen, or Mohammedan Empire, merged into the Turkish upon the taking of Bagdad, its capital, by the Turks, in 1258.

The Saracens, more than any other nation of these times, encouraged literature. The reign of Haroun al Raschid, the twenty-fifth caliph, who was contemporary with Charlemagne, was termed the Augustan Age of Saracen, or Arabic, Literature. He is said to have been the author of the "Thousand and One Nights," or "Arabian Nights."

Much as the Saracens encouraged literature, they nevertheless robbed the world of more than they furnished in that department. During the reign of Omar, from 633 to 645, he ordered the destruction of the Alexandrian Library, consisting of seven hundred thousand volumes, for the following reason, which he gave his general, Amrou, in his order for its destruction. Said he: "If these writings agree with the Koran, they are useless, and need not be preserved; if they disagree with it, they are pernicious, and ought to be destroyed."

Possibly the world at large would be as well satisfied had the Koran been burnt, and the Alexandrian Library preserved, as they are with the reverse.

FEUDALISM.

This was another element of society in the Middle, or Dark Ages, which had no small influence over the minds and affairs of the nation. It had its origin among the Goths, Vandals, Huns, Lombards, etc., that held sway in Europe on the fall of the Roman Empire. It was adopted by Charlemagne, most of the princes of Europe, and introduced into England by William the "Conqueror," so called. The relics of the system are still seen in the condition of the lands there at the present day, held by lords and tenants.

It was the very opposite of the plan pursued by the nobility of Rome, who *withheld* the public lands from the plebeians, who did the fighting, but lost the spoils. A feudal chieftain, who led out his legions, would, on the conquest of a country, make division of it into lots, on condition of rendering him military service upon demand. He first took the lion's share for himself, and then distributed the rest among his whelps, or captains, giving them portions of various sizes, as towns, or counties, which they distributed on the same conditions (of military service) to the lower animals, or *serfs*, or *villains*, as they were actually called. Thus a feudal kingdom became a military establishment — a victorious army encamped, under its officers, all over the conquered territory, — every captain, or baron, independent of his sovereign, except in time of war, and then every man and officer is sworn to support his feudal lord.

These lords came at length not only to oppress the people at times, but were often, by their immense numbers, and their strong fortresses and castles, in a condition to defy the authority of the civil magistracy, and even the crown itself. Upon the refusal of the barons to obey their feudal chief, the most turbulent wars were engendered, which shows feudalism to be adapted only to a dark age, or an age of feuds. Hence, with the dawn of light, letters, and liberty, feudalism vanishes away.

CHIVALRY.

This was also a peculiarity of the middle ages, and rather an accompaniment and softener of feudal manners. It was a strange blending of valor, love, and religion. Its origin is involved in obscurity, but it received a high finish in the times of the crusades.

The sons of noblemen, destined for chivalry, were placed, at the age of seven years, in the castle of their father, or of some neighboring noble, to receive the course of education necessary to fit them for the performance of the duties, and the enjoyment of the honors, of chivalry. At the age of fourteen they received the title of *esquire*, and were then authorized to bear arms. They were kept in constant employment, and waited upon the master and mistress of the castle, at home and abroad. They were surrounded by noble ladies and valiant knights, so that their earliest impressions were those of love, gallantry, honor, and bravery. They were taught to adore chivalry, as containing all that was noble or desirable.

"The love of God and the ladies, was enjoined as a single duty; and he who was faithful and true to his mistress, was held sure of salvation, in the theology of the castles." The virtues and endowments of an accomplished knight were, "beauty, strength, and agility of body; great dexterity in dancing, wrestling, hunting, hawking, riding, tilting, etc.; the virtues, piety, chastity, modesty, courage, loyalty, liberality, sobriety, an inviolable attachment to truth, and an invincible courage." To roam among perils was noble; and every knight was at liberty to challenge to single combat, and to fight with the utmost fury, all those of his order whom he met, if they did not acknowledge his lady-love to be the most beautiful in the world, — even if his friend had never seen her. From this foul seed of chivalry, sprang the still more foul fruit of duelling — a *dark-age plant.*

Chivalry has been much lauded for its intrinsic excellence and its noble deeds; but, from the fact that it had its origin, flourished, and decayed, in an age and under circumstances which no well-informed person, philanthropist or Christian, could wish back upon the earth again, there is no good reason why we should not repudiate chivalry also. A better faith says: "Do to others as ye would they should do to you." Chivalry says: "Be ready at all times to thrust thy sword into the belly of a heretic, as far as it will go."

Upon the fall of the Western Empire, sprang up the modern nations of Europe. The Visigoths took Spain; the Franks, Gaul; the Saxons, England; the Huns, Pannonia; the Ostrogoths, Italy, etc., etc. Most of the divisions of the East, made at that time, still continue.

MODERN NATIONS.

Among the modern nations, which arose upon the ruins of the Roman Empire, most important to be noticed, are France and England. Of those that have since arisen, none can receive extended notice, consistent with the design of this work, except the United States.

The chief points of importance connected with France and England, are the services they have each rendered the great interests of civil and religious liberty. The elements that have caused those nations to foment, have been the clashing interests of Royalty and Popery on one hand, and those of Republicanism and Protestantism on the other. They have been alternately and confusedly under the sway of one and the other, and both together, until a tolerable degree of order has been evolved from the chaos; furnishing the world with two better specimens of nations than all antiquity can boast of. And yet a third has sprung out of them, diverse from either, succored by both, and of which both may be proud. The "philosopher's stone" of civil and religious liberty was at last found, upon the virgin shores of Americus' "Columbia!"

By reference to the diagram, it will be seen that the two former nations had their origin in the "Age of War for Opinion," and have continued to the present time; while the United States had its origin wholly in the last age, or that of "Consolidation."

III.—AGE OF WAR FOR OPINION.

FRANCE—FROM PHARAMOND TO LOUIS NAPOLEON BONAPARTE.

CIVIL HISTORY.

PERIOD I. FROM PHARAMOND, 4424 A. M., AND 420 A. C., TO PEPIN, 4756 A. M., AND 752 A. C.

France, formerly called Gaul, was conquered and annexed to the Roman Empire by Julius Cæsar, 51 B. C. It received its name, "France," from a tribe of Germans, living in the districts of the lower Rhine and Weser, who assumed the name of *Franks*, or *Freemen*, from their union to resist the dominion of the Romans.

PHARAMOND.—After a great variety of the fortunes of war, the first permanent stand appears to have been made by the Franks against the Romans, under their leader, Pharamond. From this little graft, has grown the imposing nation of the French.

CLODIUS, MEROVŒUS, AND CHILDERIC.—These are said to have been the successors of Pharamond. Nothing of note is connected with them, except the second, from whom the first dynasty of the kings of France took its name,—known as the Merovingian dynasty.

CLOVIS.—He was grandson of Merovœus, and somewhat distinguished. He defeated the Romans in the battle of Soissons; next the King of Thuringia, who had invaded his kingdom; then the Germans, in the battle of Tolbiac; and, finally, the Visigoths, under Alaric, when he subdued all the south of Gaul.

In his contest with the Germans, he is said to have invoked the aid of the God of Clotilda, his wife, who was a Christian. The battle turning in his favor, he was true to his promise, that in the event of success he would embrace Christianity, and was accordingly baptized, he and three thousand of his subjects, on Christmas day, 496 A. C. His motive, however, being a sordid one, he relapsed into sin. Clovis made Paris the seat of his empire. He published the *Salic Laws*, excluding females from the throne. He died in 511 A. C.

CHARLES MARTEL.—The Merovingian kings proved themselves a race of weak rulers, being generally controlled by the "mayors of the palace," or the highest officers under the crown. Martel himself, was mayor, and held the reins of government under three kings.

After his father's death, his mother-in-law confined him in prison for a time; but, escaping thence, he triumphed over all opposition, and took the reigns of government, and ruled, with the title of Duke of France; and even when the throne became vacant, he continued in the same relation, without usurping the crown. The most signal service he rendered France, Europe, and possibly the world, was in his successful resistance of the Saracens, in 732 A. C. These furious crusaders threatened all Europe with subjugation to the Mohammedan power and religion, and but for their providential defeat by Charles Martel, might to this day have been the masters of the civilized world. He checked their invasions into France and Spain in a general battle, between Poictiers and Tours, into which he drew them, defeating them with immense slaughter. From this blow they never recovered, and were finally driven out of the country, and the terror of their name perished throughout Europe.

After some other conquests, Charles left the throne of France to his two sons, Pepin le Bref and Carloman, as mayors of the palace. Childeric III., a weak prince, was the nominal king, but of little count, as the power was in the hands of the mayors. He was the last of the Merovingian race of kings.

PERIOD II. FROM PEPIN, 4756 A. M., AND 752 A, C., TO THE END OF THE REIGN OF PHILIP IV., 5317 A. M., AND 1313 A. C.

PEPIN. — Carloman, brother of Pepin, soon retired to a monastic life, leaving the sole administration to his brother. From Carloman sprang the name of the "*Carlovingian*" race of kings,—Pepin being the first king.

Pepin, now seeing that Childeric III. was all the impediment in his way to being king, set himself at work to clear the track. Carloman, having become a good son of the church, opened the heart of His Holiness towards the aspirant for the throne of France; and Pepin, knowing the influence the favor of the Pope would have in establishing his usurpation, propounded this question to him: "Who ought to sit upon the throne of France, Childeric or Pepin?" His Holiness, Pope Zachary, replies: "You, Pepin."

Hereupon Pepin assembles a meeting of dignitaries at Soissons, in 751, where he was proclaimed king, and crowned by St. Boniface, Bishop of Mentz. Shortly after, he marched against the revolted Saxons, defeated them, and added Languedoc to the realm. Upon his return from this expedition, he was crowned a second time, by Pope Stephen II. In return for this gracious act, Pepin marched against the Lombards, who had invaded the principality of Ravenna, and threatened Rome itself. The invaders were spared, on condition they would surrender Ravenna, which Pepin bestowed on the Holy See. This raised the Pope to the rank of a temporal prince, and united the sceptre to the "Keys." Charles Martel saved Europe from the power of the Mohammedans; Pepin put it under the power of the popes. He next drove out the remainder of the Saracens from the south of France.

Pepin was only four and a half feet in height. Upon hearing that some of his courtiers ridiculed his personal appearance, he invited them the next day to witness a fight between a lion and a bull. The lion immediately leaped upon the bull, and would soon have destroyed him. Pepin, turning to his courtiers, asked them: "Who has the resolution to go and oblige the lion to let go his hold?" No one spoke. "Mine, then, shall be the task," said Pepin; and, leaping into the amphitheatre with a drawn sword, cut off the lion's head at a single blow. What Pepin lacked in *stature*, his mocking courtiers lacked in *courage*. Pepin died in 768 A. C., after a successful reign, in his fifty-fourth year, leaving his dominions to his two sons, Charles and Carloman. An observation worth remembering is this, that the popes of Rome have never received greater *favors*, nor greater *abuses*, from any potentates in the world, than they have from the kings of France.

CHARLEMAGNE. — Carloman, brother of Charlemagne, dying soon after his father, left the whole kingdom to Charles. He is called Charlemagne (*i. e.*, Charles the Great) both for his exploits and personal size. For, notwithstanding the diminutive size of Pepin, his father, he is said to have been seven feet high, of a robust constitution, and a majestic appearance. He also distinguished himself as a warrior and statesman. He had a long and bloody contest with the Saxons, overthrew the Lombards in Italy, and made extensive conquests even beyond the Danube; so that his kingdom finally included France, Netherlands, Germany, Switzerland, much of Italy, and part of Spain. But his greatest difficulty was in subduing the brave and freedom-loving Saxons. His effort to subdue their fierce spirit, in attempting to convert them to Christianity by compulsion, is most reprehensible. Several thousands of them were butchered, for refusing to receive Christian baptism. His zeal, in compelling all whom he conquered to receive baptism, won for him the distinction of "Saint," for his eminent services to the Papal Church.

In the year 800, he was crowned Emperor of the West, by Pope

Leo III. In his yearly tour from France into Germany, he used to call at Rome. On his last visit there, while on his knees at mass before the altar, the Pope came suddenly behind him, and placed on his head the crown worn by the Cæsars of Imperial Rome. This act was loudly applauded by the populace. But this did not restore ancient Rome to its former splendor. The new Western Empire of Charlemagne *arose* with its great emperor, and also *perished* with him. (See the same of Epaminondas and Thebes, page 312.) He had no particular capital of the empire, though Aix-la-Chapelle was his favorite residence for a long time.

His superintendence of the affairs of the realm was very extraordinary, — giving even personal attention to the redress of grievances, and to the execution of his orders. He discountenanced luxury, encouraged industry, and sought to elevate the social and intellectual character of his subjects, though he himself could not spell his own name. His court was frequented by Alcuin, and other learned men of the time, and he endeavored, but with poor success however, to dispel the ignorance of the times.

His frugality and simplicity of manners are seen in superintending his own farms, and in training his sons to every manly exercise. His court ladies were employed with the needle and distaff, and he took great pleasure in appearing ornamented with the needlework of his wife and daughters. He often invited his sumptuously dressed courtiers to hunting excursions, when he would lead them into the wild forests, where they would get their fine clothes badly torn. On their return, he would show them his own uninjured sheepskin cloak, in contrast with their own tattered vestments. He then, by way of advice and rebuke, would say: "Leave silks and finery to women; the dress of a man is for use, and not for show." Charlemagne died at Aix-la-Chapelle, in the seventy-second year of his age, and the forty-sixth of his reign, 814 A. C.

Louis I. — He was son and successor of Charlemagne, and a weak prince, having an inglorious reign. He left his kingdom to his three sons, 840 A. C.

Charles I. — He and his two brothers quarrelled, which involved their subjects in a bloody war, and the strife was ended by the terrible battle of Fontenay, where one hundred thousand men fell, including most of the nobility of France. A new division of the empire now followed, when Charles received the western part of France, termed Aquitaine and Neustria; Lothaire received Italy; and Louis, Germany. During the reign of Charles, the Normans invaded France, and burnt Paris. Thus the Empire of the West was soon divided.

Germany, being now lost to France, takes a separate place among the nations of Europe.

LOUIS II. — He was son of Charles I., and, in order to secure peace in his realm, was obliged to make many gifts of lands, titles, and offices to his nobles and bishops. Advantage was taken of this weakness of the king, and in those feudal times the titled grandees chose to remain in their castles, and even became so formidable as to defy the power of government, and keep the country in commotion through their feuds. He came to the throne in 877 A. C.

LOUIS III. AND CARLOMAN. — These were sons of Louis II., and were united and vigorous, and met with some success against the Normans. Louis, in pursuing a young female who fled from him, struck his head against a door, and was killed by the blow, in 882. Carloman was killed by a spear, which one of his company threw at a wild boar, 884.

CHARLES II. — He was called to the throne, in 885. He was son of Louis I., of Germany, and grandson of Charles I. He was soon rejected for his cowardice, and Eudes, Count of Paris, and brother of Louis III. and Carloman, was chosen Regent, by the nobility of France, during the minority of Charles.

EUDES. — He reigned a short time, and died.

CHARLES III. — Upon the death of Eudes, Charles came to the throne, in 898 A. C. During his reign, the Normans invaded Neustria, which was ceded to them in 911. To Pollo the king gave his daughter Giselle in marriage. From this time the country was called Normandy, from the Normans, from whom sprang the future conqueror of England. Charles died in prison, 929.

ROBERT. — Charles was deposed by Robert, brother of Eudes, in 922. Though Charles was a weak monarch, and despised by his nobles, yet he slew Robert with his own hand.

RODOLPH — Son-in-law to Robert, succeeded to the throne, 923.

LOUIS IV. AND LOTHAIRE. — The son of Charles III. He was called to the throne in 936. He was called Outremer, or Transmarine, from being brought up in England. During his reign, and that of Lothaire, the administration of affairs passed into the hands of Hugh the Great — like the mayors in earlier times.

LOUIS V. — While Louis succeeded to the throne, Hugh Capet, son of Hugh the Great, succeeded to the *control* of the government, as his father had done. Lothaire and Louis were both poisoned by their queens. Louis V. was the last of the Carlovingian dynasty.

HUGH CAPET. — He assumed the government of France in 987 A. C. Finding, upon the death of Louis, that he held in his power a vacant throne, and with the example of Pepin before him, and with far less violence, he could, so with equal safety and willingness he did, seat himself thereon.

Capet was the first of the third race, or dynasty, of the kings of France, called the *Capetian.* He was crowned at Rheims, the third of July. His reign was marked with ability, both by the enactment of salutary laws and by adding considerable territories to his kingdom. He made Paris his place of residence, though it had been deserted by his predecessors for over two hundred years. Though holding and wielding the power of France, yet Capet never assumed the insignia of royalty, — probably through fear of the jealousy of his nobles. On great occasions, even, he appeared in a plain dress.

Robert II. — He was son of Capet, and had been associated with his father in power from near the beginning of his reign. He succeeded to the empire in 996. He married Bertha, his fourth cousin, daughter of the King of Burgundy. From some motive, the Pope disapproved of the marriage, and annulled it, excommunicated the king, and put his kingdom under an interdict. Ill treatment that, to the sovereigns of France, who had done so much for the Pope! But it was doubtless, in part, a spite at the Capetian dynasty.

The confusion of affairs which followed this step was great. The king was almost forsaken by his court, such was the horror felt in those times towards an *excommunicated* person. From the extraordinary pressure upon the king, he was obliged to abandon Bertha, though much against his will. In order to please His Holiness (?), Robert married Constantia, who caused him endless trouble. She procured the assassination of the grand master of the palace; she sowed discord among the king's sons, and caused thousands of heretics (?) to be cruelly put to death. It was no crime in the Pope's eyes for Robert to live with this fiend; but to live with his fourth cousin, annoyed the holy (?) father into a righteous indignation.

It is not a little singular, that in Languedoc, the very region of this fierce persecution, the cause of Protestantism has ever since held the ascendency over Catholicism. Robert was the first king whose touch was said to cure the scrofula, or "King's Evil."

Henry I. — Upon the death of the king, his two sons, Henry and Robert, both aspired to the throne. Their meddlesome mother-in-law sought to promote Robert; but, after some bloodshed, Henry obtained his right, and became king, 1031 A. C. He was an energetic sovereign, and successful in arms, and at first joined William of Normandy, against the Norman nobles, but finally turned against William, which laid a foundation for long and disastrous wars.

In the reign of Henry I. occurred another famine, which spread desolation in France and Europe. Human flesh was not only eaten, but the dead even were dug up and eaten. At hotels, the poor were taken to furnish the tables at breakfast. Crops were cut off, pasturing failed, and cattle and men died. In Henry's time, a law was passed, called "*The Truce of God*," prohibiting duelling between Thursday and Sunday. Such was its prevalence at this time, that all classes were obliged to meet in single combat; even priests must fight when challenged, or provide a substitute. This law was a slight effort at reform, and a very commendable one, amid the darkness of the times.

PHILIP I. — He took the crown of France when seven years old, in 1060, under the Regency of Baldwin, Count of Flanders. Being rather a spectator than an actor in his reign, we look more for what *was* done, than for what he did.

In his time, Peter the Hermit preached and instigated the first crusade. In his reign also occurred the invasion of France by William the Conqueror, a king of England. This, no doubt, was done by William out of revenge for the part Henry I. had taken against him. From this time began a long-continued rivalship and hostility between the French and English monarchies.

LOUIS VI. — He ascended the throne of France in 1108. He had rather a popular reign, and was esteemed a very good king. In a war carried on with Henry I. of England, he was unsuccessful, and his army defeated at Brenneville, in 1119. In his flight, after the battle, an Englishman seized his horse's bridle, and exclaimed: "The king is taken!" When Louis replied: "The king is never taken, not even in a game of chess!" and struck his enemy down, and fled.

On his death-bed, he charged his son, who was to succeed him, thus: "Remember that royalty is nothing more than a public charge, of which you must render a very strict account to Him who makes kings, and who will judge them."

LOUIS VII. — He succeeded his father in 1137. Having been educated in an abbey, he was zealous for the religion of the age. The eminent men of the abbeys in this age, were *Suger*, a great politician, *Bernard*, famous for his eloquence and zeal in exciting the *second* crusade, and *Abelard*, celebrated for his genius and learning in scholastic theology, and for his unfortunate love for *Heloise*, and the misfortunes he suffered therefor.

Louis quarrelled with the Pope respecting the appointment of an archbishop, — the king against, and the Pope for, the appointment. Louis marched to the town of Vitry, at the head of a large army, and burnt the church, in which the rebellious people had taken refuge, when thirteen hundred perished in the flames. The king was brought to repentance for this act, and led to favor the *second* crusade.

He married *Eleanor*, heiress of the Grand Duchy of Guienne, whom he divorced for her levities and vices. In six weeks' time after, she married Henry Plantagenet, Earl of Anjou, who became, the next year, Henry II. of England; and who, by this marriage, acquired large possessions in France — nearly one-fifth of it. Louis, in his time, made several pilgrimages; among them, one to the tomb of Thomas à Becket. In one of these tours he died, and his body was deposited in a tomb in the Abbey of Barbeau. Charles IX., in 1556, visited it, and found the body in a high state of preservation; and took off the gold rings on his fingers, and a gold chain found in the tomb, and wore them. He was another of the French kings who differed with the Pope.

PHILIP II. (AUGUSTUS). — He ascended the throne in 1180, and reigned forty-three years. He was the most ambitious and enterprising monarch of France, since Charlemagne. A severe act of his was, the confiscation of the property, and expulsion of the Jews from France.

He joined Richard the Lion-hearted in a third crusade. During Richard's absence, Philip invaded Normandy; but, upon his return, the English undertook to punish the French for seizing their territory. During the war, Richard died, when John ascended the English throne, in spite of his nephew, Arthur, who was the rightful heir, and was supported by Philip.

It being suspected that John poisoned his nephew, Philip summoned him, as Duke of Normandy, to appear and answer to the charge, before a tribunal of his peers. This John refused to do; whereupon he was declared guilty of felony, and his French possessions confiscated. Philip then took forcible possession of Normandy, and added it to France, — three hundred years after it had been detached from it, by the incapacity of Charles the Third. In a short time the King of England lost all his possessions in France, except Guienne. While Philip's father quarrelled with the Pope, he, on the other hand, so far favored him, as to give the Inquisition his sanction, — which institution had a *strong leaning* towards the Papacy.

Philip left his kingdom about double the size it was when he came to the throne.

LOUIS VIII. — He came to the throne of his father in 1223. He was bold and bitter. He took most of the English possessions on the Continent, and instigated a furious persecution against the Albigenses. He was poisoned at the siege of Avignon, by the Count of Champaign.

Louis IX. ("Saint Louis") — Became king at twelve years of age, in 1226. He is styled pious, upright, and benevolent. He offered successful resistance to Henry III. of England, in his war with that king. His only fault was fanaticism. He engaged in two crusades, in the last of which he died, near Tunis.

Philip III. — He succeeded his father in 1270. He had no prominent trait of character, except for amassing wealth. He ended the crusade, in which his father died, favorably to himself. Failing in an attempt to avenge the massacre of ten thousand Frenchmen in the Island of Sicily, known as that of the *Sicilian Vespers*, he died of grief in consequence.

Philip IV. — He ascended the throne in 1285. He was called "The Fair," from the beauty of his countenance and the elegance of his person. Yet in disposition, he is represented as ambitious, deceitful, perfidious, and cruel.

In attempting to raise money of the clergy, as well as his other subjects, he was involved in a quarrel with Pope Boniface VIII., who prohibited the clergy from paying the tax, laid France under an interdict, and issued a bull, declaring, "*That the vicar of Christ is vested with full authority over the kings and kingdoms of the earth!*" Upon this haughty and intolerant claim, Philip responded by denouncing Boniface as an impostor, heretic, and simoniac, and declared the Roman See vacant. He contrived also to seize the person of the Pope, then placed His Holiness upon a horse without saddle or bridle, *and with his face turned towards the horse's tail.* This indignity, with the loss of his immense treasure, so recoiled upon the Pope, that he died of a broken heart.

In addition to this onslaught upon the "Vicar of Christ," Philip procured the election of Clement V., a Frenchman, as his successor, and transferred the seat of the Papacy from Rome to Avignon, in France, where it remained for seventy years. The Italians became indignant at these proceedings, and styled the removal, "The Babylonish Captivity of the Holy See." He also abolished the order of Knights Templars (a feudal military-religious society in the interests of Papacy), and confiscated their immense property. Violent as were his proceedings against the Pope, they checked the growing assumptions of the papal power; and from this *facing about* of Boniface, the decline of the Papal Church began, and it has never recovered from it yet; neither do its assumptions over the potentates of the earth seem to be required.

Another example of Pepinism, per contra. Philip has the honor of instituting French parliaments. He left four children, — Louis, Philip, Charles, and Isabella.

PERIOD III. FROM PHILIP IV., 5317 A. M., AND 1313 A. C., TO FRANCIS II., 5563 A. M., AND 1559 A. C.

LOUIS X.—He ascended the throne of France in 1314. The principal event in his reign was the death of his prime minister, for alleged crimes, but in reality for his wealth. He reigned only a few months.

JOHN I.—An infant son of Louis X., and born after his death. Died at four days old.

PHILIP V.—His reign was distinguished for persecution of the Jews, and of all foreigners residing in his dominion; and refused to embrace Christianity himself. The Jews were accused of poisoning the wells and springs of water.

CHARLES IV.—Philip, leaving no male heir, his brother Charles came to the throne in 1322. He was called a wise and upright prince, but reigned only five years.

BRANCH OF VALOIS.

The Capetian race of kings still continues on the throne of France, in the branch of Valois.

PHILIP VI. (OF VALOIS).—The three sons of Philip IV., leaving no male heirs, and the *Salic* law—which forbid females coming to the French throne—preventing Isabella, now Queen of England, from assuming the government, Philip VI., cousin-german to Charles IV., was acknowledged by the French nation, 1328. Upon this, Edward III. of England, son of Isabella, asserted his claim, in right of his mother. This is the ground of the claim of the English kings to the crown of France, and which gave rise to the fierce contests for it between the two nations. Edward invaded France with an army of thirty thousand men, to maintain his right by force. He gained the famous battle of Cressy, and captured Calais. The English gained some advantages by the war, but the French retained the sceptre, and Philip on the throne.

Amid his misfortunes, Philip had the pleasure of seeing the province of *Dauphiny* annexed to the crown of France, by its last count, Hubert, on condition that the king's oldest son should bear the title of *Dauphin*.

During the reign of Philip, occurred a general plague. Commencing in the northern provinces of China, it swept over Asia, Africa, and Europe, raging for eighteen months. The remotest history furnishes no account of any such calamity surpassing this in its horrors and devastations. In places, it cut down two-thirds of the inhabitants.

It was preceded by terrific earthquakes, that swallowed up whole cities.

John II. — He succeeded his father in 1350. Taking the field, with sixty thousand men, against the "*Black Prince*," he was defeated by a far inferior number, in the battle of Poictiers, and made prisoner, and carried to London.

After four years, he was permitted to return to France, upon ceding several important places to the English. John, however, soon returned to England, — it is supposed on account of a passion he had for the Countess of Salisbury. He soon after died in London.

Charles V. — The dauphin, assumed the government during the captivity of the king, and upon his death succeeded to the throne, with the title of Charles V., in 1364. To him is attributed the honor of saving France from the dominion of England. Though of a slender constitution, he was a patron of literature and a sagacious statesman. By creating *Du Guesclin*, a celebrated general, Constable of France, the tide of success which had attended the British arms in France was turned, and most of the places they had captured were retaken. It is said Guesclin could neither read nor write.

Charles V. is regarded as one of the best sovereigns France ever had, both in his public and private character. His father left him a library of twenty volumes, to which he added nine hundred, which rendered it the greatest library of the age. He is regarded as the founder of the magnificent royal library, of which Paris is still proud.

Charles VI. — He succeeded his father, Charles V., in 1380. He commenced his reign by making war upon the Flemings. The successes of his father against the English, inspired him with the desire to invade England. The fleet fitted out for this purpose consisted of twelve hundred and eighty-seven sail, of which sixty were ships of the line. In the centre of it was a wooden city, three thousand paces in diameter, provided with towers and bastions, all built on boats fastened together. It was made so as to be easily taken to pieces in a day, and put up again, and was designed for lodgings for his troops, after landing. But the wreck only of this invading citadel reached the British shore, being scattered there by a furious tempest.

During his reign, a civil war occurred between the houses of Orleans and Burgundy, concerning the regency, as Charles had become insane, and finally almost idiotic. The invention of cards occurred in his reign, and was got up for the purpose of amusing the king, to relieve the melancholy which followed his alienation of mind. Important invention, designed to amuse an insane old king, used now to amuse *sane* (?) men! In the midst of the confusion and disorders this state of things produced, Henry V. of England invaded the country, and gained the memorable battle of Agincourt. The result of this victory, and other advantages gained thereby, was the acknowledgment of his right to the French throne, upon the death of Charles, in a treaty made at *Troyes*. These sovereigns soon after died, and within two months of each other.

CHARLES VII. — He was son of Charles VI., and was crowned at Poictiers, 1422; and at the same time, the infant Henry VI. was crowned at Paris, through the agency of the Duke of Bedford, the English Regent of France.

Notwithstanding the treaty of Troyes, which gave the crown of France to England, Charles determined to recover by force what had been taken by force, and so asserted his right to the crown. This competition issued in war. The English first undertook the siege of Orleans, a place of great importance. Here an act of daring occurred, which threw the heroes of ancient Troy, Marathon, and Thermopylæ into the shade.

The affairs of Charles were continually growing worse and worse, until his council even had fled to Dauphiny in despair. At this juncture, Joan of Arc, a country girl of twenty-seven years of age, presented herself before the council, and declared that God had revealed it to her that the troops of Charles would force those of the enemy to raise the siege. An assembly of divines declared her mission to be supernatural; and, at her own request, she was clothed in male attire, and armor, and headed the troops. A noble white state horse bore her to the scene of combat, and on her banner was displayed an image of the Saviour. The peculiar circumstances of her call, her singular and courageous appearance, made the French troops, led on by the intrepid *girl*, invincible, and the English were driven to flight. She saved her king and country. Charles recompensed this service, by incorporating Joan and her whole family, and their heirs and descendants, among the French nobility.

After this, her peculiar mission, was finished, she asked leave to retire; but this request was refused, from the belief that her presence in the army would be of great service. But Joan was as sure that her mission was done, as she was of her call to it, and the sequel shows her to have been in the right. At the siege of Compeigne, not long after, she was taken prisoner by the English, tried for sorcery, and condemned to be burnt. When led to execution, the heroic maid, overcome by her emotions, burst into tears. This act, besides being an everlasting disgrace of itself, is made one of *eternal infamy* to her murderers, by *prolonging her tortures*. The place of her death was Rouen, France. The mode of her death was by a scaffolding of plaster, erected high above the fire, requiring considerable time for the flames to penetrate to her body, which was *gradually consumed.*

The tide of fortune now turned against the English, and they lost the battle of Formigny, then Paris, and finally the whole of the French monarchy came into the hands of Charles, 1450. Charles came to his grave in sorrow, from the circumstance that his son, the Dauphin, sought his life by poison. In his reign originated the assembly called "*The Pragmatic Sanction,*" composed of the nobility and clergy of the Gallican Church, to check the power of the popes, by asserting the superiority of their assemblies over the See of Rome. Another fling of France at His Holiness!

Louis XI. — He was son of Charles VII., and came to the throne in 1461. He immediately removed all his late father's ministers, and acted the tyrant in almost every respect to his subjects. He is represented as an odious compound of dissimulation, profligacy, cruelty, and superstition, and has been styled the *Tiberius of France.*

He was possessed of considerable talents, great application to business, affability of manners, the author of many wise laws and excellent regulations for commerce, and for promoting the administration of justice. His aim was to humble the nobles, and in these efforts provoked the war called "*The War of the Public Good.*" A specimen of his cruelty is seen in his causing a nobleman's children to be placed under the scaffold where he was to be executed, so that they might be sprinkled with their parent's blood.

He received from the Pope the title of "*Most Christian Majesty,*" which is still retained by the kings of France. He died a victim of superstitious terror, and remorse of conscience.

Charles VIII. — He succeeded his father, Louis XI., at the age of thirteen, under the regency of his sister, Anne of France, in 1483. Though mild and courteous, to the extent that he obtained the surname of "Affable," yet he led a life of intemperance, and was early cut off by that vice. The direct line of Philip of Valois ended with him.

Louis XII. — He was great-grandson to Charles V., and came to the throne in 1498. He was a beneficent and popular sovereign, but unfortunate in his enterprises. He retained the ministers of the late king, even those who had ill-used him. His excuse for this was, that "it was unworthy of the King of France, to punish the injuries done the Duke of Orleans." He was Duke of Orleans, and with him began the "Branch of Orleans," of the Capetian kings. He gained the title of "Father of his Country," for his frugality and care for it. His saying was: "I had rather my courtiers would laugh at my avarice, than my people weep on account of my extravagance." He is said to have procured money, however, by the improper sale of important offices. (Not peculiar, that, to Louis XII.!)

In the first of his reign, he reduced Genoa and Milan, and proceeded to enforce a claim the French kings had gained to Naples. At first he was successful, but was made the victim of the treachery of Ferdinand of Spain and Pope Alexander VI., and thereby lost Naples. After this, the wealth of the city of Venice became an object of desire to the powers around, when the *League of Cambray* was formed, consisting of Pope Julius II., the Emperor of Germany, and the kings of France and Spain.

Louis entered into the war with Venice with spirit, and gained the battle of Agnadello. But the confederates quarrelled over the spoil, and a new league was formed against France. Betrayed a second time by the Pope, on the one hand, who, with the French kings and people, on the other, blessed and cursed each other alternately, or indiscriminately, as occasion required. In his struggle with the confederates, Louis lost his best general, Gaston de Foix, in the victory gained at Ravenna. Soon followed the loss of all the French possessions in Italy. In the midst of preparations to regain his losses, Louis suddenly died. On every side the murmur was heard, "The good king is dead!"

FRANCIS I.—He was nephew of the late king, and Duke of Angouleme, and ascended the throne in 1515. Being of a romantic turn, and eager for glory, he made early conquest of the Milanese, which advantage he soon lost. In 1519, the death of Maxamilian brought Francis I. and Charles V. of Spain into competition for the crown of Germany. Charles finally succeeded in obtaining the election, which threw them into deadly hostility for nearly thirty-eight years.

The reign of Charles V. is of great importance, from the part he took in the Reformation. He threw the whole weight of his imperial power against it; yet, for all that, the mighty cause triumphed. During his reign also occurred the divorce of Catharine of Arragon, aunt to Charles, and wife of Henry VIII. of England. Two important events transpired in his reign, viz., the establishment of the Reformation, and overthrow of Popery in England.

Unfortunately for Francis, he quarrelled with his best general, the constable of Bourbon, who deserted to Charles, and was placed in chief command of his imperial forces. Francis and Bourbon soon met at Pavia, in Italy, where the French king fell into the hands of his own constable (formerly), a prisoner to Charles, and was detained for some time at Madrid. The surrounding kings, viewing the success of Charles with jealousy, a league was formed among them which checked his power. By this means, he was laid under the necessity of liberating the French king, who, reaching his own realm, exclaimed, "I am yet a king!" Charles had meanly extorted promises from him, while in bonds, which Francis felt bound to keep only with *Punic faith.* The breaking of these promises caused new wars and insulting challenges between the two sovereigns. England then joined France against Charles; and the large army he sent against the French was so badly cut off, that he withdrew into Italy, sorely beaten.

By the advice of friends, a truce of peace was concluded at Nice, for ten years, between Francis and Charles. The two monarchs soon after met at *Aigues Mortes*, in the south of France, and though they had been at war for twenty years, yet here they vied with each other in acts and expressions of respect and friendship. The next year, Charles obtained permission to pass through France, on his way to the Netherlands, and was entertained, during his stay of six days in Paris, with great magnificence. Charles had previously stipulated to grant the French king the investiture of Milan, but he departed from Paris without leaving any evidence of doing so. Upon this, war again broke out between them, with redoubled animosity. Peace was soon after concluded, Charles having all he could attend to in Germany, and Francis was willing to have the unequal contest cease; Charles being more than a match for him in policy and resources.

The elements of his character were, his open temper, beneficence, honor, generosity, and courage, mingled with rashness, negligence, fickleness, prodigality, and voluptuousness. His whole bearing, however, was that of a finished gentleman. Under his auspices, the French court received that polish and refinement in taste and manners, for which it has since been so conspicuous throughout the world. In order to polish the manners of his court, he drew to it the most respectable women and distinguished prelates of the age. He founded the Royal College and Printing-House. While he encouraged the study of the languages, he took care to have all the laws published in French. In the same manner he encouraged the fine arts; he built Fontainbleau, and began the Louvre. He died in 1547.

Henry II. — He succeeded his father in 1547; and, though brave and polite, was the slave of pleasure, and the dupe of favorites. He continued the war with Charles V. and his son, Philip II. of Spain. At first Henry gained advantage in the victory at the siege of Metz, but was terribly defeated by Philip at St. Quentin. This war, the success of which had not been very satisfactory to either party, was concluded by the treaty of Chateau Cambresis.

The greatest point gained in his reign was, the recapture of Calais from the English, which was effected by the Duke of Guise, in eight days, to the astonishment of all Europe. The blot of his reign was, the increase of the persecution of the Huguenots, which was commenced in the reign of Francis I., and which gave rise to the distracting wars of the three following reigns.

His death occurred by his attempting to amuse the ladies, at a tournament (mock fight), with a tilt between himself and the Count of Montgomery, who was considered the most dexterous jouster of his time. In their rencounter, both their lances were broken, and the count thrown from his horse. In his fall, the broken trunk of his spear, still remaining in his hand, struck the king's right eye, and produced so violent a contusion as to terminate his life.

It was during the reign of Henry II. that the all-important treaty, called "*The Peace of Religion*," was formed, at Augsburg, Germany, September 25, 1555. From that time each state proceeded in matters of religion according to its own pleasure, being responsible to no other power. Hence the cruel proceedings of the French government against the Protestants of its own realm, instigated by the diabolical spirit of Popery.

IV.

AGE OF CONSOLIDATION.

SUBJECT — CIVIL HISTORY.

PERIOD IV. FROM FRANCIS II., 5563 A. M., AND 1559 A. C., TO THE REPUBLIC, TO 5796 A. M., AND 1792 A. C.

FRANCIS II. — The son of Henry II., was raised to the throne in 1559. He was the husband of Mary, Queen of Scots, and reigned only seventeen months. In his reign the Potestants were persecuted with unabated rigor by the king, Cardinal of Lorraine, and five brothers, the Guises, at the head of the Catholics. Worried and chafed beyond endurance, they resolved upon self-defence. The Protestant cause had now become strong, embracing many of the nobility and court. Among them were the Prince of Condé and Admiral Coligny.

Unfortunately they determined to dispatch their tormentors, and the conspiracy of Amboise was formed against them. This, however, was discovered, and twelve hundred conspirators were massacred or executed, — the Prince of Condé, brother of the King of Navarre, being an abettor with the conspirators.

CHARLES IX. — The brother of Francis II., came to the throne in 1560, under the regency of Catharine de Medicis, widow of Henry II., a profligate and ambitious woman, and a bigoted Papist. She had been familiar, for a long time, with the proceedings against the Protestants, and now, having the direction of public affairs, she prepares to roll in the blood of heretics.

The Protestant cause had become so formidable, that some measure of pacification became necessary. Hence, a conference was called, at Poissy, at which both parties assembled — the young king, his queen-mother, and the whole court. The illustrious reformer, Theodore Beza, defended the Protestants, and Cardinal Lorraine the Catholics. Neither party considered itself outdone, and yet Catharine and her sycophants deemed it *politic* to grant the heretics liberty to worship outside the walls of the towns. This insignificant edict was soon after basely violated, which plunged France for a long time in misery and blood. In a war that ensued, the Protestants were headed by Admiral Coligny and Condé, and the Catholics by Guise, Montmorency, and Philip of Spain. The Protestants, though generally beaten, were found to be so strong and unyielding, that it was thought best to decoy them into a peace, that should be only the prelude to more awful scenes of atrocity and blood.

It now became the policy of the government to caress the Protestants, in order to destroy them. With such consummate art did they practise the deception, that even the prudence of Coligny was lulled to sleep. An invitation was given to the Protestants, to attend the marriage of the King of Navarre, with Margaret, sister of Charles, at Paris. This was the fatal snare. The marriage took place on Sunday, on a platform erected before the door of the Cathedral of Notre Dame, in the presence of a vast concourse of both Catholics and Protestants, for the scene had lured thousands into the jaws of death.

On Friday, the twenty-second of August, an attempt was made upon the life of Coligny. On his return to his lodgings from the Louvre, he was fired upon by an assassin (supposed to be King Charles), one ball carrying away the fore finger of his right hand, and another wounding him in the left arm.

Charles and his mother soon hastened to the bedside of Coligny, and remained to see his wounds dressed, and hypocritically proposed his being removed to the Louvre, where he could be more "*comfortably accommodated.*"

In the early part of the night of the twenty-third, the preparations had all been made, and the unsuspecting victims had retired to rest, having confidence in their king. The houses of the Protestants had all been marked with white crosses on the doors, and their murderers were stationed at their posts. The chiefs were now busily engaged in riding from post to post, seeing that all was ready for the signal; others assisting at the consultations of Catharine and Charles, still going on at the seat of the bloody plot. These unusual movements excited the curiosity of the Protestants, and some ventured out to inquire after the cause of the stir. They were told that it was in consequence of a nocturnal *fete*, about to be given. (Too true, alas!)

Even at this stage, Catharine had not got Charles up to the point she wished; and, fearing lest he would fail to order the work to begin, which was to be done at half-past two, at a signal from the great clock at the Palace of Justice (?), she, therefore, took advantage of the first moment, after Charles had signified his consent, to have the work begin, and caused the alarm to be rung from the steeple of the adjacent church of St. Germain l' Auxerrois. As the bell rang its sounds of omen over the city and its suburbs, the people everywhere started from their slumbers, but only to fall in death.

A furious rush was made into the house where Coligny was; and a German, named Beme, a servant of Guise, approached Coligny, and, with a drawn sword aimed at his breast, asked him if he was the admiral. Gazing upon him, and then at the naked blade with which he was menaced, he said: "Young man, you ought to have respected my age and infirmity; but you will only shorten my life a few days or hours." He then expressed a wish "to die like a soldier, and not by the hand of this menial." Beme then, after an oath, first thrust his sword into his breast, and next struck him several times on the head, others doing the same, until he fell. Guise then called out to know if the deed was done. He soon ordered the body thrown from the window, that he might see for himself. At first he was unable to tell; but wiping away the blood with a cloth from the face, and stooping down to see, exclaimed: "Yes, I know it now; it is he himself!" He then gave the body a kick, and left.

This over, the bell from the Palace of Justice (?) sounded, to set all the subordinate agents in motion, with one continued cry, like fiends, of "Blood! blood!" On that terrible Sabbath, August 24, 1572, blood reeked from the principal streets of Paris as from a field of battle. The horrors that then followed cannot be told. From Paris the fury spread into various parts of France; and it is estimated that one hundred thousand Huguenots perished. Charles stood by, and set on his soldiers, saying, "Take care that none escape, to reproach me." He even took the responsibility of saying, that all was done by his order. A medal was struck, commemorative of the event, with the inscription, "Piety put the sword into the hands of Justice."

When the news of the massacre reached Rome, solemn (?) thanks were given for the triumph of the church militant; and public rejoicings were held in Spain. Of this most atrocious massacre, the French historian, Thuanus, says: "No example of equal barbarity is to be found in all antiquity, or the annals of the world." And yet instigated and executed by the arch-monster Catharine.

Charles soon after died, in the bitterest remorse for this horrible transaction, aged only twenty-four. This affair only strengthened Protestantism, instead of annihilating it. Both the Bourbons, the King of Navarre (who narrowly escaped with his life, even at his wedding), and the Prince of Condé espoused the cause; and it was again found necessary to grant the Protestants liberty of conscience.

Henry III. — He was Duke of Anjou, and had just been elected King of Poland, 1574. A very unworthy king. He found the Protestants so strong, he thought it politic to grant them some privileges. This so incensed the Catholics, that he finally joined a league formed for the *avowed* purpose of exterminating the Huguenots, but also a *Jesuitical* purpose of usurping all the powers of the government.

Henry, not knowing this latter purpose of the league, now under the control of the Duke of Guise and Cardinal Lorraine, joined it, but soon saw that he was being deceived by the duke and cardinal, and so procured their assassination. This in turn incensed the Catholics, and now the king had the ill-will of all parties; and he was soon after assassinated himself by James Clement, a Dominican friar.

BOURBON DYNASTY.

HENRY IV. (THE GREAT). — Upon the death of Henry III., the Capetian race ran out by the house of Valois becoming extinct, and the sceptre of France passed to the house of Bourbon, in the person of Henry III. of Navarre, who, on becoming King of France, took the name of Henry IV. At the age of sixteen he was proclaimed the head of the party of the Huguenots; and, upon his marriage with Charles' sister, narrowly escaped death at the massacre of St. Bartholomew, but was three years a prisoner. He was unsuccessful until after the death of Charles, when he gained two important victories over the League, — one at Coutras, in 1587, the other at Argues, in 1589. But, after the death of Henry III., he defeated the League again, in the battle of Ivry, then commanded by Mayenne, brother of the Duke of Guise, who had proclaimed his uncle, the Cardinal of Bourbon, king, under title of Charles X.

Though educated a Protestant, he found, upon being king, he was exposed to all the annoyances of Jesuitical cunning, and concluded to call himself a Catholic for sake of peace. Upon this change he was crowned at Chartres, and received absolution from the Pope, in 1594. In 1596 the Duke of Mayenne submitted to him as king, and so did the nation. Yet, out of respect to his old friends the Protestants, to whom he was under obligation for aiding him to the throne, he granted the celebrated *Edict of Nantes*, by which he secured to them the free toleration of their religion, and free admission to all offices of honor and profit.

Henry's own great talents, aided by his great minister, the Duke of Sully, enabled him to put the kingdom into such a state as soon to recover from the desolations of a thirty years' war. Besides, his manifest love for his subjects inspired in them respect for their king, and general happiness was the result. He and Sully formed a project, called *The Grand Design*, for dividing Europe into fifteen states, so arranged as to prevent war, and secure permanent peace, by making these ends the great interest of each and all the states.

This was a faint dawning of civil liberty, originating with the King of France, in this dark time, the grandest scheme of state policy ever proposed hitherto, in any age. His purpose was to bring his plan about by force of arms, which he probably never could have done. While impatient to depart on his romantic errand, gloomy forebodings haunted his mind, which soon changed to realities. Passing along the street one day, his coach became entangled, when his footmen leaving it for a short time, Ravaillac, a bigoted Catholic, who had followed him for some time secretly, for the purpose, seized this opportunity, and sprang forward and stabbed the king, in the midst of seven courtiers, in the twenty-first year of his reign and the fifty-seventh of his age.

Upon showing Sully, one day, his written promise to marry an unworthy woman, Sully took the paper and tore it in pieces. "I believe you are mad!" said Henry, in a rage. "It is true; I am mad; and I wish I was the only madman in France!" replied Sully. While looking for his disgrace for such an altercation with the king, he received from him the brevet of Grand Master of the Ordnance. When asked, one time, to what the revenue of the kingdom amounted, Henry replied: "To what I please; for, having the hearts of the people, they will give me whatever I ask. If God sees proper to spare my life, I will take care that France shall be in such a condition that every peasant in it shall be able to have a fowl in his pot." Henry's private and domestic character fall far short of his *kingly* character. During the first eighteen years of his reign, four thousand Frenchmen were killed in duels, arising out of amorous quarrels.

LOUIS XIII. — He succeeded his father, in his ninth year, under the regency of his mother, Mary of Medicis, 1610. Her fondness for Italian favorites gave dissatisfaction to the French nobility, and the greatest disorders ensued. But, upon the king becoming of age, he made Cardinal Richelieu his prime minister, when things soon began to wear a different aspect. He entered into a political career with great energy and spirit.

Richelieu's first effort was to subdue the turbulent spirit of the French nobility. He caused Condé to be arrested for his intrigues against Mary; and, in turn, she was sent into temporary exile. He also subdued a rebellion excited by the king's brother, Duke of Orleans, supported by the Duke of Montmorency, by defeating their army, and executing Montmorency for treason. His next aim was to humble the power of the Protestants. Wearied and disheartened as to any peace with a Papal Government, they at last resolved to rid themselves of the yoke, or die. Rochelle was their head-quarters, and here Richelieu brought the power of the king to bear upon them. A brave resistance was maintained for a whole year, when the Protestants were forced to yield to the sinews of war wielded against them. Failing of seasonable help from England, for which they had asked, they finally yielded, after the sacrifice of fifteen thousand lives; and, with the fall of Rochelle, the Protestant power in France was crushed, and has never been able to rise above it since. His third great project was to humble the power of Austria. For this purpose, he united with the Protestant princes of Germany, and with Protestant England, to crush the power of Ferdinand of Spain, who was aiming at dominion where Richelieu himself chose to bear sway. Forgetting his hatred of Protestantism, he even, to save himself and humble his enemies, built up what at Rochelle he had trampled down.

Amid all his labors and intrigues in politics at home, and in nearly all the other courts of Europe, he found time to lend a great service to the cause of literature and science; and the *French Academy* owes its origin to the genius of Richelieu. No king of France ever appeared so little in his own character and acts as Louis XIII.; and no minister ever appeared so much in the character of the king as Cardinal Richelieu. Louis died aged forty-three.

LOUIS XIV. (THE GREAT). — He came to the throne, in 1643, at five years of age, under the regency of Anne of Austria, his mother, who chose Cardinal Mazarin as her minister. The education of the young king was confided to him, and shamefully neglected. By his avarice, he caused heavy burdens to be imposed upon the people, until a civil war was fomented, under Cardinal de Retz, supported by the aristocracy.

Upon his death, Louis, being now twenty-two years old, took upon himself the whole control of affairs. He was very fortunate in his selection of generals and ministers. Colbert regulated his finances with unparalleled skill; while Condé and Turenne were the two ablest generals of the age, and Vauban the greatest fortifier of towns. His arms were everywhere triumphant. He conquered Franche Compte, and annexed it to France; made conquests in the Netherlands; overran Alsace, and twice laid waste the Palatinate with fire and sword. The first time, from the tower of Manheim, twenty-seven towns and cities of the Palatinate could be seen in flames at once. In the second case, more than forty towns and villages were burnt, and the people reduced to the greatest extremities of cold and hunger.

In 1675 Turenne was killed by a cannon ball, Colbert died, Condé retired, and no men arose to fill their places. Louis had reduced his strength in making his conquests, so that he was unable to hold them; and, in all his exploits, he manifested such ambition as to provoke the jealousy of the other states of Europe to oppose him, which gave rise to long and bloody wars. The League of Augsburg was brought about by William, Prince of Orange; but, for a time, Louis was successful against the leaguers; and here he attained the summit of his glory. In 1697 he was obliged to conclude the Peace of Ryswick.

Soon after, however, the "War of the Succession" broke out, the avowed object of which was to put Austria in possession of the throne of Spain, in the event of the death of Charles II. without issue. This Louis was barely able to prevent, against England, Germany, and Holland, their armies being under the command of the Duke of Marlborough and Prince Eugene. Louis lost his sway in the victories of the allies in the battles of Blenheim, Ramillies, Oudenarde, and Malplaquet. One or two victories after this, on the part of France and Spain, preserved Philip, Louis' grandson, on the throne. But, at the Peace of Utrecht, 1713, Louis lost nearly all he had gained.

The baseness of Louis is manifest in the revocation, in 1685, of the "Edict of Nantes," granted to the Protestants by Henry IV. All their privileges, therein decreed, were taken away, and the exercise of them forbidden, upon penalty of death. They were outlawed, and hunted like wild beasts. By this piece of barbarity France lost eight hundred thousand of her most peaceable and industrious citizens by death and exile. In the arts and manufactures the Protestants are said to have excelled.

Louis gave much attention to public works, and patronized the arts and sciences. Besides embellishing the capital, he built the splendid palace of Versailles, and the canal of Languedoc. His is called the *Augustan Age* of French Literature; and his reign is less distinguished for military advantage, than for the noble impulse given the arts and sciences. His reign, though far from being the best, for either France or the world, was the *longest* of which we have any account in the pages of history, reaching the unparalleled length of seventy-two years. He died aged nearly seventy-eight.

Louis is said to have been the handsomest man in his kingdom, and excelled in all polite accomplishments. "The greater part of his reign may be considered as a spectacle, with grand machinery, calculated to excite astonishment. Towards the close, we behold nothing but the wrecks of that theatrical majesty, and the illusion vanishes." Louis was "the best *actor* of majesty that ever filled a throne."

Louis XV. — He was great-grandson of Louis XIV., and came to the throne in 1715 (being only five years of age), under the regency of the Duke of Orleans. This regency is noted for the Mississippi Scheme of Law, which project was to pay off the national debt, by introducing a paper currency. It proved the ruin of thousands, and sunk the finances of the state still lower. From this time no paper money could be issued under the old constitution.

Louis chose, when of age, Cardinal Fleury for his prime minister, who maintained the peace of Europe for nearly twenty years. After the death of Fleury, France was involved in the war of the Austrian Succession. Charles VI. dying, two claimants appeared for the crown, — Maria Theresa, the late emperor's eldest daughter, who married Francis of Lorraine, supported by England, was one, and Charles, Elector of Bavaria, supported by France and Prussia, the other. Hostilities were terminated by the Peace of Aix-la-Chapelle, and Maria was acknowledged.

In 1755 a war broke out between France and England, respecting their American possessions, which was terminated by the Peace of Paris, in 1763, when Canada and the territories in North America were ceded by France to Great Britain.

Louis is represented as a tyrannical and profligate sovereign, and that his government was one of mistresses. In order to furnish himself with means for supporting his profligacy, he entered into the monopoly of corn, by which he starved and oppressed his subjects, to lavish it upon his minions and mistresses. He left, in his private treasury, two hundred millions of livres, thus extorted from the bread of his people. He also quarrelled with his parliaments, until both they and his subjects began to think ill of royalty; and this feeling ripened into the terrible commotions which overwhelmed his successor. The two reigns of Louis Fourteenth and Fifteenth, make an aggregate of one hundred and thirty-one years, which circumstance is unequalled in history.

Louis XVI. — He was grandson to the late king, and ascended the throne in 1774, at the age of twenty years. He came to the throne in troublous times. He is represented as a man of correct morals, upright intentions, and desirous of reforming abuses; but was not equal, in the requisite qualities, to the emergencies of the times. The nation had become disgusted with the tyrannical and profligate career of its former kings, and were in no condition to endure the necessary changes to bring about a reform. The nobles, who had been caressed, flattered, and fattened by royal pap, were determined to maintain their privileges at all hazards; while the people had come to a similar determination, to submit to abuses no longer. Unhappy must be the king, when his *nobles* will not submit to *reforms*, and the *commons* will not submit to *abuses!*

Louis engaged some of the best men of the age as his ministers, — Targot, and then Necker, a Protestant of Geneva, and a banker; but the finances of the state were beyond the reach of recovery. Calonne then took the office, and at once abandoned reform, and made a boast of prodigality. Ruinous as was this last step to France, yet it was fortunate for the world; for, about this time, war broke out between England and the American Colonies. France, glad to have an opportunity to give England a blow, at once sent men and supplies to assist the Americans, under the gallant *Marquis de Lafayette*, and declared war with England, which still further increased her debts, and at last stopped the wheels of state.

But a more terrible blow than that upon the finances of France fell upon her when her gallant officers returned to their oppressed country, covered with military glory, and flushed with the liberty they had just aided others in obtaining. This spark set on fire the huge mass of rubbish that had been accumulating for ages from the oppressions of her rulers. Some kindlings had been prepared, meanwhile, by the progress of philosophy, free-thinking, and atheism, which the writings of Voltaire, Rousseau, and others, had so effectually aided. So that the bloody massacres in which the civil power had been involved, and wasted its substance, goaded on by Popery to the destruction of Protestantism, provoked a fourth element (infidelity) into existence, which enveloped the nation in the flames of civil war.

Upon the return of peace, the government was reduced to a *stand-still* for want of supplies. Louis, now at his "*wit's end*," by the advice of Colonne, convoked an assembly of the *Notables* (persons of the higher (?) orders), when it was proposed to raise funds by a land tax, upon both nobles and clergy, and all, in proportion; but they were not the persons to yield to such a demand. At this, Colonne resigned, for he could do no more. Recourse was next had to the Parliament, at Paris, but without success; whereupon a convocation of the *States-General* met (*i. e.*, a body composed of nobility, clergy, and the commons). The *Notables* were again convoked, and Necker proposed to them that the deputies of the Commons should be equal in number to those of the other two orders united; but in *this* they refused to concur. It was, however, sanctioned by the king, and carried into effect; and, in May 5, 1789, the assembly of the *States-General* was opened at Versailles.

The king addressed the *States-General* in a very conciliatory speech, little like a tyrannical autocrat blurting at plebeians. But questions soon arose whether matters should be decided by a majority of *orders*, or *polls*. This was the old question again, in reality; viz., *despotism* or *liberty?* At this juncture, upon the motion of Abbe Sieyes, the Commons, with such of the nobles and clergy as chose to join them, seized the legislative authority, declared themselves the representatives of the people, and constituted themselves the *National Assembly* — a body "one and indivisible." Bailly was president of it. Mirabeau, a man of brilliant talents and great eloquence, was the popular leader. The Duke of Orleans, descendant of Louis XIII., rich and profligate, was a prominent member.

The first act of the National Assembly was that of *sovereignty;* and, being *indivisible*, all orders — king, nobles, and clergy — were now at the mercy of the down-trodden Commons. At this time, the worst of all for him, the king ejected the popular Necker, at which the pent-up fury, so long in accumulating, burst forth. On the 14th July, 1789, the Bastile — a huge state prison — was demolished by the infuriated populace, even women participating, and Paris was turned into a field of blood *again*. The army joined the people; the nobility (?) emigrated for safety; and the king, queen, and royal family were driven from Versailles to the capital by the mob, and only protected there from violence by Lafayette, who commanded the National Guard.

Upon this turn of affairs, the National Assembly removed to Paris, and continued the measures of reform. The three *orders* were discontinued; the royal authority nearly annihilated; the privileges of the nobles and clergy, and the feudal system, in all its branches, abolished; religious liberty and freedom of the press established; church lands confiscated; monasteries suppressed; and France divided into thirty-eight departments. The next step of the Assembly was the formation of a *Constitution*, which gave it the name of "*The Constituent Assembly.*" During its sittings, the king undertook to make his escape, but was caught on the frontiers of the kingdom, and brought back. A constitution was formed, which established a limited monarchy, the equality of all ranks, and was accepted by the king; and the Assembly dissolved, September 30, 1791. The next Assembly, which met on the first of October, was styled *The Legislative Assembly.*

Soon after the Revolution commenced, there began to be formed various political clubs in Paris, the most influential of which was the *Jacobin Club,* — so called from holding its meetings in a convent of suppressed *Jacobin monks,* — which governed Paris and controlled the Assembly. On the twenty-first of September, 1792, a new body commenced its deliberations; and, at their first sitting, they abolished the regal government, and declared France a *Republic.* So Greece, Rome, and France dared to chastise "Royalty." A mighty struggle for regular, but free constitutions, is the thread that guides our reflections through all this confusion of the affairs of nations.

PERIOD V. FROM THE REPUBLIC, 5796 A. M., AND 1792 A. C., FORWARD, TO 5864 A. M., AND 1860 A. C.

REPUBLIC.

The views of the enemies of royalty were not yet fully satisfied. They not only suspended the regal government, but the royal family was an object of their hatred. Accordingly, the whole family was immediately imprisoned in the temple. Soon Louis was brought before the bar of the Convention, and there charged with supplying the enemies of France with money; of being the author of the war waged in the French territory; and of having conspired against the liberties of the country, etc., etc. Louis answered these charges in a self-possessed and dignified manner.

Desèze, one of the defenders of the king, made a very pathetic appeal in his behalf, rehearsing his excellent measures and purposes for his people's good. But the accumulated burdens and horrors the nation had suffered at the hands of royalty, still stung them with such poignancy, that no smooth speeches could alleviate the smart. Both the source and stream from whence these miseries came must be dried up. Louis was sentenced to suffer death, by the axe of the guillotine, by a vote of twenty-six majority, out of seven hundred and twenty-one voters. The king was carried to the place of execution, and, as he ascended the scaffold, with a firm step, his confessor said to him, "Offspring of St. Louis, ascend to heaven!" Louis began a speech, thus: "I die innocent; I forgive my enemies; and you, unfortunate people! — " At this moment the noise of the drums drowned his voice, the executioners seized him, and soon the axe of the guillotine severed his head from his body, January 21, 1793.

No doubt Louis suffered principally for the sins of his predecessors, and so far he died innocent; but vengeance for the slaughtered Huguenots, the massacre of St. Bartholomew, and the riotings of the French tyrants, must fall on somebody, and poor Louis was the victim in part. And yet no better state of things followed.

"REIGN OF TERROR."

The most conspicuous character in this reign was the notorious Robespierre.

Two factions soon arose in the National Convention, — one known as the *Mountain Party*, because they took the highest seats in the Convention hall, the other as the *Girondists*, their leaders being from the department of the Gironde. The leaders in the former were Robespierre, Danton, and Marat, depraved and cruel wretches. Those of the other party were Brissot, Vergniaud, and Condorcet. Besides the horrid massacres of the rich and nobles, and all who opposed the revolutionary fury, the different factions fell to devouring each other, and thus received at each other's hands the doom they merited. The Mountain party, having gained the ascendency, let themselves loose in cruelty. They condemned and executed Queen Maria Antoinette, October 16, 1793; also Brissot, Vergniaud, and twenty others of the Girondists. The Duke of Orleans, who did most to procure the death of Louis, also suffered death by the very party he aided to rise in power.

On motion of Gobet, Archbishop of Paris, they suppressed the *Christian religion;* decreed death to be an eternal sleep; and that the only French deities, hereafter, should be *Liberty, Equality, and Reason;* established a republican calendar; abolished the *Sabbath*, and made every *tenth day* a day of rest. The churches were plundered of their gold and silver, and the bells melted and cast into cannon. The Convention was again divided into two violent parties, with Robespierre at the head of one, and *Danton*, of the Mountain party, at the head of the other. Robespierre triumphed again, and all his active opponents were guillotined.

But as doom fell upon royalty, so also was this infidel monster overtaken at length. After his condemnation, he attempted to destroy himself, but the charge from the pistol lodged in his jaw, mangling it fearfully; and, in the midst of indescribable agony, he was led forth to execution, amidst the *unsuppressed* joy of the populace, and guillotined, with eighty-three of his associates, in July, 1794. After this the Jacobin clubs were suppressed; and on October 26th, 1795, the National Convention closed its sittings, having nearly equalled all the monstrosities before them; and, two days after, the *executive* power was vested in a Directory of five, and the *legislative* power in two consuls.

DIRECTORY.

While these commotions were going on within France, her exiled nobles and clergy were stirring up her enemies without, to reek vengeance on the nation. The energy of the Republic was equal to that of the nation at any time. Notwithstanding the confusion at home, the Republican army had conquered the Netherlands, put Holland into a dependency of France, and invaded Germany.

Austria and Prussia espoused the cause of Louis, against the Republic, for various reasons, among which was that of self-preservation. Powerful armies were marched to the borders of France, but were repulsed; for, in 1794, France, without allies, had at command a million of fighting men. The government of the Directory continued until 1799, when the executive power was vested in three consuls, the first of whom was Bonaparte, the second Cambaceres, and the third Le Brun.

NAPOLEON BONAPARTE. — Against France the powers of Europe formed six leagues, or "coalitions," to check the threatening aspect of things, growing out of the Revolution. In all these but the first, this hero of modern times was the master-spirit they had to combat, and it took all the powers of Europe several years to subdue him. William Pitt is said to have been the originator and manager of these coalitions. He anticipated the turn affairs might take, and, by British gold and perseverance, he, through the powers of Europe, floored Napoleon at last. The commerce of England at this time gave them all the gold necessary for waging this costly war.

The *first* coalition was against the Republic, under the Directory, in 1793, already noticed, including Austria, Prussia, England, Spain, and several others. Against this league France was victorious. In 1796, the command of the army was given to Bonaparte, when, by a series of rapid victories, he conquered Italy, created a new republic (the Cis-alpine), and secured the Peace of Campo Formio. After this peace, Europe furnished no field for the display of Bonaparte's talents; upon which he made an expedition into Egypt, defeated the Mamelukes at the battle of the Pyramids, and took possession of Cairo and all the Delta, in 1798.

England could not rest, and have Egypt a colony of France. Accordingly, her fleet was sent against that of France, and victory was gained over the latter, by Nelson, in the Bay of Aboukir, off the mouth of the Nile, in 1798.

The *second* coalition was formed against France in 1799, instigated by England and Russia, joined by the Austrians, headed by the Archduke Charles, and the Russians by Suwarrow. Under the Directory the allies made terrible headway. But at this juncture Bonaparte was called back from Egypt and Syria; the Directory was dissolved, a new constitution formed, and Bonaparte appointed first consul.

Bonaparte applied himself vigorously at first in restoring order in the nation, quelling factions, reforming abuses, and uniting the people. After this, he put himself at the head of the army, and marched it over the Alps, and defeated the Austrians, under Melas, at Marengo, which decided the fate of Italy. This victory, with that gained at Hohenlinden over the Austrians, under the French general Moreau, led to the Peace of Luneville, with Austria and Germany, in 1801, and to that of Amiens, with England, in 1802. Russia had previously seceded from the coalition. Thus, for the first time since the Revolution, had there been peace in Europe. Bonaparte was now raised to the summit of his glory.

Soon after peace was declared, Bonaparte restored the Catholic religion, granted toleration to all religions, and instituted the Legion of Honor. A conspiracy was formed against him, which he quickly and violently crushed. He was proclaimed Emperor of France in 1804, and crowned by the Pope. The next year he assumed the title of "*King of Italy.*"

The peace of Amiens was of short duration. War broke out, in 1803, between England and France, upon the refusal of England to give up the island of Malta, the bulwark of Egypt; and with it they held the dominion of the Mediterranean. Upon this refusal, Bonaparte seized Hanover, and threatened to invade the British Isles.

In 1805, the *third* coalition was formed against Bonaparte, by England, Austria, Russia, Sweden, and Prussia. Bonaparte led the French army on, and, by his rapid movements, gained the battle of Ulm, defeating the Austrians under Mack, taking 33,000 men prisoners; and next defeated the united forces of Russia and Austria, in the battle of Austerlitz, at which battle the three emperors were present. This closed the campaign which brought about the Peace of Presburg. A few weeks previous to the battle of Austerlitz, the English fleet, under Lord Nelson, gained the great victory, off Cape Trafalgar, over the combined fleets of France and Spain. Nelson was killed.

The King of Naples, having permitted a British and Russian army to land in his dominions, was deposed by Napoleon, and his own brother, Joseph, placed upon the throne. He also compelled the Dutch, of Holland, to receive his brother Louis as king. He next set aside the constitution of Germany, and united several states, called the "Confederation of the Rhine;" he being chosen Protector. He also raised the electors of Bavaria, Wurtemberg, and Saxony, to the rank of kings. These rapid and bold movements alarmed the powers, and immediately the *fourth* coalition was formed, of the same powers as the third. Bonaparte, in his usual haste, faced the Prussians, who began hostilities, gained over them the battles of Jena and Auerstadt, entered their capital, and commenced his "continental system," against English commerce, by publishing his *Berlin Decree;* declaring the British Islands in a state of blockade, and ordering all ports shut against them. Thence, marching into Poland, beat the Russians at Pultusk.

The following year he defeated the Russians at Friedland, and brought about the Peace of Tilsit; Russia and Prussia acceding to his continental system, of shutting out British commerce from the Continent. The provinces he took from Prussia he erected into the Kingdom of Westphalia, of which Jerome Bonaparte was made king. The English government, to meet Bonaparte's *Berlin Decree,* issued their "*Orders in Council,*" compelling all neutral vessels trading with France to stop at a British port and pay duty, or be confiscated. Upon which, Bonaparte issued his Milan Decree, by which every vessel that submitted to British search, or duty, was confiscated. Afterward, by his "mad" *Decree of Fontainebleau,* he consigned to the flames all British manufactures, from Naples to Holland, and from Spain to Germany. This hurt France more than England. Napoleon had now become intoxicated with his successes, and he began to destroy himself. Not content with all Europe at his feet, and to have the kings of Spain and Portugal acquiesce in his plans, he must invade Spain, seize the king, and compel him to give up the crown to Napoleon's brother, *Joseph Bonaparte,* whom he removed from Naples to Spain, and put his brother-in-law, Murat, upon the throne of Naples.

The Spaniards, indignant at this measure, applied to England for assistance, and not in vain. This was Bonaparte's first step to his ruin, as it opened a field of operation for the British against him on the Continent. But for this rashness the Spaniards would have kept them off the Continent. But 't was done! This step opened an abyss, that swallowed up alike the French armies and the French finances.

In 1809, while the war in Spain was raging, hostilities broke out between France and Austria. Bonaparte met with his usual success, and finally defeated the Archduke Charles at Wagram. This war ended with the Peace of *Vienna;* by which Francis II., Emperor of Austria, lost considerable territory, had to accede to the "continental system," and promise his daughter *Maria Louisa*, in marriage to his victorious enemy. Whereupon Bonaparte was divorced from his beautiful empress *Josephine*. (His next fatal step to his downfall.)

The Peace of Tilsit bound Alexander, Emperor of Russia, to Bonaparte's *great delusion*, the "*continental system.*" But he found that excluding British goods from his dominions was injurious to his subjects, and ruinous to his finances, and wished to be released from this bond. The year 1811 was spent in negotiations and discussions, but nothing satisfactory arrived at on either side. Hence, as Alexander was unwilling to keep a bad promise to his own *hurt*, and to Bonaparte's sole advantage; and Bonaparte having staked all upon his "system," he resolved to *whip* Russia into the keeping of this bad promise. So, early in the spring of 1812, Bonaparte collected, in Poland, an immense army, consisting of four hundred thousand infantry, sixty thousand cavalry, twelve hundred cannon, and, on the the 24th of June, crossing the Niemen, he invaded the Russian territories. His march was directed towards Moscow, the ancient capital of the empire, and was everywhere marked by the desolation and blood found in the trail of an invading army. He steadily beat his way into the empire, and the Russians as steadily retreated. His chief design was to get into Moscow (to winter), and theirs was as steady that he should get there (but to be defeated). At the battle of Borodino the Russians gave him a terrible resistance, thirty thousand falling on each side; but Napoleon was victor. He then rushed for his winter quarters, when, to his utter amazemement, a *tremendous fire had been made*, for the purpose of giving him a *warm* reception.

A retreat was suggested, which Napoleon at first disdained, but he soon found that the Russians were far from being subdued, and were rallying to oppose him; and, in addition to this, the more terrible horrors of a Russian winter were approaching, and, his quarters being burnt, he saw that he must retreat or perish. This move proved more destructive to the army than the *invasion*. A series of sufferings, disasters, and losses followed, amid the snows and solitudes of a Russian winter, scarcely, if ever, paralleled in the history of war. Nearly thirty thousand horses perished in a day from the cold, all the cannon were lost, and only thirty thousand, out of four hundred thousand men, survived to re-cross the Niemen! After the French army had returned to the frontiers of Russia,

Napoleon left them, and fled, in disguise, through Poland and Germany, to Paris. Still insane upon maintaining his "continental system," he resolved upon another campaign, and raised a fresh army of three hundred and fifty thousand men.

This gave rise to the *fifth coalition*, composed of Russia, Prussia, Austria, some of the "Confederates of the Rhine," Sweden, and England. Bonaparte again took the command, against Europe. He worsted the Allies at the battle of Lutzen, — defeated them at Bautzen, — repulsed them at Dresden, where Moreau was killed, — but he was utterly routed in the tremendous battle of Leipsic, with a loss of forty thousand men. In this "Battle of Nations" the combatants exceeded four hundred thousand. Bonaparte again fled to Paris, where, in his address to the Senate, he acknowledged his defeat, and said, "All Europe was with us a year ago, — all Europe is now against us." Failing to arouse the French people, he again joined the army, and gave opposition to the Allies, who had already crossed the Rhine. After a desperate struggle, they penetrated into the heart of France, and finally *entered Paris!* He who had so often dictated conditions of peace to the nations, had in turn to be dictated by them, as to his future course. He was compelled to abdicate the throne of France; but, retaining his title as emperor, he was sent in banishment to the island of Elba, on the coast of Italy, which he received with full sovereignty, and a pension of two and a half millions from the revenues of France, and a body guard of four hundred men.

Louis XVIII. — Louis XVII. died in 1795. The empire of Napoleon having fallen, Louis XVIII. was restored to the throne of his ancestors, after an absence of twenty-three years, spent in Italy, Germany, Russia, and finally England. In the same month, three other princes returned to their vacated thrones, — Pius VII. to Rome, Ferdinand VII. to Madrid, and Victor Emanuel to Turin.

In order to restore and settle the affairs of Europe, a General Congress was called at Vienna, Nov. 1, 1814. Six of the crowned heads were present, with a long and splendid list of princes, ambassadors, and ministers. While engaged in their deliberations, news came, like a peal of thunder, that Napoleon was again on the throne of France. Escaping from Elba, he landed at Cannes, March 1, 1815, and in twenty days marched to Paris, with about fifteen hundred men, and not a drop of blood shed, where he was received with unbounded enthusiasm. Having already abdicated the throne to Louis, unconditionally, the Congress at Vienna at once pronounced him an outlaw, and an enemy of the nations.

At this event, the *sixth* and last coalition was formed to overthrow the "man of destiny," composed of almost every nation in Europe, small and great.

A British-German and Prussian army was collected with the greatest possible despatch, under command of Wellington and Blucher. Bonaparte, knowing that there was no mercy in store for him now, was equally vigorous in his preparations to oppose force to force. Having an army of one hundred and seventy thousand men, he pushed on to the encounter, first meeting and forcing back Blucher, from Ligny to Wavre.

Meanwhile, the army of Wellington was drawn up at Waterloo. Here the desperate strife, that had been so long ripening, must be brought to an issue. Bonaparte commenced the attack, about noon the 18th of June, 1815, with great superiority. After a desperate conflict for some time, victory was fluctuating about evening, when Blucher came up with his auxiliaries, and decided the fate of Europe and Bonaparte, in favor of the Allies. Bonaparte fled again to Paris, abdicated in favor of his son, and finally surrendered himself to Captain Maitland, of the British ship-of-the-line Bellerophon, claiming, in a letter to the Prince Regent of England, an asylum, "like Themistocles, among the most powerful, most constant, and most generous of his enemies." By the unanimous consent of the Allied Powers, he was sent a prisoner to the island of St. Helena, where he arrived on the 17th of October, 1815; and there died, May 5, 1821, in the sixth year of his captivity, and the fifty-second of his age.

Few, if any, more wonderful characters appear in the whole history of the world, than Napoleon Bonaparte. After his second dethronement, Louis XVIII. again took the throne of France, and another peace was ratified. The Allies reduced France to its old limits before the Revolution; compelled her to give up much of the plunder at Paris, and to pay one hundred and forty million dollars as part of the expenses of the war; also to maintain, for five years, an army of occupation, consisting of one hundred and fifty thousand of the allied troops, placed in sixteen frontier fortresses. In 1817 the army of occupation was reduced to one-fifth, and in 1818 wholly withdrawn. Murat, who had been raised to the throne of Naples, and Marshal Ney, having aided Bonaparte in ascending the throne the second time, were both shot. The other principal event in the reign of Louis XVIII. was the invasion of Spain by a French army, without a declaration of war, by which measures then on foot for a more liberal form of government were overthrown, and despotism reëstablished on its old foundation.

Charles X.—He was brother of Louis XVIII., and ascended

the throne in 1824. It is said of the Bourbons, that they *learnt* nothing during their exile, and *forgot* nothing! In his reign, two enterprises of foreign war of some importance occurred: one in favor of Greece, in which France united with England and Prussia; the other was the siege and capture of Algiers by the French, on 5th July, 1830. Ever since the restoration of the Bourbons, there have been repeated contests between the ultra-royalists and liberals. The royalists seek to check the spirit of liberty, by monopolizing the elections, dissolving the Chambers of Deputies, and restraining the liberty of the press. Charles, by too strenuous a use of these royal checks, brought upon the nation the revolution of 1830.

In March 1830 the Chamber of Deputies took a strong stand against the ministry, of which *Prince Polignac* was the head; in consequence of this the chamber was dissolved by the king; new elections ordered, and the two chambers were convoked for August 3d. It being ascertained that a large majority of the newly-elected members were liberals, on the 26th July three ordinances were published by the government, — one dissolving the chamber before it had met, another suspending the liberty of the press, the third altering the election law!

The liberal press being muzzled, the banks refusing to discount bills, and the manufacturers discharging their workmen, threw Paris into a revolt against the king. The citizens attacked the royal troops, and beat out their brains with paving-stones, shot them from their windows, and on the 29th of July, the last of the "three days," obtained a complete victory over the king's guards. As the Bourbon "forgot nothing," the former revolution came to mind; and whilst he thought of the head of Louis XVI., he also thought of the head of Charles X., and so took sudden leave of absence. The deputies met, August 3d (as they were ordered), and declared the throne vacant, and took advice of Lafayette what course to pursue. He advised a limited monarchy, and suggested the Duke of Orleans for king. The deputies took his advice, and raised the duke to the throne in 1830, with the title of Louis Philip.

For a time things went on well; but a revolution broke out in 1848, in Paris, which spread all over France. In December of the same year, choice was made of the nephew of Napoleon as President.

Louis Napoleon Bonaparte. — He assumed the duties of the office immediately, and thus became the first President of the Republic of France, December 1848. It is well known that Napoleon divorced his wife Josephine, because he despaired of her furnishing an heir to the French throne. But a magnificent Providence is brought about, by which the abused Josephine is honored with that very dignity of which the short-sighted Napoleon judged her incapable. The present emperor is grandson of the beautiful Empress Josephine, being son of her daughter Hortense, by her first marriage. He is only nephew of Napoleon by the marriage of his brother Lewis with Hortense. Hence, by the divorce of Josephine, Napoleon dropped the *substance*, and grasped its *shadow!*

III.—AGE OF WAR FOR OPINION.

ENGLAND—FROM JULIUS CÆSAR TO QUEEN VICTORIA.

SUBJECT—CIVIL HISTORY.

PERIOD I. FROM ITS EARLY HISTORY, TO THE END OF THE SAXON HEPTARCHY, 3949 A.M., AND 55 B. C., TO 4831 A. M., AND 827 A.C.

Early History.—The earliest accounts of this country represent the inhabitants as rude and uncivilized,—dressing in the skins of beasts, or going entirely naked, with their bodies painted with various colors. Hence is supposed the origin of the name Britain, from the word *brit*, which signifies painted. The country was originally settled by a colony from Gaul, who were called Celts, or Gaels; the remnants of whom are still found in Wales, the highlands of Scotland, and the north of Ireland. The period of their settlement there is quite uncertain.

The Phœnicians traded very early with the inhabitants of Cornwall, for copper and tin, but were unacquainted with the interior of the country. The invasion of Julius Cæsar, 55 B. C., forms the earliest distinct period in the history of Britain. Armed with clubs, spears, and swords, they fiercely attacked the invading Romans, and were not subdued for some time. In 43 A. C., Britain was invaded by the Emperor Claudius, whose general, Ostorius, defeated *Caractacus*, the king of the Britons, took him prisoner, and sent him to Rome in 51. In the reign of Nero, 61 A. C., Suetonius defeated *Boadicea*, Queen of Iceni,—people of Norfolk and Suffolk,—slaying eighty thousand men in a single battle. She had, however, gained several victories over the Romans, by her gallantry; she committed suicide, to escape her conquerors. The dominion of the Romans was fully established in Britain during the reigns of Vespasian, Titus, and

Domitian, under Agricola, who subdued the Caledonians (Scots), and built forts about the Friths of the Clyde and Forth.

At this time the Britons, though rude, were brave. Wandering, as they did, in tribes, they had little else than their cattle and arms. Their religion was *Druidism.* The *Druids,* their priests, had great authority. They taught the transmigration of souls, and offered human victims in sacrifice in great numbers. Their places of worship, like all idolaters, were in the open air, and consisted of huge stone pillars standing in a circle, and a large stone standing in the middle, which was used as an altar.

Suetonius, the Roman general, cut down their sacred groves of oak, destroyed their temples, and threw the Druids themselves into the fires they had kindled to roast the Romans. The Romans built three walls across the island, to prevent the Scots from invading the country on the north. The first was built by Adrian, of turf, from Solway Frith to the mouth of the Tyne, 121 A. C.; the second by Antoninus, of earth and stone, from the Forth to the Clyde; the third by Severus, of stone, nearly parallel with Adrian's, in 208 A. C. In 426 A. C. the Romans abandoned Britain, four hundred and sixty-five years after the landing of Julius Cæsar, by the Emperor Valentinian withdrawing his troops from the island.

SAXON FAMILY.

The Britons had been so long subject to Rome, that when left to themselves, they were unprepared for self-defence, and fell a prey to the Scots and Picts. In this dilemma they applied to the Saxons — a race of warriors living in the north of Germany — to aid them against their enemies. An army of one thousand six hundred men was sent, commanded by two brothers, *Hengist* and *Horsa,* and the Scots were driven back to their own territories. The Saxons, finding the country a better one than their own, sent for a reinforcement of five thousand men, *Saxons* and *Anglos,* conquered the Britons, and took possession of the country. From the *Anglos,* it was called *England.* Fierce contests soon arose between the Britons and Saxons, in which Arthur, a British champion, defeated the Saxons in twelve engagements. The Saxons, however, finally triumphed, and in about one hundred and fifty years formed what is called the *Saxon Heptarchy;* i. e., England was divided into seven states, and governed by seven kings. This arrangement lasted about two hundred years, in turmoil and blood.

Egbert. — In 827 A. C., Egbert, the last of the Saxon kings, succeeded, by his valor and prudence, in uniting under one government the seven states, and making himself the king, and hence the first king, of England. In 597 Augustine, or Austin, was sent to England as a missionary. Gildas, a native of Wales, the most ancient of British writers, wrote his famous "Epistle," in 560 A. C., in which he censures the depravity of the Britons most severely.

Being the last of the descendants of the Saxon kings, Egbert looked upon their whole realm as his by right. Though successful in this scheme of monopoly, he soon found more difficult work outside to do. The Danes, or Normans, who had for fifty years molested the English coast, now became more formidable than ever, and twice, during the reign of Egbert, attempted an invasion, but were repulsed with great slaughter. Egbert was educated at the Court of Charlemagne.

PERIOD II. FROM THE END OF THE HEPTARCHY, 4831 A. M., AND 827 A. C., TO WILLIAM THE CONQUEROR, 5070 A. M., AND 1066 A. C.

ETHELWOLF. — The death of Egbert, and the yielding disposition of Ethelwolf, encouraged the Danes to renew their attacks. They were often repelled, but could not be quieted.

Ethelwolf granted titles to the priesthood, with exemption from all services and imposts. A sort of Pepin. He left four sons; to two of them he bequeathed the sceptre.

ETHELBALD AND ETHELBERT. — This joint reign was short; only from 857 to 866.

ETHELRED I. — To this third son the sceptre fell. He died in battle, bravely fighting with the Danes, 872 A. C.

ALFRED THE GREAT. — This excellent king was fourth son of Ethelwolf, and came to the British throne in 872, at the age of twenty two. He found the kingdom in a very distracted condition within, and threatened by invasions without. He set himself resolutely at work to repel and silence the Danes. In one year he defeated them in eight battles. But, by a new irruption, they extended their ravages, and forced him to solicit a peace. Alfred was obliged to seek his safety, for many months, in an obscure part of the country, disguised in the habit of a peasant, and living in a herdsman's cottage as a servant. In this humble situation, the herdsman's wife set him, on one occasion, to watch some cakes which were baking by the fire; but he forgot his charge, and let them burn, for which she gave him a severe reprimand.

Venturing from his retreat, he entered the Danish camp as a

piper, in order to ascertain their position and readiness for defence. His talents as a player excited so much interest that he was introduced to Guthrum, the Danish prince, and remained with him several days. This gave him all he sought. Finding that success had rendered them remiss, he returned to his adherents, rallied a large force, and encouraged them to the attack. Falling upon the Danes in an unguarded condition, and by a surprise he defeated them with great slaughter. Instead, however, of cutting them all off, he incorporated many of them among his English subjects.

Alfred next turned his attention to regulating the internal affairs of the kingdom. He patronized learning and the arts, encouraged manufactures, and appropriated one-seventh of his revenue to repairing public buildings, ruined cities and castles, and founded the University of Oxford. But his greatest work was in regulating the administration of justice, and establishing peace. To do this, he divided the country into counties, "hundreds" (*probably towns*), and tithings; ten householders formed a tithing, who were answerable for each other's conduct, over whom a head borough (judge) was appointed. Every man was registered in some tithing, and could not change his habitation without a certificate from the head borough.

In the decision of differences, the head borough assembled his tithing to assist him. In affairs of great moment, or of controversies between different tithings, the case was brought before the Court of the Hundred, in which twelve men were chosen to do impartial justice (the origin of juries). This court met every four weeks. The County Court met twice a year, and consisted of freeholders; to this appeals could be made from the courts of hundred (or towns). The ultimate appeal from these several courts lay to the King in Council. The institutions he founded are regarded with very high favor in England to the present day. His code of laws is considered the origin of the Common Law. And still he seems to have followed out simply the plan suggested to Moses by his father-in-law.

Alfred also spent much of his time in translating the best books of the age into the Saxon language, for the benefit of his people. Though a Catholic, he sought the good of his people in enlightening them, instead of making "ignorance the mother of devotion." He is regarded as one of the greatest and best sovereigns that ever sat on a throne. He died in 900 A. C.

EDWARD THE ELDER. — He succeeded his father in 901. His reign was a continued and successful struggle against the Northumbrians and Danes.

ATHELSTAN, — Son of Edward, succeeded him in 925. He continued the wars of his father, and was successful also against the Scots, Irish, and Welsh.

He caused the noble work of translating the Scriptures into the Saxon tongue to be done; the earliest version of the Bible in the language of Britain. He conferred the title of *thane*, or gentleman, on every merchant who made three voyages to the Mediterranean on his own account.

EDMUND I., — Son of Edward, came to the throne in 941. After reigning five years, he was assassinated by the robber Leolf.

EDRED, — Another son of Edward, began his reign in 948. He was successful against the northern invaders, but became the stupid dupe of the artful and aspiring Dunstan, Archbishop of Canterbury, afterwards canonized as saint.

EDWY, — Nephew of Edred, filled the throne, 955. He married Elgiva, a beautiful princess, nearly related to him, at which Dunstan took offence. Archbishop Odo, with a band of soldiers, seized Elgiva, burned her face with a hot iron, and forcibly carried her into Ireland. In attempting to escape to her husband, she was again taken into the custody of the brutal Odo, who ordered her to be mutilated in such a shocking manner, that she died in a few days, in the sharpest torments.

EDGAR, — Youngest brother of Edwy, ascended the throne in 959. His character was odious; but, by raising Dunstan to the archbishopric of Canterbury, and paying him a forced homage, Edgar managed to accomplish his governmental ends.

Upon hearing of the exquisite beauty of the daughter of the Earl of Devonshire, Edgar sent his favorite Ethelwold to ascertain the truth of the report, with a view of marrying her in case she proved to be possessed of the beauty described. Ethelwold, being captivated by her beauty himself, conceived the plot of returning an unfavorable report to the king, and thereby seek her for himself. Accordingly, he informed the king that her beauty had been greatly exaggerated; at the same time intimating that he had a desire to marry her himself, on account of her wealth, if the king wished to make no further suit. The king declined, and Ethelwold took the prize.

Being a little curious to know personally the truth of the case, Edgar asked an introduction to his friend's *rich* wife. Ethelwold, fearing the result, made known to his wife what happened before their marriage, and desired her to conceal her beauty while in the presence of the king. Elfrida, now finding the tables had turned in her favor, resolved to regain the crown she had lost through the treachery of her husband, who had belied her *beauty*, — a grave offence in times of chivalry. Hence, upon appearing before the king, she arrayed herself so as to set forth her charms to the best possible advantage. The king's heart was taken; and, not long after, while out hunting, *unfortunately*, (?) the king's weapon pierced the body of Ethelwold. The sad event was duly solemnized by the marriage of Edgar and Elfrida.

EDWARD THE MARTYR. — He was son of Edgar by his first marriage; but he was assassinated, at the instigation of the beautiful Elfrida, 978. From the manner of his death, he was called the martyr.

ETHELRED II. — He was son of Edgar by Elfrida, and came to the throne at eleven years of age, in 978. The murder of Edward was, doubtless, to make way for Ethelred. Elfrida made herself quite conspicuous in the affairs of the throne.

The Danes having renewed their ravages, the king proceeded to measures of severity, by massacreing, at the festival of St. Brice, all those Danes who had been incorporated into the English nation by Alfred the Great. The news of this piece of barbarity arriving in Denmark, every bosom was fired with revenge. A large army of Danes, under Sweyn, soon invaded the country.

SWEYN. — He was grandson of Beatrice, daughter of Edward the *Elder*. Ethelred fled to Normandy, when Sweyn was proclaimed King of England, 1015. Dying soon after, Ethelred was again restored; but he died, also, in a short time.

EDMUND II., IRONSIDE. — He was son of Ethelred, and was called *Ironside* from his strength and valor; but his abilities were not equal to the times that called for their exercise. Upon the death of Sweyn, his son Canute was proclaimed King of England by the Danes.

DANISH KINGS.

CANUTE I. THE GREAT. — He at once maintained his right to the crown of England by force of arms. After a severe contest, he compelled Edmund to divide the sovereignty with him. Edmund was soon after murdered by Edric his brother-in-law, and Canute became sole monarch, 1017. He proved to be the most powerful sovereign of his time. He pursued the policy of amalgamating the Danes and Saxons. In the former part of his reign he was severe and arbitrary, but more mild and pacific toward the close.

HAROLD I., HAREFOOT. — He was son of Canute, and was called Harefoot from his swiftness in running. He ascended the throne in 1036.

Canute II. — He was brother of Harold, and began his reign in 1039. These two reigns were short, unimportant, and both brothers died without issue. So ended the Danish dynasty.

Edward the Confessor. — Upon the death of Canute II., the English freed themselves from the Danish yoke, and restored the Saxon line, in the person of Edward, son of Ethelred, and grandson of Elfrida, 1041. Edward's excellence consisted in an ability to conciliate the monks, and hence he was surnamed "*Confessor*," and was canonized. He was the first English king whose touch was said to cure *scrofula*, or King's Evil. This superstition continued with the kings of England until the Revolution of 1688. Edward was the last of the Saxon kings, and died without issue, and in his will left the crown to William, Duke of Normandy.

Harold II. — In the meantime, the nobility and clergy proclaimed Harold, great-grandson of Sweyn, king, 1065. William determined to maintain his right to the crown by force of arms; and, from the greatness of the prize to be gained, he soon raised a vast army, accompanied by a large number of princes and notables of the age. With an army of sixty thousand men, he set sail for the English coast. On the field of Hastings he was met by Harold, with an army nearly as large. In that memorable battle the Normans lost fifteen thousand men, while the English army was nearly all cut off, and Harold slain. Hence William is surnamed the "*Conqueror*."

PERIOD III. FROM WILLIAM THE CONQUEROR, 5070 A M., AND 1066 A. C., TO HENRY VIII, 5513 A. M., 1509 A. C.

THE NORMAN FAMILY.

William the Conqueror. — By him the Norman family ascended the throne of England. In personal appearance William was tall and strong; hardly any one could bend his bow, or wield his armor.

Being a man of might, and having to subdue the nation whose throne had been bestowed upon him by will, he was naturally inclined to make his power felt. Hence he departed from the policy of good Alfred, and bestowed all the offices of the government upon his Norman followers, to the great disgust of the nation. He forced upon the nation the use of the Norman language in the services of the church, and in the courts of justice. He introduced the feudal system, instead of the wholesome regulations of Alfred.

For trial by jury, he substituted that of single combat, or the duel. He compelled the people to extinguish their fires at the sound of the *curfew* (fire-covering) *bell*, at eight o'clock in the evening. By his forest laws he reserved to himself the right of killing game throughout the kingdom. He formed a *New Forest* by depopulating a tract of country, thirty miles in circuit, demolishing thirty-six parish churches, and the houses of the inhabitants.

One useful act of his was the establishment of the *Doomsday Book*. In this a record was made of all the lands and estates of the kingdom, with an estimate of their value, and an enumeration of every class of persons residing upon them.

His son Robert stirred up a rebellion against his father, in an attempt to wrest from him the sovereignty of Maine. In one battle Robert and his father encountered each other, and were not aware of it, until William, being dismounted from his horse, cried for assistance, when Robert recognized his father's voice, desisted from the strife, and aided him on to his own horse. They soon became reconciled. In a war waged against Philip I. of France, to punish him for aiding this rebellion, William was accidentally killed by a fall from his horse, 1087.

William II. — He was son of the Conqueror; was called *Rufus*, from his red hair; and came to the throne in 1087. He inherited little else from his father than his vices. After a reign of thirteen years, which was disturbed by insurrections, and by quarrels with the ecclesiastics, particularly with Anselm the Primate, he was accidentally shot by Sir Walter Tyrrel, with an arrow aimed at a stag, in the New Forest. Tyrrel, from fear of the consequences, fled immediately to France, so that the king's body was not found for some days after. The great works which perpetuate the name of Rufus, are the Tower, Westminster Abbey, and London Bridge.

Henry I. — He was younger brother of William II., and ascended the throne in 1100. He was surnamed *Beauclerc*, or scholar, because he was able to write his name. His brother Robert was the rightful heir, but he being absent on a crusade, Henry seized the throne. Robert was Duke of Normandy; and, upon his return from the Holy War, Henry invaded his realm, took Robert prisoner, brought him to England, caused his eyes to be burned out, and then confined him for life in a castle in Wales.

Henry married Matilda of Scotland, a Saxon princess, great-granddaughter of Edmund Ironside, and thus united the Saxon and Norman blood. This endeared him to the English, and secured to him their support. His usurpation of the throne was singularly punished in the death of his son William. In his passage from Normandy to

England, the captain and seamen getting drunk, ran their vessel on a rock. William was saved by being put into a longboat; but, while leaving the wreck, he heard the cries of his natural sister, the Countess of Perche, and ordered the seamen to row back, in hope of saving her. But the numbers who then crowded into the boat, soon sunk it, and the prince and all his retinue perished. It is said that Henry was never known to smile, after this catastrophe.

Stephen (Blois). — He was cousin of Henry, and was crowned King of England, 1135. By right it belonged to Matilda, daughter of the late king, and her son Henry; but Stephen, being a popular and talented nobleman, and distinguished for his ambition, valor, generosity, and courtesy, seized upon the crown.

The Earl of Gloucester, natural brother of Matilda, took up arms in her behalf, defeated Stephen in the battle of Lincoln, and made him prisoner. The earl was soon after defeated, taken prisoner, and exchanged for the king, and Matilda forced to leave the country. Four years after, young Prince Henry, Matilda's son, invaded England. The aristocracy dreaded the carnage that must follow, interfered, and brought the rival princes to a negociation; and the succession was secured to Henry, after the death of Stephen, which took place the next year.

FAMILY OF PLANTAGENET.

Henry II. — He succeeded to the throne in 1154, and was the first of the Plantagenets; his mother, Matilda, having married, first, Henry V., Emperor of Germany, and afterwards she married Geoffrey Plantagenet, Earl of Anjou — Henry being her oldest son. In Henry's veins flowed the mingled blood of the Saxon kings of England and the Norman family.

Henry was called *Shortmantle*, from introducing short cloaks from France into England. Besides inheriting England, Henry obtained possession, also, of nearly half of France, by his marriage with Eleanor, heiress of the Duchy of Guienne; and, during his reign, conquered Ireland. So he had the greatest possessions of any monarch hitherto on the British throne.

Seeing a necessity for restraining the assumptions of the ecclesiastics, he framed the *Constitutions of Clarendon*, which gave prerogatives to the king. To these the bishops generally gave in their consent, except *Thomas à Becket*, first Chancellor, afterwards Archbishop of Canterbury, who refused to submit to these rules, and sought to incite the other bishops to resistance. After enduring his insults a long time, Henry at last burst into a rage at his audacity, and complained of those who had been favored by him, that "their want of zeal left him exposed to the machinations of that insolent priest." At this, four of his knights pursued Becket into the Cathedral of St. Benedict, and, while before the altar, clove his head with many blows. For this affair Henry did ample penance at Becket's grave, and submitted to scourging on the bare back by the monks. Thousands visited his tomb, condoling his martyrdom to the cause of the church.

Upon an insurrection in Ireland, Henry being solicited to render aid, did so, and then, Saxon-like, annexed the island to the English crown, in 1172. His new measures of government were, finally, at the request of the Irish nation, extended over the whole kingdom. The occasion of the greatest unhappiness to Henry was his illicit love for the "*Fair Rosamond*," reported to have been the handsomest woman ever seen in England. Indignant at his voluptuousness, Eleanor, his queen, sought revenge by instigating his four sons to revolt against him. Being assisted by the King of France (her object was to wrest the crown from Henry), she gave him infinite trouble. The rebellion broke out in Henry's French territories; but he soon quelled it, and, returning to England, soon conquered the Scots, who assisted the young princes. This peace, however, was of short duration; for his sons again revolted, and were now aided by John, the king's youngest and favorite son. Henry, distracted with care, and overcome with the ingratitude of his sons, died of a broken heart, aged 58, and 35th year of his reign.

Henry is ranked among the ablest and most useful sovereigns that ever sat on the throne of England; though he governed the kingdom better than he did his own passions. He was a patron of the arts, particularly of the Gothic style of architecture; and introduced many improvements in the conveniences and comforts of life. Though at this time even glass windows were regarded as marks of great magnificence. The houses of London, even, were made of wood, with paper or lattice windows, and the floors covered with straw, and without chimneys. It is said of Becket, that while he was Chancellor, nobody excelled him in refinement and splendor; for "every day in winter, he had his apartments strewed with clean hay or straw, and, in summer, with rushes or leaves, so that those who came to pay him court might not soil their fine clothes by sitting on a dirty floor"!

Richard I. — He succeeded his father, Henry II., in 1189. He commenced his reign by a persecution of the Jews. His greatest exploit was his campaign in the Holy Wars. He defeated the heroic Saladin, at Ascalon, where forty thousand Saracens fell. On his way homeward, being shipwrecked, he attempted to pass through Germany in disguise, but was taken, and imprisoned by the emperor, and was ransomed by his subjects for $1,500,000. He died, shortly after, of a wound received at the siege of the Castle Chaluz, France.

Richard, for his valor, was styled the modern Achilles; it being almost his only merit. Even a century after his death, his name was employed by the Saracen cavalier to chide his horse, and by the Saracen mother to terrify her children. He impoverished his kingdom to bathe his laurels in blood. No cause of humanity or righteousness was advanced by the reign of Richard I., though "*Lion-hearted.*"

JOHN.—He was brother to Richard, and succeeded him in 1199, surnamed *Lackland.* His nephew, Arthur, being the rightful heir, was supported by the King of France, but, it is supposed, was murdered by John. On this account, the French king deprived him of all his English possessions in France; hence the name *Lackland.*

In consequence of using some of the funds of the church for his own purposes, John brought upon himself the wrath of the haughty and tyrannical Pontiff, Innocent III. At first, John was obstinate; but when his kingdom was laid under an interdict, himself excommunicated, and his subjects absolved from their allegiance, John curled up, and, on his knees, before the Pope's legate, Pandulf, surrendered his kingdom to the Holy See, consenting to hold it as the Pope's vassal. As John paid over part of the tribute, the sacerdotal tyrant stamped on the money, to indicate the subjection of the kingdom.

But John, in making a friend of the Pope, made sworn enemies of his barons. Under Langton, the Primate, a confederacy was formed, and a ratification of a charter of privileges was demanded of him, formerly given by Henry I. At first, John refused, and with greater effrontery than he dared to show the Pope. At this his insulted and sold barons proceeded to open war.

To this demand of his subjects he yielded a reluctant assent; and, meeting them at Runnymede, after a few days of debate, on the 19th of June, 1215, he signed the famous deed called "*Magna Charta*" (the Great Charter). This secured important liberties and privileges to every order of men in the kingdom, and is regarded as the bulwark of English liberty. Among the most important things secured, were, stringent exemption of the people from levies, without the consent of the General Council. No person shall be tried on suspicion alone, but on the evidence of lawful witnesses; and all such trials shall be before the man's peers or equals, and the laws of the land. This step is noted as the opening scene in the long and fierce contests between the kings and people of England, respecting the prerogatives of the crown and the rights of the subjects; by which, eventually, Charles I. lost his head by the axe. Indeed, *Magna Charta* may be regarded as the shepherd's anthem, sung at the rise of the star of civil liberty; or the English baron's Declaration of Independence. It is the insignia of a batch of sentiments, which tyrants could not then, have not been able since, and never will, to all ages, be able to trample under foot. Freemen can't be enslaved! He also granted, *i. e.*, was compelled to sign, the "Charter of the Forest," which abolished the exclusive right of the king to kill game all over the kingdom. These concessions of John were, however, made in "Punic faith," as he immediately after sought revenge upon his barons through the aid of foreign mercenaries, during which time he suddenly died. He is represented as the most odious and capricious tyrant that ever sat on the British throne; adding to his cowardice, levity, licentiousness, ingratitude, and treachery. Indeed, his very perfidy opened the eyes of the nation to the fact that they were unsafe in the hands of a king.

Henry III.—He was son of John, and began to reign, at nine years of age, in 1216—the Earl of Pembroke being appointed Protector during Henry's minority. He was a weak, fickle monarch, timid in danger, presumptuous in prosperity, and governed by unworthy favorites. His long reign of fifty-six years was one of turbulence, arising chiefly from contests for sovereignty between the king and people. He violated the "Charter" by confiscating the estates of some of the nobles without a court of their peers. He justified himself in this, by referring to similar injustice practised by the nobility and clergy. To which it was replied, "You, sir, ought to set them an example." Thus royalty was made to feel that *right*, not *might*, should prevail. But he paid little regard to right other than to use his *might*, and with little reference to anybody's weal but his own.

In consequence of his disregard of his barons, they formed a confederacy, with the Earl of Leicester at their head, to take the reins of government out of the hands of their unworthy king. Twenty-four of them compelled Henry to resign the regal power to them. These divided the government offices among themselves, new-modelled the Parliament, by summoning a certain number of knights from each county.

Upon this a civil war broke out, for the purpose of restoring the king; but Leicester, at the head of a large force, defeated the royalists at the battle of Lewes, and took the king and his son prisoners. He then compelled Henry, like John, to (do what he hated to) ratify his authority by a solemn (?) treaty. Leicester then assumed the regency, called a Parliament, summoning two knights from each shire, and deputies from the principal boroughs. This being the first instance of representatives being sent to Parliament from the boroughs, is regarded as the origin of the "*House of Commons;*" *i. e.*, Representatives. Hence this important branch of a free government had its origin among the *people*, not *kings* and *nobles;* a direct fruit of the *Great Charter*.

Edward, the young prince, having regained his liberty, took the field against Leicester; defeated and slew him in the famous battle of Evesham. Henry was again restored; but the latter part of his reign was one of oppression and turbulence. Like Uriah of old, Henry was placed in the front of the battle of Evesham; but, after being wounded, he cried out, "I am Henry of Winchester, your king!" His life was spared.

EDWARD I. (LONGSHANKS).—He was crowned in 1272. He immediately set himself about correcting the disorders caused by the civil commotions during the reign of his father. His first measure, however, was one of severity; he caused two hundred and eighty Jews to be hanged at once in London, and fifteen thousand were robbed of their effects and banished from the kingdom, on charge of corrupting the coin. His next enterprise was the invasion of Wales. After killing Llewellyn, the Welsh prince, and the flower of his army, the nobility of Wales submitted to him in 1283. Wales was then added to the British crown, and Edward created his eldest son "Prince of Wales," a title ever since borne by the oldest sons of the English monarchs.

He then meditated the conquest of the whole island. The death of Alexander III., of Scotland, opened the way for this desire to be gratified. Alexander leaving no son, *Bruce* and Baliol were competitors for the crown, and Edward was chosen umpire. He adjudged the crown to Baliol, who agreed to hold it as vassal of the King of England. Baliol, soon after, renounced his allegiance, whereupon arose a war between England and Scotland, lasting seventy years, and drenched both kingdoms in blood. To punish Baliol, Edward invaded Scotland, defeated the Scots with great slaughter at the battle of Dunbar, and carried Baliol a prisoner to London.

During Edward's absence, and war in France, the Scots were aroused to the recovery of their independence by Sir William Wallace. The envy of the Scotch nobles toward Wallace as governor of the country under Baliol, divided them, and exposed them to another attack from the English. Edward in person conducted the campaign, and defeated the Scots at the battle of Falkirk. Wallace was at last betrayed, carried a prisoner to London, where he was put to death with barbarous cruelty. The Scots submitted to Edward.

Robert Bruce, grandson of the former Bruce, was raised to the throne, after having expelled the British from the country. Edward prepared for a new invasion of the country, but died, on his journey, at Carlisle.

Edward is regarded as one of England's best kings, being an eminent warrior and wise legislator. He has been styled the *English Justinian.* Still he was only a restrained tyrant. The national code, and the administration of justice, were greatly improved during his reign. Magna Charta was repeatedly ratified, and an important clause added, which protected the people from the imposition of any tax without the consent of Parliament. Since that time there has been a regular succession of *English Parliaments.* Civil liberty is a *darling* thing to the people, and a *daring* thing to tyrants. It is not a little remarkable, that while Royalty was being humbled in England, during this century, Popery was receiving its death-wound in France, under Philip IV. and the Pragmatic sanction. Thus civil and religious liberty began their dawn, in the darkest part of the dark ages, while Chivalry, Popery, and Royalty, were all at their zenith.

EDWARD II. — He succeeded his father in 1307. In compliance with his father's dying injunction, he invaded Scotland. With an army of one hundred thousand men, he was met at Bannockburn by thirty thousand Scots, under Robert Bruce. Bruce had chosen a position where his right flank was covered by a hill, his left by a morass, and in his front he had dug pits, filled them with stakes, and covered them with turf. The English, confident in their superior numbers, rushed to the conflict. Their cavalry was entangled in the pits; their ranks were broken; when the Scottish horse, pouring through the breaches, scattered slaughter and dismay on every side. The English threw down their arms, and fled. This was the most signal defeat the English had sustained since the battle of Hastings; in consequence of which Robert Bruce was established on the throne of Scotland, 1314.

The reign of Edward was characterized by the corruption of the court, and contests and war between the barons and the king. His greatest sorrow arose from his queen, Isabella, sister of the French king, who ceased to care for him, and set her affections on Mortimer, a powerful young baron. Trouble arising among the barons on her account, she and her paramour fled to France. In their absence they managed to form a party in England, so that on their return, with some French troops, they compelled the king to resign the crown to his son, then only fourteen years old. Edward was thrown into prison. At the instigation of Mortimer and the queen, he was murdered by the keepers, who thrust a red-hot iron into his bowels until he was internally consumed. The defeat he suffered by Bruce, and the desertion of Isabella, rendered the life of Edward II. keenly miserable.

Edward III. — He succeeded his father, at fourteen years of age, in 1327. A regency of twelve persons was appointed during his minority, but chiefly controlled by Isabella and Mortimer. But Edward, on coming of age, disposed of the guilty pair in a summary manner. Mortimer was condemned by Parliament, and hanged upon a *gibbet.* Isabella was imprisoned for life at Castle Risings, and continued for twenty-eight years, a miserable monument of blasted ambition. Edward was successful against the Scots in the battle of Halidown Hill.

Upon the death of Charles IV. of France, Edward claimed the throne of France, being the son of Isabella, the daughter of Philip IV. of France. But the French nation chose to have Philip of Valois, cousin of Charles, ascend the throne. Edward prepared to maintain his claim by force of arms. Setting sail from England with a fleet of two hundred and fifty sail, he encountered that of France, of four hundred sail, off the coast of Flanders, where he gained one of the greatest naval victories recorded in history: losing four thousand men and two ships, while the French lost thirty thousand men and two hundred and thirty ships.

He then invaded France, at the head of thirty thousand men, and gained the battle of Cressy, over Philip, whose army amounted to one hundred thousand men, and his loss over thirty thousand.

This is noted as the first battle in English history in which cannon were used, — the secret of the great victory. Here the Black Prince, then only sixteen years old, distinguished himself for military genius. Edward afterward besieged and took Calais, which remained in possession of the English until Mary.

While Edward was in France the Scots invaded England, under their king David, but were defeated, near Durham, by Philippa, Edward's heroic queen, and David was led captive to London. John of France took the field against the Black Prince (so called from wearing black armor) with sixty thousand men, and the prince had only sixteen thousand, when the victory of Poictiers was gained, and John taken prisoner to London, where he was kept fellow-captive with David of Scotland.

Edward, becoming indolent and dissipated in his latter days, saw all his conquests return to those from whom he had wrested them. The Black Prince, falling into consumption, had to resign the command of the army, when Charles V. recovered all the French possessions except Calais. Glittering as were the reign and victories of Edward III. and his son the prince, yet he lived to see the glitter fade. The early death of his son he survived but a short time. In his reign chivalry was at its zenith in England; and among all the virtues of the knightly train in courtesy, munificence, gallantry, and magnanimity, Edward III. and his son the Black Prince were foremost. Their court was the sun of that system which embraced the valor and nobility of the Christian world.

RICHARD II.—He was son of the Black Prince, and succeeded to the throne, at eleven years of age, in 1377.

A regency was appointed, consisting of the young king's three uncles, the dukes of Lancaster, York, and Gloucester. Their quarrels distracted the kingdom. The Duke of Lancaster, John of Ghent, was the most powerful, but became unpopular with the courtiers for being the protector of Wickliffe, the English Reformer, whose opposition to the corruptions and tyranny of Rome had made him very conspicuous.

Another measure brought on the "Wat Tyler insurrection." The kings and nobles, having wasted their resources in bootyless wars, applied to Parliament to replenish their empty coffers by levying a tax of six cents on every male and female above fifteen years of age. Complaints soon followed that it was unjust to exact an equal sum from rich and poor; but collectors were sent out. One of the brutal tax-gatherers having demanded payment from a blacksmith's daughter, the father declared her under the taxable age. He was proceeding to improper familiarities with her, when the father dashed out his brains with a hammer. The action being applauded by the spectators, a spirit of sedition spread through the kingdom, and soon one hundred thousand insurgents were assembled, under Wat Tyler, on Black-heath. The taxes being remitted, peace was restored.

About this time another battle was fought between the English, under Percy (Hotspur), and the Scotch, under Douglas, at Otterburn, in which Douglas was killed, and Percy taken prisoner. On this battle is founded the ballad *Chevy Chace.*

Richard had banished Henry, son of the Duke of Lancaster, and upon the death of the duke, had seized his estate. During the absence of Richard on an expedition against Ireland (an insurrection there), Henry returned to England; soon raised a large army, and compelled Richard, on his return, to resign the crown. The king being detested, Parliament countenanced the usurpation. Richard was thrown into prison, and starved to death.

BRANCH OF LANCASTER.

Henry IV. — He was Duke of Lancaster, and came to the throne in 1400. His father was John of Ghent, the fourth son of Edward III.; but Edmund Mortimer, son of Lionel, of the house of York, *third* son of Edward III., was the true heir.

A revolt soon followed, headed by the Earl of Northumberland, in which the enemies of the usurper were joined by the Scotch and Welsh; but their united forces were defeated at Shrewsbury, and their leader, Percy (Hotspur, so called for his fiery temper), was killed. A second rebellion followed, headed by the Archbishop of York, which was quelled by the capital punishment of its author.

While a subject, it was supposed Henry had imbibed the religious principles of his father, John of Ghent, the patron of *Wickliffe* and his followers. But when raised to power, or when he had usurped the power, he sought the favor of the court clergy, by suppressing the opinions his father had supported. And here let it stand upon the page of history, that the royal usurper, Henry IV., was the first English monarch *who burnt his subjects on account of religion.* His usurpation and despotism filled him with jealousy and remorse, the fruit of his own sowing. He *felt* what Shakspeare wrote: "Uneasy lies the head that wears a crown."

His son Henry, Prince of Wales, gave him a vast amount of trouble. One of the prince's dissolute companions, having been indicted before Chief Justice *Sir William Gascoigne* for some misdemeanor, Henry was so exasperated at the issue of the trial that he struck the judge in open court. The magistrate, mindful of the dignity of his office, ordered the prince to be committed to prison. Henry quietly submitted, and acknowledged his error. The king, on hearing of this circumstance, exclaimed, in a transport of joy, "Happy is the king who has a magistrate endowed with courage to execute the laws upon such an offender; still more happy in having a son willing to submit to such chastisement."

Henry V. — He came to the throne, after his father, in 1413. He immediately assembled his riotous companions, and informed them of his purpose of reformation in manners, and assured them that all who wished his future good-will must imitate him in the same, and made liberal presents to such as seconded his proposal. He commended the Chief Justice for his impartial conduct, and encouraged him to persevere in the strict execution of the laws. "He that keepeth his own spirit, is greater than he that taketh a city." Still, men are prone to "strain out a gnat, but swallow a camel." While Henry received the reprimand of the Chief Justice, and reformed, he followed the base example of his father, under the *pastoral* care of Archbishop Arundel, in burning heretics. (?)

The followers of Wickliffe had now become numerous in England, and had for their leader Sir John Oldcastle, *Lord Cobham*, a nobleman of distinguished talents, and high in favor with the king. This *Christian* nobleman Henry delivered (like Pilate) to the Arch-Arundel, and his "legion, for they were many," to be hung up by the middle with a *chain, and roasted alive!* For the grave offence of striking the justice, Henry repented and reformed, and was commended; but for giving up Lord Cobham, to be reduced to charcoal for his simple *faith*, he repented *not, nor reformed*, and was also *commended!* In order to be a friend to Cæsar, the just must be "crucified, *crucified*."

The claim made by Edward III., to the French throne, as son of Isabella, daughter of Philip IV., not having been yet fully established, Henry V., as great-grandson to Edward III., revived the claim, and prepared to invade France, and enforce it upon the French nation.

Henry chose a time of disorder in the affairs of France to make his attack. Proceeding thither with fifteen thousand men, he was met, on the plains of Agincourt, by the French army of sixty thousand men. The French, disdaining to attack so few, stood at repose. Henry had placed his army in a narrow pass, each flank being covered by woods. Seeing the contempt of the French, Henry ordered an attack; first, by a cloud of arrows discharged upon the enemy, then a charge with the sword upon the French horse, which turned them back upon the French infantry; then followed a charge of the English horse, which gave them the victory: they losing not five hundred men, while the French lost in killed eleven thousand, and fourteen thousand prisoners.

After this battle, Henry found it necessary to return to England and recruit his army. This done, he landed in France with twenty-five thousand troops, fought his way to Paris, and compelled the French to make the treaty of Troyes, 1420. This treaty was made between the queen of Charles (who was himself insane) and the

Duke of Burgundy. It stipulated Henry's right to the crown; that he should marry the daughter of Charles, and she to receive France as her dowry, and Henry to govern as regent until the death of Charles.

Henry then proceeded against the Dauphin, who had assumed the regency. Triumphing over him, the succession of the English king to the French throne was settled. Henry soon after died, aged thirty-four, having reigned nine years. Thus the portal of earthly fame was to him that of death, and his conquests proved to be of no benefit to his country.

HENRY VI. — He succeeded to the throne, in 1422 — only nine months of age. He was proclaimed King of England and France, simultaneously at London and Paris; his two uncles acting as protectors for the young king, viz., the Duke of Bedford for France, and the Duke of Gloucester for England. At eight years of age, Henry was crowned King of France. It only remained at that time, to complete the conquest of the country, to capture Orleans, a strong and important place. The Duke of Bedford laid siege to the place, and brought the affairs of the country to a crisis that would have given the whole kingdom to the English in a short time.

At this critical juncture appeared that very extraordinary character, *Joan of Arc*, "the Maid of Orleans." By her intrepidity, "borne as on the wings of fate," she led the French forces against the English, and compelled them to raise the siege. The French who supported the Dauphin, Charles VII., took courage at this, and finally recovered all the possessions of the English in their country, except Calais and Guienne.

Henry, on coming of age, proved to be an imbecile king. He married Margaret of Anjou, whose ambition and heroism found a space for exercise upon being associated with the "sheep's head" of her royal spouse. Her intrigues hatched for her broods of enemies. An insurrection broke out among the people, who were indignant at her crimes, headed by one *Jack Cade*, but was soon crushed. The Duke of Gloucester, a great favorite of the nation, and chief pillar of the house of Lancaster, soon disappeared in a very mysterious manner (probably Margaret knew how). He was heir presumptive to the crown, in case the king died without issue, and had opposed the marriage of Henry with Margaret; hence her deadly hatred towards him.

Margaret's intrigues brought about the change of the succession from the house of Lancaster back to the house of York. Both had descended from Edward III.; but that of Lancaster had usurped the crown, in the person of Henry IV., when the Duke of York was the rightful heir. Margaret, having a hope of furnishing an heir to the throne, from the house of Lancaster, was in a nettle to prevent the next line of heirs coming in from the side of York.

Richard, son of Lionel, third son of Edward III., stood ready to take the crown. He was unambitious, though appointed lieutenant of the kingdom. This, Margaret could not endure; and so induced Henry to annul his protectorship, and place the administration in the hands of the Duke of Somerset. This meddlesome trick of hers precipitated a civil war between the houses of York and Lancaster, of thirty years' duration, in which twelve bloody, unrelenting, fierce battles were fought. In this war over one hundred thousand of the bravest men of the nation, including eighty princes of the blood, fell in the field, or perished on the scaffold. This was called the war of the "*Two Roses;*" *i. e.*, the badges of the two houses were roses: that of York was a *white rose*, that of Lancaster a *red* one.

In the battles of *St. Albans* and *Northampton*, the Lancastrians were defeated, and the king taken prisoner; but Margaret's grit collected another large army, and gained the battle of *Wakefield*, in which the Duke of York was defeated and slain. But Edward, his son, immediately espoused his father's cause, and, at the head of a large army, entered London, amidst the shouts of the people, and was proclaimed king. But the contest was not ended yet. Margaret, losing none of her effrontery, collected another army of sixty thousand men, which was met by one of forty thousand of the Yorkists, under the command of Edward and the Earl of Warwick. A tremendous battle was fought at Towton, in which thirty-six thousand Englishmen, slain by each other's hands, were left dead on the field. (Civil wars are the most desperate of all. This instance reminds one of the war between Israel and Benjamin; Sparta and Athens; and Cæsar and Pompey.)

BRANCH OF YORK.

Edward IV. — By the victory of Towton Edward was considered as king, 1461, in the proper line of Edward III. Henry VI. was taken prisoner, and confined in the Tower. Margaret fled from her enemies, taking with her her little son, eight years old. In her flight, she got lost in Hexham forest, where she fell into the hands of ruffians, who stripped her of her jewels, and then treated her with indignity. Overcome with fatigue and terror, she sunk in despair, but was soon aroused by the approach of a robber with a drawn sword. Seeing no way of escape, she arose and presented to him her child, saying, "My friend, here is your king's son, whom I commit to your protection." The robber, pleased with this confidence, so full and unexpected, took them in careful charge through many perils, to a small seaport, whence they sailed to Flanders.

The house of York had hitherto had the assistance of *Nevil, Earl of Warwick*, the most powerful baron in England, and the greatest general of his age. But Edward having given him some offence, he turned his favor on the side of the house of Lancaster. By his exertions Edward was deposed, and Henry, after having been a prisoner six years in the Tower, was released, and again proclaimed king. Margaret's hopes were now revived, and she put forth renewed efforts for the throne. But, in the battle of Barnet, Edward prevailed, and the brave Warwick was slain. In the desperate battle of Tewksbury Margaret's hopes were finally cut off. She and her son, "the Prince of Wales," were taken prisoners.

The prince, when brought before Edward, was asked by him how he dared invade his realm? Conscious of his high birth, he replied, that he came thither to claim his just inheritance. Edward, in a very unkingly manner, struck him on the face with his gauntlet. The dukes of Clarence and Gloucester took this as a signal for further violence, hurried the prince into the adjoining apartment, and despatched him with their daggers. Henry was re-imprisoned in the Tower, and found dead in a few days after. Margaret, after all her trail of blood, was only imprisoned, but was afterwards ransomed by the King of France, whither she went, and passed the remainder of her days in obscurity and neglect.

Edward, when securely established on the throne, gave himself up to unrestrained indulgence in acts of tyranny, cruelty, and debauchery. He and his brother Richard, Duke of Gloucester, concerted together to put their brother, the Duke of Clarence, to death, and drowned him in a butt of Malmsey wine. Edward, while preparing to gratify his subjects by a war with France, died suddenly, in his forty-second year — poisoned, as was supposed, by his brother Richard. One writer says of Edward himself, "His good qualities were beauty and courage; his bad qualities, every vice." Oh, the heart-aches of royalty!

EDWARD V. — He was the older of two brothers, sons of Edward IV., and was proclaimed king, at thirteen years of age, in 1483, under the regency of his uncle Richard, Duke of Gloucester.

The diabolical Richard now unmasked his design in putting his two brothers, King Henry and his son, to death. He undertook to interest the leading men in his behalf, to assist in raising him to the throne, despite the two young princes, sons of Edward IV. Lord Hastings, and other distinguished persons, refusing to second his designs against the young princes, were decapitated, in a most summary manner, almost without even the *forms* of law. The young princes he caused to be removed to the Tower, under pretence of guarding them more securely.

Hereupon he seized the crown; declared the two princes, Edward and his brother, the Duke of York, were illegitimate; and caused himself to be proclaimed king, with the title

RICHARD III.—This plot he consummated in seventy-four days after Edward V. came to the throne, 1483. Richard then gave orders to Sir Robert Brackenburg, constable of the Tower, to put the young princes to death; but, from sentiments of honor, he refused to stain his hands with the infamous deed. The diabolical Richard then engaged Sir James Tyrrel, who chose three associates, whom he led to the door of the chamber where the young princes were lodged. Tyrrel charged them to enter and execute the terrible deed, while himself stood at the door. As they entered softly, the two boys lay in their bed, in a sweet and profound sleep. After suffocating them with the bolster and pillows, they showed the naked bodies to Tyrrel, who ordered them to be buried, deep in the ground, at the foot of the stairs.

This wretch had now filled up his cup of iniquity, and seated himself upon the throne, after wading to it through the blood of his nearest relations. Vengeance there was in store, and a hand to execute it, in the person of the Earl of Richmond, the only surviving heir of the house of Lancaster. The French supplied him with means of making war upon this detestable tyrant. The armies of the two rivals met at *Bosworth*, where a desperate battle was fought. By reason of Lord Stanley's going over to Richmond, Richard was defeated and slain. On looking over the dead, behold the body of the usurper, with the golden crown upon his head. It was immediately removed, and placed upon the head of his rival, who was proclaimed king, on the battle-field, with the title of Henry VII.

It is said of Richard, that he had a harsh and disagreeable countenance, was crook-backed, splay-footed, and his left arm withered; but his deformed body was much nearer perfection than his base mind.

HOUSE OF TUDOR.

HENRY VII.—He assumed this title August 22, 1485. His right was rather defective. He was the last male heir of Lancaster, and that only by being the son of *Margaret* (great-grand-daughter of John of Ghent), and of *Edmund* Tudor. He strengthened his claim, however, by marrying *Elizabeth*, daughter of Edward IV., thereby uniting the two houses of York and Lancaster. (So, in like manner, by marrying Margaret of Scotland, Henry I. united the Saxon and Norman families.)

The policy of Henry was pacific, though disturbed by pretenders to the throne, claiming to be the young princes of the Tower. Among these pretenders and their friends, who were executed, was the *Earl of Warwick*, the last of the Plantagenets.

Henry's prejudice to the house of York is said to have been very strong, so that he even ill-treated his wife on that account, though she was in the highest degree virtuous, amiable, and obsequious. Still, she never received in return proper affection, or even complaisance: his sullen ideas of faction prevailing over all the sentiments of conjugal endearment. He was much respected, but little beloved. He was wholly devoted to business; prudent and sagacious; little susceptible of social or generous affections; serious, reserved, suspicious, despotic and avaricious.

Epsom and Dudley, two lawyers, obtained an infamous notoriety as tools of his base schemes of extortion. He left, as the fruit of his avarice, fifty millions of dollars in ready money. Though not a popular sovereign, still his reign is considered as next to Alfred's, in point of substantial advantage to the nation. He enacted many wise and salutary laws, promoted industry, encouraged commerce, reduced to subordination a factious and insolent aristocracy, and taught the peaceful arts of civilized life to a warlike and turbulent people.

By permitting the nobles to alienate their lands, he weakened their power, raised the respectability of the lower orders, and gave a death-blow to the *feudal system* introduced by William the Conqueror. He expended fourteen thousand pounds in building a ship, which he called the "*Great Harry*," which is considered as the beginning of the *English Navy*. Before this, the government depended upon hiring or pressing merchant ships, in order to raise its fleets.

PERIOD IV. FROM HENRY VIII., 5513 A. M., AND 1509 A. C., TO THE END OF THE REVOLUTION, 5692 A. M., AND 1688 A. C.

Henry VIII.—He succeeded his father, in 1509, in his eighteenth year. No person ever came to a throne under more flattering auspices than did Henry VIII. The terrible contests between the houses of York and Lancaster had ceased, and their rival interests were happily blended in himself. The nation was at peace, and prosperous; the treasury full. He was young and beautiful, with accomplished manners, frank and open disposition, possessed of some learning, and fine talents; and was regarded by the people with affection and high expectations. *(Earthly bliss!)*

But soon, ah, too soon! the scene changed. He quickly showed himself to be destitute of wisdom and virtue; an unprincipled and cruel tyrant; rapacious and prodigal; obstinate and capricious; fickle in friendships, and merciless in resentments. Sir Walter Raleigh says of him: "If all the pictures and patterns of a merciless prince were lost to the world, they might all again be painted to the life, out of the story of this king."

One of the greatest wonders of his reign was the tame servility of the people and Parliament in submitting to his tyranny, or being made the tools of its exercise. He chose eminent men for his ministers, and they, too, felt the effects of his caprice and cruelty; Archbishop Cranmer alone retaining his favor to the last. The people had become so heart-sick of war, during the civil contests, that they had little choice between being ground to powder or torn in pieces. Henry's prodigality soon made way with the immense treasure left by his father. His military operations were few. He made war with Louis XII. of France, gaining the battle of the *Spurs*, — so called from the greater use the French made of their *spurs* than their *swords*. His general, the *Earl of Surrey*, gained a great battle over the *Scots* at *Flodden Field*, where James IV. and a great part of his nobility were slain. Henry was also, in some measure, involved in the wars of the two great rivals of the age, *Charles V.* of Germany, and *Francis I.* of France.

Before Henry was thirty years of age, he wrote a book, on the Seven Sacraments, against *Luther* the Reformer, which so pleased the Pope, that he conferred upon him the title of "Defender of the Faith;" a title still retained by the monarchs of England.

But the most remarkable events in Henry's reign were his trouble with his wives and the Pope. His first wife was *Catharine of Arragon*, widow of his elder brother *Arthur*, daughter of *Ferdinand* of Spain, and aunt of Charles V. After living with her eighteen years, he *pretended* to feel conscientious scruples about having his brother's wife. (In the meantime he had conceived a fondness for, and entered into improper intimacy with, the maid of honor, *Anne Boleyn*, whom he desired, and would be under obligation to marry.) Hence he applied to the Pope for a divorce from Catharine, under pretence of having been his brother's wife.

Cardinal Wolsey, who had pampered to the dissolute habits of the young king, was suspected of using his influence against Henry, as the divorce was delayed, and was seized on a charge of high treason. Falling sick soon after, Wolsey exclaimed, in remorse, "Had I but served God as diligently as I have served the king, he would not have given me over in my gray hairs."

Henry was advised, in his dilemma and suspense, to seek the opinion of the Universities. This done, a decision was given in favor of a divorce. A court was immediately assembled, under *Cranmer*, which pronounced the marriage invalid; and Lady Anne was soon crowned queen.

This refusal of the Pope to grant a divorce introduced a new subject of contention, no less disturbing and distressing to the nation than the war of the roses. This was the abolition of the papal supremacy in England, the suppression of the wealthy monasteries, alterations in the doctrines and forms of religion, and the king declared the supreme head of the English Church. News of this bold stroke reaching Rome, Henry was immediately declared an opponent of Christ's vicar on earth; his title of "Defender of the Faith" withdrawn; he was excommunicated, his kingdom laid under an interdict, and he himself cited to appear at Rome. Henry, however, was no King *John*, to bow to the Pope, but looked upon his raving as all idle wind. In fact, he was neither Catholic nor Protestant; for he assumed infallibility, and caused the law of the *Six Articles* to be passed, termed the "bloody statute" (Draco-like), under which he put to death all, of every name, who ventured to differ from him in opinion.

In less than three years after his new marriage he caused Anne Boleyn to be beheaded, to allow him to marry *Jane Seymour*, which he did the next day after Anne's death. Jane died in child-birth, leaving a son, *Prince Edward.* He next married *Anne of Cleves*, but soon set her aside, because she was not so handsome as she had been represented; and *Thomas Cromwell, Earl of Essex*, who helped him to get Anne Cleves, suffered death on the scaffold, because he aided in bringing about that joyless marriage. He then married *Catharine Howard*, whom he had executed for adultery. *Catharine Parr*, his sixth wife, had the good fortune to survive him.

Henry was the second king (Philip IV. of France being the first) who gave Popery a mortal wound. Not that either of them had any fellowship for a pure religion; but they thought to do the Pope harm, and they did him harm. In the first place, he lost "supremacy over kings;" in the second, he lost "*England*"! The scene of conflict now changes. Instead of "war between the two Roses," it's between the "Sceptre and the Keys." Indeed, the drama from Henry VIII. to the Revolution embraces the fearful yet successful struggle for *civil and religious liberty.*

EDWARD VI.—He was Henry's son, by Jane Seymour, and ascended the throne in 1547, in his tenth year. (Henry left two other children, daughters, viz.: *Mary*, daughter of Catharine of Arragon, and *Elizabeth*, daughter of Anne Boleyn.) Edward Seymour, Duke of Somerset, uncle of the young king, was Protector; after his fall, the Duke of Northumberland was raised to the same office.

Edward was a prince of great promise and many virtues. So opposite was he in spirit to his father, that he never signed an order for an execution against any of his subjects without shedding tears. His benevolence is exhibited in the endowments he made to Bridewell (a house of correction), St. Thomas' Hospital, and several schools, which still exist and flourish.

His reign was somewhat disturbed, from the strife for the ascendency between Protestantism and Popery. The former prevailed, and the cause of the Reformation was promoted, and the reformed liturgy was modelled under the direction of Cranmer. Just before Edward's death, the Duke of Northumberland, the Protector, induced him to set aside his sisters Mary and Elizabeth, and bequeath the crown to *Jane Grey*, a great-grand-daughter of Henry VII., who had married Lord Guilford Dudley, son of the Protector. Edward died in his sixteenth year, deeply lamented by the nation. Good kings were so rare, that their loss was a great calamity.

MARY.—She was sister of Edward VI., and began her reign in 1553. She was the first *queen* of England, and, with that honor, has also the title of "*Bloody*" Mary. Her first measure was to dispose of Lady Jane Grey. This beautiful Protestant princess (another Mariamne) was induced by her father-in-law and husband to accept of a crown, which they had also induced Edward to will her. Her youth is her *apology* for the step, and her execution the *penalty* thereof. She reluctantly accepted the peril, and by their intrigues alone was she proclaimed queen; but, after wearing the crown ten days, she resigned it, and would gladly have returned to private life. But, alas! she had gone too far.

Lady Jane and her husband were apprehended, and condemned to be beheaded. On the day of their execution, her husband requested an interview with her; but she declined, writing him that the tenderness of such a meeting would unfit them both for a greater concern. Also, that their separation would be but for a moment, when they would meet to part no more. Her husband was first brought to the block, before her eyes; but, undaunted at the sight, she addressed the spectators in a most affecting speech, and, with all her gentleness and loveliness, submitted her own neck to the fatal axe. It is said of her, that she was versed in Hebrew, Chaldee, Arabic, Latin, French, and Italian. Fuller adds, that she had "the innocency of childhood, the beauty of youth, the solidity of middle, and the gravity of old age; and all at eighteen: the birth of a princess, the learning of a clerk, and the life of a saint; yet the death of a malefactor, for her parent's offences."

"Bloody" Mary next imbrued her hands in the blood of the reformers. Being a Catholic, she attempted to restore the influence of the Pope, which her father had checked, and which was waning before the Reformation.

The leading victims (some of the most prominent reformers) who sealed their faith at the stake, at Smithfield, were Cranmer, Latimer, Ridley, Hooper, Ferrar, and Rogers. But these barbarities, and the undaunted spirit the martyrs exhibited, produced so strong a sensation in their favor, that their martyrdom tended to forward, rather than check, the Reformation. Another step that rendered Mary still more unpopular was her marriage with Philip II. of Spain. By the articles of marriage, her Parliament made provision for the independence of the English crown. It was stipulated that the administration of the government should be solely in the queen. In the last year of her reign, the French took Calais, which had been in the possession of the English for two hundred and ten years. She died soon after. This loss, together with the knowledge that she was hated by her husband and her subjects, caused her to die, of grief and vexation of heart, in her forty-third year.

IV.—AGE OF CONSOLIDATION.

Elizabeth. — She succeeded to the throne, on the death of Mary, her sister, in 1558. Her accession was hailed with joy by the nation, in the hope that the Reformation would receive favor at her hands. Her sister Mary being suspicious that Elizabeth was not a Catholic, frequently laid the trap of the "*real presence*" for her: to which she used to reply —

"Christ was the word that spake it;
He took the bread and brake it;
And what the word did make it,
That I believe, and take it."

Elizabeth favored the Protestant religion, and under her auspices the Church of England received its present form of faith. But her Protestantism was precisely after the pattern of her father's: simply, that she preferred to be head of the church *herself*, instead of allowing *His Holiness* that distinction. Hers was the Protestantism of Prelacy. The preaching of the Puritans she despised, and even prohibited it, until the meeting of Parliament. Upon its meeting, in 1559, several measures were adopted favoring Prelacy; one of which was, the "*Supremacy of the Sovereign and Uniformity of Common Prayer*." The design of the act of supremacy was to put the establishment of forms and ceremonies into Elizabeth's hands. Many of the ceremonies which she established the Puritans would not adopt, and this led to the establishment of the *Court of High Commission*. This became a *prelatical Inquisition*, resembling the *papal one* not a little. By these and other measures the peace of the nation was greatly disturbed.

Elizabeth is charged with cruelty to Mary, *Queen of Scots*, who was as beautiful as she was unfortunate. She was great-granddaughter of Henry VII., and next heir to Elizabeth to the throne of England. She had been educated, in France, a Catholic, and married, when very young, the dauphin, afterwards Francis II. Influenced by her maternal uncles, the Guises, she foolishly (like Lady Jane Grey) assumed the title of Queen of England. This excited the resentment of Elizabeth, and cost the Queen of Scots her peace and head. Upon the death of Francis, she returned to Scotland, at the age of eighteen years. At this time the *Reformation*, by the zealous labors of *John Knox*, had made great progress in the country, and the people had a strong aversion to their Catholic queen, and rather looked to Elizabeth for protection, and refused to acknowledge Mary.

She married her cousin, Henry Stuart, but soon had trouble, and he was murdered not long after. Her conduct excited against her the whole kingdom of Scotland; and, being deserted by her followers, she was compelled to resign her crown to her infant son, who was proclaimed James VI.; and the *Earl of Murray*, a friend of the Reformation, appointed regent. Escaping from her confinement, she raised an army to oppose Murray; but was defeated, and fled to England in 1568. Encouraged by the plausible professions of regard from Elizabeth, she sought her protection, and desired her to act as umpire between herself and her subjects.

Elizabeth had too much of Henry VIII. in her to allow one who had committed the offence of Lady Jane to meet with any better fate. For eighteen long years she kept Mary a prisoner in Fotheringay Castle. She was at last tried (?), and, *of course*, condemned to die. When informed that she must die, she called in all her servants, and bade them a solemn farewell. Next morning she dressed herself in a rich habit of silk and velvet, and declared her resolution to die a Catholic. When brought to the block, "she displayed the majesty of a queen, and the meekness of a martyr." She, like Lady Jane, was very accomplished. Her beauty was celebrated throughout Europe. She read and understood several languages, wrote poetry, and practised music.

In this reign the Spanish *Invincible Armada* was sent against England. This fleet consisted of 150 ships, 3000 cannon, and 27,000 men. It entered the English Channel in the form of a crescent; it was met by 108 English ships. These attacked the Armada in the night, set on fire and burned many of them, when a violent storm dispersed the rest. Only 50 vessels returned, and 6000 men. (A similar attempt met with a similar fate in the reign of Charles VI. of France.)

The reign of Elizabeth was fruitful with eminent men. It has been considered the Augustan age of English literature, and was illustrated by the great names of *Milton*, *Bacon*, *Spenser*, and *Shakspeare*.

Elizabeth early formed a purpose to "live and die a maiden queen." Notwithstanding this, her flirtations and foibles were many and ludicrous. Her greatest favorite was an accomplished young nobleman, Earl of Essex. They had many quarrels and reconciliations. On one occasion, for some affront he offered her, she angrily boxed his ear; upon which Essex clapped his hand upon his sword, swearing he would not bear such usage from Henry VIII., and left the room.

She was excessively fond of dress and show, and, feeling slighted because her beauty was fading, said, "Men will turn from the setting to the rising sun." In her extreme age she maintained her excessive desire of show and flattery. Being mortified at the sight of wrinkles on her face, she refrained from using a mirror, and trusted herself entirely in the hands of her maids of honor to arrange her toilet. In painting her cheeks, her maids of *honor* (?) used sometimes to send her into the presence of her courtiers with her *nose* painted. Her manners were haughty and overbearing, and her conversation grossly profane. She is said to have spoken Greek, Latin, French, and Spanish fluently. Her policy of government was, to secure the affections of her people, to be frugal of her treasures, and excite dissensions among her enemies. During her reign, England rose from a secondary kingdom to a level with the first States of Europe. England has had few abler sovereigns than Elizabeth.

Upon hearing of the effort of Essex, her paramour, to convey a particular ring to her, after his condemnation, in hope of moving her affection for him (which was intercepted and kept from her, until after his execution, by the Countess of Nottingham), Elizabeth fell into a profound melancholy. No efforts could arouse her, and no persuasions induce her to take either food or medicine. She threw herself upon the floor, and remained in that state several days and nights, until life became extinct. (See Cleopatra and Antony.) The "maiden" queen was not proof against the darts of Cupid; and, with all her couches and luxury, Queen Elizabeth died on the floor.

HOUSE OF STUART.

James I.—Upon the approach of death, Elizabeth nominated as her successor James VI. of Scotland, the son of her rival, Mary, Queen of Scots. He ascended the throne of England in 1603, with the title of James I., when the two crowns were united. He was the first of the Stuarts, a family whose reign was an unceasing struggle with the people for the *sovereign and divine right of kings.* (The people were unable to discover *divine* right where there was so much despotism, rashness, and "Punic" *faith*).

Scarcely had James arrived in England, when a conspiracy was discovered for placing Arabella Stuart on the throne. *Sir Walter Raleigh* suffered fifteen years imprisonment on suspicion of being concerned in the plot, and was then beheaded. James had been educated a Presbyterian in Scotland, and, upon his accession, the Puritans hoped for clemency. But, on coming to the throne, he found it expedient to "remove his relation from John Knox's church, to join Queen Elizabeth's." The Catholics, seeing that their hopes, also, were at an end, formed the famous conspiracy called the "*Gunpowder Plot.*" The object was to cut off King, Lords, and Commons at a blow, on the assembling of Parliament, so as to make a *chasm* in the administration, if not a change.

On the approach of the event, a Catholic member of Parliament received an anonymous letter, advising him to be absent at that meeting; "for," said the letter, "though there be no appearance of any stir, yet I say they will receive a terrible blow, this Parliament; and yet they shall not see who hurts them." James did not treat this letter as did *Archias* the Spartan, or Julius Cæsar one with a similar note of warning, — "*business to morrow*," — but suspected the allusion made was to gunpowder. Search being made in the vaults of the building, thirty-six barrels of gunpowder, all trailed, and *Guy Fawkes*, with the matches in his pocket to set it on fire, were found, the night previous to the assembling of Parliament. He, with eighty others, suffered death.

James, like Henry VIII., allowed himself to be guided by unworthy favorites, who were possessed of no real merits, and by their excesses became odious to the people. The Puritans anticipated the favor of the new king, on account of his early religious education, but soon found him their oppressor; his *laconic* with them was, "No bishop, no king." He loved absolute power, as Elizabeth loved flattery. The divine right of kings to govern their subjects without control, was his favorite topic in conversation, and in his speeches to Parliament. [For further particulars of his treatment of the Puritans see History of Religion, page 267].

Display was the hobby of James. He hated war, and hence his pacific reign. He was as fond of flattery as Elizabeth; and it was dealt out to him, in unmeasured bounty, by his bishops and parisites, who styled him the "*British Solomon*." An opposite opinion styled him the "wisest fool in Europe." He labored to establish the divine right of kings to absolute sway, while the people grew stronger in the belief that there was no *divine necessity* for such *divine right.*

During his reign the increase of commerce, and hence of wealth, — the diffusion of information, — the little respect cherished for the personal character of the king, — the disappointed hopes of the Puritans, — their increase, and emigration to America, in 1620, for liberty's sake, — all conspired to diffuse widely the spirit of liberty. Public opinion was now strongly set upon the *extension* of the rights of the people, and the *retrenchment* of the prerogatives of the king, the fruit of which was reaped in the next reign.

Charles I. — He was son of James I., and succeeded him at his death, in 1625. He came to the throne under the favorable auspices of an undisputed title, and the kingdom in a flourishing condition. But the state of public opinion was not so favorable for the peace of a king with the sentiments of Charles.

He had married *Henrietta Maria*, daughter of Henry IV. of France. Buckingham was retained by Charles, in the same position as under James. He was sent by Charles to assist the Protestants in France, doubtless through the influence of Henry, the king's father-in-law, who favored them. Buckingham's assistance was no help; for he left Rochelle, the last hold of the Protestants, in peril, and returned to England. He was assassinated, by one Felton, just as he was about to embark for the relief of Rochelle. The fall of Rochelle was the fall of Protestantism in France.

Charles, accompanied by Buckingham, in the latter part of the reign of James, visited the court of Spain, in order to solicit the hand of the *Infanta* in marriage; but, through the mismanagement of Buckingham, the prince "got the mitten," upon which a war ensued between England and Spain; and Parliament refused supplies to aid Charles in courting the *Infanta* with bayonets. It is said that one reason for the fitting out of the *Spanish Armada* was to gratify the resentment of Philip II. towards Elizabeth for refusing him her hand in marriage. (Oh, Helen of Troy!) For this refusal to aid *Prince* Charles, *King* Charles thought to have revenge. (Unlike Louis XII., who, in a similar case, said, "It is unworthy the *King* of France to punish the injuries done the *Duke* of Orleans.") Charles *thought*, since the Parliament *thought* to proceed or withhold, regardless of him, so he would attempt to rule, independent of Parliament.

Charles was persuaded, by the alarming emigration to America, to forbid it, as the best men were leaving the nation. Among those prevented from leaving, were John Hampden, John Pym, and Oliver Cromwell, — men Charles would gladly have let gone to America not long after, could he have done it; but the Lord and the world needed them in England to stare despotism out of countenance.

Here was his fatal mistake, — in presuming to goad the nation, where it was already sore from the same cause. The famous *ship-money tax* put the wheels of revolution in motion. This was a tax to fit out a fleet, at the king's discretion, with ships, men, and supplies, independent of Parliament. John Hampden, a prominent member of the Parliament, and popular in the nation, refused to pay it. A suit was commenced, and the *corrupted* judge gave sentence against Hampden. The nation, seeing the injustice of this proceeding, now knew that they had nothing to expect of such a king and such a court. [For attempts to introduce Episcopacy into Scotland, see History of Religion.]

In 1640, Charles convoked a Parliament, after eleven years' intermission; but the House of Commons, instead of listening to his demands for supplies, began to present the public grievances, which were, violated privileges of Parliament, illegal taxes, and persecution. He soon dissolved them, and called for a new election. This new Parliament sent Stafford and Laud to the Tower, and afterwards beheaded Stafford, and, in five years, Laud also.

Infatuation now seized the king. In the face of such a Parliament, he proceeded to light the flame of civil war. This he did by impeaching Lord Kimbolton, and five distinguished commoners,—Pym, Hampden, Hollis, Hazlerig, and Strode,—and by going himself to the House to seize them, taking two hundred armed men with him to the door! Having entered the House, he ordered the Speaker, Lenthal, to point them out. Falling on his knees, Lenthal said, "Sire, I have neither eyes to see, nor tongue to speak in this place, but as the House is pleased to direct me, whose servant I am; and I humbly ask pardon, that I cannot give any other answer to what your majesty is pleased to demand of me."

The king withdrew, without obtaining the men he sought; and as he departed, murmurs of "Privilege! privilege!" were distinctly heard. Charles found he had run against Parliament in a way that he must yield; and the moment he turned from the Speaker to leave, his degradation and downfall began. The summit of kingly insolence was then attained, and the descent must follow. The next step in his decline was the acknowledgment of his fault, in an *apology to Parliament for his conduct.* (Quite a low bow for a despot to make!)

"But the 'die was cast,'
The rubicon was past,"—

and to the sword both parties flew.

This civil war began in 1642; the cause of the king being supported by the larger part of the nobility, the bishops and friends of Episcopacy, and the Catholics; that of the Parliament, by the yeomanry, merchants, mechanics, and Dissenters. The former were called *Cavaliers;* the latter, *Roundheads*, from cropping their hair short.

The royal army was commanded by the king, the *Earl of Lindsey*, *Prince Rupert*, and *Sir Jacob Astley:* the parliamentary army by *Earl of Essex*,—then *Lord Fairfax*,—and afterwards by *Oliver Cromwell.* After the war had raged for five years, with various success, Charles fell into the hands of his enemies. For some time he was kept a prisoner, during which time the power Parliament had taken from the king was, by Cromwell's management, transferred to the army.

Presbyterianism being now on the decline, the Independents managed, by the aid of Cromwell, to get a court composed of one hundred and thirty-three members of Parliament of their own stamp. This small portion of the Parliament was called the "*Rump*," by way of derision. But, alas, for royalty! it was composed of the same class of persons as a part of the members of "Hampton Court," whom James ordered to "conform, or he would dog them out of the land, or hang them." But, in Charles' case, the "*Rump*" was judge, and the king the criminal. Charles was arraigned before this tribunal. He declined the jurisdiction of the court, and refused to plead. The sentence of the court, however, was: "Being satisfied that Charles Stuart is guilty of the crimes of which he has been charged, the court do adjudge him — as a tyrant, traitor, murderer, and public enemy to the good people of the nation — to be put to death by severing his head from his body."

In the morning of the fatal day, he arose earlier than usual, and took special pains in adjusting his dress. In preparing for the axe, he observed, to the Bishop of London, "I go from a corruptible to an incorruptible crown, where no disturbance can have place." On January 31, 1649, Charles, having laid his head on the block, one of the masked executioners severed it from his body at a blow; the other, holding it up, said, "Behold the head of a traitor!" while the lamentations of the spectators were mingled with the acclamations of the soldiery. What a lesson to tyrants who domineer over freemen!

Charles I. is reputed as an author; and in his poem entitled "Majesty in Misery," the following lines occur:

> "With my own power my majesty they wound,
> In the king's name the king himself 's uncrowned;
> So doth the dust destroy the diamond.
> Felons attain more privilege than I;
> They are allowed to answer ere they die;
> 'T is death to me to ask the reason why."

Charles' death was desired and brought about by a small part of the nation, or Parliament. Yet he brought it upon himself, by indulging in insolent despotism, and being the last man to learn that the influence of authority must ultimately bend to the influence of opinion. His duplicity with Parliament shook all their confidence in him; and, when forbearance ceased to be a virtue, he was made a "royal martyr."

Troublesome as were those times, it was the period when the problem of "despotism or liberty" was solved for the world; and to the *dissenting* interests in England, at that time, kindled and kept alive by the teachings of the Bible, do England and America owe the liberty, civil and religious, of which they boast, and are so glad to enjoy. So Greece, Rome, France, and England, have in turn upset royalty.

OLIVER CROMWELL.—Upon the death of Charles, 1649, Cromwell was borne, upon the tide of events, from being the successful defender of the Parliament, to the Protectorate of the realm. The strife between the "divine right of kings" and the *inalienable rights of the people*, threw the crown and ballot-box into his hands to manage.

As regent of a kingless nation, he had the peculiar and difficult part to act of preserving royalty and cherishing liberty. His position was, with one hand in the lion's mane, and the other hold of the unicorn's horn! Well might it be said that he was never a favorite with either royalists or republicans; they could not take care of themselves; and whilst he was quieting the row, they hated each other none the less, and loved Cromwell none the more. They had forced upon him one of the most difficult tasks of the kind any mortal ever yet had to perform. It never had been adjusted by all the heroes of Greece, nor emperors of Rome, nor kings and parliaments of England, until Cromwell, and has remained substantially as he left it ever since.

To this double and difficult work he gave himself, with due energy and tact. No sooner had he come into power, than he proceeded to recover from the Duke of Ormond, who, at the head of sixteen thousand men, in Ireland, had taken some important places from the Parliament. He passed over thither, and soon put the country into its former relation to England. The Parliament of Scotland took no part in the trial of Charles; but, immediately after his death, proclaimed *Charles II.* their sovereign, upon condition of his signing the covenant. The crowns of Scotland and England having been united in James I., this act of the Scots Cromwell looked upon as equally treasonable to the crown with the assumption of sovereignty by Mary, Queen of Scots; and so proceeded against the usurpation in order to maintain the rights of the *crown*, which he was forced to hold in trust. Accordingly, he marched into Scotland with sixteen thousand men, and defeated the Scots (which Charles I. and Edward II. *could n't do*) at Dunbar. The royal Covenanters retreating into England, were pursued by Cromwell, and in the desperate battle of Worcester nearly the whole army was killed or taken prisoners. Young Charles escaped with great difficulty, travelling in disguise, and only in the night, and passing the day in obscure cottages, living on coarse bread and milk. One day he concealed himself in the top of a large oak, his pursuers passing at the foot of it. He saw them, and heard them expressing their wish to find him. After two months of the like adventures, he found an opportunity (like Margaret) of escaping to France. Thus Cromwell took care of the rights of the crown.

The famous *Navigation Act*, passed by the republican Parliament, is considered as the foundation of the naval superiority of Great Britain. The peculiarity of this act was, the confining of the importation of all foreign merchandise to *English* vessels, and those of the country producing the commodities. A war grew out of this measure, between Holland and England, terminating in favor of the latter; the Dutch losing sixteen hundred ships.

The next attempt made to interfere with the double charge in Cromwell's hands, was by the Parliament itself. This, known as the "*Long Parliament*," had been in session twelve years, and hitherto subservient to Cromwell's policy. At last the Parliament became jealous of him, and, having lost the favor of the people, a desperate stroke of policy must be adopted. The most feasible route the Parliament could take in this dilemma (they thought), was to seize the *crown power* in Cromwell's hands, and then, being already *a* Parliament (hated by the people), they could easily have things their own way. Being aware of the influence of Cromwell with the army, their only hope of success was in weakening him at that point. To impeach him, would be to condemn themselves; to remove him, would be their execution; and to oppose him, they dare not venture. At last, with faces as long as their session, they very sagely proposed to reduce the army. This measure, they thought, would be likely to please the people, by reducing their taxes, and thus gain them to their cause; and so, without meddling in the least with Cromwell's popularity with the army, get him "shorn of his locks while asleep."

Cromwell "smelled powder" as quickly as did James I. when he read "they shall not see who hurts them." In order, however, to get ground for action, Cromwell and his council of officers sent up a petition, for Parliament to act upon, which would draw them out. While sitting with his officers, a message came, informing him of the unfavorable reply of Parliament. Rising suddenly at this, Cromwell turned to his major-general, Vernon, and with the appearance of fury, said, "I am compelled to do a thing that makes the very hairs of my head stand on end."

Indignant at Parliament (like Charles), he started for the Parliament House, leaving his soldiers at the door (like Charles, only one hundred more), and entered it with marks of violent indignation in his countenance. After listening a while to their debates (*un*like

Charles), he started up, and began to load the Parliament with reproaches. Then, stamping on the floor, he gave the signal for his soldiers to enter (unlike Charles also). Addressing himself to the members, he said—"*For shame! get you gone! give place to honester men! I tell you you are no longer a Parliament! the Lord has done with you!*"

Thus, true to his trust,—viz., the keeping of the crown and ballot-box,—whenever he found either aiming to subvert the other, Cromwell intercepts the attempt, and preserves the "prerogatives and rights" for their future heirs. Having, unlike Charles, turned the Parliament out of doors, and ordered them locked, he issued a call for one hundred and forty-four persons, in England, Scotland, and Ireland, to assemble at Whitehall, as representatives of the nation. This was styled the *Little Parliament*, and, by way of reproach, "*Barebones' Parliament*," from a prominent member who was by trade a leather-dresser—his business requiring *bones* to be *bared*; hence "*Barebones.*" (The bleeding and flaying of the nation by its kings had left little else but *bare bones.* "Can these bones live?")

The *Little* Parliament met July 4th, 1653, and, after five months deliberation, re-delivered the summons to Cromwell, by which he had called them together, and besought him to take care of the Commonwealth. The supreme power now passing into his hands, what could he do with it but keep it safely, until otherwise directed? Had he not done so, his name would have been *traitor.* Guarding the "royal prerogatives and the popular rights" against usurpers was his indisputable prerogative, even though he placed as sentinels around the sacred charge, "bulls that breathed fire, and a dragon that never slept." Upon the abdication of Parliament, Cromwell was assisted by a council of twenty-one members, by whom he was declared Protector of the Commonwealth of England, with the title, not of Majesty, but of "Highness," in 1654: an office corresponding, as nearly as possible, to that of Dictator, in the Roman Empire.

It is said that he aspired to the title of King. Not very remarkable if he did, considering that he possessed already the station and authority of one; and taking the examples of William the Conqueror, Henry I., Henry IV., and Richard III., who, under far more questionable circumstances, pushed their way to the throne through seas of blood. Finally, when the title of King was tendered him, he declined it, simply keeping, as trustee, the "prerogatives and rights" uncorrupt, for the proper owners.

The interest of the nation, however, required that the machinery of government should be put in motion, notwithstanding it was in the hands of the agent of the king and people. Hence, with the utmost propriety, and with precedents in great numbers, Cromwell entered upon the administration of the government. This he did with unrivalled energy and ability, and was the most able and powerful potentate of his time in Europe. He appointed General Monk to the command of all the forces in Scotland, and sent his own son Henry to govern Ireland. Abroad, his fleets and armies were victorious. *Dunkirk* was taken from the Spanish, and the island of Jamaica also. At home, he defeated and punished the conspiracies formed against him; granted religious toleration; caused justice to be ably and impartially administered by upright and learned judges; made himself respected and dreaded by the neighboring nations; and his friendship was sought by every foreign power,—making the period of the Protectorate one of the most brilliant in English history; not even behind Elizabeth's reign. Yet his enemies were many and fierce, among both royalists and republicans, and Cromwell lived constantly in fear of assassination. This was as might be expected. Assassins were plenty, both royal and unroyal; and the man who held them in check with bit and bridle, they *naturally* hated. Neither Cyrus the Great, Alexander the Great, Julius Cæsar, nor Philip IV., were any more raised to their high positions by the tide of an overruling Providence than was Oliver Cromwell, and *he* was found competent to his task. The "prerogatives of the king, and the rights of the people," were questions in dispute; these he did not attempt to settle, but put his administration upon the basis on which they could be settled, and afterwards were settled. So that Cromwell was *neither* a "usurper" *nor* a "subverter."

Cromwell has been represented as a dissembler in religion and politics; but, as Dr. Lingard observes, "this supposition is contradicted by the uniform tenor of his life." At his death, Cromwell simply passed the charge committed to his trust into the hands of his son Richard, without marring the questions of "prerogatives and rights." Richard *was acknowledged in all parts of the empire;* but, being neither a statesman nor a soldier, with no experience in public business, having feeble talents and little ambition, he was bought off, and lived in ease to a good old age.

The Protectorate being now dissolved, anarchy and confusion returned. General Monk, seeing a disposition in the people to have a king again, marched his army into England, and crushed the contending factions, when a Parliament was assembled, on promises made by Monk to Charles, that he would assist him in regaining the throne of his father, and Parliament was induced to recall him from exile; and on the 29th of May, 1660, Charles was restored to the English throne.

CHARLES II. — Son of Charles I. The question of rights and prerogatives now came up. Charles made great promises, and the people, through a great mistake, allowed him to assume the crown, without imposing on him any conditions; and, by this fatal step, the exciting questions which brought Charles I. to the block, were all thrown open again. Cromwell had not decided them, and the people, and their new king, were not able now to do it.

It would seem that gags, shackles, and tyrants were the favorites of the people. A number of the regicides were condemned and executed; and then the royal party, and others, turned, with *Trojan heroism*, to the grave of Cromwell, dug up his carcass, and hanged it on a gallows. (*A thing they dared not do once.*) The old theme of *passive obedience* and *non-resistance* was again revived; and the divine right of kings to rule without let or hinderance, strenuously advocated. Still, those who despised these tenets in the reign of Charles I., opposed them now; and the two parties were now distinguished into Whigs and Tories, — the latter for the crown, the former for the people.

Cromwell's religious toleration was (like the revoking of the Edict of Nantes) succeeded by an "Act of Uniformity," in which all persons were required to adopt the form of worship defined by the *Prelati-papal* church of Elizabeth. It took effect on the same day of the month as the "Massacre of St. Bartholomew" in Paris, August 24, 1662, just ninety years after. Other acts followed, known as the "Conventicle Act," and "Oxford Five Mile Act." [For an account of these persecuting edicts, see History of Religion, page 269].

The prodigality of Charles forced him to sell Dunkirk to the French for four hundred thousand pounds. During his war with the Dutch, occurred the *plague* of London, 1665, which carried off ninety thousand inhabitants; and the next year a fire occurred in the metropolis, which reduced to ashes thirteen thousand two hundred houses. The failure of the war with the Dutch, and the sale of Dunkirk, rendered the administration of Charles unpopular. The Duke of York, afterwards James II., who had the chief influence at court at this time, was an avowed Catholic; and Charles himself, caring nothing for any religion whatever, was at the same time receiving a million of dollars annually from Louis XIV. of France, for the purpose of establishing Popery and despotism in England. This state of affairs (no *better*, certainly, than under

Cromwell) excited general consternation and alarm for the Protestant religion and the public liberty.

"Prerogatives and rights" were again under discussion between the people and their king; and the latter part of the reign of Charles exhibits an uninterrupted series of attacks upon the lives, liberty, and property of his subjects, and a disgusting scene of party intrigues, plots, and conspiracies. In the midst of these turmoils and excesses, the Parliament invaded the *divine right* of kings, by passing the *Habeas Corpus* Act; *i. e.*, a personal safety act, to secure the people from oppression.

"A picture in little" of this king, by Rochester, is, that "Charles never *said* a foolish thing, and never *did* a wise one."

JAMES II. — He, upon the death of Charles, ascended the throne in 1685. The chief feature of this reign was James's attempt to establish Popery in England, and his being driven from the throne in consequence of it.

Immediately upon assuming the government, he expressed his contempt of the authority of Parliament, and his confidence in the *divine right of kings.*

The Duke of Monmouth, a natural son of Charles II., having stirred up a rebellion with a view to seize the crown, was defeated, taken prisoner, and beheaded. After the rebellion was put down, the most inhuman rigor was indulged in against those who favored it. It was in this vengeance by "divine right" (?) that the atrocious Chief Justice Jeffreys acquired his egotistical notoriety, boasting that he had hanged more men than any other judge since William the Conqueror; and King James used to give himself jocularity by styling it "Jeffreys' campaign."

As every tyrant must strike his own death-blow, James must his, of course. Charles I. struck at the Parliament; James at the Bishops. His *hobby* was the establishment of Popery in England. Having made some progress in that direction, he attempted to put on the "cap-stone," by requiring the bishops to read a Declaration, suspending the laws against Popery. *Seven* bishops refused; and for this refusal were committed to the Tower! At this atrocity the *spirit of passive obedience*, inculcated by the *divine right* of kings, broke out in a general indignation and spirit of positive resistance.

Application was then made to *William, Prince of Orange*, who had married *Mary*, eldest daughter of James, who soon landed an army at *Torbay*, in order to assume the government. The principal part of the nation immediately joined his standard. Even Anne, James's younger daughter, with her husband, Prince George of

Denmark, *forsook* the king, and joined the interest of William and the nation. King James being now deserted, fled to France.

England was now again brought to the same point as at the death of Charles I., with the benefit of a little more horrid experience. A "Convention-Parliament" declared the king's flight an abdication, and then settled the crown upon *William* and *Mary*.

The Duke of Buckingham describes the two brother-kings, Charles II., and James II., thus: "The elder could see things, if he would: and the younger would see things, if he could."

PERIOD V. FROM THE REVOLUTION, 5692 A. M., AND 1688 A. C., TO QUEEN VICTORIA, 5864 A. M., AND 1860, A. C.

William III. and Mary.—Upon the accession of William and Mary, 1688, the question of prerogatives and rights was brought to a decision. The *British Constitution* now became fixed and determined. The Protestant succession was secured; religious toleration granted; and Presbyterianism reëstablished in Scotland. This was only adopting the principles of Cromwell's administration, except that the people had now adjusted their differences with their king, which matter he reserved for them to do in their own way and time.

Some of the most important articles in the Declaration, fixing the "prerogatives of the king, and the rights of the people," were these: 1. The king cannot suspend the laws, or their execution; 2. He cannot levy money without the consent of Parliament; 3. The subjects have a right to petition the Crown; 4. A standing army cannot be kept in time of peace, but with the consent of Parliament; 5. Elections and parliamentary debates must be free, and parliaments must be frequently assembled. Many other important measures were recorded, among which was *liberty of the press*.

By favoring such measures as these, Charles I. might have saved his head, as Cromwell has his fame.

Some of the High-Church bishops refused to take oath of allegiance to William, and were deprived of their stations. Ireland still adhered to James; and the Parliament of that country declared William an usurper. Being assisted by Louis XIV. of France, James landed, with some French forces, in Ireland, where he was joined by a large number of Irishmen; but he was defeated by

William, at the river *Boyne*, when the country submitted to the new king. A large French fleet, in the service of James, was destroyed off *Cape la Hogue*, by *Admiral Russell*, after a bloody contest of ten hours. By the Peace of Ryswick, which followed, the title of William to the crown was acknowledged.

After the death of James, however, a son of his was proclaimed King of England, at St. Germaine, France, and treated as such at the Court of Versailles. Indignant at this piece of insolence, both Houses of Parliament declared their willingness to assist William to their utmost to redress such an insult; and the whole nation joined in a cry of war with France. In the midst of preparations for this event, William was suddenly removed by death. Mary died seven years before.

It was during the reign of William that the system of borrowing money on remote funds commenced, and the foundation laid for the present national debt. The sanction of Parliament was also obtained for a standing army in the same reign.

ANNE. — She was second daughter of James II. Notwithstanding the dissolute character of her father, she acquired and merited the title of "Good Queen Anne."

The reign of Anne has been termed the *Augustan Age* of England, from the literary characters who adorned the time, — among whom were Newton, Locke, Addison, etc.

In the first year of her reign England, Germany, and Holland, united in a war against Louis XIV., in order to check his ambition. The command of the allied army was given to the great *Duke of Marlborough*, *Prince Eugene* acting as the imperial general. The object of the allies was fully attained by the victories of *Blenheim*, *Ramillies*, *Oudenarde*, and *Malplaquet*. Louis was forced to ask a truce, when the Peace of Utrecht was concluded in 1713. In this treaty Spain yielded to England all right to Gibraltar and the island of Minorca, and France resigned all her pretensions to Hudson's Bay, Nova Scotia, St. Christopher's, and Newfoundland.

Another important event of Anne's reign was the *constitutional union of England and Scotland*, under her common name, *Great Britain*. In this union it was stipulated that the united kingdoms should be represented by one and the same Parliament; that Scotland should be represented by sixteen peers, and forty-five commoners; and that all peers of Scotland should be peers of England, and rank next after English peers.

The latter part of this reign was disturbed by party feuds, between the Whigs and Tories, respecting divine rights, passive obedience, etc. Queen Anne died of an apoplectic disorder, brought on by a long Cabinet Council, in which the members fell into violent altercations with one another, to the great grief of the queen.

HOUSE OF BRUNSWICK, OR HANOVER.

George I. — He ascended the throne, upon the death of Anne, 1714. He was Elector of Hanover. His accession took place without the slightest disturbance of public tranquillity. It was Protestantism that gave the throne to the house of Hanover. A son of James II. made some effort to obtain the crown, but the nation acknowledged him as only the *Pretender.*

George was unassuming in his manners; a man of great application to business; and his reign, on the whole, was pacific and prosperous.

George II. — He succeeded his father, in 1727, and, like him, favored the Whigs; he also showed too great a fondness for his German possessions, to please his English subjects.

The great Minister of State in this reign was Sir Robert Walpole.

He is represented by some as depraved, and by others as virtuous, in politics.

England became involved in the war of the *Austrian Succession*, and the king commanded his army in person on the Continent. After the "variety in war," *Maria Theresa*, by the Peace of Aix-la-Chapelle, in 1748, was confirmed in her claim to the throne. While King George II. was absent on the Continent, *Charles Edward*, the young *Pretender*, assisted by Louis XV. of France, made an effort to recover the throne of the Stuarts. Landing in Scotland, he put himself at the head of an army, and defeated the royal forces in the battles of Preston-Pans and Falkirk; but he was afterwards entirely defeated, by the Duke of Cumberland, at the decisive battle of Culloden. This was the last battle that has been fought on the soil of Great Britain, and the expiring effort of the *Stuart family* to ascend the throne they had forfeited by their egregious follies and mortal crimes.

In 1755 a war broke out between Great Britain and France, on account of encroachments made upon British territories in North America. The British finally took Louisburg, Fort du Quesne, Ticonderoga, Crown Point, Niagara; and finally, under the brave *Wolfe*, the city of Quebec was taken. Wolfe, having gained the Heights of Abraham during the night, was in battle array in the morning. By his adroitness he drew *Montcalm*, the French general, out of the city into the field. Previous to the engagement, Montcalm agreed not to bring his horse into the field, if Wolfe would not his cannon. To this Wolfe agreed. At the same time, fearing treachery, he had his guns all in readiness at his rear. No sooner had a fair opportunity (as Montcalm thought) presented itself, than he ordered his horse to charge. Upon this, Wolfe opened a brisk connonade, which frightened and turned the French horse upon their own infantry, and hastened their defeat. With this victory all was surrendered to the British.

Extensive conquests were also made at this time in India by the British.

George III.—He was grandson to the late king, and succeeded him in 1760. He was the first king of the house of Brunswick that was born in England. He came to the throne at an auspicious time. The arms of Great Britain were everywhere victorious, and the administration able and popular. This war with France was soon after brought to a close, by the Peace of Paris, and Canada and other territories were confirmed to England.

William Pitt (afterwards Lord Chatham), one of the greatest statesmen England ever had, exerted a powerful influence over the nation at this period. Where England followed his advice, she found it good; and when rejected, she had to regret it. A very striking instance of this is seen in the result of the oppressive course pursued by the British government towards the *American Colonies.* Against those impolitic and oppressive measures Pitt remonstrated, and warned the government of the sure and disastrous (to England) consequences that would follow. But Pitt could not turn the purpose of the obstinate old king; but, after George had gone through with the programme Pitt gave him, he was obliged to sign a quit claim to *Boston, etc.*,—upon the defeat of Cornwallis,—in favor of General George Washington, in 1783.

Another important affair, in the reign of George III., was the Revolution in France, in 1789, in which England and all Europe were involved. In this great struggle for the balance of power, both England and her allies, against France, were directed by the policy of William Pitt; and he, more than any other man, wrought the overthrow of Bonaparte. The prominent victories achieved by the British were those of the *Nile* and *Trafalgar*, by *Nelson*, and of *Talavera*, *Salamanca*, *Vittoria*, and *Waterloo*, by the *Duke of Wellington.* Waterloo was the last battle of nations; when the world's wars ceased, and general peace has since been maintained. And may it long remain!

In 1792 Lord Cornwallis was sent to India to settle disturbance and quell rebellion, under Tippoo, which he was successful in doing. In 1798 a rebellion broke out in Ireland, aided by France. The object of France was to wholly sever Ireland from Britain; but the attempt to land troops on the island was frustrated by storms and the naval operations of Admirals Duncan and Warren.

Lord Cornwallis brought the rebellion to a successful termination, when the favorite project of Pitt for uniting Ireland to Great Britain was consummated in 1800.

The attempt of Bonaparte to exclude British commerce from the Continent, provoked the *British Orders in Council*, which were, to impose a duty on all vessels trading with France, to be paid at some British port. To oppose this, Bonaparte issued his *Milan Decree*, confiscating all vessels that submitted to the British Orders in Council. In this dilemma, the *United States* passed a decree of *Non-intercourse* with England and France. American shipping was harassed, and this brought on the war of 1812.

By the Peace of *Ghent*, December 24, 1814, these three great nations of modern times confirmed the peace of the world: and in their hands rests now the "Ark of Power." May it be borne into the "holy of holies," and the "Temple of Janus" closed forever!

The last ten years of George III. he was afflicted with insanity, when the Prince of Wales acted as regent. The old king died in 1820, having reigned sixty-nine years — the longest of any English monarch, and second only to the longest reign on record, viz., that of Louis XIV. of France, of seventy-two years.

George IV. — He was son of George III., and was crowned king in 1820. He is represented as having great fancy and vanity for dress and show. While a prince, he favored the Whigs, but as regent and king, he united with the Tories. The principal events of his reign were the interference in favor of the Greeks in maintaining their independence, — in which the great naval victory of *Navarino* was gained over the Turkish fleet by the united powers of England, Russia, and France, — and a war in India, by which a large part of the Burman Empire was added to the English possessions in the East.

A bill was passed in his reign abolishing the disabilities of the Roman Catholics. Also the "Test Act," passed in time of Charles II., making the Episcopal sacrament a qualification for civil office and employment, was repealed in 1828, — a very important step towards religious liberty. During his regency and reign, England combated the great Napoleon.

William IV. — He was brother of the late king, and succeeded him in 1830.

The question of reform, in the representation of the people in the House of Commons, had for some time been agitated. Soon after the accession of William, the Duke of Wellington, the prime minister, expressed himself very strongly against reform. But the duke and his colleagues, finding they were not supported by the House of Commons, resigned. This brought a Whig ministry into office, headed by Earl Grey.

The great measure of parliamentary reform was brought forward by this ministry, and, after a long and violent struggle, was carried through both houses of Parliament in 1832. Slow, indeed, must have been the progress of reform, when England was not able to bring about a settled basis for constitutional liberty short of fifteen hundred years. But, happily for that nation and for the world, the problem has been solved; and, before the glorious light of freedom, which has been achieved by the toils, faith, and blood of our forefathers, the darkness of tyranny is disappearing.

The constituent parts of Parliament, under the Reform Bill of 1832, are, the king, lords, and commons.

The king (or crown) is hereditary.

The *British House of Lords, or Peers,* is composed of the Archbishops of Canterbury and York, with the twenty-four bishops of England, — called lords *spiritual,* — with the dukes, marquises, earls, viscounts, and barons (the five ranks of English nobility), — called lords temporal. To these add sixteen peers, delegated by the Scottish nobility, and four *spiritual* and twenty-eight temporal lords to represent the prelacy and peerage of Ireland.

The *British House of Commons* has five hundred representatives for England and Wales, fifty-three for Scotland, and one hundred and five for Ireland; — total, six hundred and fifty-eight.

VICTORIA. — This best of England's sovereigns, the present queen, came to the throne in 1837. It is said of her, that when one of the lord's spiritual conveyed to her the intelligence of the death of William IV., and that she was to succeed him on the throne, her request was that his reverence would immediately *offer prayer in her behalf!* Her life thus far comports with such a consecration of herself before the *throne* of high heaven ere she ascended the British throne.

The years 1857–58 of her reign are rendered memorable for the siege and capture of Sebastopol by the English, French, and Turkish forces; for the "mutiny in India," and the assumption of the government of India by the crown, superseding thereby the East India Company. In the year 1860 the Prince of Wales visits Canada.

IV.—AGE OF CONSOLIDATION.

AMERICA—FROM THE REFORMATION FORWARD.

CIVIL HISTORY.

PERIOD I. FROM THE DISCOVERY, 4990 A. M., AND 986 A. C., TO THE LANDING OF THE PILGRIMS, 5624 A. M., AND 1620 A. C.

The design of this volume does not require a very minute detail of even the leading events that have transpired in the western world. Much has already been written upon these subjects, and most readers are familiar with them. And then, again, the design of the work requires, in order to its completeness, that the "trail" of the *New World* should not be overlooked; for it is not impossible that, like the departure from the ancient custom, when "the best of the wine was reserved to the *last* of the feast," so the American nation, though *last*, may be equal to the first and best.

NORTHMEN.

The date generally assigned for the discovery of America is 1492. As to modern events it is so. But that it was inhabited previously, is a fact; and that adventurers visited it before that time, are facts generally credited. And yet, when it is claimed that the aborigines of America are descendants of the "Ten Tribes of Israel," the principal evidence that can be adduced on the point is mere conjecture, without probability.

The voyages of the "Northmen"—between the years 986 and 1015—have obtained credit in the historic world. Eric the Red, with his household, emigrated from Iceland to Greenland, and formed a settlement. Among the company was Heriulf Bardson. Their places of abode they named after themselves, as, *Erics*-fiod, and *Heriulfs*-nes.

Biarne.—This first discoverer of America, son of Bardson of Eyrar, in Iceland, was absent on a trading voyage to Norway when his father left for Greenland with Eric. Biarne, finding upon his return that his father had gone, determined to follow him.

Setting sail in the summer of 986, Biarne and his company were soon enveloped in fogs, and driven by northerly winds for many days they knew not where. At last they came in sight of a land without mountains, overgrown with woods, and presenting gentle elevations. Not knowing the land, they put to sea again. After two days' sail they came to another land, wooded and flat. Bearing away again, they came to a third land, which Biarne discovered to be an island. This was mountainous, and, looking desolate, they returned, and in four days arrived at *Heriulfs*-nes, in Greenland. This voyage excited great curiosity in Greenland.

Eight years after, Biarne visited Eric, Earl of Norway; and, in relating his adventures to him, Biarne was censured for not being more thorough in his investigations of the new countries. On his return, a "voyage of discovery" was projected.

Leif. — He was son of Eric the Red, and being anxious to know more about the lands Biarne saw, bought his ship, and, with a crew of thirty-five men, set out for the strange lands, in the year 1000.

The first land they made was the last seen by Biarne. Here they went ashore. In the distance were mountains; between them and the shore was a plain of slate (hella). This they named *Hellu*-land, and is now called Newfoundland. The next land they found was covered with wood, had a low coast, and cliffs of white sand; this they called Markland (Woodland), now known as Nova Scotia.

Sailing from this, with a north-east wind, in two days they came to an island. Passing this, they sailed westward, to the mainland, near the mouth of a river. Here they concluded to winter, and threw up some houses, which were called *Leifs*-budir (Leif's booths). In a ramble of the party, one, a German, named Tyrker, found some grape-vines, and the country, from that circumstance, was called "Vineland." In the spring the voyagers returned to Greenland. This same Vineland is now known as Massachusetts and Rhode Island.

Thorwald. — He was brother of Leif, and, anxious to explore Vineland still further, borrowed his brother's ship, and set sail in 1002. In 1003 a part of the company started from Leif's-booths, and explored still south, finding the country very beautiful. Returning in autumn, Thorwald left Leif's-booths again, going east, and then north, passed a remarkable headland, enclosing a bay. This land they called "Kialarnes" (Keel-cape), from its resemblance to the keel of their ship. By modern geographers it has been likened to a horn, and to a sickle, and is called Cape Cod.

Sailing along the east shore, they turned into a frith, and while there encountered a party of Skrellings (Esquimaux). A fight ensued, when eight of them were killed, the ninth escaping in a canoe. They were soon attacked by a large number, and in the affray Thorwald was mortally wounded by an arrow. His dying request was to be buried there, and that they should plant a cross at the head and one at the foot of his grave, and name the place Krossanes (Crossness), now known as Gurnet Point. This expedition returned to Greenland in 1005.

THORSTEIN. — He was third son of Eric the Red, and upon hearing of the death of his brother, determined to make a voyage to recover his body. He set sail in the same ship, accompanied by his wife Gudrida. But, losing their way, they were driven about all summer, and finally landed in Greenland. Thorstein soon after died. In the spring his wife went to *Erics*-ford.

GUDRIDA. — She was daughter-in-law of Eric the Red. In 1006 a new and larger expedition was fitted out. In the summer two vessels arrived at Greenland; one was commanded by Thorfinn Karlsefne, a wealthy nobleman. At a festival, where he and Gudrida were present, Thorfinn was captivated with the young widow, and, *strange to tell*, married her in the following winter. At this festival the voyage to Vineland was the subject of conversation; and again, at the nuptials, Vineland is discussed. At this latter time, Gudrida, the first female American discoverer, proposed, and prevailed upon her husband to make a voyage, and plant a colony in Vineland.

The voyage was successful, and the party landed at Leif's-booths. The bay around they called "Hop," to which situation Mount Hope's bay corresponds. Not long after, Gudrida gave birth to a son, who was named *Snorre*. Hence, Gudrida has the honor of being the first *Euro-American* mother, and *Snorre* the name of the first American boy. Hostilities with the Skrellings induced them to return to Ericksford in 1011.

FREYDISA. — This woman was *daughter* of Eric the Red. She accompanied the last expedition to Vineland; and, while the settlers were fleeing before the Skrellings, she came across the body of Snorre Thorbardson, and seeing his sword near by him, she seized it, and, turning upon the Skrellings, drove them back.

At the instigation of Freydisa, another voyage to Vineland was projected, — she having persuaded two captains of a ship to go and share equally with her in the spoils they might obtain. Each party was to have a company of thirty-five men (Freydisa managed to conceal five more for herself), and they reached Leif's-booths in 1012. This piece of treachery in Freydisa destroyed the confidence and also the peace of the expedition. She finally prevailed upon her husband to destroy the two captains and their followers. After this piece of homicide, they returned to Greenland, in 1013, with the most valuable cargo ever before carried from the New World. Thence he proceeded to Norway, sold his goods, and then returned to Iceland and purchased the Glaumboe estate, where they resided during life. Accounts of other expeditions are in existence, as late as the year 1347. And it may be further *presumed*, that the intercourse with America was continued very nearly, if not quite, to the time of Columbus.

RELICS.

An old stone cemetery, discovered about fifty years ago, on Rainsford Island, in the Bay of Boston, containing a skeleton, and a sword with a hilt of iron, points out the Scandinavians. Also a skeleton found at Fall River, Massachusetts, and with it a bronze breastplate, bronze tubes belonging to a belt, and arrow heads, none of which belong to the Indian, or modern European implements.

A Runic (Gothic) inscription, still to be seen, on Dighton Rock, on the east side of Taunton River, which is exposed and covered at every ebb and flow of the tide, points to early adventurers.

A stone tower, at Newport, Rhode Island, indicates the Goths as its builders. It is very firmly built; circular in form; twenty-five feet high. Its diameter outside is twenty-three feet; inside, eighteen feet nine inches; supported on pillars ten feet high; the arches twelve feet six inches high; and the foundation extends to the depth of five feet.

Professor Rafn concludes, from the want of indications about this tower of a warlike character, and the absence of similar structures, that it must have been built and used for a baptistry. This much, however, is plain, that the footprints of a race different from the aborigines of America, and previous to the time of Columbus, are traceable in these relics. Still, these discoveries of the Northmen are of no practical account in the subsequent history of America, as they do not appear to have any connection with the enterprise of Columbus, from which the growth of empire on this continent begins.

CHRISTOPHER COLUMBUS.

"Columbus was a sailor brave, —
The first that cross'd th' Atlantic wave, —
In fourteen hundred ninety-two,
He came far o'er the ocean blue."

This prince of discoverers was born in the territory of Genoa; and still may be seen, in the village of Cocoletto, the humble mansion — standing so near the sea that its spray is often thrown upon it — where "Colon," as the Spaniards call him, first saw the light. His attention was early directed to sea affairs; and he made himself useful in drawing charts, and thereby improved his taste and knowledge of the world. From his own observations, he early imbibed the notion that land could be found by sailing in a westerly direction.

The great desire of his times was to find a passage to the East Indies, without having to cross the Isthmus of Suez. This Columbus thought could be effected by sailing directly west. Having mastered his *theory* of discovery, Columbus could not rest until he had applied the practical test. He first made propositions to the State of Genoa, and asked aid to carry out his project, as early as 1484; but all was rejected. He then made proposals to John II., of Portugal. His enterprise was so far entertained by John, as to listen to his plans, — but for the purpose of getting his secret, and then to intercept Columbus, by sending an expedition before him, and so rob him of the honor of the new discovery. This plot failing, the king desired a second consideration; when Columbus, indignant at the treatment he had received, determined to apply for help elsewhere.

He then sent his brother Bartholomew to seek aid from Henry VII., of England (author of ship "Great Harry"), while Columbus made application to Ferdinand and Isabella, of Spain. Obtaining no favor from Henry, and meeting so many delays and insults from the Court of Spain, Columbus was about departing for France, to seek aid there, when Queen Isabella consented to assist him. The Articles of Agreement were signed at Santa Fe, in Grenada, April 17, 1492.

Three vessels were put into the service, manned and victualled for twelve months, at a cost of twenty thousand dollars. The names of the vessels were, "Santa Maria," "Pinta," and "Nina;" commanded severally by Columbus, Martin Alonzo Pinzon, and Vincent Yanez Pinzon. With a crew of ninety men, these "Argonauts" set sail from Palos, in Spain, Friday, August 3d, 1492. Steering direct for the Canary Islands, they stayed and rested as long as they dared to, from fear of three vessels the Portuguese had sent to attack them.

On the sixth of September they struck out into seas to them unknown, without a chart to direct their course. After sailing about two hundred leagues (six or eight hundred miles), the variation of the compass (a new and strange phenomenon) greatly alarmed Columbus, and nearly brought on a mutiny among the crew. After thirty days more of sailing, the crew were again clamorous to desist and return. At this time Columbus quieted them by a promise, that if no land appeared in three days, he would return. But, happily, on the night of the eleventh of October, Columbus discovered a light, and the morning dispalyed the joyful sight of *land.* A hymn of thanksgiving to Almighty God was sung by the whole crew. Their mutiny was turned into most ardent expressions of admiration for their intrepid commander, with acknowledgments of their rashness and disobedience.

No sooner were they on shore, than they kissed the ground, and returned thanks to God for his merciful preservation. Having taken possession of the island, in the name of the King and Queen of Spain, the sailors acknowledged his authority. The island first discovered was called St. Salvador, — known as Cat Island, among the group of the Bahamas. Touching afterwards Cuba and Hayti, he gave them the name *Hispaniola*. Columbus, still supposing these islands were in close connection with India, called them *West Indies*, from having come to them by sailing in a westerly course.

On his return to Spain, Columbus was greeted with all the applause the courts could bestow, — receiving the attentions even that were usually reserved for sovereigns. Isabella received him with open arms, and the courts that had spurned him, now solicited his presence, to do him honor.

Among other attentions, the Grand Cardinal of Spain, Pedro Gonzales de Mendoza, invited Columbus to a banquet. It was at this banquet that the celebrated anecdote of the egg occurred. A contemptible dunce, present at the table, full of impudence, and jealousy at Columbus' fame, asked him the brainless question, that, "if he had not discovered the Indies, whether there were not men who would have been capable of the enterprise?" Columbus, looking with proper contempt upon the senseless fop, made no reply; but, taking an egg, asked the company to make it stand upon one end. All attempted it, but in vain; when he took it and struck it upon the table, so as to flat the end, and left it standing upon the broken part, — as much as to say, "No one in this company is competent to *discover the Indies*, without first being showed how!"

Columbus made two other voyages soon after, on the last of which, in 1498, he discovered South America. His fame, however, did not shield him from the jealousies and intrigues of the Court of Spain. While on his third voyage, he was accused (falsely), deprived of the government of Hispaniola, and sent back to Spain in chains. The captain of the vessel which carried him, offered to take off his fetters; but Columbus replied, "No! I wear these irons by order of their majesties, the rulers of Spain, ... and their command alone shall set me at liberty!"

Upon his arrival in Spain in fetters, the indignation of the people was aroused; and, for a time, Ferdinand was made to feel ashamed of the (too frequent) *Punic* justice and gratitude of kings. Columbus never forgot this shameful treatment, and always carried his fetters with him, hung them in his chamber, and ordered them to be buried with him.

Intent upon finding a passage to the Indies, he made a fourth voyage, and examined the coast of Darien, and was shipwrecked on the coast of the island of Jamaica. Here he gained a great influence over the natives by taking advantage of an eclipse of the moon. He predicted that the Great Spirit would put his hand over the moon at a set time. Happening as he had told them, he was greatly venerated for his familiarity with the Great Spirit. After a very calamitous adventure, mutinies of his men, treachery, and conflicts with the natives, hunger and sickness, he returned to Spain for the last time.

Worn out with fatigue, disappointment, and sorrow, he died at *Valladolid*, Spain, May 15, 1506, aged seventy years. His bones are still preserved in the cathedral at Havana, Cuba.

VASCO DE GAMA.—He (a Portuguese) first doubled the *Cape of Good Hope*, in 1497, and sailed to India. This was the leading object of Columbus, to find a passage to the East Indies.

JOHN CABOT.—He was a Venetian by birth, though residing in Bristol, England. He received a commission from Henry VII., and sailed, in May 1497, on a voyage of discovery, accompanied by his son, *Sebastian Cabot*, by whom the *Continent of North America* was discovered.

They struck *Prima Vista* (Newfoundland), and made a trip as far south as Florida. Along the shore, at various places, they erected crosses, and took formal possession of the country in behalf of the Crown of England. (Henry's desire for a slice was greater than when Columbus sent his brother to him for aid to make the first discovery.)

AMERICUS VESPUCIUS.—He was a native of Florence, and accompanied Ojeda in a voyage to America, in 1499. He wrote an account of his voyage, claiming to have discovered the *mainland*, and claiming the right of giving his own name to the continent. Instead of *Columbia*, this continent was named, very unjustly, *America*.

MAGELLAN.—This Portuguese navigator discovered and passed through the straits that bear his name, in 1519, and sailed into the Pacific Ocean as far as the Philippine Isles, where he lost his life. But his officers proceeded, and made the *first voyage around the globe*.

FERNANDO CORTEZ.—In 1519, he sailed with a fleet of eleven ships and six hundred and seventeen men from Cuba, landed at Vera Cruz, and invaded Mexico. Having fire-arms,— which the Mexicans knew nothing about,—he made very rapid advances upon the city of Mexico, where he was hospitably received by *Montezuma*.

Cortez caused him to be seized in his palace. The Mexicans, indignant at the treachery, flew to arms, when Montezuma fell, and the

Spaniards were driven from the city. But, obtaining a reinforcement, Mexico fell into the hands of the conquering Spaniard.

PIZARRO. — A settlement of Spaniards was made at Panama in 1518. From this place Pizarro sailed, in 1525, and discovered the rich and flourishing kingdom of Peru.

He then sought, of Charles V. of Spain, and obtained a commission as governor, and a military force to subdue it. He again sailed from Panama, in 1531, with three vessels and one hundred and eighty men. He landed, and advanced to the residence of the *Inca*, or King *Atabalipa*, and invited him to a friendly interview, and then seized him as a prisoner. At the same time, Pizarro's men fell upon the defenceless inhabitants, and slew four thousand of them.

The *Inca*, in order to procure his release, agreed to fill his prison, — which was twenty-two feet by seventeen, — as high as he could reach, with vessels of gold and silver. This Pizarro promised to accept as his ransom. The treasure thus brought together amounted to over seven and a half millions of dollars. But the perfidious Spaniard, being joined by *Almagro*, kept the Inca, tried him on charge of being a usurper and idolater, condemned and executed him.

The Spanish chiefs afterwards quarrelled with each other, and a civil war ensued. Almagro was taken prisoner, condemned, and executed, and soon after Pizarro was assassinated. The Peruvians then arose to drive out the invaders, but were overcome at last.

The Mexicans and Peruvians at this time understood architecture, sculpture, mining and working the precious metals; were clothed, cultivated their lands, and had a code of laws, civil and religious. But from whom they descended, or how this continent was peopled, is yet a question.

JAMES CARTIER. — In 1534 he sailed on an expedition, entered the Gulf of St. Lawrence, and took possession of the country in the name of the French king, and styled it *New France*, afterwards changed to *Canada*.

SIR WALTER RALEIGH. — He, in 1584, under a commission from Queen Elizabeth, arrived in America, entered Pamlico Sound, and proceeded to Roanoke Island, and took possession of the country. On his return to England, he gave so fine a description of the country, that Elizabeth gave it the name of Virginia, to commemorate its discovery during the reign of a *virgin* queen.

Several attempts were made — by *Sir Walter*, *Sir Francis Drake*, and *Sir Richard Grenville* — to make settlements in Virginia, but they all proved unsuccessful.

Sir Walter was finally beheaded.

Captain Newport. — Under the patent of James I., two companies were formed for the settlement of America, dated April 10, 1606. These were the London and the Plymouth companies.

On December 10th, of the same year, the *London Company* sent out a colony to Virginia, under Captain Newport, of one hundred and five persons, to commence a settlement. This company made the first effectual attempt at settling a colony in the New World. In 1607 they sailed up the *Powhatan* River, which they named *James River*, after King James I. On a beautiful peninsula they built a fort, and commenced a town, which they called *Jamestown.*

The government of the Colony was first in the hands of a council of seven, with a president chosen from among their number. The name of the first president was *Wingfield.* The most influential man, however, in the company was *Captain John Smith*, who was the second year chosen president, and who was styled the Father of the Colony. He had before commanded a company of cavalry in the Austrian army, in a war with the Turks, was taken prisoner, and carried to Constantinople as a slave. From this condition he extricated himself.

The year in which the settlement commenced, Captain Smith was taken prisoner by two hundred Indians, while hunting. But they let him go again, being so pleased with his valor and arts. Soon after he was taken by another party of three hundred, and brought before *Powhatan*, the greatest chief of the region. He was sentenced to death, and brought to execution.

Pocahontas, the chief's daughter, only twelve years of age, had interceded in behalf of Smith, without success. But while his head was placed upon a stone, where his brains were to be beaten out with clubs, Pocahontas rushed forward, and, laying her head upon Smith's, showed that she was determined to share his fate. Powhatan relented, and Smith was set free. She rendered eminent service in protecting the colonies from the depredations of the Indians.

Pocahontas was afterwards married to a *Mr. Rolfe*, a respectable young planter. The nuptials were celebrated with great pomp. She afterwards went to England with her husband, was instructed in the Christian religion, and baptized. She died soon after returning to America, at the age of twenty-two. She left a son, from whom sprung some of the most respectable families of Virginia. Such was the "Joan" of Virginia.

Upon the return of Captain Smith to England, the Colony was almost annihilated; but the timely arrival of Lord Delevan, with one hundred and fifty men, revived their hopes and prospects. At the end of twelve years the Colony contained only six hundred persons; but in 1619 the number was increased, by the arrival of eleven ships with twelve hundred and sixteen new settlers.

Many of the planters at this time were mere adventurers, not intending to make a stay in the country only long enough to make a fortune, and then return. In order to detain them in the country, an expedient was devised for supplying them with wives. (See similar instances under Romulus, page 329; Dido, page 324; and Interregnum, page 75.) In 1620–21 one hundred and fifty unmarried females, "young and uncorrupt," were brought over and sold to such as wished to purchase, for one hundred pounds of tobacco each. The price rose to one hundred and fifty pounds as the number grew less and the competition increased,—tobacco being seventy-five cents per pound. This *sale of wives* was simply to raise the passage-money.

About the same time, twenty negroes were carried to Virginia, in a Dutch vessel, and sold for slaves.

The Colony suffered from restrictions on its trade, under *Sir John Harvey*, and again, in 1676, under Charles II., which gave rise to "*Bacon's Rebellion*," in which Jamestown was burnt. (In 1776 another rebellion occurred in America, from "restrictions in trade.")

Henry Hudson.—He was an Englishman, and in 1609, while in the employment of the Dutch, discovered the river to which he gave his own name, *Hudson*. The first settlers on this river were Dutch. They built, in 1614, two forts—one at Albany, and another on Manhattan Island, where New York city now stands. The country was called *New Netherlands*, and Manhattan, "*New Amsterdam*." The government of Netherlands was administered by three governors—*Van Twiller*, *Kieft*, and *Stuyvesant*. In 1664, in a war between Charles II. of England, and Holland, the former gave New Amsterdam to his brother, the Duke of York, and Stuyvesant was obliged to surrender to *Colonel Nicholls*, commander of an English force, when the city and country were named *New York*.

PERIOD II. FROM THE LANDING OF THE PILGRIMS, 5624 A. M., AND 1620 A. C., TO THE ESTABLISHMENT OF THE INDEPENDENCE OF THE UNITED STATES, 5787 A. M., AND 1783 A. C.

PILGRIMS.

Upon the survey of the coast, in 1614, by *Captain Smith*, from Penobscot to Cape Cod,—a map of which he presented to King

Charles, — the name of the country was by him changed from *North Virginia* to *New England.*

In 1620 a patent was granted by King James to *Ferdinando Gorges*, Duke of Lenox, and others, styled "The Council of Plymouth, in the County of Devon, for Settling and Governing New England." In the same year a company set sail, September 6th, from Plymouth, England, in the *Mayflower*, for Hudson's River. But the captain was bribed to carry them farther north, when they landed upon the famous rock known by the name "Plymouth Rock," December 22, 1620. Their number was one hundred and one at first, but one was added by birth during the voyage. This colony of the Pilgrims was soon reduced almost one-half by sickness and death.

They adopted a Republican form of government, choosing *John Carver* their first governor, who, dying in 1621, was succeeded by *William Bradford.* The governor was chosen annually. At first he had one assistant, afterwards five, and finally seven. In order to protect themselves against the Indians, they formed a military organization, and appointed *Miles Standish* their captain. They learned the culture of Indian corn from *Squanto*, a native.

In 1621, they were visited by *Samoset*, a petty sachem, who saluted them with, "Welcome, Englishmen! welcome, Englishmen!" By his assistance a treaty of peace was formed with *Massasoit*, chief of the Wompanoags, the most powerful Indian chief of the region, and from whom the State of *Massachusetts* is named. This peace lasted fifty-four years, or until "King Philip's War."

NEW HAMPSHIRE. — In 1623 two settlements were begun, by persons from England, on the banks of the Piscataqua, — one at Portsmouth, the other at Dover.

NEW JERSEY. — The Dutch and Danes began settlements here in 1625.

DELAWARE. — A company of Swedes colonized it in 1627.

MASSACHUSETTS BAY. — A colony, with this title, was commenced in 1628, by a company of adventurers, under *John Endicott*, who settled at *Naumkeag*, now *Salem.*

In 1630, fifteen hundred persons arrived, under *John Winthrop*, who was appointed governor of the colony, and soon after they commenced the settlement of *Boston* and other towns near. Ten years after the first settlement of Massachusetts Bay, Harvard College, Cambridge, was founded.

CONNECTICUT. — The towns of Windsor, Weathersfield, and Hartford were settled in 1635, by emigrants from Newton and Watertown, in Massachusetts.

RHODE ISLAND. — This state dates its settlement from the banishment of Roger Williams, in 1636, from Massachusetts, on account of his *religious opinions.* He removed with his family to *Mooshawic,* and began a plantation, which place he named "*Providence,*" in gratitude for Divine favors.

MARYLAND. — In 1637, Charles I. granted a patent to Lord Baltimore, of a tract of country on the Chesapeake Bay, which, in honor of the king's wife, Henrietta Maria, he called Maryland.

. NEW HAVEN. — This colony was formed in 1638, in consequence of the English going thither to quell the invasions of the *Pequods.*

"UNITED COLONIES OF NEW ENGLAND." — For the better security of the settlements, against the depredations of the Indians, the colonies of Plymouth, Massachusetts Bay, Connecticut, and New Haven united in a confederacy, in 1643, with the above title.

This was but the foreshadowing of a more permanent union, against a more formidable enemy, which took place in 1776.

NORTH CAROLINA. — This state was first settled by Virginians, in 1663.

SOUTH CAROLINA. — The settlement of this state followed, in 1670. The Carolinas were so named from Charles IX., King of France, under whose patronage the coast was surveyed, in 1563.

KING PHILIP. — The war waged by this Indian chief, in the years 1675–76, was the most important and savage of all the colonies had to encounter. — Just one hundred years before the Revolution.

Philip was the son of Massasoit, and the last of the Wampanoags. He, seeing the growing power of the white men, resolved to make one desperate effort to snatch from their grasp his hunting-grounds, country, and liberty. His residence was at Mount Hope, Rhode Island. He was a man of talents and courage; shrewd in politics, and a great warrior. He succeeded in enlisting most of the New England tribes in his behalf.

The greatest battle of those early times was during this war, and known as the *Swamp Fight.* It took place in December, 1675, at the Indian fortress, situated in a large swamp, in the western part of the township now known as South Kingston, Rhode Island. The English were commanded by *Josiah Winslow,* Governor of Plymouth. They were victorious, but with great loss on both sides. This broke the Indian power in the country. Philip was afterwards shot by an Indian whom he had offended.

PENNSYLVANIA. — This state was early settled by Swedes; but little was done until the arrival of William Penn, in 1681, from whom it was named. Penn acquired this tract of land from Charles II., in consideration of debts due his father, Admiral Penn, from the Crown of England, for services rendered by him.

In 1682, he laid out the plan of the city of Philadelphia. In no case in the history of the world has there been a more perfect illustration of the good result of "doing to others as we would they should do unto us," than in Penn's policy with the Indians; showing the practicability of that law (when faith is kept) in the savage, as well as the civilized breast. In this case, Penn has far outdone the old Grecian sage, Lycurgus, who trained up the Spartans to the love and practice of war.

GEORGIA. — This was the last settled of the original thirteen states, and named after George II. It was founded by General Oglethorpe, in 1732.

Civil and religious intolerance drove a large portion of the first settlers of our country from their homes, and they sought here and found what there they desired but were denied. Rhode Island, Maryland, and Pennsylvania were the first civil communities that ever incorporated religious liberty into their original constitutions; since which time, the world has been led to admit the wisdom and sound policy of such a course. No country on record ever was colonized with so great a degree of intelligence and virtue, and with so just views, in the main, of the proper sphere of organized civil government as America.

COLONIES OPPRESSED. — The sovereigns of England, who were of the despotic *Stuart family*, during the settlement of the colonies, were not satisfied with driving their subjects into the wilderness, but even there must lay upon them the iron rod of power. Anxious as were the colonists to secure charters to their new homes, from their sovereigns, thereby showing their respect and loyalty to the Crown, they began soon to see that their rights and privileges all lay in the hands of these rulers far away, and unless they rendered the most servile and implicit obedience, they would be stripped of those grants, robbed of their toils, and made homeless.

Soon it was known that secret emissaries were going to and fro, seeking every possible occasion to prejudice the king and council against the colonists. The most notorious agent in this traitorous business was *Edward* Randolph, sent over to America by Charles II., in 1676, to spy out the liberties of the land. He boasted that *he had crossed the Atlantic sixteen times in nine years, for the chief purpose of destroying the liberties of New England!* He succeeded at last, and a writ was issued against the charters of the colonies, in 1683.

Sir Edmund Andros, Governor of New York, was also appointed, by James II., Governor of New England. He arrived in Boston in 1686, and summoned the colonies to surrender their charters. That of Massachusetts was given up; but that of Connecticut was concealed by Captain *Wadsworth* in the hollow of an *oak* in *Hartford*. Sir Edmund put on the lion, and ruled in America as James did in England. But James' despotism in England drove him from the throne, and he fled to France. The news of the Revolution of 1688, and the accession of William and Mary, were hailed with ecstasy in America.

Upon this, Sir Edmund, Randolph, and fifty others, were seized by the inhabitants of Boston, and imprisoned until they were ordered back to England for trial. Connecticut and Rhode Island resumed their charters, and reëstablished their former government. Massachusetts Bay people petitioned for a new charter, which was at first refused, but finally granted, in 1692, in which Plymouth and the "Bay" colonies were united, and Maine and Nova Scotia annexed. In the old charter the public officers were chosen by the people, but in the new, appointed by the Crown. But, to make it palatable, *Sir William Phips*, a native of Maine, was appointed the first governor.

War of the French and Indians. — No sooner had the colonies obtained a little repose about their titles and lands, than a war of almost twenty-five years' duration broke out, — the French and Indians uniting to harass them. This war occurred during the reigns of *William and Mary* and *Anne*, — between 1688 and 1713.

These were the most gloomy and devastating wars the colonies had yet experienced. During these wars in the colonies of New England and New York, eight thousand of the young men, the flower of the country, fell, either by the sword, or by diseases contracted in the public service. Deep mourning, for the lost and captive, shrouded nearly every family in the country.

These depredations by the French upon the English colonies were committed out of revenge for the war England was waging against France, which were terminated by the Peace of *Utrecht*, in 1713.

Old French War. — From 1713 to 1744 the colonies had a term of comparative peace; after which, another war broke out between Great Britain and France.

The first and most important step by the colonies in this war, was the capture of *Louisburg* — on the Island of Cape Breton — by troops from New England, under command of *Sir William Pepperell*. This important place the French had rendered the *Dunkirk*, or *Gibraltar*, of America, by fortifying it at an expense of six millions of dollars. Its capture was of no small importance to the interests of New England.

General Pepperell arrived at Canso, Nova Scotia, with four thousand and seventy troops, April 4, 1745, and, in three weeks was joined by *Commodore Warren*, with four ships from England. The siege was soon after commenced, and continued until June 16, when Louisburg and the Island of Cape Breton were surrendered to the English. The news of this victory greatly elated the spirits of the colonists, and inspired them with a desire to conquer all the French possessions in North America. The French government was also aroused to retrieve their losses, and have revenge. Consequently, an ("Armada") armament, under Duke d'Anville, was sent out, consisting of eleven ships of the line, and thirty smaller vessels of war, besides transports, with three thousand regular troops, and forty thousand stand of arms for the French and Indians. The design was to retake Louisburg, and distress, and perhaps conquer, New England.

The colonists were alarmed at the news of the sailing of this fleet, but were relieved of their fears by the destruction by storms of nearly the whole of it, and the suicide of one or both of the commanders. So that, without the aid of human means, the expedition was wholly frustrated. But, at the Peace of *Aix-la-Chapelle*, Louisburg was given up to France, in 1748, to the great mortification of the colonists.

The French, upon being discoverers of the Mississippi River, based a claim to the country watered by it and its tributaries; and, during the last peace, they made great efforts to connect Louisburg and New Orleans by a line of military posts, up the St. Lawrence to Lake Ontario, thence to the Ohio River, down it, and the Mississippi.

Some persons belonging to England and Virginia, known as the *Ohio Company*, holding a tract of land, obtained by grant from the king, of six hundred thousand acres, for the purpose of settlement and fur trading with the Indians, were molested, and .some of them carried prisoners to Canada. The company made complaint of the French aggressions to the Virginia authorities, and Governor *Robert Dinwiddie* laid the case before the council of the colony, and they determined to demand, in the name of the king, that the French should desist from such intrusions upon their rights. Accordingly, *George Washington*, then twenty-one past, was sent to make this demand of *M. de St. Pierre*, the French commandant on the Ohio, who replied, that he had acted according to orders. First comes firm remonstrance, then brave resistance.

The British government next had the matter under consideration, and directed the Americans not to make *demands*, but to resist the French by force of arms. Troops were raised throughout the colonies; land and naval forces were sent from England against *Nova Scotia*, *Crown Point*, and *Niagara*. Another expedition was sent against *Fort du Quesne*, commanded by *General Braddock*, who had two regiments of English soldiers, and a body of colonial troops under Colonel Washington, in all about twelve hundred men.

Unaccustomed to ambush warfare, Braddock exposed his soldiers to be cut off uselessly, by insisting upon their fighting in platoons. A suggestion from Washington, to allow the soldiers to cover themselves by the trees, and play back upon the enemy, in their own way, was treated by him with contempt; saying, to the effect, that a British general had not come to America *to learn military tactics of a Virginia colonel.* But Braddock soon found that British generals *were not too good to be shot.* He was killed, and Washington took the command, but the defeat was such that a retreat was necessary. Washington had two horses killed under him, and four balls penetrated his coat.

The expedition against *Crown Point* failed, with the exception of a battle on the banks of Lake George, between *General Johnson* and the French, under *Dieskau*, the latter being defeated, mortally wounded, and eight hundred men killed. The one against *Niagara* was delayed and abandoned.

This informal warfare, which had now been carried on for two years, was declared in 1756. During this and the next year, no laurels were won by either party. *Marquis de Montcalm* succeeded Dieskau in command of the French, and the *Earl of Loudon*, and afterwards *General Abercrombie*, had the command of the British troops.

A change occurring in the British ministry, placed *William Pitt* at the head of the administration, when affairs assumed a vigorous turn. Being popular in America, Pitt had the fortune to arouse the spirits of the American generals to energetic action, by promises of efficient aid from England being sent them. Three expeditions were next proposed. The *first* was against *Louisburg*, with a land force of fourteen thousand men, commanded by *General Amherst*, and *General Wolfe* second in command, and a naval armament, under *Admiral Boscawen.* The place was again taken from the French. The *second* was against *Ticonderoga*, under Abercrombie, but was a failure; he was repulsed, with a loss of two thousand men. The *third* expedition was against *Fort du Quesne*, under *General Forbes*, who took the place, and changed its name to *Pitts*-burg, in honor of *Pitt.*

Another campaign was proposed in 1759, having for its object the entire conquest of Canada. The British army was divided into three parts, and destined to three points, — *General Amherst* to *Ticonderoga* and *Crown Point*, which he found evacuated; *Prideaux* was sent against *Niagara*, which the English took, but Prideaux fell three days before the conquest; *Wolfe* was sent against *Quebec.* Landing on the island of Orleans, below the city, he made some ineffectual attempts to take it. He resolved, finally, to attempt the marshalling of his troops for battle on the *Plains of Abraham*, behind the city, where it was the least defensible. This bold design he effected in the night, by scaling the steep banks, and, before *Montcalm* was aware of it, Wolfe, with his whole army of eight thousand men, was in battle array. Montcalm, with ten thousand men, was confident of success, and so hazarded a battle outside the walls of the city. A hot battle ensued, in which the French were entirely defeated, losing fifteen hundred men and their four principal commanders; the English losing five hundred men and their two first officers. *Wolfe* and *Montcalm* were both mortally wounded. With this victory followed the cession of all the French possessions in America, in the *Peace of Paris*, 1763. This gave the colonies rest from the annoying wars with the French and Indians.

Revolutionary War. — The prospect of peace and thrift were never brighter for any people than for the American colonists at the close of the "French War." They had but to hold and enjoy what their valor and industry had acquired. With no contending nations near to molest, well might they look for a "good time coming."

But, alas! never was there a people, no, never! more terribly disappointed than they were. For, after fleeing hither, that they might enjoy freedom of worship, they found, as their religion taught them, that "a man's foes are they of his own house."

The wars waged by England in behalf of the colonies, had greatly augmented the national debt; and, upon this consideration, was based that *bitter project* of taxing the *Colonies* to indemnify the mother country. The colonists replied, that Great Britain had a large personal interest in the war; she had the monopoly of the commerce of the colonies; that the achievements of the wars were of mutual advantage; and that the colonies had made greater exertions, according to their ability, to secure the present advantages than had England. They claimed, above all, their rights as English subjects: one of which was, that no subject could be deprived of his property without his own consent, expressed in person, or by his representatives.

The British Parliament maintained the *right* to tax the colonies; the latter denied that right. *Mr. Grenville*, the prime minister, proposed to Parliament, in 1764, a resolution, — "That it would be proper to impose certain stamp duties on the colonies." Early in the next year, the *Stamp Act* was passed, laying a tax on all paper used for writing deeds, notes, etc., and all contracts on unstamped materials to be null and void.

The Virginia Assembly being in session at the time the news of the passage of this Act arrived, took position against it immediately, in a number of spirited resolutions brought forward by *Patrick Henry*. At the same time, Massachusetts, before what was done in Virginia was known, had adopted measures to procure a combined opposition against the offensive measures. When the news of the *Stamp Act* arrived in Boston, bells were muffled, and rang a funeral peal. The *crown officers* were insulted, and various demonstrations of resistance were made. The *Act* was hawked about the streets of New York, with a Death's head affixed to it, and styled, "The Folly of England, and the Ruin of America." The merchants resolved to import no more goods from England, until the Act was repealed. The colonies had not forgotten the advice England gave the "Ohio Company," when *St. Pierre* oppressed them, which was, "*to resist the French by force of arms.*"

A *Colonial Congress* (similar to the United Colonies of New England, in 1643, to resist the Indians), appointed by nine of the colonies, assembled at New York (now to resist England), in 1765, and published a declaration of rights and grievances, insisting particularly upon the *exclusive* right of taxing themselves, and complaining loudly of the Stamp Act. Indeed, so determined was the opposition to it by all classes, that it was *never* enforced.

By a change made in the British cabinet, Pitt and others procured the repeal of the *Stamp Act*, in March 1766. But the repeal was prefaced by a clause, declaring that Parliament "*had, and of right ought to have, power to bind the colonies in all cases whatsoever!*" Thus the sentiments of the Colonial Congress and the British Parliament were in direct antagonism to each other. Who shall yield?

The favorite project of *taxing the colonies* was persisted in by the British ministry, notwithstanding the opposition of the colonies, and the loud warnings of Pitt and others. In June 1767, an act was passed by Parliament, imposing a duty on *tea*, *paper*, *glass*, and *painters' colors*; and, in order to carry it into effect, a Custom House was established in Boston, and a Board of Commissioners appointed for the colonies, and in 1768 two regiments of soldiers arrived in town to enforce the measure, and all who resisted in Massachusetts were to be sent to England for trial.

At these insolent measures of intimidation, the people were in the highest degree indignant. And soon quarrels began to occur between the soldiers and the populace, until, on the fifth of March, 1770, a collision took place before the Custom House, when the sentinel stationed there was insulted and threatened. *Captain Preston* hastened to the spot with soldiers to support the sentinel. He endeavored to persuade the people to disperse, but the excitement increased, until a soldier, who had been struck, fired on the multitude, his comrades following suit. Four persons were killed and several wounded. A trial ensued, when Captain Preston and his men were all cleared except two — who were found guilty of manslaughter — by a Boston jury. Samuel Adams was counsel.

At this juncture, or in 1770, news arrived that, through the influence of *Lord North*, all duties were repealed, except *threepence* per pound on *tea*. By this measure the British ministry intended to establish the *right* to tax the colonies. That was the point at issue. Neither party were tenacious about the *mode* or *extent* of taxation, but both were pertinaciously in earnest to press the question of *right* to tax.

The *East India Company*, getting into want for funds, applied to Parliament for relief, complaining that their embarrassments were owing to the disturbances in America, by which their teas had accumulated in their warehouses to the amount of seventeen millions of pounds, for the want of a market. Upon this showing, the ministry were left to choose between the alternatives of *pleasing* the company and *provoking* the colonies, by relieving the *East Indies* and oppressing the *West Indies*, or do the other way.

In November 1773, news arrived that three ships were on their way to Boston, loaded with *East India tea, to be sold at threepence a pound, tax, in Boston.* Other ships were sent with tea to New York and Philadelphia. The merchants knew that if the cargoes were landed, the sale of the tea would be inevitable; hence they resolved to prevent if possible the ships being unloaded. Those bound to New York and Philadelphia were sent back to England; but those sent to Boston were detained in the harbor, though the captains of those ships would have gladly returned also.

A meeting of the citizens of Boston voted to refuse permission to discharge the tea. Here was a tight case. The governor would not permit a clearance from the Custom House to be granted for them to depart, and, further, the *guns* at Castle William would not permit their passing out of the harbor. What then? The tea must surely go to (the tea-) pot, *if the people would not let it land, and the governor would not let it depart!* The adjourned town-meeting met December sixteenth, considered the case, and dissolved. In the evening, however, a company of *Mohawk Indians* (?) boarded the ships, and, in two hours, emptied into the harbor tea amounting in value to ninety thousand dollars! So the governor had his way, and the people theirs.

In 1774, the British Parliament chose to retaliate, rather than conciliate, and so passed the "Boston Port Bill," forbidding all ships landing at Boston, except those in His Majesty's service, until the king was satisfied that good order and obedience to the laws were restored, and the East India Company *indemnified.*

In May, *General Gage* arrived in Boston, as commander-in-chief of the British forces in North America. Shortly after, two regiments landed, with artillery and military stores. These movements indicated to the colonists that they had either got to fight or submit.

The last fatal measure adopted by the British ministry, among other things, was annulling the charter of the Massachusetts Bay Colony. The people declared that if they had *violated* the charter, measures of redress should be taken against them. But if the charter, which was the only bond of union between them and the king, was dissolved, they were set free from their allegiance, and from that moment the king could no longer reign over them, unless conquered by his armies. The colonists now saw clearly that they must assume and maintain their independence by force of arms, or make an unconditional surrender of their liberties to the tyrants of their father-land.

Upon this, a Committee of Correspondence was formed by distinguished men in Massachusetts, who entered into an agreement, called the "*Solemn League and Covenant,*" the purport of which was, to suspend all intercourse with Great Britain, until their rights should be respected. The General Court of Massachusetts resolved that a Congress of the Colonies was demanded; they also enrolled a body of men, to be prepared to march at any minute, and so called "minute-men;" appointed five general-officers to command them; formed a committee of safety; and set about collecting military stores at Concord and Worcester.

The plan for assembling a *Congress* was speedily adopted by all the Colonies, except Georgia; and, on the fifth of September, 1774, the delegates met at Philadelphia. This was no "*Rump*" *parliament*, but known as the *Continental Congress.* They chose *Peyton Randolph*, President, and *Charles Thomson*, Secretary. It was composed of fifty-five members, with heart and ability to do what was required of them. Addresses were sent to the king, to the people of Great Britain, and to the Colonies, setting forth their grievances, desires for reconciliation, and, if need be, the ultimate mode of redress. These able state-papers were highly applauded in the British Parliament by Pitt (Lord Chatham), Burke, and others, who sympathized with the Colonies. The almost infinite disparity between England and the Colonies in ability to wage war, made their cause one of the utmost contempt in the estimation of a domineering ministry, and they confidently expected the "Boston Rebellion" would be easily and speedily crushed.

When the proceedings of the Continental Congress were laid before the British Parliament, in 1775, a joint address of both Houses was presented to the king, declaring that a rebellion *actually existed* in Massachusetts, and beseeching his majesty to suppress it. The army in Boston was increased to ten thousand, which was deemed sufficient to reduce the rebellious Colonies to submission.

The last parliamentary salve that was used, was a *conciliatory proposition*, by Lord North, which was to the effect, that whenever the Colonies would contribute their proportion for the common defence, and for the support of their own civil government, England would refrain from taxing them. But this very "refraining" indicated the *right* to tax, which was the very point in dispute, and hence only irritated the sore, instead of healing it.

Affairs had now come into so excited a condition that bloodshed was the next event looked for. This expectation was realized in the execution of the order of *General Gage*, who sent troops, under *Colonel Smith* and *Major Pitcairn*, to *seize* some military stores at Concord. The march, though in the night, was discovered, and early in the morning of April 19, 1775, as they passed through Lexington, about seventy "minute-men" of that town were found on the Common, under arms.

Pitcairn rode up to them, and cried out, "Disperse, you rebels! throw down your arms and disperse!" The insulted and indignant freemen being slow to obey the little minion of despotism, he discharged his pistol, flourished his sword, and ordered his troops to fire. *They* obeyed him, *and eight Americans were killed, and several wounded.* This was the first oblation on the altar of Freedom.

Proceeding to Concord, a few military stores were there destroyed, and another encounter was had between the troops and the militia of the town, under Mr. John Butterworth. During the retreat of the troops, the "minute-men" harassed them nearly every *minute* until they reached Boston. Of the troops sixty-five were killed, and one hundred and eighty wounded. Of the Americans fifty were killed, and thirty-four wounded.

The ball was now in motion, and war was inevitable. A large body of American soldiers was collected near Boston; an additional number soon arrived from Connecticut, under General Putnam.

(Besides the story of Putnam and the Wolf, there is another told of him and a British officer. The latter being on a visit to the American camp, conversation turned upon bravery. Putnam proposed a test of this quality with the Britisher. Two powder-kegs were brought, and each was to sit upon one, and a slow match to be applied, and the one who should hold out the longer should be the bravo. As the fatal fire drew near, the officer said: "Putnam, this is murder in cold blood!" Putnam replied: "Oh, no; the kegs are only filled with *onion-seed!*")

An expedition was sent to *Ticonderoga* and *Crown Point*, in order to close against the British, as early as possible, that inlet to the Colonies, by Quebec. This was done in that memorable surrender of Ticonderoga to the intrepid *Ethan Allen.* Taking the commandant by surprise, while in his bed, early on the morning of the tenth of May, demanded of him the surrender of the fort. "In whose name?" said he. "In the name of the Great Jehovah and the Continental Congress!" said Allen.

The Provincial Congress of Massachusetts had before this despatched an account of the affair at Lexington to England, with depositions showing that the soldiers were the first aggressors, declared their loyalty to the Crown, but protested against the tyranny of the British ministry; and, after "appealing to Heaven for the justice of their cause, rather than submit, we will die, or be free!"

On the tenth of May (the day Ticonderoga was taken) the Continental Congress met, for the first time, in Philadelphia. Randolph being absent, John Hancock was placed in the chair. The Colonies had responded very promptly in sending in delegates to make up this body. At this time they assumed the title of "*United Colonies.*" The Congress also recommended a day of humiliation, to implore the blessing of Heaven on their sovereign, the King of Great Britain, and the interposition of Divine aid to remove their grievances and restore harmony between the parent State and the Colonies, on constitutional terms. At the same time recommended to the Colonies to collect saltpetre and sulphur, and manufacture powder, and raise troops, for the colonial service. (Similar to Cromwell's advice to his soldiers. Said he: "Men, trust in God, and keep your powder dry!")

Towards the end of May, reinforcements of British troops arrived in Boston, also *Generals Howe, Burgoyne*, and *Clinton*, and martial law was proclaimed. A show of clemency was made, however, by *General Gage*, in an offer of pardon, in the king's name, to all who would return to their allegiance, except *John Hancock* and *Samuel Adams* — the former, President of the Congress then in session.

On the fifteenth of June, the Congress, having resolved on measures of defence, proceeded to organize a Continental army. A point of immense importance now arose: that of selecting a suitable commander-in-chief. Fortunately they were unanimous in the choice of a man distinguished for his perseverance, prudence, bravery, good judgment, elevation of character, and purity of motives; who proved himself to be truly the "Fabius, or sword and shield," of American liberty. Such an one was *General George Washington*.

The activity of the friends of liberty in the vicinity of Boston was such, that they determined to annoy, and if possible dislodge the British from that place. Accordingly, a detachment of one thousand men, under command of *Colonel Prescott*, was ordered, on the sixteenth of June, to throw up a breastwork on *Bunker Hill*, in Charlestown. So expeditiously did they carry out the order, that by daylight next morning the redoubt was nearly completed. In the morning they were reinforced by five hundred men.

About four in the morning of the seventeenth of June, the American works were discovered by the captain of the *Lively*, sloop-of-war, lying in Charles River, who instantly began a heavy cannonade upon them, and was soon joined by the other ships, the *Falcon*, *Somerset*, and *Glasgow*, and by a battery on *Copp's Hill*, in Boston. Under a shower of balls and bombs, the Americans continued their work, and lost only one man during the morning. But, about noon, a detachment of troops from Boston, under Generals Howe and Pigot, was landed near the point of the peninsula. But, seeing the strength of the American position, reinforcements were sent for. By this time the steeples, roofs of houses, hills, etc., were covered with excited spectators, awaiting the action.

At the signal, *General Howe* advanced, at the head of three thousand men, to attack the American works. The latter had orders to reserve their fire until they could see the white of the eyes of the enemy, when they poured such a tremendous volley of bullets into the breasts of the British, as to make them recoil under it, and fall into disorder. A rally was made, and a second repulse followed. But, at this critical moment, *General Clinton* (who, with other officers, stood on Copp's Hill, viewing the scene) arrived, and succeeded in rallying the British to a third attack. At this time they entered the American lines with fixed bayonets. The colonists, having used up their ammunition, and having only common fire-arms, were unable to resist a greater number of well-armed soldiery, and were compelled to retreat.

The British lost one thousand and fifty-four men, — eight hundred and twenty-eight wounded, two hundred and twenty-six killed, — among whom was Pitcairn. The Americans lost four hundred and fifty-three, — thirty-six missing, two hundred and seventy-eight wounded, one hundred and thirty-nine killed; among the latter, General Warren, who hastened to the field as a volunteer. Being seen by a British officer — and a personal acquaintance too — to rally his men in the retreat, the officer snatched a musket, took deliberate aim, fired, and Warren fell, greatly lamented by his countrymen. Thus ended the celebrated Battle of Bunker Hill, June 17, 1775.

On the second of July, General Washington arrived in Charlestown, the head-quarters of the Colonial army.

In pursuance of a plan for guarding the frontiers, an expedition was sent against Canada, to wrest it from the British Crown. Montgomery, having taken Forts *Chamblee* and *St. John's*, advanced to *Montreal*, which surrendered without resistance. He then directed his march for Quebec, where he was joined by General Arnold, with a detachment of one thousand men, who, with incredible suffering, had come through the wilderness from Cambridge, by way of the Kennebec River. They made a desperate effort to carry the city by assault, but were repulsed, with a loss of four hundred killed, among whom was the gallant Montgomery. In the spring, Canada was evacuated.

During the year 1775, the royal Governors of Virginia, North and South Carolina, so demeaned themselves that they were obliged to yield to the people, and vacate their offices. Thus royalty began to bow. In October, General Gage left for England, when the chief command of the British forces devolved upon *Sir William Howe.*

Washington's determination now was, to drive the British from Boston. Already there were fifteen thousand men, belonging to the American army, investing the city, and his plan was, a direct attack upon Boston; but a Council of War advised occupying *Dorchester Heights.* This concluded upon, a brisk cannonade was commenced upon the city, in order to divert attention from the work on the *heights.* At the same time, a detachment was sent to throw up a fortification. So incessantly did they labor, that in the morning they had cast up two forts, and other defences, making a formidable show, and drawing from Howe the remark, "that the Americans had done more in one night, than his whole army would have done in a month." He determined to make an attack upon them, but a severe storm and heavy rain prevented him.

General Howe, feeling conscious that the position on the heights was too strong to be carried, saw no alternative for him but to evacuate the town. Accordingly, on the morning of Sunday, the 17th of

March, 1776, the troops, seven thousand in number, and some hundreds of loyal inhabitants, began to embark. As the last of the British were leaving Boston, Washington marched into it, — its deliverer from the oppressions of a British soldiery, — amidst the acclamations of the people.

The news of the battle of Bunker Hill excited astonishment in England; but neither this nor the swaying eloquence of *Pitt*, *Burke*, and *Fox*, could turn the wanton purpose of the ministry to prosecute the war. Soon an act of Parliament was passed, authorizing the employment of sixteen thousand mercenaries, the troops of the *Landgrave of Hesse*, Duke of Brunswick. Trade with the Colonies was suspended, and their ships forfeited to those who should take them.

The contest with the Colonies began about constitutional rights, not for separation; but as a steady course of oppression had been pursued up to the present time, a final rupture was seriously entertained. At this juncture, the writings of Thomas Paine, published under the signature of *Common Sense*, setting forth the necessity of separation from England, did much in preparing the public mind for such a serious step.

On the seventh of June, 1776, a motion was made in Congress, by *Richard Henry Lee*, of Virginia, for declaring the Colonies *free and independent.* A committee was accordingly appointed to prepare a Declaration of Independence, consisting of *Jefferson*, *Adams*, *Franklin*, *Sherman*, and *Livingston*, and, after a full discussion, the question was carried by a vote nearly unanimous, on the memorable *fourth of July*, 1776.

After stating their grievances, this memorable and almost unequalled instrument, the Declaration, concludes thus: "We, therefore, the Representatives of the *United States of America*, in General Congress assembled, appealing to the Supreme Judge of the world for the rectitude of our intentions, do, in the name and by the authority of the good people of these Colonies, solemnly publish and declare, that these united Colonies are, and of right ought to be, *Free and Independent States*; that they are absolved from all allegiance to the British Crown, and that all political connection between them and the State of Great Britain is, and ought to be, totally dissolved; and that as free and independent states, they have full power to levy war, conclude peace, contract alliances, establish commerce, and to do all other acts and things which independent states ought to do.

"And for the support of this declaration, with a firm reliance on the protection of Divine Providence, we mutually pledge to each other our lives, our fortunes, and our sacred honor."

Each of the members of Congress signed this great charter of American Liberty. Thomas Jefferson is its reputed author.

From this time the state of affairs wore a different aspect. No more petitions to the Crown; no more avowal of loyalty; no more laying down of arms on condition of redresses being granted, and no more complaints against a tyrannical ministry; but the assumption of national dignity, national rights, and the treatment of Great Britain as a mighty, insolent, and despotic foe; and all her armies, fleets, and minions just objects of defeat, capture, and imprisonment, until she will pledge herself. in good faith, to sign and maintain an honorable peace.

Washington anticipated the purpose of the British in leaving Boston, which was to take possession of New York, and towards that place he directed his movements. Howe, after having lain at Halifax a while to recruit his army, arrived off Sandy Hook, and was soon after joined by his brother, Admiral Lord Howe, with a large naval force. The British force now amounted to thirty thousand, and Washington's to only seventeen thousand.

Having authority to make peace, Lord Howe addressed a letter on the subject to *George Washington, Esq.* Taking this as a personal insult, as well as to the Congress that bestowed his title as *General*, and indeed to the whole cause of the Colonies, Washington returned the letter without opening it. Soon after, another came, addressed *George Washington*, etc., etc. This he refused, until his proper rank should be acknowledged. Howe had to bow, as his brother had to leave Boston.

On the twenty-seventh of August a battle ensued, between *Brooklyn* and *Flatbush*. The Americans, under Putnam, being poorly armed and disciplined, and opposed by a superior number of equipped and trained soldiery, were defeated. Loss, two thousand.

On October twenty-eighth another engagement took place, on *White Plains*, in which Washington commanded, and was defeated by Howe, leaving New York, Long Island, and Staten Island in the power of the British. Washington then made his splendid retreat across the Hudson, though New Jersey, by Newark, New Brunswick, Princeton, and Trenton, thence across the Delaware into Pennsylvania, being pursued so closely by the British, under Lord Cornwallis, that the Americans had but just got across when the British arrived on the opposite shore.

This was a dark hour to the cause of liberty; and, at this time, Howe proclaimed a pardon to all who would return to their allegiance. Many complied, which made the case still worse. The future was dark and unpromising, though Washington remained firm.

On the twelfth of December, 1776, Congress removed from Philadelphia to Baltimore; but in every hour, dark and light, they remained firm, and supported Washington to the utmost of their power. About this time, commissioners were sent to France to seek sympathy in the struggle for independence.

Washington, aware of the importance of making some decided measure tell upon the cause, so as to give it a name abroad, and raise the drooping spirits of the people, planned an attack upon the British forces. Finding that they were widely scattered about for winter quarters, "Now," said he, "is the time to clip their wings, while they are spread so wide." So, on the night of the twenty-fifth of December, 1776, he conducted a portion of his army across the Delaware, about nine miles from Trenton, fell upon the Hessians quartered there, and forced one thousand of them to surrender. *Rahl*, their commander, was slain; besides, a large quantity of arms and ammunition was secured.

This victory astonished the British, elated the colonists, gave their cause popularity in Europe, and was the entering-wedge of the war. It is said that Rahl, the Hessian commander, had a letter sent him, informing him of the plan of Washington; but, being engaged at the time in a game of cards, neglected to open the letter, and thereby lost his life, and left open the gap through which American Liberty escaped the clutches of Tyranny. (In the same negligent way *Achias* lost Thebes, and Julius Cæsar his life and the Roman Empire.)

At this very period of darkness, Congress took an important step in advance, by forming "Articles of Confederation" between the states. Also, by increasing the power of Washington, giving him supreme command; by raising an army, and enlisting them for three years, and during the war, with prospective grants of land, etc., and by arousing the energies of the people, and seeking foreign aid.

General Howe's next attempt was to get possession of Philadelphia, which he succeeded in doing after repulsing the Americans, under Washington, at *Brandywine*, where they gave a brave resistance, September eleventh. Before superior numbers, discipline, and equipments they yielded, with a loss of one thousand in all. Among the wounded was *Marquis de Lafayette.*

In the spring of 1777, an army of invasion was sent up the St. Lawrence from England, under *General Burgoyne.* In June he arrived in Lake Champlain, with a force of nine thousand men.

Ticonderoga was abandoned. He then went to Skeensborough (Whitehall), and destroyed some American flotilla and stores, and thence marched to Fort Edward, on the Hudson. From thence he sent a detachment, under *Baum*, to destroy a collection of stores at *Bennington*, Vermont. On August sixteenth, General Stark, with eight hundred Vermont and New Hampshire militia, killed and took most of them prisoners. The next day a reïnforcement arrived, of five hundred, under *Colonel Breyman*, which met the same fate.

(During these operations occurred the tragedy of Miss Jane McCrea.)

Burgoyne then removed his forces and stores to *Saratoga*. *General Gates*, who had recently taken the command of the American army in the northern department, advanced towards Saratoga. On September nineteenth, an obstinate but indecisive battle was fought at *Stillwater*. Soon after, another battle was fought, of a more decisive character. Burgoyne became entangled, with the Hudson on one side, a deep wood on the other, and the Americans before and behind him. Finding himself hemmed in, he called a Council of War, which advised to capitulate; when Burgoyne, with five thousand seven hundred and fifty-two men, besides the sick and wounded, surrendered themselves as prisoners of war to General Gates, October 17, 1777. This victory was a cause of great joy to the Americans, and decided France in forming an alliance with them, through the negotiations of *Dr. Franklin*, *Silas Dean*, and *Arthur Lee*, sent out for that purpose.

In the opening of the campaign of 1778, General Howe returned to England, and the chief command of the British forces devolved upon *Sir Henry Clinton*.

The French fleet, of twelve ships, under Count d' Estang, arrived in July, but nothing decisive was accomplished.

In 1779, *Tryon* plundered New Haven, and burnt *Fairfield* and *Norwalk*. Stony Point was also taken, in July of the same year, by *General Wayne*. General Prevost also undertook the capture of Charleston, but failed. The Americans, assisted by Count d' Estang, were repulsed in an attack upon *Savannah*, which was defended by Prevost; at which battle *Count Pulaski*, a Polish officer in the American service, was killed.

In 1780, *Clinton* attacked and took Charleston. Leaving about four thousand troops for the southern service, under *Lord Cornwallis*, he returned to New York.

General Gates was appointed to command the American army South. An engagement took place between him and Cornwallis, at Camden, August sixteenth, in which Gates was defeated; and in it *Baron de Kalb*, a Prussian officer in the American service, and second in command, fell.

As the result of a visit of *Lafayette* to France, a French fleet arrived in July, with six thousand troops, under command of *Count de Rochambeau*, for the American service. At this time a great depression in the means and hopes of the Continentals prevailed; but this arrival revived and strengthened them.

The tragedy of the Revolution was the attempt of *General Benedict Arnold* to betray the fortress of *West Point*, on the Hudson, into the hands of the British, assisted by *Major André*, the agent of the enemy. Arnold had already distinguished himself at Quebec and Saratoga, being wounded at both places. But in the performance of some of his duties at Philadelphia, he was so oppressive as to require a court-martial to investigate the matter. The decision of the court was, that he should be reprimanded. Exasperated at this, he vowed revenge. But Washington, not suspecting his intentions, entrusted him with the important command of West Point. Arnold soon after entered into a negotiation with General Clinton for the surrender of the post.

Arnold requested Clinton to send him a confidential agent, with whom a final arrangement could be made. The otherwise highly esteemed *Major André* was intrusted with this secret and dangerous undertaking.

The *Vulture* sloop-of-war had been placed at a respectful distance from West Point, by Sir Henry Clinton, soon after Arnold's appointment to the command. To this sloop-of-war Arnold sent a boat on the night of the twenty-first of September, 1780, which brought André back, when he was met on the bank of the river by Arnold.

Their interview lasted until break of day, when it was deemed prudent that André should remain concealed over the day, and return in the following night. Next night the boatmen refused to carry him back, because the *Vulture* had moved off a little, in order to get out of the reach of a cannon that had been mounted to annoy her.

Poor André had now to seek escape by land. Shifting his uniform, and taking a passport from Arnold to go to *White Plains, on public business*, he passed the American lines without difficulty, and confidently hoped all danger was passed. But, in a moment when he thought not of it, three men suddenly sprang from a covert, and one of them seized his horse by the bridle. Losing his presence of mind just long enough to betray himself, he asked permission to pass as a *British officer*, supposing them to be scouts of the British army. But, as it proved, it was a party Arnold himself had sent out to scour the country between the outposts of the two armies. Discovering his mistake, he then offered them a large purse of gold for his release. This the men refused, since his anxiety, from conflicting reasons, was so great to get at liberty again.

He was now taken before Colonel Jamieson, the commander of the scout, and made himself known as *John Anderson.* Though short-sighted for himself, André had the presence of mind to request permission to notify Arnold of his capture, thereby putting him on his guard for his own safety. After the message had gone sufficiently long not to be overtaken, André avowed his true name. Thus, Arnold's own scout prevented the loss of the fort, but ruined him.

André was tried by a board of officers, who, from the fact that he had been within their lines in disguise, declared him to be a spy, and ought to suffer death. The next day, October 2d, the sentence was executed, to the grief of both the American and British armies. Arnold had previously fled for safety to the sloop *Vulture.* He was after appointed brigadier-general in the British army.

In the autumn of 1780, General Green was appointed to the command of the army in the South, instead of General Gates.

In January 1781, *Arnold,* with about fifteen hundred men, committed wanton depredations in Virginia.

A battle between *Greene* and *Cornwallis,* at Guilford Court House, was fought on the 15th of March; — indecisive, except the British held the field. Greene then marched to *Camden,* against *Lord Rawdon.* He sallied out upon Greene, and, though a loss about equal on both sides, the British had the advantage. In September, General Greene gained a decisive victory at *Eutaw Springs,* over *Colonel Stuart,* the British losing about one thousand, the Americans five hundred and fifty. This was about the last of the war in South Carolina.

After the battle at Guilford, *Lord Cornwallis* proceeded to *Virginia,* to join the British army under General Philips; and, arriving at Petersburg, in May, he took the command of the united forces. After some unimportant manœuvres, he encamped with his army on York River, near *Yorktown* and *Gloucester Point.* Here he fortified himself, as he thought wisely, little knowing what awaited him.

Washington, Knox, Rochambeau, and other officers, had planned for combined operations against the British before this; but now, seeing Cornwallis' position at Yorktown, they thought it was time to make the effort. Word was designedly given out to the effect, that New York was to be the point of attack, for the purpose of directing the attention of the Middle and Eastern states away from him, and so deceive Sir Henry Clinton as to prevent his sending timely aid to Cornwallis. Washington wrote letters to General Greene and others, and contrived to have them intercepted by the British, which had the desired effect.

Washington, having gotten all attention directed to New York, suddenly quitted White Plains, crossed the Hudson, and, with his army, pushed on rapidly through New Jersey and Pennsylvania, and arrived at Elk River, the head-quarters of a considerable army under *Lafayette*. From here a part of the army embarked and sailed for Virginia, and a part marched by land.

Clinton, not hearing of Washington's movements until too late to pursue him, vented his rage upon *New London*, Connecticut, by sending *Arnold*, the traitor, to burn it, and massacre the garrison at *Fort Griswold*, nearly opposite.

At Chester, Washington heard the cheering news of the arrival of twenty-four French ships of the line, under *Count de Grasse*, in the Chesapeake. A body of French troops was landed, to coöperate with the Americans. Now Washington's darling object was about to be realized. He had in all a force of about sixteen thousand men, and so disposed as to make it impossible for the British to escape, either by sea or land.

Early in October the siege commenced. The advance was rapid and tremendous, the British works giving way continually, until, on the 17th, Lord Cornwallis proposed a cessation of hostilities. On the 19th October, 1781, Articles of Capitulation were signed, by which the whole British army, military stores, and shipping, fell into the hands of General Washington. The army of Cornwallis marched out, with their colors cased, and laid down their arms in a field between the positions of the two armies. Whole number, seven thousand and seventy-three. This great victory decided the war in favor of American Independence. A day of public thanksgiving was recommended by Congress, and was observed throughout the United States. Washington liberated all persons under arrest, that they might partake in the general joy.

A change in the British Cabinet took place upon the surrender of Cornwallis. General Carlton succeeded General Clinton in command in America.

November 30, 1782, *provisional* Articles of Peace were signed, — upon the new ministry advising the king to discontinue the war, — by which the independence and sovereignty of the United States were acknowledged.

On the 19th of April, 1783, — eight years, to a day, after the battle of Lexington (April 19, 1775), — the cessation of hostilities with Great Britain was, by order of General Washington, proclaimed in the American camp.

On the 3d of September, 1783, there was concluded at Versailles, France, by *Adams*, *Franklin*, *Jay*, and *Laurens*, on the part of the Americans, and *Oswald* on the part of the British, a definitive treaty of peace, by which the thirteen United Colonies were admitted to be "Free, Sovereign, and Independent States." "Disperse, you rebels!" had become obsolete *in eight years!*

Upon review of the Revolutionary War, *Mr. Pitt* (the younger) said: .... "a war which was conceived in injustice, nurtured in folly, and whose footsteps were marked with slaughter and devastation. The nation was drained of its best blood and its vital resources, for which nothing was received in return but a series of inefficient victories and disgraceful defeats; victories obtained over men fighting in the holy cause of liberty, or defeats which filled the land with mourning, for the loss of dear and valuable relations slain in a detested and impious quarrel."

PERIOD III. FROM THE INDEPENDENCE, 5787 A. M., AND 1783 A. C., TO THE PRESENT TIME, 5864 A. M., AND 1860 A. C.

ARMY DISBANDED.

Freemen, after gaining their liberty, had no more use for an army, and hence its dissolution. But, being short of means, Congress was obliged to pay off the soldiers of the Revolution in paper-money, on the credit of the country. At the close of the war, this money had lost much of its value, and hence great dissatisfaction arose in the army, — that, after fighting the battles of the nation, they were to be cheated out of their pay, of which they and their families were in great want. Besides, some mischief-makers and busy-bodies took pains, by circulating written addresses, and other means, to excite the jealousies of the soldiers, and to induce them to use violence in order to obtain their rights.

At this juncture Washington's virtues and influence were of as great service to his country as at any time before. He assembled the officers, and exhorted them to moderation; pledged himself to do all he could for them, and then conjured them, "as they valued their honor, as they respected the rights of humanity, and as they regarded the military and national character of the American States, to express their utmost detestation of the men who were attempting to open the flood-gates of civil discord, to deluge their rising empire with blood." After his speech, the officers voted him an address of thanks, and avowed their confidence in the justice of Congress and their country. The accounts of the army were adjusted, and put in a train of settlement.

The 3d of November was fixed upon for disbanding the army. The day previous, Washington issued his farewell address to his troops, replete with friendly advice, and kind wishes for their present and future welfare. After taking an affecting leave of his officers, he repaired to *Annapolis*, where Congress was sitting, delivered to the president his military commission, and declared that he was no longer invested with any public character.

After his resignation he retired to his estate at *Mount Vernon*, — followed by the gratitude of his country, and the applause and admiration of the world, — where he applied himself to the peaceful pursuits of agriculture. Greater than *Cincinnatus* art thou, *Washington!*

CONSTITUTION ADOPTED.

After the dangers of war were over, the "*Articles of Confederation*" were found to be insufficient for the proper administration of government. Congress had no revenue, could not redeem its paper, and much of it was sold for a sixth or eighth of its nominal value. Thus the soldiers of the Revolution at last saw their expectations of pay cut off.

In accordance with a proposition by the Legislature of Virginia, commissioners from several of the states met at *Annapolis*, to form a general system of commercial regulations. But, feeling their authority too limited to accomplish what was needed, they adjourned, with instructions to advise the states to appoint delegates, with more ample powers, to meet the next year in *Philadelphia*.

In May 1787 those delegates met in that city, and organized by choosing *Washington* (delegate from Virginia) President. After *four months* deliberation, the *Federal Constitution* was *unanimously agreed to by the members of the Convention*, on the 17th of September; and being presented to Congress, it was by that body transmitted to the several states for their consideration. Being accepted and ratified by eleven of the states, it became the Constitution of the United States in 1788, North Carolina and Rhode Island dissenting; but the former adopted it in 1789, and the latter in 1790.

FIRST PRESIDENT.

George Washington. — According to the Constitution, the several states elected their delegates to Congress, and by a *unanimous* vote chose for the first President of the United States *General George Washington.*

Bidding adieu reluctantly to *Mount Vernon*, to private life and domestic felicity, he proceeded without delay to *New York*, where Congress was assembled.

In this journey no Roman conqueror ever received the honor of so glorious a triumph as did the "Father of his Country." The more glorious, because it was spontaneous, enthusiastic, and merited, — the gushing forth of the nation's heart in gratitude to its deliverer.

On the 30th of April, 1789, he was inaugurated President of the United States. The ceremony was performed in the open gallery of the City Hall, in *New York*, where the oath was administered, in the presence of a vast multitude of spectators. Great was the event of that day to hitherto troubled America.

At the same time *John Adams* was chosen Vice-President; *Thomas Jefferson*, Secretary of State; *Alexander Hamilton*, Secretary of the Treasury; *Henry Knox*, Secretary of War; *Edmund Randolph*, Attorney-General; and *John Jay*, Chief Justice of the United States.

Washington administered the government during eight years, — the same length of time he commanded the armies of the nation. During his administration France called upon America for assistance, under the *Directory;* but Washington's policy was that of neutrality.

Declining a second reëlection as president, — after a valedictory address to the people, replete with political wisdom, and breathing the warmest affection for his country, — he withdrew again to *Mount Vernon.*

During Washington's administration the State of *Vermont* was admitted into the Union, in 1791; Kentucky, in 1792; and Tennessee, in 1796.

John Adams. — He was chosen second president, in 1797. During his administration France entered into hostilities and aggressions towards the States for refusing to assist her. The American government assumed the attitude of defence, and General Washington was again made commander-in-chief.

Not long after accepting this office, Washington died suddenly, at *Mount Vernon*, on the 14th of December, 1799, in the sixty-eighth year of his age. The death of this *great American* produced an impression without a parallel. The people, upon a recommendation of Congress, wore a badge of black crape on the left arm for thirty days, as a token of spontaneous and unaffected grief. Eulogies were pronounced, funeral processions formed, and a general aspect of mourning was put on throughout the country,—a nation mourning for its revered Father and Deliverer.

In Adams' time, parties ran high. Those for the Constitution were called *Federalists;* the opposition men, *Anti-Federalists*—afterwards, *Federalists* and *Democrats.* The former charged the Democrats with partiality for France. This was retorted upon the Federalists with the same for Great Britain.

After a term of four years, Adams was succeeded by

THOMAS JEFFERSON.—He was third president. During his term—which commenced in 1801—the attempt to preserve neutrality in the war raging between Britain and France failed, from the jealousy of the two nations, lest *neutrality* should take liberties.

In consequence of Bonaparte's excluding all English goods from the Continent, by his "*Continental System,*" the British, to offset that, declared all the ports and rivers from Elbe in Germany, to Brest in France, to be blockaded, and all American vessels trading thither liable to seizure and condemnation.

In November after, Bonaparte, in his *Berlin Decree,* declared the British Isles blockaded, and no trade allowed with *them.*

In November 1807, by the *British Orders in Council,* all neutral vessels trading with France were obliged to stop and pay duty at some British port.

To meet this, Bonaparte issued, in December, his *Milan Decree,* declaring all vessels confiscated that should pay any duty to the British.

Seeing no alternative but to be devoured by either France or England, President Jefferson recommended an *embargo* to be laid on American shipping, and so keep it at home. But, in March 1809, that was removed, and *Non-intercourse* with France and England substituted. This, of course, brought all three of the interests into collision.

An amusing incident occurred during these troubles, in a case where a British man-of-war came upon a French merchant-ship. The captain was taken, the ship plundered and sunk. While on board the British ship, at a dinner, toasts were proposed, when the insolent British captain gave for his, in presence of the French captain, "Britannia rules the wave."

In due time, an American man-of-war came in sight. A battle

ensued, when the British man-of-war was scuttled, and sent down with the French merchantman, and the two captains taken on board the American man-of-war. Another dinner was given, and toasts prosposed, when the French captain gave his, in presence of the British captain, "*Britanny rule de wave!*"

The impressment of American seamen, and the search of American vessels, by the British, irritated the Americans to the highest pitch.

The State of *Ohio* was admitted into the Union in 1802. The Territory of *Louisiana* was purchased of France in 1803.

James Madison. — He was next elected, and was fourth president, in 1809 — Jefferson declining a reëlection, having served eight years.

Under a variety of complaints, President Madison recommended to Congress the declaration of war with Great Britain. The bill passed the House by a vote of seventy-nine to forty-nine, and the Senate by nineteen to thirteen; and on the next day, June 18, 1812, was signed by the president.

Canada was again made a point of attack. The Americans were unsuccessful in Upper Canada, though at the battle of Queenstown, the British general *Brock* was killed. The American flag was, however, successful on the ocean.

In 1813 there was considerable severe fighting in various parts of Upper Canada. The victory of *Commodore Perry*, on Lake Erie, over the British, was very much eulogized. *General Harrison* gained quite a victory over the British, under *General Proctor*, near the Thames. The Indian chief *Tecumseh* was slain at the same time. The Americans gained a decisive victory at *Chippewa*. The repulse of the British at Fort Erie was about the last of the war in that quarter.

General Prevost, receiving a reïnforcement of fourteen thousand men, began an offensive war on the United States by an attack upon *Plattsburg*. The naval and land forces coöperated. The British naval force, under *Commodore Downie*, with ninety-five guns, and one thousand and fifty men, was defeated by the Americans, under *Macdonough*, with only eighty-six guns, and eight hundred and twenty-six men. While the fleets were engaged, *General Prevost* attacked the forts of *Plattsburg*, but was effectually repulsed by the Americans, under *Macomb*. The British lost two thousand five hundred, while the American loss was only two hundred and thirty-one.

A British fleet entered the Chesapeake Bay in August 1814, advanced, and landed the forces about forty miles from Washington.

This army entered the city, and burnt the capitol, the president's house, and other public buildings, and retired without molestation, under *General Ross.*

On the 24th of December, 1814, a treaty of peace was signed at Ghent, by which the great European quarrel, in which America became involved, was put at rest. Before this was known, however, in America, a British armament, under *Sir Edward Packenham,* fitted out to attack New Orleans, arrived at that place. After suffering great hardships, the British finally made an assault upon the works (bags of cotton) thrown up for the defence of the city, on January 8th, 1815, when they were dreadfully cut to pieces and repulsed by the Americans, under General Jackson. The British lost in all two thousand six hundred, *Packenham* being among the killed; while the Americans lost only seven killed, and six wounded. Thus closed the war of 1812.

The State of *Louisiana* was admitted into the Union in 1811. *Indiana,* admitted in 1816. After a term of eight years, Madison was succeeded by

James Monroe.—He was inaugurated fifth President of the United States in 1817. During his term of eight years the following states were admitted into the Union: *Mississippi,* in 1817; *Illinois,* in 1818; *Alabama,* in 1819; *Maine,* in 1820; *Missouri,* in 1821; and *Florida* ceded to the United States in 1821, by Spain.

John Quincy Adams.—He was sixth president; inaugurated in 1825. Tariff Law enacted, putting duties on imports.

On the 4th of *July,* 1826, while the people of the United States were celebrating the Fiftieth Anniversary of the American Independence, *John Adams* and *Thomas Jefferson* both died, in their ninety-first and eighty-fourth years of age. They stood first and second on the committee to prepare the "Declaration," in 1776. Jefferson was its author, and Adams its powerful advocate. They afterwards held in succession the office of president; were at the head of the two opposite parties in politics; and, after retiring to private life, lived on the most friendly terms, and passed out of the world together, on the Fiftieth Anniversary of American Independence.

Andrew Jackson—Suppresses nullification in South Carolina; thwarts the United States Bank project. *Arkansas* admitted in 1836.

Martin Van Buren.—He was eighth president; inaugurated 1837.

William Henry Harrison.—He was ninth president; inaugurated in 1841. He died in one month's time after;—the first death of a president while in office.

John Tyler.—He succeeded to the office of president, from that of vice-president.

James K. Polk.—Inaugurated 1845. During his term occurred the war with Mexico. *Texas* admitted 1845.

Zachary Taylor.—Inaugurated 1849, and died in one year and four months.

Millard Filmore.—He succeeded, as vice-president, to the office of president, in 1850. *California* admitted 1850.

Franklin Pierce.—Inaugurated, as fourteenth president, in 1853. "Missouri Compromise" repealed, and Kansas excitement arose.

James Buchanan.—Inaugurated 1857, and present incumbent of that high office of the United States of America.

GOVERNMENT OF THE UNITED STATES.

The Government of the United States is usually styled a Confederation, or Federal Republic.

Each State makes its own laws for its internal government; but what relates to foreign commerce, the coinage of money, the Post-Office Department, Army and Navy, etc., are confided to the General Government.

The United States Government is administered by a President, Senate, and House of Representatives,—the last two forming a "Congress."

The Executive duties are divided between the six Departments of State: Treasury, Interior, War, Navy, and Post Office. The head of each of these departments, except post office, is called Secretary.

The five Secretaries, with the Post-master General and the Attorney General, constitute the Cabinet of the President. Before recommending any important measure to Congress, for their adoption, the President lays the matter before his Cabinet, and asks their advice.

The members of the Cabinet are selected by the President, and by him nominated to the Senate, which alone has the power of confirming their appointment.

Besides the power to *make* laws, which is vested in Congress, and the power to *execute* them, which is vested in the President, there is a third power, called the *Judicial*.

The Judicial power of the United States Government is vested in the Supreme Court, the Circuit courts, and the District courts of the United States. The duties of these courts are, not only to adjust differences between individuals, and to punish violations of the laws, but also to decide upon the justness of the laws made by Congress. The decision of the highest, or Supreme Court, is always final.

The judges of these courts are nominated by the President, and confirmed by the Senate. They hold office during good behavior.

Each State is entitled to two senators to Congress, who are chosen by their several legislatures, for a term of six years.

Representatives to Congress are chosen by the people, for a term of two years. Every ninety-three thousand seven hundred and sixteen inhabitants can send one.

The President and Vice-president hold office four years. Their election is made by a Convention of Electors, who are chosen by the people.

The Vice-president presides in the Senate, by virtue of his office. In case of the absence or death of the President, the Vice-president officiates in his stead.

The salary of the President is twenty-five thousand dollars per annum; that of the Vice-president, five thousand dollars; that of the members of Congress is three thousand dollars a year, and eight dollars for every twenty miles' travel to and from Congress.

LIST OF IMPORTANT BATTLES, AND THEIR COMMANDERS.

BATTLES.	VICTORS.	VANQUISHED.
Red Sea,	Moses,	Pharaoh.
Gibeon,	Joshua,	Adonizedec.
Troy,	Achilles,	Hector.
Elah,	David,	Goliath.
Babylon,	Cyrus,	Belshazzar.
Marathon,	Miltiades,	Darius.
Thermopylæ,	Leonidas,	Xerxes.
Arbela,	Alexander,	Darius Codo.
Zama,	Scipio,	Hannibal.
Pharsalia,	Cæsar,	Pompey.
Actium,	Octavius,	Antony.
Rome,	Alaric,	Honorius.
Hastings,	William,	Harold.
Heights of Abraham,	Wolfe,	Montcalm.
Waterloo,	Wellington,	Bonaparte.
Yorktown,	Washington,	Cornwallis.
New Orleans,	Jackson,	Packenham.

CONCLUSION.

A review of what is presented in the foregoing pages may not be out of place, now that we have followed the "trail" of the generations past through the dark wilderness of experiment, trials, conflicts, and triumphs, into the open fields of truth, civilization, liberty, and religion. The "spotted" way is *plainly* marked; but oh, such marks as along this pathway are found! Were the reader assured at the outset that a throng of demons had gone along that way, he would be often reässured that such was the case, and the danger of finding out his mistake would not be at all serious. But when told that this is the trail of a people of one common origin; that one Supreme God made of one blood all nations to dwell on all the face of the earth; that these were brothers, and *our* brothers, the reader of history may justly be appalled and confounded. Well may he say, If this be our fathers' *trail*, as for the *spots*, an enemy hath done this, either before or after the fathers had passed. But hold, confounded reader! stand amazed! let thy limbs shake, and thy knees smite! believe or be damned! — these are the fathers' spots! What! BLOOD and— Silence, man! an unbeliever's hell awaits thee unless thou receive it; the fathers' spots are these! Ah me! with faith as a grain of mustard-seed, I believe! Well hast thou done to take it in! And learn thou from this not to do as they have done, that none after thee may have to say of thy *spots*, Ah me!

Yet, oh! with what tears of joy we behold amid the throng the worthies walking in the midst of these fiery trials, yielding nothing but their bodies to be burned and their goods to be spoiled, "keeping the faith once delivered to the saints." To these martyr-heroes of the Lord we owe, under Him, all that in church and state is worthy the name of religion or right; and, with them, our motto should be, "To live is Christ, and to die is gain!"

The principal feature of this work is its division into two parts, which treat respectively of Religion and Empire. These two great branches of human interest are all-absorbing, and have been elaborately treated by other historians, but in a mixed form. To the theologian the mixed account of the world's affairs presents the great subjects of sacred and ecclesiastical history in such a tangle, that it requires a large amount of reading to *find* the facts he would learn, and then no small amount of study and reflection to arrange them in their proper relation to each other and to contemporary history. The same may be said, and with equal propriety, of the statesman who is in search of facts pertaining to empire. And of the general reader it may also be safely said, that he will be aided more directly to an understanding of history by this than by the mixed style of writing. And finally, without undue egotism, and truthfully it may be said, that no other work now before the public treats these great subjects in the separate and parallel form — a fact that must go for what it is worth in the estimation of enlightened readers. Here it is, the ways of God with man, and the ways of man with God, are themes of wonder and instruction; and whoever by their contemplation is inspired to a holy faith, or aroused to a noble patriotism, must be amply repaid for a perusal of the past, and better fitted for the discharge of his duty to his God and to his country.

For general readers, then, this work must have a particular adaptedness, since they have but little time to read, and hence a compact, systematic arrangement of the great body of history in this form will exactly meet their case. Neither can it be any impediment to the student of history who wishes to take a wider range than this volume embraces. The leading points herein set forth will not bewilder him for further research. In the Sabbath school, the Bible-class, yea, everywhere, may it have a mission for good to the causes of Christianity and freedom.

Another important division is that of Ages. This sets clearly before the reader (see Diagram) the definite portions of the world's history, when particular sentiments controlled the public mind. The Patriarchal Age embraces that portion in which society was formed upon the sentiment that the parental model should be preserved. This continued until Moses' time, when the popular fancy took in the idea of transforming the head of a tribe or family into a chief, king, or hero; and so grew up the "Age of War for Power." During this long season — from Moses to Christ — the nations of the earth were absorbed with the one idea of "Who shall be king?" The decision of this question lay in the ability of each party to wield the sword. No great cause of humanity or philanthropy moved the nations to action, but all interests were merged in the love and acquisition of power. Julius Cæsar felt the spirit of the times, and was often heard repeating a sentiment from Euripides, "that if right and justice were ever to be violated, they were to be violated for the sake of reigning." Behold an age spent in *violating right and justice* for the sake of reigning!

The introduction of Christianity engrafted a new feature upon the sentiments of the world; or, in other words, introduced the "Age of War for Opinion." The question now was, not wholly

Who shall rule? but, with that, whoever rules shall have the right also to coërce all the ruled into the same faith as the ruler or the party in power. This, instead of lessening the occasions and abating the lust for war, increased the number of disputes, and intensified the fury with which all parties flew to arms. Hence the fiendish barbarities of the dark ages; hence the holy (?) wrath of men fighting for the faith; hence the terrible meaning of the terms *Catholic* and *Heretic.* But these very abominations wrought their own overthrow; for, while men were thus engaged, the discovery was made that it was all wrong, and a better way was sought and found. Yea, in the times of fiercest priestly persecution and most oppressive kingly tyranny, the great doctrines of Civil and Religious Liberty sprang up, were promulgated, and signally triumphed; and so was introduced the fourth age.

The Age of Consolidation dates from the establishment of the Reformation. The peculiarity of this portion of the world's history is the tendency to separation of civil and ecclesiastical affairs, or the rendering "to Cæsar the things that are Cæsar's, and to God the things that are God's." And yet all the while this separation is going on, a process of consolidation is also working like leaven in the whole mass of mind, in all lands of free Bibles, schools, and presses. The form this process is assuming is that of the perfect and triumphant working of the affairs of both church and state. In the United States, where the principle has been most fully applied, the result is, we have a healthy, vigorous church, unpampered by government pap and untrammelled by state fetters; and, on the other hand, a free, prosperous, and powerful government, ranking first among the nations of the earth, unburdened of excessive church rates, and liable to no papal interdicts. Thus we have the Patriarchal Age, represented by the chief magistrate of the nation; the Age of War for Power, seen in the civil government of the country; and the Age of War for Opinion, gleaming forth in the religious liberty enjoyed by all peoples and tongues under the whole heaven. Thus the peculiarities of the three former ages, embracing so many thousands of years, are harmoniously blending, or *consolidating,* to form the fourth, which is and is yet to be infinitely superior to all that have gone before. This pattern of things must yet be applied to other than this nation, and is even now being rapidly done. The advantage of such a state of things to this "wide, wide world" let the thoughtful ponder and estimate.

Another item in the arrangement of the present work can be noticed by the reader with profit, viz., the Periods into which the work is divided. These have no particular reference to the Ages, but are, so to speak, the "spotted trees" along the trail of history. For example, the period from the Flood to the death of Joseph is a very definite section of history; and it will be found, by a little attention, that most of the other periods, though less familiar, are not less pertinent and instructive. They have for the most part reference not to individuals simply, but to them as representative characters in the important events with which they stand connected.

Another matter, which is not distinctly treated in the work, deserves notice; that is, the relative distances and similarity of certain great events before and after Christ. The coming of Christ, and the ascendency of the Roman emperors, form the most important epochs in the history of Religion and Empire. From this point go back three hundred years (see Diagram), and we find the time of Alexander the Great, "conqueror of the world," moving the sceptre of power, for the first time, from Asia over into Europe. Come down three hundred years after Christ, and we find Constantine the Great, "emperor of the world," dividing the Roman world into East and West, and thereby changing the whole current of human affairs. Both these events pertain to empire, and are quite similar.

Go back before Christ six hundred years, and we come to the captivity of the Jews. Here a lordly potentate assumed to stand between God and his people, and coërce them to bow to his mandate, and image even, and so change times and laws. Come down six hundred years after Christ, and we find the first Pope, or the captivity of the church. Here a lordly prelate assumed to stand between God and his people, and coërce them to bow to images, and thus change the worship of God into idolatry. Both these events pertain to religion, and are quite similar.

Go back before Christ one thousand years, and we come to the time of Solomon's Temple, or the highest state of prosperity to which the Jewish nation ever rose. Come down one thousand years after Christ, and we find the "Dark Ages," or the state of the greatest depression Christianity ever saw. In this case the events are similar, but in the sharpest contrast, hence easy to remember;—the Jews at the summit, and Christianity at the base, of the mount of prosperity.

Go back fifteen hundred and fifty-five years before Christ, and we find Moses delivering the people from Egyptian bondage and the yokes of their oppressors. Come down fifteen hundred and fifty-five years after Christ, and we meet with the triumph of the Reformation, and the church making its exodus from the dark ages and throwing off the papal yoke. Religious events both of them, and strikingly similar.

Go back eighteen hundred and sixty years before Christ, and we are with Abraham, Isaac, Jacob, Shem, and Job. Come down eighteen hundred and sixty years after Christ, and we are literally in the midst of our own peculiar, wonderful time.

Go back two thousand three hundred and forty-eight years, and we come to the destruction of the world by *water*. Look forward to two thousand three hundred and forty-eight years after Christ, and what impropriety is there in suspecting that then will come the destruction of the world by *fire*. There is no positive proof on this point, but the former was foretold and came to pass: the latter is foretold and will come to pass. By the contrasts we have made, we find such and such events, and of a *similar kind*, occurring at such and such intervals. Without, therefore, turning aside from this drift of thought, but rather forced along by the irresistible tide of facts, the mind is driven mightily towards the conclusion that *then* will be the consummation of all things. But again, the question returns, If God has turned and overturned, ruled and overruled, lo, these five thousand eight hundred years, to bring the world into a "consolidated" state for proper action, and as infancy is to age, so, will he not yet take a corresponding time to display his works and ways before countless millions yet unborn? This query also presses us with such force, that between the two we are obliged to admit that "secret things belong to the Lord."

By fixing the foregoing points distinctly in the mind, as seen upon the Diagram, any person can easily, rapidly, and retentively store away a vast amount of important historical knowledge.

"Westward empire makes its way." This statement is made strikingly true by all movements of the nations. That empire began in the East all admit; and that Asia held sway over Europe until the time of Alexander the Great, is a very plain case. By the triumph of the Greeks over the Persians at that time, military prowess was yielded to the Western conquerors. The sceptre of power was next borne west by the triumphant Romans — Greece, Persia, and all the East lying prostrate at their feet. Upon the fall of the Western Empire, the sceptre of power was set afloat among the Goths, Vandals, and other Western tribes, until France and England attained the ability to lead in power; and so westward again empire made its way.

Empire having reached westward as far as the "Pillars of Hercules," even, could not there be stayed; but, with marvellous strides, now proudly stands on the western verge of earth, and watches the setting sun. With France, England, and the United States the ark of power now reposes; and, as no other three powers on earth can do, they together can dictate terms to the whole world.

Westward religion makes its way also. The westward march of the Bible is as plainly marked as the footsteps of empire. In the extreme East also did God plant the Garden of Eden, and there and about there dispense his law. From thence it was removed west to Jerusalem, until "Shiloh should come."

Just at the point of time when the Jewish nation failed to be able to serve as the trustees of the Lord's dispensation, a faithful band of apostles was sent forth west, even to Greece, Rome, Spain, and to Britain, preaching the everlasting gospel. Soon Christianity is made the religion of the Roman State. This fostering degenerates into the Papacy, when lo! France, Germany, and England rise and reject the Pope. The land of Palestine had fallen long before under the sway of the false prophet, and so the "Ark of the Covenant" was borne to the precints of the Pillars of Hercules also. After its rout at Jerusalem, the Ark of God continued among the "Philistines," until it was safely, sacredly, and triumphantly placed upon the *Rock of Ages*, in Providence, Rhode Island.

Religion and Empire having completed their westward tour, and in their course evolved the great doctrines of civil and religious liberty, and being "monarchs of all they survey," are gloriously advancing in all that pertains to the pomp and circumstance of state; and in church learning daily better and better how to "render to Cæsar the things that are Cæsar's, and to God the things that are God's." Besides this internal work, they are rolling along back, in the pathway of nations, an influence for good on the Old World that, like leaven, is destined to leaven the whole lump.

The present movements in the East indicate very strikingly what impulse is seizing the masses; and the day is coming when civil and religious liberty will triumph over the despotisms of Europe, or when heathenism, Mohammedanism, and Popery, must fall before the dominion of "the King of the Jews," our Messiah.

We are now living beyond Bible prophecies, and have no programme of what is about to be; but that a great Age is near, many voices unite in saying, "Lo, He comes!"

THE END.

www.ingramcontent.com/pod-product-compliance
Lightning Source LLC
LaVergne TN
LVHW021317110826
845150LV00003B/602

* 9 7 8 1 4 2 5 5 5 7 8 1 2 *